German-American Names

German-American N·A·M·E·S

George F. Jones

3rd Edition

1st Edition 1990
2nd Edition 1995
3rd Edition 2006
Copyright © 1990, 1995, 2006
Genealogical Publishing Co., Inc.
3600 Clipper Mill Rd., Suite 260
Baltimore, Maryland 21211
All Rights Reserved
Library of Congress Catalogue Card Number 2005934662
International Standard Book Number 0-8063-1764-7
Made in the United States of America

Acknowledgments

I wish to thank Bertha Butler of the University of Maryland Computer Science Center for many years of expert and patient help in devising computer programs. One of these, a system of reverse-alphabetical listing, served to assemble the names in this book according to their last roots and thus shed much light on their meanings and relationships. I also wish to thank Carol Warrenton, likewise of the University of Maryland Computer Science Center, for composing the program for printing this book.

G. F. J.

Der Schmidt.

CHAPTER ONE

Given Names - Significance and Origin

Many Americans with German names know the dictionary meaning of the corresponding German word without realizing that their name, being a name, may have an entirely different meaning. For example, the German dictionary tells us that the word *Kuss* means "kiss," but it does not tell us that the name Kuss is most often a shortened form of Dominicus and that, while the word *Mass* means "measure," the name Mass or Maas is usually a shortened form of Thomas, unless the first bearer of the name lived near the Maas (Meuse) River.   (1)

Unfortunately, onomastics (the science of names) is not an exact science, as is proved when experts disagree as to the meaning of a name. Only the parents of a child know what they think a name means, and often they do not know. While interning in an obstetrics ward, an acquaintance of mine once delivered a worn-out mountain woman of her tenth child. When the grateful woman asked him to think up a name, he suggested Decimus Ultimus; and she was delighted with the choice, which she did not understand. The name meant "the tenth and the last." He was right: he had tied her tubes.   (2)

When my wife's parents chose the name Joyce for their daughter, they probably associated it with "joy " and "rejoice," little realizing that it once denoted a Goth; and the same thing was repeated when Joyce named our daughter Jocelyn (little Goth). Such misunderstandings are called popular etymology or folk etymology, etymology being the study of *etyma* or roots of words. A good example of folk etymology is the common expression "planter's wart," which suggests that planters were most exposed to it, whereas it is really a "plantar wart" or a wart on the sole of the foot, as I learned recently.   (3)

Old Germanic names were misunderstood already a thousand years ago by scholars who tried to interpret them. For example, Ratmund was rendered as "counsel + mouth" instead of as "counsel + guardianship;" and Adalramus was rendered as "noble ram" instead of as "noble raven." This study will make every effort to avoid folk etymologies, but some are inevitable, and the author will appreciate hearing of any the reader might find.   (4)

Sometimes the researcher must risk an educated guess. For example, the German-American name Hass could derive from German *Hass* (hate) or from German *Hase* (hare), most certainly (but not absolutely certainly) from the latter, which is found in many American names such as Hashagen (hare hedge) and Hasenjaeger (hare hunter). A half century ago one of my sisters had a gentleman caller named Hass, who had the misfortune of having the first name Jack. When Jack Hass was spoken quickly, it said just what we brothers thought of him.

Sometimes the context makes it clear which of two homonymous roots is the correct one: in the name Sauerbier the root *sauer* means "sour," while in Sauerland it means "southern." Among the scores of homonymous root-pairs (having the same sound and spelling), we find *gehl* (yellow), *gehl* (swamp); *ger* (spear), *ger* (swamp); *han* (rooster), *han* (swamp); *reh* (roebuck), *reh* (marsh); and *sud* (muddy), *sud* (south). In some cases there are even triplets: *ahl* (eel), *ahl* (noble), *ahl* (awl); *dick* (thicket), *dick* (dike), *dick* (fat); and *hart* (strong), *hart* (stag), *hart* (forest).   (5)

It is easy to define the term "German-American name," once we decide on the meaning of "German name"; for a German-American name is any name derived from the German language or its dialects, even if changes in pronunciation and spelling have rendered it unrecognizable. For our purpose, both Beam and Dice are German-American names, even if we do not easily identify them with Boehm and Theiss.   (6)

Defining "German names" is somewhat more difficult. For example, the Netherlands were originally a part of the Holy Roman Empire (i.e. the German Empire); and the people there speak Low Franconian, Low Saxon, and Frisian. The first two of these are German dialects, while the third is an independent language, which is also spoken in Germany. Since Dutch is now a national language, we will not include obviously Dutch names such as de Gruyter and van Horn, even if they may have been borne for centuries by families in Berlin.   (7)

On the other hand, even though Dreyfuss was a loyal Frenchman, his name (meaning "tripod") was German and is therefore included. When I first visited Paris, I rented a room from a woman who pronounced her name Oh-mess-air, which I took to be French. I later discovered that it was Haumesser, an

Alsatian word meaning "hackknife" or "meat-cleaver," so it is also included. Also included are the names Kirchhoff and Stockmann, even though they are best known to us as the names of a Russian physicist and of the protagonist in Ibsen's *Enemy of the People* and also (with one *n*) of a precocious American economist who ridiculed Reaganomics. In other words, we are interested in the linguistic origin of the name, not in the nationality of its bearers. The word "German" refers to the German language, whether the name in question came from West or East Germany, Alsace, Switzerland, Austria, the South Tyrol, or any other German-speaking areas of Europe.   (8)

It is not always possible to ascertain from which language a name is derived: Horn could be German, English, Dutch, or Scandinavian. Therefore some American names discussed below may actually have been brought here by non-German families, but all do exist in Germany. A few well-known Latin and Greek names like Astor, Faber, Melanchthon, Mercator, Neander, Praetorius, Sartorius, and Stettinius are included because they have now become German names. There are also a few names of French origin, like Tussing for Toussaints, and a few names of Slavic derivation, like Kretschmer, Lessing, and Nietzsche. Some German-looking names appearing below may have been Slavic names shortened or germanized at Ellis Island by officials who knew German better than the various Slavic languages.   (9)

Because the word "philologist" will appear many times in this book, now might be a proper time to explain the word, even if it is hard to explain the profession. As the Greek roots *phil* and *logos* suggest, a philologist is one who loves words, one who cherishes them for their own sake, not for the sake of gain. No philologist ever became rich, not one ever built a bridge, removed a tumor, or won a battle; and it is difficult to explain what good they serve, unless, perhaps, to disabuse us of much misinformation. Nevertheless, some of the world's greatest minds have devoted themselves to this unproductive study, two splendid examples being Jacob and Wilhelm Grimm, scholars known to the public for their fairy tales but to the scholarly world for their collection of legal antiquities and, above all, for the "Grimms' Law," an explanation of the development of the various Germanic languages. The observations made by the

Grimm brothers and other philologists of their day make it possible for us to understand the origin of German names, and therefore their contributions will be described in some detail a bit later.   (10)

Most philologists write for each other, affecting an arcane jargon to exclude everyone else. Unfortunately, this study will have to use a few technical terms, but these will be explained. At the Day of Judgment I shall have to confess to having devoted a half century of my life to Germanic philology, whereas I could have been serving my Maker in some more productive way. However, unlike most Germanic philologists in their ivory towers, I am aware that there are many perfectly decent, hardworking, law abiding people out there who have never studied Germanic philology. It is for them that this book is written.   (11)

"In the beginning was the word." St. John was not alone in this belief; it was the opinion of most of his contemporaries, especially of his Greek ones, who had a word for everything. It was centuries before Goethe's Faust, as the first Modern Man, refuted St. John and argued that "In the beginning was the deed." Today most people would agree with the *New English Dictionary* that a word is merely "Speech, utterance, or verbal expression." The ancients, on the other hand, and not only those of our culture, knew that a word was more than a mere utterance. It was a living spirit with inherent power to do good or evil, as is so evident in the blessings and curses of the Old Testament. Noah's curse of Canaan and Isaac's blessing of Jacob were not just words but were forces direct from Jehovah. Words had power not only for the ancient Hebrews but also for the ancient Germanic peoples, for whom an insult was a malevolent spirit, a relentless demon that clung to a man until washed off with blood.   (12)

What has been said about words naturally holds for names too, since they are proper nouns, even in the few instances when they are formed like adjectives or verbs, as in the case of Lionhearted or Lackland. The very term "proper nouns" (*nomina propria*) is significant; for a name, be it given or earned, is proper to, or the property of, the bearer. This is especially evident in the German word *Eigennamen*, or "own names." One's name is, of course, more than just a possession, like land or gold; it is the immortal part of the person, as Othello's ensign Cassio avowed. It is the part that lives after the body dies, possibly borne by children of the deceased, or perhaps by many children of his admirers. Or perhaps his name is carved in stone or borne by a city or a symphony. (13) Even the Old Testament taught the value of a good name, and this is one reason that, during the Middle Ages, to be "nameless" (*namenlos* or *ungenant*) was most tragic. Proverbs 22:1 tells us that "A good name is rather to be chosen than great riches," and Ecclesiastes 7:1 preaches that "a good name is better than precious ointment." (Cf "to leave a living name behind," and "their bodies are buried in peace, but their name liveth for evermore.") (14) It has been said that "your name is who you are." Indeed, before social security numbers, a name was most people's only identity. This attitude is deeply ingrained in the Christian Church, which accepts a new member only when he receives a Christian name and ignores his surname; and it helps explain the emphasis on the Feast of the Holy Name on New Year's Day. In some cultures a change of name indicates a change in nature: the Indian youth receives a new name when he becomes a brave, and a British commoner receives a more fitting name when he is ennobled. When Lawrence Olivier was knighted, he became Sir Lawrence, not Sir Olivier. (15) That such obsession with names was only a holdover from ancient word-magic is suggested by the ease with which modern men can change their names, without any great metamorphosis in their person. Indeed, one does not even have to go to the legislature, as was necessary in my father's childhood. When his nextgate neighbors tired of being teased because of their name, which was Hogg, they changed it to Howard. The next day some jokester put a sign on their gate: "Hogg by name, and hog by nature, changed to Howard by legislature." What the public did not know was that Hog was a respectable name as long as it denoted the young of most animals, including sheep. A Highland lassie cared little whether her laddie called her "my little lamb" or "my little hog." (16) There are many tales of name changes, usually apocryphal but sometimes illuminating. From the '30s comes the tale of Franklin Delano Stink. When the judge agreed to let him

change his name and asked which name he had chosen, he answered "Theodore Roosevelt Stink." Then there was the Mr. Murphy of South Boston who wished to change his name to O'Reily. When the judge asked why he wished to exchange one Irish name for another, he answered: "Venn I say my name iss Murphy, people aks me vut it vuss before it vuss Murphy."
(17)

The ancient Germans had no firm faith in a hereafter, despite what latter-day mythologists tell us about Valhalla, which must have developed late and probably through analogy with the Christian heaven. Long after they had become nominal Christians, Germanic warriors were far more concerned with their posthumous good name than with their souls. *Beowulf* is nominally a Christian poem; yet, when the hero dies, the poet is concerned not with his soul but only with his good name, for he eulogizes him as *leofgernost*, or "most eager for fame." (18)

This obsession with one's good name lasted throughout the Middle Ages. Despite Christ's injunction to turn the other cheek, men of honor preferred to risk their immortal souls in duels rather than risk their worldly honor by declining a challenge. Today we can say "Sticks and stones may break my bones but names can never hurt me," but in those days names hurt far more than mere broken bones. Turning the other cheek would have been incomprehensible to the ancient German, the medieval knight, or the Southern Gentleman, who knew that he would enjoy no respect or esteem if he failed to gain satisfaction for an insult. (19)

The New English Dictionary says that a name is "the particular combination of sounds employed as the individual designation of a single person, animal, place, or thing." It is to be noted that the name consists of sounds, not letters. Now that most people of the Western World are literate, we think of names as groups of letters, as in a signature. Yet even today the sound is foremost, extremely varied spellings are legally recognized only if they sound the same (*idem sonans*). MacIntire, McIntire, and McIntyre are the same name, even if differently spelled, as are Cramer, Craemer, and Kraemer. (20)

When the ancient Germans formed their names, they, like the ancient Hebrews, knew that a name was more than a mere designation: like a word, a name had inherent power and was part and parcel of the person himself. It was believed that a man's virtues were influenced by his name and were in turn transmitted to his namesake. This belief lasted long after the introduction of Christianity, and Christian parents continued to select godparents whose names would contribute to their children's virtue.   (21)

Because the God of the Old Testament was created in man's image, He was a jealous God, especially jealous of His name; and it should be noted that He performed most of His great works "for His name's sake," or to enhance His reputation among the various tribal gods of the time. ("Thou shalt have none other god before me.") Woe unto anyone who took the name of the Lord in vain! In fact, the Hebrews dared not utter His name; they had to resort to all sorts of circumlocutions such as Adonai and Elohim. Sacred names are taboo in many other religions as well: for example, the Hairy Ainu of Hokaido are afraid to utter the name of the bear. The early Germans, who were also shamanists, must have shared this fear, for they avoided the inherited Indo-European name for "bear," which would have been similar to Latin *ursus*. Instead, they beat around the bush with words like *bruin* and *berin*, both of which meant "brown" and gave us names such as Bruno, Bernhard, and Bermann. It should be noted that the name Beowulf meant "bee wolf," a circumlocution for the bear, which relishes honey.   (22)

With such a long tradition of name-magic behind us, it is not surprising that people are still so touchy about their names. Goethe was wise in saying that we should never make a play on a person's name. For some twenty-five years, whenever I have been introduced to someone, he was likely to answer with a hearty chuckle, "Oh, one of the Jones boys!" I have always tried to be diplomatic and laugh along with my tormentor, as if I had not been subjected to the same stupidity a thousand times before, realizing that he really thought he had said something clever and original. (Strangely enough, I still do not know who the Jones boys were.)   (23)

How did names arise? According to the Bible, after God created Adam:

> Out of the ground the Lord God formed every
> beast of the field, and every fowl of the air; and

brought them unto Adam to see what he would
call them: and whatsoever Adam called every
living creature, that was the name thereof.
This occurred just before God created Eve from Adam's rib.
When Eve heard that Adam had named the hippopotamus hippopotamus, she asked why he had done so; and he answered
that it looked more like a hippopotamus to him than any other
animal God had shown him.   (24)
Just as one could injure his enemy by driving nails into
his image, one could gain power over him by abusing his name.
As Stith Thompson's *Motif-Index of Folk-Literature* proves, this
belief has been strong in all cultures, including our own. For
example, in the Grimm's tale of Rumpelstiltskin, the queen's
daughter gains power over her captor by learning his name.
Belief in the power over names still lingers in our subconscious
as either a positive or a negative factor. In discussing Johann
Adam Treutlen, the first elected governor of Georgia, Henry
Melchior Muhlenberg praised him for having Adam's natural
intelligence and ability to give a name to every animal. Despite
St. John's faith in the precedence of the word, many medieval
scholars agreed with Genesis that the thing preceded the name:
Nomina sunt consequentia rerum (names are the consequence
of things).   (25)
To understand early German names, we must keep in mind
that the ancient Germans, like the Latins, Celts, Slavs, Greeks,
and many more peoples, were descended from one speech
community, one we now call the Indo-Europeans. When I was
in college, we learned that this linguistic community had
developed its language in India and had gradually spread it
westward to Europe. However, during the Hitler regime, when
the terms "Aryan" and "Indo-European" were confused and
abused, German philologists began to argue that the Indo-
Europeans, or Indo-Germans as they called them, first developed their language in eastern Central Europe, in what is now
more or less East Germany and Poland, from where they
gradually carried it eastwards into Iran (Parsee) and India
(Sanskrit), as well as into all of Europe, except where Finnish,
Estonian, Hungarian, and Basque are spoken.   (26)
The languages resulting from these Indo-European invasions
in Europe were the Celtic languages in the west and south,

Latin and Greek in the south, the Slavic languages in the east and south, and German in the old homeland and also to the north. Perhaps the least changed of all these languages were Old Prussian, Lithuanian, and Latvian, all of them near and just north of the old cradle. This new theory, which smacked of blatant racism, first met with ridicule; yet the linguistic evidence has now convinced most philologists, be they ever so anti-Nazi. (27)

The Germanic tribes, which were among the last to leave the old homeland, were excellently described in the year 98 A.D. by the Roman historian Cornelius Tacitus in a little area-study called the *Germania*, which may have been the foreword to a never-written history of the German wars. Tacitus describes a barbarian culture centered mainly on war; and, as we shall see, early German names bear him out. The language of the ancient Germans was not recorded, but we can reconstruct it by comparing words from old and modern Germanic languages, and also by comparing Germanic names recorded in Greek and Latin writings. From these we can learn much about the ancient Germans' life-style. We know, among other things, that they had cattle, horses, wagons, plows, grains, cloth, and a means of inscribing words, names, and incantations. (28)

All languages are in constant flux. Children do not speak exactly like their parents and grandparents; and today we have difficulty in understanding Chaucer, or even Shakespeare. The remarkable thing is not that languages change, but that they change so slowly. As the various Indo-European peoples left their homeland, their dialects developed independently until they became mutually unintelligible languages. It was the great work of the Grimm brothers, especially of Jacob, to comprehend and codify the mutations that distinguished the Germanic languages from all other Indo-European languages. These mutations are now known as the Germanic sound shift. (29)

The phrase "sound shift" sounds ominous, like the Andreas Fault, or the Tower of Babel, as if any moment we might not be able to communicate. Actually, sound shifts occur so slowly that the speakers who perpetrate them are unaware of the havoc they are wreaking. There even seems to have been a sound shift, although not yet recorded, since we Americans broke off from our linguistic motherland: we pronounce words like "latter" and "bitter" the same as "ladder" and "bidder." Some Americans deny obstreperously that they do so; but, if they didn't, they would sound like Englishmen with their "clipped accent." Imitating the Brothers Grimm, I will formulate the Jones law as follows: "In American English intervocalic voiceless dental stops have become voiced." Or, put simply, *t* has become *d* between vowel sounds. "Voiceless" stops like *p*, *t*, and *k* do not cause the vocal chords to vibrate as the voiced stops *b*, *d*, and *g* do. In "this" the *th* is voiced, in "thistle" it is not. A "stop" is a consonant that interrupts the breath, like *p*, *t*, and *k*, whereas a "spirant" is spoken while air is being exhaled as in the case of *th*, *f*, and *s*. An "affricate" combines a stop and its corresponding spirant, as in *pf* and *ts* (which is written as *z* in German).

(30)

To explain the Germanic sound shift simply, yet sufficiently for our purpose, we might say that the voiceless stops *p*, *t*, and *k* became the voiceless spirants *f*, *th*, and *ch* (which soon became *h*), while the voiced stops *b*, *d*, and *g* became the voiceless stops *p*, *t*, and *k*, thus replacing the lost consonants. Consequently the Indo-European roots that gave the Latin words *piscis*, *tenuis*, and *cornus* also gave the English words *fish*, *thin*, and *horn* as well as the German words *Fisch*, *duenn*, and *Horn*, while Latin *turba*, *duo*, and *genu* are cognate with (related to) "thorpe," "two," and "knee."   (31)

The language produced by the Germanic sound shift, which is called Proto-Germanic, was subsequently subdivided by various mutations into many Germanic dialects, including Alemannic, Anglian, Bavarian, Danish, Dutch, Frankish, Hessian, Norwegian, Saxon, Swedish, and Thuringian, as well as by many extinct languages such as Burgundian, Cimbric, Gothic, Lombard, and Vandal. Of the modern dialects, some have become national languages, such as Dutch and Flemish (from Low Franconian), and English from Anglian and Saxon.   (32)

This might be a suitable time to remind the reader that one should distinguish between the words "German" and "Germanic" rather than confuse them as many genealogical societies do. The word "Germanic," like *germanique*, *germanico*, and *germanisch*, denotes all the languages resulting from the Germanic sound shift, including English, Dutch, Swedish, Pennsylvania Dutch, etc. Since English is a Germanic language, one cannot distinguish between the English and Germanic elements in Pennsylvania. The recent popularity of the word "Germanic" seems to have begun during the Hitler regime, perhaps because it sounded less Nazi than "German" did. Correctly speaking, the inhabitants of Tacitus' *Germania* should not be called "Germans," since the German nation did not develop until after the invasions of the fourth to the seventh centuries. However, since it is awkward always to say "Germanic" and "Germanic peoples," we will sometimes just say "Germans" and "ancient Germans." (33)

A language is a culturally independent dialect with its own rules. Pennsylvania German and Afrikaans, with only a million or two speakers each, are languages, while Bavarian and Swabian, with many millions of speakers, are only dialects of German. No one can complain that the Pennsylvanians are speaking incorrect German or that the Afrikaners are speaking incorrect Dutch; yet a speaker of standard German can scold a Bavarian or a Swabian for distorting the German language. We will soon see that many German and German-American names were taken from dialects and do not conform to standard German spelling or pronunciation. The dialect form of the name might be much older than the standard language and is not really a deviation, merely an alternate form not chosen by Luther and other language standardizers. Behm is merely a dialect variant of Boehm (Bohemian), whereas the American form Beam is a new development in both pronunciation and spelling. Because the vowels, like the consonants, varied from dialect to dialect, the names Naumann, Niemann, and Neumann are one and the same. (34)

The dialects sometimes caused differences in the meaning of names. Although *Fuss* means "foot" in standard German, the name Streckfus originally meant "Stretch leg," not "Stretch foot." Some South German colonists in Georgia told their pastor that one of his parishioners had suffered an injury to his *Fuss* when a bear he had treed and shot fell on him. The pastor reported in his journal that the man's foot had been injured, but later he was more specific, the man's thigh had been dislocated. I had a similar experience in Bavaria when a man's ski stuck in the wet snow and, with his foot held high up by the ski, he began screaming in his dialect *mein Fuoss ist gebroche, mein*

Fuoss ist gebroche. In trying to loosen his foot from the ski, I handled it ever so gently, while quite ignoring his thigh, even though it was really his femur that was broken.   (35)

Like the ancient Hebrews, but unlike the Romans, the Germans were content with one name, a name made of two syllables. We cannot call this name a "first" name, because there was no second one; and we cannot call it a "Christian" name, since the Germans were still heathens. Therefore we must call it a "given" name, or, for the present, just a "name." The Germanic system of name-giving seems to have been derived from Indo-European practices, for similar systems were used by the Celts and Greeks. Some scholars think this system was limited to the Celts, Greeks, and Germans; others think that it was once universal among the Indo-Europeans but was later discarded by many of the tribes after their dispersal. For our purpose such a dispute is irrelevant: it is enough to know that the ancient Germans, like the Celts and Greeks, chose names composed of two roots. For example, the Greek name Thrasybulos combines the concepts "brave" and "counsel," just as the German name Conrad does. The concepts, but not the Indo-European roots, were identical.   (36)

The roots used in primitive Germanic names were general concepts. For example, *rik (cognate with Latin *rex* and *regnum*) could mean either "rule" or "ruler," as could the root *wald (cognate with English "wield"). Likewise, *athel could mean "noble," "nobility" or "nobleman." The asterisks (*) in the above examples signify that the words have not been preserved in their given form but have merely been reconstructed or postulated from later linguistic evidence. A few Germanic name-roots survived intact long enough to be recorded more or less unchanged, for example, *athel and *hrotho appeared in many Anglo-Saxon names such as Aethelraed the Unready, king of Wessex, Aethelstan, king of Mercia, and Hrothgar, the lord and kinsman of Beowulf.   (37)

If these last three names had been preserved in southern Germany instead of in England, they would have appeared as *Edelrat, Edelstein,* and *Ruediger.* To understand these changes, we must consider the High German sound shift, a second sound shift that followed the first almost a millenium later. This sound shift, also described by the Grimm brothers, distinguished the South German dialects from all the other Germanic languages. This High German sound shift, which altered most consonants, began soon after the Alemanni and Bavarians reached the Alps following the collapse of the Roman Empire.

(38)

The High German soundshift gradually spread northward into central Germany and affected standard German, while the North Germans clung to the unshifted consonants of the other Germanic languages such as Dutch and English. Thus the German dialects were divided into High German in the south and Low German in the north. Many of the names we shall discuss were North German and were therefore unaffected by the High German sound shift. On the other hand, with the increase of literacy and the spread of the High German written standard language into northern Germany, many Low German names have taken on standard spelling. For example, the spellings of Kock, Groote, and Schaper have often become Koch, Grosse, and Schaefer; and the names are pronounced according-ly.

(39)

Once a gentleman named Holthusen asked me the meaning of his name, and I explained that it meant "forest house," being the Low German form of Holtzhausen. He was highly indignant when I said "Low German" and assured me that his people had been perfectly respectable. What he did not understand was that "High German" refers to the southern highlands of Germany, while "Low German" refers to the low coastal plain in the north. Boats go down the Rhine in a northwesterly direction from Basel to Rotterdam and down the Elbe in a northwesterly direction from Dresden to Hamburg. Because maps often hang on walls with north at the top, we say "up north" and "down south," just as the Germans say "up in Schleswig" (*oben in Schleswig*) and "down in Bavaria" (*unten in Bayern*), so it is sometimes hard to remember that High Germany is in the south and Low Germany is in the north.

(40)

Of greatest interest to us in the High German sound shift are the changes of the new voiceless stops *p* and *t* (when initial) into the voiceless affricates *pf* and *ts* (written *z*) and the changes of *p*, *t*, and *k* (when medial or final) into *f*, *s*, and *ch* (pronounced as in Bach). Also important were the changes of the voiced stops *b*, *d*, and *g* to the voiceless stops *p*, *t*, and *k*. Because of this shift, the English words "plow," "hope," "toe," "water," and "break" are cognate with German *Pflug, hoffen, Zeh, Wasser*, and *brechen*; and English "door" is cognate with the High German word *Tor*. At the end of a syllable *k* was shifted to *ch* in all dialects; but at the beginning of a syllable it was shifted only in Switzerland, and there only in pronunciation, not in spelling, so it did not change the standard spelling of names beginning with *k*. As a result, "King" and *Koenig* are cognates, whereas in the Germanic root **rik* the final *k* was shifted in High German to *ch* (*rich*). This shift of *k* explains the different endings of English "book" and German *Buch*. The *b* and *g* shifted only in the Upper German dialects of the far south, where they are reflected in variants such as Pichler-Buehler and Kugel-Gugel. (41)

Simultaneously with the sound shift in some areas, and soon thereafter in others, the *h* was dropped before *l* and *r*, as it was also in English. Likewise, *w* was dropped before *r* as in English pronunciation, but not in spelling (Cf. "wretch" and *Recke*). Starting in the south a short time later was the change of *th* to *d* (*thing* became *ding*). The *th* in modern German names should always be pronounced as *t* because the *h* in the digraph *th* was introduced into spelling in the sixteenth and seventeenth centuries in an attempt to gain elegance, since *th* appeared in many words taken from the Greek via Latin. Therefore the *h* should be ignored in pronouncing German names like Walther and Goethe. (42)

Soon after the High German sound shift *sl, sm, sn*, and *sw* became *schl, schm, schn*, and *schw* so that *schlecht, schmal, schnee,* and *schwarz* are cognate with "slight," "small," "snow," and "swart." *St* and *sp* also acquired the *sh* sound, but it is not indicated in the spelling. By chance, many German-American names reverted to the older Germanic pronunciation through the influence of English, which had not gone through the High German sound shift. For example, Schwartz sometimes became Swarts, Schnell sometimes became Snell, and Stein was pronounced as Stein instead of as "Schtein." There were, of course, also changes in many vowels; but they played a lesser role in identifying names.

Both the Germanic sound shift and the High German sound shift were infinitely complicated, with many apparent exceptions, most of which were explained by the Danish philologist Karl Verner. The simplified account given here serves only to clarify those changes that will help explain the present forms of German names. For example, as a result of the High German sound shift there are many pairs of German names that are similar except that one of them (or its roots) was altered by the sound shift, while the other was not. Examples are the Low German names Dormann, Dierdorp, and Timmermann as opposed to the High German names Thormann, Tierdorf, and Zimmermann. (43)

It would be impossible, and certainly unrewarding, to try to reproduce all names under discussion in the exact form they had at a given date in their given area, because the changes took place at different times in different places. We will therefore give all German names in their classical Middle High German form, the form in which they appeared in South German literature from the eleventh through the thirteenth centuries. As a result of the High German sound shift, the Proto-Germanic roots *athel*, *hari*, *hrotho*, *rik*, and *theod* became *edel*, *her*, *ruod*, *rich*, and *diet*. Therefore *Hludowics became Ludwig, *Hrothgar became Ruedeger, Hrothoberacht became Ruoprecht, Theodoric became Dietrich, and Hariman became Herman. (44)

Now that we have explained the origin of the roots used in German names, we might list some of them. It was mentioned that the Germans were a warlike people. Consequently, it is not surprising that their names often referred to war, weapons, and martial virtues, as well as to armies, victory, protection, and domination or rule. It is significant that the common German words *Schwert* (sword), *Schild* (shield), and *Speer* (spear), which were non-Indo-European, do not appear in old Germanic names. This confirms the theory that the old Germanic names were already composed in Indo-European times, before the Germans borrowed these three words, along with many maritime terms, from non-Indo-European neighbors. (45)

Among the name-roots designating battle were *badu*, *gund*, *hadu*, *hilti*, *not*, and *wic*, while *wal* designated a battleground. Among weapons we find *bart* (battle ax), *bil*, *brand*, and *ecke* (sword), *ger* (spear), *gies, giesel* and *ort* (point of spear or sword), *grim* (mask, helmet), *helm* (helmet), and *lind* and *rand* (shield). Among martial virtues we find *bald* (bold), *hart* (strong), *kuni* (brave), *mut* (courage), *neid* (hate), and *wille* (determination). *Macht* and *Megin* both meant "power" (as in "might and main"), as did *ellen* and *kraft*. *Diet* meant the folk, therefore Dietrich was the ruler of the folk, while Dietmar was famous among the people and Dietbald was brave among the people. *Liut*, related to English "liege," meant retinue and *volk* meant "people"; but, because all peoples were armed, *volk* also signified "army," as did *her*. It is to be noted that the ancient Germanic word for "folk" was the source of the Russian word *polk*, meaning "regiment."   (46)

Victory was expressed by *sieg*, protection by *burg, fried, wart,* and *wern*, and guardianship by *mund*, while mastery or rule was suggested by *wald* and *rich*. Pride in possessions is suggested by *arbi* (inheritance), *od* (treasure) and *uodal* (inherited lands). Since fame, the purpose of life, was best won on the battlefield, we find the roots *hruod* (illustrious), *mar* (renowned), *brecht* (bright), and *luod* (loud or illustrious). *Regin* (mind, intelligence) and *rat* (both council and counsel) can be classed as military terms, since councils were usually councils of war. Among the few peaceful concepts we find E *(law)*, *fruot* (wise), *hein* (home), *hold* (loyal to one's lord, cognate with "beholden"), *trut* (dear), *hug* (mind), and *win* (friend); and we also find *ans* and *god* (god) and *alb* or *alf* (elf).   (47)

Certain predatory animals and birds also deserved namesakes: *ar* or *arn* (eagle), *ram* and *hraben* (raven), *ber* (bear), *wolf* (wolf), and *lint* (dragon). Thus we get Arnold (*arn + hold*), Wolfram (*wolf + hraben*), Bermut (*ber + mut*). The wild boar (*ebur*), even though not predatory, was extremely brave and therefore offered the root found in Eberhart and many other names. Strangely, the harmless little hedgehog, the *igel*, also furnished the root in Igelhart, perhaps because of some shamanistic affinity, as was the case of *hirsch* (hart). Igelhart could, to be sure, derive from *igel* (hedgehog) and *hart* (stag), combining two creatures as are found in the names Wolfram (wolf + raven) and Arnolf (eagle + raven), but this is unlikely. The swan, although inoffensive, furnished the name-root *swan*, but at first only for women, as in Swanhild. The non-European

lion, when finally introduced by the Bible and literature, and
perhaps by royal menageries, supplied the first root in Leonhart, probably formed through analogy with Bernhart and
Wolfhart.   (48)

From the small sample of name-roots listed above we can
make innumerable compounds, such as Albwin, Ansgar,
Anshelm (St. Anselmus), Baldwin, Dietbald, Dietmar, Friedrich,
Gunther, Hadubrand, Helmbrecht, Helmut, Heribrand, Hildebrand, Luther, Meinhart, Reinhart, Siegfried, Sigismund,
Volker, Walther, Wernher, Willebald, and many more. Most of
these roots could occupy either the first or the second place in
the compound, for example, we find both Friedgund and
Gundfried and Gundhild and Hildegunde. However, some, like
diet, edel, and *sieg* could only occupy the first place, while some,
like *mund* (guardianship), could only occupy the second. As a
result, we find Siegmund and Dietrich but not Mundsieg or
Richdiet. Two popular roots, *engel* and *land,* now mean "angel"
and "land." If Engelhart was a pre-Christian name, then *engel*
must have had another meaning, perhaps the tribal name
"Angle." In Lambrecht *(landberacht)* and Roland *(Hrodoland),*
the root *land* must have had some meaning other than "land,"
perhaps "brave," or else it may have been corrupted from *nand*
(risk).   (49)

Not only men, but also women, bore warlike names, such as
Gertraut (spear + beloved), Gerwig (spear + battle), Gundhilt
(battle + battle), Hildegunde (battle + battle), Kriemhild (helmet
+ battle), Kunigunde (brave + battle), and Waltraut (battlefield
+ beloved). To be sure, Germanic women did not actually fight;
but in his *Germania* Tacitus tells us how the women accompanied their men into battle and acted as cheer leaders, war being
the chief sport of the time. Besides that, women could transmit
warlike virtues to their sons through their names; for, as we
have seen, names exerted a power of their own. Today most
Germans assume that Rosamund and Roselind mean Rose-
mouth and Rosegentle; but, in actuality, they are composed of
the root *hros* (warhorse) combined with *mund* (guardianship)
and *lind* (dragon or shield). The name Roswitha is now usually
interpreted as Rosewhite, whereas it really consisted of *hrodo*
(famous) and *switha* (swift, brave). A medieval dramatist nun
by that name was aware of the true meaning, for she called

herself *Clamor Validus*. Familiar with Latin, the clerics assumed that Rosamunda came from *rosa munda* (pure rose) and referred to the Virgin Mary. We will, however, devote little time to feminine names because this study is concerned only with surnames, which patriarchal societies generally derive from male progenitors. Nevertheless, some feminine names and words did produce place names, which, in turn, formed surnames. For example, the Virgin Mary gave the city name Marienborn (Mary's spring), which in turn gave the surname Marienborner; and the Nonnengasse (convent alley) gave the surnames Nonngasser and Nunnengasse.   (50)

In ancient days the two roots of an Indo-European name had usually reflected some mental association as in Adelbrecht (illustrious through birth), Wolfhart (as strong as a wolf), Sigismund (guardianship resulting from victory), and Dietrich (ruler of the people). In some cases the root *fried* would seem to contradict its partner, for example in Gundfried (battle peace) and Friedgund (peace battle). However, we should remember that war was the normal state: as Tacitus put it, a nation not at war was stagnating. Therefore we should not think that **frithu* (the earlier form of *fried*) had anything in common with the Christian concept of peace, rather it meant "protection" and even "defensive alliance." Consequently, Gundfried would suggest "security won through battle" and Friedrich would suggest "ruler of an alliance." Today most people think that a *Friedhof* (cemetery) is a place of peace, but actually it is a "protected yard," the German word *fried* in this context meaning "walled," as in *bergfried* (belfry). When I was a graduate student in Zurich, I took a room at a pension called the Fried-egg (pronounced freet eck and meaning walled field). The other Americans knew it only as the Fried Egg.   (51)

Whereas the name roots had once been meaningfully combined, in time the roots were chosen with no thought of logical connection. Each family had its favorite roots, which it attached at random to other roots, perhaps to those featured by the family with whom it was being allied through marriage. If a man named Wolfhart married a woman named Gertraut, they might name their son Wolfger, even though wolves do not use spears. Likewise, we find names like Arnolf (eagle + wolf) and Wolfram (wolf + raven), even though these creatures had different virtues. Also, there were tautologies like Richwald (ruler + ruler) and Hildegunde (battle + battle). Eventually the roots were combined entirely mechanically. Some of the old Germanic roots eventually coalesced; both Gerwalt (spear + rule) and Gerhold (spear + loyal) became Gerold. (52)

While Germanic names originally consisted of two roots, they were often shortened. For example, Adolf, Arnold, Bernhard, Gerhard, and Konrad could be shortened to Alf, Anno or Arnd, Benno or Bernd, Gert, and Kurt or Kunz. Likewise, Dietrich, Eberhart, Rudolf, and Uodalrich could give Dirk, Ewert, Rolf, and Uozo. Often a shortened form could have derived from any one of several longer forms: Otto might come from Otfried, Otmar, or Otward; Brand could have represented Hildebrand, Hadubrand, or Heribrand; and Wolf could have derived from Wolfbrecht, Wolfhart, or Wolfram. Often the shortened form of a name provided compound names. For example, Benshoff (Bernhard's farm) was derived from Bernhard via Benno. Names like Arnsdorf and Wolfshausen could mean "eagle village" and "wolf's houses," but they more likely mean "Arno's village" and "Wolf's village," being named for the founders rather than for animals. (53)

The shortened form was often a pet name (*Kosename*), yet it was officially valid even in the case of emperors. Surprisingly, Attila, the scourge of God, was known by a pet name, it being a diminutive of the Gothic word *Atta*, "father." After passing through the High German sound shift, it became the name Etzel, which has been brought to America as a surname. While Attila was a bogeyman in Western Europe, the Etzel of German legend was a generous overlord, whom it was an honor to serve, a sort of Arthur and Charlemagne combined. Pet names are often so far removed from their base forms as to be unrecognizable. One could hardly guess that Peg is a pet name from Margaret or that Ted and Teddy are pet names from either Edward or Theodore. Such metamorphoses did not occur in one fell swoop. Margaret was shortened to Marg, Marg became Meg, and then Meg became Peg. Similar steps occurred in forming pet names like Theiss from Matthias (via Thiass and Thiess) and Bartel from Bartholomaeus. In time these pet names became surnames. Sometimes the shortened form is not immediately recognizable because it went back to an earlier form of the name. The English name Hank and the German name Heink do not look like Henry and Heinrich, but they do look somewhat like the earlier forms Henrik and Heinrik. Likewise, Utley scarcely resembles Ulrich, whereas the older form Utli does have something in common with *Uod* in the older form *Uodalrich*.   (54)

The very terms "pet name" and "shortened form" must be used advisedly. When one says Bill instead of William, it may show affection, but it may also show mere laziness, in which case it is actually only a shortened form. It would be difficult to ascertain the precise nature and degree of affection expressed by the names in the well-known lines, "Father calls me William, Mother calls me Will, Sister calls me Willie, but the fellows call me Bill." Heintzelein can hardly be called a "shortened" form of Heinrich. In my childhood gang there was a boy named John, but we called him Johnny with the Nubbin on the End of his Nose "for short." In the early stages of this book I used the term "pet name," but gradually I replaced it with the symbol < , meaning "derived from," thus leaving it to the reader to decide whether or not the shortened form indicated affection. It will be noted that pet names are often diminutives: a small man may refer to his wife as "the little woman" (*die Kleine*), where the diminutive denotes endearment, not stature. In German the main diminutives are *ke, kin,* and *je* in the far north, *chen* and *gen* in the central regions, *lein* and *le* in the south, and *li* in Switzerland.   (55)

As the Roman Empire crumbled in the fifth and sixth centuries and the northern barbarians invaded Britain, Gaul, Spain, and Italy, they brought their names with them to the lands they conquered. The names of the invaders, as the ruling class, were soon adopted by many of the conquered populaces, with dire results for the names. Most of all, the Romanized Celts in France could not master the harsh consonants of the invaders' names and dropped many of them. Thus Henrik became Henri, Theodoric became Thierry, and Willihalm became Guillaume. Most of the names that we consider typically French today were once Germanic: Albert (Athalbrecht), Arnaud (Arnhold), Bertram (Berachtram), Gautier (Walthari), Louis (Hludowics), Renault (Reginwald), Robert (Hrothoberacht), Roger (Hrothgar), Roland (Hrotholand), and Thibault (Dietbald).

The same held for Italy, where we find Alberto, Arnoldo, Enrico, Gualtieri, Guido (Wido), Gulielmo, Leonardo (Leonhard), Ludovigo, Orlando, Ottone (Otto), Rinaldo (Reginwald), Ruggiero (Hrothogar), Umberto (Hunberacht or Helmbrecht), and a host of others. In Spain, the most common names, such as Alfonso (*athel + fons*, noble + ready) and Hernandez (*fardi + nantha*, journey + risk) were inherited from the Gothic invaders. (56)

After the Norman invasion of England in 1066, most Anglo-Saxon names (still clearly Germanic) were replaced by French cognates. These were no longer so clearly Germanic as they had been after being introduced into Gaul by the Frankish invaders. Instead of Hrothgar, Athelbrecht, and Reginwald, we therefore find Roger, Albert, and Reynold. (57)

CHAPTER TWO

Surnames - Their Need and Origin

As the population increased after the migrations, it became necessary to distinguish between the various individuals in the community who shared a common name. This could be done, among other ways, by reference to a person's parentage, his residence, a terrain or topographical feature near his dwelling, his profession, his employer, his appearance, or his behavior.

(58)

In Scandinavia, a man was often designated as the son of his father. Niel, the son of Lars, would be called Niel Larson, but his son Peer would be Peer Nielson, not Peer Larson. The same system of patronymics was once common in Germany. Arnold's son Berthold might have been designated Arnolds Berthold or Berthold Arnolds, just as Hinrich's son Hans might have been called Hans Hinrichs or Hans Hinrichssen. In the case of names like Arnolds and Hinrichs, the *s* eventually became a fixed part of the name and no longer suggested first generation descent. In other words, Heinz Hinrichs may have been the son of Hinrichs and the grandson of Hinrich, just as Felix Mendelssohn was the son of Mendelssohn, not of Mendel. Names sometimes indicated employment rather than descent, as in the case of the ecclesiastical names Pabst, Bischof, and Moench. The same was sometimes true of other names that could be mistaken for patronymics. While Hubers Hans, or Hans Huber, was probably Huber's son, he might also have been Huber's hired hand, as everyone in the village would know. (59)

As family names became fixed, Huber's Hans may have adopted the surname Huber and transmitted it to his children, even if they served other families. A similar phenomenon occurred in the American South after emancipation. The slaves had no surnames; they were known as "the Pinckney's Jim" or "the Middleton's Jupiter." As freedmen, these two may have become Jim Pinckney and Jupiter Middleton, unless they preferred to choose the names of neighboring planters. The surname Hubers could possibly come from the place name Hubers, a shortened form for Hubershof (Huber's farm). Although patronymics were the rule, there were a few cases of metronymics, or surnames from the mother, perhaps from a widow or an unwed mother. Examples are Elsohn (Else's son), Figge (Sophia's son), Grett (Margaretha's son), and Anneshansli (Anna's Hans).   (60)

Noble families customarily assumed the name of their chief castle, as was the case of the Hapsburgs and Hohenzollerns. The owners of Wolkenstein Castle were the von Wolkensteins, or the Wolkensteiners. However, if they sold Wolkenstein Castle and moved elsewhere, they dropped their old appellative and took on the name of their new seat. Even humble people could sometimes be identified by the names of their residences: for example, the Josef who lived in Straatmannshaus was sometimes called Josef Straatmann, but only as long as he lived there. If he sold the house, the buyer received the name Straatmann along with the house. Already in the thirteenth century a German poet named Heinrich Hessler explained that Heinrich was his right name and that Hessler was the name of his house. It is understandable that the inventor of moveable type wished to be known by the name of his house, Gutenberg (good mountain), rather than by his true name, Gensfleisch (goose flesh).   (61)

The name of the house sometimes appeared on a shield in front of the house with an illustration for the benefit of illiterates. These illustrations often had religious significance: not only the angel but also the eagle, lion, lamb, and ox had religious significance, they being the creatures that accompanied the four Evangelists in church art. If the house sign hung before a business establishment, it often designated the wares sold or the services rendered; and this explains many German names such as Fisch (fish) or Tuchscherer (cloth shearer).   (62)

Sometimes a man was named for his place of business. If a tavern were called *zum Goldenen Loewen* (to the Golden Lion), *zum Rothen Hirsch* (to the Red Stag), or *zum Schwarzen Adler* (to the Black Eagle), the proprietor might have been called Loewe, Hirsch, or Adler. Regardless of the name of the establishment, the proprietor (*Wirt*) might be called Wirt or Wirth, or else Krug, Krueger, or Krieger, since the word *Krug* (pitcher) often designated a pub. Regardless of what the dictionary might say about the word *Krieger*, the name Krieger did not designate a soldier. Since taverners hung out a sprig of greenery to announce the arrival of new wine, they might be called Zweig (branch), or Busch (bush). According to popular wisdom, such advertisement should be unnecessary because "good wine needs no bush." (63)

Many years ago a German colleague of mine named Busch, seeing my interest in names, suggested that I run an advertisement in the *New York Times* offering to interpret names. I did so; and the first request I received was from a widow named Busch. Suspecting that she might not care to have had a husband descended from tavern keepers, I answered that the name Busch could be either the sprig hanging in front of a tavern or else the *Helmbusch*, or crest on a knight's helmet. It is easy to guess which interpretation she preferred. (64)

The words *Haus* (house) and *Haeuser* (the occupant of a house) provided many names. Since most people lived in houses, these simple words would have had little power of differentiation, so we can assume that the present names Haus, Haeuser, and Heuser are usually shortened forms of compounds such as Althaus (old house), Neuhaus (new house), or Scheraus (house where cloth or sheep are sheared). The American forester family Weyerhaeuser once lived in a house by a *Weiher* or fish pond (from Latin *vivarium*). Whereas the word *Haeuser* is now the plural of *Haus*, it used to denote the occupant, not the plural, of *Haus*. The plural used to be the same as the singular (*hus*), as is indicated by dative plural place names like Holthusen, Schaffhausen (sheep houses) and Niederhausen (lower houses). If one dwelled on a road, one might be called Gass, Gassner, or Gessner, or else Bahn or some name ending in *weg*. (65)

In parts of Germany *aeu* and *eu* are pronounced like English "eye" (remember the Tannenbaum, a branch of which *freut* [gives joy] even in winter when it *schneit* [snows]). Therefore Haeuser is often pronounced Hizer, as in the case of James Lighthizer (from Leithaeuser), a county executive in Maryland, and also in the name Anhaeuserbusch, which recalls the ditty:

A boy fell off Anhaeuserbusch
And tore his pants to Schlitz.
He rose a sad Budweiser boy.
Pabst yes and Pabst no.

The baseball player Orel Hershiser's name derived from Hirschhaeuser, or "stag houses." Since the American name

Rukeyser would make no sense if divided into *ru* and *keyser*, it must have been Ruckheyser, meaning the occupant of a house on a ridge.   (66)

As in the case of Rukeyser, families were often designated by the terrain features near which they lived, such as hills, dales, mountains, valleys, fields, and forests. If a Johann lived near a *buehl* (hill), he might be called Johann Buehl, or Buehler (and in America Beeler or Bealer). Or if, as was usually the case, the hill was more precisely defined, such as Kraehbuehl (crow hill), then the resulting name would be Kraehbuehl (in America, Craybill, Greybill, and some forty other forms). If a man lived at, but not on, the *Buehl*, he might be called Ambuehl (in America, also Ample). Another kind of hill is a *kofel*, a sort of monticule or projection jutting up from the slope of a mountain, which might give a man living on it the name of Kofler. If there were two such chimney-like projections, an upper one (*Oberkofel*) and a lower one (*Unterkofel*), they might furnish the names Oberkofler and Unterkofler or Oberkaufer and Unterkaufer.
                                                                    (67)

Far more numerous, of course, are names derived from *berg*, the commonest name for mountain. In addition to many families named Berg and Berger, there were far more named for specific mountains, such as Oberberg, Unterberg, Gruenberg, Silberberg, Koenigsberg, Heidelberg, and hundreds of others. In Switzerland, Austria, and Bavaria, where there are many mountains, names in *berg* and *berger* are especially frequent. The peak of the mountain was the *Horn*, as in Berghorn and Matterhorn, and the ridge was the *kamm* (comb) or the *ruecken* (back).   (68)

The surnames based on terrain features or place names had at first been preceded by the preposition *von*, as in von Oberberg; but in time the preposition was dropped in most of Germany by all but the nobility and became a sign of rank. Commoners were satisfied with the name Oberberg or Oberberger. Nevertheless, some people, especially in Switzerland and along the Netherlands border, retained the *von* with no pretensions to nobility, as in the case of Von der Weit and Vonholt. Other prepositions, like *in* and *zu* were also usually dropped, though they occasionally remain as in Indorf and Inhoff. In dem Winkel (in the wooded valley) became Winkel or Winkler, and zem Stege (at the sty) became Steg or Steger. The name Austermuehle means "out of the mill," not "Oyster Mill." (69)

Sometimes the preposition was not entirely lost, as when zum Eichelsweg (at the acorn path) became Meichelsweg and when in den Eichen (in the oaks) became Neichen (just as in English "a nadder" became "an adder" and "an ickname" became "a nickname"). In the case of Admiral Zumwald the preposition has remained, as it has also in the names Vomberg (from the mountain) and Vormwald (before the forest). The preposition and article have regularly remained in Dutch names like Vandergrift, Vanderbilt, and van der Ren. Similar phenomena appear in English names like Attenborough and Atterbury, both meaning "at the borough." (70)

Since most flat lands in Germany are cultivated, the forests are largely on mountain ranges. As a result, the word *wald* (forest) usually designates a mountain range, as is the case of the Schwarzwald (Black Forest), Boehmerwald (Bohemian Forest), and Thueringer Wald (Thuringian Forest). In and near Austria a steep slope is a *Leite*, a word giving the names Leite, Leitner (Lightner in America), Hangleitner, etc. This name has an exact English equivalent in the name Banker, which denotes not a financier but a man who lives on a bank or slope. A person occupying a house on a *Leite* would be a Leithaeuser (the previously mentioned Lighthizer). Other names for slopes are *Fuhr, Gaeh, Gand, Halde, Ruetsche, Schief, Schrudde,* and *Stechen.* A man residing on or near a *Stade* (landing) might be called Stade, just as a man living near a bridge might be called Brueckner and a man living near a church might be called Kircher or Kirchner. (71)

There are relatively few name roots denoting forests. The most frequent is the root *wald* (cognate with English "wold" as in the Cotswolds). While *wald* always means "forest" in later names like Waldhausen, it must be differentiated from the older root *wald* meaning "rule," as in Walther (rule + army). A low or scrubby forest was a *busch*, as in Buschmann or Buschkirch (dweller or church in the low woods). A *horst* (cognate with the place-name root *hurst* in Lakehurst and Pinehurst) was a general word for a small forest or grove, whereas now it suggests an aerie or even a small military airbase, as in

Fliegerhorst. A *hain* or *hein* was a grove, as in Hainmueller and Heindorf.   (72)

A rocky summit or crag was a *Stein* (stone), which was a good position for a castle, so we find castles with names like Steinfels (stone cliff), Steinburg (stone castle), and Altenstein (old mountain). In most names of this kind the root *stein* refers to a mountain, and therefore it is so translated in our appended list even though, in some cases, the root *stein* could have referred to the castle itself, which was inevitably built of stone. Logic suggests that *Steinberg* means "stone mountain," whereas *Bergstein* means "mountain rock." A man dwelling on or near a *Stein* might be named Stein or Steiner (in America often Stine, Stone, and Stoner). Whereas the ancient German fortress had been made of wood, the medieval castle (*burg*) was always of stone.   (73)

In the name Steinert the last consonant is not part of the root: it is merely an excrescent *t*, that is, a *t* that formed to interrupt the *r*, which was still trilled in Germany at the time surnames were being introduced. In some names the root *stein* does not designate a cliff or crag, but merely a mineral substance, as in Steinhauer (stone carver) and *Edelstein* (noble stone, jewel). Other terms for hills, mountains, peaks, and ridges are *Boll*, *Brink*, *Gipfel*, *Huebel*, *Huegel*, *Kamm*, *Knoll*, *Kopf*, *Kuppe*, *Nase*, and *Stauf.*   (74)

This might be an appropriate time to explain why there is so often a dative ending on the adjective describing a terrain feature, such as the *en* suffixed to the *alt* in the name Altenstein. This goes back to the previously mentioned days when place names were still preceded by a preposition, as was formerly the case in English tavern names such as "To the Red Rose." Originally, one would have said "at the old stone" (*zum alten stein* or *am alten stein*); and in both cases the place name would end up as Altenstein. The same would hold of Breitenbach (*zum breiten bach*, "at the broad brook") and Neuemburg (*zur neuen burg*, "at the new castle.")   (75)

Names were suggested not only by hills and mountains, but also by valleys, the most frequent root being the *Tal* (formerly *Thal*) which is found in Rosenthal, Lilienthal, and Thalmann. In Alpine regions a bowl-like valley is a *gruob*, and a man dwelling in one might be dubbed Gruber. A narrow gorge is a

Schlund, so the Heinrich living in or near one may have been called Heinrich Schlund. (76)

People were often designated by the stream or creek on which they lived. As in the case of the name Berg, the name Bach (brook) was often a shortened form of a compound name. The appended list of names contains scores of compounds containing *bach*, examples being Auerbach, Bacher, Bachmann, and Rauschbach. In Pennsylvania the name Bach and its compounds are often written as Baugh because the English scribes knew the sound *ch* only in Scots names. These still retained the sound and indicated it with *gh*, whereas the sound had long since ceased in English and survived only in the archaic spelling of words like "through" and "though." Unfortunately, the first syllable of these Pennsylvania names with *baugh* are often corrupted beyond recognition. In Pennsylvania the names Bach and Bacher also appear as Pack and Packer. (77)

A *Bach* is sometimes larger than a brook: one would translate *Forellenbach* as "trout stream," rather than as "trout brook," just as a *Rauschbach* would be a "rushing stream" rather than a "rushing brook." An *Altmuehlbach* would surely be an "old mill stream" rather than an "old mill brook." In personal names, the ending *bach* was practically interchangeable with *becker*. A family living on the Winsbach could call itself either Winsbach or Winsbeker. (As we shall see, when standing alone the name Becker most often meant a baker.) The foot-crossing through a brook was a *furt* or *fort*, as in Frankfurt. (78)

The word *Ach*, which is cognate with Latin *aqua* (water) and designates a river, is found in many place names such as Charlemagne's capital Aachen and in Achebach and Anderach. This ending *ach* has now coalesced with the ending *ach* from *achi* (terrain) as in Steinach (stone terrain) and Dornach (thorny area) and also with *ach* from Latin *acum* (estate) as in Breisach and Andernach. Other words for streams are *born* and *bronn*, both of which appear in American names such as Aalborn (eel stream) and Bornemann (stream man). The word *brunnen*, which designated either a spring or a well, is found in the names Brunner and Brunnholtz. Many people took the name of the river near which they resided, as in the case of Johannes Tauber and Rembrandt van Ryn. An island in a river

is a *Werde* (also written Wert and Woerth), which is cognate
with the English root *worth*.   (79)

Although Germany has been well drained for the last few
centuries, it was, as Tacitus reported, a land of vast swamps. As
a result we find many name-roots referring to marshes, bogs,
and swamps such as *Bruehl, Bruch, Lache, Mar, Mies, Moor,
Moos, Ohl, Pfutze, Pfuhl, Schlade, Schlier, Siech, Seifen, Struth,*
and *Sutte.* Unfortunately, it is not possible to translate names
containing these roots precisely without knowing from which
areas their bearers came. For example, the word *bruch* (in Low
German spelled *brock, broek,* and *brook,* and cognate with
English "brook" and "brake") had various meanings, but it
usually meant a damp clearing in a swampy forest. Since that
definition is too cumbersome, we will translate it as "brake" as
in "canebrake." The same name, Bruch, can also designate a
quarry. The root *mar* meaning "swamp," as in Marbach and
Marburg, should not be confused with the root *mar* meaning
"famous," as found in Dietmar and Marbold. It is to be remem-
bered that a surname like Marbach may commemorate a place
that had long been drained before the name was assumed.(80)

A marsh or bog is often indicated by a root meaning reeds or
bullrushes, as in the case of *riet* and *reth* in Riet and Rethmeyer. The concept of "marsh mountain" sounds contradictory,
yet we find it expressed by the names Hallenberg, Kellenberg,
Marberg, Mosberg, Morsberger, Moersberger and many more.
The name suggests a hill rising out of a marsh or swamp, as is
expressed by our Southern word "hammock" (for hummock).
However, in some areas there are actually marshes (*moor*) on
the tops of mountains, as in the Sauerland Mountains of
Westphalia. The word *mor* should not be confused with English
"moor," which usually denotes a dry heath, which in German is
a *Heide.*   (81)

To drain the many marshes, one had to dig many ditches and
build many dams and dikes (*dam, dick, diek*). The High German
cognate *Teich* means not the dike but the pond behind it, or any
pond. A *lache* can be a pond as well as a bog, and a *fizer* or
fuetze (from Latin *puteus*) could be either a pond or a puddle. A
See is not a sea, but a lake. In marshy areas the word *Berg* is
only relative. In Alpine regions it designates a sizeable pile of
rocks and earth, but on the North German coastal plain it

might be more modest, as in the case of Koenigsberg and Wittenberg. Similarly the root *brink* is translated here as "hill," while it may mean an area in a marsh elevated just enough to remain dry and arable. (82)

A large number of surnames may be based on river names even if they have other meanings as well. For example, the name Tauber could suggest the raiser or seller of pigeons, but it may also designate a dweller on the River Tauber. Like many other rivers in western and southern Germany, the Tauber may have derived its name from a Celtic word. Just as most American rivers have Indian rather than European names, many German rivers have pre-Germanic names, mostly Celtic, some of which, in turn, derived from earlier Ligurian names. The Germanic invaders learned the names of the streams, swamps, hills, etc. from the Celtic inhabitants of the areas they occupied, but they did not understand their meanings. Therefore they added the words for stream, swamp, and hill to the native name. This gave forms like *albach, ascbach,* and *erbach,* which were eventually folk-etymologized into Allenbach (eel brook), Eschbach (ash tree brook), and Erlbach (alder brook). Of course, some brooks named Allenbach, Eschbach, and Erlbach may have first been named by German-speaking people and therefore not be a case of folk-etymology. (83)

Many names were based on words for fields or pastures. The words *Acker* and *Feld* (field) supplied many American names such as Acker, Ackers, and Ackerman, as well as Feld, Felder, Feldman, and Rheinfelder. Low land, usually lying along a body of water, was an *au,* as in Reichenau on Lake Constance and also in the surnames Aumann and Aumueller. A man living on an *au* was an *auer,* as in Reitenauer and Rheinauer. Another word for meadow was *Wiese,* and a man living on it was a Wiessner or a Wiesmann. Only in Switzerland does one find *matt* (cognate with English mead and meadow), which designated a meadow that was mowed and is found in the surname Durrenmatt. The word *Weide* denoted a pasture, as in the name Fuellenweide (foals meadow); and so did the word *Anger,* as in names like Anger, Angermann, and Angermeyer. Smaller than a field is a *Garten* (garden), which may be a *Baumgarten* (orchard), two words that furnish many names such as Gaertner

and Baumgaertner. If the field was fenced in, it gave names like
Bantner, Bunde, and Painter.   (84)

One very common root is hard to define, namely, *eck* (corner),
as in the previously mentioned *Friedegg*. Although the meaning
"corner" is often acceptable, the root *eck* (or *egg*) often has a
vague meaning of "place," as in the expression *in allen Ecken*
(cf. "In every corner under the sun"), where no angle is implied.
Therefore, it will be rendered as "place" in the following list. A
man's name sometimes reflected the direction in which he lived
from the major town, such as Nord (north), Nordhoff (northern
farm), Ost (east), Ostberg (eastern mountain), Sudler (southerner), Sudhoff (southern farm), Westdorf (western village), and
Westenfeld (western field).   (85)

The reader is reminded that onomastics is not an exact
science but sometimes requires an educated guess. While *eck*
clearly means "corner" in the word *Eckstein*, the name Eckhof
could mean either "corner farm," or more likely, "oak farm," the
latter being more likely because of varients like Eichhof,
Eickhof, and Eykhof. In the old Germanic name Eckhard, *eck*
definitely means "sword."   (86)

It will be noted that many surnames based on terrain features
end with the agent suffix *er* (from Latin *arius*). This was
especially common in South Germany, especially in Austria,
with the result that, when the Salzburger Protestants were
banished in 1731 and settled in East Prussia, the natives there
assumed that all people whose names ended in *er* must be
Salzburgers. Names like Acher, Bacher, Gruber, Kofler, and
Steiner usually implied that the bearer was the proprietor of a
farm at the said terrain feature: if he sold the farm, he left the
name with it and took on the name of his new abode. The *er*
ending often developed an excresent *T*, as in Bachert and
Steinert.   (87)

In English it is easy to distinguish in writing between a
terrain feature and a proper name, because only the latter is
capitalized. For example, we say "he went to the white oaks,"
but also "he went to White Oaks." The difficulty in distin-
guishing between *Flurnamen* (terms for terrain features) and
proper names is well illustrated in the boundary descriptions
(*Markbeschreibungen*) found in medieval documents describing
the lands donated to monasteries and other religious organiza-

tions. Most of these descriptions were written in Latin, only the terrain features and place names being left in German; the Wurzburg boundary descriptions are an exception, being written solely in German. In tracing the boundaries of the donated lands, these valuable documents name numerous terrain features that now appear in American names, including: *acha* (river), *berg* (mountain), *brunno* (spring), *buohha* (beeches), *clingo* (rapid stream), *furt* (ford), *gruoba* (round valley), *houc* (hill), *loh* (low forest), *ror* (reeds), *seo* (lake), *sol* (pond), *stein* (mountain), and *struot* (swamp). (88)

Rural people often derived their names from the kind of trees they lived among or near. If one of two Josefs lived near the oaks while the other lived near the linden, then the first might have been called Josef Eichner or Aichner and the second Josef Linde or Lindner. Similarly, a man named Erlenhaus must have lived in a house among the alders, while a man named Eschenbach may have lived on a brook with overhanging ash trees, if not one containing *Aesche* (graylings). A farmer living among the birches might be called Birkenmeyer, or just Birk, Birker, or Birkli. A man named Ulmer may have lived near the elms, unless possibly his forebears had come from the city of Ulm. The word *Tanne* (fir), which is found in names like Tannenbaum and Tanhoeffer, also appears as in Dannenbaum and Danhoeffer. Because firs are the dominant tree in some areas, the root sometime merely connotes a forest of any kind, not just of firs. Although the word *Kiefer* denotes both a pine tree and a jaw bone, the name Kieffer, as we shall see, most often meant a barrel maker. In the case of fruit trees and fruit, like Apfelbaum and Birnbaum, the name probably signifies the pertinent orchard owner or fruit dealer. Only a few names are derived from blossoms and flowers, such as Ahle (honey-suckle), Blum (flower), Eisenhut (monk's hood), and Mohn (poppy).(89)

When I was swimming on the University of Heidelberg swimming team shortly after the Berlin Olympics of 1936, the latest and most popular backstroke was the "Kieffer stroke." Seeing no connection with pine trees, we concluded that the stroke got its name from the fact that the swimmer had to thrust up his chin in order to lower his head and thereby raise his legs for a flutter kick. Years passed before I learned that the stroke was named for its innovator, an American swimmer at the '36 Olympics, who had inherited his name from some German barrel maker. And this leads us to names derived from professions. (90)

The two oldest professions, for men, were hunting and fishing, which have given the names Jaeger and Fischer (Yeager and Fisher in America). In the late Middle Ages, when surnames were first being assumed, the fundamental profession was agriculture, which occupied about ninety-five percent of the population, rather than the five percent it occupies today in the developed nations. Consequently, many families were named Ackermann (field man), Bauer and Baumann (farmer), Felder or Feldmann (field man), and Pflug or Pflueger (plowman). The farmer's name might have derived from the nature of his farm. If he had one *huob* (hide of land), then he was a Huber; if he cultivated a *Schweighof* (cattle farm), then he was a Schweiger, Schwaiger, Schweighof, or Schweighofer (in America Swiger, Swiggert, or Swaggert, again with excrescent *t*). The name is not related to the noun *Schweiger*, meaning a silent man. A farmer might be named after the major crop he grew, such as Gerste (barley), Haffe (oats), or Weitzen (wheat). A husbandryman was often named for the kind of beast or fowl he raised: for example Gais (goat), Kalb (calf), Lamm (lamb), Ochs (ox), Stier (steer), Stehr (wether), and Ziege (goat) or Ante or Entemann (duck raiser), Huhn (chicken), and Gans or Goos (goose). As mentioned, all of these could have been house names with signs illustrating the occupant's profession. (91)

Many families received their names from the word *Hoff*, which originally meant a farmyard. The ancient Germanic king, who was merely the foremost peasant of the kinship, also had a *Hof*, which was larger than the other *Bauernhoefe*. Eventually the king's court, or *Koenigshof*, became more elegant, with many a *Hofmann*, or courtier, in attendance, such as the *Hofmeister,* or steward of the royal household. These words are now spelled with one *f* to show that the *o* is long (as in "hope"); but they used to have double *f*, as still found in most American names derived from them, such as Althoff, Althoffer, Hoffmann, and Neuhoff. (92)

Perhaps the most common name designating a farmer was Meyer or Mayer, which also had many other meanings. The word derived from the Latin word *major domus*, or the keeper of the household. At first it referred to an important official who was more or less the business manager of the kingdom or the castle. Later it also referred to the bailiff who managed an estate or farm. Eventually it denoted any large farmer. Since this was the most usual meaning at the time that surnames were being formed, that is the way it is rendered in the appended list of names. A thirteenth-century Austrian tale called *Meier Helmbrecht* tells of a peasant lad who wished to become a knight but met a sad end. The story is misnamed, the lad is not a *meier:* his father, who is casually mentioned at the beginning, is the *meier*, a position the son would have inherited only at his father's death or retirement. (93)

The name Meyer was so common that it became the equivalent of *mann*, in fact, even interchangeable with it, so that a man could be called either Kuhlmann or Kuhlmeyer. In a few cases, the suffix *mann* still designated a vassal or follower. It will be seen that many Jews took the name Meyer, perhaps because of its similarity with the Hebrew name Meir, the name of a famous medieval scholar. Sometimes *mann* had no significance at all: Til and Tilmann were the same name, as were Litz and Litzmann, all of them having been derived from Dietrich and Ludwig. Likewise, *mann* and *er* were equivalent in names like Bacher--Bachmann, Felder--Feldmann, and Aicher--Aichmann. Names like Neumeyer and Neumann do not imply that the farmer was new but rather that he was the proprietor of the Neuhoff, or New Farm. Likewise, a Waldmeyer or Waldbauer did not have to live in a forest, he may have been the proprietor of the Waldhoff, which had once been in the woods before the surrounding forests had been cleared. Another word for farmer was *Hausmann*, literally "house man." That this word meant "farmer" was proved when the Dutch humanist Roelof Huysman latinized his name as Agricola. (94)

If a countryman owned no land, he may have been a *Schaefer* (shepherd), *Hirt* or *Hirte* (herdsman), or, in Switzerland, a *Senn*. Or else he many have been a *Holtzhacker* (woodcutter), *Kohlenbrenner* (charcoal burner), or *Aschenbrenner* (ash burner). There were many other professions open to landless people, such as finding wild honey (Zeidler) or gathering faggot (Ast). But this leads to the subject of more specialized trades. The ancient Germans lived in large family units, which provided most of their domestic needs. The non-warriors, meaning the women, children, elderly men, and serfs, not only farmed but also produced most of the goods and artifacts needed in their culture. Gradually, certain individuals became adept at certain crafts and supplied goods not only for their own family group but also for neighbors and even strangers, with the result that the craft became a full time profession. In this case the person practicing the profession often assumed the name of the trade he practiced. (95)

Because of constant warfare, smiths were essential for making and repairing weapons; and secret powers were ascribed to them so that the name Schmidt was held in awe. Later there were other smiths, such as the *Hufschmidt* (blacksmith), *Nagelschmidt* (nailsmith), *Blechschmidt* (sheet metal smith), and *Messerschmidt* (knife smith or cutler). As a consequence there were many names including the root *eisen* denoting the people who produced or sold iron. Among other surnames designating professions we find Brauer (brewer), Binder, Fassbinder, or Boettcher (cooper), Gerber (tanner), Reeper and Seiler (rope maker), Schneider and Schroeder (tailor), Schumacher (shoemaker), Wagner (wainwright), Weber (weaver), and Zimmermann (carpenter). In addition we find hosts and taverners (Wirth and Kruger) and musicians and entertainers such as Geiger (fiddler), Trommer (drummer), Harfner (harpist), Tanzer (dancer) and Gauckler (acrobat). (96)

As time passed, the trade could become more specialized, the brewer could be *Bierbrauer* (beer brewer) and the tanner could be a *Weissgerber* or a *Rotgerber*, depending on whether he cured white or red leather. This might be cut into straps or belts by a *Riemenschneider*, or strap cutter. As the weaver became more specialized, he might employ a *Scherer* or *Tuchscherer* (cloth shearer) to cut off the Irish pennants protruding from his cloth. While the tanner prepared raw hides, the *Kirschner* or *Kuerschner* (furrier) prepared fine furs. In all these cases the profession was originally in apposition to the person and required a definite article: Peter der Schuster (Peter the shoemaker), Hans der Schneider (Hans the tailor), etc. (97)

The ancient Germans built their houses of wood, as is proved by Germanic roots in American names like Ahle (awl), Hammer (hammer), and Naegel (nails). Other names from carpentry are

Drexler or Drechsler (turner), Tischler (cabinet maker), and Zimmermann (carpenter). The *l* in *Tischler* is not part of the root as it is in *Drechsler* and *Sattler* (saddler), which are composed of *Drechsel* and *Sattel* and the agent ending *er*. By error, names (and words) like Drechsler and Sattler were wrongfully divided into Drechs-ler and Satt-ler, thus causing people to think that *ler* was a functional agent-ending to be added to other roots like *tisch* (from Latin *discus*). The same faulty division was made of names like Gaert-ner (from *Garten*) and Oef-ner (from *Ofen*), thus producing a new agent-ending *ner,* which appeared in the recently mentioned names Lindner and Kirchner. As we have seen, the same phenomenon occurred in English when "a nadder" was erroneously divided into "an adder" and "an ickname" became "a nickname." (98)

Whereas most carpentry terms were of Germanic origin, the Germans did borrow the Roman word *scrinarius*, which designated a skilled joiner and later became the word and name Schreiner. In old Germanic sagas and ballads, the *burg* or borough was always made of wood, with the result that many feuds ended in a *Saalbrand* (hall fire), when the defenders chose to die in the flames rather than come out and surrender. After suffering raids from the Magyars in the tenth century, the Germans learned how to build stone fortifications like those of the Mediterranean and Arabic nations. (99)

Masonry was one of the most important skills learned from the Romans. The Latin word *murus* (wall) gave German *Mauer*, which in turn gave the word for a mason (*Maurer*), who might also be called a *Steinmetz*. (On the other hand, Hans Maurer may not have been a mason, he may have just lived on, or against, the city wall, in which case he would first have been called Hans auf der Mauer.) The Germans did, however, coin words from their own language for these imported skills: a stone cutter was a *Steinhauer* (stone hewer), a quarryman was a *Steinbrecher* (stone breaker), and a brickmaker was a *Steinbrenner* (stone burner). The ending *hauer* (cognate with English "to hew"), usually denoted someone who hacked or chopped, such as an Eisenhauer (metal cutter, armor smasher), Fleischhauer (butcher), and Holtzhauer (wood cutter); yet in some cases the basic meaning of to hack was lost and the ending *hauer* merely denoted a maker or manufacturer, as in Fadenhauer (thread-maker), Fasshauer (barrel maker), Haushauer (house builder), and Schildhauer, which means either the maker or breaker of shields.   (100)

Upon occupying old Roman territory, the barbarian invaders learned many other skills they had never known or had practiced only crudely; and they often kept the Roman word, which in many cases went through the High German sound shift along with their native vocabulary. This was the case of the Latin word *cuparius* (barrel + maker), which gave the English name Cooper. Altered by the High German sound shift, it became Kuefer or, in southern dialects, Kiefer or Kieffer, as in the aforementioned "Kieffer stroke." When the Latin word *catila* (kettle) went through the soundshift, it came out as *kessel*, which gave the name Kessler (maker or repairer of kettles). Likewise, the Latin word *tegula* (tile) passed through the soundshift to become *Ziegel*, which gave the professional name Ziegler (tiler or brickmason).   (101)

Perhaps Roman cooks were more skilled than German cooks, for the present German word for cook, *Koch*, is derived from Latin *coquus*, just as the name Pfister (baker) is derived from Latin *pistor*. The Germans also acquired two new words for "butcher": *Metzger* (from *matiarius*) and Metzler (from *macellarius*). A *Kellner* was the keeper of the wine cellar (*Keller*, from Latin *cellarium*). Tacitus tells us that the Germans had no wine, so they must have acquired all their art of viticulture from the Romans. The German word *Wein* was derived from Latin *vinum*, and the word *Winzer* (vintner) from *vinitor*, while the seller of wine, the *vinumcaupo*, ultimately gave the names Weinkauf and Weinkop. Tacitus makes it clear that, while the Germans had no wine, they did have beer. Nevertheless, the German word *Bier*, like English "beer," is derived from Latin *bibere* (to drink).   (102)

The name Mueller (from Latin *molinarius*) also reflects the Romans' more advanced technology, for the ancient Germans still had only the *quirn* (English "quern") or hand mill. Because there were so many kinds of mills, the name Miller was as common as the name Meyer. The millers often acquired their names from the spot along the stream where their mills were located, such as Aumueller (mill on the meadow), Waldmueller (mill at the forest), etc. Apparently meaningless miller-names may have been shortened forms. While a Weissmueller ground white flour and a Braunmueller ground brown flour, it is unlikely that Schwartzmueller ground black flour (even if his brown flour became blackbread). It is more likely that his mill stood on the Schwartzbach and that he had first been called the Schwartzbachmueller. (103)

Before the advent of store-bought clothes and shoes, tailors and shoemakers were in great demand and supply. The word *Schneider* originally meant "cutter," being analogous with the Old French word *tailleur*, from which we get "tailor." Another word for tailor was *Schroeder*, so that there are many American families named Schneider, Snyder, Shroder, and Schroeder (usually pronounced, and sometimes written, as Shrader). The most usual word for a shoemaker (and the source of the English word) was *Schumacher*, while the words *Schumann* and *Schubert* were also common. The Latin word *sutor* gave the German word *Schuster*. A man trained only to repair shoes, but not to make them, was a *Flickschuster*, which gives the American name Flick. As in the case of surnames based on place names and house names, professional names were not fixed initially. If Hans Schuster's son Heintz became a baker, he would become Heintz Beck or Heintz Becker, not Heintz Schuster. In time, however, professional names, like other names, became fixed and the cooper Carl Zimmermann may have inherited his name from his great-grandfather, the last carpenter in the family. Such non-correlation of names with their bearers must have been overlooked by the Englishman who was impressed by New York egalitarianism when he heard that a department store was being run by a lord and a taylor. (104)

When we speak of "Roman" arts and crafts, we should remember that the word is used in a general sense of everything from the Roman empire. The Romans were not the world's best craftsmen; they let their slaves, mostly foreigners, do much of their work for them. Therefore the "Roman" skills or sciences we praise may have come from Egypt, Cappadocia, Greece, Spain, or any other part of the far-flung Roman empire. For example, the Roman traders who visited the ancient Germans often came from Syria or Greece. Traders from the Roman world dominated trade in ancient Germany, just as the English and Scots did among the American Indians, who, like the ancient Germans, were warriors and disdained mercenary pursuits. Hence it is not surprising that the Latin word *caupo* (merchant), in its High German form *Kauf*, served as a root in the word *Kaufmann* (merchant). Later on, small retailers were Haacker, Hackermann, Hoeker, Haendler, or Kraemer, and the shopkeeper on the corner (Winkel) might have been called Winkel or Winkler. Often the merchants were given the names of the wares they sold. (105)

Like the Roman wine seller (*vinumcaupo*), many medieval German merchants took their name from the wares they sold, for in the highly regulated and guild-minded commerce of the Middle Ages merchants usually specialized in a single item. A seller of pepper (from Latin *piper*) was Pfefferick or Pfeffermann, the seller of salt was Salzer, Selzer, or Saltzmann, and the seller of sugar was Zucker or Zuckermann, the word *Zucker* having come from Arabic via Spanish *azucar*. The seller of herrings (usually caught in the Baltic Sea and salted) was called Hering. Numerous items supplied names for the people who manufactured them, sold them, or used them. Typical of the resulting names are Beil (ax), Gabel (fork), Kamm (comb), Kunckel (distaff), Loeffel (spoon), Messer (knife), and Teller (dish). A Hutzler sold dried fruit. Whereas medieval merchants were usually specialists, we need not think that they always sold only one item. A fishmonger whose shield bore a pickerel may also have sold bass and perch. The artist may have chosen the most available fish as his model. Because craftsmen usually sold their wares in the front of their shop, we cannot really distinguish between craftsmen and shop keepers. (106)

Men who served in the military often gained their surnames from their military occupation or rank. At the time surnames were first being taken, most recruits became pikemen (*Landsknechte*, lansquenets), whereas the more fortunate ones became *Reuter*, or cavalrymen. The word *Reuter* and its synonym *Reiter* both came from the verb to ride (*reiten*), whereas the word *Ritter* first meant "trooper," being a member of a *rit* or cavalcade. In time *ritter* became the equivalent of French *chevalier* (knight) and was used only of the gentry. Those who served for pay were *Soeldner* (mercenaries, from Latin *solidarius*). (107)

The crossbow (*Armbrust,* folk etymology from Latin *arca balestra*) was still an effective weapon and gave the name Armbruster to both the user and the manufacturer of the weapon. The same was true of the *bogener,* who could either shoot or make bows. The *panzer* and the *bruenner* were the makers, rather than the wearers, of armor. A soldier who excelled and survived might become a *Webel* (sergeant), *Faehnrich* or *Faenner* (ensign), a *Hauptmann* (captain), or *Oberst* (colonel), or even *Marschall* (*marah,* horse + *scalc,* servant). A man who served a knight was a *Schildknecht,* or squire (literally, "shield knight"). (108)

The foremost man in a rural village was the *Bauernmeister* or village head man, also called the *Schultz, Scholz,* or *Schultheiss.* A larger town would have a *Burgermeister* and council of *Ratherren,* which gives the American name Rather, as in the case of Dan Rather. A surname referring to the higher offices usually indicated not descent, but rather employment. A man named Kaiser (emperor) was probably in imperial service, while a man name Koenig (king) was probably in royal service, unless perhaps he was persistently the *Schuetzenkoenig,* or winner of the markmanship contest. Employment is also suggested by the names Herzog (duke), Graf (count), Vogt (governor), Probst (provost), and Witzthum (vice-governor), the last three of these being from Latin *advocatus, propositus,* and *vice-dominus.* In addition to the higher officials, there were many more modest public servants such as public criers (Bellmann), bell ringers (Glocke) and official weighers (Waeger or Wagemann). Some of these services were rendered by "dishonorable" people, those who had no legal standing, like the skinner (Schinder or Abzieher) and court bailif (Scherg). (109)

Employment obviously produced the names Pabst (pope), Bischof (bishop), Abt (abbot), Pfaff (priest), and Moench (monk), since clergymen did not leave legitimate children to carry on their names. On the other hand, the sextons Sigrist, Mesner, Kirchner, and Kuester (think of Custer's last stand) may have had families with surnames taken from their profession, as might a lay brother such as a Beghard (Beckhardt), Palmer, or mass attendant (Messmann). A Kentucky gentleman once named his sons Bishop, Commodore, Dean, and Major, with the result that later generations respected his family for having had so many titled members.   (110)

The name Gott (God) was most often a shortened form of some name like Gottfried, Gotthelf, Gotthold, Gottlieb, or Gottschalk; but in some cases it may have been the nickname given to the actor who regularly played the role of God in a miracle play. Miracle plays may have contributed to the popularity of the names Adam and Eva, Maria Magdalena, Caspar, Melchior, and Balthasar (the Three Kings who brought gifts to Jesus), and other favorite roles in the plays. This was surely true of Puntzius (Pontius Pilate), who was hardly an exemplary character.   (111)

People often gained their surnames from nicknames. (As mentioned, the word "nickname" is a false division of "an ickname," or an added name.) A common type of nickname comes from hair color or style, such as Red, Curly, Goldy, etc. In German we find the names Schwarz (brunet), Braun (brown haired), Roth (red haired), Weiss (blond), Krause, Kraus (curly), and Kraushaar (curly haired); and the name Gold may have sometimes referred to hair color, just as the name Kahl (bald) betokened the absence of hair. The name Rotbart, like its Italian form Barbarossa, could designate a man with either a red or a blond beard. As in the case of names from professions, all these nicknames had once been preceded by a definite article: Hans der Schwarze (Hans the brunet), and Klaus der Kraus (Klaus the curly haired). Nicknames could also result from the clothes one wore, especially if they were unusual or indicated the wearer's profession or status. Examples are Lederhos (leather breeches) and Bundschuh (laced footwear), both meaning peasant, Weisskittel (white smock), meaning miller or baker, and Gelbrock (yellow gown), meaning a Jew. People could also be teased about the food they ate, especially if it revealed their social status or rural tastes as in the case of turnips (Rueb), sour beer (Sauerbier), or porridge (Brey). (112)

Physical stature gave names such as Kurtz (short), Lang (tall), Gross (large), and Klein (small). and age gave names like Alt (old), Jung (young), Juengling (youth), and Greis (greybeard). A name like Kleinhans was appropriate when little Johnny was a child, but less so when he grew up and surpassed his father in height. I had two cousins called Big Julia, the mother, and Little Julia, the daughter, and Little Julia retained her name even after she had outgrown her mother. The physical cruelty of the Middle Ages is well attested by instruments of torture and by the popular merriment caused when they were used publicly, so it is not surprising that mental cruelty is suggested by some of the nicknames inflicted at that time. A man with a twisted body might be called Krumm (crooked) or Krumbein (crooked leg), one with arthritic joints could be called Steiff (stiff), one with a misshapen head might be called Breithaupt (broad head) or Groskopf (bighead), and one who squinted might be called Schiele (squint). Sometimes a nickname was facetious: a large man might be called Small, and vice versa. On Quadalcanal my troopers called me Curly (behind my back) because of my prematurely bald pate.   (113)

Kropf (goiter) was a fitting name for anyone so afflicted, and Spitznas suited anyone with a pointed nose, just as Finkbein (finch leg) suited a man with skinny shanks. A fat man might be called Feiss, Fett, or Dick (thick) or perhaps Bauch (belly). In fact, any part of the anatomy might suggest a nickname, provided it were sufficiently deformed or unusual, such as Nase (nose), Schnaebele (little snout, in America Snaveley), and Kehl (throat, unless he came from Kehl across the Rhine from Strassburg). Originally, such names had been prepositional phrases such as *mit dem bart* (with the beard), *mit dem bauch* (with the belly), and *mit der nase* (with the nose).   (114)

Nicknames could also result from personal behavior: a man might be serious (Ernst) or jovial (Froehlich), courtly (Huebsch) or crude (Rauh, Grob); or, if he vacillated, he might be called Wankel or Wankelmut. Even more vituperative were Greul (atrocity), Greulich (dreadful), and Grausam (cruel). Less frequent were positive terms, such as Schoen (beautiful), Klug (clever), and Kuhn (brave). Comical nicknames could also be taken from our furry and feathered friends, such as Fuchs (fox), Has (hare), Gans (goose), Fink (finch), Amsel (ousel, blackbird), and many others. Names were also suggested by fish, such as Aal (eel), Barsch (perch), Hecht (pickerel). In some cases the names of such creatures may have signified that the person involved trapped, raised, or sold them. This was true even of songbirds, for it was not unusual for four-and-twenty blackbirds to be baked in a pie, and thrushes and finches fared no better.

A man named Kaefer (beetle) may have had the perseverence of that insect, and a man named Frosch (frog) may have eaten frogs, as Frenchmen do in American fancy. Even extinct animals such as the *Wissent* (bison) and *Auer* (aurochs) survive as surnames. (115)

Nicknames were sometimes imperatives, such as Bleibtreu (Remain loyal!), Fuerchtegott (Fear God!), Haltdichwohl (Keep well!), Hoerauf (Stop it!), Kaufdasbier (Buy the beer!), Streckfuss (Stretch a leg!), Schwingschwert (Swing the sword!), and Siehdichum (Watch out!). Such names were often given to new guild members at their initiation. Some of these imperative names were commands given in tasks no longer known to us. For example, Schudrein means "Shove it in!," but we do not know what was being shoved into what. If Samuel Clemens had not told us, we would not know the meaning of "Mark Twain." (116)

Some nicknames derived from a man's favorite expression, as was the case of Jasomirgott (so help me God!), as Henry II, the first duke of Austria, was called because he used that oath so often. Similarly derived names may include Garaus (bottoms up!), Fruehauf (early up!), Glueckauf (safe return!, probably a miner's term), Gottbehuet (God forbid!), Herr Gott (Lord God), and Amen. The names of small coins sometimes serve to suggest parsimony or miserliness, examples being Dreier (thrupence), Grosch (penny), and Heller (worthless coin). On the other hand, a large coin like a Gulden (guilder), Mark (mark), or Thaler (reichsthaler) might suggest magnanimity. Many names were "initiation names," names given to new members when they joined a guild or brotherhood. These could be complimentary like Goldfuss (gold foot) or defamatory like Ochsenreiter (ox rider), or Galgenschwank (gallows bird). (117)

Some nicknames lasted for a long time, long after the reason for them had been forgotten. One of my fellow Boy Scouts rightfully acquired the name Asparagus Tips, which plagued him for years but was, fortunately, not passed on to his children to the third and fourth generation. Having run out of supplies on a mountain hike and half starved, we resolved to send a relief party down to the valley to find food. With many empty stomachs and only a few dollars, we could not decide between baked beans and hominy grits with gravy. At that point our friend suggested asparagus tips. Many of the names listed below can no longer be explained, even if their literal meanings are known. The best we can sometimes do is to translate the roots literally and leave the significance to the reader's fancy.

(118)

Before the Germans borrowed and imitated the French words for grandparents, aunts, uncles, and cousins, they had their own very intricate vocabulary for blood relationships, bonds which were much more binding then than now. These relationships have left American names such as Ahn (grandfather), Base (female cousin), Eidam (son-in-law), Enkel (grandchild), Ohm and Oheim (mother's brother), Schnur (daughter-in-law), Schwager (brother-in-law), Schwiegermutter (mother-in-law), Tochtermann (son-in-law), and Vetter (male cousin, kinsman). Although *Kegel* now means ten-pin, it used to mean an illegitimate child, as in the misunderstood expression *mit Kind und Kegel*.

(119)

Since very few people traveled in ancient days, a stranger was most easily identified by his tribal origin, and therefore we have surnames such as Bayer (Bavarian), Francke (Frank), Hess (Hessian), Preuss (Prussian), Sachs (Saxon), Thueringer or Duerringer (Thuringian), and Schwab or Schwob (Swabian, sometimes Swopes in America). Naturally, a person was not called by a tribal name until after leaving home, for such a name would not distinguish him as long as he remained among his nationals. Because dialects differed so strongly, a stranger's accent immediately identified him even a few miles from home. At first, the words Sachsen, Bayern, and Schwaben referred not to the provinces but to the tribes themselves, regardless of where they were at that moment in their migratory wanderings. The terms were dative plurals and meant "to or among the Saxons," etc. The same held true later in the American colonies: traders and missionaries did not go to Iroquoia, but to the Iroquois, who might have been in transit.

(120)

Among other territorial names that have furnished American surnames are Baden, Brandenburg, Durlach, Holstein, Oldenburg, Pfaltz, Schweitz, Silesia (Schlesinger), and Wuerttemberg.

The name Deutsch does not refer to a tribe or territory, it is the name of the common language spoken by the various German tribes. Originally it just meant the vernacular or the

tongue of the people (*zunga thiudisca*), this being a translation
of the Latin term *lingua vulgaris,* or the vulgar language, as
opposed to the *lingua latina,* the Latin language. Any German-
speaker in an alien land may have been named Deutsch,
Duetsch, or Daitsch. In Russia, on the other hand, he was called
Niemitz (the dumb one) because he could not speak (Russian).

(121)

People often bore the name of the city of their origin. Some
just took the name of the city itself, such as Rosenheim or
Bamberg, but most took the designation of the inhabitants of
the town, as in the case of New Yorker as opposed to New York.
Consequently, we find the American names Basler, Bamberger,
Berner, Bremer (Bremen), Frankfurter, Hamburger, Mainzer
(and Mentzer), Posner (Posen), Rosenheimer, Strassburger, and
legions more. A Frankfurter need not have come from the large
city on the Main, he could have come from the smaller Frankfurt on the Oder or from any of many places where the Franks
forded a stream.   (122)

Not only cities, but even small hamlets and villages supplied
surnames. Some of these ended in the Germanic roots *dorf* (village, compare English "thorp"), *heim* (homestead, hamlet, cf.
English "ham"), *hagen* (enclosure, hedge), and *ingen,* a root
referring to a group of followers, as in the case of Sigmaringen,
the place where Sigmar's people lived. A secondary meaning of
ing is a vague concept of belonging, for example, Huelzing
(belonging to a forest) and Aiching (belonging to the oaks).

(123)

Whereas *dorf* and *heim* originally designated small clusters of
dwellings, some so-named places have grown into large cities,
like Duesseldorf and Mannheim. Among place names and
surnames ending in *dorf* and *heim* we find Altdorf, Altdorfer,
Pappenheim, and Pappenheimer. The root *heim* sometimes
appears as *ham* as in English Birmingham, for example in
Mosshammer, an inhabitant of Mossham, who has nothing to do
with hammers. The ending *heimer* finally lost most of its
meaning and just meant an inhabitant in general, and therefore
Burgenheimer did not have to have come from Burgenheim but
could have come from Burgen.   (124)

A *hag* or *hagen* was an outlying settlement protected by a
hawthorn hedge. Single sons often lived in such enclosures, with

the result that a bachelor is called a *Hagestolz*. The root *hag* (hawe) appears in many names like Hashagen (hare hedge), Hagenbeck (enclosure brook), and Hagedorn (hawthorn); and a man living in a *hag* might be called Hagen, Hager, Hagmann, Hagemann, or even Hackmann. The Low German root *rode*, meaning a clearing, is found in Minnegerode and Wernigerode, while its High German equivalents *reit* and *reut* are found in Reitenbach and Reutlingen. (125)

A name often misunderstood is Roland, of whom there is a statue in Bremen holding a gigantic sword. Most people assume that it commemorates the hero of the *Chanson de Roland* (from *Hrotho and **land)*, but this was not the case. Roland was not a name: it was a corruption of the legal term *rodoland*, or "reclaimed land." If a ruler undertook to clear *(roden)* unclaimed and uncultivated land, he could assert jurisdiction over it. To attest his juridical rights over this *rodoland*, he might stake his claim by erecting a marker, often in the shape of a man holding a sword as a symbol of jurisdiction. Because of the popularity of the hero Roland, people supposed that the markers represented him; and thus we have another case of folk etymology. A whole category of names derived from the act of clearing land, among which are *brand*, *reut*, *rod*, *sang*, and *schwand*. The name Waldbrand does not denote a forest fire, but a clearing in the woods. In America the root *schwand* sometimes appears as *schwang*, as in the name Neiswanger and Neuswanger (new clearing).(126)

In addition to the place names ending in *dorf, heim, hagen, rod*, and *reut*, there were also many towns, especially in Switzerland, that ended in *weil* (also written *weiler, wil*, and *wyler*. These derived from the Latin word *villa*, which meant a large farm or estate and gave us the word "village." The first component of names ending in *weil* was often the name of the owner. For example, Wittenweil was a Roman villa appropriated by a Germanic invader named Witto, whose descendants were later called Wittenweiler. Among American names stemming from *weil* we find Weil, Weiler, and Hofwyl. At some time, already in Switzerland, names like Ebers-wil were wrongly divided and resulted in forms like Eber-schwil or Eberschwyl. Another root designating a town that is largely restricted to Switzerland is *ikon* (from *inghofen*), which is found in Ruemlikon, Rueschlikon, Russikon, Stallikon, Fuellikon, and many

more. A less common ending, found mostly in north central
Germany is *leben*, originally meaning "inheritance" but later
just meaning property in general, as in Eisleben. The Slavic
root *witz*, meaning village, appears in names like Bonnewitz.
(127)

Inghofen is not the only ending that has been mutilated. By
tracing successive documents mentioning a place, we find that
they have often dropped many unstressed syllables, so that from
Udilscalckesberge all that remains is Uschelberg. Similar
contractions occur in England, even if not always indicated by
the spelling. When an American stated that he was going to St.
Magdalene Church to catch a bus for Lancashire in order to call
on Lord Cholmondeley, his British friend corrected him,
pronouncing the names as Maudlin, Lancsha, and Chumly.
When the Englishman said he would like to see Niagara Falls,
the American corrected him with "Niffels." Because some long
German names like Hruodinesheim, Autmundistat, and
Heribrachtshusen have been shortened to Rudisheim, Umstadt,
and Herbstein, we cannot always be certain of the etymology of
place names unless they appear in very old documents. (128)

As Tacitus mentioned, the ancient Germans did not care to
live in cities; during the invasions they often camped around the
old Roman settlements and left the inhabitants at peace. The
result was that many South German cities, towns, and villages
retained their names, even if these names were sometimes
altered by the High German sound shift and by the inability of
the invaders to pronounce them properly. Most of these names
were Celtic names that had long been latinized, such as
Turicum (Zurich), Tavernae (Zabern), and Moguntia (Mainz).
These Romanized Celtic place names provided the American
names Zuricher, Zaber, Maintzer, and Mentzer.   (129)

There were also genuine Latin names such as Confluencia
(Koblenz, at the confluence of the Rhine and Moselle) and
Colonia Agrippina (Koeln, a colony named in honor of Nero's
mother, which we call Cologne).   (130)

CHAPTER THREE

Christian Names

As we have seen, early German names were all pagan and mostly warlike. Names containing the roots *ans* and *god*, like Ansgar (god + spear) and Godwin (god + friend), referred to pagan gods. While the Germanic names were the most popular ones in Western Europe throughout the Middle Ages, Christianity introduced new names, mostly of Hebrew, Greek, and Latin origin. These names, often those of saints, were first found in the monasteries, where the monks shed their warlike Germanic names in favor of names more pleasing to God. Gradually, some of these names were assumed by royalty also; and we find rulers named John (Jehan, Jean, Johann, Jan, etc.), Georg, Stephan, and Philip. Some Christian names joined the older pagan names more easily because they resembled them. For example, Philip could have been confused with Filibert (very bright), Simon with Siemund (*sigi*, victory + *mund*, guardian), and Pilgrim with Biligrim (*bil*, sword + *grim*, helmet). Later converts often received names such as Christ, Christian, Karst, Kirst, and Kressmann, names which should protect their bearers from the devil. The devil, incorporating the qualities of Satan and of various pagan gods, became a very important personage with many names and circumlocutions such as Helmann, Helmeister, and Deubel. (131)

The names of saints gradually took root also among secular people who, following ancient pagan beliefs, wished to gain the personal support of certain saints by naming their children for them, since namesakes had a moral claim on the protection of the people for whom they were named. The Virgin Mary's name was so popular that it was even borne by men, as in the case, later, of Karl Maria von Weber, Rainer Maria Rilke, and Erich Maria Remarque. (Few people know that Voltaire's real name was Marie Francois Arouet.) (132)

Despite the intrusion of saints' names, the old Germanic names still predominated until the Counter Reformation of the sixteenth and seventeenth centuries. In a group of ballads by a thirteenth-century Austrian poet known as Neidhart von Reuwenthal, we find many rustic names. The first fifty-seven names are Adelber, Adelheit, Adelhune, Adelmar, Ave, Berchtel,

Diethoch, Eberhart, Elena, Engelbolt, Engelmar, Engelprecht,
Eppe, Ermelint, Etzel, Frideger, Friderich, Friedliep, Friderun,
Gisel, Giselher, Gotelinde, Gozbrecht, Gumprecht, Gunthart,
Gundrat, Hadwig, Heilken, Hilde, Hiltburg, Hiltrat, Holengaere,
Irenwart, Irmgart, Kuenzel, Randolt, Kuenegunde, Kuenz,
Megenbolt, Liuthart, Megenwart, Richilt, Ruoze, Ruoprecht,
Sibant, Sigehart, Uodalhilt, Uolant, Uoze, Vrena, Vriderun,
Vromuot, Walfrit, Waregrim, Werenbolt, Wierat, and Willebolt.
It will be noted that all but three of these peasants have old
Germanic names, mostly expressing warlike concepts, and most
of these names were composed of the roots discussed earlier.
Only Ave, Elena, and Vrena (St. Verena) have any Christian
significance.   (133)

Among the most popular holy names were those of certain
popes, including Adrian, Alexander, Benedict, Clement, Fabian,
Hildebrand, Johannes, Mark, Martin, Nicholas, Paul, Stephen,
Urban, and Victor. A modern German named Hildebrand
probably owes his name to Pope Hildebrand rather than to the
hero of the old German *Lay of Hildebrand*, who had to fight his
own son. Many of these foreign names gave two sets of deriva-
tives. The common people followed native speech patterns and
stressed the first syllable, whereas the Church retained the
Latin accent. Thus we get JOhann and JoHANNES, from which
arose Jahn, Jahnke, and Jantz as well as Hans, Hannes, and
Hansel. Likewise, Jacobus gave both Jack and Kopp.   (134)

After Luther revolted against Rome, most of his followers
limited themselves to the names of scriptural saints such as
Andreas, Johannes, Marcus, Matthaeus, Lucas, Petrus, and
Paulus, while dropping the names of local and otherwise
dubious saints. In place of the discarded saints, they often chose
the names of Old Testament characters such as Abel, Abraham,
Adam, Benjamin, Daniel, David, Jacob, Joachim, Jonas, Samuel,
and Solomon. All of these were the source of German-American
surnames in numerous variants. Because Old Testament names
began to smack of heresy, they were forbidden in 1574 by the
Synod of Tournai in France.   (135)

Meanwhile, during the Counter Reformation, the Roman
Catholic Church required all parents to name their child for a
saint, which was usually the saint on whose day it was born.
Consequently, most of the old Germanic names fell into disuse,

except for those of popular emperors such as Carl, Conrad, Friedrich, Heinrich, Leopold, Ludwig, Otto, Siegmund, and Wilhelm. Among the most popular masculine saints in Germany, as elsewhere in Europe, were Johann, Joseph, Matthaeus (or Matthias), Sebastian, and the archangels Michael and Gabriel. It is not clear why the archangels Raffael and Uriel were less popular. Once a child had a hagiographic name, the parents could add a secular one too; and this custom continued in Protestant lands, as in the case of Johann Wolfgang Goethe.

(136)

While most of the saints had Aramaic, Greek, or Latin names, there were some Celtic and even a few Germanic names on the list. Among the latter the Germans cultivated Conrad (brave + counsel), bishop of Augsburg, Meinrad (power + counsel), abbot of Einsiedeln, Oswald (god + rule), an Englishman, Rupertus (usually Ruprecht, from *hrodo* + *beracht*, famous + bright), who established Christianity in Salzburg, and Hubertus (mind + bright), the patron saint of hunters. Very popular was St. Francis of Assisi, whose name, derived from Germanic *frank*, appears in German as Franz or Frantz, but is pronounced Frantz in both cases. Less popular was St. Anselmus (god + helmet), also an Italian. Among the saints who contributed names to many German-American families were Anthony (Thoeni, Denny), Bartholomaeus (Bart, Bartel), Marcus (Merk, Merkel), Martin (Marti, Maertens), and Matthias (Matt, Matz, Thiess, Thyssen, and, in America, Tyson and Dyson.)

(137)

Christianity brought a slight softening of manners: to use Nietzsche's terms, a *Herrenmoral* (master morality) gave way somewhat to a *Sklavenmoral* (slave morality); and the ethics of the monastery were gradually imposed on society at large. Old names took on new meanings, while new names were introduced. The adjective *vrum* had once denoted effectiveness, a *vrumer ritter* was a capable knight, a *vrumer bauer* was a productive peasant, and a *vrumer munich* was a pious monk. Gradually the word dropped its first two meanings and kept only the last, and thus the name Frommhold, instead of meaning "effective and feudally loyal," took on the new meaning "pious and dear" for all classes. *Tuechtig* and *bieder*, which once meant doughty in battle, acquired for some people the meaning of capable and diligent, for example in business. In the new bourgeois society, respectability was more important than fame, so people adopted names like Ehrenmann (man of honor), Ehrlich (honest), and Ehrsam (respectable).   (138)

Gutmann, like French *bonhomme* and English Goodman, first meant "landowner" but was gradually understood to mean "good man." Among these new Christian names were Sanftmut (gentle disposition) and Demut (humility), which had literally meant "servant-disposition" (from *thius*, servant, and *mut*, disposition). The name is pronounced "day moot" in German, but is pronounced mostly as DeMUTH in America. This is one of the many cases in which the English sound *th* (thorn), long since dead in Germany, has been falsely introduced into German-American names. Since it is more Christian to serve than to be served, we begin to find names like Diener (servant) and Dienst (service). The christianizing of German culture is shown in place names like Marienborn (Mary's well) and Theresienstadt (Theresa's city), which in turn became surnames. The Swiss city and surname Frauenfeld, which is now interpreted as "Field of our Lady," may have originally been Fronfeld "the field of our lord," or field where the peasants could perform their corvee service, or *Frondienst* (cf. *Fronleichnam*, Corpus Christi). However, most names like Frauenmann, Frauenhof, etc. do designate men or farms belonging to a convent.   (139)

The names Gottfried, Gotthelf, Gotthilf, Gotthold, Gottlieb, Gotthlob, and Gottschalk, which had once belonged to the monasteries, gradually crept out into the world and became especially popular in Lutheran parsonages, where they were joined by new coinages like Fuerchtegott (fear God), Ehregott (glorify God), Leberecht (live right), Christfried (Christ peace), and Himmelreich (kingdom of heaven). The old name Friedrich (ruler of the **frithu*) was interpreted as "Prince of Peace" and was equated with the Hebrew name Solomon. Ulrich Zwingli misinterpreted his first name as Huldreich (full of grace), whereas it had actually been Uodalrich and had meant "rich in allodial (inherited) lands," again a case of folk etymology.(140)

During the period of humanism in the sixteenth century, scholars often signed their Latin writings with Latinized names. Georgius Agricola, the great humanist, was actually named

Bauer; and the ancestors of the pencil manufacturing family
Faber derived their name from the Latin word for smith, their
name having been Schmidt. The map maker Gerhard Kremer
signed his Latin maps with his Latin name, Mercator, while
Francis Praetorius, the founder of Germantown, bore a latinized
form of Schultheiss. In like manner Fischer (fisherman), Weber
(weaver), Schumacher (shoemaker), Jaeger (hunter), and
Schneider (tailor) gained prestige by calling themselves Pisca-
tor, Textor, Sutor, Venatus, and Sartor, or, the even more
elegant, Sartorius. The prestigious ending *ius* was quite
superfluous in Praetorius and Sartorius, since the Latin forms
were complete as Praetor and Sartor.   (141)

Some Latinists latinized their names by retaining or adding
the suffix ending *us*, which was still commonly used until
modern times in Biblical names like Petrus, Paulus, Martinus,
etc. It should be noted that the common German name Christ
is not blasphemous, since it merely means "Christian," the
Lord's epithet always being Christus. Hans, the son of Martinus
was Hans Martini, that being the Latin genitive, not an Italian
name as is sometimes believed. In like manner, Paulus' son
Niklas was Niklas Pauli or Pauly, while Jacobus' son Heinz was
Heinz Jacobi or Jacoby. Scholars with names ending in *e*
preferred the ending *ius*. The pastor of the Georgia Salzburgers
bore the name Boltzius, a latinization of either Bolte or Boltze,
while a con-artist who fleeced him called himself Curtius,
although his real name was Kurtz. A Moravian teacher who
served in Georgia and Pennsylvania was named Schulius,
surely from Schule. The name Stettinius came from Stettin on
the Baltic.   (142)

Some scholars were not satisfied with mere Latin names but
preferred Greek ones, such as Neander for Neumann (new
man). This was the case of Luther's friend Melanchthon, who
incorrectly interpreted his name Schwarzerd as "Black earth."
Actually the name may have been only Schwarzer (brunet), to
which an excrescent *T* had been added. Excrescent *T*s appear in
numerous names, among which are Braunert, Craemert,
Daubert, Dickert, Dobert, Pabst, Obst, and Schweigert. Some
people were named for the day of their births, such as Freitag
(Friday), Sontag (Sunday), Maytag (May Day), and Oster
(Easter). Obviously, descendants of such people bore those

names without being born on those days. It is possible that a man named Freitag received his name because he owed corvée service on Fridays. (143)

Many German names had originally been French, often Huguenot. Literate French immigrants could preserve the correct spelling of their names because they associated with educated people who understood them, as was the case of the family of the German author Friedrich Heinrich Carl de La Motte Fouqué. On the other hand, the names of the working-class and peasant immigrants were usually germanized, and one would scarcely recognize Tussing as a rendering of Toussaints. In one instance the reverse took place: the accent on the North German name Guder Jan (Good John) was shifted to the second syllable, forming the name Guderian, which is usually assumed to be French. German names were sometimes gallicized when Germans settled in francophone areas, examples being Blancpain, Chupart, and Grenier from Weissbrodt, Schubart, and Greiner. (144)

In the South German language area the Romance-speaking Celts survived the Germanic invasions and lived alongside the invaders, even to the present in the Engadin. The first Celts the Germans met when crossing the Rhine were the Volcae, which gave them the noun *walch* and the adjective *welsch*. In England the Saxons gave the cognate word *welsh* to the Celts of Wales. When the Volcae became romanized, the Germans on the Continent began to use the word *welsch* to designate Romance-speaking people, as the German Swiss still call their French-speaking countrymen. Because the romanized Celtic pockets remained among the Germanic invaders, we find place names like Wallensee, Wallenstein, and Wallis, where the older inhabitants survived. (145)

The number of germanized Slavic names is high everywhere east of the Elbe, which served as a linguistic frontier between Germans and Slavs after the latter had occupied the lands abandoned by the former during their migrations westward and southward. Ever since the thirteenth century there had been a persistent *Drang nach Osten* (drive toward the east), which was finally reversed in 1944 at the Battle of Stalingrad. During the drive toward the east the Germans had often retained, even if altered, Slavic names such as Bogatzky, Cernak, Kretschmer,

Lessing, Nietzsche, and Leibnitz. They also kept many East German place names such as Berlin, Breslau, Danzig, Dresden, Fehrbellin, and Leipzig, which have given us American surnames. Many names could be of either Germanic or Slavic derivation. If they are frequent in western Germany but rare in the east, then they are probably Germanic; if they are frequent in the East but rare in the West, then they are probably Slavic. (146)

There are not really any German-Jewish names. There are Hebrew names, such as Chaim, Cohen, Levi, and Me'ir, the last of which, as mentioned, may have predisposed some Jews to adopt the name Meyer. A few German-language names were borne mainly by Jews, such as Langrock and Gelbrock, which referred to the long and yellow garments they were required to wear. Otherwise, there is no distinction between the names borne by Christians and Jews, except that certain names were more frequently adopted by the latter. In many of our Eastern inner-cities, names like Evans, Davis, Robertson, White, Williams, Wilson, etc. are borne mostly by blacks; yet they remain British, not African, names. (147)

Within the Jewish community, or ghetto, simple names usually sufficed; if not, the father's name could be added. When the Jews were emancipated at the end of the eighteenth and beginning of the nineteenth centuries, they were required to take surnames for the purpose of taxation. If they had their choice many chose common German names that began with the same consonant as their "holy" or "synagogue" name. Thus, Menachem might choose Mendel just for its initial sound, and Nathan might choose Nadler for the same reason, not because he made needles. Some merely re-arranged the letters, so that Lewi became Weil. Even after assuming gentile-sounding *Decknamen* (cover names), religious Jews still considered their synagogue names to be their true names, for which they felt an emotional attachment. When given a choice, some Jews chose romantic names such as Morgenthau (morning dew), Blumenthal (flower valley), Lilienthal (lily valley), Rosenberg (rose mountain), Silberstein (silver stone), and their like. Although Americans often consider such names to be Jewish, they are straight German names, for such names were current in sentimental novels at the time that Jews were taking civil names. The name Rosenkranz (rosary) is certainly more appropriate for a Catholic than for a Jew, and the name Rosenberg was borne by the Nazi ideologist who wrote *The Mythos of the Twentieth Century.* Shakespeare was not suggesting Jewish descent when he named two of Hamlet's colleagues Rosencrantz and Guildenstern. Some "fantasy" names were composed with as little logic as were many of the ancient Germanic names composed of two unassociated roots. Examples of typical *Fantasienamen* are Feinstein, Goldfein, Himmelfarb, Loewenstern, and Morgenroth.   (148)

Like their gentile neighbors, the Jews often took the name of their trade, so many bore names like Kuerschner or Kirschner (furrier), Kraemer (shopkeeper), Schlechter (slaughterer), or Wechsler (money-changer). On the other hand, the chosen name did not necessarily designate trades associated primarily with the Jews, for we also find Ackermann, Bauer, Forster, Gaertner, Gerber, Jaeger, Wirth, and Zimmermann. When required to assume surnames for purposes of taxation, the Jews often used their house names, by which many families had been known for generations. Typical examples were Adler, Drache, Fisch, Fuchs, Gans, Hecht, Mandelbaum, Rose, Rosenstock, and Rothschild. Many Jews took the names of cities, often of large and imposing cities like Frankfurt and Hamburg, without having ever lived there.   (149)

It is said that the Jews often had to bribe the officials to obtain desirable names. A tale, surely apocryphal but no less significant, tells of a Jew who was in the tax collector's office for a long time while getting his name. When he finally emerged, his friends asked what name he got. "Schweiss" (sweat) was his answer. "Very good," his friends remarked. "Yes, but the *w* cost me half my fortune!" Since puns cannot be translated, the story should be altered in English: he received the name Shirt, but the *r* cost him half his fortune. To know what names the German Jews received or selected, one has only to look at any list of donors to cultural and charitable undertakings. When I was studying at Heidelberg, the main building, which had been donated by American benefactors, bore a large bronze plaque listing the names of the donors, more than half of whom were clearly Jewish. When I arrived there in 1936, all Jewish professors had just been dismissed.   (150)

CHAPTER FOUR

The Americanization of German Names

In looking through the following list, it will be noted that, while German-American names differ widely from the standard written form of the German words, they differ far less from the dialect variants brought to this country. Nevertheless, many names did become altered significantly through English influence.When the immigrants boarded their ships at Rotterdam, the English captains had difficulty in writing their manifests or ships lists. Knowing no German, and unfamiliar with German dialects, the scribes wrote down the names as they heard them, sometime in the form of the English names most resembling the sound. In this way Theiss, Weiss, and Weidmann became Dice, Wise, and Whiteman, while Albrecht, Leitner, and Leithaeuser became Albright, Lightner, and Lighthizer. The reason that so many eighteenth-century German immigrants could not sign their names and merely made an X was not that they were illiterate, because Protestant Germans had a higher literacy rate than their British contemporaries. The reason was that they could write only in German script, which the British authorities could not read. It occasionally appears that the immigrants tried to spell their names but did so with the German sounds of the letters. If a man named Diehl spelled his name as *"day, ee, ay, ha, ell,* the scribe may have understood it as Deahl. (151)

In a few cases the writer of the ship list gave up and asked the meaning of the name; and thus Becker, Koch, Schneider, Soeldner, and Zimmermann became Baker, Cook, Taylor, Soldier, and Carpenter. Often the translation was advantageous. When two brothers named Zwetschen (plum) stood in separate lines at Castle Garden (prior to Ellis Island and therefore used by most German immigrants) they were handled by different clerks. One, being conscientious, struggled with the unfamiliar name and wrote it Tsvetshen. The other soon gave up and asked the meaning, and then he assigned the name Plum. It is not hard to guess which brother was more successful in business in America. (152)

In the eighteenth century it was customary to translate Christian names, just as we still do today in the case of royal

names when we say Frederick the Great and William the
Second instead of Friedrich der Grosse and Wilhelm der Zweite.
Common names like Johann, Georg, and Wilhelm were regularly anglicized into John, George, and William; but the scribes
failed to recognize the roots of some names. Therefore they
failed to see that Ruprecht was the· equivalent of Robert and
that Ludwig was the equivalent of Lewis, and the result was
that they sometimes rendered them as Rubright and Ludowick.
The same situation could occur in the case of surnames that
were identical with Christian names: Paulus Franz might
become Paul Francis and Johann Wilhelm might become John
Williams. Sometimes only a part of the name was translated, as
in the case of Newbauer, Newhart, and Blackwaelder (for
Schwartzwaelder).   (153)

Only a few German first names have taken root in the United
States, most of them still being found in families who cherish
their German heritage. Among those that are still popular are
Carl, Ernst, Herman, Hubert, and Otto, all of which also serve
as surnames. Among girls' names we find Heidi, Gretchen,
Liese, and Minna. A test of whether or not such names have
really taken root is their presence or absence in non-German
families, for example, among our African-American populace.
                                                            (154)

It should be noted that, while the first few generations of
Germans in America continued to choose German first names
to honor their parents and grandparents, later generations
joined the mainstream in naming their children for national
heroes and non-German friends. The reverse was also true: the
black mayor of Baltimore is named Kurt Schmoke, and a lovely
black bank teller in Savannah, Georgia, is named Zeagler (from
Ziegler). My own grandfather, who had no German blood and
bore the surname Meldrim, was christened Peter Wiltberger in
honor of his father's commanding officer.   (155)

In a few cases the German immigrant willfully changed his
name for professional reasons. The dancer Frederick Austerlitz
preferred to perform under the stage name Fred Astaire, which
sounded more elegant to American ears after World War I; and
Allan Konigsberg and Doris Kappelhof acted under the names
Woody Allen and Doris Day. It has been mentioned that
religious Jews cherished their synagogue names more than their

cover names, and that explains why it was easy for some of them to discard their cover names and choose more suitable ones after reaching America. (156)

Some Germans tried to gain prestige by giving a French flavor to their names, French being fashionable at the time. August Schoenberg, a Jew, translated his surname to Belmont and thus entered circles formerly closed to him. Some people merely shifted the accent to the second syllable to make it sound French. A few North Germans whose names ended in an *e*, like Bode (messenger) and Gode (good), had already added an acute accent (Bodé, Godé) so that South Germans would not drop the final vowel. In America such names were thought to be French and were pronounced, and sometimes written, as Boday and Goday. In Charleston the early Lutheran silversmith Johann Paul Grimké left many "Huguenot" descendants named Grimké. (157)

A name like Dusel (pronounced DOOzel and meaning "silly") sounds very French when the accent is shifted to the second syllable and the name is pronounced as DuSELLE, and the same is true of Mandel (almond) and Mantel (coat) when they are pronounced ManDELLE and ManTELLE (which Mickey Mantle did not choose to do). The same principle was at work in the change of accent in the word "tercel," meaning a thrice-moulted male falcon. The word should be accented on the first syllable, but the automobile manufacturer knew that the car would be more stylish if pronounced TerCELLE. Even the seventeenth-century English composer Purcell suffers his name to be murdered by Francophiles as PurCELLE. (158)

Some immigrants altered the spelling of their names to preserve the correct pronunciation, which would have been mispronounced if they had kept the original spelling. Families named Erhardt, Gerhardt, and Igelhard saved the correct sound (the true component of a name) by changing the spelling to Earhardt, Gearhard, and Eagleheart. Many German-American names deviated greatly from the standard German form without being americanizations. The apparently "wrong" letters may not have resulted from American pronunciation or spelling: they may represent a dialect variant or a relic of a bygone age. For example, Rhylander and Schwytzer are not American corruptions: they are the authentic Swiss forms of those names. It is evident that names like Mince, Minehart, Rice, Tice, and Troy are American phonetics for Maintz, Meinhart, Reiss, Theiss, and Treu. On the other hand, it is not always possible to ascertain whether names like Isemann, Wigel, and Wiler are corruptions of the standard forms Eisemann, Weigel, and Weiler or whether they derive directly from old dialect forms. The same is true of the use of umlauts, which varied greatly from region to region. Sometimes the corruption of a German name was due to a false breaking of the name, as we have seen in the case of Ebers-wyl and Eber-schwyl. Roth-schild (red shield) has become Roths-child, which has no meaning. Rat-her (council gentleman) has become Ra-ther, a rather meaningless name; and the Kraus-haar (curly hair) Auditorium in Baltimore is often pronounced Kraw-shower.   (159)

World War I extinguished, or hopelessly disguised, many German names. Because British propaganda convinced most Americans that the Germans cut off the hands of all Belgian boys and impaled little girls on the projections of the Gothic cathedrals, some German Americans renounced their origins in order to escape public opprobrium, and even sauerkraut had to take on the name "liberty cabbage." I was born during "the War to End all Wars," and for years afterwards we knew scarcely any Germans. Among our acquaintances the Ottos were Norwegians, the Balls were Alsatians, the Altstaetters were Swiss, and the Holsts were Danish. Some others had rectified their spellings from Schmidt to Smith and from Henrichsen to Henderson. Strangely, German shepherd dogs remained German, except when they were called police dogs, and Dachshunds remained "dash hounds."   (160)

The chief value of the appended list of German-American names for genealogists is to help them continue their search of a family's antecedents when the line seems to come to an end. A friend of mine in Atlanta was proud of his descent from a prominent New England family named Capp. However, when he tried to document the descent, the line came to an abrupt halt in the mid-nineteenth century in Ohio and could not be pursued until it was discovered that the father of the earliest known Capp had previously been named Kapp. Therefore, if a genealogist comes to the end of an Anglo-Saxon line, it may be worth his while to search under the nearest German names.   (161)

To be sure, not every Miller used to be a Mueller, in fact the spelling Miller was common in South Germany and Switzerland, as in the case of Johnny Weissmiller, the original Tarzan. In many cases the source of an apparently Anglo-Saxon name must have been Continental, usually German, because the name does not appear, or seldom appears, in England. Among these are Albright (Albrecht), Fulbright (Vollbrecht), Height (Heyd, Heid, or Heidt), Lightner (Leitner), Lighthizer (Leithaeuser), Yonce (Jantz), and Youngblood (Juengbluet, not young blood but young blossom). It is generally known that Firestone was an anglicization of Feuerstein, but it has not been mentioned that Firestone's greatest rival, Goodyear, may have had a similarly formed name. I have never known an Englishman named Goodyear, but Johannes Gutjahr of Linzingen arrived in America aged sixteen in 1864, just as Rudolf Feuerstein had done one year earlier; and it is likely that other Gutjahrs had arrived before Charles Goodyear vulcanized rubber.   (162)

CHAPTER FIVE

Suggestions for Using the Name-list

In searching for a German-American name, particularly an early one, the reader should keep several things in mind. Being unfamiliar with German names, the English ship captains sometimes wrote them phonetically. Thus they sometimes spelled the sound represented in German by *ie* as "ee" or "ea", as was the case with Keefer and Keafer for Kiefer and with Reeser and Reaser for Rieser. Unfamiliar with the trigraph *sch*, the scribes usually wrote only "sh" as in English. Thus Schneider appears as Shnyder (or Snyder), Schultz as Shults, and Schueler as Shiele. In searching for a German-American name beginning with *sh*, the reader is advised to search under the *sch* spelling, since the *sh* list has been greatly shortened to avoid unnecessary duplication. (163)

The digraph *pf*, unfamiliar to the scribes, appeared as *f*, as in Fleeger and Fleager for Pflueger and in Fister for Pfister. Whereas there had been only a few German surnames ending in *s* (indicating the genitive case), the English scribes often added a spurious *s* to German surnames, so that Bauer, Meyer, and Hyde (Heidt) also appeared as Bauers or Bowers, Meyers or Myers, and Hydes. Perhaps the scribes heard of these families mentioned in the plural, as in the case of the Smiths or the Blacks, and thought the *s* to be part of the name. (164)

Umlauts, the diacritical marks over *a*, *o*, and *u*, were seldom used by German Americans and therefore do not appear here. They were originally the letter *e* superimposed over the vowel to modify its pronunciation, changing an *a* to *e* (rhyming with "say"), an *o* to the vowel sound in "girl" or "hurt," and the *u* to the sound of a French *u* (or, in South German names, to the sound *ee*). Instead of being superimposed, the *e* could follow the vowel, as in names like Goethe and Goetz; and that is the method used in the following list, even when the Standard German name has umlaut, as in the case of Schoen instead of Schön. In many cases the umlaut was eventually dropped. Therefore, when seeking a name with an *ae*, *oe*, or *ue*, the researcher should also search under *a*, *o*, and *u*, and vice versa. There is also a correlation between *e* and *oe*. A Germanic *e* like that in "hell" and "twelve" may be rounded to *oe* (ö) in German, as in the case of *Hoelle* and *zwoelf*. The reverse also appears: Goetz becomes Getz and Boehm becomes Behm.   (165)

The following compilation was begun in the naive belief that it could be complete, or even almost complete. Although not of German descent, I have competed for half a century against German thoroughness and have striven for *Vollstaendigkeit*, or completeness. Innocently expecting to find all German-American names, I have added list after list; yet, like Achilles, whenever I have almost caught up with the tortoise of completion, the tortoise has moved on; and now the list, still incomplete, is as much as my readers, or my publisher, will bear. While this is a partial list, I cannot claim that it is an impartial list, for I have included all eligible friends, acquaintances, and colleagues lest they think I did not have them in mind while compiling the list. Originally based on eighteenth- and nineteenth-century ship manifests, this list also includes German names from American telephone books, newspapers, and TV programs.   (166)

Although this study cannot pretend to list all the thousands of American variants of German names, it is hoped that the reader can deduce most unlisted names by observing the various roots and the way they are combined in the names that are listed. For example, the name Auerstein is not listed (because I have found no American by that name), but the roots are found in Auerbach and Steinfeld and many other names so that the reader should be able to ascertain the meaning without finding the exact name itself. Likewise, the index sometimes refers to paragraphs (not pages) in the introduction that do not list the precise name in question but which do explain related names.   (167)

If the researcher cannot find a name where it belongs alphabetically, he should look for several lines above and below. Also, he should remember that, because of the High German sound shift, *b*, *d*, and *g* are sometimes interchangeable with *p*, *t*, and *k* and *p* and *t* are sometimes interchangeable with *pf*, *f*, and *z*. Also, many names can begin with either *C* or *K*, *T* or *Th*, or *Sch* or *Sh*.   (168)

The reader will note that the translations often do not concur with modern dictionaries. Since most surnames were adopted in the fourteenth to the seventeenth centuries, they were based on older meanings of the roots, often as they appeared in Middle

High German. For example, since there were still no street cars, umbrellas, alarm clocks, or computers, the names Schaffner, Schirm, Wecker, and Rechner are rendered as "steward," "protection," "waker," and "teller" rather than as "conductor," "umbrella," "alarm clock," and "data processor." It will also be noted that many German-American names, especially of the earlier families, differ in spelling from modern German forms of the same names. This is because in the nineteenth and early twentieth centuries many German families altered the spelling of their names to concur with current orthographic reforms, which attempted to simplify and standardise spelling. The early immigrants, being safely in America, were unaffected by these reforms. Therefore many American families still use the older spellings; for example, we still find the spellings Carl, Schwartz, and Cunckel in place of the newer spellings Karl, Schwarz, and Kunkel. (169)

Every effort has been made to avoid folk etymology, or the popular but mostly incorrect interpretations of the names, but instances surely appear. The English renditions are merely transliterations, not interpretations. The reader is free to interpret a definition such as "marsh dweller" as "a person who lives near a marsh," " at a marsh," or "in a marsh," as he sees fit. The reader is reminded that fr means "from," the symbol < means "derived from," and OT and NT mean Old and New Testament. (170)

In the case of surnames derived from place names, space has sometimes been saved by explaining only the place name. The item "Altdorf, Altdorfer (old village)" explains the place name Altdorf as "old village"; it is assumed that the reader will understand that an Altdorfer is an inhabitant of that place. The same is true of "Frankfurter" (the Franks' ford), which explains only the name of the city, not that of the inhabitants. Places sufficiently populated to appear on maps and in gazetteers are marked with a raised 122, which follows the entry unless there may be confusion, in which case the 122 follows immediately after the pertinent name. It will be noted that old Germanic names like Eckhard and Anslem are rendered as (sword + strong) and (god + helmet) to indicate that there need be no conceptual relation between the two roots. Some names seem to be listed twice; for example, Forstreiter (forest rider, gamekeeper) is listed separately from Forstreiter (dweller in a forest clearing). Although the two appelations share the same spelling and pronunciation, they have different sources and different meanings and are therefore treated as separate names. (171)

Foreword to the Third Edition

I wish at this time to thank all the reviewers who judged the first two editions of this work favorably and all the readers who sent letters suggesting additional names, all of which, I hope, appear below. I also wish to thank all those who bought copies and thus encouraged the Genealogical Publishing Company to publish this revised and expanded edition.

George Fenwick Jones

Der Müller.

Reminder: Numbers following items refer to paragraphs, not to pages, of the introduction. OT and NT = Old and New Testament, fr = from, < = derived from.

A

Aach, see Ach
Aachen (city) 79, 122
Aal, Aahl (eel, eel catcher) 115, 106
Aal, Ahl (awl, cobbler) 98
Aalborn, see Ahlborn
Aalrep (eel catcher) 91
Aar, Ahr (eagle)
Aarau (meadow on the Aar) 83, 84
Aargauer, Aargeyer (fr Aargau, Swiss region on the Aar) 121
Aarmuehle (mill on the Aar) 83, 103
Abaler, see Abele
Abbriter (from the clearing) 69, 124
Abbuehl (from the hill) 69, 67
Abderhalden (from the slope) 69, 71
Abegg (from the ledge) 69
Abel 53 (diminutive for Abraham, OT name)
Abel, Abell, Abele 53 < Albrecht
Abel, Abell, Abels (brother of Cain) 135
Abele (poplar tree, fr Latin *albus*) 89
Abelmann (dweller near the poplars) 89
Abend (evening, one who lives toward the south) 85
Abendroth (evening red) 148
Abendschein, Abenschein (evening glow) 148
Abendschoen, Abenschoen (as beautiful as the evening) 148

Abendstern (evening star) 148
Abenroth (Abbo's clearing) 124, 125
Abens (pre-Germanic river name) 23
Abenschein, see Abendschein
Abenteuer (adventure) 118
Aber, see Albrecht
Aberbach, see Auerbach
Aberhard, see Eberhard 151
Aberholt (hostile, offensive) 115
Aberle, Aberly < Albrecht, see also Aeberli
Abert < Albrecht
Abich 53 (left, averse) 115
Abich < Albrecht
Abicht, see Habicht
Ablass (floodgate guard) 96
Able, see Abel
Ableiter, Ableitner (fr the slope) 69, 71
Abraham (OT name) 135
Abram, Abrams 59 (OT name) 135
Abrecht, see Albrecht
Abrell (April, period of corvée duty) 143
Abschatz (tax, tax collector) 109
Abscherer, see Scherer
Abschlag (steep slope) 71
Abschlag (excise collector) 109
Abschlag (scrap wood) 118
Absolon (OT name) 135
Abt, Abts (Abbot, fr Latin *abbas*) 110
Abtsreiter, Abstreiter (abbot's clearing) 110, 125, 126
Abzieher (skinner) 96, 109
Abzug (gully, drain) 79
Abzug (copy-sheet, printer) 96
Ach, Ache, Achen, Acher (river, cog. Latin *aqua*) 79, 122
Achabach 159, Achebach, Achenbach 122 Achenbacher, Achenback (brook coming fr a spring) 79, 77

Achen (fr Aachen) 79, 122

Acher (dweller on a river), see
also Acker

Achermann, see Ackermann

Achilles (Greek name) 143

Achim 53 < Joachim

Achleiter (land sloping down to
water) 79, 71

Achmann (dweller on a river) 79,
94

Achsel, see Axel

Achsteller (stable on a stony
terrain) 79

Achterholt (behind the forest) 69,
72

Achterkirchen (behind the
church) 69

Achtermann (dweller behind [the
village, hill, etc.]) 69, 94

Achtschilling (one who pays 8 sh.
dues) 143

Achtung (attention) 117

Achtziger (eighty-year-old, born
in the year '80)

Achzehner (the eighteenth) 118

Ackenbach, see Achebach

Acker, Ackers 59, Ackert 74
(field) 84

Ackerhaus (house on a field) 84,
65

Ackerhof (small farm) 84, 92

Ackerknecht (field hand) 84, 95

Ackermann, Akermann (farmer)
84, 91, 94

Ackmann, see Achmann

Acuff, see Eichhoff

Adalmann, Addleman 159, see
Edelmann

Adam, Adams 59 (husband of
Eve) 135, 111

Adami (son of Adam) 142

Adamsweiler (Adam's village)
135, 127

Adde < Adolf

Ade, Adde, see Adam

Adel, abbreviation of one of the
following:

Adelbald (noble + bold) 47, 46

Adelberg 122, Adelberger (noble
mountain) 47, 68

Adelbert, see Albrecht

Adelbrich, Adelbrecht (noble +
bright) 47, 51

Adeler, see Adler

Adelger (noble + spear) 47, 46

Adelhard, Adelhart, Adehart,
Adelhardt (noble + strong) 47,
46

Adelheid, Adelhyt (noble +
quality) 47, 133

Adelheim (noble hamlet) 47, 124,
122

Adelmann, Adelman (nobleman)
47, 94

Adelolt < Adelwald (noble + rule)
47, 47

Adelram (noble + raven) 47, 48

Adelsberg, Adelsberger (fr
Adelsberg, nobility mountain)
47, 68, 122

Adelsdorfer, Adelsdoerfer (fr
Adelsdorf, nobility village) 47,
124

Adelstein, see Edelstein

Ader (vein, well, blood letter) 96

Ader (crossbow string) 108

Adich 53, Adichs 59, Adix < Adolf

Adleberg 159, see Adelberg

Adleman 159, see Adelman

Adler (eagle, fr noble + eagle,
often a house name) 48, 63

Adolf, Adolph (noble + wolf) 46,
48

Adoremus (Let us adore Him)
116, 138

Adrian (Christian saint, name of
several popes) 134

Advent (fr church calendar) 143

Aeberli, Aeberlj, Aberley, see
Eberle

Aebersold (hog wallow) 118
Aebischer (dweller near ash trees) 89
Aegidi (St. Aegidius) 135
Aelbragt, see Albrecht
Aeppli, Aepplj (little apple), see Apfel
Aesch (ash tree) 89
Aeschbach (brook among ash trees) 89, 79
Aeschbach (brook containing *aesche* [graylings]) 79, see Aschenbach
Aescher, Aeschleman, Aeschlimann 94 (dweller near ash trees) 89
Afeld, Afeldt, Affeldt (river field) 79, 91
Aff (ape) 115, 116
Affenschmaltz (false praise) 115
Afferbach, Afflerbach (appletree brook) 89, 77
Affolter, Affholter (apple tree) 89
Affolter (apple tree) 89
Agatstein, Agetstein (agate, magnet) 73
Agede, see Eigenter
Agilbert (sword + bright) 46, 47
Agricola (Latin for farmer) 141
Agstein (amber, amber cutter) 96
Agster, see Elster
Agtermann, see Achtermann
Ahl (eel, catcher of, or dealer in, eels) 105, 115
Ahl, see Ahle
Ahlbach (eel brook) 115, 77, 83
Ahlberg (noble mountain) 47, 68
Ahlborn (nobly born) 47
Ahlborn (eel spring) 79
Ahlbrand, see Albrand
Ahle (awl, shoemaker) 98
Ahle (honeysuckle) 89
Ahlemann, Ahlmann, see Alemann
Ahlenstiel (awl, cobbler) 104

Ahler 55, Ahlers 59, Ahlert 74 < Albrecht
Ahlf, see Adolf
Ahlfeld, Ahlfeldt (honeysuckle field) 89, 84, 122
Ahlgrimm < Adelgrim (noble + mask) 47, 46
Ahlhelm < Adelhelm (noble + helmet) 47, 46
Ahlhorn (place name) 122
Ahlinger (fr Ahling) 122
Ahlmann (dweller at a fen or swamp) 80, 94
Ahlrep, see Aalrep
Ahlschlaeger, see Ohlschlaeger
Ahlstrom (eel stream) 115, 78
Ahlwardt < Adelward (noble + guardian) 47, 47
Ahn, Ahner (grandfather or ancestor) 119
Ahn (dweller at a fen) 80
Ahn 53 < Arnold
Ahneman (kinsman) 119, 94
Ahnsorge, see Ansorge
Ahorn (maple) 89
Ahrbeck (eagle brook) 48, 77, 122
Ahrberg, see Arberg
Ahrenbeck (eagle brook) 48, 78
Ahrenberg 122, see Arberg
Ahrend, Ahrends, Ahrens, see Arend, Arends
Ahrendorf, Ahrensdorf, see Arendorf
Ahrenholtz, see Arenholtz
Ahrenhorst (eagle hurst) 48, 72
Ahrens, Ahrend, Ahrendt, Ahrends, see Arnd
Ahrensfeld (eagle field) 46, 84, 122
Ahrensmeyer (dweller at the Ahrenshoff, Eagle Farm) 92, 93
Aich 122, Aicher, Aichner (dweller among the oaks) 89
Aichach (oak place) 89, 79, 122

Aichbichler (oak hill) 89, 67

Aichel, Aichele (acorn), see
Eichel, Eichelmann

Aichelberg (acorn mountain) 89,
68, 122

Aicher (dweller near the oaks) 89

Aichholtz (oak wood) 118

Aiching (belonging to the oaks)
89, 122

Aichmann (dweller among the
oaks) 89, 94

Aichroad 159 (oak clearing) 89,
124

Aidt, see Eid

Aierstock (Nickname for egg
dealer) 105

Aigel, see Eigel

Aigner, see Eigne

Aik, see Aich

Aikenbrecher (oak cutter) 89, 95,
100

Ainbinder (cooper) 96, see
Einbinder

Airheart 159, Airhart, see Erhard

Aisch (river name) 83

Aisenberg, see Eisenberg

Aisenstark (as strong as iron)
115

Aisner, see Eisner

Aist (place and river name) 122,
83

Aker, Akermann, see Acker,
Ackermann, also Eckert

Aker, Akers 59 (metal container
for liquids) 106

Akkerman, see Ackerman

Aland (a kind of fish) 115

Alard, Allard (noble + strong) 44

Alb, see Alp

Albach, see Ahlbach

Alban (St. Albans) 135

Albaugh 159, see Ahlbach

Albeisser, see Altbuesser

Alber, Albers (poplar tree, fr
Latin *albulus*) 89

Alber < Adelbero (noble + bear)
47, 48

Alberg, Alberger, Albirger 159 (fr
Adelberg, noble mountain) 46,
68

Albern, see Alber

Albersheim (poplar hamlet) 89,
124

Alberstein (poplar hill) 89, 73

Albert 159, see Albrecht

Alberti, Alberty, son of Albert 59,
142

Albertus (Latin for Albrecht) 141

Albinus (Latin: white) 141

Albold (noble + bold) 44, 46

Alborn, see Ahlborn

Albrand (noble + sword) 46, 47

Albrecht, Albracht, Albraecht
(noble + bright) 47, 47

Albrechtsdorf (Albert's village)
47, 124

Albright 159, 162, Albrite 159 <
Albrecht

Albwin (elf + friend) 48, 48

Aldag (weekday, also Adaldag,
noble day)

Alde (the old man, senior)

Aldefeld (old field) 84

Alder, Alders 59, see Alter

Alderfer 159, see Altdorfer

Alderman, see Altermann

Aldhaus, see Althaus

Aldorf, see Altdorf

Aldorfer, Alldorfer (fr Aldorf 122),
see Altdorfer

Aleberger, see Alberger

Aleman, Alleman, Allman,
Alemann (a German, fr
French *allemand*) 121

Alewyn <Adelwin (noble + sword)
47, 46

Alexander (name of several
popes) 134

Alf 53, Alfs 59, Alfing 55 < Adolf

Alfers 53, 59 < Adolf

Algeier, Algeir, Algeyer, Algire 159, Algyer 159 (fr Allgaeu in Austria) 121

Alias 159, see Elias

Alkire 159, see Algeier

Allbach, Allenbacher, see Ahlbach

Allbrecht, see Albrecht

Allbring 53, Albrink < Albrecht

Alldach, see Aldag

Alldorfer, see Altdorfer

Allebracht, see Albrecht

Allemann 121, Allman, Allimann, Allimang, see Aleman

Allenbach, Allebach, Allenbaugh 159 (eel brook) 77, 83, 151

Allendorf (old village) 124, 122

Allendorf (river village) 79, 124

Aller, Allers 59 (name of river) 83

Allerhand (all kinds of, exclamation) 117

Allerheiligen (All Saints) 135

Alletag (every day) 118

Allewelt (All the world! exlamation) 117

Allex < Alexander

Allgeier, Allgaier, Allgire 159, see Algeier

Allhelm, Alhelm (noble + helmet) 47, 46

Allman, Alimann, Allmang, see Aleman

Allmendinger (fr Allmendingen, public common) 122

Allp, see Alp

Allschbach, Allschpach, Allspach, see Alsbach

Alltschul, Alltschuler, see Altschul

Alltstatt, Alstadt, see Altstadt

Allwein, Allwin, Allwine 159, see Alwin

Allzeit (Any time!, nickname) 117

Alm (alpine pasture) 84

Almbach (brook through pasture) 84, 77

Alman, Almann, see Aleman

Almende (common forest or pasture) 84

Almer <Adelmar (noble + famous) 47, 47

Almstedt (alpine meadow 84, Almsteadt 151)

Alp (fr Alpe 122, alpine pasture) 84

Alpenbauer (alp farmer) 68, 91

Alpaugh 159, see Ahlbach

Alpenbaur (peasant on the mountain pastures) 84, 91

Alper, Alpers 59, Alpert 74, Alphart (elf + strong) 47, 46

Alper, Alpers 59, see Albrecht

Alperstein (Albrecht's mountain) 73

Alphart, see Alper

Alps 59, see Alp

Alram < Adelram (noble + raven) 47, 48

Alraune (mandrake, pharmacist) 96

Alrich (noble + rule) 47 + 47

Alsbach 122 (pre-Germanic river name + *bach*, brook) 83

Alspach (eel brook 77, 122), see Ahlbach

Alsentzer (fr Alsenz) 122

Alstadt, see Altstadt

Alster (river at Hamburg) 83

Alster (magpie) 89

Alt, Altz, Ault, Alter (old man, the elder, senior) 113

Altaker (old field) 84

Altbuesser (shoe repairer) 96, 104

Altdorfer (old village) 124

Altecken (old corner, old field) 85

Altemeyer, Altemeyer (previous owner of a farm) 93

Altemueller (fr the *Altmuehle*, old mill) 93, 94

Alten (place name) 122
Altenbach (old brook) 77, 122
Altenberg, Altenberger (old mountain) 68, 122
Altenburg, Altenburger (old castle) 73, 122
Altendorf (old village) 124, 122
Altenhein (old grove, or old hamlet) 124, 122
Altenhoefer (fr Altenhoefen) 122, 92
Altenhoff 122, Altenhoefer, see Althoff
Altenkirch (old church) 71
Altenstein (old mountain) 73, 122
Alter, Alther, Alters (old man) 59
Alterman 94 (old man, senior, guildleader) 113
Altevogt (old governor) 112, 109
Altfather 159, see Altvater
Altfeld (old field) 84
Altgelt (old money, money changer) 117
Altgenug (old enough) 117
Althage (old enclosure) 123
Althans (old Johnny, John the elder) 113
Althaus, Althauser (old house) 65, 122
Altheinz (Heinrich the elder) 113
Altherr, Alther (old master) 113
Althoff, Althof 122, Althoffer (old farm, old court) 92, 122
Altholz (old wood) 72, 122
Althous 159, Althouse 153, see Althaus
Altig, Altik, see Aldag
Altland 122, Altlandt (opposed to Neuland, or land recently reclaimed fr forest or swamp) 125
Altman, Altmann (old man) 113, 94
Altmark (German province, old march, old boundary) 120

Altmeister (senior guildsman) 113
Altmeyer, Altmeier (fr the Althoff) 92, 94, see Altemeyer
Altmuehl (corruption of pre-Germanic word for "swamp water") 83
Altmueller, see Altemueller
Altoff, see Althoff
Altona (fr pre-Germanic word for swamp, folk-etymologized to "all too near," town near Hamburg, cf. Too Nigh in Georgia) 122
Altorffer, see Altdorfer
Altreiter, Altreith, Altrith, Altruth (old clearing) 125
Alts 59, see Alt
Altschuh (old shoe, cobbler) 106
Altschul (old school, old synagogue) 71
Altschwager (father-in-law) 119
Altstadt, Altstaedt, Altstaetter (old city) 122
Altstein (old stone, old mountain) 73
Altvater (grandfather, patriarch) 113
Altweck, Altwegg (old bun, baker) 96
Altweg (old path) 65
Altwein (good wine, vintner) 102
Altwein (old friend) 48
Altwobner (old weaver) 113, 96
Altz (fr pre-Germanic river name) 7, see Alt, Alts
Alumbaugh 159, see Allenbach
Alvater, Alvather, see Altvater
Alwig < Adelwig (noble + battle) 47, 46
Alwin (noble friend) 47
Alzheim, Alzheimer, Altesheim (old hamlet) 124
Amacker, Amacher (at the field) 69, 84

Aman, Amann, see Amman

Amand, see Amend and Aman

Ambach 122, Ambacher (on the brook) 69, 77

Amberg 122, Amberger (on the mountain) 69, 68

Amberman, see Ammermann

Ambinder, see Ainbinder

Amboldt, see Ambos

Amborn, Ambron (at the spring) 69, 79

Ambos (anvil, blacksmith), 96

Ambrister, Ambrust, Ambruster, see Armbrust

Ambros, Ambrose, Ambrosius 141 (St. Ambrose of Milan) 135

Ambrosi (son of Ambrose) 142

Ambrust, Ambruster, Ambrister 159, see Armbrust

Ambuehl (at the hill) 67, 69

Amburn, see Amborn

Amecker (fr Amecke 122, at the corner) 69, 85

Ameis, Ameise (ant, industrious person) 115

Ameis (deforested area) 71

Amelsberg (mountain of the Amelungs), see next entry

Amelung, Ameling (a Germanic tribe or dynasty) 120

Amen (Amen) 117, see Amman

Amend, Amende, Amendt, Ament, Amment (at the end of the road, field, etc.) 69

Amenhauser, Ammenheuser, Ammenhewser 159, see Ammenhauser

Amereihn, see Amrhein

Amerman, see Ammerman

Amersbach (yellow hammer brook) 77

Ametsbichler (fr Ametsbichl, ant hill) 67, 122

Amhyser (at the houses) 69, 65, 66

Amlehn (at the fief) 69, 84

Ammacher, see Amacher

Amman 94, Aman, Ammeister (Amtmann, Swiss official) 109

Ammen (nurses, see also Amman)

Ammend, see Amend

Ammenhausen (the nurses' houses, the officials' houses) 65, 122

Ammer (yellow-hammer) 89

Ammer (pre-Germanic river name) 83

Ammerheim (yellow-hammer village) 89, 124

Ammerheim (village on the Ammer) 83, 124

Ammermann (bucket maker, fr Latin *amphora*) 94, 96, 101

Ammlung, see Amelung

Ammon, Amon (OT name) 135, see also Amman

Amort (at the end of the village), see Amend

Ampel (swinging lamp, fr Latin *ampulla* 106), or see Ambuehl

Ample 159, see Ampel

Ampler (maker of lamps) 96

Amrein, Amrain, Amrhein, Amrhine 159 (on the Rhine) 69, 83, 122

Amrain (on the footpath) 69, 72, 65

Amsbacher, Amsbaugh 159 (dweller on the Amsbach, inhabitant of Amsbach) 83, 122

Amsel, Amsl (ousel, blackbird, fond singer) 115, 106

Amsler (blackbird catcher) 91

Amspacher, see Amsbacher

am Stein (on the crag) 69, 73, 122

Amstutz, Amsturtz (on the steep slope) 71

Amtag (by day) 143

Amthor (at the gate) 69

Amtman (official) 94, 109

Amueller, see Aumueller

Amwache, see Amweg

Amweg (on the path) 69, 65, 122

Anacker (without a field) 84

Anacker (on the field) 69, 84

Anastasius (name of a pope) 134

Anbinder, see Ainbinder

Ancker (butter, butter maker) 96

Anczel 53 < Johann

Andenrieth (at the reeds, marsh) 69, 81

Anderach (on the river) 69, 79

Andereas, Anders, Anderle 55, see Andreas

Andereck, Andereg, Anderich (at the corner) 69, 85

Andermath (on the meadow) 69, 84

Anders, Andersen, Anderson (son of Andreas) 59

Anderschat (in the shade) 69

Andersnicht (In no other way!, exclamation) 117

Anderwiese (at the meadow) 69, 84

Andlau (pre-Germanic river name in Alsace) 83

Andoni, see Anton

Andre, Andrea, Andraes, Andrea, Andres, Andress, Andries (St. Andrew) 135

Andresen, Andresson, Andrewsen 159 (son of Andreas) 59

Andrew 159, see Andre

Anekost (laborer without meals) 91

Anfeld (on the field) 69, 84

Anfeld (without a field) 84, 91

Anfeld (fr Anfelden) 122

Anfield 159, see Anfeld

Angebrant (field cleared by fire) 84, 125

Angel, Angels 59, Angell (fishhook, hinge, Angle), see Anger

Angel (pre-Germanic river name) 83

Angelbach, Angelbeck (fishing brook, or see Engelbach) 77

Angelberger, Angleberger (fr Amelberg 122), see Engelberg

Angenendt (dweller at the end) 69

Anger 122, Angert 74 (small meadow, pasture) 84, 122

Angerbauer (small farmer) 84, 91

Angerhoffer (small farmer) 84, 92

Angermann (dweller on the meadow) 84, 94

Angermayer, Angermeier, Angermair (farmer dwelling on or at a pasture) 84, 93

Angermueller (miller on the field) 84, 103

Angersbach (meadow brook) 84, 77, 122

Angerstein (field marker) 84, 73, 122

Angle 159, see Angel

Angst (fear) 115

Angst (dweller in narrow part of valley) 76

Angstmann (executioner) 109, 94

Angstmann (timid man) 115, 94

Anhaeuser (fr Anhausen 122, at the houses) 69, 65

Anhalt (German city and state) 121, 122

Anheisser, see Anhaeuser

Anhorn (at the peak) 69, 68, 122

Anhut (without guard) 115

Anhut (hatless) 112

Anke, Anken (butter) 112

Ankenbauer (butter farmer) 91

Anker, Ankermann (anchor maker) 96, 101

Ankerberg (mountain on the water) 68

Ankerbrand (clearing on the water) 125

Anlauf (assault) 118

Anmuth (grace) 115

Annacker, see Anacker

Annbacher (St. Anne's brook) 135, 77

Annecker, see Anaker

Annen (short for Annenberg, etc.) 53

Annenberg (St. Anne's mountain) 135, 68, 122

Anneshansli 55 (little Hans, son of Anna) 60

Annewallt, see Anwalt

Anno 53 < Arnold

Anoker 159, see Anacker

Anreiter (clearing on the An River) 83, 126

Ansbach, Ansbacher (fr Ansbach 122, brook of the gods, or *ans* pre-Germanic word for "river") 48, 77, 83

Anschutz, Anschuetz (one who turns on the water at a mill) 96

Ansel, Ansell, Anssel, Ansler, see Anselm

Anselm, Anshelm, Anselmus 141 (god + helmet) 47, 48, 46, 135, 137

Anselmi (son of Ansel) 142

Anske 55 (little god) 47

Ansorge (without worry) 115

Anspach, Anspacher, Anspack (fr Anspach 122, god + brook) 47, 47

Anstadt, Ansteadt, Anstet < St. Anastasius 135

Anstadt (town on the *Ans*, pre-Germanic river name) 83

Anstein (at the mountain) 69, 73, 122

Anstine 159 (fr Anstein) 122

Answald (god + rule, god + forest) 47, 46, 72

Ante, Antemann 94 (dweller on the boundary, at the end), see Amend

An Weide (on the meadow) 84

Antemann (duck raiser) 91, 94

Antenberg (duck hill) 115, 68

Antenbrink (duck hill) 115

Anters 53, Antes, Anthes < Andreas

Antli, Antley 159 (little duck) 91, 115

Antlitz (face, countenance)

Anton, Anthon (St. Anthony) 135

Antoni, Anthoni (son of Anton) 142

An Weide (on the meadow) 84

Antwerck (siege machine, mechanic) 108

Antwort (answer at court, lawyer) 96

Antzengruber (fr Anzengrub) 122

Anwalt (attorney) 109

Anwaerter (candidate) 109

Apel, Appel, Apelt 74, Apfel (apple) 89, 105

Apel, see Albrecht

Apelberg (apple hill) 89, 68

Apelman, see Appelmann

Apfel (apple) 89, 105, 122

Apfelbach, Apfelbeek (apple brook) 89, 77, 122

Apfelbaum (apple tree) 89

Apfelhaus (apple house) 89, 65

Apitz 53, Apitsch < Albrecht

Apke (little Albrecht) 53, 55

Apotheker (druggist) 96

App 53 < Albrecht

Appel 89, Appelt 74, Appelbaum, see Apel, Apfelbaum

Appel (pre-Germanic river name) 83

Appelbome, see Apfelbaum

Appeldorne (apple thorn) 89, 122

Appelmann (apple grower or seller) 89, 106, 94

Appelstein (apple seed) 89, 151

Appenzeller, Appenzellar 159
    (Swiss fr Canton Appenzell)
    121
Appert 53 < Albrecht
Apple 53, 159 < Adelbert
Applefeld 159 (apple field) 89, 84
Applegarth 159 (apple orchard)
    89, 84
Appler (apple grower or seller) 89
April (April, term of corvée duty)
    143
Apteher, see Apotheker
Apteker (druggist) 98
Arant, see Arnd
Arb (heir, see Erb) 47
Arbaugh 159 (fr Arbach 122,
    eagle brook 48, 77)
Arbaugh (fr *ar*, pre-Germanic
    word for "river") 83, 77
Arbegast, see Arbogast
Arbeiter, Arbetter (worker) 91
Arbengast, see Arbogast
Arberg (eagle mountain) 48, 68
Arberg (mountain on the Aar) 83,
    68
Arbesman (heir) 47
Arbogast (heir + guest, name of a
    saint) 47, 135
Arbor, Arbort 74 (fr Latin *arbor*
    for tree) 141
Arburg (eagle castle) 48, 73
Arcularius (Latin, casket maker)
    141
Arehart 159, see Erhard
Arenberg, see Arensberg
Arend 53, Arends 59, Arendt,
    Arenth, Arentz, Arens, see
    Arnold
Arenholtz (eagle forest, Arnold's
    forest) 48, 72, 122
Arensberg, Arensberger (eagle
    mountain) 48, 68, 122
Arenstein, see Arnstein
Arf, Arfmann (heir) 46, 94

Arg (mean, stingy) 115
Argabright 159, Argenbright,
    Argubright < Erkanbrecht
    (genuine + bright) 46, 151
Argast, see Arbogast
Argire 159, Argauer, see
    Aargauer
Arisman 159, see Ehrismann
Arlt 53 < Arnold
Armbrust, Armbruester,
    Armbreast 159, Armbreaster
    (crossbow, fr Latin
    arcubalista) 108
Armel, Aermel (sleeve, tailor) 104
Armenbeter (one who prays for
    poor) 138
Armentraut, Armentrout,
    Armontraut 159 (friend of the
    poor) 138
Armgast (poor stranger) 120
Armistead 159 < Armistaed
    (place name) 122
Armknecht (poor servant) 138
Armpriester 159, see Armbrust
Armstark (arm strong) 115
Armstrong, see Armstark
Armut, Armuth (poverty) 118
Arnau (eagle meadow) 46, 84
Arnbuehl (eagle hill) 46, 67
Arnd 53, Arndt < Arnold
Arndald, Arnswald (eagle forest)
    48, 72
Arndorf (eagle village) 46, 124,
    122
Arndt, see Arnd
Arner (harvester) 91, 96
Arnheim (eagle hamlet) 46, 124
Arnhelm (eagle + helmet) 46, 46
Arnhoff (eagle farm) 46, 92
Arnholt, Arnholtz, see Arnold
Arno 53 < Arnold
Arnold, Arnolt, Arnholt, Arnolds
    59, Arnoldus 141 (eagle + loyal
    or eagle + rule) 48, 58, 47

Arnoldi (son of Arnold) 142

Arnreich (eagle + rule) 46, 47

Arnsdorf, Arnsdorfer, see Arndorf

Arnsmeyer (occupant of the Arnshoff, eagle farm, Arnold's farm) 93

Arnstein (eagle mountain) 46, 73, 122

Arnt, see Arnd

Arnulf (eagle + wolf) 46, 48

Arnwine 159 (eagle + friend) 48, 48

Arold, see Arnold

Aronstein, see Arnstein

Artmann, Artmeier (proprietor of tilled fields) 84, 93

Arzberger (fr Arzberg 122), see Erzberger

Arzt, Artz, Arts 159 (doctor, fr Latin *arciater*) 96

Asang (burned clearing) 126

Asbach, Asbacher (pre-Germanic *as*, meaning "dirty water" + *bach*, brook) 83

Asch, Asche, Ash 159 (ash tree, ash forest, see Esch) 89, 122

Asch (ashes, ash burner) 95

Asch (vessel) 106

Aschbacher (fr Aschbach 122), see Eschbach

Aschberg, Ascheberg, Aschberger (ash tree mountain) 89, 48

Aschemeier (farmer among the ash trees) 89, 93

Aschenbach (ash tree brook) 89, 77

Aschenbrand (clearing in the ash trees) 89, 126

Aschenbrenner (ash burner, for glass and soap) 96

Aschendorf (ash tree village) 89, 124, 122

Aschenfelter (ashtree fields) 89, 84

Aschenmoor (ash fen) 89, 80

Aschenreiter (clearing in ash woods) 89, 84

Ascher, Aschman 94, Aschmann (maker of tanner's lime, soapmaker's ash) 95

Asendorf (grazing village) 122

Ash 159, Ashe, see Asch

Ashauer 159 (ash tree cutter, dweller on a meadow in the ash trees) 89, 95

Ashbaugh 159, Ashbaugher, see Aschbacher

Ashenfelter 159 (ash tree field) 84

Asher 159, see Ascher

Ashliman, see Ascher

Ashman 159, see Asher

Asman 53, Asmann, Assmann, Asmus, Assmus < St. Erasmus 135

Aspe, see Espe

Aspeck, Aschbeck (ash brook) 89, 77

Aspel (fen) 80

Aspelhof (farm on a fen meadow) 80, 92

Aspelmeyer (fr the Aspelhof, fen farm) 80, 93, 94

Aspin (aspen) 89

Aspinwall < Espenwald (aspen forest) 89, 72

Assenmacher (wainwright) 96

Asser, Assmann (wainright) 96

Asshauer (wainright) 96

Assheim (carrion hamlet) 124, 122

Assmann < Erasmus

Ast (branch, wood cutter, difficult person) 95, 115, 122

Astheim (east hamlet) 85, 124, 122

Astholz (branch wood, faggot gatherer) 95

Astor (astor, fr the Greek 9, or
    perhaps *Aster*, magpie 89, or
    astore, Italian: hawk 89)
Astroth (branch clearing) 125
Aswalt, Answald, see Oswald
Atlikon (Swiss village) 127
Atteborn (at the well) 70, 79
Atterholt, Atherholt (at the
    forest) 69, 72
Atler 159, see Adler
Atz, Attz (donkey) 115
Atz, see Albrecht
Atzbach (pre-Germanic *at*, river
    + *bach*, brook) 83, 77, 122
Atzel, see Elster
Atzelstein (magpie mountain) 73
Atzman (follower of Albrecht) 94
Atzrodt, Atzrott (donkey clearing)
    125
Au, Aub, Aue (meadow, usually
    shortened fr compound word)
    84, 122
Aube (wet land) 80
Aubel 53 < Albrecht
Auberg (meadow hill) 84, 68
Aubitz 53 < Albrecht
Aubrecht, see Albrecht
Auburg, Auburger (castle on the
    meadow, or castle at Au) 84,
    73, 122
Auch, Auchmann 94 (night
    shepherd) 95
Auchenbach, Auchenbaugh 159,
    Auchinbaugh 159, see
    Achebach
Auchtmann, see Achmann
Aue, Auen, see Au
Auenbrugger (dweller near the
    bridge at the meadow) 84, 71
Auer (dweller on a meadow,
    usually shortened fr
    compound word) 84
Auerbach (muddy water brook)
    84, 77
Auer (auerochs) 115

Auerbach 122, Auerback (brook
    through meadow, possibly
    bison [*auerochs*] brook, or else
    based on pre-Germaic *ur*,
    muddy water) 84, 77, 115, 122
Auerhahn (grouse) 84, 115
Auerswald (meadow wood) 84, 71
Auerweck (meadow path) 84, 65,
    Auerweck (meadow village, fr
    Latin *vicus*) 84, 124
Aufderheide (on the heath) 69, 81
Auffahrt (Ascension Day) 143
Aufleger (mover, transporter) 96
Aufrecht (upright) 115
Auge, Augen (eye, eyes) 114
Augenbaugh, Aughenbaugh 159,
    see Achebach
Augestein (St. Augustine) 135
Aughinbaugh 159, see Achebach
Augsburg, Augspurg, Augsburger
    (Swabian city) 122
Augst, see Augstein
August, Augustus (Latin,
    Augustus) 141
Augustin, Augustinus 141 (St.
    Augustine) 135
Auhagen (enclosure on the
    meadow) 84, 123
Aul, Auler, Aulner (pot, potter, fr
    Latin *olla*) 96
Aulbert, see Albert
Auld, see Alt
Aule (jackdaw) 115
Aulebach, Aulenbacher (fr
    Aulenbach) 122
Aulenbaecker (potter) 96
Aulmann (potter) 96, 94
Aulmend, see Amend
Aulner, see Aulmann
Ault, see Alt
Aulthaus, see Althaus
Aultland, see Altland
Aultmann, see Altmann
Auman, Aumann (meadow man)
    84, 94

Aumend, see Amend

Aumiller, see Aumueller

Aumueller (fr the Aumuehle, mill on the meadow) 84, 103

Auner, see Auman

Aungst 159, see Angst

Aurich (place name) 122

Ausdemwalde (out of the forest) 69, 71

Ausderau (out of the meadow) 69, 84

Ausdermuehle (out of the mill) 69, 103

Ausfresser (glutton) 115

Ausheim (outside the village) 69, 124

Ausherman 159, see Ascher

Auslander (outlander, foreigner) 120

Auspurger, see Augsburg

Aust, Austen, Austin (St. Augustine) 135

Auster, see Oster

Austerlitz (town in Bohemia) 122

Austermann, Austmann (easterner) 85, 94

Austermuehle, see Ausdermuehle

Austrich, Austria 153, see Oestrich

Auwaerter (meadow guard) 96

Avernarius (Latin for Habermann) 141

Averbach, see Auerbach

Averbeck (beyond the stream) 77

Averdieck (beyond the dike) 70, 82

Averhart, see Eberhard

Avig 151, see Ewig

Awald 151, see Ewald

Awl 151, see Ahl

Ax, Axe, Axt 74, Axmann 94 (ax, ax maker, carpenter) 96

Axel 53 < Absolon (OT name, Absalom) 135

Axelbaum (axel shaft, wainwright) 96, 106

Axelmann (cartwright) 96, 94, 106

Axelrad, Axelrod (axle wheel, cartwright) 106

Axenmacher, see Assemaker

Axt 74, Axtman 94 (ax, woodcutter) 95

Ay, Aye, Ayer, see Ei, Eier

Ayd, Aydt, see Eid

Ayrer, Ayers 59, see Eier

Ayzenberg, see Eisenberg

Azenweiler (donkey village) 127

Azman (donkey man) 115, 94

B

Baacke, Baake, see Baak

Baaden, Baader, see Baden, Bader

Baak (horse, horse dealer) 105

Baar 122, see Bahr

Baarsch, see Barsch

Baart, Baartz, see Bart

Baas (master, chief, boss) 109

Baasche, see Basch

Baase, see Base

Baasler, see Basler

Babbes, Babst 74, Babest, see Pabst

Babst, see Pabst

Baccus, see Backhaus

Bach 122, Bache, Bachs 59 (brook, dweller on a brook) 77

Bacharach, Bachrach (city on the Rhine) 122

Bachaus, see Backhaus

Bachdold, Bachdolt, Backdolt, see Bechtold

Bache (brood swine, female wild boar) 91, 115

Bache (ham, hog) 91, 82

Bachenheimer (fr Bachenheim 122, brook hamlet) 77, 124

Bacher, Bachert 74, Bachner, Bachart 74 (dweller on a brook) 77, 87, 122

Bacher (wild boar) 115
Bacher (Jewish, *bachur*, Talmud student) 147
Bachfeld (brook field) 122, 84
Bachhoffen, Bachofen 122, see Backof
Bachhuber (farmer on the brook) 77, 92
Bachmann, Bachman (dweller on the brook) 77, 94
Bachmeyer, Bachmeier, Bachmaier, Bachsmeyer (farmer on a brook) 77, 93
Bachmeyer (occupant of the Bachhof, brook farm) 77, 93
Bachner, see Bacher
Bachofen, see Backofen
Bachrach, see Bacharach
Bachrodt (clearing by the book) 77, 126
Bachschmidt (the smith on the brook) 77, 96
Bachstein (brook hill, brook stone) 77, 73
Bachstein, see Backstein
Bachtel, Bachtell, Bachtler, see Bechtel
Bachthal (brook valley) 77, 76, 122
Bachus, see Backhaus
Back, see Baak
Back 159, see Bach
Back, Backe (jowl) 114
Backebrandt (baker's fire, baker) 96
Backer 159, Backert 74, see Bacher, Becker
Backfisch (fish for frying) 115
Backhaus, Backhus, 159 (bakehouse, bakery) 65, 122
Backhoffer, Backhofer, see Backof
Backler (baker) 96
Backley 159, see Bechtle
Backman, Backmann (baker) 96, 94

Backmeister (master baker) 96
Backner (baker) 96
Backof, Backoff, Backofen, Backhoffer, Backoven (baker's oven, baker) 96
Backstrom (brook stream) 77, 78
Backus, see Backhaus
Bacmeister, see Backmeister
Bad, Bade, see Bader
Badder, see Bader
Badecker, see Boettcher
Badedorfer, Badendorfer (bath village) 96, 124
Bademann (bath attendant) 96, 94
Baden (baths, any one of many South German places) 121, 122
Badenhamer, Badenheimer (fr Badenheim 122, bath hamlet) 124
Bader (bath attendant, surgeon) 96
Badertscher (surgeon) 96
Badmann, Badner, see Bademann
Badstuber (bath room, bather) 96
Baecher, Baechert, see Becher, Bechert
Baechle 53 (little brook) 77
Baechtel, see Bechtel
Baeck 122, see Becker
Baecker 122, see Becker
Baedeker, see Boettcher
Baehler, see Buehler
Baehm, see Boehm
Baehr, Baehre (bear) 48
Baehring, Baehringer, see Behrens
Baehrle 53 (little bear) 48
Baehrmann, see Berman
Baehrwolf (bear + wolf) 48, 48
Baender, see Bender
Baeninger, see Peninger

Baenisch, Baensch, see Benesch

Baenk (bench, bench maker) 96, 106

Baentzler 53 < St. Benedictus 135

Baer, Baehr (bear, usually a shortened form) 48

Baer (wild boar) 48

Baerenburg (bear castle) 48, 73, 122

Baerenreuth (bear clearing) 126

Baerenreuth (fr Berenreuth 122, burned clearing) 126

Baerenwyl (bear village) 48, 127

Baerger, see Berger

Baerhold (bear + loyal) 48, 48

Baeringer, see Behrens

Baerli 53, Baerley 159 (little bear) 48

Baerman, Baermann (bear man, bear trainer) 48, 96, 94

Baerstein (bear mountain) 48, 73

Baertlein 55, Berlein (little beard) 114

Baertschi, see Bertsch

Baerwald (bear forest) 48, 71

Baeseke, see Beseke

Baesel, Baesler, see Basler

Baetger, see Boettcher

Baetje, Baetjer, see Boettcher

Baetz, see Betz

Baeumer, Baeumler (expert on fruit trees) 89, 96

Baeuml 53 (little tree) 89

Baeurele, Baeurlein, Baeuerlein (little peasant) 91, 55, 122

Baeyerlein 55, see Baeuerle

Baez, see Betz

Bagger (dredger) 96

Bahl 53, Bahle, Bahler, Bahls 59, Bahlmann 94, Bahler < Baldwin

Bahn, Bahne, Bahnlein 55 (path, track, road) 65

Bahner, Bahnert 74 (weaver's tool, weaver) 106

Bahnke 55 (little path) 65

Bahnmueller (miller on the path) 65, 103

Bahr (bear) 48

Bahre, Bahremann 94 (stretcher bearer) 96

Bahrenburg, see Barenburg

Bahrlein 55 (little bear) 48

Bahsel, see Basler

Baier, Baierman 94, see Bayer

Baierlein 55, Baierline 159, see Bayerle, Baeurele

Baiersdorf 122, see Bayersdorf

Bail, Baile, Bailer, Bailor 159, Baylor 159, see Beil, Beiler

Bain, Bainn, see Bein

Bainhauer, see Beinhauer

Bainter, see Painter

Bair, Bairer, see Baer, Bayer

Baisch 53 < St. Sebastian 135

Baitmann 94, Baitz, Baizner (falconer) 91

Bakenhus 122, see Backhaus

Baker 159, Bakker, see Becker, Bacher

Baketel 159, see Bechtel

Bakhoffer, see Backhov

Balbier, Balbierer (barber) 96

Balcer, see Baltzer

Balch (kind of game fish) 115, 106

Balck, see Balk

Bald, Balde, Baldt, Balt (bold 46, river name 83)

Bald (soon) 118

Baldauf, Balldauf, Balduf (brave + wolf) 48, 117

Baldauf ("soon up," perhaps a greeting to miners) 117

Baldemar (bold + famous) 46, 47

Baldewein, see Baldwin

Baldhauer, see Waldhauer

Baldinger 122 (fr Balding, belonging to Baldwin) 46, 59

Baldrich, Baldrick (bold + rule) 46, 47

Baldwin, Baldewin (brave + friend) 46, 48, 50

Balg (hide, skinny person) 114

Balk (beam, carpenter) 96

Balke (beam, carpenter) 96

Ball, Balls (ball, dance, hunting sound) 59

Ball 53, Ballmann 94 < Baldwin

Ballauf, see Baldauf

Ballenberg, Ballenberger (fr Ballenberg) 122

Ballenger, Baller 53 < Baldwin

Ballenhausen (town name) 122

Ballerstadt (fr Ballerstaedt) 122

Balling 53, 55, Ballinger < Baldwin

Ballman 53, 94, Ballmann < Baldwin

Ballwein, see Baldwin

Balmer, Ballmer, Ballmert (dweller under a cliff, see also Palmer) 74

Balmtag (Palm Sunday) 143

Balsam (balsam) 106, 115

Balsbaugh 159, see Pfaltzbach

Balser 53, Balsor 159 < Balthasar

Balsgrove 159, see Pfaltzgraf

Balsinger, see Bellsinger

Balster, see Balthasar

Balt, Balter 53 < Balthasar

Balthasar, Baltasar, Balthhauser, Baltzar, Baltzaer (one of the Three Kings) 135, 111

Balthauer, see Waldhauer

Baltz, Balz, Baltze, Baltzer, Baltzel, Baltzell, Baltzer, Baltzar, see Palts, Paulser, Balthasar

Baltzer, see Balthasar

Bambach 159, see Bombach

Bamberg, 122, Bamberger, Bamesberg (fr Bamberg)

Bamler, Baemler (idler, loafer) 115

Bammert, see Bannwart

Bancalf 159, see Bannkauf

Band (hoop maker) 106

Bandel, Bandell, Bandele, Bandli (ribbon maker) 106

Bandhagen, Bandhaken (cooper's hook, cooper) 106

Bandholt, Bandtholtz (wood for barrel hoops, cooper) 96, 106

Bandmacher (ribbon maker) 96

Baner, Banner, see Bahner

Bang, Bange, Bangs 59, Banger, Bangers 59, Bangert 74 (timid) 115

Banger, Bangart, Bangert, Banghart, Bangerth, see Baumgart

Bangratz, see Pankratz

Banholtz, Banholtzer (proscribed forest, forester) 72, 109

Bank 122, Banke, Banker, Banks 59 (bench, workbench, bench maker) 106

Bankamper (field on a road, proscribed field) 65, 84

Bankard, Bankhart, Bankerd, Bankert (illegitimate child) 119

Bankert (illegitimate child)

Bankwirt (taverner) 96

Bann (ban) 122

Bannat (Banat, German area in Hungary) 121

Banne, Bannmann (crowd, mob) 118

Banner (banner, ensign) 107

Bannerman, Bannertraeger (ensign) 107, 94

Banninger (fr Banningen) 122

Bannkauf (proscribed sale) 118

Bannwardt (forest guard) 109

Bansch, Banscher, Baensche (pot belly) 114

Banse, Bansen (store room, granary, woodpile, storekeeper) 96

Bantel, Bantell, Bantle 159, Bantli 55 (little band, ribbon maker) 106

Bantel, Bantele 53 < St. Pantaleon 135

Bantner (dweller in a fenced area) 84

Bantz, Banz, Banzel 55 (small child) 115

Banwarth (forest guard) 65, 47

Banzer, see Panzer

Banzhaf (barrel, barrel maker) 96

Baptista, Baptiste, Baptisto (John the Baptist) 135

Baranhardt, see Bernhard

Barb, Barbe (kind of river fish, fisherman) 115, 106

Barbel 53, Baerbel < Barbara 60

Barbelroth (Barbara's clearing) 126

Barch (barrow hog) 91

Barchell (fr Barchel) 122

Barchent (fustian weaver) 96

Barchmann (swineherd) 95, 94

Barcket (weaver of Barchend, rough cloth) 96

Bard, see Bart

Bardelman, see Bartel

Bardenhagen (halbard enclosure) 124, 122

Bardenheuer (halbard maker) 108

Bardenwerter (halbard maker) 108

Bardman, see Bartmann

Barenbaum, see Birnbaum

Barenburg (bear castle) 48, 73, 122

Barensteker (bear killer, hunter) 91

Barfknecht (honest vassal) 119

Barfuss (barefoot, barefoot friar) 114, 110

Barg (castrated swine) 91, see Barmann

Barg, see Berg

Bargar, Barger, see Berger

Bargfeld 122, see Bergfeld

Barghan, see Berghan

Barghoff, see Berghoff

Bargholtz, see Bergholtz, Berkholtz

Bargmann, Bargman, see Bergmann

Barmann (swine castrator) 95, 94

Barhausen (bear houses) 48, 65

Barhorst (bear hurst) 48, 72

Baringer, see Baehringer

Bark, Barke 122 (birch tree) 89

Bark, Barke (ship, boatman) 96

Barkamp (bear field) 48, 84

Barkdoll, see Bergdoll

Barkewitz (mountain village) 127

Barkhaus, Barkhausen 122, Barkhauser, Barkhouse 153, Barkhouser, see Berghaus

Barkheimer, Barkhimer 159, see Bergheimer

Barkhorn, see Berghorn

Barkmann, see Bergmann

Barmann, Barmeyer (half-free peasant) 91, 94, see Bermann

Barnd, see Bernd

Barner, see Berner

Barnhard, Barnhardt, see Bernhard

Barnhaus 122, Barnhauser (bear house) 48, 65

Barnheart 159, see Bernhard

Barnholt, see Bernholt

Barnhouse 153, Barnhouser 159, see Barnhaus

Barnscheier (bear barn) 48

Barnstein (fr Barnstein 122), see Bernstein

Barpfennig (money changer) 96

Barnstorf (bear village, or
Bernhard's village) 48, 124,
122
Baron, Barron (warrior, baron)
107
Barr (cash) 115
Barr 159, see Baer
Barrabas (NT name) 111
Barringer < Berenger (bear +
spear) 48, 46
Barringer 159, see Behringer
Barsch, Barss (perch, fish dealer)
115, 105
Barsch 53 < Bartholomaeus
Bart, Barth, Barthel 55, Bartz 74
< Bartholomaeus, Barthold,
Bartolf, etc.
Bart, Barth (beard, barber) 112,
96
Bartal 159, see Bertel
Bartasch (fringed purse) 106
Barte (butcher's ax, butcher) 106
Bartel, Bartels 59, Barthels,
Barttel, Bartelmes <
Bartholomaeus
Bartenschlager, see Bardenheuer
Barth 122, see Bart
Barthel, see Bartel
Barthelheim (Barthel's hamlet)
123
Barthels, see Berthold
Barthelm (battle-ax + helmet) 46,
46
Barthelmes, see Bartolomaeus
Bartholomaeus, Bartholoma,
Bartholomae, Bartholome,
Bartholomes, Bartholomei,
Bartholomy, Bartholomus (St.
Bartholomew) 135
Bartholt (battle-ax + loyal) 46, 48
Bartkuss (beard kiss) 112
Bartle 159, see Bartel
Bartlebaugh 159 (Bartel's brook)
77
Bartling (fr Bartlingen) 122

Bartmann (thick stone jug) 106
Bartmann (beard wearer) 112, 94
Bartol, Bartold, see Bartholt,
Bartholomaeus
Bartolomaeus, Bartolome, see
Bartholomaeus
Bartosch, see Bartasch
Bartram (battle-ax + raven) 46,
48
Barts 59, see Bart
Bartsch 53 < Bartholomaeus
Bartsch, see Bertsch
Bartscher, Bartscheer,
Bartscherer (beard shears,
barber) 96
Barttel, see Bartel
Bartz 53, 59, Barz, see Bart,
Bartholomaeus
Barzmann 53, 93 <
Bartholomaeus
Basch (sharp, as of spice) 115
Base, Basemann 94 (cousin,
gossip) 119
Basel 122, Basler, Bassel (fr
Basel) 122
Bass (boss) 109
Basse (one-masted boat) 122
Basselmann, see Basel
Bassler, see Basel
Bast, Bastian, Bastmann,
Bastien < St. Sebastian 135–
136, 53
Bast (hunting term, breaking up
of stag) 91
Bastert (bastard) 119
Bate (help), see also Pate
Bates 159, see Betz
Bateman 159, see Bethmann
Bath, see Bad
Bathmann, Batmann (bath
attendant) 96, 94
Batt (emolument), also St.
Beatus 135
Batt (St. Batt, Beatus) 135

Batten, Battenberg, Battenfeld (place names fr *bat*, swamp water) 80, 122

Battermann (wooden spade) 106

Battermann (boaster) 115, 94

Battist (John the Baptist) 135

Batts 159, Batz, Batze, Batzer, see Patz

Batty 159, see Battist

Batz (a small coin) 117

Bau (construction, cultivation) 122

Bauch (belly, glutton) 114

Bauchmann (man with big belly) 114

Bauer, Bauers 59, Baur, Bauerdt 74 (farmer) 91

Bauerfeld, Bauernfeld, Bauersfeld (peasant field) 91, 84

Bauerle 55, Bauerlein, Bauerlien 159, Bauerline 159 (little peasant) 91

Bauermann (same as Bauer) 91, 94

Bauermeister, Bauernmeister (village head) 109

Bauernfeind, Bauernfiend 159 (peasant enemy, probably initiation name) 117

Bauernschmidt (peasant smith) 91, 96

Bauernschub, Bauernshub 159 (peasant overcoat) 112

Bauers 59, see Bauer

Bauerschmidt, Bauernschmid (village smith) 91, 96

Bauersfeld, see Bauerfeld

Bauershaefer (peasant oats) 91, 92

Bauerwein (peasant wine) 91, 102

Baugh 159, Baugher, Baughman, see Bach, Bacher, Bachmann

Baughman 159, see Baumann

Baughtall 159, see Bechtold

Bauhaus (shelter at construction site) 65, 122

Bauholzer (seller of building wood, builder in wood) 72, 106

Bauk, Bauker (drum, drummer) 96, 106

Bauknecht (construction helper, field hand) 96

Bauknight 159, see Bauknecht

Baum, Baums 59 (tree) 89, 122

Bauman, Baumann (farmer, see Bauer) 91, 94

Baumbach (tree brook) 89, 77, 122

Baumberger (fr Baumberg 122, tree mountain) 89, 68

Baumbusch (tree busch) 89, 72

Baumeister (builder, agricultural manager) 96

Baumel 55 (little tree) 89

Baumer, Baumert 74 (horticulturist) 84, 143

Baumer (manager of, or dweller near a toll gate)

Baumgaert, Baumgaertel, Baumgaertner (orchard, orchardist) 84

Baumgarden, Baumgarten 122, Baumgardner, Baumgartner, Baumgaertner, Baumgarthner, Baumgartel, Baumgartner, Baumgart, Baumgarth (orchardist) 84

Baumhacker, see Baumhauer

Baumhard (strong as a tree) 89, 46

Baumhard (uncultivated, tree-studded area) 89, 84

Baumhauer, Baumheuer (lumber jack) 95

Baumheuer (tree cutter) 91

Baumhof, Baumhoefer (tree farm) 89, 92, 122

Baumiller (miller at a *Bauhof*) 103

Baumler (tree guard) 89, 96, see also Baumer

Baummer, see Baumer

Baumoehl (tree cutter) 95, see also Baumohl

Baumohl (olive oil seller) 106

Baumrin, Baumrind (collector of bark for tanning) 95

Baumstark (strong as a tree) 115

Baumstein (tree stone) 89, 73

Baumwoll (cotton) 105, 106

Baur, see Bauer

Baurmeister, Bauernmeister (village mayor) 109

Baus, Bausch, Bauscher (bolster) 106

Baus (bruise, swelling) 114

Bausback (chubby cheek) 115

Bausch, see Busch

Bauschenberger (bush mountain) 72, 68

Bauser, Bausermann (heavy drinker) 115

Baustian, see Bast, Bastian

Bauth, Bauthe, Bauthner (building, beehive) 95

Bauthz (fr Bautzen) 122

Baverungen 159, see Beverungen

Bawman 159, see Baumann

Bayer, Bayr, Beyer, Bayermann 94 (Bavarian) 121

Bayerfalck (Bavarian falcon) 120, 91, 115, 62

Bayerhoff (Bavarian farm) 122, 121, 92

Bayerle 55, Bayerlein 55 (little Bavarian, see Baeuerle) 120

Bayersdorf (Bavarian's village) 120, 124

Baylor 159, see Beiler

Bayrle, see Bayerle

Baxstrasser, see Bergstrasser

Bazermann, see Patz

Beacher 159, see Buecher

Beachler 159, see Buechler

Beadenkof 159, Beadenkoef, Beadenkopf, see Biedenkopp

Beagle 159, see Buegel

Beahm 159, see Boehm

Beahmesderfner 159 (Bohemian villager) 122, 124

Beal 159, Beals 59, Beall, see Buehl

Bealefeld 159, Bealefield 153, see Bielefeld 122

Bealer 159, Beeler 159, see Buehler

Beam 159, Beamer, see Boehm, Boehmer

Beamsderfer 159, Beamesderfer, see Beahmesderfner

Bean 159, Beane, see Bohn, Bohne

Bear 159, Bearman, see Baehr, Baehrmann

Beardorf 159 (bear village) 48, 124, 151

Beaver 153, see Bieber

Bebel, Bebler, Beber (something or someone small) 113

Bech, Bechmann (pitch gatherer) 95

Bechel (little brook) 77, 55

Bechdold, Bechdolt, see Berchthold

Bechelmeier (fr the Bechelhof, little brook farm) 77, 93, 92, 94

Becher, Bechermann 94, Bechler (maker of mugs, fr Latin *bicarium*) 106

Becher (tarheeler, tar maker, fr Latin *pix*) 95

Becher (dweller on a brook) 77

Becher, Bechler (drinker, tippler) 115

Bechhoffer (pitch farm) 92

Bechler (dweller by a stream) 77

Bechlinger (fr Bechlingen) 122

Bechmann (tarheeler, tar maker) 95, 94

Bechold, see Bechthold

Bechstein (pitch stone) 73

Becht, Bechte, Bechtel, Bechtler (New Year revelry), see also Bechthold

Bechthold, Bechtolt, Bechtoll, see Berchthold

Beck (brook) 77, 122

Beck, Becks 59, Becke (baker) 96

Beck (snout) 114

Beck (basin, Latin, *bacinum*) 106

Beckel (helmet) 108

Beckelheimer 55, Beckelhimer 159 (fr Beckelheim 122, little brook hamlet) 77, 124

Beckemeyer (brook farmer) 77, 93

Beckenbach (Becco's brook) 77

Beckendorf (brook village) 77, 124, 122

Beckenhaub (helmet maker) 108

Beckenholt (brook wood) 77, 72

Beckenschlager (coppersmith) 96

Becker, Beckert 74 (baker) 96, 104, 143

Becker (dweller on a brook) 78

Beckerbach, see Beckenbach

Beckermann, Beckmann (baker) 96, 94

Beckeweg (brook path) 77, 65

Beckhardt (Beghard, lay brother) 110

Beckler (tippler) 115

Becklin 55, Beckley 159, see Boekle

Beckman, Beckmann (baker) 96, 94

Beckmann (dweller on a brook) 77, 94

Beckner, see Becker

Beckolt, see Berchtold

Beckstein (brook stone) 77, 73, 122

Beckstein (brick maker) 100, 122

Beckstrom (brook stream) 77, 78

Beech 159, see Buech, Buecher

Beechener 159, see Buechner

Beehler 159, see Buehler

Beek (brook) 77

Beeker 159, see Buecher

Beekmann, see Bachmann

Beel 159, see Buehl

Beeler 159, Beehler, see Buehler

Beem 159, Beemer, see Boehm, Boehmer

Been, see Bein

Beer, Beermann, see Baer, Baermann, Bier, Biermann

Beer, Beers 59, see Ber, Behr, Bier

Beerbach (bear brook, boar brook) 48, 77, 122

Beerbohm (dweller near a pear tree) 89

Beerends, see Behren

Beerger, see Berger

Beermann, see Baehrmann

Beerschank (pub, taverner) 96

Begabock 159, see Beckenbach

Begemann (dweller on the Bega) 83, 94

Begstein, see Beckstein

Begtel, Begtoll, Begtolt, see Bechtel

Behagel (affable) 115

Behl, Behle, Behler, Behlert 74, see Buehl

Behling (fr Behlingen) 122

Behm, Behme, Behmer 34, see Boehm

Behn, Behne, Behner, Behnemann 94 < Bernhard

Behnke 55, Behnken (little bear), or < Bernhard

Behr, Behre, Behrs 59 (bear, boar), or < Bernhard

Behren 53, Behrens 59, Behrend, Behrendt < Bernhard

Behrens < Bernhard

Behrenstengel, see Birnstengel

Behringer (fr Behringen, the descendants or people of Behr) 124, 122

Behrmann (bear + man, bear trainer) 48, 94

Behrman, Behrmann (beer handler) 96, 94

Behrnhard, see Bernhard

Behse, see Besen

Beichel 55, Beichl (little belly) 114

Beichler, Beichmann 94 (slope dweller) 71

Beichley, see Beichel 151

Beichtel, Beichter (confessor) 110

Beidel, Beidler, see Beutel

Beidelmann, Beidelman, see Beutelmann

Beiderwieden (dweller by the willows) 69, 89

Beier, Beiermann, see Bayer

Beierlein, see Baeuerlein, Bayerlein

Beiersdort (Bavarian's village) 121, 124

Beigel, see Buegel

Beightel 159, Beightol, see Beichtel, Bechtol

Beights 159, see Beitz

Beikler, see Beichler

Beil, Beiler (ax maker or seller) 106

Beilfus (ax foot) 114

Beiling (fr Beilingen) 122

Beilke 55 (little ax) 106

Beilstein (ax stone, old hunting grounds) 73

Beimel, Beimler, see Baeumel, Beumer, Baeumler

Beimford (by the ford) 78

Bein, Beine, Beinn, Beinle 55 (leg, bone) 114

Beinhauer (butcher, not leg hacker) 96

Beinhorn (river name, swamp corner) 80, 83

Beinike, Beinle 55 (little bee) 115

Beinkampen (by the fields) 69, 84

Beinstein (by the mountain) 69, 68, 122

Beischwanger (adjacent clearing) 125

Beisel, Beissel, Beissler (tool for splitting wood) 106

Beisner (one who hunts with falcons) 91

Beispiel (example) 118

Beisser (falconer) 91

Beisser (one who bites) 115

Beiswenger 159, see Beischwanger

Beitel 122, Beittel, Beitle 159, Beitler, Beitelmann (purse maker) 106, see Beutel, Beutler, Beutelmann

Beitz, Beitzel, Beitzell (falconer) 91

Beker, see Becker

Bekkenbach, see Beckenbach

Bekker, see Becker

Bekerer (mug maker) 96

Bekmann, see Beckmann

Beler 159, Beeler, see Buehler

Belfield 153, see Bielefeld

Belitz (place name) 122

Bell, Belle (part of a ship) 118

Bell, Belle (white poplar) 89

Beller (watch dog, quarreler) 115

Belling, Bellinger (fr Belling) 122

Bellmann (public announcer) 109, 94

Bellmer, Bellner (public announcer) 109

Belman, Bellmann, see Bellmann

Belmont 17, see Schoenberg

Belser (swamp dweller) 80

Belsner, see Beltz

Beltz, Belz, Beltzer, Beltzner, see Peltz

Beltzenhagen (place name) 124, 122

Bemer 159, see Boehmer

Bemiller, see Buehlmueller

Bence 159, see Bentz

Benck, Benke, see Benk

Benck, Bencke < Bernhard

Bendel (ribbon maker or seller) 96, 106

Bendel, Bendler (barrel hoop maker, cooper) 96, 106

Bender, Benders 59, Bendert 74 (cooper) 96

Benderoth (swamp clearing) 80, 125

Bendewald (swampy forest) 80, 71

Bendex, Bendix < St. Benedict

Bendorf (Bernhard's village) 124

Bendt < St. Benedict 135

Benedict, Benedick, Benedikt (St. Benedict, name of several popes) 134

Beneke 53, Bennecke < Bernhard

Bener 53 < Bernhard

Benesch, Bensch, Benisch < Czech, Benedict 146

Bengel (club, fool) 115

Bengert, see Benkert

Benhof, Bennhoff (Bernhard's farm) 92, 122

Benighoff, see Benninghoff

Benisch, see Benesch

Benisch < Benedictus

Benjamin (OT name) 135

Benk, Benke, Benker, Benkner, Benkert 74 (bench, cabinet maker 96, from Benk 122)

Benkert, Benkart (bastard) 119

Benn, Benning, Benninger 53, 122 < Bernhard

Benner 159, see Bender

Benninghoff, Benninghof 122, Benninghove (peat bog farm) 80, 92

Benno 53 < Bernhard

Benroth, Benrath 122 (a city, stream clearing) 126

Bens, see Bentz

Bensch, see Benesch

Bense, Bensen 122, Benser, Bensing, Bensinger (place where bullrushes grow) 81

Bensehaffer (reed farm) 81, 92

Bensel, Benseler (dweller among the reeds) 81

Benshoff (reed farm) 92

Benshoff (Bernhard's farm) 53, 92

Bensing, Bensinger, see Bentzinger

Benson, see Bentzen

Bentell, Bentels 59, see Bentler

Benter, see Painter

Bentheim (name of city, marsh hamlet) 122

Bentler < St. Pantaleon 135

Bentli, Bentley 159, see Bantli

Bentsen, son of Bentz 59

Bentz 53, Benz, Benze, Benzel 55, Bentzel < Bernhard Benedict, or Berthold

Bentzen, son of Bentz 59

Bentziger, Bentzing, Bentzinger (fr Bentzingen) 122

Benweil (Benz's village) 127

Benz, Benzle, Benzelius 141, see Bentzel

Benzenhof 122, Benzenhoffer, Benzenhafer 159 (reed farm) 81, 92

Benzinger, see Bentziger

Beohmer 159, see Boehmer

Ber, see Baer

Berach (bear river) 48, 83

Berbisdorf (Berbi's village) 124, 122

Berch, see Berg

Berchelbach, Berckelbach (birch brook) 89

Bercher, see Berger and Bircher

Berchner, see Bergner

Bercht, Berchtel, see Berchthold

Berchthold (bright + loyal) 46, 46

Berchthold < Berchtwald (bright + rule) 46, 46

Berck, Bercker, see Berg, Bercker

Berckhaeuser, Berckheiser 66, Berckhyser 66 (occupant of mountain house) 68, 65

Berckheimer (mountain hamlet)

Berckman, Berckmann, see Bergmann

Berdahl (bear valley) 48, 76

Bere 53, Berele 55 < Bernhard

Berenbach (bear brook) 48, 77, 122

Berenberg 122, Berenberger (bear mountain, berry mountain) 48, 68

Berend, Berends 59, Berents, see Baehrend

Berenger (bear + spear) 48, 46

Berenhaus (bear house) 48, 65

Berenholtz (bear forest) 48, 72

Berenstecher (boar castrator) 95

Berfeld (boar field) 48, 84

Berg, Berge, Bergs 59, Bergen (mountain) 68, 82

Bergbauer (mountain farmer) 68, 91

Bergdoll 159 (mountain valley) 68, 76

Bergdoll, see Berchtold

Bergdorf (mountain village) 68, 124

Bergenbach (mountain brook) 68, 77

Bergenslott (mountain castle) 68

Bergenstine 159 (fr Bergenstein 122, mountain stone) 68, 73, 151

Bergenthal (mountain valley) 68, 76

Berger (mountain man) 68

Bergfeld (mountain field) 68, 84, 122

Bergh, Bergher, see Berg

Berghaus (mountain house) 68, 65, 122

Berghauser, Berghaeuser, Berkhaeuser, Berckheiser, Bergheiser 66 (fr Berghausen 122, house on a mountain) 68, 65

Bergheimer (fr Bergheim, mountain hamlet) 68, 124, 122

Berghof, Berghoff, Berghoeffer (mountain farm) 68, 92, 122

Bergholtz (mountain forest) 68, 72, 122

Berghorn (mountain peak) 68, 68

Berghuis, see Berghaus

Bergk, see Berg

Bergkirch (mountain church) 68, 122

Bergland (mountain country) 68, 49

Bergler, Bergner (mountain man) 68

Bergmann, Bergman (miner, mountain man) 68, 96, 94

Bergmeister (mine supervisor) 68, 96

Bergner (mountain man, miner) 68, 96

Bergold < Berchtold

Bergschmidt (mountain smith) 68, 96

Bergschneider (mountain tailor) 68, 104

Bergstein (mountain stone) 68, 73, 122

Bergstrasser 122, Bergstresser, Bergstrosser (dweller on a mountain road, fr Bergstrasse) 68, 65

Bergstrom (mountain stream) 68, 78

Bergtold, Bertoll, see Berchtold

Bergweiler (mountain village) 68, 127, 122

Berhart, see Bernhard

Bering, Beringer (fr Beringen 122; see Behring)

Berk, Berke, see Berg and Birck
Berkelbach (birch brook) 89, 77
Berkemeyer, Berkenmeyer, see
  Berkmeyer
Berkenbusch (birch bush) 89, 72
Berkenfeld (birch field) 89, 84
Berkenhauer (birch chopper) 89,
  95
Berkenkamp, Berkenkaempfer,
  Berkenkemper (birch field) 89,
  84
Berkenmayer, see Berkmeyer
Berkenstock (birch trunk) 89
Berker, see Berger
Berkey 159, see Buerki
Berkhan, see Birkhan
Berkhausen, see Berghaus
Berkheim 122, Berkheimer (birch
  hamlet) 89, 124
Berkheiser, see Berghauser
Berkhof, Berkhoff, Berkoff (fr
  Berghof, mountain farm) 89,
  92, see Berghoff
Berkholtz (birch wood) 89, 72,
  122
Berkman, Berkmans 59, see
  Bergmann
Berkmeyer, Berkmeyer (fr the
  Berkhoff) 68, 93, 92, 94
Berkner (mountain man, miner)
  68, 96
Berkstresser, see Bergstrasser
Berlanstein 159 (pearl mountain)
  68
Berlein 55 (little bear) 48
Berlin, Berliner (German city)
  122, 146
Berman, Bermann, Bermant 74
  (bear trainer) 48, 22, 94
Berman, Bermant (swineherd)
  95, 94
Bermut (bear + disposition) 48,
  114
Bern 122, Berne, Berner, Berns
  59 (fr Bern)

Bernard, see Bernhard
Bernauer (fr Bernau, swamp
  meadow) 80, 84, 122
Bernd 53, Berndt, Berends 59 <
  Bernhard
Berner (Swiss fr Bern) 122
Bernfeld (swamp field) 68, 80, 84
Bernhard, Bernhardt, Bernard
  (bear + strong) 22, 48, 46
Bernhardi (son of Bernhard) 142
Bernhauser (swamp house) 80,
  65
Bernheim, Bernheimer (swamp
  hamlet) 68, 124
Bernheisl 55, see Berninghaus
Bernhold, Bernholt (Bernhold,
  bear + loyal) 48, 48
Bernhold < Bernwald (bear +
  rule) 48, 47
Bernholt (bear forest) 48, 72
Berning (belonging to the bear)
  48, 59
Berninghaus (Berning's house)
  65, 122
Bernolt, see Bernholt
Bernsohn (son of the bear, son of
  Bern) 48, 59
Bernstein (bear mountain) 48,
  73, 122
Bernstein (amber, amber worker)
  106, 122
Bernt 53, see Bernhard
Bernwinkler (bear + wooded
  valley) 48, 76
Berodt (bear clearing) 48, 125,
  122
Bersch, see Barsch
Berschneider (hog castrator) 96
Berstein (bear mountain) 48, 73
Berstroser 159, see Bergstrasser
Bert 53, Bertz 59 < Bertram,
  Berthold, etc.
Bertel 53, Bertell, Bertels 59 <
  Berthold
Bertha < Brecht

Berthel, see Bertel

Berthold, Bertholdt, Bertold,
    Berthhoud (brilliant + loyal)
    46, 48

Bertline 159, see Bert

Bertling, see Bartling

Bertman, see Bartmann

Bertold < Brechthold, illustrious
    + loyal) 47, 47

Bertoldi, son of Bertholdus 142

Bertram, Berteram, see Bartram

Bertrand (brilliant + shield) 46,
    47

Bertsch 53, Bertschi, Bertschj <
    Berthold, etc.

Bertz, Berz, see Bert

Berwage, Berwanger (fr
    Berwangen, bear field) 48, 71,
    122

Berwald (bear forest) 48, 71

Berwig (bear + battle) 48, 46

Berwin (bear + friend) 48, 48

Besch 53 (St. Sebastian) 135

Beschorner (shorn one,
    clergyman) 112, 110

Beseke (fr St. Basilius) 135

Besel (broom maker) 96

Besemann (broom maker) 96, 94

Besinger, see Bessing

Besner (broom maker) 96

Besold 159, see Betzold

Besse (swamp) 80

Bessener (swamp dweller) 80

Besser, Bessert (better, collector
    of fines) 74

Besserdich (Better yourself!
    initiation name) 116

Bessing, Bessinger (fr Bessingen)
    122

Bessmann (repairman) 96, 94

Best (best) 115

Best 53 < St. Sebastian 135

Beste (river name, muddy water)
    83

Bestenholtz (for Westenholtz,
    western forest) 85, 72

Besterfeldt (west field) 85, 84

Bestgen < St. Sebastian 135

Bestheimer (for Westheimer,
    western hamlet) 124

Betcher, see Boettcher 151

Betenbaugh 159, see Bittenbach

Beter (prayer) 110, see Peter

Bethge 55, Bethke, Betke <
    Bertram

Bethman, Bettmann (payer of
    landlord's "requests") 109, 94

Betram, see Bertram

Betrand, see Bertrand

Bettendorf (town name) 124, 122

Bettenhausen (tenant house) 65,
    122

Better, Bettermann 94 (rosary,
    rosary maker) 106

Bettger, see Boettcher

Bettler (beggar) 110

Betts 151, see Betz

Betz 53, Betts 159, Bates 159,
    Pates 159 < Bernhard

Betzinger, Betzner (fr Betzingen)
    122

Betzold, Petzold, Betzel, Betzler
    < Peter

Beuchel (little belly) 114

Beucher, Beuchert 74, see
    Buecher

Beuckelmann 94, see Buechner

Beuel (bruise) 114, 122, see Beul

Beuer, Beuermann 94 (peasant)
    91

Beuerle, see Baeuerle

Beuke, see Buche

Beul, Beuler, see Buehl, Buehler

Beulshausen (place name) 65,
    122

Beumler, see Baeumler

Beunde (private fenced-in area)
    84

Beurlein 55, see Baeuerlein

Beusch, see Baus

Beuschlag, see Beyschlag

Beuschlein 55 (little bush) 89, 72

Beutel, Beutler (purse, sack, purse maker) 96

Beutel (wooden club) 114, 118

Beutelmann (purse maker) 96, 94

Beutelsbach, Beutelspacher (fr Beutelsbach, sack brook) 77, 122

Beuthler, Beutler (purse maker) 96

Beutner (honey gatherer) 95

Bever, Bewer, Beeber 151, see Bieber

Beverung, Beverungen (a city, the people on the Bever) 122

Beyder (possibly short for name like Beiderwieden) 69

Beyer, Beyers 59, Beyern, see Bayer

Beyerle, Beyerley 55, Beyerlein, Beyerling, see Bayerle, Baeuerle

Beyermeister, see Bauernmeister

Beyersdorf (Bavarians' village) 121, 124, 122, see Bayersdorf

Beyl, Beyhl, see Beil

Beylstein, see Beilstein

Beyrer, see Bayer

Beyrodt (adjacent clearing) 125

Beyschlag (small piece of a field) 84

Beyschlag (illegitimate child of a ruler) 119

Beyth (hesitation) 115

Bez, see Betz

Bezold, see Betzold

Bibelhimer 159 (Bible hamlet) 124

Biber, see Bieber

Bichel, see Buehler

Bichell, Bichler, see Buehl, Buehler

Bicher, Bichert 74, see Buecher

Bichler, see Buehler

Bickel, Bickle 53, Bickell < Burkhart, see Pickel

Bickel, Bickler, see Pickel

Bicksler (box maker, gun maker) 96, 151

Biddel 159, Buettel (beadle) 109

Biddenbach, see Bittenbach

Biddinger (fr Bidingen) 122

Biddle 159, see Biddel

Biderman 159, see Biederman

Bie, see Biene

Biebel, Bieble 159, Biebel (Bible)

Bieber (beaver) 115

Bieberbach (beaver brook) 77, 122

Bieberbach (swamp-water creek) 80, 77

Biecheler, Biechelar, see Buechler

Biedekopp, Biedenkopf (boundary lookout) 122

Biedenbach, Biedenback (fr Biedenbach 122, boundary brook) 77, 122

Biedenbuender (boundary fence) 84

Biederkep, see Biedekopp

Biederman, Biedermann (doughty man, respectable citizen) 138, 94

Biegel, see Bichel, Buehel

Biegel, Biegler (ax maker) 96, see Buegler

Biegeleisen (stirrup, pressing iron) 96

Biehl, Biehler, see Buehl, Buehler

Biehlmueller (hill miller) 67, 103

Biehn, see Bien

Biel, Bieler, Bieller, see Buehl, Buehler

Bielefeld, Bieleveld (city name) 122

Biemann (bee keeper) 95, 94

Bien, Bienemann 94, Bieneman (bee keeper) 95

Bienenfeld (bee field) 84

Biener, Bienert 74 (bee keeper) 95

Bienfang (bee catcher) 95

Bienkorb (beehive) 95

Bienlein 55 (little bee) 115

Bienstein (bee stone) 73, 118

Bienstock, Bienenstock (beehive, beekeeper) 95

Bier, Bierr (beer, brewer) 96, 106

Bierach (beaver river, bear river) 83, 122

Bierbach (mud creek) 80, 77

Bierbauer (farmer on muddy creek) 80, 91

Bierbaum 122, see Birnbaum

Bierbrauer (beer brewer) 97

Bierenbaum, see Birnbaum

Bierenberg (pear mountain) 89, 68

Bierenbrodt (bread and cheese, victualer) 96

Bierhagen (bear enclosure), 48, 124

Bierhagen (pear tree enclosure) 89, 124

Bierkenbeyl (birch ax) 89, 96

Bierley 159, see Bayerle

Bierman 94, Biermann, Biermeyer 93, Bierwirth (taverner) 96

Biernbaum, see Birnbaum

Biersack (taverner) 96

Biersack (beer belly) 114

Biersdorf (beer village) 124, 122

Biersdorf (swamp village) 80, 124, 122

Bierstadt (place name, swamp city) 80, 122

Bierwage, Bierwagen (beer wagon, beer distributor) 96

Bierwirt, Bierwirth (beer host) 96, also < Berwart (bear + guardian) 46, 47

Biese (bull rush, broom maker) 96

Biesenbruck (bullrush brake) 80

Bietendüvel (Beat the devil! exclamation) 117

Biettel, see Buettel

Biewer, see Bieber

Bigel, Bigler, see Buegel, Buegler

Bihl, see Buehl, Beil

Bihlmeier, Beylmeyer, see Buehlmayer

Bilauer (hill meadow) 67, 84

Bilderbach, Bilderback, Bilderbeck, see Wilderbach

Bildhauer (sculpter) 96

Bildstein 122, see Wildstein

Bile 159, see Buehle, Beil

Bilfinger (having six fingers) 114

Bilfinger (fr Bilfingen) 122

Bilger, see Pilger

Bilheimer, see Buehlheimer

Bilig, see Billig, Bille

Bilk, Bilker (region in Rhineland) 121

Bill, Biller, Bills 59 (hill) 67

Billauer (swamp meadow) 80, 84, see Bilauer

Bille, Biller, see Buehl, Buehler

Bille (battle ax) 108

Biller, see Buehler

Billerbeck (hill brook) 67, 77, 122

Billheimer, Billhimer 159, see Buehlheimer

Billig (fair, as in *recht und billig*) 115, 122

Billing, Billings 59, Billinger (fr Billing 122, hill dweller) 68

Billman, Billmann, see Buehlman

Billmann (maker or user of battle axes) 107, 108, 94

Billmeyer, Billmeier (hill farmer, see Buehlmeyer) 67, 93

Billmire 159, Billmyer, see Billmeyer

Billroth (hill clearing) 67, 125

Billstein (hill stone) 67, 73

Billstone 159, see Billstein

Bilse (henbane) 89

Biltz, Bilitz, Bilz, see Piltz

Bimeler 159, see Baeumler

Bimmiller, see Buehlmueller

Binau (bee meadow) 84, 122

Bince 159, see Bintz

Bindbeutel (fastenable purse) 96, 106

Bindel (bundle)

Binder (cooper) 96

Binder, Bindermann 94, Bindler (sheaf binder, cooper, bookbinder) 96

Bindschaedler (cooper) 96

Bindseil (cord maker, roper) 96, 106

Binebrink (bee hill) 74

Bineke, Bineker, see Beneke

Binfield 153, see Bienefeld

Bingel, Bingle 159, Bingley 159, see Bengel

Bingen, Binger (city on the Rhein) 122

Binkert, see Benkert

Binning, Binninger, Bininger (fr Binningen 122), see Benning

Binnix < St. Benedict 135

Binns, see Bintz

Binsbacher (reed brook) 81, 77

Binstock (rush stem) 81, see Bienstock

Binswanger (fr Binswangen, reed field) 81, 125, 122

Binz, Bintz, Binzen, Bintzel (fr Binz 122, bull rushes) 81

Birbaum, Birenbaum, see Birnbaum

Birch, Birchen, see Birk

Birchbauer, Birchbaver 159 (fr the Birchhof, birch farm) 89, 91, 94

Birchfield, see Birkenfeld

Birchhoff (birch farm) 89, 92

Birchler, Birchner (dweller among the birches) 89

Birchwil (birch village) 89, 127

Birck, Birk, Birke (birch) 89

Birckelbach (birch brook) 89, 77

Birdsong 152, see Vogelsang

Birely 159, see Baeuerle

Birgel (place name) 122

Birger, see Berger, Buerger

Birk, Birkel 55, Birkelein 55 (little birch) 89

Birk 53 < Burkhart

Birkbach, Birkenbach (birch brook) 89, 77, 122

Birkborch (birch bark) 89, 73

Birkelein 55, see Birk

Birkenberg (birch mountain) 89, 68

Birkenfeld (birch field) 89, 84, 122

Birkenhauer (birch cutter) 89, 95, 100

Birkenstock (birch trunk) 89

Birkenthal (birch valley) 89, 76, 122

Birkhan (black grouse) 115

Birkholt (birch wood) 89, 72, 122

Birkholz, Birkholtzer (birch wood) 89, 72, 122

Birkle 55 (little birch) 89

Birkle 55 < Burkhard

Birkmann 94, Birkmeyer 93, Birkmaier, Birckenmayer (farmer among the birches) 89

Birkner, see Birchler

Birman, see Berman

Birnbach (pear tree brook) 89, 77, 122

Birnbaum (pear tree) 89, 122

Birner 159, see Berner

Birnstengel (pear stem) 89, 114, 118

Birnstiel (pear stem) 89

Birstaedt 159, see Bierstadt

Birtha 159, see Bertha

Birx, see Birck

Bisant, Biszant (Saracen coin)

Bischberg 122, see Bischoffsberger

Bischoff, Bischof, Bischop (bishop) 59, 110

Bischoffsberger, Bischopberger (bishop's mountain) 110, 68

Bishof 159, see Bischoff

Bishop 159, see Bischoff

Bisinger (fr Bising) 122

Bismark, Bismarck 122 < Bischofsmark (bishop's boundary)

Bisschop, see Bischoff

Bissel, Bissler (bite, small quantity) 118

Bisser (fr Bissen) 122

Biswanger, Biswangen 159 (adjacent clearing) 125

Bitel, see Buettel

Bitinger, Bittinger (fr Bittingen) 122

Bitman, see Buettner

Bitner, see Buettner

Bittel, see Buettel

Bittenbach (barrel brook) 77

Bittenbender (barrel maker) 96

Bitter, Bitterlich, Bitterley 159 (bitter, bitterly) 115

Bitter (public announcer, beggar) 109

Bittermann (barrel maker) 96, 94

Bittle 159, see Buettel

Bittmann 94, see Buettner

Bittner, Bitner 159, see Buettner

Bitz, Bitzel (fenced area) 84, 122

Bitzelberger (fenced hill) 84, 68

Bitzer (dweller on the Bitiz) 83

Bixler (box maker, gun maker), see Buechsler 96

Blaas < St. Blasius 135

Black 152, see Schwartz

Blacker, Blackert 74, Blackner, Blackman 94 (bleacher) 96

Blackwelder 153, see Schwarzwaelder

Blaetterlein (little leaf) 55

Blahut (blue hat, show-off) 112, 115

Blaich, Blaicher, Blaik (bleacher) 96

Blakmann, see Blech

Blamberg (place name) 122

Blanck, Blank (shining white)

Blanckenberg (white mountain) 68, 122

Blancpain 144, 152, see Weissbrodt 152

Blank, Blancke, Blank, Blanke, Blanken (white, clean) 118

Blankemeier, see Blankmeyer

Blankenbaker 159, Blankenbeckler (baker of white bread) 96

Blankenburg (white castle) 73, 122

Blankenheimer (fr Blankenheim, white hamlet) 124

Blankenhorn (white peak) 68

Blankenmeier (proprietor of the White Farm) 93

Blankensee (white lake) 82, 122

Blankfeld (white field) 84

Blankmann (white man, bleacher) 96, 94

Blankmeyer (fr the Blankhof, white farm) 93, 94

Blankner (bleacher) 96

Blasebalg (bellows, blacksmith's helper) 96

Blaskopf (bald head) 115

Blass, Blasse, Blasser, Blaser (bald) 112

Blass (pale) 114

Blass 53, Blasse < St. Blasius 135

Blatman, Blatner, see Blatter

Blatt (leaf) 89

Blatt (hunter's decoy call) 91

Blattberg (leaf mountain) 68

Blattberg (swamp mountain) 80, 68

Blatter, Blatterman 94, Blattermann, Blattner (armor smith) 108

Blatz, Blatzer (wedge for breaking stone) 106

Blatz, see Platz

Blau, Blauer, Blauert 74 (blue) 112

Blau, Blauer, Blauert 74 (credulous) 115

Blaufeld (blue field) 84, 122

Blaufuss (kind of falcon, falconer) 115, 96

Blaume, Blaumen, see Blumen

Blaurock (blue coat, dandy, coat maker) 112, 96

Blaustein (blue stone, blue mountain) 73, 122

Blaxberg 159, see Blocksberg

Blay, see Blei

Bleacher 159, see Bleicher

Blech, Bleche, Blecher, Blecker, Blechmann 94, Blechschmidt (sheet metal, tinsmith) 96, 106

Bleck, Blecke, Blecker, Bleckmann 94, Bleckenschmidt, see Blech

Bleek, Bleeker (bleacher) 96

Blei (lead, lead worker) 96, 106

Blei (kind of fish) 105, 115

Bleiberg (lead mountain, lead mine) 68

Bleibtreu (Remain true!) 116

Bleich, Bleicher, Bleichner (pale) 113

Bleich, Bleicher (bleacher) 96

Bleier, Bleiler (lead worker) 96

Bleiker, see Bleicher

Bleistein, Bleisenstein (lead stone, pencil) 96

Blekmann, see Bleck

Blendermann (prestidigitator) 96, 94

Blendermann (swamp dweller) 80, 94

Blenker, Blenkner (dweller in a barren spot)

Blesch (blow)

Bless, Blesse, Blessmann (blaze, bald head) 113, also < Blasius

Blessing, Blessinger 53 < Blasius

Bletz (patch, tailor) 96

Bleucher, see Bleicher

Bley, Bleyer, Bleuer, see Blei, Bleier

Bleystein (lead mountain) 73

Bliede (blithe, cheerful) 115

Bligh 159, see Blei

Blimke, see Bluemke

Blimline 55, 159 (little flower) 89

Blimmer 55, 159 (little flower) 89

Blind, Blinder (blind) 114

Blitstein 159, see Blitzstein

Blitz, Blitzer (lightning) 118

Blitzstein (lightning mountain) 73

Blob, see Blau

Bloch, Block, Bloech, see Block

Blocher (jailer) 109

Block (block, trunk, stocks) 118

Bloed, Bloede (weak, shy, weak) 115

Bloem, Bloemen, Bloemeke, Bloemer, Blom, Blohm, Blohme (flower seller) 89, 106

Bloes, Bloess < St. Blasius 135

Blomeyer (flower farmer) 89, 93

Blond, Blondell, Blonder (blond) 112

Bloom 152, Bloomer, see Blum

Bloomberg 153, see Blumberg

Bloomfield 152, see Blumenfeld

Bloomgarden 152, see Blumgaertner

Bloomingdale 152, see Blumenthal

Bloss, Blosse, Blosser (bare, naked, unarmed) 113

Bloss 53 < Blasius

Blotenberg, Blottenberger (swamp mountain) 80, 68

Blotkamp (swamp field) 80, 84

Blotner 159, see Blatner

Blough 159, see Blau
Blubaugh 159, Bluebaugh 159
(blue brook) 77
Blubaum 159 (blue tree) 89, 151
Blucher, Bluecher (Slavic place
name) 122, 146
Bluefeld 153, see Blaufeld
Bluehe (blossom) 89
Bluehtner (flower seller) 106
Blueme, Bluemel 55, Bluemelein
(little flower) 89, 106
Bluementhal, see Blumenthal
Bluemke 55 (little flower) 89, 106
Bluestein 153, Blustein, Blue-
stone 152, see Blaustein
Bluetner (florist) 96
Bluh, see Bluehe
Bluhdorn (blossom thorn) 72, 89
Blum, Blume, Bluem, Bluhm,
Blumen (flower) 89, 106
Blumbach (flower brook) 89, 77
Blumberg, Blumenberg (flower
mountain) 89, 68
Blumann (florist) 96
Blume, see Blum
Blumenauer (flower meadow) 89,
84, 122
Blumenberg, see Blumberg
Blumenfeld, Blumenfeldt,
Blumfeld (flower field) 89, 84,
147, 122
Blumenschein (flower brilliance)
89, 148
Blumenstein (flower mountain)
89, 73, 148
Blumenstiel (flower stem,
skinny) 89, 114
Blumenthal (flower valley) 89,
76, 147, 122
Blumentritt (florist) 96
Blumer, Blumert 74, Blummer
(flower seller) 89, 106
Blumfeld (flowerfield) 148
Blumgart (flowergarden, florist)
96

Blumingdale 152, see
Blumenthal
Blumlein (little flower) 55, 89
Blumner (flower seller) 106
Blunt (blond) 112
Bluntschli (fat man) 114
Blusten 159, see Blaustein
Bluth (blood) 118
Bluth (blossom) 89
Bly 159, see Blei
Blyer 159, Blyler, see Bleier
Blyman 159, see Bleimann
Blyweiss 159 (lead white) 118
Boarman 159, see Borman
Boas, Boaz (OT name) 135
Bobenheisser 66 (upper house,
see Oberhaeuser)
Bobenhyser 66, see Bobenheisser
Bobenriet (upper marsh) 81
Bober (dweller by the Bober) 83
Bobst, see Pabst
Boce 159, see Bos
Bocher (insistent person) 115
Bock, Bocks 59, Bocker (buck,
often a house name) 63
Bock (beech tree) 89
Bockhaus, see Backhaus
Bockholt, see Buchholtz
Bockhorst (beech grove) 41, 72
Bockman, Bockmann (dweller
among beech trees) 89, 94
Bockmiller (fr the Bockmuehle,
beech mill) 89, 103
Bockner, see Buechner
Bod, Bode (messenger), 96, 157,
see also Boede
Bodamer, see Bodener
Boday 157 < Bode
Bodefeld (swampy field) 80, 84
Bodeke, see Boettcher
Bodemeyer (farmer in the
swamp) 80, 93
Boden (soil, bottom, valley) 76
Bodenbender (cooper) 96
Bodenberger (valley mountain)
76, 68

Bodener (valley dweller, cotter) 76 see also Buettner

Bodenhamer, see Bodenheimer

Bodenheimer (valley hamlet) 76, 124

Bodenschatz (duty on wine)

Bodensieck (valley swamp) 76, 80

Bodenstab (barrel maker) 96

Bodenstein (valley stone) 76, 73, 122

Bodiker, Bodker, see Boettcher

Bodmer (tabulator) 96

Bodmer (dweller on the plain) 67

Bodner, Bodnar 159, see Bodener

Bodtker, see Boettcher

Boeck, Boecker, Boekker, Boeckh, Boeker, Boekel, Boekl, Boekler, Boekner, see Bock, Beck, Becker

Boecker, see Boettcher

Boeckler (shield bearer) 108, 109

Boecklin (little buck) 55

Boeckman, Boeckmann, see Beckmann

Boede, Boedde (wooden tub) 106

Boedeker, see Boettcher

Boegel, see Buegel

Boeger, Boegner, see Bogener

Boeggerman, see Beckermann

Boehl, Boehler, Boehling, Boehlke 55, see Buehl, Buehler

Boehler (cloister official) 109, 139

Boehm, Boehme, Boehmer, Boehmlein 55, Boem (Bohemian) 34, 121, see also Baeumer

Boehme (pre-Germanic river name) 83

Boehmke (little tree) 89

Boehne, Boehner, Boehnert 74 (bean dealer) 105

Boehning, see Benning

Boehnisch, see Benesch

Boehnlein 55, Boehneke 55 (little bean) 118

Boehringer, see Behringer

Boeke (beech) 89

Boekel 55, Boeckl, Boekle, Boeklin, Boekelmann, Buckley 159 (little buck)

Boekenheide (beech heath) 89, 81

Boeker, see Boettcher

Boekman, Boeckmann, see Beckmann, Buchmann

Boelker (howler, bellower) 115

Boelker 53 < Baldwin

Boellner see Bellner

Boem, see Boehm

Boender, see Bender

Boener, Boenert, see Behner

Boening, Boenning, Boeninger, Boenniger, see Benning

Boer, Boeren, Boern, see Bauer

Boerger, Boergert 74 (burgher)

Boerghausen, see Burghause

Boermann (peasant) 91, 94

Boermann, see Baermann

Boemer, see Boehmer

Boerner, see Berner

Boernstein, see Bernstein

Boerries 53 < St. Liborius 135

Boes, Boese, Boesser (angry, mean) 115

Boesch 53, see Sebastian

Boese (small stag) 91

Boessel (place name) 122

Boessner (repairman) 96

Boethius (Latin for Boie, Boysen)

Boettcher, Boetcher, Boether, Boettge, Boettger, Boetjer, Boettiger (barrel maker, fr Latin *apoteka*) 96

Boettinger, see Boettcher

Boettner, Boetter, see Buettner

Bogen, Bogener, Bogner, Bognar 159 (bowman or bow maker) 108

Bogensberger (bow mountain) 68

Bohde, see Bode

Bohl, Bohle, Bohlen, Bohls 159, Bohlken, Bolsen (plank) 118

Bohlander, see Polander

Bohlen 53, Bohler, Bohling, Bohlinger, Bohlmann 94 < Baldwin

Bohltz, see Boltz

Bohm, Bohme, see Baum

Bohm, Bohmer, see Boehm, Boehmer

Bohmann, see Baumann

Bohmfalk (tree falcon) 89

Bohmgarden, see Baumgarten

Bohmheuer, see Baumheuer

Bohn, Bohne, Bohner, Bohnert (bean dealer) 105

Bohn 53, Bohne < St. Urbanus 135

Bohnenberg (bean hill) 68

Bohnenstengel (bean stalk) 113

Bohnewald (bean forest) 72

Bohnsack (bean sack) 96, 106

Bohr 53 < St. Liborius 135

Bohrer (borer) 96

Bohrmann, see Bormann

Bohrmester, Bohrmister 159, see Bauernmeister

Bohse, see Boos

Bokmann, see Buchmann

Boland, Bolandt, Bolander, see Poland, Polander

Bolderman, see Poldermann

Boldt (bold) 46

Boldt (bolt, crossbow bolt) 108

Bolenbaugh 159 (fr Bolenbach, swamp brook) 80, 77

Bolender, see Polander

Boler, see Bohlen

Boll, Bolle (hill) 67

Boll (river name, swamp water) 83

Bollack, see Pollak

Bolland (hilly country) 67

Bollbach (dirty brook) 80, 77

Bolle (plump person) 114

Bollenbach, Bollenbacher (swampy brook) 77

Boller, see Bohlen

Bollhorst (hill hurst) 67, 72

Bolling 112, Bollinger (hill dweller) 67, see also Buhle

Bollman, Bollemann (small heavy-set youth) 114, 94

Bollmann (dweller on a hill) 67, 94

Bollwagen < Baldwin

Bollweg (hill path) 67, 65

Bollwinkel, see Bullwinkel

Bolner (hill dweller) 67

Bolster, see Polster

Bolt, Bolte, Bolter, Bolth, Bolten, see Boltz

Boltz, Boltze, Bolz, Boltzius 141, Poltz (bolt, maker of crossbow bolts) 108, also < Baldwin

Boltzmann, see Boltz

Boman, see Bauman

Bombach, Bomback, Bombeck (swamp brook) 80, 77

Bomberg, Bomberger (fr Bomberg 122, tree mountain) 89, 68

Bomer, Bomert 74, see Baumer

Bomgartner, see Baumgaertner

Bongardt, see Baumgarten

Bomhardt (tree forest) 89, 72

Bomhoff (tree farm) 89, 92

Bomstein (tree stone) 89, 77

Bonacker (bean field) 84

Boner, see Bohner

Bongart, Bongartz, see Bomgartner

Bonhag, Bonhage (forbidden enclosure) 124

Bonhoff (bean farm) 92

Bonifacius (name of a pope) 134

Bonmueller (bean miller) 103

Bonn, Bonner (inhabitant of Bonn) 122

Bonner, see Bonn

Bonnewitz (place name, swamp village) 127

Bonsack (bean sack) 96, 106

Bonse 159, see Buntz

Bontrager (bean carrier) 118

Bontz, see Buntz

Bonzer, see Panzer

Boode, see Bote

Book ..., see Buch ...

Book, Booker, see Buch, Bucher

Bookhultz, see Buchholtz

Bookman, Bookmann, see Buchman

Bookmiller, see Buchmueller

Bookoff, see Buchhoff

Bookstein (beech mountain) 89, 73

Bookwalther (beech forest) 89, 71

Boom, see Baum

Boonce, 159, see Buntz

Boone, see Bohne

Boor (peasant) 91

Boos (wicked, evil) 115

Boos 159, see Buss

Boot, Boote, see Bote

Booterbaugh 159, see Butterbaugh

Booth, see Bote

Borch, see Burg

Borchart, Borchardt, Borchert, see Burkhart

Borcher, Borchert 143, Borchers 59, see Burger, Burkhart

Borcherding (belonging to Borcher) 59

Borchgrave, see Burggraf

Borchholder, Borckholder, see Burghalter

Bordelmay, see Bartholomes

Bordemann (lace maker) 96, 94

Bordner (gate keeper) 96

Bordorf, see Borgdorf

Borenstein, see Bernstein

Borg, Borger, see Burg, Buerger

Borg (swamp) 80

Borgdorf, see Burgdorff

Borgenicht ("Don't borrow," or "I don't borrow") 116

Borger (borrower) 115

Borger (castle dweller) 73

Borgfeld (castle field) 73, 84

Borgfeld (swamp field) 80, 84

Borggreve, see Burggraf

Borghard, see Burkhard

Borgholte (castle wood) 73, 72

Borgmann, Borgman (castle man, burgher) 73, 94

Borgmeier (castle bailif) 73, 93

Borgstrom (castle stream) 73, 77

Borgstrom (swamp stream) 80, 77

Boris, see Borries

Bork, Borke (bark, bark gatherer) 91, 95

Bork, see Burg, Burkhard

Borkart, Borkhardt, see Burkhard

Borkholz (castle wood) 73, 72

Borkmann, see Borgmann

Bormann 53 < St. Liborius 135, see also Bornemann

Born, Borne, Borner, Borns 59 (spring) 79

Borneman, Bornemann (spring + man) 79, 94

Bornfiend 159, see Bauernfeind

Borngesser (spring road) 79, 65

Borngraeber, Borngreber (well digger) 79, 96

Bornhausen (spring house) 79, 65, 122

Bornheim (spring hamlet) 79, 124

Bornhoefte (spring farm) 79, 84

Bornholt, Bornholtz 59 (spring forest) 79, 72

Bornhorn (spring peak) 79, 68

Bornhorst (spring hurst) 79, 72

Bornkessel (spring kettle) 79

Bornman, see Bornemann

Bornscheuer (spring barn) 79

Bornsdorf (spring village) 79, 124, 122

Bornstein (spring mountain) 79, 73, see Bernstein

Borntraeger (water carrier) 96

Borries, Borrus 53 < St. Liborius 135

Borsch 53, Borscher < St. Liborius 135

Borsdorf, see Burgdorf

Borst (bristle) 114, 106

Bortner, Bortmann, see Pfortner

Bortz, Borz, see Portz

Bosch, Bosche (bush, brush, branch) 72

Boschert 74, Boschel, Boschmann 94, Boschenmeyer 93 (dweller in the bush) 72

Bose, see Boos

Bosemann (evil man) 115

Boskind (naughty child) 115

Bosler, see Basler

Bosman, see Bosemann

Boss (barrow hog) 91

Boss (wicked) 115

Bossard, Bosshard, see Bussart

Bosse 53 < Burckhart

Bosshard, Bosshart, Bossert (Strike hard!) 116, also see Bussart

Bossler, Bossle, see Basler

Bossner (striker, ten pin player)

Bostian 159, see Bastian

Bot, Bote, Both, Bothe, Boat 159 (messenger) 96, 157

Bottcher, see Boettcher

Botterbusch (butter bush) 89

Bottermann (butter dealer) 105

Bottich, Bottiger (barrel, barrelmaker, fr Latin *apotheca*) 96

Bottmann (court messenger) 109, 94

Bottner, see Buettner

Bottomstone 153, see Bodenstein

Botts 159, Botz, Botzler (bogeyman) 115

Botzenhard, Botzenhart (scarecrow, bogeyman) 115

Botzmann (scarecrow, bogeyman) 115, 94

Bouch 159, see Bauch

Bouck, see Buch, Bock

Bouerman 159, see Bauermann

Bough 159, see Bau, Bauch

Bougher 159, Boughers 59, see Bauer, Bauers

Boughman 159, see Bachmann, Baumann

Boughner 159, see Bachner

Boughtall 159, see Bechtold

Boughwalter, see Buchwalder

Bouknight 159, see Bauknecht

Bouman 159, see Baumann

Boumgarter, see Baumgardner

Bounds 159, see Buntz

Bourgholtzer, see Burkhalter 151

Bouse 159, Bousman 159, see Baus, Bausemann

Boush 159, see Busch

Bouthner 159, see Bauth

Bouwkamp 159 (cultivated field) 84

Bowden 159, see Boden

Bowel 159, see Paul

Bower 159, Bowers 59, see Bauer

Bowerfind 159, see Bauernfeind

Bowerman 159, see Bauermann

Bowermaster 159, see Bauernmeister

Bowersack 159, Bowersock, Bowersox (peasant bag) 91

Bowker 159, see Bauker

Bowman 159, see Baumann

Bowmaster 159, see Baumeister

Bowscher 159, Bowsher 159, see Baus

Boyer, see Bayer

Bozman, Bozemann, see Botzmann

Braaten, Braatz (roast, cook) 96

Brabant, Brabandt, Brabender
(province in Belgium) 121

Brach (fallow land) 122

Brachfeld (fallow field) 84, 122

Brachmann (dweller on a fallow
field) 94

Bracht (river name) 83, 122, see
Brecht, Pracht

Brachvogel (a kind of bird) 115

Brack, see Brach

Brack, Bracke (small tracking
hound, huntsman) 91, 115

Brackbill, Brackbuehl (fallow
hill) 67

Bracker (dweller on fallow land)
91

Brackhahn, Brachhahn (plover)
115

Bracklein 55 (small hunting dog)
115

Brackmann, Brackemann
(hunter leading hounds) 91, 94

Brachtmann, see Brachmann

Bradenbaugh 159, see
Breitenbach

Brader (roast, cook) 96

Bradfisch (fried fish) 112, 106

Bradscherer 159, see
Brettschneider

Bradt, see Brot

Braechbuehler (fallow hill) 67

Braehmer, see Bremer

Braeger, Brager, see Prager

Braendle, see Hildeband

Braeuer (brewer) 96

Braeunig, Braeuniger, see
Brauninger

Braeutigam (bridegroom) 119

Braf, Brafman, Braffmann, see
Bravmann

Brager, Bragher, see Prager

Brahl, see Prahl

Brahm, Brahms 59 (swamp) 80

Brahm, Brahms 59 < Abraham
135

Brahm (broom plant) 89

Brahmeier (swamp farmer) 80,
93

Braid, Braidman, see Breit,
Breitmann

Braitenbah, see Breitenbach

Brake, Bracke (fallow, brackish)

Brakebill, see Brackbill

Brakebusch (fallow scrub land)
72

Brakefield 153, see Brachfeld

Brakenhoff (fallow farm) 92

Brakhage (fallow enclosure) 125

Brakmann, see Brachmann

Brambeck (thorn brook, swamp
brook) 80, 77

Bramer (hornet) 115, see also
Bremer

Bramkamp (thorn field) 84, 122

Brammeyer (fr the Bramhoff,
thorn farm) 93, 94

Bramstedt (thorn place)

Brand 53, Brandes 59, Brandt,
Brant (sword) 46, also <
Hildebrand

Brand, Brant, Brandt (forest
clearing) 5

Brandau (clearing meadow) 125,
84, 122

Brandecker, Brandegger (fr
Brandeck 122, clearing) 125,
85

Brandeis, Brandies 159, Brandis
(cauterizing iron) 106

Brandel, see Brander

Branden < St. Brenden 135

Brandenberg 122, see
Brandenburg

Brandenburg, Brandenburger (fr
Brandenburg) 121

Brandenstein (torch mountain)
73, 122

Brandenstein (burned-off
mountain) 125, 68

Brander, Brandner (occupant of a
clearing) 125

Brander, Brandler (distiller) 96
Brandes 5, 59 < Hildebrand
Brandfas (fire bucket) 96
Brandhaver 159, Brandhover, see Brandhoff
Brandhoff (cleared farm, burned off farm) 125, 92
Brandhorst (burned off hurst) 125, 72, 122
Brandjes, Brandl, see Brander
Brandkamp (burned field) 125, 84
Brandl, see Brandel
Brandland (burned off land) 125
Brandmueller (miller at the burned clearing) 103, 125
Brandner, Brandtner, Brantner (occupant of a forest clearing, fr Branden) 125
Brandstaedter, Brandstetter (cleared place, burned off place) 125, 122
Brandstein (brick) 106, 122
Brandt, see Brand, Hildebrand
Brandwein, Brandtwein, Brantwein (brandy, distiller) 96, 106
Brandywine 159, see Brandwein
Brang, see Prang
Branoff, see Brandhoff
Brant, Brantl 55, see Brand
Brantz, see Brand
Brasch, Brasher, Brash 159 (impudent) 114
Brasch 53 < Ambrosius 135
Brasse (broom plant) 89
Bratfish 152 (fried fish) 115, 105
Bratmann, see Brotmann
Bratt (roast, cook) 96, 106
Brauch, Braucher (use, custom, recipe) 118
Braucht 159, see Pracht
Brauer, Braue (brewer) 96
Braukhoff, Brauckhoff (brake farm) 80, 92

Braukmeyer (farmer on the brake) 80, 93
Braumann (brewer) 96
Braumbart (brown beard) 112
Braumueller, see Braunmueller
Braun, Brauns 59, Braune, Braunert 74 (brown, fr Braunau) 112
Braunbach, Braunbaugh (brown brook) 77
Braunbaugh 159, see Braunbach
Braunbeck (brown brook) 77
Braunbeck (baker of brown bread) 104
Braunberg, Braunberger (brown mountain) 68
Braunfeld, Brauenfeld (brown field) 84
Braungart (brown garden) 84
Braungreber, see Brungraeber
Braunhof (well farm) 92
Brauning, Brauninger, Braunigger (having brown hair) 112
Braunmueller, Brownmueller 159 (miller of brown meal) 103
Braunscheidt, Braunscheidel (brown log) 118
Braunschweiger (person fr Brunswick, "Bruno's village," fr Latin *vicus*) 121, 122
Braunspan (brown chip) 118
Braunstein (brown stone) 73
Brauntuch (brown cloth) 105, 106
Braunwald, Braunwalde (brown forest) 72
Braus, Brause, Brausen (noise, confusion) 115
Brautigan, see Braeutigam
Brautlacht (wedding, wedding song)
Bravermann (brewer) 96, 94
Bravmann (well-behaved man) 115, 94
Brawn 159, Brawner, see Braun

Bray, see Brey

Braymer 159, see Bremer

Breakfield 159, see Brachfeld

Brech, Brecher (breaker, flax breaker) 95

Brechbill, Brechbiel, Brechbuel, see Brackbill

Brecheisen (Break iron! blacksmith) 96, 116

Brechenmacher (maker of threshing tools) 106

Brecht (bright) 47

Brecht 53 < Albrecht

Brecht (a clearing) 125

Brechtel 53, 55 < Brecht, Albrecht

Breckbuehl, Brechtbuehler (fallow hill) 68

Brecker, see Brecher

Brede, Breden (swamp) 80

Bredehoef (marshy farm) 80, 92

Bredehoeft, Bredehoft, see Breithaupt

Bredekamp (marshy field, broad field) 80, 84

Bredemeyer (marsh farmer) 80, 93

Breden (marsh) 80

Bredenburg (marsh castle) 80, 73

Bredhorst (marsh hurst) 80, 72

Bredt, see Brett

Bredthauer, see Brethauer

Breeback (marsh brook) 80, 77

Breemer, see Bremer

Bregenzer (fr Bregenz, town and river name) 83, 122

Brehm, Brehmer (deer fly, restless person) 115, see also Bremer

Brei (porridge) 112

Breidbach, Breidenbach 122, Breidenbeck, see Breitbach

Breidenbaugh 159, see Breitbach

Breidenstein 122, Breidenstine 159, see Breitenstein

Breier, see Braeuer

Breigher 159, see Braeuer

Breiner, Breighner 159 (pottage maker), 112, see Breun

Breining, Breininger, see Brauning

Breis, see Preis

Breit, Breiter (broad) 113

Breitacker (broad field) 84

Breitbach 122, Breitenbach, Breitenbaecher (fr Breitbach 122, broad brook) 77

Breitbart (broad beard) 112

Breitbart (broad battle-ax) 46

Breitenbach 122, see Breitbach

Breitenberger (fr Breitenberg 122, broad mountain) 68

Breitenbuecher (broad beeches) 89

Breitenecker (broad place) 85

Breitenfeld (broad field) 84

Breitenherdt (broad hearth, mason) 100

Breitenstein (broad stone, broad mountain) 73, 122

Breitfus (broad foot) 114

Breithaupt (broad head) 114

Breithof (broad farm) 92

Breitkopf, see Breithaupt

Breitmann (fat man) 114, 94

Breitmeyer, Breitmier 159 (occupant of the Breithoff, broad farm) 93

Breitmoser, Breitenmoser (broad marsh) 80

Breitschnaid (broad pieces of firewood) 96

Breitschneider, see Brettschneider

Breitschwerd, Breitschwerdt (broadsword) 108

Breitstadt (broad city) 122

Breitstein, see Breitenstein

Breitwieser (broad meadow) 84

Breivogel (porridge eater) 112

Brem, Bremer, Bremehr,
Bremen, Bremmer,
Bremermann 94 (fr Bremen)
122
Bremhorst (gadfly hurst) 72
Brendel 53, 55, Brendl, Brendle
159, Brendler < Hildebrand
Brenizer 159, see Brenneiser
Brenker, see Brinker
Brennecke (burned field) 85
Brenneisen (poker, brand) 106
Brenneiser (blacksmith) 96
Brenner 122, Brennermann 94
(burner of charcoal, etc., or
distiller of brandy) 95
Brennholtz, Brenholts 159
(firewood) 72, 105
Brennwald (burned forest) 72
Brentz 122, Brentzer, Brentzel,
Brentzinger (dweller near the
river Brenz) 83
Breslau, Breslaw, Breslauer,
Bresslauer (fr Breslau 122)
Bresler, Bressler, Bresslers 59,
see Breslau
Breslow, see Breslau
Breth, Bretter (board, board
cutter) 98
Brethauer, Bretthauer (board
cutter, cabinet maker) 98, 100
Brethholz (board, board sawyer)
98, 105
Brethower 159, see Brethauer
Brett, Bretz 59 (board) 105, see
also Bretzel
Brettschneider, Brettscheider
(board sawyer, cabinet maker)
98
Bretzler (pretzel maker, fr Latin
bracillum) 96
Breuel (swamp) 80, see Brauer
Breuer, see Brauer
Breun, Breune, Breuner, see
Braun, Braune
Breun, Braeunig, Breuninger, see
Brauning, Brauninger

Breusscher (dweller on the
Breusch 83), see Preuss
Brewbaker 159, see Brubach
Brewer 153, see Brauer
Brey (pottage) 112
Breyer, Breyere, see Brauer
Breymayer, Breymeyer (brew
master) 93
Breyvogel (porridge eater) 112
Brezler, see Bretzler
Briar 159, see Braeuer
Brick 159, see Brueck
Brickbauer, see Brueckbauer
Brickel 55, Brickell (little bridge)
71
Bricker, Brickerd 74, see
Bruecker
Brickhouse 159, Brickous, see
Brueckhaus
Brickhus, see Brueckhaus
Brickmann, see Brueck
Brickner, see Brueckner
Bridaheart 159, see Breitenherdt
Bridegam 159, see Braeutigam
Bridenbach 159, Bridenbaugh
159, see Breitbach
Bridner 159 (dweller on the
Briede) 83, see Breitner
Briedenstein 159, see
Breitenstein
Brief, Brieftrager (letter carrier)
96
Briefel 55 (little letter)
Brieftraeger (letter carrier) 96
Brieger (fr Brieg) 122
Brieger (malt maker) 96
Briel, Brieler (fr Briel) 122, see
Bruehl
Brier 159, see Breuer
Briest 122, see Priest
Brigenz, see Bregenzer
Briggeman, Briggemann,
Brigermann, see
Brueggemann
Brigger, see Bruecker
Brighoff (farm at the bridge) 92

Bright 159, see Breit, Brecht
Brightback 159, see Breitenbach
Brightbeil (broad ax) 96, 108
Brightbill 159 (broad hill) 67,
    151, see also Brechbill
Brightman 159, see Breitmann
Brightstein 159, see Breitstein
Brigman, Brigmann, see Brugge
Brik, Rikner, see Brueckner
Brill (eye glass) 114, 106, 122
Brine 159, Briner, see Braun,
    Brauner
Bringenberg (grassy mountain)
    68
Bringhurst (grassy hurst) 72, 151
Bringmann, see Brinkmann
Brink 122, Brinke, Brinck,
    Brinks 59, Brings (grassy
    raised ground) 74
Brinker, Brinkmann 94,
    Brinkmeyer 93, Brinkmayer,
    Brinkmeier (small farmer) 74
Brinkerhoff (small farm) 74
Brinkhof, Brinckerhoff (farm on
    raised ground) 74, 92
Brinkschulte (village mayor) 74,
    109
Brinksitzer (owner of small
    parcel of land near village)
    74
Brintzenhoff (prince's farm) 92
Britenstein 159, Britenstine 159
    (swamp mountain) 80, 73, see
    Breitstein
Brixner (fr Brixen) 122
Broadbeck 159, see Brotbeck
Brobeck (bread baker) 104
Brobeck, see Brombeck
Broberg, see Bromberg
Brobst, see Probst
Broch 122, Brochmann 94 (brake
    dweller) 80
Brocht, see Pracht
Brock (brake, swamp) 80, 122
Brockdorf (brake village) 80, 124

Brockelhorst, Brochelhurst,
    Brockelhurst (brake hurst) 80,
    72, 122
Brockelmann (fr Brockel) 122, 94
Brockhage, Brockhagen 122
    (brake enclosure) 80, 124
Brockhase (rabbit in the briar
    patch) 118
Brockhaus, Brockhausen 122,
    Brockhus (brake house) 80, 65
Brockhoff (brake farm) 80, 65,
    122
Brocklebach 159 (brake brook)
    80, 77
Brockman, Brockmann (brake
    dweller) 80, 94
Brockmeyer, Brockmeier (brake
    farmer) 80, 93
Brockner (brake dweller) 80
Brockschmidt (brake smith) 80,
    96
Brocksmith, see Brockschmidt
Brod, Brode, Brodt, Brodte
    (bread, baker) 96
Brodbaeker, Brodbeck (bread
    baker) 96
Brodkorb (breadbasket, baker) 96
Broeder, see Bruder
Broek, see Brock
Broemm, see Brehm
Broening, see Brening
Broenner, see Brenner
Broenstein, see Braunstein
Broger (boaster) 115
Brohm, see Brahm
Broich, see Brock
Brokhus, see Brockhaus
Brokman, see Brockmann
Bromann (swamp dweller) 80, 94
Brombach 122, Brombeck
    (swamp brook) 80, 77
Bromberg, Bromberger (swamp
    mountain) 80, 68
Bromberg (thorn mountain) 68,
    122
Bromer (swamp dweller) 80

Brondenberg 159, see
Brandenburg

Brondenburg 159, see
Brandenburg

Bronholz 159, see Brunnholtz

Bronkhorst, see Brunkhorst

Bronner (dweller near a well) 79

Bronstein (spring stone) 79, 73

Brook, Brooks 59, see Bruch,
Brock

Brooker (brake dweller) 80

Brookhard (brake forest) 80, 72

Brookhiser, see Brockhaus 151

Brookhover, Brookover, see
Brockhoff

Brookland (marshy ground) 80

Brookmann, see Brockmann

Brookmeyer, see Brockmeyer

Brose, Brosi 53, Brosius < St.
Ambrosius 135

Bross, Brossmann, see Brose

Brot, Broth (bread, baker) 96

Brotbeck (bread baker) 96

Brotman, Brotmann, Brotzmann,
Brotsman 159 (baker) 96, 106,
94

Broun 159, Brouner, see Braun,
Brauner

Brounmiller 159, see
Braunmueller

Brouse 159, see Braus

Brouwer 159, see Brauer

Brower 159, Brouwer, see Brauer

Brown 159, Browner, see Braun,
Brauner

Brownbach 159, see Braunbach

Browning 159, see Brauning

Brownstein 159, see Braunstein

Broyle, Broyles, see Breul 151

Brubach, Brubaker, Brubacher,
Brubeck (swamp brook) 80, 77

Bruch (quarry) 122

Bruch (bog, swamp) 80, 122

Bruchman, Bruchmann (bog
dweller) 80, 94

Bruchmann (quarry worker) 96,
94

Bruck 122, Brucker, Bruckmann
Brueckmann, 94, Bruckmeyer
93, Bruckner, Bruekener
(dweller by a bridge) 71

Bruckbauer, see Brueckbauer

Bruckhard, see Burkhard

Bruder (brother, priest) 119

Brueck, Bruecker, Brueckner
(dweller by a bridge, bridge
builder) 71

Brueckbauer (bridge builder) 96

Bruecker, Brueckmann 94,
Brueckner (dweller near
bridge) 71

Brueckhaus, Brueckhausen
(house near a bridge) 71, 65,
122

Brueckhoff (farm at the bridge)
71, 92

Bruederlein 55 (little brother)
119

Bruedigam, see Braeutigam

Bruegge, Brueggemann 94,
Bruegemann, Bruegger, see
Bruecker

Brueggermeyer (farmer at the
bridge) 93

Bruehl (scrub-covered marsh) 80,
122

Bruekbauer, Brueckenbauer
(bridge builder), 96

Bruekbauer (farmer near bridge)
71, 92

Bruening 53 < Bruno

Bruenner (maker of burnies) 108

Bruennings 59 (fr Bruening) 122

Bruens, see Bruns

Bruestle (little breast) 114

Brugge, Bruggeman, Brugaman,
Bruggemann, Brugger, see
Bruecker, Brueckmann

Bruhl, see Bruehl

Bruhn, see Bruno, Braun

Bruich, see Bruch

Bruker, see Brueckner

Brukhaffer 159 (farm by a
bridge) 71, 92

Brumann, see Braumann

Brumback, Brumbaugh 159, see
Brombach

Brumm, Brummer (loud noise,
maker of loud noise) 115

Brun, Brune, Bruner, Brunert
74, see Braune

Bruner, see Brunner

Brungard, Brungardt (well
garden) 79, 84

Brungreber, Brungraber,
Brungraeber, see
Brunnengraeber

Brunhoefer (well farm) 79, 92,
see also Braunhof

Brunholtz, see Brunnholtz

Bruning, Brunjes < Bruno

Brunk 53, 55, Brunke, Brunken,
Brunker < Bruno, see also
Prunk

Brunkhorst (swamp hurst) 80, 72

Brunn 122, Brunner,
Brunnemann, Brunnermann
93 (person living near a spring
or well) 77, see Bruenner

Brunnenmueller (miller at the
spring) 79

Brunngraeber, Brunnengraeber
(well digger) 79

Brunner (dweller by a well) 79

Brunner (burnie maker) 108

Brunnholtz, Brunnsholtz (forest
by a spring) 79, 72

Bruno, Brunno (brown, bear) 22

Bruns, Brunsmann 94 (brown),
see also Bruno

Brunst (ardor, heat) 115

Brunstetter (well site) 79

Brupbacher 159, see Brubacher

Brusch (low growth, backwoods)
72

Bruschmueller (brush miller) 72,
103

Bruschweiler, Bruschwiler,
Bruschwiller, Bruschwitz
(brush village) 72, 124, 127

Brushwiler 159, see Bruschweiler

Brust (breast, chest) 114

Bruun, see Brun, Bruhn

Bryfogal 159 (porridge bird,
porridge eater) 112

Bryl, see Brill

Bryner 159, see Breiner

Bryte 159, see Breit

Bub, Bube (boy, servant) 118

Bubeck (butterfly) 118

Buberl 55 (little boy) 118

Buccolz 159, see Buchholtz

Buch (book, scribe) 96

Buch, Buchs 59, Buchler,
Buecher, Buechner (dweller
near the beeches) 41, 89

Buchacker (field by the beeches)
89, 84

Buchalter, see Buchhalter

Buchbinder (bookbinder) 96

Buchdahl (beech valley) 89, 76

Buchdrucker (book printer) 96

Buchel 55, Buchal 159, Buchle
(little beech) 89

Buchel 55, Buechel (little book)
106

Buchenauer (beech meadow) 89,
84

Buchenmeyer, Buckenmayer, see
Buchmeyer

Buchenroth (beech clearing) 126

Buchenwald 122, see Buchwald

Bucher (dweller among the
beeches) 89

Buchhalter (dweller on a beech
slope) 89, 71

Buchhalter (book keeper) 96

Buchholtz (beech forest) 89, 72

Buchhorst (beech hurst) 89, 72

Bucher 122, Buchert 74, see
Buechner

Buchhagen (beech enclosure) 89, 124, 122

Buchhalter (bookkeeper) 96

Buchhalter (beech slope) 89, 71

Buchheimer, Buchheim 159 (beech hamlet) 89, 124

Buchhoff (beech farm) 89, 92

Buchholtz, Bucholz (beechwood) 89, 72, 122

Buchler, see Buechler

Buchman, Buchmann, Buchman, Buchner (dweller near the beeches) 89, 94

Buchmeyer, Buchmaier, Buchmoyer (fr the Buchhoff) 89, 93, 94

Buchmueller (miller near the beeches) 89, 103

Buchner, see Buechler

Buchoff, see Buchhoff

Bucholz, see Buchholtz

Buchs, Buchsbaum (boxwood) 89

Buchstab (letter, schoolmaster) 96, 109

Bucht (bay) 118

Buchwald, Buchenwald, Buchwalter, Buckwald, Buckwalder (beech wood) 89, 71, 122

Buchwalt, Buckwalter 159, see Buchwald

Buck, see Bock, Buche, Burkhard

Buckbinder 159, see Buchbinder

Buckdorfer (beech village) 89, 124

Buckel, Buckelman 94, Buckleman 159 (humpback) 114

Bucker, Buckert 74 < Burkhart

Buckhalter 159, see Burkhalter, Buchhalter

Buckhard 159, Buckert, Bucker < Burkhard

Buckhaults 159, see Buchholtz

Buckholtz 159, Buckholz, see Buchholtz

Buckler (shield, fr Latin *buccula*) 108

Buckman 159, see Buchmann

Buckmeyer 159, Buckmeier, Buckmeir, see Buchmeyer

Buckner 159, Bucknor 159, see Buechner

Buckreus 159 (beech branch) 89

Budde (cooper) 96

Buddecke (vat maker, cooper) 96

Buddemeier, Buddemeyer, Buddemyer (bog farmer) 80, 93

Buddenbohm, Buddenbohn (bog tree) 80, 89, 122

Buddenbrook (bog brake) 80, 80

Buddenhagen (bog enclosure) 80, 125, 122

Budecker, Budicke, Budke (cooper) 96

Budelman, Budelmann (purse maker) 96, 94

Buechel 55 (little book) 118

Buechel 55 (little beech) 89, 118

Buechel, Buechler, Buehler (hill dweller) 67

Buechenau (beech meadow) 89, 84, 122

Buecher, see Buechner

Buechner, Buechler (dweller among beeches) 89

Buechsenmacher, Buechsler (gun smith) 96

Buechsenschuetz (sharpshooter) 107

Buechsler 98, Buechsel, Buechsmann 93 (box maker, gun maker) 96

Buecker, Bueckler 159, see
  Buechner

Bueckmann, see Buchmann

Bueckster (gun maker) 108

Buedel, see Buettel

Buegler (stirrup maker) 96

Buehl, Buehler, Bueler (fr Buehl
  122, hill) 41, 67

Buehlheimer (hill hamlet) 67,
  124, 122

Buehlman, Buehlmann (hill
  dweller) 67, 94

Buehlmayer, Buehlmeyer (hill
  farmer) 67, 93

Buehr, Buehre, Buehrer,
  Buehrmann, see Bauer

Buekler, see Buckler

Buel, Buell, Bueller, see Buehl

Buende (fenced in land)

Buendtner, see Painter

Buendtner (inhabitant of
  Graubuenden) 120

Buenger, see Binger

Buerger (castle dweller, burgher)
  73

Buergi 55, Burgy, see Birck

Buerhaus (peasant house) 91, 65,
  122

Buerk, Buerkie, Buerklein 55,
  159 (peasant) 91

Buerki < Burghalter, etc.

Buermann, see Bauermann

Buesche, Buescher, see Busch,
  Buscher

Bueschel (bundle) 118

Bueschner (bush dweller) 72

Buetefisch (plaice, fishmonger)
  115, 106

Buettel (beadle) 109

Buettel (homestead) 118

Buettemeyer (householder) 93

Buettler, Buettner (barrel maker,
  fr Latin *buttis*) 96

Buettner (cooper) 96

Buetzel (scarecrow, bogeyman) 115

Buetzenberger, see Pitzenberger

Bugher 159, see Bucher

Buhl, Buhle, Buhler, Buhlert 74,
  Buhlman 94, Buhlmann (lover,
  suitor, see also Buehl)

Buhmann, see Baumann

Buhr, Buhrmann 94 (peasant) 91

Buick (beech) 89

Bulger (Bulgarian) 121

Bulle, Bull (cattle dealer) 91, 105

Bullerich (shouting, screaming)
  115

Bullermann 53, 94 < Baldher
  (bold + army) 46, 46

Bullhausen (bull houses) 65, 91

Bulling, Bullinger, see Bollinger

Bullwinkel (attic space) 118

Bulman, see Buhlmann

Bultman, Bultmann (mattress
  seller) 106, 94

Bultmann (dweller on a hill) 72,
  94

Bumann, see Baumann

Bumbaugh 159, see Bombach

Bumgardner, Bumgartner,
  Bumgarner, see Baumgaertner

Bummel (stroll, promenade) 118

Bunce 159, see Buntz

Bunde (fenced meadow) 84, 122

Bundschuh (laced boot, peasant
  revolt) 112

Bungartz, see Baumgart

Bunger, Bungerts 74, 59
  (drummer) 96

Bunt, Bunte, Bunter (colorful)
  115

Bunte (fish box) 118

Buntrock (coat of many colors
  112, kind of crow 115)

Bunts 159, see Buntz

Buntz, Bintz (sleeping birth)

Buntz (fat man) 114

Burack, Buracker (peasant's
  field) 71, 84

Burbach (peasant brook) 91, 71

Burch, see Burg
Burchard, Burchhards 59,
    Burckhardt, see Burghart
Burchland (castle land) 118
Burck, see Burg
Burckhalter, see Burghalter
Burdorf 122, see Burgdorf
Burenfeind, see Bauernfeind
Burenhagen (peasant's enclosure)
    91, 125
Buresch, Buresh (Slavic:
    peasant) 146
Burg (fortress, castle) 46, 73, 122
Burgalter, see Burghalter
Burgard, Burgartz 59, see
    Burkhard
Burgdorf (castle village) 73, 124,
    122
Burgemeister, see Burgermeister
Burger, Burgers 59, Burgert 74
    (burgher, castle dweller,
    townsman) 73
Burgermeister (mayor) 109
Burggraf (burgrave) 109
Burghalter (castellan) 73, 109
Burghard, Burghardt, Burghart,
    see Burkhart
Burghauser, Burgheiser 66 (fr
    Burghausen 122, castle
    houses) 73, 65
Burgheimer (castle hamlet) 73,
    124, 122
Burgherr (castellan) 73
Burghoff (castle courtyard) 73,
    92, 122
Burgholder, see Burkhalter
Burgman, Burgmann (burgher)
    73, 94
Burgstiner (castle mountain) 73,
    93
Burgtorf, see Burgdorf
Burgunder (Burgundian) 121
Burgwin (protection + friend) 47,
    48
Burhard, Burhart, see Burkhart

Burhorst (peasant forest) 91, 72
Burk, Burke, see Burg
Burkard, Burkart, see Burkhard
Burker, Buckert 74, see Burger
Burkhalter, see Burghalter
Burkhamer, Burkheimer, see
    Burgheimer
Burkhard, Burkhardt, Burckhart
    (protection + strong) 47, 46
Burkhoff, Burkoff, see Burghoff
Burkholder, see Burkhalter
Burkhouse 153 (castle house) 73,
    65, 151
Burkman, see Burgman
Burkmeyer, Burkmire 159 (castle
    bailiff, castle farmer) 93
Burlein 55 (little peasant) 91
Burmann, see Bauermann
Burmeister, Burmester, see
    Bauernmeister
Burnemann, see Bornemann
Burrichter (village magistrate)
    109
Bursch, Bursche (youth, servant)
    109
Burt (birth, burden) 118
Busch, Busche, Buscher (bush,
    tavernkeeper) 72, 63
Buschel, Buschell (bunch,
    bundle) 118
Buscher, Buschert 74, Busching,
    Buschling (dweller in the
    bush) 72
Buschfeld (bush field) 72, 84
Buschgans (bush goose) 72, 115
Buschkemper (bush field) 72, 84
Buschman, Buschmann,
    Buschmeyer (farmer in the
    brush-land) 72, 93, 94
Buse (pocket) 118
Bush ..., see Busch ...
Bushart 159, Busshart, see
    Bussard
Bushbaum 159 (bush tree) 72,
    89, 151

Bushert 159, 74 see Buscher

Bushman 159, Bushmann, see
Buschmann

Bushrod 159 (bush clearing) 72,
125, 151

Bushyeager 159 (bush hunter)
72, 91, 151

Buskirk (bush church) 72

Busler (penitent) 115

Buss, Busse (penitence, penance,
fine, see also Busch) 118

Bussard, Bussart (soaring hawk)
115

Busse 53 < Burkhard

Busser (one doing penance) 115

Busser, Bussler, Bussmann 94
(repairman) 96

Bussman, Bussmann (heavy
drinker) 115, 94

Bussmann (handyman) 95, 94

Buterbaugh, see Butterbaugh

Butke, see Boettcher

Butner, see Buettner

Butt (plaice, fishmonger) 115

Butter (butter dealer) 105, see
also Butz

Butterbaum (butter tree) 89

Butterbaugh 159 (butter brook)
77

Butterbrot (buttered bread) 112

Butterfass (butter keg) 91

Butterfuss (butter foot) 114

Butterhof, Butterhoff (butter
farm) 92

Buttermann (butter dealer) 105

Butterweck (butter role, baker)
96

Buttmann (paice dealer) 105, 94

Buttner, see Buettner

Butts 159, see Butz

Butz, Butze, Butzer, Butzner,
Butts 159 (scarecrow) 114,
also < Burkhard

Butzke (little Burkhard) 54, 55

Buxbaum (boxwood) 89

Byer 159, Byers 59, see Bayer

Byerly 159, Byerley, see Baeuerle

Byle, Byler 159, Beyler, see
Beiler

Byrle 159, see Bayerle

Byroade 159 (by the clearing) 69,
125

C

Note: In the eighteenth and
nineteenth centuries many
German words began with a "C,"
and thus they were imported to
America. At the end of the
nineteenth century a spelling
reform in Germany changed most
of them to a "K," and thus they
were brought in by later arrivals.
Therefore words should be
searched under both spellings. A
few words begin with a "C" in
Upper German dialects whereas
they begin with a "G" in standard
German. In this book they are
listed under the standard form.

Cabel, Cabell, Cabler, see Kabel,
Gabel

Cace 159, see Kaes

Cade, see Kade

Caemmerer, see Kaemmerer

Caesar (Roman emperor) 109

Cagle 159, see Kegel

Cahler, see Kahl, Koehler

Cahn, see Kahn

Calb, see Kalb

Caldmeyer, Caldemeyer 159 (fr
the Kalthof, cold farm) 93, 94

Cale, see Kehl 151

Calehuff 151, see Kehlhoff

Calfmann 159, see Kaufmann

Calk, see Kalker

Call, see Kall, Gallus

Callbaugh 159, Callbeck, see
Kaltenbach

Callenius (Latin for Callen) 142
Calp, see Kalb
Cam 159, Camman, see Kamm
Cammerhof (farm belonging to
    the royal chamber) 92
Cammermeyer (manager of the
    Cammerhof, see above) 93
Camp, Campe, Campen, see
    Kampe
Camper, see Gamper, Kamper
Campf, Campher, Camphor 159,
    see Kampf, Kaempfer
Camphir, Campfor, see Kaempfer
Canegieser, see Kannengiesser
Canisius (probably Latin for
    hunt) 142
Cansler 159, see Kantzler
Cantor (Latin, singer) 142
Cantzler, see Kantzler
Canz, see Ganz
Cap, see Kapp
Capehart 159, see Gebhard
Capeheart, see Gebhart
Caplan (chaplain) 110
Capp, Cappe, Cappes 59, see
    Kapp
Cappel, Cappele, Cappeler,
    Capele, Cappelmann 159, 94
    (chapel servant, person fr
    Cappel) 109, 139, 122
Carbaugh 159, Carbauh,
    Carbach, Carbeck (possibly
    carp stream) 115, 77, 151
Carber 159, see Gerber
Carcher 159, see Karch
Carcker, see Karcker
Carhart 159, see Gerhard
Carl, Carle, Carel, Carll, Carls
    59, Carolus 141 (man)
Carlberg (Charles' mountain) 68
Carling (follower of Charles) 119
Carlsen, son of Carl 59
Carman 159, see Garmann
Carner, see Garner
Carolus (Latin for Carl) 141

Carpenter, see Zimmermann 152
Carrel 159, Carril, see Carl
Carrickhof, see Kerkhof 151
Carsten, Carstens 59, Carstensen
    (Christian) 135
Carthaeuser (Carthusian 110, or
    fr Carthausen 122)
Cartman 151, see Gaertmann
Carver 151, see Gerber
Casch 53 < Karl
Cascorbi < Kaesekorb
Case 151, see Kaese
Caser, see Kaese
Casman 151, see Kaesemann,
    Gasmann
Casner 151, see Gessner
Caspar, Casper, Caspers 59
    Casperl 55 (one of the Three
    Kings) 135, 111
Caspari (son of Caspar) 142
Cassel, Cassell, Casseler, Castle
    159 (fr Cassel, fr Latin
    castellum) 121, 122
Casselberry, see Kesselberg
Castleman 94, 151, see Kassel
Castner, see Kastner
Castor (Latin, beaver, patron
    saint of Koblenz) 141, 135
Cather, see Kater
Catz, see Katz
Cauf, see Kauf
Caufler, see Kaufler
Caufman, Cauffmann,
    Caughman 159, 94, see
    Kaufmann
Caulberg 159, see Kalberg
Caulk 159, see Kalk
Cayce 159, see Kaes
Caylor 159, Cayler, see Kehler,
    Koehler
Cedarbaum 159 (cedar tree) 89
Cellarius (Latin for Keller, cellar
    master) 141
Centner, see Zentner
Cerber 159, see Gerber

Cerf (French, stag) 144
Cerst, see Gerst
Charles < Karl
Chaser 159, see Kaese
Chel 159, see Kehl
Chevalier (French for cavalier) 144
Chonrat 159, see Conrad
Chorengel 152 (choir angel) 115
Chresman 159, see Kressmann
Chrisman 159, see Christmann
Christ 151 (Christian) 135, 142
Christbaum (Christmas tree) 143
Christer, Cristel (Christian) 135
Christfried (Christ peace) 140
Christgau (Christian district)
Christhilf (Christ's help) 139
Christi, Christy 159 (son of Christian) 139, 142
Christian (Christian) 135
Christiani (son of Christian) 142
Christler (see Christ)
Christman, Christmann (Christian), see Kressmann
Christof, Christoff, Christoffel, Christoph (St. Christopher) 135
Chrypfius (Gryphius, griffin, housename) 141, 142
Chrysler, see Kreisel
Chupart 144, see Schubart
Chur (person fr Chur in Switzerland) 122
Cider, see Seider
Claar, see Klar
Claas, Classen, see Clas
Clabaugh 159, see Kleebach
Clain 159, see Klein
Clap, Clapp, see Klap, Klapp
Clarmann, see Klarmann
Clas, Class, Clasen, see Nicolaus
Clatenbaugh 159, Clattenbaugh, Clatterbaugh, Clatterbuck, see Gladbach
Claudfelter, see Klotfelder 151

Clauer, see Glauer
Claus, Clauseer, see Klaus, Klauser
Clause, Claussen (hermitage, cell) 122
Clausenius 141, see Klaus
Clauser, see Klause
Clausey 159, Clawsey, see Klause
Clawes 53 < Niklaus
Claybaugh 159, see Kleebach
Clayman 159, see Klehmann
Claypool 159, Claypoole, see Kleepuhl
Cleaver 159, see Cleve
Cleh, see Klee
Clem 159, see Klemm
Clemens, Clementz, Clement (name of several popes) 134
Clemmer, see Klemmer
Cleve (fr Cleves) 121
Clevenstine 159, see Kliebenstein
Clever, see Kleber
Click, Clickner, see Glueck
Cline 159, Clien 159, see Klein
Clinedienst 159, Clinedinst, Clindist, see Kleindienst
Clinefelter 159, see Kleinfeld
Clinetopp, Kleintopp (small forelock) 112, 151
Clingenpeel 159, see Klingenbuehl
Clinger, Clingler, see Klinger
Clingman, Clingermann, see Klingmann
Clise 159, see Gleis
Cloates 159, see Klotz
Clocke, Clocker, see Glocke, Glocker
Clodfelter (log field) 84
Clontz 159, see Glantz
Clos, Closs, Close, Closse, see Kloss, Klosse
Closterbecker (Cloister baker) 96
Clostermann, see Klostermann
Clotfelter, see Clodfelter

Clouse 159, Clouser, Clowser, see
    Klaus, Klause
Clower 159, Clowers 59, see
    Glauer
Clutts 159, Clutz, see Klott
Coal 159, Coale, see Kohl
Cobach, Cobaugh 159 (cow brook)
    77
Coben, see Koben
Cober, see Kober
Coberg (German principality) 121
Coble 159, see Goebel
Coblenz, Coblenzer, see Koblenz
Coch, see Koch
Cockel 159, see Kachel
Coder 159, see Koeder
Cody, see Kothe
Coen 53, Coene, Coenen <
    Conrad
Coerper 159, see Koerber
Coffelt, Coffield 153 (cow field)
    84
Coffer, see Koffer
Coffman, see Kaufmann
Cogle 159, see Kugel
Cohen, Cohn (Hebrew: priest)
    110, see also Kuhn
Cohler, Coler 159, see Kohler
Cohnen, see Koehn
Cokenour 159, see Kochenauer
Coker, see Kocher 151
Colb, see Kolb, Kalb 159
Colbeck, see Kohlbecker
Colberg, see Kohlberg
Coldiron 153, see Kalteisen
Cole, see Kohl
Colebrunn, see Kaltenborn 151
Colefelt, Colfelt (cabbage field) 84
Colehaus 159, Colehouse 153, see
    Kohlhas
Coleman 159, see Kohlmann,
    Kuhlmann
Coler, see Koehler
Colflesh 159, see Kalbfleisch
Colhower 159, see Kohlhauer

Colhower 159 (coal digger) 96
Collar 159, Coller, see Kohler,
    Koller
Collin 53 < Nickolaus
Collin (place name) 122
Collitz (place name) 122
Collmann 159, Colman, see
    Kohlmann
Collmeyer, see Kohlmeyer
Colmar (fr Colmar in Alsace) 122
Colter, see Kolter
Comb 152, see Kamm
Compher 159, see Kaempfer
Cone, see Kohn
Conkel, Conkle 159, see Kunckel
Conrad, Conrads 59, Conradt,
    Conrath, Conradus 142 (brave
    + counsel) 36, 46, 46, 136
Conradi, Conrady, son of
    Conrad(us) 142
Conselman 159, see
    Kuenzelmann
Conz 159, see Kunz
Conzelman 159, see
    Kuenzelmann
Cooble 159, see Kuebel
Coogle, Coogler 159, see Kugel,
    Kugler
Cook 152, Cooke, see Koch
Cool 159, Cooll, see Kuhl
Coolbaugh 159, see Kuhlbach
Cooler 159, see Kuhler
Coolmann 159, see Kuhlmann
Coomer 159, see Kummer
Coon 159, Coons 59, Coonce 159,
    59, Coonts, see Kuhn, Kuhns
Coope (merchant, fr Latin *caupo*)
    105
Cooper 159, see Kupfer, Kuper
Cooperman 94, 159, see
    Kupfermann
Coopersmith 153, see
    Kupferschmidt
Cooperstein 159 (copper
    mountain) 151

Coopman, see Kaufmann

Coos 159, see Kuss

Copeman 159, see Kaufmann

Copenhaver, Copenheaver 159,
see Koppenhaver

Copman, see Kaufmann

Coppel, Coppele, see Koppel

Coppersmith 152, see
Kupferschmidt

Coradi, see Konradi

Corber, see Koerber

Corbman 94, see Koerber

Cordes, see Kordes

Cordesmann (Conrad's vassal)
53, 94

Corn, see Korn

Corenblith, see Kornblith

Corfman 94, see Korff

Cornbach (corn brook) 77

Cornberger (fr Cornberg 122,
grain mountain) 68

Cornblath, Cornblatt, see
Kornblatt

Cornbrook, Cornbrooks 59 (grain
brake) 80

Cornelius (Roman family)

Cornelius (Roman name [crow],
name of pope) 141, 134

Cornell, see Cornelius

Cornfield 152, see Kornfeld

Cornman, see Kornmann

Cornmesser (grain measurer) 109

Correll 159, see Karl

Corthes, Cortes, see Cordes

Corvinus (Latin for Kraeh) 141

Cossaboom, see Kassebaum 151

Cost, see Kost

Coster 159, see Kuester

Cott, Cottman, see Gott,
Gottmann

Cotz 159, see Goetz

Couchenuour 159, Coughenour,
see Gauchenauer

Coughman 159, see Kaufmann

Cougle 159, see Kugel

Couler 159, see Kuehler

Coulter 159, see Kolter

Coun 159, see Kuhn

Counce 159, see Kuntz

Councel 159, Council, Counsul,
Counselman 94, Councilman,
see Kuenzel, Kuenzelman

Counterman 159, Countryman,
see Guenthermann

Counts 159, see Kuntz

Couper 159, see Kupfer

Couts 159, Coutts, see Kauz

Cowell 159, see Kaul

Crabbe (crab) 114

Crabill 159, see Kraebuehl

Crable 159, see Kraehbuehl

Craemer, Cramer, Cramert 74,
see Kraemer

Craesman 159, see Kressmann

Craft, see Kraft

Crall, see Kral

Cram (retail trade, huckster's
cart) 105

Cramer, see Kraemer

Crance 159, see Krantz

Crank, see Krank

Crass, see Grass

Crater 159, see Kraeuter

Cratsar 159, see Kratzer

Cratz, see Kratz

Crau, see Grau

Crauel 159, see Graeul

Craumer 159, Crawmer, see
Kraemer

Craus, Crause, see Kraus,
Krause

Cravenstine 159, see
Graffenstein

Craver, see Graeber

Crawf 159, see Graff

Craybill 159, Crebil, see
Kraehbuehl

Crayenbuehl, see Kraebuehl

Creager 159, see Krueger

Creamer 159, see Kraemer

Crebbs, Crebs, see Krebs
Creek 159, see Krueg
Creff 159, see Graf
Creger 159, Creeger, Cregar, see
     Krueger
Creiner 159, see Greiner
Creitz, Creytz, Creitzer, see
     Kreutz, Kreutzer
Crell, see Grell
Cremer, see Craemer
Crentzer 159, see Grentzel
Cress, Cresse, see Kress, Kresse
Cressman, Cressmeyer, see
     Kressman
Creutz, Creutzer, see Kreutz,
     Kreutzer
Crever 159, see Grueber
Crews 159, see Kruse
Creyts 159, see Kreutz
Crick, Crickman 159, see Krug,
     Kruegmann
Crickenberger 159,
     Crickenburger, see
     Krueckenberger
Crider 159, Cridler, see Kraeuter,
     Kreider
Crigger 159, see Krueger
Crimm, see Grimm
Criner 159, see Greiner
Cripe 159, see Greip
Crisman, Crissmann, see
     Kressmann
Crist, Criste, Cristner, see Christ
Crites 159, Critz, Critzer, Crizer,
     Critzman, see Kreutz,
     Kreutzer, Kreutzmann
Croesman, Croessman, see
     Kressmann
Croft, see Craft
Crogg 159, see Groff
Croll, see Groll, Kroll, Krall
Crolus 159, see Carolus
Crombach, see Grumbach
Crombholts 159, see Krumbholtz
Cromer 159, see Kraemer

Cromm 159, see Krumm
Cron, Crone, see Kron, Krone
Cronauer, see Gronau
Cronberger, Cronenberg,
     Cronenberger, Croneberge, see
     Kronberg
Cronemeyer (royal bailiff) 93, 109
Cronjager 159 (royal hunter) 91,
     109
Cronk 159, see Krank
Cronkite 159, see Krankheit
Cronmiller (crown miller) 103
Cronrad, Cronrath (crown
     council), see Konrad
Crook 159, see Krug
Crosman 159, see Grossmann,
     Kressmann
Crossbart, see Grossbart
Crosse, Crossman, see Grosse,
     Grossmann
Crossman 159, see Kressmann
Crotser 159, see Kreutzer
Crounse 159, see Krantz
Crouse 159, see Kraus
Croushore 159, see Kraushaar
Crout 159, see Kraut
Crouthamel 159 (herb hamlet)
     124
Crow 153, see Kraehe
Crowder 159, Crouther, see
     Krauter
Crown 159, see Kron
Crownen 159, see Kronen
Crowninshield 159, see
     Kronenschild
Croyter 159, Croyder, see
     Kraeuter
Crueger, see Krueger
Cruess, see Gruess
Cruise 159, see Kruse
Crull, see Krull
Crum, Crumm, Crumber, see
     Krumm
Crumbacker, Crumbaker,
     Crumbaugh 159 (crooked
     brook) 77

Crumling (misshapen person)
113
Crump, see Krumm
Crupe 159, see Krup
Cruse 159, see Kruse
Crusse 159, see Gruss
Crute 159, see Kraut
Crybile 159, see Kraehbuehl
Crybile, see Kraebuehl
Cryder 159, see Kreider
Cryer 159, Cryor, see Kreier
Crynes 159, see Grein
Crytz, Crytzer, see Kreutz,
    Kreutzer
Cuffman 159, see Kaufman
Cugel, see Kugel
Cuhn, see Kuhn
Culler, see Koller, Koehler
Culman, Cullmann 159, see
    Kuhlmann
Culp 159, see Kulp, Kalb
Cumberbatch 159, Cumberpatch,
    see Kummerbach
Cumprecht 159, see Gumbrecht
Cunkel, see Kunkel
Cunrad, Cunratt, Cuonrad,
    Cunred 159, see Conrad
Cunradi, son of Cunrad 142
Cuntz 159, Cunz, Cuntze,
    Cuntzer, see Kuntz
Cunzeman 159, Cuntzmann, see
    Kuntzemann
Cuper, see Kupfer
Cupp, see Kopp
Curland, Curlander (fr the
    Kurland) 121
Curtius 141, see Kurtz
Custer, see Kuester
Cutchall 159, see Gottschalk
Cutlip 159, see Gottlieb
Cyfret, Cyphert, see Seyfert

D

A name beginning with a "D" in
one dialect may begin with a "T"
in another and be so listed below.

Daab (swamp) 80
Dabelstein (dice, gambler)
Dabler, see Doebler
Dach (clay, mud) 118
Dachenhausen, Dachhausen
    (thatched houses) 65
Dacher (thatcher, roofer) 96
Dachhausen, see Dachenhausen
Dachler, Dachl, see Dacher
Dachler (swamp dweller) 80
Dachs (badger, badger hunter)
    115, 91
Dachslager (badger lair)
Dackerman 94, Dackermann,
    Dackman, Dackmann, see
    Dacher
Daehn, Daegen, see Degen
Daehn, Daehnert < Degenhard
Daehnick 53, Daehnike, Daehnke
    < Degenhard
Daeneke 53, 55 < Degenhard
Daengler, see Dengler
Daescher, Daeschner, see
    Taescher
Daettlikon (swamp village) 80,
    127
Daeuber, see Taeuber
Daeubler, see Taeubler
Daeumler (thumb, Tom Thumb)
    113
Dafner, Daffner (taverner, fr
    Latin *taberna*) 96
Dagenbeck (baker who bakes
    daily) 96
Dagenhart 159, see Degenhart
Dagher, see Dacher
Dahl 122, Dahle 122, Dahler,
    Dahlmann 94, Dallmann
    (valley man, see Thalmann) 76

Dahlberg (valley mountain) 76, 68

Dahlhaeuser (valley houses) 76

Dahlheim, Dahlheimer (fr Dahlheim 122, valley hamlet) 76, 124

Dahlhoff, Dalhoff (valley farm) 76, 92

Dahlinger (fr Dahlingen) 122

Dahlke 55 (little valley) 76

Dahlmann, see Thalmann

Dahlmeyer, see Thalmeyer

Dahm 53, Dahms 59, Dahme, Dahmer < Adam 135

Dahm, Dame 53 < Damian 135

Dahm (dweller near the Dahme River) 83, 122

Dahmke (little Dahm) 55

Dahn, Dahne (forest) 72

Dahniel, see Daniel

Daiber, see Teuber

Daichler, see Deigler

Daigel, Deigle, see Deigler

Daimler (thumb screwer) 96

Daisch (cow dung, peasant) 91

Dalhoff, see Dahlhoff

Dalke, see Dahlke

Daller (moist, cool place) 80

Dallmeyer, see Thalmeyer

Dallwig, see Dalwig

Dalman, see Thalmann

Dalmeyer, see Dahlmeyer

Dalsheimer, Dalshimer 159, Dalsemer (valley hamlet) 76, 124

Dalwig (valley village) 76, 124

Dam 53 < St. Damian 135

Dam 53, Dame, Damser < Adam 135

Dam (stag, hunter) 91

Daman, Damen, see Dahm

Damasus (name of a pope) 134

Damewald, see Dannewald

Damian (patron saint of physicians) 135

Damkoehler (forest collier) 89, 95

Damm 122, Damme, Dammes 59 (causeway, dike) 81

Dammann, Dammermann, Dammsmann (dweller on or near dike) 81

Dammann 53 < Thomas

Dammermut (dike, causeway, dweller on the dike) 81

Dammeyer 93, Dammeier, Dammyer (farmer on or at the dike) 81

Dammsmann (dweller at the dike) 81

Dampf (steam) 118

Damrosch (forest slide) 89, 71

Dan (forest, fir) 89, 71

Danaker, see Danecker

Danbach (brook through firs) 89, 77

Dance 153, see Tanz

Dancel 159, see Dantzel

Danckert, see Dankwart

Dandorf (fir village, forest village) 89, 124

Danecker, Danecke, Daniker, Danegger (place in fir trees) 89, 85, see Tannecker

Daneman, Danemann (forest dweller) 89

Danenhauer, Danhaur (fir chopper, wood cutter) 89, 95, 100

Dange 53 < St. Anthony 135

Dangel, Dangle 159 < Daniel 135

Dangler, see Dengler

Danhower 159, see Danenhauer

Danick, Danicke, see Danecke

Daniel, Daniels 59 (OT name) 135

Dankelmann 94 (marsh dweller, cf. English "dank") 80

Dankelmeyer (marsh farmer) 80

Danker, Dankers 59, Dankert < Dankwart 48, 47

Dankmar (thought + famous) 48, 47

Dankmeyer, Dankmeier 93, see Dankelmeyer

Dankwart (thought + guard or watch) 48, 47

Danmeyer, Danmyer 159 (forest farmer) 89, 93

Danmiller (forest miller) 89, 103

Dannecke, Dannecker, Dannecker, Dannegger, see Danecker or Denecke

Dannehauer (wood chopper) 89, 96

Dannemann (dweller near the pine trees)

Dannenbaum 122, Dannebaum, see Tannenbaum

Dannenberg (forest mountain) 89, 68, 122

Dannenfeld, Dannenfeldt, Dannenfelder, Dannenfeltzer (forest field) 89, 84

Dannenfelser (wooded cliffs) 89, 84

Dannenmann (forest dweller) 89, 94

Danner, Dannermann 94 (forest dweller) 89

Danner < Giessendanner

Dannewald, Damewald, see Tannenwald

Dannewitz (fr Danewitz 122, forest village) 89, 127

Dannhaeuser, Dannheisser 122, see Tannhaeuser

Dannhoeffer, see Tannhoeffer

Danninger (fr Danningen) 122

Dannwolf (forest wolf) 89, 48

Danoff, see Dannhoeffer

Dansberger 159, Danzberger (forest mountain) 89, 68

Danser, see Tantz 159

Dansicker 159, see Dantziger

Dansler, see Densler

Dantz, Danz, Dantzer, Dantzler (dancer) 96

Dantzenbecker, Tanzenbecker (dancing brook) 77

Dantzic, Dantzig, Dantziger (Baltic city) 122

Dantzler, Danzler, see Dantz

Danz, Danzer, Danzel, see Dantz

Danzig, Danziger, see Dantzic

Dapfer, Dapper, see Tapfer

Darmstadt, Darmstaet, Darmsteadt, Darmstaedter (fr Darmstadt) 122

Dasbach (swampy brook) 79

Dasch, Dascher, Dasher 159, Dashner, see Taescher

Dasinger (fr Dasing) 122

Dattelbaum (date tree) 89, 149

Datwyler, Dattweiler, see Dettwiler

Daub, Daube, Dauber, Daubert 74, Daubner, see Taub, Taube

Daube, Daubler (barrel stave, cooper) 96

Daubenberger (dove mountain) 115, 68

Dauberman, see Taubermann

Daublein 55 (little dove) 115

Daudt (swamp, reeds) 80

Dauenhauer (cooper) 96

Dauer (duration) 118

Dauer (barrelstave maker) 95, 96

Dauernheim (place name) 124, 122

Daught 159, see Daudt

Daum (thumb, short person) 113

Daumenlang (thumb long) 113

Daumer (thumbscrew, torturer, tool for cutting rock) 106

Daun, Daunn, Dauner (goose down, dealer in feathers) 105

Daun (down, swamp) 80, 122

Dauner (swamp dweller) 80

Dausch (mother swine) 91

Davis 159, see Dewes

David, Davit (OT character) 135
Davids, Davidssohn (son of
David) 59
Daymude 159, see Demuth
Deaderick 159, see Dederick
Deagler 159, see Diegler
Deal, Deahl 159, see Diehl
Dealbone 159 < Thiel Bohn
Dealy, see Diele
Deamer 159, see Dietmar
Deamud 159, see Demuth
Deaner 159, see Diener
Deangler 159, see Dengler
Deardorf 159, Deardorff, see
Tierdorf, Duerrendorf
Dearholt 159, (animal forest) 72
Dearing 159, see Duering
Dearman 159, see Diermann
Dearstine 159 (animal mountain)
73
Dearwaechter 159, see
Thuerwaechter
Deasel 159, see Diesel
Deatrich 159, see Dietrich
Deats 159, see Dietz
Debald, Debold, Debolt, see
Dietbald
Debelbesin 159, see Teufelbiss
Deboer (the peasant) 91
Debold, Deboldt, see Dietbold
Debs 53 < Matthias
Dechan, Dechant (tithing man,
tithe collector) 109
Decher, Dechert 74 (roofer) 92,
143
Decher (set of ten, tenth child)
Deck, Decke (blanket) 106
Deckdenbron (Cover the well!)
116
Decker, Deckert 74, Deckner
(thatcher, roofer) 96
Decker, Deckert (blanket maker)
96
Deckler, Deckelman 94 (maker of
bedclothes) 96

Deckman, Deckmann (thatcher)
94, 96
Deckner (blanket weaver) 96
Dedekind 53 < Dietrich
Dedemeyer (Dietrich + farmer)
93
Dederer (stutterer) 114
Dederick, Dedrich, Dedrick, see
Dietrich
Deeck 53, Deeken < Dietrich
Deemar 159, Deemere, see
Dietmar
Deener 159, see Diener
Deer 159 ..., see Tier ...
Deering, see Thueringer
Dees 53, 159, Deese, see Thiess
Deeter, Deeters 159, see Dieter
Deetje, 53, 55 Deetjen < Dietrich
Deets 159, Deetz < Dietrich
Defenbau 159, Defenbaugh,
Defibaugh, Deffibaugh,
Deffinbaugh, see Tiefenbach
Defriece 159, see Devries
Degen (thane) 46
Degen, Degener (dagger, dagger
maker) 108
Degenhardt, Degenhart (thane +
strong) 46, 46
Degenkolb (hero + club) 46
Degering 53, Degerink <
Degenhard
Degner, Degener (dagger maker)
108
DeGraffenried, see Graffenried
Degrote, Degroot, DeGroat 159
(the large) 113
Dehle 53, Dehles 59, Dehls 59,
Dehler < Dietrich
Dehlenbeck (Dietrich's brook) 77
Dehlke 53, 55 < Dietrich
Dehm, Dehmann, Dehmel, 94,
Dehmert 74 < Thomas,
Damianus 135
Dehn, Dehne, Dehner, Dehnert <
Degenhard

Dehrenbach (animal brook) 77
Dehrenkamp (animal field) 77
Deibel (devil) 135
Deibert < Dagebert
Deibler, see Teubler
Deibler, see Taeubler
Deich, Deicher, Deichert 74
(dweller on a dike) 81
Deichgraber, Deichgraeber (ditch
digger, dike digger) 81
Deichgraff (dike supervisor) 109
Deichman, Deichmann,
Deickmann, see Teichmann
Deichmann, Deikmann, see
Teichmann
Deichmiller, Deichmueller (pond
miller, miller on the dike) 81,
103
Deicke, Deickman 94 (dweller at
or on the dike) 81
Deigler (maker of wooden water
pipes) 96
Deimler, see Daeumler
Deimling, see Daeumling
Deiner, see Deinert, Diener
Deinert, Deinhart, see Degenhar
Deinhard, see Degenhard
Deinhardt, see Degenhardt
Deininga 53, Deininger <
Degenhard
Deinlein 53, 55 < Degenhard
Deis 159, Deise, see Theiss
Deisinger (fr Deising in Bavaria)
122
Deisler (wainwright) 96
Deisroth (manure clearing) 126
Deiss 159, see Theiss
Deissel, Daissler (wainwright) 96
Deist, Deister, Deistler (wooded
ridge) 72
Deisterberg (wooded mountain)
68
Deistermann (dweller on a
wooded ridge) 72, 94

Deisteroth (clearing on a wooded
ridge) 72, 125
Deitsch, Deitscher, Deitschman
94, Deitch 159, see Deutsch
Deitelbaum, see Dattelbaum
Deiter 159, Deitermann,
Deitrich, Deitrick, see Dieter,
Dietrich
Deitz, Deitzel, see Dietz, Dietzel
Deken 53 < Dietrich
Dekker, Dekher, see Decker
Delikat (delicate) 115
Delinger, Dellinger, see Dillinger
Delius (Latin for Dehl)
Dem < Damianus 135
Dem, Dehm, see Demm
Demback (Tom's brook) 77
Demeling, see Daeumling
Demke 53, 55, Demeke, Dempke
< Thomas
Demm 53, Demme < Thomas
Demmler, Demler (glutton) 115
Dempewolf (Kill the wolf!) 116
Demus (St. Nicodemus) 135
Demuth (humility) 139
Denbeck (fir brook, forest brook)
89, 77
Denburg (forest castle) 89, 73
Dencker, Denker (thinker, left-
handed person) 114
Dencler 159, see Dengler
Denecke 53, 55, Denicke <
Degenhard
Dener 159, see Diener
Dengler (one who repairs blades
by hammering them) 96
Denhard, Denhardt < Degenhard
Denk (left, left handed) 114
Denker, see Dankwart
Denlein, see Dennelein
Denmeyer (fr the Denhoff, forest
farm) 89, 92, 93
Dennard < Degenhard
Denneger 53 < Degenhard
Dennelein 55, Dennerlein (little
fir tree) 89

Dennemann (dweller among the firs) 89, 94

Dennenberg 122, see Tannenberg

Denner, Dennler, see Tanner

Dennewitz 122, see Dannewitz

Dennstedt, Daennstaedt (forest place) 89

Denny 159, sometimes < Thoeni

Densler, Denzler (dancer) 96

Dentz, Denz, Dentzer, Denzer, see Tants, Tantz

Dentzel, Dentzler, Dentzner (dancer) 96

Denys (St. Dionysius, name of a pope) 134

Denzinger (fr Denzing) 122

Deobald, see Dietbald

Depenheuer (wooden tub maker) 96

Depfer, see Tepper

Deppendal, Dependahl (deep valley) 76

Deppisch, Deppish 159 (foolish, clumsy) 115

Derenberger (animal mountain) 68

Derenkamp (animal field) 84

Derflinger 159 (villager) 124

Derhammer (fr Derheim) 122, 124

Derheim (animal hamlet) 124

Derick 53, Derrick < Dietrich

Derling 159, see Deuerling

Dermeyer (occupant of the Derhoff, animal farm) 93

Derr (dry, dour, see Duerr) 115

Derrenbacher (animal brook) 77

Derrenberger, see Derenberger

Derrick < Friedrich

Derring, Derringer, see Thueringer

Dersch (foolish) 115

Derst 159, see Durst

Derstein, Derstine (dry stone, dry mountain) 73

Derwart (game warden) 96

Derwin (animal friend) 48

Desch, Descher, Deschner, see Tischler

Deschler, Deschner, see Taescher

Desel 159, see Diesel

DeShong (French, Deschamps, fr the fields) 144

Dessau, Dessauer (German city) 122

Dester, Destler, see Textor, Dexter

Detenbach (swamp brook) 80, 77

Deter, Deters 59, Detert 74, Deterd, Dettermann 94, Detterer < Diethard

Dethloff, Dettlof < Dietloff (folk + wolf) 44 + 48

Detje 53, 55, Detjen, see Dietrich

Detmer, Detmar < Dietmar

Detmold (place name, "people's assembly" or else "swamp place") 46, 80, 122

Detner, Detters 59, see Dettner

Detrich, see Dietrich

Dettelbach (swamp brook) 80, 77, 122

Detter, Dettermann, see Dettner

Dettingen, Dettinger (fr Detting) 122

Dettmann (swamp dweller) 80, 94

Dettmar, Dettmer, see Dietmar

Dettmeyer (swamp farmer) 80, 93

Dettner, Dettler (swamp dweller) 80

Dettweiler, Dettwiler, Detwiler, Dettwyler (swamp village) 80, 127

Detzel 53, 55 < Dietrich

Detzner (manurer) 95

Deubel (devil) 135

Deuber, Deubler, Deubert 74, Deuberts 59, see Tauber, Taubert

Deubner, see Taubner

Deuchler (maker of wooden water pipes) 96

Deuerling (darling) 115

Deufel, see Deubel

Deumlich, see Daeumling

Deurer, see Duerer

Deuss < Matthaeus

Deutch, Deutcher 159, see Deutsch

Deutelmoser (reed bog) 81, 80

Deutermann (expounder) 94

Deutsch, Deutscher, Deutschman 94, Deutschmann (German) 121

Deutschendorf (German village) 121, 124

Devil 159, see Teufel

Devilbiss 159, De Villbiss, see Teufelbiss

Devriend (the friend) 7

Devries (the Frisian) 7, 121

Dewalt, Dewald < Dietwald (people + rule) 46, 46

Deward < Dietward (folk + guardian) 44, 47

Dewes, see Matthaeus

Dewitz (Slavic place name) 146, 122

Dexter (Latin, right hand), see also Textor

Deyck, see Deich

Deys, see Theiss

Diamant (diamond)

Dibel, see Teufel

Dibelius (Latin for Diebold) 141

Dibert < Dietbrecht

Dice 159 < Theiss

Dichmann, see Dickman

Dichter (poet, fr Latin *dictare*) 96

Dichter (grandchild)

Dick 122, Dicke 122, Dicks 59, Dix, Dicker, Dickert 74, Dueck (dweller near a thicket) 142

Dick, Dicker, Dickert 74 (fat, thick) 114, 143

Dickenberger (thicket mountain) 72, 68

Dickerhoof, see Dickhoff

Dickhans (fat Johnny) 114

Dickhaus, Dickhouse (dike house) 82, 65, 151

Dickhaut, Dickhout (thick skin) 114, 115

Dickhoff, Diekhof, Dieckhof, Dyckhoff (dike farm) 81, 92

Dickhut, Dickhout (tanner, hide dealer) 105

Dickman, Dickmann, Dickermann, see Teichmann

Dickmer, see Dickmeyer

Dickmeyer (dike warden) 81, 93

Dickopf (thick head, obstinate) 114

Dicks 53 < Benedictus 135

Didrichs, see Dietrich

Diebald, see Dietbald

Diebel, see Teufel

Diebelius (Latin for Dietbald) 141

Diebendoeffer, Dieberdoeffer (thieves' village) 124, see Dubendorffer

Diebert, see Dietbrecht

Diebold, Dietbolt, see Dietbald

Diechmann, see Teichmann

Dieck, Diecks 59 (dweller on or near the dike) 81

Dieckgreber, see Teichgraeber

Dieckhaus (dike house) 81, 65, 122

Dieckhof (farm by the dike) 81, 84

Dieckkrueger (tavern on the dike) 81, 96

Dieckmann, Diekmann, Dieks 59, see Teichmann

Diederich, Diedrich, Diedrichs 59, see Dietrich

Diefenbach, Dieffenbach, Dieffenbacher, see Tiefenbach

Diefenbacher (deep brook) 78

Diefendoerfer (deep village) 124

Dieffenthal (deep valley) 76

Diegel, Diegler, Diegelman 94 (potter) 96

Diegmann, see Teichmann

Diehard 159, see Diethard

Diehl, Diehle, Diehlmann 94, Diel (wall or floor of planks)

Diehl 53 < Dietrich

Diehlbeck, see Dillenbeck

Diehm, Diehmer 53, see Dietmar

Diek, Dickhart, see Teichmann

Diek, Diekmann, see Teichmann

Diekkrueger (tavern on the dike) 96

Diel (swamp brook) 80, 77

Diel, see Diehl

Diele, Dielen, Dieler (board, board sawyer) 96

Dielius (Latin for Diehle) 141

Dielschneider (board cutter) 96

Diener (servant) 119

Dienhart < Degenhard

Dienst (service, servant) 109, 139

Dienstag (Tuesday) 143

Dienstknecht (servant) 109

Dienstmann (vassal, ministerial) 109

Diepolt, see Dietbald

Dier, see Tier

Dierauer (animal meadow) 84

Dierbaum (animal tree) 89

Dierdorf 122, Dierdorff, Dierdorp (swamp village) 80, 43, 124, see Tierdorf

Dierenberger, see Duerrenberger

Dierhoff (animal farm) 92, 43

Diering (Thuringian) 121

Dierk, Dierks 59, Dierkes, Dierksen 59, Dierchs 59 < Dietrich

Dierkoff (Dierk's farm) 92

Diermann (animal man) 94

Dierstein (deer mountain, animal mountain) 73

Diesbach (swamp stream) 80, 77

Diesch < Dietrich

Diesel 53, 55 < Matthias

Diesing < Matthias

Diess < Theiss

Diestelhorst (thistle brake) 80

Dietbald, Dietbold (folk + bold) 46, 46

Dietbald, Dietbold < Dietwald (folk + rule) 46, 46

Dietbrecht (folk + illustrious) 46, 47

Dietel 53, 55, Dietler, Dieteler, Dietle 159 < Dietrich

Dieter, Dieder, Diether, Dieterle 55, Dietermann 94 < Dietrich or Diethard

Dietgen 53, 55 (little Dietrich)

Dietgenrode (Dietgen's clearing) 125

Diethard, Diethart (folk + strong) 46, 46

Diethelm (folk + helmet) 46, 46

Diethof (swamp farm) 80, 92

Diethold (people + rule) 46, 48

Dietmann (folk + man) 46, 94

Dietmar (folk + famous) 46, 47, 49

Dietram (people + raven) 46, 48

Dietrich, Dieterich, Diederich, Dietrichs 59, Diettrich, Dietrick (folk + rule) 44, 46, 47

Dietsch 53 < Dietrich

Dietter 53 < Dietrich

Dietwald (folk + rule) 46, 47

Dietwein (folk + friend) 46, 47

Dietz 53, Dietze, Diez, Dietzel 55, Dietzer < Dietrich

Dietz (swamp) 80

Dietzius (latinized form of Dietze) 141

Diewald, Dietwald (folk + rule) 46, 47

Diffenbaugh 159, Diffenbach, see Tiefenbach

Diffendal, Diffendall (deep valley) 76, 151

Diffenderfer 159, see Tiefendorf

Diffrient, see Devrient

Digler, Digelmann 159, see Degeler

Dihm, see Thiem

Dikhoff, Dikoff (fr the Dickhoff, dike farm) 81, 92, 94

Diktes < St. Benedictus 135

Dilger (son of Ottilie) 60

Dill, Diller (board, board sawyer) 96

Dill, Diller (fr Dill) 122

Dillenbeck (board creek) 77

Dillenberger (board mountain) 68

Dillenseger, Dillenschneider (board sawyer)

Diller (plank sawyer) 96

Dillfelder (board field) 84

Dillinger (fr Dilling) 122

Dillmann 53, 94, Dillman < Dietrich

Dimeler 159, see Daimler

Dimler, Dimling (acrobat) 96

Dimling, Dimmerling, see Daeummling

Dimot 159, see Demuth

Dinckelacker (spelt field) 84

Dinehart, see Degenhardt

Diner 159, see Diener

Dingbaum (council tree) 89

Dingedal (council valley) 76

Dingell, Dingelmann, see Dengler

Dinger (judge, arbiter) 109

Dingfelder (parliament field) 84

Dingler, see Dengler

Dingwall < Dingwald (parliament forest) 72

Dinkel, Dinkle 159 (spelt, see also Duenkel)

Dinkelmann (spelt dealer) 105

Dinn, see Duenn

Dinnis (St. Dionysisus) 135

Dinsman, see Dienstmann

Dintenfass (inkwell, scribe) 96, 106

Dinter (ink maker) 96

Dippel, Dipple 159, Dipper, Dippmann 94, Dippold, see Dietbold

Diring 159, see Thuering

Dirk 53, Dirker, Dirks 59, Dirkes, Dirksen 59 < Dietrich

Dirr, see Duerr

Dirrwaechter (doorkeeper) 96

Dirschedl < Duerrschaedel (gaunt skull) 114

Dirstein, see Dierstein

Dirzuweit (too far from you) 116

Disch, see Tisch

Discher, Dischler, Dischel, Dischart 74, see Tischler

Dischman, Dischner, see Tischmann, Tischner

Dischner, see Tischler

Dischong, see DeShong

Dishman 159, see Tischmann

Dissler, see Tischler

Distel (thistle) 89

Ditericks 159, see Dietrich

Dithart, see Diethard

Ditmann, see Dietman

Ditmar, Dittmer, see Dietmar

Ditrich, see Dietrich

Dittenbrand (swamp clearing) 80, 126

Dittenhafer, Dittenhoefer, Dittenhoffer (swamp farm) 80, 92

Dittmann (swamp dweller) 80, 94

Dittmar, Dittmer, see Dietmar

Dittrich, see Dietrich

Dittweiler, see Dettweiler

Ditz, Ditzel, Ditzell, see Dietz, Dietzel

Divilbiss 159, Divilbess, see Teufelbiss

Diwall, see Dietbald

Dix 53 < Benedictus, also see
　　Dick
Doarnberger 159, see Dornberger
Doarnfeld 159, see Dornfeld
Dober, Doberer, Dobert 143
　　(pigeon raiser or seller) 96
Doberstein (dovecote mountain)
　　73
Dobert < Theodoberacht (folk +
　　bright) 46, 46
Dobler, Dobeler, Doebeler, see
　　Tobler
Dochman, see Tuchmann
Dochterman, see Tochtermann
Dock (kind of fish, fishmonger)
　　106, 115
Dock (dry dock) 118
Dockstade (fish landing) 71
Dockweiler (marsh village) 80,
　　127
Doctor (teacher, professor) 96
Dode (swamp, reeds) 81
Dodenhof (swamp farm) 81, 92
Doderer, Dodderer (stutterer) 114
Doebberstein, see Doberstein
Doebel, Doebler, Doebling, see
　　Tobler
Doecker, see Decker
Doefler, see Dorfmann
Doehl 53, Doehle, Doehlen,
　　Doehler < Adolf
Doehl, Doehle (place names) 122
Doehling (fr Dehling in
　　Wurttemberg) 122
Doehn < Anton 135
Doehrer, Doehrling, Doehring,
　　see Thueringer
Doelfel 53, 55 < Adolf
Doell, Doelle, Doeller (marsh
　　water, dweller in a marsh) 80
Doellfeld (marsh field) 80, 84
Doelling (kind of perch,
　　fishmonger) 106, 115
Doellinger (fr Doelling) 122, see
　　also Doehling

Doellinger, see Doehling
Doemling < Domarich (judgment
　　+ rule) 46
Doenges 53 (fr Anthonius) 135
Doeninger (dweller on damp
　　terrain) 80
Doepfer, Doepner (potter) 96
Doerer 53 < Theodor 135
Doerfer, Doerfler, Doerfling,
　　Doerflinger (villager) 124
Doerflein 55 (little village) 124,
　　122
Doering, Doeringer (Thuringian,
　　"hering-nose" attributed to
　　Thuringians) 121, 113
Doerle 55 (little door, dweller by
　　city gate) 71
Doermer (tower keeper, fr Latin
　　turris) 96
Doernberg (thicket mountain) 72,
　　89
Doerner (thicket dweller) 72
Doerr, Doerre (dry, withered) 114
Doerrbaum (dead tree) 118
Doerrer, Doerrmann 94 (dryer)
　　96
Doescher (thresher) 96
Doetsch, Doetscher, see Deutsch
Doggendorf (bulldog village) 124
Dohl, Dohle 122, Dohlen,
　　Dohling, Dohler, Dohlert 74
　　(daw) 115
Dohm 53, Dohme, Dohmke <
　　Thomas 135
Dohm (cathedral) 118
Dohn, Dohnke 53, 55 < Anton
　　135
Dohr, Dohrman, Dohrmann, see
　　Thor, Thormann
Dohrn, see Dorn
Dolch (dagger) 108
Dold 53, Dolde < Berthold
Doleman, see Dollmann
Doles 159, 59, see Dohl
Dolf 53, Dolfi, Dolfs 59 < Adolf

Doll, Dolle (mad) 115

Doll (valley) 76

Dollenberg (valley mountain) 76, 48, 122

Doller, Dollar 159 (valley dweller) 76

Doller, Dollar 159, see Thaler

Dollfuss (club foot) 114, or < Adolphus, Rudolfus

Dollkey 159, see Dahlke

Dollinger, Dolinger (fr Dolling) 122

Dollmann (madman) 115, see Tollmann

Dollmann (valley dweller) 76, 94

Dolmetsch (Slavic: interpreter) 146

Dolph 53, see Adolf

Dom, Dohm, Dohme, Dohmer (dweller near a cathedral) 71

Domaas, Domas, Domaschke 53 < Thomas 135

Dome, Domes, Dohm, Dohme < Thomas 135

Domhoff (cathedral court) 92, 122

Dommermut (simple minded) 114

Domnick < Dominicus

Donat, Donatt, Donath < St. Donatus (Latin grammarian) 135

Donawerth, fr Donauwerth (city on Danube island) 79

Dondorf, see Dandorf

Donecker, see Danecker

Donge 53, Donges, Dongis < St. Anthonius 135

Donhauser, see Tanhauser

Donicht (Do nothing!, lazy person)

Donies, see Anthon

Donnenberg, see Tannenberg

Donner, Donner, Donnerlein 55 (thunder, thunderer) 115

Donnerstag (Thursday, day of corvée duty)

Donnewitz, see Dannewitz

Doober, see Dober

Door 159, see Thor

Dopmann (potter) 96, 94

Doppler (gambler)

Dopsch (Tobias, OT name) 135

Doran 159, see Dorn

Doremus < Adoremus (Let us adore [Him]!) 117

Dorenfeld (thorn field) 72, 84

Dorf, Dorff, Dorfman 94, Dorffmann, Dorfler (villager) 124

Dorfzaun (village fence) 124

Dorman, Dormann, see Thormann

Dorn (thorn, thicket) 72, 122

Dornbach, Dornbeck (thorny brook) 72, 77, 122

Dornberger (thorn mountain) 72, 68

Dornburg (thorn castle) 72, 73, 122

Dornbusch, Dornbush 159 (thorn bush) 72, 72, 122

Dorneck (thornfield) 72, 84

Dornenburg (thorny castle) 72, 73

Dorner (dweller among the thorns) 72

Dornfeld (thorn field) 72, 84

Dornheim (thorn hamlet) 72, 124, 122

Dornkamp (field with thorn hedges) 72, 84

Dornseif (thorn bog) 72, 81

Dorp (village) 124, 122

Dorr, see Thor

Dorsch (codfish seller) 115, 106

Dorst 159, see Durst

Dorward, Dorwarth, see Thorwart

Dosch, Dosche, Dosh 159 (bush, tavern keeper) 96

Doster (thyme seller, spice seller) 106

Dotter, Dotterweich (yolk soft) 115

Dottweiler, see Dettweiler

Doub 159, see Taub 113

Dove (deaf)

Dower 159, see Dauer

Dowhauer 159, see Tauhauer

Downer 159, see Dauner

Drach, Drache, Dracke (dragon, house name) 62, 149

Drachenbert (Bert of the Dragon House) 62, 149

Drachman (occupant of the Dragon House) 62, 149, 94

Drachsel, Drachsler, see Drechsler

Drake, see Drach

Drakenfeld (dragon field) 84

Drath (wire, wire drawer) 96

Dratz, see Trotz

Draut, Drautmann 159, see Traut, Trautmann

Drayer 159, see Dreher

Dreber 53, Drebert < Andreas 135

Drechsel, Drechsler, Drexler (turner) 98

Dreck (filth) 118

Dreer, see Dreher

Drees 54 < Andreas 135

Dreher, Drehmann (potter) 96

Dreher, see Drechsler

Dreier (thrupence) 117

Dreier (potter) 96

Dreifus, Dreifuss, Dreyfuss (tripod) 8

Dreifus, Dreyfuss (fr Trier) 122

Dreis, see Andreas

Dreisbach, Dresbach, see Troestbach

Dreiser, Dreist (audacious) 115

Dreiss (swamp water) 80

Dreissigacker (thirty acres) 84

Dresch, Dresh 159, Drescher, Dreschler (thresher) 95

Dresden, Dresner (fr Dresden) 122

Dressel, Dressler, Dresler, see Drechsel

Dresselhaus (fr Dresselhausen 122, turner's house) 96, 65

Dreus 53, Drewes, Drewing < Andreas 135

Drexel, Drexler, see Drechsel

Dreyer, Dryer 159 (potter, see Dreier) 96

Dreyfus, Dreyfuss (tripod)

Dreyfuss (inhabitant of Trier) 122

Driebenbach (murky brook) 77

Driehaus (fr Driehausen) 122

Dries 53, Driesslein 55 < Andreas 135

Driesch (uncultivated field) 84, 122

Drieschbach (pasture brook) 84, 77

Driessen (son of Andreas) 59, 135

Driessheim (pasture hamlet) 84, 124

Driessler, see Drechsel

Drinkhouse, see Drinkhaus 151

Drisch (Thrash!) 116

Droege (dry)

Droegmyr 159, Droegemeyer (dry farmer) 93

Droesch, Droescher, see Dresch

Drommelhausen, Drommelhauser (drummer houses) 65

Drommeter (trumpeter)

Drossel (thrush) 115

Drost, Droste (steward) 109

Droy 159, see Treu

Druckenbrod, see Trockenbrod

Drucker, Druecker, Druker 159 (cloth presser) 96

Drucker (printer) 96

Drueckhammer (hammer maker) 96, 106

Drueckscherf (penny pincher) 115

Druessel (throat, gullet) 114

Drummer (drummer) 96

Drusch (uncultivated, as of land) 72

Drussel (trunk, snout) 114

Drutz (defiance) 115

Dryer 159, see Dreier, Dreyer

Dubendorffer, Diebendoerfer (swamp village, thieves' village) 80, 124

Dubenhorst (swamphurst) 80, 72

Duchmann, see Tuchmann

Ducker (diving duck, devil) 115

Dude (bagpiper) 96

Duden (blockhead) 115

Duden 53 < Ludolf

Dudenhoffer, Dudenhoefer (fr the Dudenhoff, Ludolf's farm) 92

Duebel, Duefel (devil) 135

Dueffenbach, see Tiefenbach

Duehr, see Teuer

Duehring, see Duering

Duell (stubborn) 115

Duemmling (mute, fool) 115

Duenn (thin) 115

Duensing (Duden's swamp) 80

Duerbeck (dry brook) 77

Duerenberger, Duerrenberger (region in Austria, dry mountain) 121

Duerer (door keeper) 96

Duering, Dueringer (Thuringian) 121

Duerkop (expensive purchase) 118

Duermueller (water miller) 103

Duerr (dry, skinny) 114

Duerrbaum (dry tree) 89

Duerrenmatt (dry meadow) 84

Duerrfuss (dry foot) 114

Duesenberg (silent mountain) 68

Duester (gloomy) 115

Duesterdiek (gloomy dike) 82

Duetsch, Duitscher, see Deutsch

Duffner (fr Teufen in Wurttemberg) 122

Duhm, see Daum

Duhrmann, see Thormann

Dulde 53 < Berthold

Dulheuer (knife maker) 106

Dumbaugh 159 (fr Dumbach 122) 77

Dumernick < St. Dominick 135

Dumler (inexperienced, noisy) 114

Dummann (stupid person)

Dunbaugh 159, see Danbach

Dunckel, see Dunkel

Dundorf, see Dandorf

Dunge 53 < St. Anthonius 135

Dunger (manure) 118

Dunger (dweller on a hummock) 68

Dunhouer, see Danenhauer 151

Dunkel, Dunkle 159 (dark) 113

Dunkel, see Dinkel

Dunkelberg (dark mountain) 68

Dunker, see Dunkel

Dunkhorst (low-hill hurst) 68, 72

Dunmire 159, Dunmyer, see Danmeyer

Dunst (vapor, steam, bather) 118

Dunstmann (bath attendant) 96

Duppe (pot, potter) 96

Duppengiesser (pot maker) 96

Durban (St. Urbanus) 135

Durbaum (dead tree) 89

Durcholtz (through the forest) 69, 72

Durenberger, see Durrenberger

Durer, see Duerer

Durfeld (dry field) 84

Durholtz (dry wood) 98

During, Duringer (Thuringian) 121

Durlach (dry pond) 80

Durlach (principality on Rhein) 121, 122

Durman, see Thurmann

Durnbaugh 159 (dry creek) 77

Durner, see Turner

Durr, see Duerr

Durrenberger, see Duerenberger

Durschlag (colander, sieve) 106

Durst (thirst) 115

Durst (daredevil) 115

Dusel (silly, cf. English "dizzy") 115, 158

Dusenberry 159, see Duesenberg

Dussel, Dussler (stream near Dusseldorf) 83

Dusseldorf (German city) 122, 124

Dussing (ornamental belt 106), see also Tussing

Dusterhoff (dreary farm) 92

Dutsch, Dutscher, Dutschler, see Deutsch

Dutweiler 122, see Dettweiler

Duve (dove, dove raiser) 96

Dwerg (dwarf) 113

Dyce 159, see Theiss

Dycker, Dyckmann, see Teichmann

Dynhart, see Deinhard

Dyson 159, see Theissen

Dyssgen 53, 55, Dyssli < Dietrich

E

Eagel 159, Eagle, Eagler < *Igel* (hedgehog) 48, 159

Eagleburg 159 (hedgehog castle) 48, 73, 159

Eaglehart 159, see Igelhart

Eakel 159, Eakle 159, see Eichel

Eaker 159, Eakers 59, see Eicher

Ealy 159 (Eli, OT name)

Earhart 159, Earhardt, Earehart, see Erhard

Earl 159, Earle, Earley, see Erle, Ehrlich

Earlbeck 159, see Erlenbach

Earlick 159, see Ehrlich

Earman 159, see Ehrmann

Earnest 159, see Ernst

Earnhard 159, Earnhardt, see Erhard

Earp 159, see Erb

East 152, see Ost

Eastberg 152, see Ostberg

Easter 152, see Oster

Easterday 152, see Ostertag

Eastwood 159, see Ostwald

Ebaugh, see Ibach

Ebbe, Ebbeke 53, 55, Ebbeling < Eggebrecht

Ebberle, see Eberl

Ebbert 53, Ebberts 59, Eggebrecht

Ebbinger, Eppnger (fr Ebbingen, plain), also see Eggebrecht

Ebbinghause, Ebbinghauser (house on the plain) 65

Ebe, see Eberhard

Ebel 53, Ebele, Ebell, Ebelein 55, Ebelt 74 < Albrecht

Ebelding (belonging to Ebel) 59

Ebeling 53, 55, Ebelke < Ebel 59

Eben, Ebener, Ebner (whiffletree, planer) 96

Eben, Ebener, Ebner (fr Eben 122, dweller on a plain) 68

Ebenhack (level enclosure) 124

Ebenreiter, Ebenreuther (flat clearing) 125

Ebensberger (mountain on a plain) 68

Ebentheuer (knight errant) 118

Eber, Ebers 59, Ebert 74, 143 (wild boar) 48, or < Eberhard

Eberbach, Ebersbacher, Eberbeck (reed brook) 81, 77

Eberding (fr Eberding 122, belonging to Ebert 59)

Eberfeld (boar field) 48, 84

Eberhagen (wild boar enclosure) 48, 124

Eberhard, Eberhardt, Eberharde, Eberhards 59, Eberhart (wild boar + strong) 48, 46

Eberl 55, Eberle, Eberlet, Eberli, Eberly 159, Eberlein, Eberlin, Eberling (little wild boar) 48, or < Eberhard

Eberman (wild boar hunter, Eber's vassal) 48, 94

Ebersbacher, Eberspacher (fr Ebersbach 122, boar brook) 48, 77

Ebersberg, Ebersberger (fr Ebersberg 122, boar mountain) 48, 68

Eberschwein (wild boar) 48

Eberschwyl, Ebertschwyl 74 (boar village) 48, 127

Ebersmann (Eber's vassal) 48, 94

Ebersol, Ebersolt (hog wallow) 48, 81

Eberstein (boar mountain) 48, 73, 122

Ebert 53, 74, Eberts 59, Eberth, Ebertz, see Eber, Eggebrecht

Ebertsbach (Ebert's brook) 48, 77

Eberwein, Eberwine 159 (boar + friend) 48, 48

Ebinger (fr Ebing) 122, see also Eppinger

Ebinghausen (place name) 65, 122

Ebler 53 < Albrecht

Ebner, see Eben, Ebener

Ebrecht (law + brilliant) 47, see also Eggebrecht

Ebright 159, see Ebrecht

Ebstein, see Epstein

Eccard 159, see Eckhard

Eccles 159, 59, see Eckel

Eche, Echeman, see Eiche, Eichmann

Echerd, Echard, see Eckhard

Echt (lawful, genuine) 115

Echtermann (man living behind the village) 70

Echternacht (name of Swiss town) 122

Eck, Ecken, Ecker (fr Ecke 122, corner, place) 86

Eckard, Eckhardt, Eckhart, Eckharte, see Eckhard

Eckbert (sword + bright) 46, 47

Ecke, see Eckehard

Ecke (peak) 68

Eckeberger (oak mountain) 89, 68

Eckeberger (sword + protection) 89, 68

Eckel, Eckell, Eckels 59, Eckelt 74, see Eickel

Eckel, see Ekel

Eckelhof (oak farm) 89, 92

Eckelmann (dweller among the oaks) 89, 94

Eckelmeyer (fr the Eckelhof, oak farm) 89, 93, 94

Eckenauer (oak meadow) 89, 84

Eckenfelder, see Eckfeld

Eckenrode, Eckeroth (oak clearing) 89, 125

Eckensberger, Eckensbarger, see Eckeberger

Ecker (river name) 83, see Acker

Eckerd, Eckert, Eckardt, see Eckhard

Eckerle 55 (little field) 84

Eckermann (dweller on the Ecker) 83, 94, see Ackermann

Eckert, see Eckhard

Eckes 59, see Eck

Eckfeld, Eckfield 153 (oak field) 89, 72, 122

Eckhard, Eckehard, Eckhardt, Eckert (sword + strong) 46, 46

Eckhaus (corner house) 85, 65, 122

Eckhoff (oak farm) 89, 92, 122

Eckholt, Eckholdt (oak forest) 89, 72, 122

Eckholt (sword + loyal) 46, 48

Eckinger, Eckler, Eckner, Eckmann 94 (dweller on the corner) 85

Eckmann, see Eckinger, Eichmann

Eckmeyer (fr the Eckhoff, oak farm) 89, 93, 94

Eckner, see Eckinger, Eichner

Eckof, see Eckhoff

Eckrich (sword + rule) 46, 47

Eckroad 159, Eckrodt, Eckrote, Eckroth (oak clearing) 89, 126

Eckstein, Eckstine 159 (corner stone) 89, 73

Eckstrut (oak swamp) 89, 80

Eckwart (sword + guard) 46, 47

Eddel, Eddleman 159, see Edel, Edelmann

Edel, Edell, Edele, Edeler, Edler, Edeling, Edling (noble) 47

Edelberg (noble mountain) 47, 68

Edelblute (noble blood) 47

Edelbrock, Edelbrook (noble brake) 47, 80

Edelen (noblemen) 47

Edelheiser (noble houses) 47, 65, 66

Edelman, Edelmann (nobleman) 47, 94

Edelmeyer (fr the Edelhof, noble farm) 4, 93, 94

Edelmut (noble disposition) 47, 115

Edelsberg (noble's mountain) 47, 68, 122

Edelstein (jewel) 38, 47, 74

Eden, Edens 59

Edenbaum (tree of Eden) 135, 89

Edenfeld, Edenfield 153 (Eden field) 84, 135

Eder, Ederle 55, Edert 74 (dweller on barren soil) 122

Eder (dweller near the Eder) 83

Edgar (treasure + spear) 47, 46

Eding, Edinger, see Ettinger

Edler, see Edel

Edmund, Edmunds 59 (treasure + guardian) 47, 47

Edsell, Edsall, see Etzell

Edward, Eduard, Edwards 59, (guardian) 47, 47

Efeldt (place name) 122, 84

Effert < Everhard

Effinger (fr Effingen) 122

Effler, Effner, Effland (dweller among the elms) 89

Effler (smith, tool repairer) 96

Effner, see Oefner

Efland, see Effler

Egbert, Egbertsen 59 (sword + brilliant) 46, 47

Ege, Egge (harrow) 106

Egeberg (harrow hill) 68

Egel (leech, bloodsucker) 115

Egelberg (swamp mountain) 68

Egenberger, see Eckenberger

Egenhoeffer (oak farm) 89, 92

Eger 122, Egert 74 (fr the Eger) 83

Egg, see Eck

Eggebrecht (sword + bright) 46, 47

Eggelmann 53, 94 < Eggebrecht

Eggemann 94, Eggermeyer 93 (harrower) 95, see also Eckmann

Eggenberger 122, see Eckeberger

Egger, Eggers 59, Eggert 74 (harrower) 95,

Egger < Agiheri (sword + army) 46, 46

Egger, Eggers 59 (dweller on the corner, shopkeeper) 96

Eggert, see Eckhard and Eggebrecht

Eggs 59, see Eck

Eghard, see Eckhard

Egidy, Egyde < St. Aegidius 135

Egiloff (sword + wolf) 46, 48

Eginhard (sword + strong) 46, 46

Egli, Eglin (kind of perch) 115

Egli (a place in Switzerland) 122, see Egloff

Eglisau (perch meadow, place in Switzerland) 84, 122

Egloff, see Egiloff

Egloffstein (Egloff's mountain) 68, 73

Egmont, Egmund (sword + protection) 46, 47

Egner, Egnert 74, see Eigen, Eigner

Egolf, see Egloff

Ehard, see Ehart

Ehardi (son of Ehard) 142

Ehart (law + strong 47, 46), see also Erhard

Ehbauer (peasant under contract)

Ehebrecht (law + bright 47, 46), see also Eggebrecht

Eheman, Ehemann (lawful husband) 47

Ehemann, see Ehbauer

Ehemann (contracted peasant) 93

Ehinger (fr Ehingen) 122

Ehle, Ehlen, Ehles 59 (alder) 89, see also Ehrler

Ehler, Ehlers 59, Ehlert 74, Ehrlermann 94 (sword + army) 46, 46

Ehling, Ehlinger (fr Ehlingen) 122

Ehly (Eli, OT name) 135

Ehman, Ehmann, see Ehemann

Ehmer, Ehmert < Agimar (sword + famous)

Ehnert < Eginhardt

Ehninger (fr Ehningen) 122

Ehr, Ehren (honor, honors) 47, 138

Ehregott (Glorify god!) 116, 140

Ehrenbeck (honor brook) 77, 138

Ehrenberg, Ehrenberger (honor mountain) 77, 138

Ehrenfeld (field of honor) 138, 84

Ehrenfried (honor + victory) 138, 46

Ehrengut (honor and good) 138, 47

Ehrenheim (honor's hamlet) 138, 123

Ehrenholt (herold) 109

Ehrenkranz (wreath of honor) 138

Ehrenmann (man of honor) 138, 94

Ehrenpforten (Gates of glory) 138

Ehrenpreis (prize of honor) 138

Ehrenreich (rich in honor) 138

Ehrensperger, see Ehrenberg

Ehresmann, Ehrismann (man of honor) 138

Ehrhard, Ehrhardt, see Erhard

Ehrich, Ehrichs 59, Erich, Ehrichs, see Ehrreich

Ehringer (fr Ehringen) 122

Ehrle, see Erl

Ehrlerding (belonging to Ehrler) 59

Ehrlich, Ehrlichs 59, Ehrlicher, Ehrlick 159 (honest) 138, 115

Ehrling, Ehrlinger (fr Ehrlingen) 122

Ehrman, Ehrmann, see Ehrenmann

Ehrmannstraut (honored man's beloved) 138

Ehrmannstraut (the beloved of Irmin, the chief god) 51

Ehrreich (rich in honors) 47, 46, 138

Ehrsam (respectable) 138

Ehrstein (honor stone) 47, 73, 138

Ei (egg, egg seller) 106

Eib (yew, crossbow) 89, 108

Eibach (fr *ib*, pre-Germanic word for brook) 77, 122

Eibel 53, 55, Eibl, Eibner, Eibling < Albrecht

Eiben, Eibner (yew tree) 89, 122
Eiberger (yew mountain) 89, 68
Eibler (dweller near the yews) 89
Eich, Eiche, Eicher (oak) 89
Eichach, Eichacher (fr Eichach
   122, oak river, oak forest) 89,
   79
Eichacker (oak chopper) 95, 96
Eichbach (oak brook) 89, 77, 122
Eichbauer (oak farmer, occupant
   of the Eichhoff, oak farm) 89,
   91
Eichbaum, Eichelbaum (oak tree)
   89
Eichberg 122, Eichenberg,
   Eichberger (oak mountain) 89,
   68
Eichborn (oak spring) 89, 79
Eichbuechler (dweller on an oak
   hill)
Eichel (acorn, acorn gatherer) 96
Eichel (pre-Germanic river name)
   83
Eichelberg, Eichelberger (fr
   Eichelberg 122, acorn
   mountain) 68
Eichelhart (acorn forest) 89, 72
Eichelkraut (acorn herbs) 89
Eichelmann 94 (acorn gatherer)
   89, 91
Eichelsbeck (acorn brook) 89, 77
Eichelstein (acorn mountain) 89,
   73
Eichen (oaks) 89, 122
Eichenauer (oak meadow) 89, 84,
   122
Eichenberg 122, Eichenberger,
   see Eichberg
Eichenbrunn 122, Eichenbrunner
   (oak well) 89, 79
Eichenfeld (oak field) 89, 84, 122
Eichenfels (oak cliffs) 89
Eichengruen, Eichengrien 159
   (oak green) 89
Eichenherr, see Eigenherr

Eichenhoffer (oak farm) 89, 84
Eichenlaub (oak foliage) 89
Eichenmeyer, Eichenmoyer (fr
   the Eichhoff, oak farm) 89, 93,
   94
Eichenmueller (miller at the
   oaks) 89, 103
Eicher, Eichert 74, Eichler
   (dweller near the oaks) 89
Eichermann, see Eicher
Eichfelder (oak fields) 89, 84, 122
Eichhacker (oak chopper) 95
Eichhammer (oak village 89, fr
   Eichheim oak hamlet) 89, 122
Eichhauer (oak chopper) 95, 100
Eichhoff (farm surrounded by
   oaks) 89, 92, 122
Eichholm (oak island) 89
Eichholtz, Eichholz (oak wood)
   89, 72, 122
Eichhorn (squirrel) 115
Eichhorst (oak hurst) 89, 72, 122
Eichinger (fr Eichingen) 122
Eichler, Eichinger, Eichlinger, see
   Eicher
Eichmann (dweller among the
   oaks) 89
Eichmeyer (fr the Eichhoff, oak
   farm) 89, 93, 94
Eichmueller, Eichmiller (miller
   in the oaks) 89, 103
Eichner, see Eicher
Eicholz, see Eichholtz
Eichorn, see Eichhorn
Eichrodt (oak clearing)
Eichstadt, Eichstaedt, Eichstedt
   (oak city, oak place) 89, 122
Eichstein (oak mountain) 89, 73
Eichwald (oak forest) 89, 72
Eick ..., see Eich
Eick, Eicke, see Eich, Eiche
Eickel, see Eichel
Eickelberg, Eichelberger (acorn
   mountain) 89, 68
Eickemeyer, see Eichmeyer

Eickenberg (oak mountain) 89, 68

Eickhammer, see Eichhammer

Eickhoff 122, see Eichhoff

Eickholt 122, see Eichholtz

Eickmann, see Eichmann

Eickmeier, see Eichmeyer

Eickrot (oak clearing) 89, 126

Eid, Eide (oath)

Eidam, Eydam (son-in-law) 119

Eidel, see Eitel

Eidelberg 122, see Heidelberg

Eidelmann, see Edelmann

Eidemiller (miller on the Eide) 83, 103

Eidenberg (mountain on the Eide) 83, 68

Eidenwald (forest on the Eide) 83, 72

Eidenweil (village on the Eide) 83, 127

Eidinger (fr Eidingen) 122

Eidler, see Edler

Eidman, Eidner (oath taker) 94

Eier, Eiers 59, Eyers, Eirler, Eierman 94, Eiermann (egg seller) 105

Eif, Eife (fr Eife) 122

Eifel, Eifler (fr the Eifel region) 121

Eifert 74, Eiffert, Eifner (zeal) 115

Eifrig (zealous) 115

Eigel, see Egel

Eigelbach (leech brook) 77, 122

Eigelberger, see Eichelberger

Eigen, Eigner (fr Eigen 122), see Eigenmann

Eigenberg (private mountain) 68

Eigenbrod, Eigenbrode, Eigenbrodt (one's own bread, an independent man) 92

Eigenbrun (private well) 79

Eigenherr, Eigenheer (independent landowner, freeholder) 92

Eigenholt (vassal + loyal) 48

Eigenholt (private forest) 72

Eigenmann 94 (serf, vassal) 119

Eigensatz (dwelling on his own land)) 92

Eigner, Eigert 74 (smallholder) 92

Eik ..., see Eich ...

Eike (oak) 89

Eikenberg, see Eichenberg

Eikenberry 159, see Eickenberg

Eiker, see Eicher

Eikhoff, Eikof, Eickhoffe, see Eichhoff

Eikmann, see Eichmann

Eikmeyer (fr the Eikhoff, oak farm) 89, 93, 94

Eikner, see Eichner

Eikstein (oak mountain) 89, 68

Eiland, Eilander (island)

Eilbach, Eilbacher (rapid stream) 77

Eilbach (swamp brook) 80, 77

Eilberg (place name, swamp mountain) 80, 68, 122

Eildeberger, see Eidelberger

Eiler, Eilers 59, Eilert 74, Eilermann 94 (hurrier), see also Euler, Eilhart

Eilertsen (son of Eilert) 59

Eilhart (sword + strong) 46, 46

Eilhauer (potter) 96

Eilrich < Agilrich (sword point + powerful) 46, 47

Eimer (bucket, fr Latin *amphora*) 106

Eimer < Agilmar (sword + famous) 46, 47

Eimke (little bucket) 55, 96

Einaugler, Eineigel (one-eyed) 114

Einberg (place name 122, swamp mountain) 80, 68

Einbinder (book binder) 96

Einbrod, see Eigenbrod

Einegger 122, Einecker (owner of private field) 92, 84

Einenkel (grandchild) 119

Einerhand (one-handed) 114

Einert, see Einhardt

Einfalt (simplicty) 115, 139

Einfeldt, Eigenfeld 122 (private field) 92, 84

Einhardt, see Eginhard

Einhaus (private house) 65, 92, 122

Einholt, see Eigenholt

Einhorn (unicorn, a house name) 62

Einig (united) 118

Einiger (single, solitary) 115

Einmueller (independent miller) 92, 103

Einoeder (fr the waste land) 72

Einolf (sword + wolf) 46, 48

Einsiedler (hermit 110, fr Einsiedeln, hermitage 122)

Einsporn (one spur, spur maker) 96

Einspruch (objection, protest)

Einstein (place encompassed by a stone wall) 73

Einwaechter (single guard) 96

Einzig (alone) 115

Eirich, see Eurich

Eis (ice) 118

Eis (iron, ironmonger) 96

Eischberger (ice mountain) 68

Eischberger (iron mountain) 68

Eisdorfer (ice village) 124, 122

Eise, Eisele, Eiseley 159, Eiseler, Eiselen, Eiselt 74, Eiseman 94 (iron monger) 96

Eiseman, Eisenmann, see Eise

Eisen (iron, ironmonger) 96

Eisenach 122, Eisenacher (German city, iron springs) 79, 122

Eisenauer (fr Eisenau 122), see Eisenhauer

Eisenbach (iron brook) 96, 77, 122

Eisenband (iron band) 106

Eisenbart < Eisenberacht (iron + bright) 96, 46

Eisenbeil (iron axe) 96, 106

Eisenbein (piece of armor over shin, armorer) 108

Eisenbeis, Eisenbeiss (iron bite, bully) 115

Eisenberg, Eisinberg 159, Eisenberger (fr Eisenberg 122, iron mountain) 96, 68

Eisenbiss, Eisenbiess, see Eisenbeis

Eisenblaetter (armorer) 108

Eisenbrand (iron fire, smith) 96

Eisendraht (iron wire) 96, 106

Eisenfeld (iron field) 96, 84, 122

Eisenfels (iron cliff) 68

Eisenfress (iron eater, turbulent person) 115

Eisenfuehrer (metal dealer) 105

Eisengrein (iron + mask, helmet) 46

Eisenhand (iron hand) 114, 115

Eisenhard, Eisenhardt, Eisenhart (iron + strong) 96, 46

Eisenhaub (helmet) 108

Eisenhauer, Eisenhower 159 (iron hacker, perhaps based on Fr. Taillefer) 100

Eisenhaupt (iron head, house name) 114

Eisenhauser (iron house) 65

Eisenhaut, see Eisenhut

Eisenhoefer (iron yard) 96, 92

Eisenhour 159, Eisenhower, see Eisenhauer

Eisenhut, Eisenhuth, Eisenhueter (fr Eisenhut 122, iron hat, helmet, helmet maker) 96, 108

Eisenhut (monk's hood, a flower) 89

Eisenklam (iron clamp) 106

Eisenkolb (iron club) 106

Eisenkraemer (iron monger) 96, 94

Eisenloeffel (iron spoon) 106

Eisenlohe, Eisenlohr (iron flame, smith) 96

Eisenman, Eisenmann (ironmonger) 96, 94

Eisenmann (jailer) 109, 94

Eisenmenger, Eisenmenger (iron monger, fr Latin *mango*) 96, 105

Eisenmeyer (fr the Eisenhof, iron farm, ice farm) 93, 94

Eisenrauch (iron smoke, smith) 96

Eisenreich (rich in iron) 118

Eisenring (iron ring) 106

Eisenschmid, Eisenschmidt (iron smith) 96

Eisenstadt (iron city, iron place) 122

Eisenstein (iron stone, iron mountain) 73

Eisentraut, Eisentrout 159 < Isandrut (iron + beloved) 60

Eisenzieher (wire drawer) 96

Eisenzoph (iron top) 106

Eiser, Eisert 74 (iron worker, metal dealer) 105

Eisermann, see Eisenmann

Eisfeld, Eisfelder, Eisfeldt (ice field) 84, 122

Eisgrau (iron grey) 112

Eisgruber (iron miner) 96

Eisinger (fr Eising) 122

Eisler, see Eiser

Eisloeffel, see Eisenloeffel

Eisman, Eismann (ironmonger) 96, 94

Eisner (ironmonger) 96

Eiss, see Eis

Eisvogel (ice bird, tricky person) 115

Eiswald (iron forest) 72

Eiswald (ice forest) 72

Eit, Eith (oath) 118

Eitel, Eitler (empty, having no first name) 114

Eitemiller (miller on the Eite) 83, 103

Eitermann (dweller among the nettles) 89, 94

Eiting, Eitner (fr Eiting) 122

Eitner (burner, stoker, smelter) 96

Ekard, Ekhard, Ekhardt, Ekert, see Eckhard

Ekel 112, Ekels 59 (disgust) 115

Ekelberry 159, see Eichelberg

Eken (oaks) 89

Ekenhoffer (oak farm) 89, 92

Ekenroth, Ekerroth (oak clearing) 89, 126

Ekert, Ekhard, see Eckhard

Ekestein, see Eckstein

Ekhard, see Echkhard

Ekhoff, see Eickhoff

Ekman, see Eckmann

Elbaum (alder tree) 89

Elbe, Elbthal (German river, Elbe valley) 83

Elbeck, Elbek (alder brook) 89, 77

Elberg (alder mountain) 89, 68

Elbers 59, Elberth, Elbrecht, Elbright 159 (sword + bright) 46, 47

Elbert < Agilbrecht (sword + illustrious) 46, 47

Elbing (fr Elbingen) 122

Elbrecht, Elbright 159, see Elbers

Eldemann, see Eltermann

Elend (exiled, miserable, wretch) 114

Elenzweig (alder branch) 89

Elermann, see Ellermann

Elers, see Ehlers

Elert 74, see Eller

Elfenbein (ivory) 106

Elfers 59, Elfert 74 < Alfheri (elf + army) 48, 46

Elflein 55 (little elf) 48

Elfring 53, Elfringer (son of Elvert)

Elg, Elgg, Elger, Elgert 74, Elgart (foot path) 65

Elgast <Agilgast (sword + guest) 46, 47

Elger < Agilger (sword + spear) 46, 46

Elhardt, see Eilhart

Eli (OT name) 135

Elias (OT name) 135

Eliasberg (Eli's mountain) 135, 68

Elich, Elik, Eliker (lawful) 115

Eliel (OT name) 135

Eling, Elinger, see Elling

Elkmann (elk + man) 94

Elkmann (swamp man) 80, 94

Ell, Ells 59 (yard, measure, tailor) 96

Ellbrecht, see Elbrecht

Elldorfer (alder village) 89, 124

Elle (ell, tailor, mercer) 96

Ellekamp, see Ellenkamp

Ellemann, see Ellermann

Ellen (prowess) 115

Ellen (alders) 89, 122

Ellenbach, Ellenbeck (alder brook) 89, 77

Ellenberg, Ellenberger (fr Ellenberg 122, alder mountain) 89, 68

Ellenbogen (elbow) 114, 122

Ellenburg (alder castle) 89, 73

Ellenhardt, Aljanhard (prowess + strong) 46, 48

Ellenkamp (alder field) 89, 84

Eller, Ellers 59 (dweller by the alder trees) 89, 122

Ellerbach (alder brook) 89, 77

Ellerbrock, Ellerbrook 159, Ellerbruch (alder brake) 89, 80, 122

Ellerhorst (alder grove) 89, 72

Ellerkamp, see Ellenkamp

Ellermann (grandfather) 119, 94

Ellerrot (alder clearing) 89, 126

Ellestad (elder place, alder shore) 89

Ellewin, see Alwin

Ellg, see Elg

Ellgass (alder street) 89, 65, 122

Elling, Ellinger (foot path) 122

Ellinghaus, Ellinghausen, Ellinhuyzen (fr Ellinghausen 122, house on foot path) 65

Ellingrod, see Ellroth

Ellmer, see Elmer

Ellner (dweller among the alders) 89

Ellrich (prowess + strong) 46

Ellroth (alder clearing) 89, 126

Ellsaeser, see Elsass

Ellwanger (alder field) 89, 84

Ellwanger (fr Ellwangen, elk trap) 122

Ellward < Agilward (sword + guardian) 46 + 47

Elm, Elms 59, Elman 94 (dweller among the elms) 89

Elm, Elms 59 (swamp) 80

Elmendorf (elm village) 89, 124, 122

Elmenhorst (elm grove) 89, 72

Elmer, Elmar (noble + famous) 46, 47

Elmhorst (elm grove) 89

Elmshaeuser (swamp houses) 89, 65

Elpert, see Albrecht

Elrich, Elrick (noble + rule) 46, 46

Elrod, see Ellroth

Elsass, Elsasser, Elsaesser, Elsassor 159 (Alsatian) 121

Elsbach, Elsbacher (shad brook, swamp brook) 80, 77, 122

Else, Elsen, Elser, Elsner (dweller on the Els) 83

Elsenbach (alder brook) 89, 77

Elsenhans (Hans, son of Else) 60

Elsenheimer (alder hamlet) 89, 124

Elsensohn (Else's son) 60

Elserode, Elseroad 159 (clearing on the Els) 83, 126

Elserode (clearing in the alders) 89, 126

Elsfeldt (alder field) 89, 84

Elshof, Elshoffer (alder farm) 89, 92

Elshorst, Elsinghorst (swamp hurst) 80, 72

Elshorst (alder hurst) 89, 72

Elsing, Elsinger (fr Elsing 122, alder place) 89

Elsner, see Else

Elsohn, see Elsensohn

Elsroad 159, see Elserode

Elstein (alder mountain) 89, 73

Elster (magpie, talkative person) 115

Elster (village senior) 113

Elterman, Eltermann (senior) 113, 94

Eltermann (dweller on the Elter) 83

Elteste (village senior) 113

Eltzroth, see Elserode

Elvers, see Elfers

Ely 159 (OT name) 135

Emanuel (OT name) 135

Embach (beyond the brook) 69, 77, 122

Emberger (beyond the mountain) 69, 68, 122

Embs (ant) 115

Emde, Emden 122, Emder (German city) 122

Emer 53, Emert 59, Emmer, Emmert, Emmart < Emerich

Emerich, Emerick, Emerik (fr Amelrich, ruler of the Amelungs, or fr Irmin, "world king") 46

Emery 159, see Emerich

Emmel 53, 55, Emmell, Emmelmann 94 < Emerich

Emmen (place name) 122

Emmendorf (place name) 124, 122

Emmerich, Emmrich, Emmerik, see Emerich

Emmermann (follower of Emerich) 94

Emmermann (bucket maker) 96

Emmheiser (ant house) 65

Emminger (fr Emmingen) 122

Emrhein, see Amrhein

Emrich, Emrick, Emmerich, see Emerich

Ems 122 (fr the Ems River) 83

Emshof, Emshof (farm on the Ems) 83, 92

Emsweiler, Emswhiler 159 (village on the Ems) 83, 127

Emund < Emunt (law + protection) 47

Enck, Encke (accurate, perspicacious) 115

Enck (hired hand) 95

Enckhause (hired hands' shelter) 65

End, Ende, Ender, Endter, Endemann, see Amend

Endelman 53, 55, 94, Endelmann < Andreas

Ender 53, Enders, Endres, Endress, Endris, Enderis, Endriss < Andreas

Enderich (drake) 115

Enderle 53, 55, Enderli, Enderly 159, Enderlin, Endler, Enderlein < Andreas

Endler, see Amend

Endlich (finally!) 117

Endres, see Andreas

Endrich, see Enderich
Enenkel (grandchild) 119
Eng, Enge, Enger, Engermann 94
(dweller in a narrow valley) 76
Engass (narrow street) 65
Engbart (narrow beard) 112, 122
Engbert, see Engelbert
Engeberg (swamp mountain) 80,
68, 122
Engebrecht, see Engelbrecht
Engel, Engle, Engeln, Engels 59,
Engeli 55, Engeler, Engler
(angel, probably house name)
62
Engeland (England) 121
Engelbach (angel brook) 77, 122
Engelberg (angel mountain) 68,
122
Engelbert, Engelberth,
Engelberts 59, Engelbrecht
(angel + bright) 49, 47
Engeler, see Engler
Engelfried (angel + peace) 138
Engelhard, Engelhart,
Engelhardt, Engelhart,
Engelharth, Engelhaart
(angel + strong, angle +
strong) 49, 46
Engelhaupt (angel head, house
name) 62, 149
Engelhaus, Engelhausen (angel
house, house name) 65, 149
Engelhoff (angel farm) 92, 122
Engelke 53, 55, Engelken,
Engelking, see Engelbert
Engelkraut (angel herb) 89
Engelman 94, Engelmann
(occupant of Engelhaus 65 or
Engelhoff 92)
Engelman 53, 94 < Engelbert
Engelmann (Englishman) 121, 94
Engelmeyer (fr the Engelhoff,
angel farm) 93, 92, 94
Engels, see Engel
Engelsberg, see Engelberg
Engelschalk (angel servant) 109

Engelskirche (angel church) 71,
122
Engemann (dweller in a narrow
valley) 76, 94
Engenhoefer (narrow farm,
swamp farm) 92, 76
Enger, Engers 59, Engert 74 (fr
Engen 122)
Engermann, see Engemann
Engesser, Engass (dweller on a
narrow street) 65
Enghaus (house on a swamp) 76,
65
Enghause, Enghausen,
Enghaussen, Enghauser
(narrow house) 65
England, Englander, Englaender
(Englishman) 121
Engle.... 159, see Engel...
Englebach 159, see Engelbach
Englebrecht 159, see Engelbert
Englehart 159, Englehardt, see
Engelhart
Englehaupt 159, see Engelhaupt
Engleman 159, see Engelman
Engler, Englert 74, Englerth
(angel + army) 46, 49
Engli 55 (little angel) 118
Englischer (Englishman) 121
Engman, Engmann, see
Engemann
Engmeyer (fr the Enghof, narrow
farm) 93, 92, 94
Engnoth (difficult straits) 118
Engstrand (narrow beach) 118
Engwall (narrow wall) 100
Enk, Enke, Enker (hired hand) 95
Enkel (grandchild) 119
Enker (anchor, house name) 62,
149
Enker (farm hand) 96
Ennesfeldt (Enno's field) 84
Enninger (fr Enning) 122
Enrick, see Heinrich
Ensel, Enslin 55, Ensslin,
Enslein < Anselm

Ensinger (fr Ensingen) 122

Ensminger 159, see Eisenmenger

Ent, Ente, Enten, Entemann, Entenmann, Entelmann 94 (duck raiser) 91

Ente (duck, poultry dealer) 105

Entermann (duck raiser) 91, 94

Entner, see Ent

Entres, see Andreas

Entstrasser (dweller across the road) 69, 65

Entz, Enz, Enzman (fr Enz or fr the Enz) 122, 83

Entzbacher, Entzenbache (fr Enzenbach) 77, 122

Enzinger (fr Enzingen) 122

Ep 53, Epp < Eberhard

Epelbaum, Epelboim, see Apfelbaum

Epenstein, Eppenstein, Epstein, Eppstein, see Epstein

Eple, Epple, Eppli (little apple) 53, 55, 89

Epp, see Eberhard

Eppel, Epple, Eppler, Epler, Eppelmann, see Appel, Apfel

Eppelsheim, Eppelsheimer (fr Eppelsheim 122, apple hamlet) 89, 124

Epperle 53, 55, Epperley 159 < Eberhard 53

Eppert 53 < Eggebrecht

Epping, Eppinger (fr Epping) 122

Eppley, see Eppel

Epps 53 < Eberhard

Eprecht, Epprecht (law + bright) 47, 47, see also Eggebrecht

Epstein, Epsteine, Epstien 159 (wild boar stone) 48, 73, 118

Erard, see Erhard

Erasmi (son of Erasmus) 142

Erasmus (saint) 135

Erb 122, Erbe, Erber, Erbin, Erben (heir, inheritance) 47

Erb 53 < Erwin

Erb, Erbe, Erbes 59, Erbsen (pea) 105

Erbach 122, Erbacher (swamp brook) 80, 77, see Erdbach

Erblich (inheritable) 118

Erbsland (inherited land) 47

Erbstoesser (pea dealer) 106

Erck, see Erk

Erd 53 < Erhard

Erd, Erde (earth, or fr *ard*, swamp) 80

Erdbach, Erdesbach (earth stream, swamp stream) 80, 77, 122

Erdbeer (strawberry)

Erdbrink (earth + grassy hill) 74

Erdel (arable land) 84

Erdenbrecht (earth + brilliant) 47

Erdheim (swamp hamlet) 80, 124

Erdman 94, Erdmann (earth man, modeled on Hebrew *Adam*) 135

Erdmeyer (swamp farmer) 93

Erdreich (kingdom of earth), see Erdmann

Erdroth (swamp clearing) 126

Erenheim (honor hamlet) 138, 47, 124

Erfmeyer, Erffmayer (farmer on the water) 80, 93

Erfurt 122, Erffurth, Erfuerth (German city) 122

Ergelet (grape bucket, fr Latin *arca*) 106

Ergenbright 159 < Erkanbrecht (genuine + bright) 46

Ergler (grape picker) 95

Ergott (Glorify God!) 117, 140

Erhard, Erhart, Erhardt (honor + strong) 47, 46

Erich, Erichs 59, Erig, Erick (law + rule) 47, 47

Eriksen (son of Erick) 59

Erischmann, see Ehresmann

Erismann, see Ehresmann

Erk 5 < Erkenbrecht (genuine + brilliant) 47

Erkmann 53, 94 < Erkenbrecht

Erl, Erle (alder) 89

Erlach (swamp pond) 89, 81, 122

Erlanger (fr Erlangen) 122

Erlebach, Erlbeck (alder brook) 89, 77, 122

Erlemann (dweller among the alders) 89, 94

Erlen, Erler (alder) 89, 122

Erlenbach 122, see Erlebach

Erlenheiser (inhabitant of house among the alders) 89, 65, 66

Erlenmeyer (occupant of the Erlenhoff, alder farm) 89, 92

Erler, see Erlen

Erlewyn, Erlwein (freeman + friend) 48

Erlich, Erlichman, see Ehrlich, Ehrlichmann

Ermann, see Ehrmann

Ermattinger (fr Ermattingen) 122

Ermbrecht < Irminbrecht (sky god + illustrious) 47

Ermel, Ermling, Ermeling (sleeve, tailor) 96, 106

Ermrich < Ermenrich (ruler + powerful) 47

Ermut (honor + disposition) 115

Erna 53, Erne, Erni, Ernel < Arnold

Ernest, see Ernst

Ernesti (son of Ernest) 142

Ernhut (guardian of honor) 138

Ernsperger, Ernsberger, see Arnsperger

Ernst, Ernest (vigor, earnestness) 115

Ernstein 122, see Arnstein

Ernsthausen (Ernst's houses) 65, 122

Ernte (harvest) 91

Erp, see Erb

Erpel (drake, duck raiser) 96

Erpenbach, Erpenbeck (heirs' brook) 47, 77

Erpenstein (heirs' mountain) 47, 68

Errmann 159, see Ehrmann

Ertel, Ertell, Ertle 159, Ertelt 74 < Ortlieb

Ertz, see Erz

Ertzberger (ore miner, man fr Erzberg) 96, 122

Ervin, see Erwein

Erwein, Erwin (honor + friend) 47, 48

Erz (ore, miner) 96, 106

Erzbischof (archbishop) 110

Erzgraeber (ore miner) 96

Esbach 122, see Eschbach

Esbaugh 159, see Eschbach

Esbenschade, see Espenscheid

Esberg (ash tree mountain) 89, 68

Esbrandt (clearing in the ash trees) 89, 126

Esch, Esche (ash tree) 89, 122

Eschauer (fr Eschau 122, ash meadow) 89, 84

Eschbach, Eschenbach, Eschbacher, Eschelbach, Eschbeck, Eschelbeck (fr Eschenbach 122, ash tree brook, or fr pre-Germanic river term) 83, 89, 77, see Aeschbach

Eschborn (ash tree spring, or see Eschbach) 89, 79, 122

Eschelmann, Eshelman, see Escher

Eschenbrenner, see Aschenbrenner

Eschenfelder (fr Eschenfelden 122, ash tree field) 89, 84

Eschenhagen (ash tree enclosure) 89, 4

Eschenmosen, Eschenmoser (ash bog) 89, 80

Escher, Eschler, Eschmann 94 (fr
  Escher 122, swamp) 80
Eschmeyer (farmer among the
  ash trees) 89, 93
Eschrich, Escherich (rich in ash
  trees) 89
Eschwege (path through the ash
  trees) 89, 122
Esel (ass, fool) 114
Eselkopf (donkey head, house
  name) 114, 62
Esenberg (ash mountain) 89, 68
Esendal (ash dale) 89, 76
Eser (back pack, also see Escher)
Eshbaugh, Eshbach 159, see
  Eschbach
Eshelmann 159, see Eschelmann
Esher 159, Eshler, see Escher
Eshman 159, see Escher
Esksteyn 159, see Eckstein
Esler, see Escher
Eslin, Esslin (jenny) 91
Eslinger (fr Eslingen) 122
Esner, see Eschner
Espe, Espen (aspen) 89, 122
Espenhain (aspen grove) 89, 72,
  122
Espenlaub (aspen leaves) 89
Espenschade (aspen shade) 89
Espenscheid, Espenschied (aspen
  log) 89
Espich (aspen bush) 89
Ess (forge, hearth, smith) 96
Essegern (I like to eat, glutton)
  115
Essel, Esselmann 94 (fr Essel)
  122
Essendorf (forge village, chimney
  village, swamp village) 80, 122
Essenfeld (forge field, swamp
  field) 80, 84
Essenhaven (forge farm, swamp
  farm) 80, 124
Esser, Essers 59 (axel maker,
  wainright) 96, 106

Esser (glutton) 115
Esserwein (wine drinker) 115
Essig, Essich (vinegar, fr Latin
  acetum) 105
Essig (pre-Germanic word for
  swamp) 80
Esskuchen (Eat the cookie!,
  pastry baker) 117
Esslin, see Eslin
Essling, Esslinger (fr Esslingen)
  122
Essner, Essner (forge worker,
  hearth worker) 96
Ester, Esters 59 (OT name) 135,
  122
Esterly, Esterling (easterner) 85,
  151
Estermann (field man) 96, 94
Estermann (Ashkenazic
  metronym for Esther's
  husband) 60, 94
Estermyer 159 (fr the Esterhof,
  eastern farm) 85, 93
Estinghausen (eastern houses)
  85, 65, 122
Estreicher, see Oestreich
Estrich (flooring, parquet layer)
  96
Etchberger 159, see Etschberger
Etel ..., see Edel
Etsch, Etschmann 94 (Adige,
  dweller on the Adige) 83
Ettenhausen, Ettenhoffer,
  Ettenhuber 122 (farmer on the
  Ett) 83
Etter (dweller on the Ett, dweller
  in a wattled enclosure) 83
Ettinger (fr Ettingen, village on
  the Ett) 83, 122
Ettlinger (fr Ettlingen, village on
  the Ett) 83, 122
Ettwein < Otwin (wealth +
  friend) 47, 48
Etzel, Etzler (pet name of Attila
  the Hun) 54

Eubel 53 < Albrecht
Eugel (little eye) 114
Eugen (name of Pope) 134
Eulbacher (swamp brook) 77
Eulbeck (swamp brook) 77, 122
Eulberg (owl mountain) 68
Eulberg (swamp mountain) 80, 68
Euler, Eulers 59, Eulert 74, Eulner (potter) 96
Eurich (sword + rule) 46, 47
Eva (wife of Adam) 135
Ever ..., Evers ..., see Eber..., Ebers
Everet 159, see Eberhard
Everhard, Everhardt, Everhart, see Eberhard
Everley 159, see Eberli
Everman, see Ebermann
Evers (wild boar) 48
Eversberg (boar mountain) 48, 68
Eversburg (boar castle) 48, 73, 122
Eversfield 153 (wild boar field) 48, 84
Eversmann (Ever's vassal) 109, 94
Eversmeier (fr the Evershof, Ever's farm) 73, 94
Eversol, Eversole, Eversull (hog wallow) 118
Everstein 122, see Eberstein
Evert, Everts 59, Evertz, see Ebert
Ewald, Ewalt (law + keeper, priest) 47, 47
Ewart, Ewartz 59 (guardian of the law, priest) 47, 47
Ewers 59, Ewert 74, Ewertz, see Eber, Ebert
Ewig (eternal) 138
Exler, Exner, see Oechsler, Oechsner
Exley 159, see Oechsele
Exner (ox raiser) 91

Ey, Eyer, see Ei, Eier
Eyb (pre-Germanic river name) 83, see Eib
Eybel, see Eibel
Eyc, Eych..., see Eich...
Eychler, see Eicher
Eyck (oak) 89
Eyckhof (oak farm) 89, 92
Eydam (father-in-law) 119
Eydelman 159, see Eitelman
Eyder (eider) 105, 106
Eyer, Eyermann, see Eier, Eiermann
Eygenbrod, see Eigenbrod
Eyler, see Eiler
Eymann (egg man) 105, 94
Eyrich, see Eurich
Eyring, see Eurich
Eysel (iron monger) 96
Eysemann, Eysenman, see Eiseman
Eysen ..., see Eisen
Eytel, see Eitel
Eyth, see Eid
Ezell, Ezzel, see Etzel

F

Faas < Gervasius, Servatius 135, see Fass
Faatz (St. Boniface) 135
Fabal, Fabel < St. Fabian, name of a pope 134
Faber, Fabert 74, Fabor (Latin: smith) 141
Fabian (name of a pope) 134
Fabricius, Fabritzius (Latin name for Schmidt) 141
Fabrikant (manufacturer) 96
Fach (compartment, pigeonhole, fishtrap) 106
Fach (swamp water) 80
Fachler (swamp dweller) 80
Fack (swine) 91
Facker, Fackert 74, Fackeret (flax breaker) 95

Fackert (joyful) 115

Fackler (flax breaker) 95

Fadem, Faden (thread, tailor) 96

Fadenhauer (thread maker) 96, 100

Fader (dweller in a fenced area) 84

Faecher (fan) 106

Faeger, see Feger

Faehner, Faehnle (ensign) 107

Faelten, see Felten

Faerber (dyer) 96, 122

Faerli, see Fehr

Faernbacher, see Farbach

Faesch 53, Faesche < St. Servatius 135

Faessle, Faessler (cooper) 96, 106

Faeth, Faetke 55, see Fader

Faeustlin 55 (little fist, little dog) 114

Faff, see Pfaff

Fahenstock, see Fahnenstock

Fahl, Fahle, Fahler, Fahler (pale, swamp)

Fahl (swamp)

Fahland (devil)

Fahlbusch (pale bush, swamp bush) 80

Fahlfeder (pale feather)

Fahlteich (swamp pond) 80

Fahn (swamp) 80

Fahn < Stephanus (St. Stephen) 135

Fahn, Fahnen (flag) 108

Fahnestock (flag staff)

Fahr, Faehr (ferry landing, ferryman) 122, 96

Fahrbach, Fahrenbach, Farenbach (*vornebach*, before the brook) 69, 77

Fahrencorn (before the grain field) 69

Fahrenhorst (before the hurst 69, swamp hurst 80) 72, 122

Fahrenwald (before the forest 69, swamp forest 80) 71

Fahrmann (ferryman) 96

Fahrmeyer (fr the Fahrhoff, ferry farm) 93, 94

Fahrner (fr Fahrn) 122

Faid (shirt, shirt maker) 96

Faig, see Faigel

Faigel, Faigle 159 (timid) 115

Failer (file maker) 106

Fainberg, see Feinberg

Fair, see Fehr

Fairbaugh 159, see Fahrbach

Fairchild 152, see Schoenkind

Faiss, Faist 74, Faister, see Feiss, Feist, Feister (fat, corpulent) 114

Fakler, see Fackler

Falbausch, see Fahlbusch

Fale, Fales, see Fehl

Falk, Falke, Falck (falcon, falconer, fr Latin *falco*) 91, 115

Falkenau (falcon meadow, swamp meadow) 91, 84, 122

Falkenberg (falcon mountain) 68, 122

Falkenburg 122, Falkinburg 159 (falcon castle) 73

Falkenhahn, Falkenhain (falcon's grove) 72

Falkenheimer (falcon hamlet) 124

Falkenhorst (falcon's grove) 72

Falkenklaus 159 (Klaus the falconer) 91

Falkenmeyer, Falenmayr (fr the Falkenhoff, falcon farm) 93, 94

Falkenstein 122, Falkenstine 159 (falcon's crag) 73

Falkewitz (falcon village) 127

Falkner, Falker, Falker (falconer) 91, see Volker

Fallentin (St. Valentine) 135

Falsenmayer (cliff farmer) 93

Falten 53 < St. Valentine 135

Falter (butterfly) 115

Falter (apple tree, fr *apfelter*) 89, 122

Falter, Faltor (dweller by a portcullis, gatekeeper) 96

Faltin (St. Valentine) 135

Falz 159, see Pfalz

Fandrich (ensign) 108

Fang, Fanger, Fangman, Fangmann 94 (catcher) 96

Fannacht, see Fasnacht

Farabaugh 159, see Fahrenbach

Farb (color, dyer) 96

Farbach, see Fahrbach

Farbenblum (colored flower) 89

Farbenstein (colored stone, jeweler) 73, 96

Farber, Farbman 94, see Faerber

Farch, Farke (little pig) 91, 115

Farenholtz, Farenholz (before the forest) 69, 72

Farenhorst, see Fahrenhorst

Farenwald (before the forest) 69, 72

Farinholt, see Farenholtz

Farn, Fahrne (fern) 89

Farnbacher, see Fahrbach

Farr (young bull)

Farrenkopf (steer head) 62, 113, 149

Farver, see Faerber

Fascher (bandager) 96

Fasching (Mardi Gras, Carnival) 143

Fasel (draft animal, breeding animal) 91

Fasenfeld (pheasant field) 84

Fasman, Fassmann (barrelmaker) 96, 94

Fasnacht, Fassenacht, Fastnacht (Mardi Gras, Shrove Tuesday) 143

Fass, Fasse, Faas (vat, barrel, barrel maker) 96, also pet name for Servatius, Gervasius

Fassbach (barrel brook) 77

Fassbinder, Fassbender, Fassbindler (barrel maker) 96

Fasshauer (barrel maker) 96, 100

Fassel, Fassell, Fassler (barrel maker) 96

Fassnacht, see Fasnacht

Fastabend, see Fastnacht

Fate 159, see Veit

Fatthauer, Fathauer, see Fasshauer

Fatz 53 < St. Bonifatius 135

Fatzenbacher (St. Boniface brook) 77

Fauch, Fauck, Faucker (bellows, smith) 96, 106

Fauenbach (peacock brook) 115, 77

Fauerbach, see Feurbach

Faught 159, see Vogt

Faul, Fauler (lazy) 115

Faulbach (stagnant brook) 77, 122

Faulert (dweller near stagnant water) 74

Faulhaber, Faulhaffer (oat farmer)

Faulhuber (farmer near stagnant water) 91

Faulker 159, see Volker

Faulkinberry 159, see Falkenberg

Faulkner, see Falkner

Faus, Fausel, Fauser (puffed up) 115

Fausnacht, Fausnaugh 159, see Fasnacht

Faust, Fausten (fist) 114, 115

Faust (fist, dog) 114

Faut 159, Fauth, Fautz, Fautzen, Fautzer, Fautter, see Vogt

Fawler 159, see Fauler

Fawst 159, see Faust

Fay < St. Sophia 135, 60

Fayerbach, see Feuerbach

Faygenblat 159 (fig leaf) 148

Fayler, see Feil

Faynshteyn 159, see Feinstein

Fayst, see Feist

Fazenbacher, see Fatzenbacher

Fearer 159, see Fuehrer

Fease, see Fues

Feaster 159, see Pfister

Fecher, see Faecher

Fechheimer (fr Fechheim) 122

Fechler, Fechner (furrier) 96

Fecht, Fechter, Fechtner, Feght 159, Feghtmann 94, 159, Fegter 159 (champion) 96, 107

Feckel 53, 55 < Frederick, Friedrich

Fecker (tailor)

Fedder, see Vetter

Fedderwitz (feather village) 124

Feder, Federer, Federler, Federmann, Feddermann 94 (feather seller, goose down dealer, pillow maker) 105, 96

Feder, see Vetter

Feder (scribe) 96

Federbush 159 (crest on helmet) 64

Federkeil (quill, scribe) 96

Federlein 55 (little feather) 118

Federspiel (trained raptor, falconer) 91

Federwitz, see Fedderwitz

Fee 159, see Vieh

Feer 159, Feehr, see Fehr

Feerer 159, see Fuehrer

Feffer, see Pfeffer

Fegebeutel (steal purse)

Feger, Fegert 74 (cleaner, burnisher) 108

Fegler, Feglear 159, Feggeler, see Feger

Fegley, see Voegele

Fegt ..., see Fecht...

Fehl, Fehle, Fehler (swamp dweller) 80

Fehlbaum (swamp tree) 80, 89

Fehlbier (much beer, drunkard) 113

Fehleisen (file maker) 96

Fehlhaber (much oats, oat farmer) 91

Fehn (swamp) 80, 122

Fehr, Feehr, Feer (ferryman) 96

Fehrenbach, Fehrenbacher, Fehrbach (fr Fehrenbach 122, swamp brook) 80, 77

Fehrenecke (fir field) 89, 85

Fehrenkamp, Fehrkamp (fir field) 89, 84

Fehrhof (ferryman's homestead) 92

Fehrle (pig raiser)

Fehrlinger (fr Fehrlingen) 122

Fehrmann (ferryman) 96

Fehsenfeld (spelt field) 91, 84

Fei < St. Sophia 135, 60

Feichtner 159, see Fechtner

Feidler, see Pheidler, Fiedler

Feierabend (quitting time) 117, 122

Feierstein, Feiersten, see Feuerstein

Feiertag (holiday) 143, 117

Feig, Feige, Feigel, Feigeler, Feigelman 94 (doomed to die, cowardly) 115

Feig, Feigmann (coward) 115, 94

Feige, Feigel, Feigl (violet) 89

Feigenbaum (fig tree) 89

Feight 159, see Veit

Feik, see Feig

Feil 122, Feiler, Feilner, Feihl, Feillmann 94 (file, file maker) 96

Feil (violet) 89

Feilenschmidt (file smith) 96

Feiler, Feilner (file maker) 96

Feilinger (fr Feilingen) 122

Fein (fine, elegant) 115

Feinaigle (pretty eye) 115

Feinberg (fine mountain) 68, see Weinberg

Feinblatt (fine leaf) 89

Feinblum (fine flower) 89
Feind, Feindt (enemy) 118
Feinfrock, Finfrock (fine gown) 96, 112
Feinglas (fine glass, glazier) 96
Feingold (goldsmith) 96
Feinkohl (fine cowl, cowl maker)
Feinleib (fine loaf, baker) 96
Feinman, Feinmann (elegant man) 115, 94
Feinstein (fine mountain) 73, 148
Feinstein (precious stone, jeweler) 96
Feinster 159, see Finster, Fenster
Feintuch (fine cloth, weaver) 106, 96
Feirtag, see Feiertag
Feiss (fat) 114
Feist, Feister (fat, fertile) 114
Feistenau (fertile meadow) 84, 122
Feit, Feitel, Feitler, Feith, Feitz, Feiz (St. Vitus) 135
Felbach (swamp brook) 80, 83, 77
Felbaum (willow tree) 89
Felber (dweller near willow trees) 89
Felbinger (fr Felbing) 122
Feld, Feldt, Felder, Felders 59, Felden (field) 84
Feldbach (field brook) 84, 77
Feldbaum (field tree) 84, 89
Feldbausch, see Feldbusch
Feldberger (fr Feldberg 122, field mountain) 84, 68
Feldbursch (field lad) 84
Feldbusch (field bush) 84, 72
Felder, Feldner (fieldman, farmer) 84, 91
Felderstein, see Feldstein
Feldhamer, see Feldheim
Feldhaus 122, Feldhausen (field house) 84, 65
Feldheim 122, Feltheim, Feldheimer (field hamlet) 84, 124

Feldhofer (fr Feldhof 122, field farm) 84, 92
Feldhusen, see Feldhaus
Feldkamp (field field) 84, 84, 122
Feldman, Feldmann (field man, farmer) 84, 91, 94
Feldmeier (field farmer) 84, 93
Feldmesser (surveyor) 84, 96
Feldmueller (field miller) 84, 103
Feldner, see Felder
Feldpausch, see Feldbusch
Feldscher, Feldsher 159 (army surgeon) 96, 108
Feldschuh (field shoe, bootmaker) 96, 112
Feldstein (field stone) 84, 73
Felger, Felgenhauer, Felgenmacher (felly maker, cartwright) 96, 100
Felgner, see Felger
Felhauer, see Felger
Felinger (fr Feling) 112
Felix (Latin, joyful) 115, 141, name of a pope 134
Felk 53, Felkel 55, Felker, Felkner, Felkmann < Volkmar
Felker, see Voelker
Fell, Felle, Fellman 94, Fellmann, Feller, Fellner, Fellers 59, Felleret 74, Fellermann (worker in hides) 96, 106
Felleisen (traveling bag) 106
Fellenbaum (Fell the tree!, forester) 96, 116
Fellenstein (Hew the rock!, quarryman) 116
Fellger, see Felger
Felman, see Fell
Felmar < Volkmar
Felner, see Fell, Feldner
Fels (cliff, crag) 68
Felsberg (cliff mountain) 68, 122
Felsch (false) 115
Felscher, see Feldscher

Felsecker (cliff field) 68, 85
Felsen (cliffs) 68
Felsenberg (cliff mountain) 68
Felsenheld (cliff hero)
Felsenstein (cliff mountain) 68, 73
Felsenthal (cliff valley) 68, 76
Felser, Felsing, Felsinger (fr Felsen 122, cliff)
Felt, Felts, Feltz, see Filtz
Feltberger, see Feldberger
Felten, Feltkin 55 < St. Valentin 135
Feltenbarger, see Feldberger 151
Felter, see Felder
Felthaus (field house) 84, 65
Feltheim, see Feldheim
Feltmacher (felt maker) 96
Feltman, see Feldmann
Feltmeyer (field farmer) 84, 93
Feltner, see Felder
Feltz, see Filtz
Feltzmann, see Feldman
Feltzner, see Felder
Fenchel (spice dealer) 105
Fendrick, see Faehnrich
Fengfisch (Catch fish!, fisherman) 91, 116
Fenhagen (marsh enclosure) 80, 124
Fenkel (spice dealer, fr Latin *foeniculum*) 105
Fenker (millet dealer) 105
Fenkhoff (millet farm, fr Latin *panicum*) 92
Fenn 122, Fennemann 94 (bog dweller) 80
Fennel (fennel, fr Latin *foeniculum*) 91
Fenner (ensign) 108
Fennhof, Fennhoff (fen farm) 80, 84
Fennig, see Pfennig
Fennigwerth (pennyworth) 117

Fenster, Fensterer, Fenstermacher, Fenstermaker, Fenstamaker 159 (window maker, fr Latin *fenestra*) 96, 106
Fensterwald, see Finsterwald
Fentz, Fenzel, see Wentzel
Ferber, Ferbert 74, see Faerber
Ferch (fir tree) 89
Ferckel (shoat, pig raiser) 115, 91
Ferdig, see Fertig
Ferdinand, Fernantz (Gothic: journey + risk) 49, 56
Feredag, Feredag, see Feiertag
Ferembach, Ferenbach, Ferenback 159, see Fehrenbach
Ferg, Ferge, Ferger, Ferges 59 (ferryman) 96
Ferhman, see Fehrmann
Ferhorst, see Fahrenhorst
Ferkel, Ferkler (shoat) 91
Ferman, see Fehrmann
Fernbach, see Fehrenbach
Ferne (glacier) 68
Fernhaber, see Firnhaber
Fernhoefer (fern farm) 89, 92
Fernholtz, see Fahrenholtz
Fernkorn (last year's corn) 118
Ferrenbach, see Fehrenbach
Fersch, see Pfirsich
Ferschbach (swamp brook) 80, 77
Fersner, see Foerstner
Ferst 159, see Fuerst
Ferster 159, Ferstner, Ferstermann, see Foerster
Fertig (ready to travel, skillful) 115
Fertner 159, see Pfoertner
Fese, Fehse (chaff, spelt) 91
Fesenfeld, Fessenfeld (spelt field) 91, 84, 122
Fesmeier (spelt farmer) 91, 93
Fessel, Fesseler, Fessler, Fesler (fetter maker) 96, 106

Fessel (barrel maker) 96
Fest (firm) 115
Fest (firm, fat) 114
Fester 53, Festerling 55 <
    Sylvester 134
Fester, Vester < Pope Silvester
Festerman (vespers singer) 110
Fett, Fette (fat, fertile) 114
Fetter, see Vetter
Fetter, Fetters 59, Fetterle 55,
    see Vetter, Vetterli
Fetterhof (fertile farm) 92
Fettig, Fetting, see Fett
Fetting (wing)
Fetz, Fetzer (executioner,
    quarreler) 115
Fetz 53 < St. Boniface 135
Feucht, Feuchter (damp, moist)
    122
Feucht (fir tree) 89, 122
Feuchtenberger (fir mountain)
    89, 68
Feuchtenwange, see
    Feuchtwange
Feuchtner (dweller by the firs)
    89
Feuchtwange (swamp field) 80,
    84
Feuer, Feurer (fire, fireman) 96
Feuerbach 122, Feurbach
    (swamp brook) 80, 77
Feuerberg (swamp mountain) 80,
    68, 122
Feurborn (swamp spring) 79
Feuereisen (fire iron, poker) 106
Feuerhacken (poker) 106
Feuerhardt, see Feuerherd
Feuerherd (fire hearth, smith) 106
Feuerleim (fire clay) 106
Feuerlein 55 (little fire, smith) 96
Feuermann (fireman, stoker) 96
Feuermann (flint dealer) 105
Feuerstein, Feuerstine 159 (flint
    dealer) 105
Feuler, Feulner, see Feiler

Feuerthaler (swamp valley)
    76
Feurer (stoker) 96
Feurmann (stoker) 96
Feursang (burned clearing)
    126
Feust, Feustel, Feustle 159, see
    Faust
Fey, Feye, see Fay
Feyerabend, see Feierabend
Feyerbaugh 159, see Feurbach
Feygelman, see Feig
Feyl, Feyler, see Feil, Feiler
Fichandler 159, see
    Fischhaendler
Ficht 122, Fichtel, Fichter,
    Fichtner (dweller among the
    fir trees) 89
Fichtelberg (fir mountain) 89, 68
Fichtmeyer, Fichtemayer (farmer
    in the fir trees) 89, 93
Fick 53, Ficke, Ficks 59, Ficken,
    Ficker, Fickert 74 < Friedrich
Fickenscher (Cut the purse!) 116
Fickus (fig, fr Latin *ficus)* 89
Fickweiler (Friedrich's villa) 127
Fidel, Fidler, Fidelman, Fiddlke,
    see Fiedel, Fiedler
Fiebach, Viehbach (cattle brook)
    77, 151
Fiebelcorn (grain infested by
    weevils) 118
Fieber (fever) 113
Fiebig, Fiebiger, see Viebig
Fiedel, Fiedler, Fiedeler,
    Fiedelman (fiddler) 96, 106
Fiedelmeyer (occupant of the
    Fiedelhoff, fiddle farm) 93
Fiederer (fletcher) 108
Fiedler (fiddler) 96
Fiege, Fiegner (overseer) 96
Fiegenbaum, see Feigenbaum
Fiehmann 159, see Viehmann
Fieken, Fiekers 59, Fiekert 74 <
    Sophia 60

Fieldhouse 153, see Feldhaus

Fienberg 159, see Feinberg

Fierer 159, see Fuehrer

Fierschnaller (four buckles) 112

Fierstein 159, see Feuerstein

Fiess (violent person) 115

Fiessler, Fiesler (womanizer) 115, see Fuessler

Fiester, Fiestner 159, see Pfister

Fietzen < St. Vincent 135

Fifer 159, see Pfeifer

Figge (son of Sophia) 60

Fighte 159, Feight, see Veit

Fikus (fig, Latin *ficus*) 89, 141

Filbert < Volkbrecht

Fildhut (felt hat, peasant) 112

Filer 159, see Feiler

Filibs, see Phillips

Filler (flayer) 96

Filtz (pasture) 84

Filtz (course farmer) 115, cf. "wool hat" and *filtzgebur*

Filtzer, Filzer (hatter, felt maker) 96

Filtzinger (fr Filtzing) 122

Filtzmeier (farmer by a high marsh) 80, 93

Filz, see Filtz

Finck, see Fink

Finckel, see Finkel

Finckelstein, see Finkelstein

Finckenstedt (finch city) 122

Findeisen (bloodletter) 96

Findeisen (Find iron! blacksmith) 96, 116

Findekeller (Find the cellar!, heavy drinker) 116, 115

Finder, Fintler (finder in a mine) 96

Findling (foundling) 119

Fine 159, see Fein

Fineberg, Fineblum, Fineman, Finestone, see Feinberg, Feinblum, Feinman, Feinstein 159

Finfrock (five gowns) 112

Finger, Fingern (finger 114, also ring maker 106)

Fingerhut, Fingerhuth, Fingerhood 159 (thimble, tailor, thimble maker) 106

Fingerle (little finger) 118

Fingernagel (finger nail) 114

Finglas 159, see Feinglas

Finister 159, see Finster

Fink, Finke, Fincke, Finken, Finks 59 (finch, carefree person) 115

Finkbein (finch leg) 114

Finkel, Finkle 159, Finkelman 94 (blacksmith 96), see also Fuenkel

Finkelstein (sparkling mountain, pyrite) 68

Finkemeyer, see Finkmeyer

Finkenauer, Finknauer (finch meadow) 84

Finkenbeiner, see Finkbein

Finkenstein (finch mountain) 68

Finkernagel 159, see Fingernagel

Finkmeyer (fr the Finkhof, finch farm) 93, 94

Finkstedt, Finkenstedt (finch city) 122

Finkweiler (finch hamlet) 124, 122

Finnefrock, see Fuenfrock

Finster (dark, gloomy) 115

Finsterbusch (dark bush) 72

Finsterwald (dark forest) 72

Finzel < Wentzel, Vincentius 135

Firebaugh 159, see Feuerbach

Fireman 159, see Feuermann

Firestone 152, Firestine 159, see Feuerstein

Firkel 159, see Ferkel

Firmwald, see Vormwald

Firne, see Ferne

Firneisen (old iron, iron dealer) 105

Firnhaber (last year's oats, oat dealer) 105

Firor 159, see Fuehrer

First (mountain ridge) 68, see also Fuerst

Firstenberg, see Fuerstenberg

Firstman, see Fuerstmann

Firstnau (ridge meadow, prince's meadow) 84

Fisch, Fische, Fischer (fish, fishmonger) 62, 105, 114

Fischart, see Fisher

Fischauer (fish meadow) 84

Fischbach, Fischbeck (fish stream) 77, 122

Fischbein, Fischbein, Fishbein 159 (whale bone, not fish leg!) 105

Fischborn (fish stream) 79, 122

Fischdorf, Fischendorf (fishing village) 124

Fischel, Fischell, Fischelt 74, see Fischer

Fischenthal (fish valley) 76

Fischer, Fisscher (fisherman, fishmonger) 91, 106

Fischgrund (fish bottom, fishing hole) 91

Fischhaber 159, Fischhof (fish farm) 92

Fischhaendler (fish monger) 106

Fischle (little fish) 118

Fischlein 55 (little fish) 114

Fischler (swamp dweller) 80

Fischmann (fish seller) 105

Fischmann 94, Fischner (fishmonger) 91, 106

Fischmeyer (fr the Fischhof, fish farm) 93, 94

Fischner, see Fischer

Fise 159, see Feise

Fishbach 159, Fishbeck, Fishbaugh 159, Fishpaugh, Fishpaw, see Fischbach

Fishbein 159, Fishbone, see Fischbein

Fisher 153, see Fischer

Fishter 159, see Fichter

Fisler, Fissler, see Fuessler

Fister, see Pfister

Fite 159, see Veit

Fitschner 53 < Friedrich

Fitten (place name) 122

Fitter, Fitterman, see Vetter, Vetterman

Fitts 159, Fitz, Fitze, Fitzell, Fitzer, Fitzner (artistic weaver, tailor) 106

Fitzberg, Fitzenberg, Fitzenberger (pond mountain) 81, 68

Fitzenreiter (pond clearing) 81, 126

Fitzlert 74, see Fitts

Fitzner (artistic weaver) 96

Fitzthum (governor, fr Latin *vice-dominus*) 109

Fix < St. Vitus 135

Fizner (dweller near a pond) 81, see Fitts

Flach, Flacher (flat, plain) 67

Flachmueller 103, Flachmeyer 93 (miller, farmer on the Flach) 83, 103, 93

Flachs, Flaxman (flax, flaxenhaired) 112

Flachs (flax grower or dealer) 91, 105

Flachsbart (flaxen beard) 112

Flachshaar (flaxenhaired) 112

Flachsmann (flax dealer) 95

Flacht (woven fence) 84

Flack, see Flach

Flack (swamp) 80

Flacks 159, see Flachs

Flad, Fladd, Flade (flat cake, cake baker) 96, 112

Flaechsner (flax dealer) 105

Flaesch, see Fleisch, Flaschner

Flagel 159, Flagler, see Flegel, Flegler

Flager < *Pfleger*, governor 109, 151

Flagge (flag, colors) 118

Flaks 159, see Flachs

Flamholtz (fire wood, wood cutter or dealer) 96, 105

Flamholtz (swamp forest) 80, 72

Flamm (flame, blacksmith) 96

Flammenkamp (swamp field) 80, 84

Flammer (smith) 96

Flander, Flanders (a Belgian province, a mercenary fr there or who served there) 121

Flanz (crooked mouth) 114, see also Pflantz

Flaschenriem (flask strap) 106

Flaschner (bottlemaker) 96

Flasharr, see Flachsharr

Flashhauer 159, see Fleishhauer

Flashman 159, see Fleischmann

Flashner 159, see Flaschner

Flath, Flather, Flater, Flathman, Flathmann 94 (swamp dweller) 80

Flaum (feathers, down) 105

Flaum, see Pflaum

Flautt (flute player) 96

Flax, Flaxman, see Flachs

Fleager 159, see Pflueger

Fleagle 159, see Fluegel

Flechner, Flechtner (basket weaver) 96

Flechsenhar (flaxenhaired) 112

Flechsner, see Flaechsner

Fleck, Flecke (speck, spot, stain, cobbler, tailor) 96, 104

Fleckenstein (spotted mountain) 68

Fleckner (cobbler, tailor) 96

Fleckner (fr the Fleckhof, stain farm) 118

Fleddermann (cake baker) 96, 94

Fleder, see Flader

Fleegle 159, see Fluegel

Fleetmann 94 (dweller by running water) 83

Fleg, see Pfleger

Flegel, Flegler (flail user or maker, thresher, fr Latin *flagellum*) 106

Fleig (fly, lively person) 115

Fleisch (meat), Fleischer, Fleischmann 94, Fleischner (butcher) 96

Fleischbein (flesh leg, meat bone, butcher) 96

Fleischer (butcher) 96

Fleischhacker (butcher) 96

Fleischhauer, Fleischouer 159 (butcher) 96, 100

Fleischhaus, Fleishhous 159 (butcher shop)

Fleischman, Fleischmann, Fleishman 159 (butcher) 96

Fleischner (butcher) 96

Fleisener 159, see Fleischner

Fleisher 159, Fleishmann, see Fleischer, Fleischman

Fleiss (industry, diligence) 115, see also Fleisch

Fleissner (fr Fleissen), see Fleischner

Flekstein, see Fleckstein

Fleming, Flemming, Flemmings 59 (Fleming, Flemish mercenary, cloth maker) 121

Flender (flighty person) 115

Flensberg (fr Flensberg) 68, 122

Flersheim, see Floersheim

Flesche, Flescher, Fleschmann, see Fleisch, Fleischer, Fleischmann

Fleschner, see Fleischner, Flaschner

Flesher 159, Fleshman, Fleshow, see Fleischer, Fleischmann, Fleischhauer

Flettner (dweller near rushes) 81

Flettner, see Floetner

Flexer, Flexner, see Flaechsner

Flick, Flicken, Flicker, Flickner (patch, short for *Flickschuster*, cobbler) 104, 106

Flickinger (fr Flicking) 122

Flieder (elder, lilac) 89

Fliedner (bloodletter) 96

Fliegel, see Fluegel

Flieger (restless person) 115, see Pflueger

Fliessbach (flowing brook) 77

Flinchbaugh 159 (pebble brook) 77

Flink, Flinke, Flinkman (quick, nimble) 115

Flins, Flint (flint, flint worker) 96

Flintenfeld (flint field) 84

Floch, Flock (flake)

Flockshaar, see Flachshaar

Floegel, see Fluegel

Floegel, see Flegel

Floerscheim (fr Floersheim) 122

Floesser, Floetzner (raftsman) 96

Floetner, Pfloetner (raftsman) 96

Floery < St. Florian 135

Floetner (flute player) 96

Flohr 53, Flor < St. Florian 135

Florey, Flory < St. Florian 135

Florian < St. Florian 135

Florscheim, see Floerscheim

Florschutz (field guard) 109

Flossman (rafter) 96

Flott, Flotz (river, pond) 79, 81

Flottmann (dweller on a river) 79

Flougar 159, see Pflueger

Flucht (flight) 118

Fluck, see Fluegge

Fluegel (wing, jutting piece of land) 84

Flueger, see Pflueger

Fluegge, Fluegger, Flueggert 74 (fledged, lively) 115

Flueh (precipice) 72

Fluers (field guard) 95

Flug, Fluge (flight), see also Pflug

Flugel, see Fluegel

Flugfelder (plowed field) 84

Flugelmann (wing man, model soldier) 107

Fluh (steep stone slope) 71

Fluhr, Flur (meadow) 84

Fluhrer (field guard) 95

Fluke, see Flug

Flumenbaum, Flumbaum (plum tree) 89

Fluss (river) 83

Fluth (flood) 77, 83

Focht 159, Fochtmann, see Vogt

Fock 53, Focke, Focken < Volkwart, Volker, etc.

Fockeroth < Volkerodt (folk + clearing) 126

Fockhausen < Volkhausen (folk + houses) 65

Foederer (furtherer) 118

Foehl (file maker) 96

Foehr, Foehrs 59 (fir tree) 89

Foehrkolb (fir club) 89

Foelix, see Felix

Foelke, Foelker, see Voelke, Voelker

Foerg (ferryman) 96

Foerst (pre-Germanic river name) 83, see Fuerst

Foerstel, Foerstler, see Foerster

Foerster, Foerstner, Foerstiner, Foerstermann 94 (forester) 96

Foerstermann (fr Foerster in the Harz 122) 94, see also Foerster

Foertner (dweller by a ford) 71

Foertsch, see Pfirsich

Foertschbeck (peach brook) 89, 77

Fogel 159, Fogal, Foegel, Fogaler, Fogler, see Vogel, Vogler

Fogelberg 159, see Vogelberg

Fogelman 159, see Vogelmann

Fogelsanger 159, Fogelsong 159,
    see Vogelsang
Foght 159, see Vogt
Fohl (foal, young horse) 91
Fohlk, see Volk
Fohn, Foehn (south wind) 118
Fohr (fir) 89
Fohr (ferryman, dweller by the
    ferry) 96
Fohrbach (fir brook) 89, 77
Fohring, Fohringer (fir) 89
Fohrman, see Fuhrman
Foht 159, see Vogt
Folck, Folk, Folke, Folker,
    Folkert 74, see Volk, Voelker
Folckemer, Folckemmer,
    Folkemar, see Volkmar
Folendorf, Folenweide, see
    Fuellendorf, Fuellenweide
Folger (follower) 109
Folk, Folke, see Volk
Folkart 74, see Volker
Folkman, see Volkmann
Foll, Follen (foal) 91
Follendorf (foal village) 124
Foller, Foeller < Volkhart (folk +
    strong) 46, 46
Follhart, see Foller
Follman, see Volkmann
Follmeyer (foal farmer) 91
Folmer, Follmer, Fulmer, see
    Volkmar
Folter (torturer) 96
Folter (portcullis)
Foltin < St. Valentin 135
Foltmann (torturer) 96, 94
Foltz, Folz < Volkmar
Fontain, Fontaine, Fontane (fr
    French Fontaine, fountain)
    114
Fooks 159, see Fuchs
Foos 159, Foose, see Fuss
Forbach 122, Forbeck, see
    Fahrbach
Forch, Forchel (fir) 89
Forchenbach (fir brook) 89, 77

Forchenbach (trout stream) 77
Forchheimer, Forchhenner (fr
    Forchheim, fir hamlet) 122
Forchner (dweller among the firs)
    89
Forcht (fear) 115
Forchtenicht, see Fuerchtenichts
Fordemfeld, Fordemfeldt (in
    front of the field) 69, 84
Fordenbach, Fordtenbacher, see
    Vorbach
Forderer, see Foerderer
Forelle (trout) 115
Foremann, see Formann
Forgang, see Vorgang
Forhel (trout) 115
Forhoff, Fornnoff, Fornhof, see
    Vorhoff
Fork, Forke, Forkel 55 (pitchfork)
    106
Formann (drayman) 96
Formhals (before the pass) 69
Formwalt, see Vormwalt
Fornadel (fir needle) 89
Forner (dweller among the ferns)
    89
Forsberg, see Forschberge
Forsch, Forschlern, Forschner,
    see Forst
Forschberge, Forshberge 159
    (forest mountain) 72, 68
Forschlager (forest lair) 72
Forscht, see Forst
Forsh 159, see Forsch
Forsman, see Forst
Forst 122, Forster, Forstmann
    94, Forstner (forester, dweller
    in the forest) 72
Forster (see Foerster)
Forstreiter, Forstreuter (forest
    clearing) 72, 126
Forstreiter, Forstreuter (forest
    rider) 72
Fortenbaugh 159 (brook with
    ford) 78, 77, 155
Forth, see Furth

Forthofer (farm at the ford) 78,
92
Forthuber (farmer at the ford)
78, 91
Fortkamp (field at the ford) 78,
84
Fortman, Fortmann (dweller at
the ford) 78, 94
Fortmeier (farmer at the ford)
78, 93
Fortmueller, Fortmuller 159
(miller at the ford) 78, 93
Fortner, Fortney, see Pfortner
Fortwengler, see Furtwanger
Fosbrink (fox hill) 74
Fosbrok, Fosbroke, Fosbrook (fox
brake) 80
Fosburg (fox castle) 73
Fosler, Fossler, see Vossler
Fosnaught 159, Fosnot, Fasnot,
see Fasnacht
Fosnot 159, see Fastnacht
Foss, Fosse, Fosz, see Voss
Foster, see Forster
Foth, see Fuss
Fourhman 159, see Fuhrmann
Foust 159, see Faust
Fout 159, Fouts, Foutz, see Faut
Fow 159, see Pfau
Fowl 159, Fowle, see Faul, Faule
Fox 153, see Fuchs
Fraalich 159, see Froehlich
Fraas (glutton) 115
Frack (full dress) 112
Fraemdling, see Fremdling
Fraenkel 55, Fraenkle 159 <
Frank
Fraenzel 55 < Franz, St. Francis
135
Frage, Frager (food dealer) 105
Fralich, Frailey, Fralick, Fraley
159, Fraleigh 159, see
Froehlich
Frambach, see Frombach
France 159, Frances, Francis, see
Frantz

Franck, Francke, see Frank,
Franke
Franckfurther, see Frankfurter
Franckhauser, Frankhuyse (the
Franks' house) 121, 65
Frank, Franke, Franken, Franks
59 (Franconian) 120. Franken
may be short for Frankenberg,
etc.
Frankel 55, Frankle 159, Frankl
< Frank
Frankenbach (Franks' brook, the
Franks' brook) 121, 77
Frankenberg, Frankenberger,
Frankenberry 159
(Franconian mountain) 121,
68
Frankenfeld, Frankenfelder (fr
Frankenfeld 122, the Franks'
field, or Frank's field) 121, 84
Frankenfield 153, see
Frankenfeld
Frankenhausen (city) 122
Frankenheim (the Franks'
hamlet) 121, 124
Frankenstein (Franconian
mountain) 121, 73
Frankenthal (Franconian valley)
121, 76, 122
Frankfelder, see Frankenfelder
Frankford, see Frankfurter
Frankfurter, Franckenfurther (fr
Frankfurt) 122
Frankl, Frankle 159, see
Fraenkel
Frankland (Franconia) 121
Frankouse 159, Frankhouser (the
Franks' houses) 121, 65, 155
Franks, see Franck
Franz, Frantz, Frantzen,
Fransen, Franssen (St.
Francis) 135, 137
Franzmann (Frenchman) 121
Fras, Frass (glutton) 115
Fratz (grimace, rascal, glutton)
115

Frauenberg (Mountain of Our Lady) 139, 68

Frauendienst (service of the ladies, service to Our Lady) 118

Frauendoerfer (fr Frauendorf 122, Our Lady's Village) 139, 124

Frauenfelder (fr Frauenfeld 122, "Field of our Lady," or "corvée field") 139, 80

Frauenholtz (convent woods) 139

Frauenknecht (servant to Our Lady's convent) 139, 119

Frauenlob (praise of ladies) 118

Frauenpreis (praise of ladies) 118

Frauenschu (maker of ladies' shoes) 96, 104

Frauenstadt (City of Our Lady) 139

Frauke 55, Fraucke (little lady) 118

Fraumann (vassal of or worker at a convent) 139

Fraundorf, see Frauendoerfer

Fraunfelder, see Frauenfelder

Fraunhoffer (convent farm) 139, 84

Fraunholtz (probably Fronholtz, corvée forest) 139

Fray, see Frey

Frayberg, see Freiberg

Fraylick 159, Fraylich, see Froehlich

Freas, Frease 159, see Fries

Frebel, see Frevel

Freburger 159, see Freiburger

Frech (impudent, bold) 115

Freck, Frecker, Freckmann 94 (bold), also < Friedrich

Frede, Freder (fr Frede 122, swamp) 80, also < Friedrich

Fredekin (little Friedrich) 55

Fredel < Friedrich

Fredenstein (peace stone) 73

Frederic, Frederick, Frederica (feminine of Friedrich), see Friedrich

Fredericki, son of Frederick 142

Fredericksen (son of Fredrick) 59

Fredhoff 159, see Friedhoff

Fredrica, see Friedrich

Freeauf 159, see Fruehauf

Freeberger 159, Freeburger, see Freiberger, Freiburger

Freebour 159 (free peasant) 92, 151

Freed ... see Fried ...

Freed 159, Freede, see Friede

Freedberg 159, Freedbergh, Freedburg, see Friedberg, Friedburg

Freedlander 159, Freedlender (fr Friedland) 121, 151

Freedman 159, see Friedmann

Freeh, see Frueh

Freehauf 159, see Fruehauf

Freehof 159, see Friedhof

Freehold 159, see Freiholt

Freeland 159, see Friedland

Freehling 159, see Fruehling

Freemann 159, see Freimann

Freemire 159, see Freimeyer

Frees, Freese, Freeze 159, Freesen, Freesemann (Frisian) 121

Freesmeyer (Frisian farmer) 121, 93

Frei, Freie, Frey (free, freeman) 115, 109

Freiberg, Freiberger (fr Freiberg 122, tax exempt mountain) 68

Freiburger (fr Freiburg) 122

Freid ..., see Fried ...

Freidag, see Freitag

Freidel 159, see Friedel

Freidenberger 159, see Freudenberger

Freidenreich, see Freudenreich

Freidenstein 159, see Freudenstein

Freidhof, see Friedhof
Freier (wooer) 119
Freihard, Freiheit (vagabond) 115
Freihauf, see Fruehauf
Freihof (independent farm) 84, 92, 122
Freiholt, Fryholtz (public forest) 72
Freihuber (freehold, freeholder) 92
Freihuber, see Freihof
Freilich, Freligh 159 (Freely! to be sure!) 117, see Froelich
Freimann 94, Freiling (freedman) 92
Freimeyer (tax exempt farmer) 93
Freimueller (tax exempt miller) 103
Freimut, Freimuth, see Freyermuth
Freind, Freint, see Freund
Freinstein, see Freudenstein
Freis, Freise, Freisen (Frisian), see Fries
Freischmidt (independent blacksmith) 96
Freistat, Freishtat 159 (free city) 122
Freistueler, Freisthuhler, Freistuler (official of Vehmgericht) 109
Freitag (Friday, day of corvée duty) 143
Freivogel (free bird, outlaw) 109
Fremd, Fremder (stranger) 120
Fremdling, Froembdling (stranger) 120
Frendt 159, see Freund
Frene, Frehner < St. Verena 135
Frenkamp (swamp field) 80, 84, see Fehrenkamp
Frenkel, see Fraenkel

Frens, Frensel, Frenz, Frenzel 55 < Franz
Frenssen (son of Franz) 59
Frentz, Frenzel 55 < Franz
Frerich, Frerichs 59, see Friedrich
Frese, Fresen, see Fries
Fresenburg (Friesian castle) 120, 73
Fress (glutton) 115
Freter, see Fress
Fretz, see Fritz
Freud, Freude, Freuden (joy) 115
Freudemann (jolly fellow) 115
Freudenberg, Freudenberger (fr Freudenberg, joy mountain) 68, 122
Freudenberger (one who has seen the *Mons Gaudium*)
Freudenburg (joy castle) 73, 122
Freudenhammer (fr Freudenheim 122) 124
Freudenreich, Freudenrich (joyful) 115
Freudenstein (joy montain) 73, 122
Freudenthal (joy valley) 76, 122
Freudhafer (joy farm) 92, 159
Freudig, Freudigmann (happy fellow) 115
Freudweiler (happy village) 127
Freund, Freundt, Freint, Freundel 55 (friend) 119
Freuntlich, Freunlich (friendly) 115
Frevel (theft, evil doer) 115
Frey, Freye, Freyer (free) 92
Freyberger (fr Freyberg 122, free mountain), see Freiberger
Freyburger (fr Freyburg 122, free castle), see Freiburger
Freydel, see Friedel
Freydig, see Freitag
Freyer, see Freier
Freyermuth, Freymuth, Freymuht (free spirit) 115

Freyhofer (independent farm) 92
Freyling (free man) 92
Freyman (free man) 92
Freymeyer (free farmer) 92
Freysinger (fr Freising) 122
Freytag, see Freitag
Freyvogel (free bird, outlaw) 109
Frez, see Fritz
Friand 159, see Freund
Friauf 159, see Fruehauf
Fric 159, see Frick
Frichi 159, see Fritschi
Frichtenicht, fr Fuerchte nicht!
    (Fear not!) 116, 151
Frick 53, Fricke, Frickel 55 <
    Friedrich
Frickenhaus (house on the Frick)
    83, 65
Frickenstein (mountain near the
    Frick) 83, 73
Fricker, Frickert 74 (dweller on
    the Frick) 83
Frickinger (fr Fricking 122,
    belonging to Friedrich) 59, 124
Frickmann (dweller on the Frick)
    83, 94
Frickmann (follower of Friedrich)
    94
Fridag, Fridy 159, Friday 153,
    see Freitag
Fridel, see Friedel
Frideric, Friderick, Friderich,
    Fridrich, see Friedrich
Fridley 159, see Friedlich
Frie, see Frei
Friebach (public brook) 77, see
    Friedbach
Friebe (fr Slavic *vrba*, willow
    tree) 89, 146
Frieberger, see Freiberger
Fried, Friede, Frieds 59 (peace),
    also < Friedrich
Friedag, see Freitag
Friedbach (foamy brook) 77
Friedbald, Friebald (peace +
    bold) 47, 46

Friedberg, Friedberger (fr
    Friedberg 122, peace
    mountain) 47, 68
Friedburg (peace castle, walled
    castle) 47, 73, 122
Friedel 55, Friedle 159, Friedl
    (friend, sweetheart) 119
Friedemann, see Friedmann
Friedenberg, see Friedberg
Friedenheim, see Friedhaim
Friedensthal (peace valley) 76
Friedenwald (peace forest) 47, 72
Friederic, Friederick,
    Friedericks, see Friedrich
Friedgen 53, 55 < Friedrich
Friedhaber (peacemaker) 138
Friedhagen (walled enclosure)
    47, 124
Friedhaim (fr Friedheim 122,
    peace hamlet, walled hamlet)
    47, 124
Friedhof, Friedhoffer (cemetery)
    47, 92
Friedke 53, 55 > Friedrich
Friedland, Friedlaender (fr
    Friedland) 121
Friedle 159, Friedly 159,
    Friedler, see Fried
Friedlein 55, Friedline 159 <
    Friedrich
Friedlich (peaceful) 115
Friedlieb (peace lover) 115
Friedman, Friedmann (peace
    man) 115, also < Friedrich
Friedrich, Friederich, Friedrichs
    59, Friederick, Friedericks,
    (peace + ruler) 47, 46
Friedrichsson (son of Friedrich)
    59
Frieling 159, see Fruehling
Friemann, see Freimann
Friemuth, see Freimuth,
    Freyermuth
Friend 153, Friendlich, see
    Freund, Freundlich

Friermood 159, see Freyermuth
Fries, Friess, Friese, Frieser,
　　Friesche, Friesner (Frisian,
　　often a false plural of Frey)
　　121
Frieschknecht (Friesian servant)
　　121, 109
Friesenhahn (fr Friesenhagen
　　122, Frisian hamlet 121)
Frietag 159, see Freitag
Friethrick 159, see Friedrich
Frietsch 53 < Friedrich
Frigh 159, see Frey
Frik, Frike, see Frick, Fricke
Friley 159, see Freilich
Frind 159, see Freund
Fring, Fringe, Frings, Frinken 59
　　< St. Severin 135
Frisch, Frische (fresh, lively 115),
　　also < Friedrich
Frischbier (fresh beer, brewer,
　　taverner) 96
Frischeisen (fresh iron,
　　blacksmith) 96
Frischholtz (fresh wood,
　　woodcutter) 96
Frischkorn, Frishkorn 159 (fresh
　　grain) 106
Frischman, Frischmann, see
　　Frisch
Frischmut (fresh courage) 115
Frischolz (wood cutter) 95
Frishcorn 159, see Frischkorn
Frist (period, time limit)
Fritchey, Fritchi 53, Fritsch,
　　Fritschi, Fritsche, Fritscher,
　　Fritschel 55, Fritschler,
　　Fritschner, Fritzsch <
　　Friedrich
Fritz, Fritts 159, Fritze, Fritzel,
　　Fritzges, Fritzsche, Frizzel,
　　Fritzius < Friderizius, Latin
　　for Friedrich 141
Fritzmann 94, Fritzner <
　　Friedrich

Fritzweiler (Friedrich's villa,
　　peace village) 124
Froberg, see Frohberg
Frock 159, see Frack
Froeb, Froeber (willow, fr Slavic:
　　vrba) 89, 146
Froebel (undaunted) 115
Froehlich, Froehlicher, Froehlig,
　　Froelig, Froeli, Froehly 159
　　(joyful) 115
Froehling, see Fruehling
Froehlke, see Froehlich
Froelich (happy) 115
Froembdling, see Fremdling
Froeschle 55 (little frog) 115
Froese, see Fries
Froh (merry) 115
Frohbart (merry beard) 112, 115
Frohberg (merry mountain) 68
Frohboese (quick to anger) 115
Frohlich, Frolic, Frolick, Frohligh
　　159, see Froehlich
Frohling (merry person) 115
Frohm, see Fromm
Frohmader (corvée mower) 91, 96
Frohman, Frohmann (merry
　　man) 115, 94
Frohn, Frohne, Frohner,
　　Frohnert 74 (court messenger,
　　corvée payer) 139
Frohnder, see Frohn
Frohnmayer (overseer of corvée
　　service) 93
Frohsinn (merry spirit) 115
Frohwein (merry friend) 115
Frohwirt (jolly host) 115, 96
Frolich, Frolick, Frohligh 159,
　　see Froehlich
From, Frome, see Fromm
Froman, see Frohmann
Fromberg 122, see Frommberg
Fromknecht (faithful servant)
　　139
Fromm, Fromme, Frommer
　　(useful, capable, pious) 138

Frommberg (swamp mountain) 80, 68

Frommeyer (industrious farmer) 138, 93

Frommholt (pious dear) 138, 48

Fronacker (lord's field, corvée field) 139

Froneberger (corvée mountain) 139, 68

Froner, see Frohn

Fronfelder, Fronfelter (corvée field) 139, 84

Fronheuser, Fronhyser 159 (corvée houses) 137, 65, 66

Frosch, Frosh 159 (frog, house name) 62

Froschauer (fr Froschau 122, frog meadow) 84

Froschheiser (fr the froghouse) 65, 149

Frost, Frostz 59 (frost) 118

Frostdorf, Frostdorp (frost village) 124

Frowenfelder 159, see Frauenfelder

Frucht (crop, fruit) 106

Fruchtbaum (fruit tree) 89

Fruchtel 55, Fruchter, Fruchtmann, Fruchterman (fruit dealer) 105

Fruden 159, see Freuden

Fruechte (crops, fruit dealer) 105

Frueh (early riser) 115, see also Frey

Fruehan (early cockcrow) 143

Fruehauf (early riser) 115

Fruehauf (child sired before marriage) 119

Fruehbrot (breakfast) 118

Fruehling (spring) 143

Fruehsang, Fruesang (early song) 118

Fruehstueck (breakfast) 118

Fruehwein (early wine) 118

Fruendt, see Freund

Fruetag (morning, Friday) 143

Fruetrank (early drink) 118

Fruh, Fruhling, see Frueh, Fruehling

Fruhwirth (early host) 96

Fruke, see Frauke

Frum, see Fromm

Fruman (worthy man) 138, 94

Fruth (intelligent) 115

Fry 159, Frye, Freyer, see Frey

Fryberger, see Freiberger

Frydag, see Freitag

Frydman 159, see Friedmann

Frydryck 159, see Friedrich

Fryer, see Freier

Freyermouth 159, see Freyermuth

Fryfogel, see Freivogel

Fryhafer, see Freihoffer

Fryling, see Freiling

Frymyer, Frymire 159, see Freymeyer

Fuchs (fox, furrier, house name) 96, 149

Fuchsberger (fr Fuchsberg 122, fox mountain) 68

Fuchsloch, Fuchslocher (fox den) 118

Fuchsmann (furrier) 96

Fuchsschwanz (fox tail, furrier) 96

Fuderholtz (wood carter) 96

Fuechtner, see Fichtner

Fuegel, Fuegli, Fueglin (skilful) 115

Fueger (public administrator)

Fuehrer (leader, carter) 96

Fuelle, Fuellen (foal) 91

Fuellendorf (filly village) 124

Fuellenweide (foals' meadow) 84

Fueller (glutton) 115

Fuellgrabe (Fill-the-grave!, grave digger) 116

Fuenfrock (five cloaks) 112

Fuenkelstein, see Finkelstein

Fuentling, see Findling

Fuerchtegott (Fear God!) 116, 140

Fuerchtenicht (Fear not!) 116

Fuerenschild (Bear the shield!) 116

Fuersicht (caution) 115

Fuersprech (advocate) 118

Fuerst (prince) 109

Fuerstein 159, see Feuerstein

Fuerstenberg (prince's mountain) 68, 122

Fuerstler, see Foerstler

Fuerstmann (prince's follower) 109, 94, see Forst

Fuerstner, see Foerstner

Fues, Fuess, Fuos, see Fuss

Fuesser (pedestrian, infantryman) 107

Fuessler (one who works for the *Barfuessler*, Barefoot Friars) 110

Fuetter (fodder) 105

Fuetze (pond, puddle, fr Latin *puteus*) 80

Fug, Fuege (pleasant) 115

Fuge, Fuger, Fugman (overseer) 96

Fughs 159, see Fuchs

Fugler, see Vogler

Fuhlroth (rotted clearing, swampy clearing) 80, 126

Fuhr 159, Fuhrer, see Fuehrer

Fuhr (dweller by a ferry or ford)

Fuhrman, Fuhrmann, Furman (carter) 96

Fuhrmanneck (carter's place) 96, 85

Fuks 159, see Fuchs

Fuksman 159, Fuksmann, see Fuchsman

Fulbright 159, 162, see Volkbrecht

Fulcher, Fulker, see Volker

Fulda (name of city) 122

Fuldner (fr Fulda) 122

Fulenbacher (swamp brook) 80, 77

Fulenwider 159 (foal's meadow) 84

Fulenwider 159 (swamp meadow) 80, 84

Fulger, see Folger

Fulk, Fulker, see Volker

Fullbrake 159, see Vollbrecht

Fulle, see Fuellen

Fullenkam, Fullenkamp (foal's field) 84

Fuller (fuller, fr Latin *fullare*) 96

Fullewiler (foals' hamlet) 127

Fullmer, Fulmer, see Volkmar

Fults 159, Fultz, Fultze, see Voltz

Funderburk < von der Burg (from the castle) 69, 73

Funk, Funck, Funke (spark, unstable person) 115

Funkel (spark, smith) 106

Funkenstein (spark mountain) 73

Funkhauser, Funkhouser 159 (fr Funkhaus 122, spark house) 65

Furch (furrow) 118

Furcht (fear) 115

Furchtgott, see Fuerchtegott

Furman (ferryman) 96, see also Fuhrmann

Furrenbauer (furrow farmer, plowman) 91

Furst 159, see Fuerst

Furstenberg, see Fuerstenberg

Furstmeyer, Furstmeier (manager of prince's farm) 93

Furth (ford, suburb of Nuernberg) 122

Furthemeyer (ford farmer) 78, 93

Furtmiller (ford miller) 78, 103

Furtwanger (sloping meadow at the ford) 78, 71

Fusel, fuseler (bad liquor, taverner) 96

Fuselbach (bad liquor creek) 77

Fuss, Fuess (foot, leg, foot of mountain, see also Fuchs) 114, 68

Fusselbaugh 159, see Fuselbach

Futerer, Futter, Futterer, Futerman 96 (feeder, fodder dealer) 105

Fux, Fuxe, see Fuchs

Fuxmann, see Fuchsmann

Fyfer, see Pfeiffer

G

Gaas, Gaass, see Gas

Gabble 159, see Gabel

Gabe (gift) 118

Gabel 122, Gabell, Gabler, Gabeler, Gabelmann (fork, fork maker) 106

Gabel, Gabell, Gabler, Gabelmann 94 (dweller at a road fork) 65

Gabelsberg (fork mountain) 68

Gaberle 55 < St. Gabriel 136

Gabhart 159, see Gebhard

Gable 159, Gabler, see Gabel, Gebel

Gabriel, Gabriels 164 (an archangel) 136

Gach (quick, turbulent) 115

Gack (silly, foolish) 115

Gackenbach (swamp stream) 80, 77, 122

Gackenback (shepherd's hut) 77

Gade, Gaden (chamber, room) 118

Gade 53 < Gottfried, Gottschalk, etc.

Gade (miner) 96

Gadermann (dweller by the village gate) 65

Gadjohann (handsome John) 115

Gaeb (pleasant, welcome) 115

Gaebel (skull) 114

Gaebler, see Gabel, Gabler

Gaedeke, Gaedtke, see Goedeke

Gaehring, see Goering

Gaengel (leadstring, horse trainer) 96, see Gangel

Gaensbauer (goose raiser) 91

Gaensebein (fenced yard for geese) 84

Gaensebein (goose leg) 114

Gaenshirt (goose herder) 95

Gaenslein 55, Gaensle, Gennsli (gosling) 91

Gaensler (goose raiser) 95, 91

Gaerber, see Gerber

Gaerstener, see Gerstner

Gaertel 55 (little garden, gardner) 84, 98

Gaertner, Gaertener (gardner, fr Garden or Garten) 84, 98

Gaes, Gaesser, see Gaessner

Gaessler, see Gass

Gaestel 55 (little stranger, little guest) 120

Gaetge 55, see Goetz

Gaetz, see Goetz

Gafke 55 (little gift) 118

Gager (fr Gagen) 122

Gahl, Gahler (fr Gahlen) 122

Gahr, Gahre, Garht 74 < Garmann (spear man) 46, 94, 53

Gahraus, see Garaus

Gahs, see Gas

Gaier, see Geier

Gaiger, Gaigler, see Geiger

Gail, Gailing, see Geil

Gainer 159, see Gehner

Gairing 159, see Gehring

Gais (goat) 91

Gaisel, Gaiselmann, see Geisel, Geiselmann

Gaiser, see Geiser

Gaister, see Geister

Galander (lark) 115

Galgenschwank (gallows bird, initiation name) 117

Gall, Galle, Gallen < St. Gallus 135, (fr St. Gall) 122, 139

Galler, Gallner (servant at St. Gall) 139

Gallinger (fr Galling) 122

Gallman, Gallmann (servant of St. Gall) 139, 94

Gallmeyer (bailiff at St. Gall) 93, 139

Gallster (incantation, warlock) 96

Gallus (St. Gall) 135

Galm (noise) 115

Galster, see Gallster

Gambach, see Gandbach

Gambel, Gamble 159, see Gamber

Gamber, Gambert 74, Gampert (acrobat, entertainer) 96

Gambler, Gambolt 159, see Gambel

Gamerman, see Kammerman

Gamertsfelder (field on a ridge) 84

Gamp, see Kamp

Gamper, Gampffer, Gampert 74, see Gamber, Kaempfer

Gams, Gamse (chamois, chamois hunter) 91

Gamstetter (fr Gamsstaedt, chamois place) 122

Gand, Gandel, Gandelman 94 (pebble field) 71, 84

Gandbach (swamp brook) 80, 77

Gandenberg (stony mountain) 71, 68

Gander, Gandermann (swamp dweller) 80

Gangel (huckster) 105

Gangenmeyer (farmer on a stream) 93

Gangler (stream) 77

Gangloff, Ganglof (gait + wolf, cf. Wolfgang) 48

Gangmueller (miller on a stream) 77, 103

Gangolf (St. Gangolf) 135

Ganke 55, Gankel 55 < Janke (Johann) 134

Gann (magic, magician) 96

Gans, Ganss, Gansman (goose, goose herder) 91, 115

Gansberg, Ganzberger (goose mountain) 68, 122

Gansbichler (goose hill) 67

Gansburg (goose castle) 73, 122

Gansel 55, Gaensel (little goose) 91, 115

Ganser, Gansler, Gansner, Gansert 74 (goose raiser) 91, 115

Ganshorn, Gantzhorn (goose field) 84

Ganskop (goose head) 114

Ganten, Gantner (goose raiser) 91, 115

Ganter, Ganther (auctioneer) 96, also see Guenther

Gantzer (goose raiser) 91, 96

Ganz, Gantz, Gantze, Gantzer, Ganzert 74 (whole, complete), see Ganser

Ganzemueller, Gantzenmueller (goose miller) 91, 103

Gaphard 159, Gapehard, Gapehart, see Gebhard

Gapp, see Gabe

Gar (spear) 46

Garaus (Bottoms up!) 117

Garbe, Garben, Garbes (sheaf) 164

Garben, see Gerwin

Garber, Gaerber < Garbrecht, see also Gaerber

Garbrecht (spear + brilliant) 46, 47

Gardenhour 159 (fr Gartenau, garden meadow) 84, 84, 151

Gardenhour 159 (garden digger) 84, 151

Gardner 159, see Gaertner

Garecht, see Garrecht

Garfinkel, Garfinkle 159, Garfuenkel (carbuncle, fr Latin *carbunculus*)

Garg, see Karg

Garhard, Garheart 159, see Gerhard

Garinther, see Kaerntner

Garke 53, 55, Garken < Gerhard

Garlach, see Gerlach

Garling, see Gerling

Garman, Garmann (spear + man) 46, 94

Garmes 53, 164, Garms < Garmann

Garmhausen (Garmann's houses) 65, 122

Garn (yarn, snare, fish or fowl netter) 106, 91

Garner (snarer, fish netter) 91, 96

Garrecht (Quite right!) 117

Garreis, see Garaus

Garrel 53, Garrels 164, Garrelt 74, Garrelmann 94 < Gerhold (spear + loyal) 46, 48, 53

Garrel (place name, swamp) 80, 122

Garst, Garster, see Karst

Garstener, see Gerstner

Gart, Garth, see Geert, Garthe

Gartelmann (gardener) 84, 94

Garten (garden, gardener) 84

Gartenhaus (gardenhouse) 84, 65

Gartenhoff, Garthoff (garden yard) 84, 92

Gartmann (gardener) 84

Gartner, see Gaertner

Garver, see Gerber

Garwin, see Gerwin

Garz, see Geert

Gasel 159, see Gesell

Gasner, see Gass

Gaspar, Gaspars 164, see Caspar

Gass 122, Gasser, Gassert 74, Gassner, Gasmann 94, Gassmann (dweller on a street, shortened form) 65

Gassinger (dweller on a road) 65

Gassel, see Kassel

Gassel, Gasser, Gassler, Gasser, see Gass

Gassenheimer (hamlet on a road) 65, 124

Gassmann, see Gass

Gassmeyer (farmer on the road) 65, 93

Gassner, see Gass

Gast, Gastmann (stranger, guest) 120

Gasteier, Gasteiger (dweller on a steep mountain path) 71

Gastgeber (host, inn keeper) 96

Gastmeyer (newly arrived farmer) 120, 93

Gastorf (village on the high land) 124, 122

Gastreich, Gastrich (hospitable) 115

Gattermann, Gattener (dweller by a rail fence) 84

Gattling, Gatling (kinsman, comrade) 119, 151

Gatz, Gatzke 55 (fr Gatzen 122), see Katz

Gau (district, countryman)

Gaubatz (Slavic place name) 146

Gauch (cuckoo, fool) 115

Gauchenauer (fools' meadow) 84

Gauckler, Gaukler (juggler) 96

Gaudenberger (one who has seen the *Mons Gaudium*), see Freudenberger

Gauer (countryman) 91, 109

Gauf, see Kauf

Gaug, Gauger (gadabout) 115

Gaugle 159, Gaugler, see Gauckler

Gaugh 159, see Gauch

Gaughund (stray dog) 115

Gaul, Gauler (horse, carter) 96

Gaum (gum) 114

Gaum (man) 109

Gauman (country dweller) 91

Gaumer (overseer) 96

Gaus, Gause, Gauss, Gausman 94, Gauslin, Gaussmann, see Gans

Gausebeck (goose creek) 77

Gausepohl (goose pond) 80

Gautz, see Kautz

Gaver 159, see Geber

Gawff 159, see Kauf

Gayer, see Geier

Gayger 159, see Geiger

Gayheart 159, Gayhardt, see Gerhard

Gayle 159, Gayler, Gaylor see Geil, Geiler

Gaylor 159, see Geil

Gayring 159, see Goering

Gazell 159, see Gesell

Gearheart 159, see Gerhard 151

Geartner 159, see Gaertner

Geas, see Giese 151

Geating 159, Geeting, Geedig, see Gueting

Gebaur, Gebauer (peasant) 91

Gebbe 53, Gebberd < Gebhard

Gebeke 53, 55 < Gebhard

Gebel 53, 55 Gebele, Gebelein 55 < Gottfried 53

Gebel 159, see Giebel

Geber, Gebers 164, Gebert 74, Geeber (giver)

Geber 53, Gebers 164, Gebert 74 < Gebhard 53

Gebhard, Gephardt, Gebhart (gift + strong) 46

Gebhauer 159, see Gebauer

Geble 159, see Gebel 151

Gebrecht (gift + bright) 47

Gebwein (gift + friend) 48

Gebwein (Give wine!, taverner) 117

Gecht, Gechter (impetuous person) 115

Geck, Gecke, Geckel 55, Geckler, Geckeler (fop, dandy) 115

Gedance 159 (fr Danzig) 122

Geddoecke 53, 55 < Gottfried

Gedion (OT Gideon) 135

Gedult (patience) 115, 139

Geebel 159, see Gebel

Geeber, see Geber

Geehreng, see Gehring

Geelhaar (yellow haired) 112

Geer, Geers 164, see Gehr

Geerdes 164, Geerdert 74, see Geert

Geerdsen, see Geert

Geerke 53, 55, Geerken (little Gerhard)

Geerling 53, 55 < Gerhard

Geert, Geerts 164, Geertsen 59, Geertke 55 < Gerhard

Gees, Geesman 94, Geesmann, Geesaman 159, see Gieseke

Geesler 159, see Giessler

Geest (dweller on high dry ground) 68

Gefeller (dweller by a waterfall) 77

Geffert < Gebhard

Geffinger < Gebhard

Geffken 53, 55, Gefken < Gebhard

Gefuege (skillful) 115

Gegenbach, see Geigenbach

Gegenwart (presence) 118

Geger, Gegner (opponent, dweller outside of village or across the street) 65

Gehau (forest) 72

Gehauf (Go up!) 116

Gehaut (Go out!) 116

Gehl, Gehle, Gehler, Gehlert 74, Gehlmann 94 (yellow haired) 112

Gehlbach (swamp brook) 80, 77

Gehlharr (yellow haired) 112

Gehlhose (yellow breeches) 112

Gehman 94, Gehmann, Gehner (dweller on a slope) 71

Gehr, Gehres 164, Gehret 74 < Gerhard, Gerwin, Gerbert

Gehrhard, Gehrhardt, see Gerhard

Gehrich 53, Gehrig, Gerick < Gerhard, Gerbrecht, etc.

Gehring, Gehringer, see Goering, Goeringer

Gehrke < Gerhard, Gehbrecht, Gerwin, etc.

Gehrke 53, 55, Gehrken, Gehrlein < Gerhard, Gerbrecht, etc.

Gehrkensmeier (Gehrken's farmer) 93

Gehrman, Gehrmann, Geermann (spear + man) 46, 94

Gehrt, see Geert

Gehse (speer) 46

Geib, Geibe, Geibig (filth) 115

Geidel (braggart, spendthrift) 115

Geidt (greed, desire) 115

Geier (gerfalcon, vulture) 115, see Allgeier

Geierman (falconer) 91, 94

Geiersbach (vulture brook) 77

Geiersbuhler (vulture hill) 67

Geiershofer (vulture farm) 92

Geifuss, see Geilfuss

Geigel, Geiglein 55 (little fiddle, little fiddler) 96

Geigenbach (fiddle brook) 96, 77

Geigenberger (fr Geigelberg 122, fiddle mountain) 96, 68

Geigenmeyer (occupant of the Geigenhof, or farmer on the Geigenbach) 96, 73, 77, 94

Geigenmueller (miller on the Geigenbach) 96, 103, 83

Geiger, Geigert 74 (fiddler) 96

Geigerheim (fiddlers' hamlet) 96, 124

Geigermann (fiddler) 96, 94

Geigmueller, see Geigenmueller

Geil, Geils 164, Geiler, Geilert 74 (lively, wanton) 115

Geil (swamp) 80

Geilenkirchen (swamp church) 80, 122

Geilfuss, Geilfuess (lively foot, lively person) 115

Geilhaar (yellow haired) 112

Geimer (spearpoint + famous) 46, 47

Geis, Geise, Geiss (goat, goatherd) 95

Geisbert (noble scion + brilliant) 47, 47

Geisdoerfer (fr Geisdorf 122, goat village) 124

Geisel, Geisler, Geissler, Geisselmann (hostage) 94

Geisel, Geisler (whip, flagellant) 110

Geiselbrecht (point of spear + illustrious) 46, 47

Geisemeyer (goat farmer) 91, 93, 95

Geisenheimer (fr Geisenheim 122, goat hamlet) 124

Geisenrotter (goat clearing) 126

Geisenstein (goat mountain) 73

Geiser, Geisser (goatherd) 91

Geisfel (goat skin) 106

Geishirt, Geissert, Geisshard (goat herder) 91, 95

Geising, Geisinger (fr Geising) 122

Geisler < Giselher (hostage + army) 46, 46

Geisler (goat raiser) 91

Geismann (goat man) 91

Geismar (swamp pond) 80, 122

Geisreiter (goat clearing) 126

Geisreiter (goat rider, nickname for tailor) 104, 117

Geiss, see Geis

Geissberg (goat mountain) 68

Geissblatt (honeysuckle) 89

Geissbuehl, Geissbuehler (goat hill) 68

Geissel, Geissler, see Geisel, Geisler

Geissendorfer (goat village) 124

Geissheimer (fr Geissheim 122, goat hamlet) 124

Geissinger (fr Geissing) 122

Geissler (flagellant) 110, 122

Geist (spirit) 122, see Geest

Geist (dregs, sediment) 118

Geister (spirits) 118

Geisthardt (spirit + strong) 46

Geistlich (spiritual, clerical) 110

Geistmeyer (goat farmer) 91

Geisweiler (goat hamlet) 127

Geiswinckler (goat forest) 69

Geisz, see Geis

Geit, Geite, Geithe (greed) 115

Geitdorfer (fr Geitdorf 122, goose village) 124

Geiterling (greedy person) 115

Geitz, Geiz, Geize, Geitzer (greed) 115

Geitzmann (greedy man) 115

Gelb, Gelber (yellow, blond) 112

Gelbach (swamp brook) 80, 77, 122

Gelbart (yellow beard) 112

Gelbaugh, see Gelbach

Gelbert, Gelberdt, see Gilbert

Gelbke 55 (little blond) 112

Gelblum (yellow flower) 89

Geldemeister (guild master) 109

Gelder, Geldern, Geldermann 94, Gelderlaender (fr Geldern in the Netherlands) 121

Geldhaeuser (money changer) 65, 96

Geldmacher (goldmaker, alchemist, minter) 96

Geldman, Geldmann (money man) 96, 94

Geldreich, Geldrich (money rich)

Geldschlaeger (minter) 96

Gelerter (scholar, savant) 96

Gelfert < Gelfrat (merry + counsel) 47

Gelfrat (challenge + counsel) 47

Gelhaus (yellow house) 65, see Gellhaus

Gelhose (yellow stockings) 112

Gelinek, see Jellinek

Gelke 53, 55 < Gelmar (wanton, cocky) 115

Geller (sacrifice + army) 46

Geller (town crier) 109

Geller, Gellert 74, Gellermann 94 (yellow haired) 112

Gellermann, see Geldermann

Gellhaus, Gellhausen (guild house) 65

Gellinger (fr Gelling) 122

Gellmann, Gelman, see Geldmann

Gellner, Gelner (goldsmith) 96

Gellwasser (marsh water) 80

Gelpke 55 (marsh brook) 80

Gelriche, Gelricke, see Geldreich

Geltman, see Geldman

Geltner (goldsmith) 96

Geltzer (hog castrator) 96

Gembler, see Gamber

Gemeinbauer (farmer on the common) 91

Gemeiner (private soldier) 107

Gemp, Gempp, Gemper, see Gamper

Gems (chamois) 91, 115

Gemuendt (mouth of stream) 79

Genau (exact) 115, 117

Gencel 159, see Gaensel

Gender (auctioneer) 96

Gender 159, Genderman 94, see Guenther, Guentherman

Gengel, Gengler (huckster) 105

Gengrich (Slavic for Heinrich) 146

Gens (goose) 91, 115

Gensel 55, see Gaensel

Gensheimer, Genshemer (goose hamlet) 124

Gensler (goose raiser) 91

Gensli 55, Genslin, see Gaensel

Genter, Gentermann, see Guenther, Guentherman

Gentsch, Gentzsch, Gentz < Johannes

Genung (Enough!) 117

Genz, Genzler < Johannes

Genzer, see Gensler 151

Georg, George, Georges (St. George) 135

Georgi, son of Georg 142

Gephard, Gephardt, see Gebhard, Gebhardt

Geppel < Gephard 53, 55

Geppert < Gebhard

Gerach, Gerack < Georgius 135

Geradwohl, see Gerathewohl

Gerald (spear + rule) 46, 47

Gerald (spear + loyal) 46, 47

Gerard, see Gehrhard

Gerathewol, Gerathewold (May it turn out well!, guild name) 116

Gerbel < Gerbald (spear + bold) 46, 46

Gerben < Garwin, Gerwin

Gerber, Gerbert 74, Gerbler (tanner) 96

Gerberg (spear mountain) 68

Gerbert, Gerbracht, Gerbrich (spear + brilliant) 46, 47

Gerbig < Gerwig (spear + battle) 46, 46

Gerbrand (spear + sword) 46, 46

Gercke 53, 55, Gereke < Gerhard

Gerd, Gerde 53, Gerdes 164, Gerts, Gerdts, Gerding < Gerhard

Gerecht, Gerechte, Gerichten, Gerichter (righteous, just, skillful) 115

Gereuth (clearing) 126

Gerhard, Gerhards 164, Gerhardt, Gerhart (spear + strong) 46, 46

Gerhing 159, see Gehring

Gerhold, Gerholz 164 (spear + loyal) 46, 48, 52

Gerig 53, Gerich, Gerick, Gericke 55 < Gerhard 53

Gering 53, 55, Geringer < Gerhard or Gerold

Gerisch 53 < Georg, Gerhard

Gerke 53, 55, Gerken, Gerkens 164 < Gerhard, Gerwin, Gerbod, etc.

Gerker 53, 55, Gerkle 159 < Gerhard

Gerlach, Gerlak (spear + play) 46

Gerland < Gernand (spear + brave) 46, 49

Gerlicher, see Gerlach

Gerling 53, 55, Gerlinger < Gerhard, Gerhold, etc.

Gerling, Gerlinger (fr Gerling) 122

Germann, German (spear + man) 46, 94

Germanus (Latin, cousin) 141

Germar, Germer (spear + famous) 46, 47

Germershausen (swamp houses) 80, 65

Germersroth, Germerroth (swamp clearing) 80, 126

Germeyer, Germyer (swamp farmer) 80, 93

Germroth (swamp clearing) 80, 126

Germund (spear + protection) 46, 47

Germuth (spear + disposition) 46, 46

Gern, Gerne, Gerner, Gerners 164, Gerns, Gerndt 74, Gernt, Gernerdt (desirous) 115

Gernand (spear + brave) 46, 56

Gerngross, Gernegross
(ambitious, aggressive) 115

Gernhard, Gernhardt, Gernhart
< Gerner (desirous) 115

Gernot (spear + battle) 46, 46

Gerold, Gerould 159, see Gerhold

Gerolstein (Gerold's mountain)
73, 122

Gerrard 159, see Gerhard

Gerrecht, see Gerecht, Garrecht

Gerring, Gerringer, see Gehring

Gerrsmann (Gerhard's follower)
94

Gersbach (Gerhard's brook) 77,
122

Gersch, Gersh 159, Gerschmann
(barley farmer) 91

Gerschberg, see Gerstenberg

Gerschheimer (barley hamlet)
124

Gerschwiller (barley village) 127

Gersdorf (barley village) 124

Gersh 159, Gershman, see
Gersch

Gershengorn 159, see
Gerstenkorn

Gershman 159, see Gerstman

Gerst, Gersten (barley) 91, 106

Gerstaecker, Gerstacker (barley
field) 84

Gerstbrein (barley porridge) 112

Gerstel 55, Gerstle 159, Gerstler,
Gerstner (barley dealer) 105

Gerstemeyer, Gerstenmeier,
Gerstemeir, Gerstenmeyer
(barley farmer) 91, 93

Gerstenacker (barley field) 84

Gerstenberg, Gerstenberger (fr
Gerstenberg 122, barley
mountain) 91, 68

Gerstenblith (barley blossom) 89

Gerstendoerfer (barley village)
124

Gerstenfeld, Gerstenfield 153
(barley field) 84

Gerstenhaber (barley farmer) 92,
91

Gerstenkorn (barley grain) 91,
106

Gerstenschlaeger (barley
thresher) 96

Gerstman, Gerstmann (barley
dealer) 105, 94

Gerstmeyer, Gerstmyer (barley
farmer) 159

Gerstner (barley dealer or raiser)
105, 91

Gert 53, Gerth, Gerthe, Gertz
164 < Gerhard

Gerteisen (goad) 106

Gertel (switch) 106

Gertelmann, see Gartelmann

Gerthner, Gertner, see Gaertner

Gertler 159, see Guertel

Gertz 53, 164, Gertzmann 94 <
Gerhard

Gerung 53, 55 < Gerold

Gerver, see Gerber

Gervinus (Latin for Gerwin) 141

Gerwart (spear + guardian) 46,
47

Gerwer, see Gerber

Gerwig (spear + battle) 46, 46

Gerwin (spear + friend) 46, 48

Gesche, see Giese

Gescheidt (clever, prudent) 115

Geschke 55 (clever, cunning) 115

Geschwind, Geschwinds 164,
Geshwend (swift) 115

Gesell, Gesele, Geseller
(companion) 119

Geselschap (company) 119

Gesinder (following) 119

Gess, Gesser, Gessler, Gessner,
Gessel, see Gasner

Gessmann, see Gasner

Gestl 55, see Gast

Getrost (confident, optimistic)
115

Gettel, Gettle 159, Gettleman
(kinsman, peasant youth) 119

Gettenberg (swamp mountain) 80, 68

Gettenmueller (miller near the swamp) 80, 103

Getter, Getner, Gettermann (caster, founder) 96

Gettman, Gettmann (caster, founder) 96

Getts 159, Getz, Getze, see Goetz

Getty 159, see Goette

Getz, see Goetz

Getzenberg (foundry mountain) 68

Getzendanner, see Giessendanner

Geuter, Geutert 74, Geutner, see Geit

Gevantmann (mercer) 96

Gevers < Gebhard

Gewand (cloth, mercer) 96

Gewehr (warranter, sponsor) 96, 109

Gewert, see Gebhard

Gewinner (winner) 118

Gewirtz (spice dealer) 105

Gex 164, see Geck

Geyer, see Geier

Geyger, see Geiger

Geyler, see Geiler

Geys, see Geiss

Geyser, see Kaiser

Geysler 159, see Geissler

Gezelle 159, see Gesell

Gfeller, Gefeller (waterfall, steep valley) 77, 76

Gibe 53, Giebe < Gilbert

Gibler 159, see Kuebler, Giebler

Gibrich < Giperich (gift + rule) 47

Gice 159, see Geiss

Gichtel (gout) 114

Gichtel (confession) 118

Gideon (OT name) 135

Giebel, Giebler, Giebeler (skull, head) 118

Giebel (gable) 118

Giebelhaus (gabled house) 65

Giefer 159, see Kieffer

Gieger 159, Giger, see Geiger

Gielbert, see Gilbert

Gier, Gierer (desire) 115, see also Geier

Gierhard, see Gerhard

Giering, see Gehring

Gierke 53, 55 < Gerhard

Gierlach, see Gerlach

Giers, Giersch, see Gerisch, Kirsch

Gies, Giese 53, Gieseke 55, Gieschen, Giesecke, Gieske, Gieseking < Giesebrecht

Giesbert, see Giesebrecht

Giesebrecht (scion, or hostage + brilliant) 47

Giesel 53, Giessel, Giesler, Gieseler < Gieselher (scion or hostage + army) 46

Gieselbrecht (point of sword + bright) 46, 47

Giessbach, Giessbacher (swamp stream) 80, 77

Giesselbrecht, see Gieselbrecht

Giesselmann, see Geisel

Giessendanner (swamp forest) 80, 72

Giesser (founder) 96

Giesshof (swamp farm) 80, 92

Giessler (dweller near a swamp) 80

Giessler (foundryman) 96

Giezendanner, see Giessendanner

Giffert, see Gebhard

Gilbart (scion + battle ax) 46

Gilbert (scion + bright) 47

Gildemeister (guildmaster) 96, 109

Gildhaus, Gildehaus (guildhouse) 65

Gildner (guild member) 109

Gilfert, see Gelfert

Gilg, Gilgen (St. Aegidius) 135
Gilgen (lilly) 89
Gille 53, Giller < Gilbert
Gilljohann (Gilbert-Johann) 118
Gillmann 53, 94 < Aegidius 135
Gilner, see Gildner, Geldner
Gilsdorf (Gilbert's village) 124
Gilsemann 94 (dweller near the
    Gilse) 83
Gilstein (swamp mountain) 80,
    73
Giltner, see Gildner, Gelder
Gimpel, Gimbel, Gimpel
    (bullfinch) 115, see also
    Gumprecht
Ginder 159, see Guenther
Ginrich, Gingrich, Gingerich
    (Slavic for Heinrich) 146
Ginsberg (Guenther's mountain)
    68
Ginsburg (Guenther's castle) 73
Ginter 159, see Guenther
Ginthard (battle + strong) 46, 46
Gintling (belonging to Guenther)
    59
Ginz < Guenther
Gippe (jacket), 96, 106, 112
Girard, see Gerhard
Girbach (vulture brook) 77
Girdner 159, see Gaertner
Girke 53, 55 < Gerlach
Girsch, see Kirsch
Gise 159, see Geiss
Gissel, Gissler < Gieselbrecht
Gisselbrecht, see Gieselbrecht
Gisselbrecht (hostage + bright)
    47
Gisseldanner, Gissentanner, see
    Giessendanner
Gisselman, see Geisel
Gissendanner, Gissentanner, see
    Giessendanner
Gissner, see Giessler
Gist (dregs, sediment), see also
    Geist

Gitting, Gittings 164, Gittinger
    (fr Gitting) 122
Givler, see Kuebler
Glaas, see Glas
Glaatz, see Glatz
Gladbach (swampy brook) 80, 77,
    122
Glade, Gladen (shining) 115
Glade (swamp) 80
Gladfelder, see Glatfelder
Glaenz (brilliance) 115
Glaenzer (shining) 115
Glaeser, Glaesener, Glaesmann,
    Glasman, see Glas
Glahn (dweller on the Glan) 83
Glaiber 159, see Kleber
Glance 159, see Glantz
Glantz, Glanz (brilliance, show
    off) 115
Glaris < St. Hilarius
Glarner (fr Glarus in
    Switzerland) 121
Glas, Glaser, Glaeser (glazier) 96,
    106
Glasbrenner (glass maker) 96
Glasemeyer 93, see Glassmeyer
Glasenap (glass bowl) 96
Glaskopf (glass cup, maker of
    glass cups) 96, 106
Glass, Glasser, Glassler, Glassner
    (glazier) 96, 106
Glassbrenner, Glassmann (glass
    maker) 96
Glasshof (glass factory) 96
Glassmeyer, Glasmeier,
    Glasmyer 159 (manager of the
    glass factory) 96, 93
Glatfelder, Glattfelter, Gladfelder
    (smooth field) 84
Glatfelder (swampy field) 80, 84
Glatt (smooth) 115
Glatthaar (smooth hair) 112
Glatz, Glaz, Glatzer (bald man)
    112
Glaub (faith) 118

Glauber (believer, creditor) 115

Glaubitz (Slavic place name) 146

Glauch, Glaucher (fr Glaucha) 122

Glauer (clever) 115

Glauner (cross-eyed) 113

Glaus, Glauser, see Klaus, Klauser

Glaz, Glazer, see Glatz, Glatzer

Gleich (shapely) 115

Gleichauf (prompt) 115

Gleim (swamp) 80

Gleisbach (shiny brook) 77

Gleissner (hypocrite) 115

Gleit, Gleitsman 94, Gleitsmann, Gleitzmann (mounted guard) 107

Glendemann, Glindemann (fr Glinde 122, swamp) 80

Gleser, see Glaser

Glessner (glazier) 96

Glick, see Glueck

Glicksman, Glicksmann (lucky man) 115, 94

Glickstern, see Glueckstern

Glimph (sport, fun) 115

Glind (fenced area) 84

Glindeman (dweller in a fenced area) 84, 94

Glindeman, Glindemeyer (swamp dweller) 80, see Glendemann

Glitman, see Gleit

Glitsch (spear) 46

Glitzenberg (glittering mountain) 68

Glitzenhirn (bald shiny pate) 114

Glock, Glocke, Glocker, Glockner (bell ringer) 109

Glockengeter (bell caster) 96

Glockmann (bell ringer) 109, 94

Gloecker, Gloeckner, Gloekler, see Glock

Glor < St. Hilarius 135

Gloss, see Glass

Glossbrenner, see Glasbrenner

Gloster, see Kloster

Gloth, see Glatt

Glotz, Gloetzel 55, see Klotz

Gluck (luck) 117, 118

Gluckstern (lucky star) 117

Glueck, Gluck (luck, fortune) 117

Glueckauf (miner's greeting) 116

Glueckhaft (lucky) 115

Glueckselig (blissful) 115

Glug, see Klug 115

Glut, Gluth (fire) 118

Gmeiner (commoner, community leader, private soldier) 107

Gmeinwieser (user of common pasture) 84

Gnade (mercy, grace) 138, 116

Gnaedig (gracious) 115, 138

Gnann, Knann (cousin, namesake) 119

Gnau, see Genau

Gnuesleben (life of enjoyment) 115, see Sanftleben

Gob 53 < Jacob 135

Gobel, Gobbel, see Goebel

Gobrecht < Godebrecht (god + bright) 47

Gochenauer, Gochenour 159, Gochnauer (fools' meadow) 84

Gockeler, see Gaucer

God, Godt, see Gott

Gode, Goday 159 (good) 115, 43, 157

Godebrecht (god + bright) 47

Godehard < Gotthard

Godeluck (Good luck!) 117

Godeschalk, see Gottschalk

Godewald (god + rule) 48, 46, see Gottwald

Godfried, Godfrey 153, see Gottfried

Godlove 153, see Gottlieb

Godman 153, see Gottmann, Gutmann

Godschalk, Godschall, Godschalks 164, see Gottschalk

Godt, see Gott

Goebel 53, 55, Goebbel, Goebels 164, Goebeler, Goebling 55 < Godebrecht

Goecke 53, 55, Goeckeler < Gottfried

Goedeke 53, 55, Goedike < Gottfried

Goedhart, see Gotthardt

Goegel, Goegell, Goegelmann, Goeggelmann (juggler, jokester) 96

Goehke 53, 55 < Gerhard

Goehl, Goehler, Goehlert 74 (swamp dweller) 80

Goehmann (dweller on the Goe) 83

Goehre (swamp dweller) 80, see also Goehring

Goehring 53, 55, Goehringer < Gerhard

Goeldener, Goeller, Goellner, Goellman (gold miner) 96

Goeller, Goellner, see Gellner

Goellnitz (Slavic place name 122) 146

Goeltner, see Goldener

Goeltz (animal castrator) 96

Goenner, Goeners 164 (patron) 118

Goepel, Goepell, see Goebel

Goepfert < see Gebhard

Goeppinger (fr Goeppingen) 122

Goeppner (jacket maker) 96

Goerg, Goergen, Goerges, see Georg

Goering, Goerung 53, 55 < Gerhard

Goerner, see Gerner

Goerres < St. Gregorius 135

Goertler, see Guertler

Goertz 53, 164 < Gerhard

Goertzhain (Gerhard's grove) 72

Goesch, Goscher < Gottschalk

Goessler, see Gessler

Goessling (gosling) 91, 115

Goessling (fr Goesslingen) 122

Goesswein, see Gooswein

Goetche (barrel maker) 96

Goetel, Goethals 164, 159, see Goettel

Goethe < godfather 119

Goethe, see Goedeke

Goetsch 53, Goetsche, Goetschi < Gottfried

Goetschalk, see Gottschalk

Goetschy, see Goetz

Goette (baptized child) 119

Goettel 53, 55, Goettig, Goethler, Goetting, Goettling 55 < Gottfried, Gotthard

Goetz 53, Goetze, Goettschi < Gottfried, etc.

Goetzel 53, 55, Goetzelman, Goetzelmann < Gottfried

Goetzendanner, see Giessendanner

Goetzendorf (Gottfried's village) 124, 122

Goetzinger (fr Goetzing) 122

Goetzke 53, 55 < Gottfried

Gogel (relaxed, merry) 115

Gohde 53 < Gottfried

Gohl (Slavic for bald), 146, see also Kohl

Gohn, see Kohn

Gohr, Gohrmann 94 (fr Gohr) 122, see Gormann

Gohr (swamp) 80

Gohres < St. Gregory

Gohring, see Goering

Gohs, Gohse, Gohsman 94, see Gans

Gold, Golde, Golden (gold, goldsmith) 96

Goldacker (gold field) 84

Goldammer, see Goldhammer

Goldbach, Goldbeck, Goldbeker (fr Goldbach 122, gold brook) 77

Goldband (gold band) 106

Goldbaum (gold tree) 89, 148

Goldberg 122, Goldenberg, Goldbergh, Goldberger, Goldeberger (gold mountain) 148

Goldblatt (gold leaf, goldsmith) 96

Goldblum, Goldbloom (gold flower) 89, 148

Goldcamp (gold field) 84

Goldeisen (gold iron) 148

Goldenbaum, see Goldbaum

Goldenberg, see Goldberg

Goldenblum, see Goldblum

Goldencrown 153, see Goldenkron

Goldenstein, see Goldstein

Golder, Golderman 94 (goldsmith) 96

Goldfarb (gold color) 148

Goldfeder, Goldfedder (gold feather) 148

Goldfine 159, (gold fine) 148, 159

Goldfinger (gold finger, ring maker) 96

Goldfuss (gold foot) 148, 117

Goldgeier (golden vulture, house name) 62, 149

Goldhaber (gold possessor) 117

Goldhammer (yellowhammer, house name) 62, 149

Goldhammer (yellow hammer) 115

Goldhar (golden hair) 112

Goldhirsch (golden stag, housename) 62, 149

Goldhofer (proprietor of the Goldhof, gold farm) 92

Goldhorn (gold horn, house name) 62

Goldklang (sound of money) 117

Goldman, Goldmann (gold man, goldsmith) 96, 94, 117

Goldmeyer, Goldmeier (occupant of the Goldhof) 93, 94

Goldner (gold worker) 96

Goldreich, Goldrich (rich in gold) 117

Goldschlager (goldsmith) 96

Goldschmidt, Goldschmitt (goldsmith) 96

Goldstad (gold city) 122

Goldstein (gold stone, topas, jeweler) 73, 122

Goldstern (gold star, house name) 62, 149

Goldstick (gold piece) 159

Goldstrom (gold stream) 77

Goldvogel (golden bird) 62, 117

Goldwasser, Goldwater 153 (Danzig cognac) 106

Goldwein, Goldwine 159, Goldwyn (gold friend) 48

Goll (bullfinch, fool) 115

Goller (collar) 106

Gollmenz (fr *Kalmincz*, Slavic place name) 146

Gollner, see Goldner, Gellner

Gollnitz (fr Golnitza 122, Slavic place name) 146

Gollstadt, see Goldstad

Golltermann, Goltermann (quilt maker) 96, 94

Golltermann 94, (fr Goltern) 122

Golt, see Gold

Goltze, Golz (fr Goltzen 122, Slavic place name) 146

Gombert, see Gumbert

Gommel 53, 55 < Gumbert

Gompf, see Kampf, also Gump

Gompertz 164, Gomprecht, see Gundbrecht

Gonce 159, see Gans

Gonder 159, Gonderman, see Guenther, Guenthermann

Gonder, see Gander

Gondorf (pre-Germanic place name) 122

Gongloff 159, see Gangloff

Gonnerman 159, see Guentherman

Gonsman 159, see Gans, Gansman

Gonter 159, Gontert, see Gunther

Gontrum 159, see Guntram

Good ..., see Gut...

Goodbrood 153 (good bread, baker) 96

Goodchild, see Gottschalk

Goodhard 153, see Gotthard

Goodknecht, Goodknight 153, see Gutknecht

Goodman 153, see Gutmann

Goodmuth 153, see Guthmuth

Goodnight 153, see Gutnacht

Goodyear 153, 162, see Gutjahr

Goontz 159, see Kuntz

Goos (goose) 91

Gooswein, Gautawin (Goth + friend) 119

Gorenberg (bog mountain) 80

Goring 159, see Goering

Gorman, Gormann (dweller near a bog) 80

Gorn 159, see Korn

Gorr 53 < Gregorius 135

Gorth, see Gurth

Gortler, see Guertel

Goschen (OT Goshen) 135

Gosdorfer (fr Gosdorf, goose village) 124, 122

Gosdorfer (fr village on the Gose) 83

Gosmann, see Goss

Gosner (goose raiser or dealer) 91, 105

Goss, Gossmann (Goth) 120

Gosse, Gossen, Gosser (drainage ditch) 81

Gossler, Gosseler (fr Goslar, dirty water) 122

Gossweiler (goose village, swamp village) 127

Gosswein (Goth + friend) 121, 48, 119

Got ..., see Gott

Gotcher 159, see Goettcher

Gotfried, see Gottfried

Gothe, Gothen (place name) 122

Gotlib 159, see Gottlieb

Gotsch, see Gottfried, Gottschalk

Gotschall, Gotshall 159, see Gottschalk

Gott, Gotte (God, usually fr Gottfried, etc., or actor in miracle play) 111

Gottbehuet (God forbid!) 117

Gottberg (swamp mountain) 68, 80, 122

Gottdiener (God's servant) 140

Gottemoeller (monastery miller) 139

Gotter 53 < Gottfried

Gottesfeld, Gottfeld (God's field, glebe land) 84, 139

Gottesman (convent or monastery worker) 139, 94

Gottfried (God + peace) 138, 140

Gotthard (god + strong) 46, 46

Gottheimer (God hamlet) 124

Gotthelf, Godhelf (God + help) 140

Gotthold (dear to God, god + rule) 140

Gottleben (life in God) 140

Gottleben (swamp village) 80, 127

Gottlieb, Gottliebs 164, Gottleib 159 (God + love) 140

Gottmann (man of God, monastery worker) 139, 140, 94

Gottschalck, Gottschalk, Gottschall, Gottsalk 159 (God + servant) 140

Gottsegen, Gottsagen 159 (divine blessing) 140

Gottskind (child of God) 140

Gottsmann, Gottesmann (God's man, vassal or employee of a monastery) 140, 139, 94

Gottstein, see Goldstein

Gottwald, Gottwalt, Gotwalt, Gottwalts 164, Gottwals (God + rule) 140

Gotz 53, Gotze, Gotzen < Gottfried

Gotzmann (God's man, clergyman) 110

Gouchenauer, Gouchenour 159, Gouchnour (fools' meadow) 84

Goucher 159 (dweller on a meadow) 84

Goucker 159, see Gauger

Goughenour 159, see Gauchenauer

Gouldman 159, see Goldmann

Gouse 159, see Gauss

Graaf, see Graf

Graas, see Grass

Grab, Grabe, Grabs 164, Graben (grave, grave digger) 96

Grabau (grave meadow) 84, 122

Grabb, Grabbe (grabber, seizer), see Grab

Grabel (rivulet) 79

Grabeman (grave digger) 96

Graben (ravine) 76

Grabenheimer (ravine hamlet) 124

Grabenkamp (grave yard) 84

Grabenstein (gravestone) 73, see Graffenstein

Graber (engraver) 96

Graber, see Graeber

Grabill 159, see Kraehbuehl

Grable 159, see Kraebuehl

Grabmann (dweller near a ditch) 80, 94

Grabner (dweller near a ditch) 80

Grad (dextrous, skillful) 115

Graebe, Graeber, Graebner, Graebener (grave digger) 96

Graef, Graefe, Graeff, Graeffe, see Graf

Graefinstern 159 (the count's star) 109

Graeper (maker of earthen pots) 96

Graeser, see Graser

Graeul, Grauel (atrocity) 115

Graf, Graff, Graffe, Graef, Grave, Groff (count) 109

Graffenperger (fr Grafenberg, count's mountain) 68, 122

Graffenried (count's marsh) 81, 122

Graffenstein (count's mountain) 73

Graffmann (count's man) 94, 109

Grafstein, see Graffenstein, Grabstein

Graft, see Kraft

Grahl, Grahls 164 (chalice) 106

Grahmann (graybeard) 112

Grahn, Grahne, see Kran

Graim, see Greim

Grall, see Grahl

Gram, Gramm, Gramer, Grammer, see Kraemer

Graman, Gramann, Grammann, see Graumann

Gramberg (fr Grambergen, muddywater mountain) 68, 122

Gramm, Grams 164 (angry), see Gram

Gramueller (gray miller) 103

Grandadam (big Adam) 113, 135

Grander, Grandner, Grandfield 153, see Grantner

Grandt (trough) 122, see Grant

Graniwette, Granwetter (juniper tree) 89

Grannemann (dweller near the junipers) 89, 94

Granroth (clearing in the juniper trees) 89, 126

Grans (beak) 114

Grant, Grantner (gravel, pebbles) 118

Grantfeld, Grandfield 159 (gravel field) 84

Grantmeyer, Grantmire 159,
Grantmyer 159 (fr the
Granthoff, pebble farm) 93
Grantner (dweller on gravel)
Grantzau (gravel meadow) 84
Granz, see Grant, Krantz
Grap, see Grab
Gras, see Grass
Grasberger (grass mountain) 68
Graser (official mower) 95, 109
Grashof (grass farm) 92
Grasmaeder (grass mower) 95
Grasmann (grass mower) 95
Grasmeher (grass mower) 95
Grasmick, Grasmueck (hedge
sparrow) 115, 117
Grass, Grasse, Grasser,
Grassmann (grass, meadow
guard) 96, 95, 109
Grassau (grass meadow, meadow
guard) 84, 122
Grassman, see Grass
Grassmick, see Grasmick
Grat (ridge) 68
Gratewohl, see Gerathewol
Gratz, Gratze (fr Graetz, Slavic
for castle) 122, 146
Gratz 53 < Pancratius 135
Grau, Graue, Grauer, Graumann
94 (graybeard) 112
Graubach (gray brook) 78
Graubart (graybeard) 112
Graubuenden (the Engadin in
Switzerland) 121
Grauel, Graull 159, see Graeul
Graulich, Grauling (dreadful) 115
Graumann, see Grau
Grauper (barley peeler) 96
Graus (gray) 112, see also Kraus
Grausam (cruel) 115
Graustein (graystone) 73
Grave, 159, Graves, 164, see Graf
Gravenhorst (the count's grove)
109
Graver, see Graeber

Grawber 159, see Graeber
Grawe, see Graf
Graybach 159, see Graubach
Graybill 159, Graybeal 159, see
Kraehbuehl
Grayligh 159, see Greulich
Grayning 159, see Groening
Greanawald 159, Greenawalt,
Greenwalt, Greanalt, see
Gruenwald
Greathouse 153, see Grothaus
Greaver 159, see Graeber
Greb, Grebe, Greber, Grebner
(official of a free community)
109
Grebill, Grebuehl 159, see
Kraehbuehl
Greef, see Graf
Green ..., Greene ..., see Gruen
..., Gruene
Greenbaum 159, Greenebaum,
see Gruenbaum
Greenbeck 159, see Gruenbeck
Greenberg 159, see Gruenberg
Greenblat 159, Greenblatt, see
Gruenblatt
Greenblum 159, see Gruenblum
Greenfeig 159, (green fig) 89
Greenfeld 159, Greenfelder, see
Gruenfeld, Gruenfelder
Greenhaus 159, see Gruenhaus
Greenholtz 159, see Gruenholtz
Greenhut 159, see Gruenhut
Greening 159, see Gruening
Greenspan 159, Greenspon, see
Gruenspan
Greenstein 159, see Gruenstein
Greenwald 159, see Gruenewald
Greesman 159, see Kressman
Grefe, see Graf
Grefenkamp (swamp field) 80, 84
Greger, Gregerman 94, Gregorius
(St. Gregory), name of a pope
134
Greider, see Kreider

Greif, Greiff (griffin, house name) 62

Greifenhagen (griffin hedge) 124, 122

Greifenstein, Greyfenstein (fr Greifenstein, griffin castle) 73, 122

Greifzu (Grab it!, Help yourself!) 116

Greil, see Greul

Greilsamer, fr Crailsheim

Greim, Greims 164 (helmet, mask) 46, 112

Grein, Greiner (quarreler, complainer) 115

Greip, see Greif

Greis, Greisel 55, Greiser, Greisman 94 (graybeard) 112

Greisler, see Kreisel

Grell, Grelle, Greller (shrill, angry) 115

Grellenschmidt (spear smith) 108

Grempel, Grempler (retailer) 105

Grendelmeyer (farmer at the swamp) 80, 93

Grenier 144, see Greiner

Grentzel, Grenzel, Grentzer, Grenzer (dweller on a frontier) 146

Greschke < St. Gregorius 135

Gresemeyer, see Gress

Greser, Gresser, see Grass

Gress, Gressler, Gressmeyer, see Grass

Gressmann, see Grass, Kressmann

Gret (bog) 80

Grett, Gretter (son of Margaretha) 60

Gretz, see Gratz

Greubler, see Griebel

Greul, Greuel, see Graeul

Greulich (frightful) 115

Greuth, Greuther (dweller in a clearing) 126

Greutz, Greutzer, Greutner, see Kreutz, Kreutzer

Greve, Greven (swamp) 80, see Graf

Grevenkampen (swamp fields) 80, see Grafenkamp

Grewe, see Graf

Greybill, see Kraehbuehl

Greyder 159, see Kreider

Greyerbuehl, see Kraehbuehl

Grice 159, see Greis, Kreis

Grider 159, see Kreider, Kraeuter

Grieb, Griebe (greaves) 112

Griebel, Griebner (dweller in a hollow) 76, see Gruber

Griebler, see Gruebler

Grief, Griefe, see Greif

Grieg, Grieger, see Krieger, also < Gregorius

Griem, Grieme (fr Griemen) 122, 108

Griem (mask, helmet) 46, 108

Griener 159, see Greiner

Griep, see Greif

Griepenkerl (Grab the rascal!) 116, 117

Griepentrog (Grab the trough!) 116, 117

Gries (gravel, sandy bank) 118

Griesacker (gravel field) 84

Griesammer, Griesamer, Griesemer, Grieshammer (fr Griesheim 122, gravel hamlet) 124

Griesbach (gravel brook) 77, 122

Griesbaum < Kriesbaum (cherry tree) 89

Griesbaum (gravel tree) 89

Griesbeck (gravel brook) 77

Griese, see Greis

Grieshaber (rough-ground oats) 112

Griesheim (gravel hamlet) 124, 122

Grieshoff (gravel farm) 92, 122

Griesing, Griesinger (fr
    Griesingen) 122
Griesmar (gravel swamp) 80
Griesmeyer, Griesmyer 159 (fr
    the Grieshof, gravel farm) 93
Griess, Griesse, Griessler,
    Griessmer (dweller on sandy
    soil) 118
Griessmann, see Griesmeyer
Grievogel (griffin) 62
Griffe (marsh ditch) 122
Gril, Grill (cricket, whimsical
    person) 115
Grillenberg 122, Grillenberger
    (cricket mountain) 68
Grim, Grimm, Grimme (grim)
    115
Grimbacher 122, see
    Grumbacher
Grime 159, see Greim, Grimm
Grimké 55 (little Grimm) 157
Grimmel, see Krimmel
Grimmelman (crooked man) 113
Grimmiger (fierce) 115
Grimpe (gudgeon, fisherman) 91
Grinberg 159, Grinblatt, see
    Gruenberg, Gruenblatt
Grindel 122, Grindler,
    Grindlinger (swamp dweller)
    80
Grindelwald (forest in
    Switzerland) 72
Grindle 159, see Grindel
Griner 159, see Greiner
Grinspun 159, see Gruenspan
Gripinkerl, see Griepenkerl
Gripp, see Griepp
Grisbach, see Griesbach
Grise 159, see Greis
Grist, see Christ
Gritz, Gritzner (grist maker) 96
Grob, Grobb, Grobe (crude) 115
Grob, Grober (swamp dweller) 80
Grobbacher, Grobbaker (swamp
    brook) 80, 77

Grobecker (rye bread baker) 96
Grobleben (swampwater
    settlement) 80, 122
Groce, see Gross
Groegger 53 < Gregorius 135
Groen, Groene, Groener,
    Groenest (green)
Groenewald, see Gruenewald
Groenheim (green hamlet) 124
Groenig, Groening, Groeninger
    (fr Groeningen) 122
Groening (yellow hammer) 115
Groenthal (green valley) 76
Groenwood 153, see Gruenewald
Groeschel (small silver coin) 117
Groesser (larger) 113
Groessinger (fr Grossingen) 122
Groethausen, see Grosshaus
Groff, Groffe (crude, rough) 115,
    see also Graf
Groft, see Groff
Groh, Grohe (gray) 112
Grohmann (graybeard) 112
Grohn (green) 112
Grohskopf, see Grosskopf
Grojan (gray Johnny) 113
Groll (anger) 115
Groll, Grollman 94 (grassy
    marsh) 80
Groller (sulker) 115
Gromann (graybeard) 112, 94
Grombein 159, see Krummbein
Gron, see Gruen
Gronau, Gronaw 159 (green
    meadow) 84, 122
Gronberg, see Gruenberg
Grondt, see Grund
Grone, see Krone
Groneck, see Kroneck, Grueneck
Gronemeyer (dweller on the
    Gronhoff) 93
Gronewold (green wood) 72
Gronhaeuser (occupant of a green
    house) 65
Gronhagen (green hedge, green
    enclosure) 124

Gronheim (green hamlet) 124
Gronhoff (green farm) 92, 122
Gronholz (green wood) 72
Groninger (yellow hammer) 115
Gronloh (green forest) 71
Gronweg (green path) 65
Grooman, see Grohman
Groon (swamp) 80, see Gruen
Groos, see Gross
Groote 39, see Gross
Groover 159, see Gruber
Gropp, Groppe, see Grob
Grosbusch (large bush) 72
Grosch, Groschel (penny) 117
Groscup 159, see Grosskopf
Grosfeld, Grosfield 153, see
    Grossfeld, Grossfield
Grosh 159, see Grosch
Grosholtz (big forest) 72
Grosmueck, see Grasmick
Grosnickle 159, see Grossnickel
Gross, Grosse, Gros, Grose,
    Grosz, Groos (large) 113
Grossarth (grandeur) 115
Grossbach (large brook) 77
Grossbart (big beard) 112
Grossberg (big mountain) 68
Grossblat, Grossblatt (large leaf)
    89
Grosscup 159, see Grosskopf
Grossenaker (large field) 84
Grossfeld, Grossfield 153 (large
    field)
Grossgebauer (big farmer) 91
Grossgeorg (big George) 113
Grosshandler (wholesaler) 105
Grosshans (Big Johnny) 113
Grosshart, Grosshard (large
    forest) 72
Grosshaupt (bighead) 114
Grosshaus, Grosshauser (fr
    Grosshausen 122, large house)
    65
Grosskopf (bighead) 114

Grosslicht (big light, big clearing)
    126
Grossman, Grossman (big + man)
    113, 94
Grossnickel, Grossnickle 159 (Big
    Nicholas, Nicholas the elder)
    113
Grossweiler, Grosswiler (fr
    Grossweil 122, large hamlet)
    127
Grosz, see Gross
Grote, Groth, Grothe, Grotte, see
    Gross
Grotegut (large estate) 92
Grotendick, Grotendiek (big dike)
    82
Grotewohl, see Gerathewohl
Groteyahn 159, see Grotjan
Grothaus, Grothhaus, Grothusen
    (large house) 65
Grotheim (large hamlet) 124
Grothof (large farm) 92
Grothman, see Grossman
Grotjan (Big John, John the
    elder) 113
Grotkop (big head) 114
Grousaam 159, see Grausam
Grove 159, see Grob, Grab
Grovejan (course John) 115
Grovenstein 159, see
    Graffenstein
Grover 159, Groover, see Gruber
Grub, Grube (hollow, pit,
    mountain cove) 76
Grube (pitfall, bear trap) 91
Grubel, see Gruebel
Grubenhoff (farm in a hollow) 76,
    92
Gruber, Grubert 74 (dweller in a
    Grube or hollow) 76
Grubmeyer (farmer in the dell)
    76, 93
Grueber, Gruebel, Gruebler
    (brooder) 115, see Gruber
Gruel 159, see Greul

Gruen, Gruene, Gruener (green) 112

Gruenast (green branch) 89

Gruenau (green meadow) 84

Gruenbacker 159 (green brook) 77

Gruenbaum (green tree) 89

Gruenbeck (green brook) 77

Gruenberg, Gruenberger (green mountain) 68, 112

Gruenblatt, Greenblat (green blade, leaf) 89

Gruenburg (green castle) 73

Gruendel, Gruendl (swamp) 80

Gruendelberger (swamp mountain) 80, 68

Gruender (founder), see Grund

Gruender, Gruendler (valley dweller) 76

Gruendling (kind of fish, fisherman) 91, 96

Gruene, Gruener, Gruenert 74 (green) 112

Grueneck, Grueneckle (greenfield) 84

Grueneklee (green clover) 89

Gruenewald 122, Gruenwalt (green forest) 72

Gruener, see Grueninger

Gruenfeld (green field) 84, 122

Gruenholt (green wood) 72

Gruenhut (green hat, housename) 112, 62

Grueninger (yellow hammer) 115

Grueninger (fr Grueningen) 122

Gruenspan (green chip, verdigris)

Gruenstein (green mountain) 73, 122

Gruenthal (green valley) 76, 122

Gruenwald 122, see Gruenewald

Gruenzweig (green + twig, host's sign) 63

Gruess (greetings) 116

Gruesser (greeter, blower of hunting horn) 91

Gruetter (fr Gruett) 122

Gruetzner (grits grinder, dealer) 96, 106

Gruhl (place name) 122

Grumbach 122, Grumbacher (swamp brook) 84, 77, see Krumbach

Grumbine 159, Grumbein, Grumbine 159 (crooked leg) 114

Grumm, see Krumm

Grunau (green meadow) 84, 122

Grunbaum 159, see Gruenbaum

Grunberg 159 (green mountain) 68

Grunburg (green castle) 73

Grund, Grunder (bottom, valley) 76

Grundherr (landlord)

Grundlach (valley lake) 76, 80

Grundman, Grundmann (valley dweller) 76

Grundmueller (valley miller) 76, 103

Grundner, see Grundmann

Gruner, Grunert 74, see Gruener, Gruenert

Grunewald 122, Grunwald, see Gruenewald

Grunsfeld, see Gruenfeld

Gruntal, see Gruenthal

Gruntman, see Grundman

Grupe, Grupp (grouper fisherman) 115

Grupenhoff, see Grubenhoff

Gruse 159, see Krause

Gruss, Grusz, see Gruesse

Gruve, Gruver, see Grube, Groover

Gruver, see Gruber

Gruylich 159, see Greulich

Gryder 159, see Kreider

Gryner 159, see Greiner

Grys, see Greis

Gschwandel, Gschwantner (dweller in a clearing) 126

Gschwind (quick) 115
Gschrey (shouter, yeller) 115
Gschwindt (swift, fast) 115
Gsell, see Gesell
Gubler (ridge dweller) 68
Guckel (rooster) 115, 91
Guckenberger, Guckelsberger
  (rooster mountain) 68
Gucker, Guckert (lookout) 74
Gude (swamp) 80, see Gut
Gudekunst, see Gutkunst
Gudeman, see Gutman
Guderian, Guder Jan (Good
  John) 144
Gudermuth, see Gutermuth
Gudikunst, see Gutkunst
Guedemann, Guedermann, see
  Gutmann
Guelberth, see Gilbert
Gueldenpfennig (golden penny)
  117
Gueldner (gilder) 117
Guelich, Guellich (Juelich,
  principality on the Rhine) 121
Guelther (debtor)
Guembel, Gumbold < Gundbald
  (battle + bold) 46, 47
Guempel, see Gimpel
Guendel < Gundram, Gundhart,
  Gundolf, etc.
Guendelach, see Gundlach
Guender, see Guenther
Guengerich, see Gingrich
Guenst (favor) 117
Guenter, Guentert 74, see
  Guenther
Guenterberg (Guenther's
  mountain) 68
Guenther (battle + army) 46, 46
Guentherman (follower of
  Gunther) 94
Guenz 53, Guentzer, Guntzel 55,
  Guenzler, see Guenther
Guenzburg (Guenther's castle) 73
Guering, see Goering

Guertel, Guertler, Guertner (belt
  maker) 106
Guertelmeyer (proprietor of the
  Guertelhof) 92
Guess 159, see Gess
Guetemann, see Gutmann
Gueth, Guethe, Guether, see Gut
Gueting (man of substance,
  dweller on an estate) 92
Gugel, Gugle 159 (cowl wearer or
  maker, fr Latin *cuculla*) 112,
  96, 106, see Kugel
Guggenbuehler (fr Guggenbuehl
  122, swamp hill or cuckoo hill)
  67
Guggenheim (swamp hamlet or
  cuckoo hamlet) 124
Gugler (cowl maker or wearer, fr
  Latin *cuculla*) 96, 110, 112, see
  Kogler
Guhl, Guhler (fr Guhlen) 122, see
  Kuhl
Guinter 159, Guinther, see
  Guenther
Gulde, Gulden (guilder) 117
Guldenfuss, see Goldfuss
Gulich, Gulick, see Guelich
Gull (swamp dweller) 80
Gullberg (swamp mountain) 80,
  68
Gumbert, Gummert, see
  Gundbrecht
Gump, see Gundbrecht
Gumpel < Gundbold (battle +
  brave) 46, 46
Gumpelman (acrobat) 96
Gumpert, see Gumbert
Gumpost (sauerkraut) 112
Gundacker < Gundwaker (battle
  + brave) 46
Gundbrecht (battle + bright) 46,
  47
Gundel 53, 55 < Gundolf,
  Gundrum, etc.
Gundelach, see Gundlach

Gundelfinger (fr Gundelfingen)
122, or < Gundolf
Gunder, see Gunther
Gunderberger (Gunther's
mountain) 68
Gunderdorf, Gundersdorf,
Gunderstorff (Gunther's
village) 124
Gunderman, see Guentherman
Gundersheimer (Gunther's
hamlet) 124
Gundert, see Gundhart
Gundhart (battle + strong) 46, 46
Gundlach (battle + play) 46
Gundlach (stagnant pond) 80
Gundolf (battle + wolf) 46, 48
Gundrum, see Guntram
Gunkel, Gunkle 159,
Gunkelmann, see Kunkel
Gunn 159, see Kuhn
Gunselman 159, see Kuntzelman
Gunst (favor) 118
Gunter, see Gunther
Guntermann 94 (follower of
Guenther) 94, 119
Gunteroth (Gunther's clearing)
126
Gunther (battle + army) 46, 49
Guntram (battle + raven) 46, 48
Guntrum, see Guntram
Guntzel 53, 55 < Gunther
Guntzenhauser (fr
Gunzenhausen 122,
Guenther's houses) 65
Gunzelman, see Kuntzelman
Gunzenheimer (fr Gunzenheim
122, Guenther's hamlet) 124
Gurth (girth, girdel) 106
Gurtner (girth maker) 96
Gurts, see Kurtz
Guss, Gusman 94, Gussmann
(founder, caster) 96
Gusstein (sink) 73
Gust, Gustl 55 < Augustus 141
Gustav < Swedish, Gustaf (for
Gustavus Adolphus)

Guster, see Kuster
Gut, Gutt, Guth, Gute (good,
property, estate) 92
Gutbier (good beer, brewer) 96
Gutbrodt (good bread, baker) 96
Gutekunst (good skill) 115
Gutenberg (good mountain) 68
Gutenbrunner (fr Gutenbrunnen
122, good fountain) 79
Gutenkunst (good art) 96
Gutenschwager (good in-law,
good kinsman) 119
Gutensohn (Guda's son) 60
Gutermann (good man) 115, 94
Gutermuth (good disposition) 115
Gutfleisch (good meat, butcher)
96
Gutfreund (good friend) 119
Gutgesell (good fellow) 119
Guth, see Gut
Guthaber (estate owner) 92
Guthart, Guthardt, see Gotthard
Gutheim (estate hamlet) 92, 123
Guthhard, Guthardt (good +
strong) 46
Guthman, see Gutmann
Gutjahr (New Year's Day) 143
Gutke 55 (small estate) 92
Gutkind (good child) 115
Gutknecht, Gutnecht 159
(worker on an estate) 92, 96
Gutkunst, Gutekunst (good skill)
115
Gutmann, Guthman, Gutman,
Gutzler (good man, man
owning an estate) 92, 138
Gutschall, Gutschke, see
Gottschalk
Gutschmidt (smith on an estate)
106
Guttenberger, see Gutenberg
Guttentag (Good day!) 117
Guttmann, see Gutmann
Gutwald, see Gottwald
Gutwasser (good water) 118

Gutwein (good wine, taverner) 96
Gutwillig (affable) 115
Gutwirt, Gutwirth (good host) 96
Gutzeit (Good times!) 117
Gutzel, see Gut
Guyer, see Geier
Gwinner (winner) 118
Gwirtzman, see Gewirtz
Gyger, see Geiger
Gyser, see Kaiser, Geiser
Gysler, see Geisel

H

Haab, see Hab
Haacke, see Hacke
Haacker (retailer) 105
Haaf, see Haff
Haag, Haage, Haagen, Haager,
    see Hag, Hager
Haak, Haake, Haackel (fr Haak
    122, hook) 106
Haakmann (user of a hook) 106
Haan, see Hahn
Haanecam (cock's comb) 84
Haar, Haare, Haars 164 (hair)
    112
Haar (flax) 91, 106
Haarbleicher (flax bleacher) 96
Haardt, see Hardt
Haarer (flax dealer) 96, 105
Haarhaus (fr Haarhausen 122,
    marsh house) 80, 65
Haarmann (marsh dweller 80),
    see also Hermann
Haarmeyer (marsh farmer) 80,
    93
Haart, see Hart
Haartz, see Hartz
Haas, Haase (fr Haas 122), see
    Hase
Haaseler, see Hassler
Haasmann, see Hasmann
Hab (possessions) 118
Habacher, Habacker (fr Halbach)
    122

Habbeck, Habbecker (hawker) 91
Habbecker (fr Habbecke, swamp)
    122
Habben < Hadebert (battle +
    bright) 53, 46, 47
Habber, Habberle (oat grower) 91
Habecker, Habegger, see
    Habbeck
Habedank (Many thanks!) 117
Habeger, Habegger, see Habbek
Habel (Slavic for St. Gall) 146
Habenicht (Have not! 116, or I
    have not 117)
Haber, Habers 164, Habert 74
    (oats, oat dealer) 105
Haberacker (oatfield) 84
Haberberger (oat mountain) 68
Haberbosch (oat bush) 72
Habercam, see Haberkam
Haberecht (Be right!, Know-it-
    all) 116
Haberer (oat dealer) 105
Habergans (oat goose) 115
Haberger (fr Haberg) 122
Haberkam, Haberkamp (oat
    field) 84
Haberkorn (oat grain) 106
Haberl, Haberle, Haberly 159
    (oat farmer) 91
Haberland, Haberlander
    (oatland) 122
Haberling 122, see Haberl
Haberloh (oat forest) 72
Habermaas (oat measure) 106
Habermann (oat dealer) 105
Habermayer (oat farmer) 91
Habermehl (oat meal) 106, 112
Habersack (oat sack) 118
Habersat (newly sowed oatfield)
    84
Habersieck (oat fen) 80
Haberstad (oat landing) 83
Haberstamm (oat stalk, skinny)
    114
Haberstich (oat hill) 67

Haberstock (oat stalk, skinny) 114

Haberstroh (oat straw) 106

Habich, Habicht, Hebicht (hawk, hawker) 115, 91, 96

Habight 159, see Habich

Habighurst (hawk hurst) 72

Habluetzel, Habluezel (Have little!, or I have little) 116, 117

Habmann, see Habermann

Hach, Hache, Hachen (youth) 112

Hachelbach (muddy brook) 77

Hachenberg (hawk mountain) 68, 122

Hachenburger (fr Hachenburg, hawk castle) 73

Hacher (flax hackler) 95

Hachlage (swamp water - lair) 80

Hachmann (dweller by swamp water) 80, 94

Hachstein (swamp mountain) 80, 73

Hacht, Hachtmann 94, see Habich

Hachthal (swamp valley) 80, 76

Hack, Hacke (rake) 106, see also Hag

Hack (huckster) 96

Hackbart (rake beard) 112

Hackbusch (swamp bush) 80, 72

Hackenberg (swamp mountain) 80, 68, 122

Hackendorf (swamp village) 80, 124

Hackenfeld (swamp field) 80, 84

Hackenmueller (swamp water - miller) 80, 103

Hackenschmied (rake smithy) 96

Hackenshmit 159 (rake smith) 96

Hackenteufel (Hit the Devil!) 116

Hacker, Hackert 74 (raker) 96, see also Haacker

Hackermann, Hackler (huckster, retailer) 105

Hacklander (swamp land) 80

Hackmann, see Hagmann, Hackermann, Hakenschmied

Hackmeister (master of the enclosure) 124

Hackstiel (rake handle) 106

Hadamar (battle + famous) 46, 47, 122

Hadamar (swamp marsh) 80

Hadd 53 < Hadeward (battle + guard) 46, 47

Haddenhorst (swamp hurst) 80, 72

Hadebold (battle + brave) 46, 46

Hadebrecht (battle + illustrious) 46, 47

Hadel, Hadeler (bog dweller) 80

Hadepohl (swampy pond) 80, 80

Hader, Haderman 94, Haderle 55, Hadler, Hadner (quarreler) 115, 122

Hadwig (battle + battle) 46, 46

Haeberle 55, Haebbeler, Haeberling, Haeberlein (young goat) 91

Haebler (yeast dealer) 105

Haech (pot hook, cook) 96

Haechel (hook, hook maker, cook) 96, 106

Haechler (flax hackler) 96

Haeckler (vineyard worker) 96

Haeckel, see Fleischhacker

Haefell, Haefele, Haeffele, Haffeli, Hefley 159, Haeffler, see Hafner

Haefer, Haefner, Haeffner, see Hafner

Haeg 122, Haege, see Hag

Haeger, Haegler, Haegele, Haegmann 94 (dweller in an enclosure) 124

Haehl, Haehle (swamp) 80

Haehn 122, Haehner, Haehnert 74 < Haginher (master of the enclosure) 124

Haehnel, Haehnle, Haehnlein (little rooster) 115

Haehnel, < Johannes 55
Haekel, see Haechel
Haelblein (ha'penney) 117
Haeling (swamp dweller) 80
Haell, see Haehl
Haemel (sheep castrator) 95
Haemmer, see Hammer
Haemmerer, Haemmerle 55
    (hammerer, smith) 96
Haen, Haenes 164, Haenle 55,
    see Haehn
Haendel (fight) 115
Haendel, Haendler (trade) 105
Haendler (merchant, huckster)
    105
Haener, see Haehn
Haenkel, see Henkel
Haenle 55, see Haehnel
Haensel, Haensli (little John) 55
Haentschel 55, see Hensch
Haerdel 55, see Hert
Haering, see Hering
Haertel 55, Haertele, Haertle,
    see Hert
Haerter, Haertter (communal
    herdsman, communal
    shepherd) 95
Haertz, see Hertz
Haesemeyer, see Hasemeyer
Haesle, Haesler, Haeseler,
    Haessler, see Hasel
Haeubt, see Haupt
Haeuser, Heuser, see Haeusler
Haeusler, Haeussler
    (householder, cotter) 65
Haeussli 55 (little house) 65
Haf, Haff (harbor, bay) 118
Haf, Haff, Haffen (oats) 91, 106
Hafele 55, see Hafner
Hafemeyer, Hafemaier (farm
    overseer) 93
Hafemeyer (oat farmer) 93
Hafen, Haffen, Hafenmeister
    (harbor master) 109
Hafendoerfer (oat village) 123

Hafer, see Hoefler
Hafer, Haffer, Hafers 164, Hafert
    74 (oats, oat dealer) 91, 105
Haferkamm, Haferkamp (oat
    field) 84
Haferkorn (oat grain, oat seller)
    106
Hafermann (oat dealer) 105
Haff, Haffen, see Haf
Haffentraeger (oat carrier) 96
Hafferstock (oat stalk)
Haffmann, see Hoffmann
Hafner, Haffer, Haffner, Haeffner
    (potter) 96
Hafstaetter, see Hofstetter
Haft (custody, bailiff) 109
Hag, Hage, Hagen (fr Hag 122,
    enclosure, hedge) 124
Hagberg, see Hackenberg
Hagdorn (hawthorn) 89
Hagebaeke (hedge stream) 77
Hageboek (hedge beech) 124, 89
Hagebom (thornbush) 124, 89
Hagedorn (hawthorn, hedge) 124,
    89, 122
Hagel, Hagle 159, Hagler, Hagele
    (fr Hagel 122, hail)
Hagelauer (hail meadow) 84
Hagelberg (hail mountain) 68,
    122
Hagelgans (snow goose) 115
Hagelmaier (enclosure farmer)
    93
Hagelstein (hailstone, a name for
    the devil) 122, 135
Hagemann (enclosure dweller)
    125, 94
Hagemeier, Hagemeyer,
    Hagmaier (manager of the
    enclosure) 125, 93
Hagemeister (master of the
    enclosure) 125
Hagemueller (miller by the
    enclosure) 125, 103
Hagen, Hagens 59 (fr Hagen 122,
    enclosure, hedge) 125

Hagenauer (enclosed meadow)
124, 84

Hagenbach, Hagenbeck (hedge
brook) 125, 77

Hagenbach (swamp brook) 80,
77, 122

Hagenberg (enclosure mountain)
125, 68, 122

Hagenbruch (enclosure quarry)
125, 80

Hagenbuch, Hagenbucher,
Hagenbucker 159 (hornbeam)
125, 89

Hagendorf (enclosed village 125,
124, village on the Hagen 83)

Hagendorn, Hagedorn
(hawthorn) 89, 125

Hagenhoff, Hagenhoffer
(enclosed farm) 125, 92

Hagenkamp (enclosed field) 125,
84

Hagenkotter (cotter in an
enclosure) 125

Hagenkotter (cotter on the
Hagen) 83

Hagenleite (enclosed slope) 125,
71

Hagenmeyer, Hagenmayer,
Hagmaier (enclosure farmer)
125, 93

Hagenmeyer (farmer on the
Hagen) 125, 93

Hagenmueller (miller at the
enclosure 125, 103

Hagenmueller (miller on the
Hagen) 83, 103

Hager, Hagers 59, Hagert 74,
Hagermann 94 (dweller in an
enclosure) 125

Hagerleben (enclosed property)
118

Hagerskamp (field belonging to a
Hager) 125, 84

Hagius (latinized form of Hage)
141

Hagmann, Hagimann (dweller in
an enclosure) 125, 94

Hagmauer (enclosure wall) 125,
100

Hagner, see Hager

Hahn, Hahne, Haan (rooster,
house name) 115, 62

Hahnberger (rooster mountain)
68

Hahnberger (swamp mountain)
80, 68

Hahner (swamp dweller) 80

Hahner (poultry farmer) 96

Hahnfeld (swamp field) 80, 84

Hanke (little rooster) 55, 115

Hahnstein (rooster mountain) 73

Hahnstein (swamp mountain) 80,
73

Hahr, see Haar

Hahrtman, see Hartmann

Haibler (hood maker) 96

Haid, Haidt, Haide, see Heid,
Heide

Haidbrueck (heath bridge) 81, 71

Haidler, Hailer, Heiler (castrator)
96

Haidler (heath dweller) 81

Haight 159, see Heid, Heide

Haigler, see Hegel

Hail, Hailer, Hailler, Hailmann,
see Heil, Heiler, Heilmann

Hailfinger (fr Heilfingen) 122

Hailgen, see Heiligen

Hailmann, see Heilemann

Haimbaugh, see Heimbach

Hain (grove, copse) 72, see also
Hagen

Hain, see Hoehn

Hainemueller (miller at the
grove) 103, 72

Haines, see Heintz

Hainle 55, see Heinle

Hains, Hainz, Haintz, see Heinz,
Heintz

Haiser, see Heiser

Haisler, see Heussler

Haiss < Matthias 135

Haiter (swamp) 80, see Heiter

Haitz 164, see Heid

Hake, see Haak

Hakenkamp (swamp field) 80, 84

Haker, see Hoeker and Hacker

Halbach (swamp brook) 80, 77, 122

Halbacker (half acre) 84

Halbauer (half-owner of a farm, sharecropper) 91, 92

Halber (ha'penny) 117

Halberstadt (German city) 122

Halbfass (half barrel, tenant farmer) 91

Halbfoerster (half-owner of forest rights) 92

Halbgewachs, Halbgwachs (half grown) 113

Halbhuber (peasant owning half a hide of land) 91

Halbkat, Halbkath, see Halbmeyer

Halbmeyer (half-owner of a farm) 92, 93

Halbright 159, see Albrecht

Halbritter (half-knight) 107

Halbrunner (swamp spring) 79

Halbscheffel (payer of half a bushel for rent) 91

Halde, Haldemann, Haldiman (dweller on a slope) 71

Halden (slopes) 71, 122

Halder, Halderman 122, see Haldemann

Halfacre 159, see Huffacker

Halfadel (half-noble) 46

Halfmann (share cropper) 91, 92, 94

Halikman 159, see Heiligmann

Hall (Swiss town) 122

Hallbauer, see Halbbauer

Halle (hall, German city) 122

Hallebach, Hallenbeck (brook along a slope) 71, 77

Halleman (swamp dweller) 80, 94

Hallenbach (swamp brook) 80, 77

Hallenberger (fr Hallenberg 122, swamp mountain) 81

Hallenburg (swamp castle) 81, 73, 122

Hallendorf, Hallendorff (swamp village) 80, 124

Haller (fr Hall or Halle 122), see also Heller

Hallfrisch 159, see Helfrich

Hallick, Hallig, see Heilig

Hallmann, see Hellmann, Heilmann

Halls, see Hals

Hallwachs, see Halbgewachs

Hallweg (swamp path) 80, 65

Halm (blade, stalk) 89

Halman, see Hallmann

Halper, Halpert, see Alper, Alpert

Hals (throat) 114

Hals (mountain pass) 68

Halt (halt) 116

Haltdichwohl (Keep well!) 116, 117

Haltemann, see Haldemann

Haltenberg (steep mountain) 68

Haltenhof (slope farm) 71, 84

Haltenmeyr (slope farmer) 71, 93

Halter, Haltermann 94 (owner, proprietor) 118

Halter, Haltmann, see Haldemann

Haltwanger, Haltiwange (sloping field) 71, 84

Halverstadt (city name) 122

Halwig, see Helwig

Ham 159, see Hamm

Hamacher, Hamacker, see Hammacher

Hamann, Hamannt 74 < Johann

Hambach, Hambacher (fr Hambach 122), reed brook 81, 77, see also Hagenbeck

Hamberg, Hamberger (fr
    Hamberg 122, reed mountain)
    81, 68, see also Hagenberg
Hambrecht, Hambrick 159,
    Hambrach (body + bright) 124,
    47
Hambright 159, see Hambrecht
Hambruck (reed bridge) 71
Hamburg, Hamburger (fr
    Hamburg 122, reed brook
    castle) 81, 73
Hamel, Hamelmann 94 (fr
    Hameln, Hamlin, swamp) 122
Hamer, see Hammer
Hamermann, see Hammermann
Hamfeld (swamp field) 80, 84
Hamfstengel (hemp stalk) 114
Hamlin (fr Hameln) 122
Hamm, Hamms 164 (horse
    collar) 106
Hammacher (horse collar maker)
    96
Hammann 53 < Johann
Hammecker, see Hammacher
Hammel, Hammel (wether) 91,
    see Hamel
Hammelgarn (fish net) 106, 91
Hammelmann, fr Hamlin
    (Hameln) 122, 94
Hammer 122, Hammers 164,
    Hammermann 94, 94,
    Hammerer (hammer, hammer
    maker, smith, carpenter) 96,
    106
Hammer, Hammermann 94,
    Hammerer (maker of horse
    collars) 96, 106
Hammer < Hadumar (battle +
    famous) 46, 47
Hammerbacher, Hammerbacker
    159 (hammer brook) 77
Hammerbauer (fr the
    Hammerhoff, hammer farm)
    91
Hammerberg (hammer
    mountain) 68

Hammerlein 55 < Hammer
Hammerschlag (hammer blow,
    smith) 96
Hammerschmidt, Hammersmith
    152 (hammer smith) 96
Hammerstedt (hammer city) 122
Hammerstein (hammer stone,
    mountain) 73, 122
Hammeyer, see Halbmeyer
Hammler, see Hamelmann
Hammon, Hamon (OT name) 135
Hampe, Hampel 55 <
    Hagenbrecht (enclosure +
    bright) 124, 46
Hampf, see Hanf
Hampfling (hemp grower or
    dealer) 91, 105
Han (reeds or swamp) 81, also
    see Hahn
Hanauer, Hannauer (fr Hanau,
    marsh meadow) 122
Hanawalt (marsh wood) 80, 72
Hanback, Hanbeck (marsh creek)
    80, 77
Hance 159, see Heintz
Hand (hand) 114
Handel, Handle 159, Handler,
    Handelsman 94, Handelman
    (trade, trader) 105
Handel < Johannes
Handschlegel (hand mallet) 106
Handschuh, Handshu 159 (glove,
    glover) 112, 106
Handschumacher (glover) 96
Handtke 55 (little hand) 114
Handwerk, Handwercker,
    Handwerger (craft, craftsman)
    96
Hanengrath (chicken bone) 117
Haner (poultry dealer) 105
Hanf, Hanff, Hanft (hemp) 91,
    106
Hanfeld (marsh field) 80, 84
Hanfling (hemp grower or dealer)
    91, 105

Hang, Hange, Hangg, Hanger (slope dweller) 71

Hangarter (slope orchard) 71, 84

Hangleiter, Hangleitner (dweller on a steep slope) 71, see Hagenleitner

Hangner (fr Hangen 122, slope dweller) 71

Hangsleben (slope property) 71, 127

Hangstorfer (slope village) 71, 124

Hanitsch 53 < Johannes

Hank 53, Hanke, Hankel 55 < Johannes

Hanmann, Hannemann, see Hahnmann, Hahnemann < Johann

Hann, see Hahn

Hanna, Hannah < Johann 53

Hannauer, see Hanauer

Hanneman, Hannemann (follower of Hanna) 94

Hanner, see Haener

Hannes, Hanns 53 < Johannes

Hannibal (Carthaginian general)

Hanover (Hannover) 121

Hans, Hansi, Haensel, Hansel, Hanselmann, Hansemann < Johann 55, 94

Hansa (Hansa, city league) 118

Hansberger, Hansberry (Hans' mountain) 68, 159

Hanschel, Hanschke < Johannes 53, 55

Hanschildt, see Hanschel

Hansel, Hansele, Hansell, Hanzel (little John) 53, 55

Hanselmann (brownie) 134, see Heinzelmann

Hansen (son of Johann) 59, 134

Hanser, Hanssener, Hansser, Hanssers 164 (member of Hanseatic league)

Hansing < Johannes 53, 55

Hansle, see Hansel 55

Hansman (follower of Hans) 94

Hanson (son of Hans) 59

Hanstein, see Hahnstein

Hantske (Little John) 53, 55

Hanz, Hanzel, see Hans, Hansel

Hanzer, see Hanser

Hapacher (fr Happach 122, enclosure brook) 124, 77

Hapelbach (nightshade + brook) 89, 77

Hapelfeld (nightshade + field) 89, 84

Happel, Happolt < Hadebold

Happenmacher (sickel maker) 106

Harbach, Harback, Harbeck, Harbecker, Herbach (fr Harbach 122, swamp brook) 81, 77

Harbarth, Harbert, Harbertz 164, see Herbert

Harbaugh 159, see Harbach

Harbeck, Harbke (swamp brook) 80, 78

Harbers 164, Harbert, Harberts 164, Harbrecht, see Herbert

Harbold < Haribald (army + bold) 46, 46

Harbst, see Herbst

Harburger (fr Harburg, army castle) 46, 73, 122

Harcke (rake) 106

Hard, Hardt, Hart, Harth (strong) 46

Harde (herdsman) 95

Hardekop, Hardekopf (hardhead) 115

Harden 53, Hardelen < Hartwig

Hardenberg (wooded mountain) 72, 68

Hardenstein (forest mountain) 72, 73

Harder, Harders 164 (forester) 96

Hardeward (strong + guard) 46, 47

Hardewig, see Hartwig

Hardmann, see Hartmann

Hardner, see Hartner

Hardrich, Hardrick < Hartrich (strong + rule) 66, 66

Hardt (forest) 72, 122

Hardt, Hardtke 55, see Hirsch

Hardtmann, see Hartmann, Hirschmann

Hardwig, see Hartwig

Harebeck (swamp creek) 80, 77

Haren (swamp) 80, 122

Harenberg (swamp mountain) 80, 68

Harenmann (swamp dweller) 80, 94

Harf, Harff (harp, harpist) 96, 106

Harf (man fr Harff in the Rhineland) 122

Harfner (harpist) 96

Harfst (harvest, autumn) 118

Haring (herring, herring dealer) 115, 105

Harje 55, Harjes 164, Harjis < Hermann, Herwig, etc.

Harkabus (harquebusier) 107, 108

Harke, Harkmann 94 (rake, raker, rake maker) 96, 106

Harkel 55 (little rake) 106

Harkelroad 159 (little rake clearing) 126

Harm, Harms 164 (weasel) 115

Harm 53 < Hermann

Harm (ermine, furrier) 96

Harman, see Hermann

Harmar (army + famous) 46, 47

Harmening 53, Harming < Hermann

Harmon, see Herrmann

Harmsdorff 122, see Hermsdorf

Harmsen (son of Harms) 59

Harnisch, Harnish 159 (armor, harness) 108

Harnischfeger (armor burnisher) 108

Harniss (armor, harness) 108

Harold, see Herold

Harpe (harp, harpist) 96, 106

Harpst, see Herbst

Harr, see Haar

Harre 53 < Hermann, Herwig, etc.

Harsch (military troop) 107

Harsch (iced snow) 118

Harschberger, see Hirschberger

Hart (stag) 62

Hart, Hardt, Harth (fr Hart 122, wooded mountain) 72

Hart, Harte, Harter, Hartel, Hartsel, Hartzel, Hartzell, Hartzler (strong), also short for names beginning in Hart 55, 94, 46

Hart, Hartmann (dweller on a wooded mountain) 72, 94

Hartel, Hartle 159, see Hart

Hartenbach (muddy brook) 77

Hartenberg (wooded mountain) 68

Hartenstein, Hartstine 159 (wooded mountain) 73, 122

Hartfeld, Hartfelder (fr Hartfeld 122, stag field) 84, see Hirschfeld

Hartge (little stag) 55, 62

Harth 122, see Hart

Harthause, Harthousen 159 (stag house) 62

Harthkopf, see Hartkopf

Hartig, see Hartwig

Harting 53, 55, Hartting, see Hartwig

Harting, Hartinger (place name) 122

Hartje 53, 55, Hartjen, see Hartwig

Hartkopf (hard head) 115

Hartkopf (stag head, house name) 62

Hartleb, Hardleff, see Hartlieb

Hartlager (fr Hartlage) 122

Hartlaub (forest foliage) 72

Hartleb (forest property) 72, 127

Hartlein, Hartline (little stag) 159, 55

Hartlieb (strong + dear) 46

Hartlieb, see Hartleb

Hartmaier, Hartmeyer, Hartmayer (farmer in the woods) 91, 93

Hartmaire, see Hartmeyer 151

Hartmann (strong + man) 46, 94

Hartmeyer (forest farmer) 72, 93

Hartmueller (forest miller) 72, 103

Hartmut, Hartmuth, Hartmutz 159, 164 (strong + disposition) 46, 46

Hartnagel (nailsmith) 96

Hartneid = Neidhart

Hartner (forest dweller) 72

Hartog, see Herzog

Hartranft (hard crust, baker) 96

Hartrath (strong + counsel) 46, 47

Hartsel 55, see Hart

Hartshorn (stag horn) 62, 106

Hartsock 159, Hartsook, see Herzog

Hartstein (wooded peak) 72, 73

Hartstein (hard stone) 73

Hartsuck 159, see Herzog

Hartung (strong man) 46

Hartway 159, see Hartweg

Hartweg (path through forest) 72

Hartwig, Hartwigsen 59 (strong + battle) 46, 46

Hartwild (forest game) 72, 91

Hartz, Hartze (fr the Harz Mountains), see also Hart

Hartzel 55, see Hart

Hartzfeld (field in the Hartz) 84, see also Hirschfeld

Hartzog, Hartzok, see Herzog

Harwig (army + battle) 46, 46

Harz, see Hartz

Hasch, Hasche (Slavic for Johannes) 134

Hascher, Haschert 74 (policeman) 109

Hascup 159, see Hasenkopf

Hase, Has (hare) 5, 115

Hasekamp, Hasenkamp (hare field) 115, 84

Hasel, Hasele (hazel) 89

Haselbach (hazel brook) 89, 77, 122

Hasenbalg (hare skin, skinner) 96

Haselbauer (hazel farmer) 89, 91

Haselberger (hazel mountain) 89, 68

Haselbrug (hazel bridge) 89, 71

Haselhorst (hazel hurst) 89, 72, 122

Haselkorn (hazel nut) 89

Haselman, Haselmann (dweller in the hazel) 89

Haselmeyer (farmer in the hazel trees) 89, 93

Haselwander (hazel slope) 89, 71

Hasemann (fr the Hase River)

Hasemeyer (occupant of the Hasehoff, hare farm) 115, 93

Hasenau, Hasenauer (hare meadow) 115, 84

Hasenbalg (hare skin, furrier) 106

Hasenbein (hare leg, quickfooted) 114, 115

Hasenberg (hare mountain) 68, 112

Hasenbusch (hare bush) 118

Hasenclever (fr Hasenclev, rabbit clover) 122

Hasenei (rabbit egg) 118

Hasener (hare raiser or catcher) 91, 96

Hasenfeld (hare field) 84, 122

Hasenfratz (hare face) 113
Hasenfus, Hasenfoth (hare leg) 114
Hasenjaeger (hare hunter) 5, 91
Hasenkamp (hare field) 84
Hasenkopf (hare head) 114
Hasenlauer (hare catcher) 91
Hasenmeyer (proprietor of the Hasenhof) 92
Hasenohr (hare ear) 113
Hasenpflug (Hate the plow!, guild name) 116
Hasenschart (hare lip) 113
Hasenzahl, Hasenzagel (rabbit's tail) 115
Hashaar (rabbit hair) 115
Hashagen (hare hedge) 5, 124
Haskamp, see Hasenkamp
Haslack (hare lake) 80
Haslbeck, see Haselbach
Hasler, Hassler (dweller among the hazels) 89
Hasli 55 (little hare) 115
Haslinger, Hasslinger (fr Hasling) 122
Hasman (hare + man) 94
Haspel (yarn reel, windlas, spool maker) 106
Haspelhorn (turnstile arm, toll collector) 109
Hasper, Haspert 74 (swamp water) 80
Hass, Hasse (hate) 115
Hass, see Hase
Hasse < Hadebrecht
Hassel (fr Hassel 122, swamp) 80, see also Hasel
Hasselbach, Hasselbacher, Hasselbaecher (fr Hasselbach 122, brook running through hazel trees, swampy brook) 89, 80, 77
Hasselhoff (hazel farm) 89, 92
Hasselmann, see Haselman
Hasselmeyer, see Haselmeyer

Hasselwanger (hazel slope) 89, 71
Hassenau, see Hasenau
Hassenkerl (Hate the rascal!) 116
Hassenkrug (Hate the pitcher!) 116
Hassenpflug (Hate the plow) 116
Hassinger (fr Hassingen) 122
Hassler (dweller among the hazel trees) 89
Hasslinger (fr Hasslingen) 122
Hassmann, see Hasmann
Hassner, see Hasmann
Hasso 53 < Hartmann
Hatman, Hatmann, Hattsmann (dweller in the fen) 81, 94
Hatt (fen, bog) 81
Hattendorf (fen village) 80, 124
Hattenberger (hill in a fen) 81, 68
Hatto 53 < Haduwulf (battle + wolf) 46, 48
Hatz, see Hetz
Hau (Chop, hew!) 116
Hau (timber area) 72
Haub, Haube (cap, hood, helmet) 106, 108
Haubeil (hewing axe, woodsman) 91, 106
Haubensack (clothing quartermaster) 107, see Hobensack
Hauber, Haubert 74 (cap or hood maker) 96
Hauberger (deforested mountain) 68, see Heuberg
Hauboldt, see Hugbold
Hauch (breath, hunting cry) 91, also < Hugo
Hauck 53, Haucke < Hugo
Haudt, see Haut
Haueisen (mattock) 106
Haueisen (Hack the iron!, blacksmith) 116, 96
Hauenschild, see Hauschild

Hauenstein (Hew the stone!) 116, 122, cf. Steinhauer

Hauer, Hauers 164, Hauert 74 (hewer, chopper) 96

Hauer (wild boar tusk, hunter) 91

Hauf, Hauff, Haufmann (heap, military detachment) 107

Hauf, Hauff (place names) 122

Haufler (trooper) 107

Haug, Hauge, Haugg, Haugk, Haugs 164, Hauk, Hauke < Hugo

Hauhn, see Huhn

Haukamp (deforested field) 84

Haumann (hay dealer) 105, 94

Haumeister (hay ward) 109

Haumesser (hackknife) 8, 106

Haunschild (Hack the shield!, mercenary) 116

Haupt, Haubt (head) 114

Hauptman, Hauptmann (captain) 107

Hauptvogel (bird dealer) 105

Haus, Hauss, Hausz, Hause, Haussen (house, usually a shortened form) 65

Hausberger (fr Hausberg 122, house mountain) 65, 68

Hauschild, see Haunschild

Hausdorf (house village) 65, 124

Hausemann, Hausener, see Hausmann

Hausen (houses, probably shortened fr some name like Hagenhausen) 65, 122

Hausenbeck (brook among the houses) 65, 77

Hausenflug, see Hasenpflug

Hauser, Hausermann 94 (householder) 65

Haushalter (householder) 65

Haushauer (house builder) 65, 100

Hausknecht (domestic servant) 119

Hausleiter (house slope) 65

Hausler, see Haeusler

Hausman, Haussmann (house owner, farmer) 65, 94

Hausner (house owner) 65

Hausrat, Haussrad (household belongings) 65

Hausser, Haussner, see Hauser, Hausner

Hauswald (house forest) 65, 72

Hauswart, Hauswarth (house guardian) 65, 47

Hauswirt, Hauswirth (master of the house) 65

Haut, Hauth, Hautz 164 (skin, hide, skinner) 96, 106

Haut, Hauth, see Hut, Huth

Hauver 159, see Huber

Havel, Havelmann 94 (dweller along the Havel, marsh) 80, 83

Havemeyer (oat farmer) 93

Havener, Havenner, see Hafner

Haver (oats) 91, 106

Haverkamp, see Haberkamp

Haverland, see Haberland

Haverle, see Haberle

Havermehle, see Hafermehl

Haverstein (oat mountain) 68

Haverstick, see Haberstich

Havervass (oat barrel) 106

Hawffman 159, see Hoffmann

Hawn 159, see Hahn

Hayd, Hayde, Hayden, see Heidt, Heide, Heiden

Hayduck, see Heiduk

Hayer (caretaker, warden) 96, 109

Hayl, see Heil

Hayler, see Heiler

Haym, see Heim

Haymaker < Heumacher, hay maker 105, 151

Hayn, Hayns 164, see Hain

Hayner, see Heiner

Hayser, see Haeuser, Heiser

Hax, see Hack

Heaberlin 55, 159, see Haeberle

Headrich 159, Headrik, see
Heidrich

Heagler 159, see Huegler

Heald 159, see Held

Healer 152, see Heiler

Hearl 159, Hearle, see Hoerl

Hearsey, see Hirshi

Heartman 159, see Hartmann

Heatterich 159, see Heidrich

Heavener 159, Heavner, see
Hafner

Heaver 159, see Hueber

Hebenstreit, Hebstreit (Start the
fight!) 116

Hebbel, see Hebel

Hebeisen (crowbar) 106

Hebekerl (Catch the fellow!) 116

Hebel, Hebeler (lever) 106

Hebel (sourdough, yeast, baker)
106, 96, 122

Hebenstreit, Hebstreit (Start the
fight!, belligerant person) 115

Hebentheier, see Abenteuer

Heber 122, Heberer, Hebeler,
Hebener, Hebert 74,
Hebermann 94, see Hafer,
Hafermann

Heber, Heberer (loader, carrier)
96

Hebermehl, see Hafermehl

Hebich, Hebigt, see Habicht

Hebnagel (nailsmith) 96

Hebner 159, see Huebner

Hebsack (Lift the sack! perhaps a
miller) 116

Hebstreit, see Hebenstreit

Hech, Hechel, Hechler (flax
hackler) 95

Hechekbart (hacklebeard) 113

Hechelberger (hackle mountain)
68

Hechmann (flax heckler) 96

Hecht (pickerel) 115, 106

Heck, Hecke (hedge) 124, 122

Heckart, see Hecker

Heckel, Heckle 159, Heckler
(vineyard worker) 96

Heckel, see Heck

Heckenberg (hedge mountain)
124, 68

Heckendorf (hedge village) 124

Heckendorn, Heckedorn,
Heckethorn 153 (hedge thorn)
125, 72

Heckenlaub (hedge leaves) 125,
89

Hecker, Heckers 59, Heckert 74,
Heckler, Heckner, Heckener,
Heckmann 94 (enclosure
dweller) 125

Heckner (huckster) 96

Heckrote, Heckerotte (hedge
clearing) 125, 126

Heckscheer, Heckscher (hedge
shears) 106

Heckwelder (fr the Heckenwald,
hedge forest) 125, 72

Heckwolt 159 (hedge wood) 125,
72

Hector (Greek hero) 143

Hedemann, see Heidenman

Hederer (ragman, old clothes
dealer) 105

Hedrich, Hederich, Hedrick,
Hedricke, see Heidenreich

Hedwig, see Hadwig

Heebner 159, see Huebner

Heede, see Heide

Heer (army) 46 or < Hermann

Heerbrandt, see Herbrand

Heerdt, see Herd

Heerhorst (swampy hurst) 80, 72

Heering, see Hering

Heerwagen (army cart) 107

Heeter 159, see Hueter

Hefentraeger (yeast seller)

Hefer, Hefler, Hefner, Heffer,
Heffler, Heffner, Hefermann
(yeast dealer) 105, 94

Heffertschwyl (yeast dealers village) 105, 127

Heffner, see Haefner

Heflebower 159 (yeast farmer) 91

Hefright 159, see Hilfreich

Heft, Hefter (clasp maker, buckle maker) 96, 106

Hegberg (hedge mountain) 125, 68

Hege, Hegeman, Heggeman, see Hag, Hageman

Hegel, Hegl, Hegeler, Hegler (enclosure dweller) 125

Hegelmaier, Hegemeyer (proprietor of an enclosed farm) 93

Hegen (see Hecke)

Hegenauer, see Hagenauer

Hegendorn, see Heckendorn

Heger, Hegner, Heggler, Hegmann, see Heckmann

Heger (gamekeeper, forester) 109

Hehl, Hehle, Hehler (concealer, fence) 96

Hehr (sublime), see also Heer

Hehr (jay) 115

Hehring, see Hering

Hehrmann, see Hermann

Heibel 159, see Huebel

Heiberger, see Heuberger

Heibly 159, see Hueble

Heicher, see Heucher

Heichler (hypocrite) 115

Heickel (fastidious, critical) 115

Heid, Heide, Heidt (heath, heath dweller, heathen) 81

Heidebrecht (swamp thicket) 80, 72

Heidecker, Heideke < Heidenreich

Heidegger, see Heidecker

Heidel (blueberry) 89

Heidel, see Heidenreich

Heidelbach, Heidelbaugh (blueberry brook) 89, 77

Heidelbauer (blueberry farmer) 89, 91

Heidelberg (blueberry mountain) 89, 68

Heidemeier, Heidemeyer, Heidmayer (dweller at the Heidehof, heath farm) 81, 93

Heidemueller (miller on the heath) 81, 103

Heidenberger (heath mountain, heathens' mountain) 81, 68

Heidenman (heath dweller) 81

Heidenreich, Heiderich, Heidrich (heathen, heath + rule) 81, 46

Heidkamp (heath field) 81, 84

Heidner (dweller on the heath) 81

Heidt, Heidts 164, see Heid

Heidtman, see Heideman

Heiduk (Magyar infantryman) 107

Heidwolf (heath wolf) 81, 48

Heier, Heiert 74, see Heger, Hauer

Heierman, see Heuerman

Heiger (heron) 115

Height 159, 162, see Heid

Heikel, see Heickel

Heil, Heill (fortune, prosperity, blessing) 138

Heiland (the Savior) 140

Heilbrunn, Heilbrun, Heilborn, Heilbronn 122, Heilbronner, Heilbrunner (holy + spring, healing spring) 138, 79, 122

Heilemann (healer) 96, 138

Heiler (healer) 96, 138

Heilig (holy) 138

Heiligenberg (saints' mountain) 138, 68

Heiligendorf (saints' village) 138, 124

Heiligentag (All Saint's Day) 143

Heiligenthal (saints' valley) 138, 76

Heiliger (saint) 135
Heiligmann (holy man) 138
Heilkamp (holy field) 138, 84
Heilmann, see Heilemann
Heim, Heimer, Heimert 74
  (home, hamlet, a shortened
  form) 124
Heimann < Heinrich
Heimbach (hamlet + brook) 124,
  77, 122
Heimbaugh 159, see Heimbach
Heimberger (fr Heimberg 122,
  hamlet mountain) 124, 68
Heimbert, Heimbrecht (home +
  bright) 124, 47
Heimburg (home castle) 124, 73,
  122
Heimfahrt (Ascension) 143
Heimgarten (home garden) 124,
  84
Heimlich (furtive, secretive) 115
Hein 53, Heine < Heinrich
Heinbaugh 159, see Hagenbach
Heinberg, Heineberg, see
  Hagenberg
Heinbuch, Heinbuck 159, see
  Hagenbuch
Heindorf, see Hagendorf
Heinefeld, Heinefield 153, see
  Hagenfeld
Heineke 53, 55, Heinecke,
  Heinecken < Heinrich
Heinel, Heinl, see Heiner
Heineman 53, 94, Heinemann <
  Heinrich
Heiner 53, Heinert 74 < Heinrich
Heinfelder, see Heinefeld
Heinhauser (fr Heinhaus 122,
  grove house) 72, 65
Heinickel 53, 55, Heinkel <
  Heinrich
Heining 55, 124, Heininger <
  Heinrich
Heinke 53, 55 < Heinrich
Heinle 53, 55, Heinlein <
  Heinrich

Heinmann, see Heinemann
Heinmeyer (farmer in the grove)
  72, 93, see Hagenmeyer
Heinmueller (miller at the grove)
  72, 103
Heinolt, Heinoldt < Heinholt
  (home + loyal) 47, 48
Heinrich, Heinrichs 164,
  Heinrick (home + master) 47,
  46
Heinritz < Henricius, Latin for
  Heinrich 141
Heinroth (Henry's clearing) 126
Heins, Heinsmann (son of Hein)
Heintz, Heintze, Heintzen,
  Heinz, Heinze, Heintzler
  (diminutive of Latin
  Henrizius, for Heinrich)
Heintzel, Heintzler,
  Heintzelmann < Heinrich
Heinzer (follower of Heinz)
Heinzeroth (Heinz's clearing) 126
Heinzmann 94 < Heinrich
Heis, Heiss 122, Heise (hot), see
  also Heidenreich
Heisch (hellish) 135
Heischman (devil) 131
Heisel, see Haeusel
Heisemann, Heissmann, see
  Hausmann
Heisenberg (scrub forest
  mountain) 68, 122
Heisenbuettel (scrub forest
  house) 65
Heisenstein (scrub forest
  mountain) 73, 122
Heiser (hoarse) 114, see also
  Haeuser
Heiser 53 < Heidenrich
Heisler, see Haeusler
Heisner, Heisman, see Hausner,
  Hausman
Heiss, Heisse, Heisser (hot) 115
Heisser, Heissler, see Haeusler
Heist, Heister (young beech tree)
  89, 122

Heisterhagen (beech enclosure)
89, 124
Heisterman (dweller among the
beeches) 89
Heit, Heith, Heitz 164, see Heidt
Heitecke (heath field) 81, 84
Heitemeyer (heath farmer) 81,
103
Heitereiter (heath rider) 81, 107
Heitereiter (clearing on the
heath) 126
Heitkamp (heath field) 81, 84,
122
Heitmann, Heitzmann (heath
man) 81, 94
Heitmeyer, see Heidemeyer
Heitz, Heitzler (stoker, fireman)
96
Heizer (stoker) 96, see Haeuser
Hejduk, see Heiduk
Hejl, see Heil
Hejn, see Hain, Hein, Heine
Hejne, see Heine
Hekenturm (tower surrounded by
hedge, *turm* from Latin *turris*)
124
Helbert, see Elbers
Helbig, Helbing, Helbling
(ha'penny) 117
Helbrand, see Hildebrant,
Hellebrandt
Held, Heldt, Heldmann (hero) 46
Heler, see Hehler
Helf, see Helfer
Helfeier, see Hellfeier
Helfenbein (elephant bone, ivory
worker) 96
Helfenstein (Stone of Help) 140,
122
Helfer, Helfert 74 (helper) 119
Helfrich, Hilfreich (helpful) 138
Helge (healthy, fortunate) 155
Helgenmacher (maker of wooden
saints) 96
Hell, Helle (brilliant, bright) 115

Hellauer (rocky meadow) 84
Hellbach (bright brook or rocky
brook) 77
Helldorfer (bright village or
rocky village) 124
Hellebard (halberd) 107, 108
Hellebrand, see Hildebrand
Hellebrandt (hell's fire) 117, 115
Helleman, Hellemanns 164, see
Heilmann, Helmann
Hellenbrecht, see Helmbrecht
Heller, Hellert 74 (small coin fr
Hall) 117
Hellerbran (Hell's fire!) 117
Hellfeier, Hellfair (Hell's fire!)
117
Helling, Hellinger (fr Helling)
122, see Helbling
Hellinghausen (place name) 122
Hellmann (dweller on a steep
slope) 71, see Heilmann
Hellmer, Hellmers 164 (dweller
on a steep slope) 71, see
Helmer, Helmers
Hellstern (bright star) 118
Hellstrom (bright stream) 77
Hellvogt (hell's governor, devil)
131
Hellwage (hell's chariot, the
Great Bear, the Big Dipper)
118
Hellwege (army road, *strata
publica*) 65, 122
Hellwig, see Helwig
Helm, Helms (helmet) 108
Helman, see Heilmann
Helman (devil) 135
Helmbacher (fr Helmbach 122,
helmet brook) 46, 77
Helmbarth (helmet + battle axe)
46, 46
Helmbold, Helmboldt (helmet +
brave) 46, 47
Helmbrandt (helmet + sword) 46,
46

Helmbrecht, Helmbright 159
(helmet + brilliant) 46, 47

Helmeister (the devil) 131

Helmer, Helmers 164, Helmert
74 (helmet maker) 46, 108

Helmer < Hildemar (battle +
famous) 46, 47

Helmholtz (shaft wood, for
spears, etc.) 46, 96, 108

Helmholtz < Helmhold (helmet +
loyal) or Helmwald (helmet +
rule)

Helmkampf (swampy field) 80,
84

Helmke 55, Helmken (little
helmet) 46, 108

Helmle 55, Helmy 159 (helmet,
helmet maker) 108

Helmrath (helmet + counsel) 46,
46

Helmreich, Helmrich (helmet +
rule) 46, 46, see Himmelreich

Helmschmiedt (helmet smith)
108

Helmschrot (helmet smasher,
soldier) 108

Helmstaetter (fr Helmstadt) 122

Helmuth (helmet + disposition)
46, 46, 49

Helpenstine 159, see Helfenstein

Helschein, Helshine 159 (bright
sheen) 118

Helsel 55 (little throat) 114

Helser (lover) 119

Helt, see Held

Heltzel (forest dweller, woodman)
96

Heltz, Heltzel 55 (hilt, hilt
maker) 108

Helvenston 159, Helvenstone
153, see Helfenstein

Helveti (Helvetian, Swiss) 121,
141

Helwig, Helwick, Helvig, see
Hiltiwic

Helzer 159, see Helser

Hembrick 159, see Hambrecht

Hemd, Hembt (shirt) 112, 106

Hemecker, see Hammacher

Hemelright 159, see
Himmelreich

Hemerich, see Emerich

Hemerlein 55 (little hammer),
see Hammer

Hemler, see Himmler

Hemmenger (fr Hemmingen) 122

Hemmer (swamp dweller) 80

Hemmerichs 164, see
Himmelreich

Hemmerle 55, see Hemerlein

Hemming, see Hambrecht

Hemminghaus (Hemming's
house) 65

Hemmingway < Hemmingweg
(Hemming's path) 65

Hemmler, see Himmler

Hempel, Hempele, Hemple,
Hemperley 159, Hempelmann
< Hambrecht

Hempel, Hempelmann 94,
Hempfling (hemp grower or
dealer) 91, 105

Hempsath (hemp seed) 118

Hench 53, Henchell < Johann

Hench, see Hentsch

Hencke 53, 55 < Heinrich

Henckel 53, 55, Henkel, Henkle
159, Henckels 164, Henckler,
Hinkel < Heinrich

Henckeljohann (Henry John)

Henckelman 53, 94,
Henckelmann < Heinrich

Hendel, see Haendel

Henderer, see Hinderer

Hendler, see Haendler

Hendrichs 164, Henricksmann 94
< Heinrich

Hendrick, Hendricks 164,
Hendriks, Hendrikse <
Heinrich

Henecke (Little Henry), see Henn 55

Heneger, see Heinecke

Henel 53, 55 < Heinrich

Henf, see Hamf

Hengel, Hengler, see Henkel

Hengst (stallion, horse breeder) 91, 106

Hengstebeck (stallion brook) 77

Hengstenberg (stallion mountain) 68, 122

Henig 53, 55 Hening, Heninger < Johannes

Henke (little Henry) 53, 55

Henkel, Henkle 159, Henkels 164, Hinkel, Henkelman 94, Henkelmann (handle, see Henckel)

Henker (hangman, executioner) 96

Henn, Henne, Hennlein, Henny 159 (hen), or < Heinrich

Henne < Johannes

Henne (place name) 122

Henneberger (fr Henneberg 122, chicken mountain, Johann's mountain) 134, 68

Hennecke, Henneckes 164, Henneken, see Heinecke

Henneforth (John's ford) 78

Hennel, see Henel

Hennemann < Johann

Hennes 53 < Johannes

Hennig 53, 55, Henniger, Hennick, Henning, Hennings 164, Henninger < Johann

Hennighausen (John's house) 65

Hennlein (little John) 55

Henrech, see Heinrich

Henrich, Henrichs 164, Henrick, Henricks, Henricksen 59, see Heinrich

Henritz, Henrici (son of Henricius, Latin for Heinrich) 141

Henry 153, see Heinrich

Hensch, Henschel 55, Henschen, Henschle, Henschke 159, Henshel 159, see Hentsch

Hensel 53, 55, Hensler, Henseler < Johannes

Hensle, see Hensel

Henss 53, Henssel 55, Henssler, Henssmann < Johannes

Hentsch, Hentscher, Hentzschel, Hentscher (glove maker) 96, 106

Hentsch, Hentscher, Hentzschel < Johann or Heinrich

Hentz, Henz, Henze, Henzel 55, Henzell, Hentzel, Henzler, Hentzelmann < Heinrich

Hepel, Heppel, Heppler (pruning knife, vintner) 106

Herald, see Herold

Herb, Herber (bitter, harsh) 115, see Herbert

Herbach (swamp brook) 80, 77, 122

Herberg, Herberger (army + shelter, inn) 46, 47

Herbert, Herberts 164, Herberth (army + bright) 46, 47

Herbig, see Herwig

Herbold, Herbolt (army + bold or rule) 46, 46

Herboldtsheimer (Herbold's hamlet) 124

Herbord < Heribord (army + rim of shield) 46, 46

Herbrand, Herbrandt (army + sword) 46, 46

Herbrecht (army + bright) 46, 47

Herbst (harvest, autumn) 143

Herd (hearth) 118

Herd, Herde, Herdt, Herdte (herd) 95

Herdegen (army + thane) 46, 47

Herder (herder) 95

Herdt (strong, hard) 115

Herfahrt, Herfert (military
　　expedition) 107
Herford 122, Herfurth (army
　　crossing) 46, 78
Hergenrother (fr Hergenroth)
　　122
Herger, Hergert 74 (army +
　　spear) 46, 46
Hergesell (army + companion) 46
　　+ 119
Herget, see Herrgott
Hergott, see Herrgott
Herguth (army + wealth) 46, or
　　see Herrgott
Herholt (swamp forest) 80, 72,
　　see Herold
Herich, Herig, see Hering
Hering (herring, seller of
　　herrings) 115, 106
Herkimer (fr Herkheim) 122, 124
Herl 53, 122, Herle, Herlein 55 <
　　Hermann
Herliberg (glorious mountain) 46
Herling 53, Herlinger <
　　Hermann
Herman, Hermann, Hermans
　　164, Hermanus 141 (army +
　　man) 46, 94
Hermsdorf, Hermannsdorfer
　　(Herman's village) 124
Hermsen (son of Hermann) 59
Hernberger (the Lord's
　　mountain) 139, 122
Herold 122, Heroldt (army +
　　ruler 46, 46, herald in miracle
　　play 111)
Herr, Herre, Herrn (hoary, senior,
　　master) 113
Herrand (army + shield) 46, 46
Herrdegen (army + thane) 46
Herrenbauer (the Lord's peasant,
　　monastery servant) 139
Herrgott (Lord God!) 117
Herrimann, Herrmann, see
　　Hermann

Herring, Herrink, see Hering
Herrisperger, see Hirschberger
Herrlich (Splendid!) 117
Herrman, Herrmann, see
　　Herman
Herrnbrot (subsisted by a lord,
　　see Eigenbrot) 109
Herrnknecht (the Lord's servant,
　　monastery worker) 139
Herrold, see Herold
Herrwig, see Herwig
Hersberger, see Hirschberger
Hersch, see Hirsch
Herschbach, see Hirschbach
Herschberger (fr Herschberg
　　122), see Hirschberg
Herschbrunner (stag fountain) 79
Herschel 55, Herschell (little
　　stag) 115
Herscher (ruler) 109
Herschfeld, Herschfield 153 (stag
　　field) 122, see Hirschfeld
Herschfenger (deer catcher) 91
Herschman, see Hirschman
Herse, Hersen (millet) 91, 106
Hersh 159, see Hirsch
Hershey 159, see Hirschi
Hert, Herte, Hertel 55, Herthel,
　　Hertlein, Hertle 159 < various
　　names beginning in *Hart*
Herter (shepherd) 91
Herts 159, see Herz
Hertsch, see Hirsch
Hertter 53, Hertler < Hartwig,
　　Hartlieb, etc.
Hertweck, Hertweg (hard roll,
　　baker)
Hertwig, see Hartwig
Hertwin (strong + friend) 49
Hertz (heart) 118
Hertzbach, see Hirschbach
Hertzberg (rosin mountain) 68,
　　see Hirschberg
Hertzel, Herzels 164 (little
　　heart), see also Hert

Hertzfeld (fr Herzfeld 122, stag field) 84, see Hirschfeld

Hertzstein (heart mountain) 68

Hertzstein (stag mountain) 73

Herwagen (army wagon) 46

Herwald < Hariwald (army + rule) 46, 47

Herwig, Herweck (army + battle) 46, 46

Herz, see Hertz, Hirsch

Herzag, see Herzog

Herzberg, Hertzberger (fr Herzberg 122, heart mountain) 68, see also Hirschberg

Herzel, Herzelein, see Hertzel

Herzer, Herzner (resin gatherer) 95

Herzfeld 122, see Hertzfeld

Herzig (sweet, charming) 115

Herzog, Hertzog (duke, army leader) 46, 109

Herzogin (duchess, man in duchess's employ) 109

Herzstein (rosin mountain) 73

Hesekiel (Ezekiel, OT name)

Heselbach, see Haselbach

Hesler, see Hassler

Heslin 55 (little hare)

Hess, Hesse, Hessen (Hessian) 121, also < Hermann

Hesselbach 122, Hesselbacher, see Haselbach

Hesselberg (hazel mountain) 89, 68, 122

Hesselgesser (dweller on the hazel road) 89, 65

Hessler, see Hassler

Hessling, Hesslinger (fr Hesslingen) 122

Hessenauer, see Hasenauer

Hetler, Hettler (goatherd) 91, 95

Hetman, Hettmann (Polish, captain, fr Hauptmann) 107, 146

Hetrich, Hettrich, Hetterrich, see Heidrich

Hettel, Hettler, Hettelman (goat, goatherd) 91

Hettich < Hadebert, battle + bright 46, 47

Hettinger, Hettner (fr Hettingen) 122

Hettmann, see Hetmann

Hetz, Hetzel, Hetzler, Hetzner (beater on hunt) 91

Hetz, Hetzold 53 < Hermann

Hetzel, see Hermann

Hetzer (master of the hounds)

Heu (hay, hay farmer) 106

Heubach, see Heubeck

Heubaum (hay tree) 89

Heubeck (hay brook) 77

Heuberger (fr Heuberg 122, hay mountain) 68

Heubner (cap maker) 96

Heubusch (hay bush) 89

Heucher (dweller on a fen) 80

Heuer (this year's wine, vintner) 96, fr Heue 122

Heuer, Heuermann (hay dealer, hay raiser) 91, 105

Heuermann (vintner) 96

Heugele, see Huegel

Heule (howl) 118

Heuman, Heumann (hay dealer) 105, 94

Heuschreck (grasshopper) 113

Heuse, Heuser, Heuss, see Haus, Haeuser

Heusler, Heussli 55, Haeussler, see Haeussner, Haeusler

Heusman, see Hausman

Heusser, see Hauser

Heuwarth (hay ward) 96, 109

Hevener, Hevner, see Hafner

Hever, see Hefer

Heyd, Heyde, Heydt, Heyden, see Heid

Heydeke, see Heidecke

Heydel, see Heidel

Heydeman, see Heideman

Heydrick, Heydricks 164, see Heidrich

Heyduk, see Heiduk

Heyer, Heyerman 94, see Heuer, Heuerman

Heyl, Heyler, see Heil, Heiler

Heyland, see Heiland

Heyliger, see Heiliger

Heylmann, Heylemann, see Heilmann

Heyman, Heymann, see Heinemann

Heyn, Heyne, Heyner, see Hain, Hein, Heine

Heynemann, see Heinemann

Heyrat, Heyroth (hay clearing) 126

Heys, Heyse, see Heiss

Heyschreck, see Heuschreck

Heyser, see Heiser, Haeuser

Hezel, see Hetzel

Hibler 159, Hible, Hiblein 55, Hibbler, see Huebler

Hibscher, Hibschman, see Huebscher, Huebschman

Hice 159, see Heiss

Hickelmann, see Huck

Hickman, see Heckmann

Hide 159, Hides 164, see Heidt

Hiebel, Hiebler, see Huebler

Hieber, Hiebert, see Hueber, Huebert

Hiebner, see Huebner

Hiegel, see Huegel

Hienreik 159, see Heinrich

Hiepler, see Huebler

Hierl (sword) 46

Hierl 53 < Hermann

Hiernmeyer, Hiermeyer (swamp farmer) 80, 93

Hieronymus, Hieronimus (St. Jerome) 135

Hiersfeld, see Hirschfeld

Hiester, see Heister

High 159, see Hoch

Highberger 153, see Heuberger

Highfield 153, see Heufeld

Highler 159, see Heiler

Hight 159, see Heid

Hilberg, Hilberger (hill in swamp) 80, 72

Hilbers 164, Hilbert, Hilbricht, see Hildebrecht

Hilbert < Hildebrecht (battle + illustrious) 46, 47

Hilbolt, Hildebold, Hilboldt, Hilbolt < Hildebald (battle + bold) 46, 46

Hilbrand, see Hildebrand

Hild 53, Hildt, see Hildebrand

Hildebrand, Hildebrant, Hildenbrandt, Hiltenbrandt (battle + sword) 4, 46, 46, 49, name of pope 134

Hildebrecht (battle + bright) 46, 47

Hildeger (battle + spear) 46, 46

Hildemar (battle + famous) 46, 47

Hildemut (battle + disposition) 46, 47

Hilderich, Hildrich (battle + powerful) 46, 47

Hildesheimer, Hiltzheimer (fr Hildesheim 122, marsh hamlet) 80, 124

Hildeward (battle + guardian) 46, 47

Hildewig (battle + battle) 46, 46, 52

Hildewin (battle + friend) 46, 119

Hildihart (battle + strong) 46, 46

Hildner (swamp dweller) 80

Hildt, see Held

Hildwein (battle + friend) 46, 119

Hile 159, Hiler 159, Hilmann 159, see Heile, Heiler, Heilmann

Hilfman (helper) 119
Hilfmirgott (Help me God!) 117
Hilfrich (helpful) 138
Hilgartner (swamp garden) 80, 98
Hilgenberger, see Heiligenberg
Hilger 122, Hilgers 164, Hilgert 74 < Hildeger
Hilke (diminutive of Hill) 54, 55
Hilkebrook (Hilke's brake) 80
Hill, Hille, Hiller < Hildebrand, Hildeger, etc.
Hillebrand, Hillenbrandt, see Hildebrand
Hillegas, Hillegass, Hilligass (swamp road) 80
Hillemann (swamp dweller) 80, 94
Hillen (swamp) 80
Hillenbrand, see Hildebrand
Hillenburg (castle in swamp) 80, 73
Hillferding (fr Hilferding) 122
Hillgard, Hillgartner, Hillgaertner, see Hilgartner
Hilliger, see Heiliger
Hillikman, see Heiligmann
Hillmann 53, 94, Hillikman < Hildebrand, Hildebert, etc.
Hillmer, 53, Hillmar, see Hildemar
Hillmeyer (swamp farmer) 80, 91
Hillmuth, see Helmuth
Hillsee (holly lake, swamp lake) 89, 81
Hillsinger (fr Hillsing) 122
Hillstrom (swamp stream) 80, 77
Hilmer, see Hildemar
Hilnbrand, see Hildebrand
Hilpert < Hildebrecht (battle + bright) 46, 47
Hilscher (swamp dweller) 80
Hilse, Hilsmann (dweller near the holly trees, or near the swamp) 89, 80

Hilseberg (holly mountain) 89, 68
Hilsenbeck (holly brook, swamp stream) 89, 77
Hilsenrad, Hilsenrath (holly clearing) 89, 126
Hilspach (swamp brook)
Hiltiwic (battle + battle) 46, 46
Hiltner (attic) 118
Hiltz (swamp) 80, 122
Hiltzheimer (swamp hamlet) 80, 124, see also Hildesheimer
Himbeer (raspberry) 118
Himebaugh 159, Himebook 159, see Heimbach
Himel 159, see Himmel
Himelfarb 159, see Himmelfarb
Himelmann 159, see Himmelmann
Himelright 159, see Himmelreich
Himelsbach 159, see Himmelsbach
Himler 159, see Himmler
Himmel (heaven, sky, probably a house name) 62, 122
Himmelberger (fr Himmelberg 122, heaven mountain) 68
Himmelfarb (sky color) 148
Himmelmann, see Himmler
Himmelreich, Himmelrich (kingdom of heaven) 140
Himmelsbach, Himmelsbacher (swamp brook) 80, 77
Himmelserb (inheritor of the kingdom of heaven) 140
Himmelwright 159, see Himmelreich
Himmer 159, see Hubmeier
Himmler (occupant of Haus zum Himmel) 61
Himpel, Himple 159, Himpler, see Hempel
Hinaman 159, see Heinemann
Hince 159, see Heintz
Hinck, Hincke, Hinckel 55 (limper) 113

Hinck 53 < Heinrich

Hinckel, Hinkelmann 94 (baby chick) 115, 91

Hinde, Hinda (hind) 115

Hindeleuthner (fr the backslope) 69, 71

Hinderberger, see Hinterberger

Hinderer, Hindermann 94 (dweller behind the village) 69

Hinderhoffer (occupant of the Hinderhoff, farm out back) 69, 84

Hinderleiter (beyond the slope) 70, 71

Hindriks, see Hendriks

Hine 159, Hinelein 55, see Hein, Heinlein

Hinebaugh 159, see Heimbach

Hineman 159, see Heinemann

Hineline, see Heinle 151

Hines 159, see Heinz

Hinkel, Hinkle 159, Hinkelmann 94, see Hinckel

Hinnen (dweller "back there") 69

Hinrich, Hinrichs 164, see Heinrich

Hinsch 53, Hinsche < Heinrich

Hintenach (in pursuit) 69

Hinter, see Hinderer, Hinnen

Hinterberger (fr Hinterberg 122, fr behind the mountain) 69, 68

Hinterer (one living out back) 118

Hintz 53, Hintze, Hintzel 55, Hinz, Hintzman 94, Hintzmann, Hinzman < Heinrich

Hiob (OT Job) 135

Hipner, see Huebner

Hipp, Hippe, Hippmann 94 (pruning knife) 106

Hipp 53 < Hildebert 46, 47

Hippel, Hipple 159, Hippler, Hippelmann (waffle seller) 106

Hippenstiel (pruning knife handle) 106

Hippert 53, see Hildebrecht

Hipsch, Hipscher, see Huebsch, Huebscher

Hipskind 159 (well-mannered child) 115

Hipsman 159, see Huebschmann

Hire, Hires, see Heuer 151

Hirnschal, Hirnschael (skull) 114

Hirsch, Hirsche (stag, hart) 48, 62, 63, 149

Hirschbach (stag brook) 77

Hirschbein (deer bone) 48, 106

Hirschberg, Hirschberger (fr Hirschberg 122, stag mountain) 48, 68

Hirschbiehl, Hirschbuhl, Hirschbuehler (stag hill) 48, 67

Hirschblond (stag blond) 112

Hirschburg (stag castle) 48, 73

Hirschenfang (stag catch) 91

Hirschfeld, Hirschfield 153 (stag field) 48, 84, 122

Hirschhausen (stag house) 48, 65, 122

Hirschheimer (stag hamlet) 48, 124

Hirschhizer 66, see Hirschhausen

Hirschholtz (stag forest) 72

Hirschhorn (antlers, deer horn) 48, 62, 106

Hirschi, Hirschy 159 (little stag) 48

Hirschkind (little stag) 48

Hirschle, Hirschlein 55 (little stag) 48

Hirschler, Hirschner (stag hunter) 48, 91

Hirschman 94, Hirschmann (stag man) 48

Hirschstein (stag mountain) 73

Hirse (millet) 91, 106

Hirsh 159, see Hirsch

Hirshauer 159 (fr Hirschau 122, stag meadow) 48, 84

Hirshbein 159, see Hirschbein

Hirshberg 159, Hirshfeld, see Hirschberg, Hirschfeld

Hirshi, Hirshy, see Hirschi

Hirshizer 159, see Hirschhizer

Hirt 122, Hirth, Hirtz 164 (shepherd, herdsman) 95

Hirtenstein (shepherd's mountain) 95, 68

Hirtz, Hirtzel 159, Hirzel, see Hirsch

Hirtzach (stag stream) 77

Hirtzbach (stag brook) 77

Hirtzwanger (shepherd's clearing) 95, 126

Hiser 159, see Heiser, Haueser

Hisle 159, Hisler, see Haeusle, Haeusler

Hiss 159, Hisser, see Heis and Heuss

Hite 159, see Heidt

Hiter 159, see Heiter, Hueter

Hitner, see Huettner

Hitter, see Huetter

Hitz (heat) 118

Hitz (goat) 91

Hitzelberger (fr Hitzelberg) 122

Hitzler, see Hutzler

Hivner, see Hueber

Hixenbaugh 159 (Hick's brook) 77

Hizer 159, 66, see Haeuser

Hoak, see Hoch

Hobach, Hobeck (high brook) 77

Hobell, Hobelmann 94 (carpenter's plane, carpenter) 98, 106

Hobensack (hops sack, hops dealer) 105

Hober, Hobert 74, Hobart, Hoberman 94 < Hadebracht (battle + bright) 46, 47

Hoberg, see Hochberg

Hobler (planer, carpenter) 98

Hoblitz, Hoblitzell (Plane little!, cabinet maker) 116, 96

Hobman, Hobmann, Hobner, see Hoffmann

Hobt, see Haupt

Hoburg (fr Hochburg 122, high castle) 73

Hoch (high, tall man) 113

Hochberg (high mountain) 68

Hochbrueckner (fr Hochbruck 122, dweller by the high bridge) 71

Hochdanz (dancing master) 96

Hochermut (high spirits)

Hochfelden, Hochfellner (fr Hochfeld 122, high fields) 84

Hochgenug (High enough!) 117

Hochhalter (dweller on a high slope) 71

Hochhaus (tall house) 65, 122

Hochheim, Hochheimer (high + hamlet, a city and famous wine) 124, 122

Hochheiser, Hochhiser 159 (dweller in a high house) 66

Hochherz (hearty, cordial) 115

Hochhut (high hat) 112

Hochkeppel (high cap) 122

Hochlander (highlander) 118

Hochman, Hochmann, see Homann

Hochmut (high spirits, arrogance) 115

Hochnadel (high needle) 118

Hochrein (high path) 65

Hochreuter (fr Hochreute 122, high clearing) 126

Hochschild (high shield) 62

Hochstadt, Hochstettler, Hochstaedtler (fr Hochstadt 122, high city, high shore) 71

Hochstein (high crag) 73, 122
Hochstetter, Hochstettler, see
    Hochstadt
Hochwald (high forest) 72 122
Hochwart (high lookout) 122
Hock, Hocke, Hocken (retailer,
    huckster) 105
Hockenbrock (fr Hockenbroich)
    122
Hockhaus 159, see Hochhaus
Hockstein 159, see Hochstein
Hodel (wagon cover, huckster
    with wagon) 105
Hodemacher (hat maker or
    dealer) 105, 116
Hodler (huckster, ragman) 105
Hoebecke (from Hoebeck) 122
Hoebel, Hoebeler (hill, hill
    dweller) 67
Hoebener, see Huebner
Hoeblich, see Hoeflich
Hoebling (courtier) 92
Hoechst (high place, ridge, name
    of city) 122
Hoeck, Hoeckel 55, Hoekeler
    (huckster) 105
Hoecker, Hoeckert 74 (seller of
    foodstuffs) 105
Hoef... , Hoeff.... , see Hof, Hoff
Hoefer, Hoefner, see Hofer
Hoefle 159 (small court, small
    farm) 92
Hoefler, Hoeffler, Hoefner
    (farmer) 92
Hoeflich (courtly, courteous) 115
Hoefling (courtier) 118
Hoefnagel, see Hufnagel
Hoefner, see Haffner
Hoeh, Hoehn, Hoehne, Hoehner
    (heights)
Hoehenholtz (forest on the
    heights) 72
Hoehl (cave) 118
Hoehler (dweller near a cave)
    118

Hoehllander, see Hollander
Hoehn, Hoehner, see Hoeh
Hoehn, Hoehner (scorn) 115
Hoehster (highest) 118
Hoelle (hell) 131
Hoelscher (maker of wooden
    shoes) 96
Hoeltmann, see Holzmann
Hoeltz, Hoeltzer, Hoelter,
    Hoeltzel, Hoeltzle, Hoelzl, see
    Holtz
Hoener (scorner) 115
Hoenig, see Honig
Hoenstein, see Hohenstein
Hoeper, see Hoepfner
Hoepfel, Hoepflinger (hops
    dealer) 105
Hoepfner, Hoepke (hops dealer)
    105
Hoepke (hops dealer) 105
Hoeppel, Hoeppner, see Hoepfner
Hoerauf (army + wolf) 46, 48,
    folketymology: "Stop it!" 116
Hoerder, see Herder
Hoerger, Hoeriger (serf) 109
Hoerger (fr Hoergen) 122
Hoerich, Hoericks 164, see
    Hering
Hoering (place name 122), see
    Hering
Hoerl 53, Hoerle 55, Hoerli,
    Hoerlein < Hermann
Hoermann, see Hermann
Hoerner (horn maker) 96
Hoernle 55, Hoernlein (little
    horn) 118
Hoersch, see Hirsch
Hoerst (place name) 122, see
    Horst
Hoertz (place name) 122, see
    Herz
Hoesler, Hoessler, see Hessler
Hoetz (place name) 122, see Hetz
Hof, Hofe, Hoff (yard, court) 92,
    122

Hofacker, Hoffacker, Hoffecker (fr
Hofacker 122, field belonging
to farm or court) 92, 84

Hofbauer, see Hoffbauer

Hofer, Hoffer (farmer) 92

Hofer (fr Hof) 122

Hoff (court, farm) 92

Hoffart, Hoffarth (pride,
arrogance) 115

Hoffart, Hoffwart (keeper of the
court) 109

Hoffbauer (peasant working for
court) 92, 91

Hoffberg, Hoffberger, Hoffenberg
(court mountain) 92, 68, 122

Hoffecker, see Hofacker

Hoffeiser 159 (farm houses) 92,
65, 66

Hoffeld (court field or high field)
92, 84, 122

Hoffer, Hoffert 74, Hofferth,
Hoffhers 164 (manager of a
cloister farm 92, fr Hofe 122)

Hoffheintz, Hoffheins (hired
hand) 95

Hoffheiser (occupant of the
Hoffhaus, farm house) 92, 65,
66

Hoffherr (gentleman of the court)
92

Hoffman, Hofmann, Hoffmanns
164 (courtier, manager of a
cloister farm) 92

Hoffmantel (court cloak) 112

Hoffmaster 153, Hoffmeister, see
Hofmeister

Hoffmeyer (court farmer, estate
manager) 92, 93

Hoffnagel, see Huffnagel

Hoffnar, see Hofnar

Hoffner, see Hofer

Hoffpauir, see Hoffbauer

Hoffschlaeger (blacksmith) 96

Hoffstadel (farm stable, court
stable) 92

Hoffstatt, Hoffstaetter,
Hoffstetter, Hoffstaedler (fr
Hoffstadt, court city) 122

Hofgaertner (court gardener) 96

Hofius, Hoffius (latinized Hoff)
141

Hoflich 159, see Hoeflich

Hofmann, see Hoffmann

Hofmeier, see Hoffmeyer

Hofmeister (manger of cloister)
92

Hofmeyer, see Hoffmeyer

Hofmiester 159, see Hofmeister

Hofnagel, see Hufnagel

Hofnar (jester, court fool) 96

Hofner, see Hoffer

Hofrichter (court judge) 109

Hofstadter, Hofstetter,
Hofstettler (fr Hofstadt 122,
farmstead) 92

Hofweil, Hofwyl (fr Hofweiler,
farm belonging to court) 92,
127

Hogedorn, see Hagedorn

Hogel, see Hagel

Hogemann (prominent person)
115

Hogendorf, see Hagendorf

Hogenkamp, see Hagenkamp

Hoheisel, Hoheiser, see
Hochheiser

Hohemeyer (farmer on the
heights) 93

Hohenberger (high mountain) 68,
122

Hohenbrink (high hill) 74

Hohenhaus (high house) 65

Hohenholtz (high forest) 72, 122

Hohenloh (high forest) 72, 122

Hohenschilt, see Hochschild

Hohenstein (high crag) 73, 122

Hohenthal (high valley) 76

Hohl, Hohler, Hohlmann (fr Hohl
122, hollow), see Hollmann

Hohlbaum (hollow tree) 89

Hohlbein, see Holbein
Hohlfelder (sunken field) 84
Hohlsteiner (fr Holstein) 121
Hohlweg (sunken way) 65
Hohlwein (Fetch wine!)
Hohman 94, Hohmann (tall man, prominent man) 113, 115, see Hofmann
Hohmeister, see Hofmeister
Hohmeyer, see Hoffmeyer
Hohn, Hohne (contempt) 115
Hohn (heights) 122
Hohnecker (high field) 84
Hohnholz (high forest) 72
Hohr (place name 122), see Haar
Hoit, see Heid
Holand, Holland, Hollander (Holander) 121
Holbach, Holback 159 (swamp brook) 80, 77, 122, see also Hollebach
Holbein (bowlegged) 114
Holbrunner (elder tree spring) 89, 79
Hold, Holdt, Holt, Holder (loyal, beholden, dear) 48
Holdeman, see Haldeman
Holderbaum, Hoelderlin (elder tree) 89
Holderieth (elder marsh) 89, 81
Holdermann, see Hollmann
Holdorf (elder village) 89, 124, 122
Holemann 159, see Hollmann
Holfeld, Holfelder (swamp field) 80, 84
Holl, Holle (elder tree) 89, 122
Holland, Hollandt, Hollander, see Holand
Hollebach, Hollenbach (swamp tree brook) 80, 77, 122
Holleman, Holliman 159, see Hollman

Hollenbach, Hollenback 159, Hollenbeck (swamp brook) 80, 77, 122
Hollenbaugh 159, Hollabaugh, Hollobaugh, see Hollenbach
Hollender, see Hollander
Hollenschade (elder shade) 89
Hollenschein (elder sheen) 89
Hollenstein (elder mountain) 89, 68
Holler 159, see Haller
Hollerbach (elder brook) 89, 77
Hollinger (fr Hollingen) 122
Hollinger (swamp dweller) 80
Hollkamp (sunken field) 84
Hollman, Hollemann, Holloman, Hollomann (swamp dweller) 80, 94
Hollman (dweller among the elders) 89
Holloway, see Hohlweg 151
Hollstein 122, see Holstein
Hollwein (Fetch the wine!, taverner) 96, 116
Holm (crossbeam) 118
Holm (island) 122
Holmann, see Hollman
Holschuh, Holsche, see Holtzschuh
Holser, see Holtzer
Holsinger, see Holtzinger
Holst, Holste (forest dweller) 72
Holst (fr Holstein) 121
Holstein, Holsteiner, Hollstein, Holsten (fr Holstein) 121
Holster 159, see Holtzer, Holtser
Holston, see Holstein
Holt, Holte, Holth, Holtzer (forest) 72, 122
Holt, Holter, see Hold
Holtapfel, see Holtzapfel
Holtgreve (forest warden) 72, 109
Holthaus, Holthausen (forest house) 72, 65, 122
Holthoff (forest farm) 72, 92

Honecke, Honegger, see
Hunecker
Honeyman 153, see Honig
Hong 159, see Hang
Honig, Honigs 164, Hoenig,
Honik, Hoenik (honey,
beekeeper) 95
Honigsberg, Honikberg (honey
mountain) 68
Honnold, see Hunold
Hons 159, Honts, see Hans
Honsa 159, see Hansa
Honstein, see Hohenstein
Hoober, Hoover, see Huber
Hoobler 159, see Huebler
Hooch, see Hoch
Hoof, Hoofman, see Hoff,
Hoffmann
Hoofnagel, Hoofenagel, see
Hufnagel
Hoogstraten (high street) 65
Hook (point) 118
Hookheim 159, see Hochheim
Hoon 159, see Huhn
Hoop, Hoope, Hoopen, see Hoff,
Hauf, Hopf
Hoope (hops grower or dealer)
105
Hoopengardner, see
Hopfengaertner
Hooper 159, Hoopert 74, see
Huber
Hoosen, see Hose
Hooser 159, see Hauser (Huser)
Hoover 159, see Huber
Hoovler 159, see Huebler
Hopack, Hoppacher (hops brook)
77
Hopf, Hopff, Hopfe (hops) 91, 106
Hopfensack (hops sack) 106
Hopffeld (hopsfield) 91, 84
Hopfgaertner (hop grower) 91, 98
Hopfgarten, Hopfengaertner
(hops garden) 98, 122

Hoppe (hops grower or dealer)
91, 105
Hoppenfeld (hops field) 84
Hoppensack, see Hopfensack
Hoppenstein (hops mountain) 73
Hoppler, Hoppner, Hoppmann
(hops dealer) 105
Hopsack (hops sack) 106
Hora (Slavic: forest) 146
Horath (place name) 122
Horbach, Herbach (swamp creek)
80, 77, 122
Horberg (swamp mountain,
wooded mountain) 80, 68
Horcher (listener, hearer) 115
Hord, Horde (treasure) 118
Horein (high path) 65
Horenberg (swamp mountain) 80,
68
Horenkamp (swamp field) 80, 84
Horenstein (swamp mountain)
80, 73, see also Hornstein
Horger, see Hoerger
Horich, Horichs 164, see Hoerger
Horlacher (fr Horlach 122,
swamp pond) 80
Horlander (swamp land) 81
Horlbeck (swamp stream) 81, 77
Horn, Hoerner (fr Horn) 122
Horn (horn, mountain peak,
promontory) 68
Horn (wedge of field projecting
into forest) 84
Hornbach, Hornbacher, Hornback
159, Hornbake 159, Hornbeck,
Hornbecker (brook near peak,
swamp brook) 80, 68, 77, 122
Hornberg, Horenberg,
Hornberger (fr Hornberg 122,
peaked mountain) 68, 68
Hornbogen (bow maker) 108
Hornburg (castle on the peak) 68
Horner, Hoerner, Hornemann
(horn blower) 96

Horner (dweller near mountain peak) 68

Horner (at end of field) 84

Horner (comb maker) 96

Hornig, Horniger, Hornick, Horning 55 (probably fr Slavic *hora*, mountain) 68, 146

Hornisch 159, see Harnisch

Hornle 55, Hornlein (little horn) 68

Hornsperger (peak mountain) 68, 68

Hornstein (peak mountain) 68, 73, 122

Hornung (frost, February) 143

Hornung (bastard) 119

Horst (hurst) 72, 122

Horstkamp (hurst field) 72, 84

Horstman, Horstmann (dweller in a hurst) 72, 94

Horstmeyer (farmer at a hurst) 72, 93

Hort, Horter, see Hart, Harter

Horter, Hortmann, Hortel (treasure keeper) 109

Hosbach (hare brook) 115, 77

Hose (chainmail leggings, hose) 108

Hospel, Hospelhorn 159, see Haspel, Haspelhorn

Hoss, Hosse, Hossen, see Hess

Hossbach, Hossbeck (Hessian brook) 121, 77

Hosselrode (hazel clearing) 89, 126

Hossler 159, see Hassler

Hostetter 159, Hostetler, Hostettler, see Hoffstetter

Hoth, Hotter, Hotler, Hottmann 94 (milliner, hat maker) 96

Hotop, Hotopf (Hat off!) 116

Hottenbach, Hottenbacher (swamp brook) 80, 77, 122

Hottendorf (swamp village) 80, 124

Hottenroth (swamp clearing) 80, 125

Hottenstein (swamp mountain) 80, 73

Hotzinger (fr Hottzingen) 122

Houch 159, see Hauch

Houck 159, Houk, see Hauk

Houderscheldt 159, see Haunschild

Houer 159, see Hauer

Houf 159, Houff, see Hauf

Hough 159, see Hauch

Houpt 159, see Haupt

Hour, see Auer 151

House 153, see Haus, Hauss

Householder 152, see Haushalter

Houseknecht 153 (domestic servant) 119

Housely 159, see Haeusle

Houseman 153, see Hausmann

Housen 159, see Hausen

Houser 159, see Hauser

Housewart 159, see Hauswart, Housewird 159, see Hauswirth

Housewright 159, Houseright, see Hauswirth

Housman 159, Housmann, see Hausmann

Houtman 159, see Hauptmann

Houts 159, see Haut

Hovere 159, see Huber

Howarth, see Heuwarth

Hower 159, see Hauer

Howse 159, Howser, Howze, Howzer, see Haus, Hauser

Hoy 159, see Heu

Hoyden, see Heid

Hoyer (guard, watchman) 96, 109

Hoylmann 159, see Heilmann

Hoyt, see Heid

Hreeder, see Reeder

Hub, Hube, Huben (fr Hub 122, hide of land) 91

Hubbach, Hubacher (farm brook) 91, 77

Hubbe 53 < Hubert
Hubbel, Hubel (hill) 72
Huber, Hueber, Hubers 164,
    Huberd 74, Hubbert 74,
    Hueber (cultivator of one hide
    of land) 91
Hubert, Huberts < St. Hubertus
    (mind + bright) 47, 135
Hubmeier, see Huber
Hubner, Huebner, see Huber
Hubsch, Hubscher, Hubschman,
    see Huebsch, Huebschmann
Hubschmidt, Hubsmith 153
    (smith owning one hide of
    land) 91, 95
Huch 53 < Hugo
Hucht (thicket) 72
Huck, Huckel, Hucker (marsh
    dweller) 80
Huckestein (marsh mountain) 80,
    73
Hudepohl (hut pond) 81
Hudt, see Hut
Huebel, Huebler (hill) 67
Huebenthal (Hueben Valley 76,
    Hueben 122, prehistoric name
    of brook) 83
Hueber, Huebner, see Huber
Huebsch, Huebscher, Huebschert
    74 (courtly, handsome) 115
Huebschmann (courtier) 92
Huegel, Huegler, Huegeler (hill)
    67, 122, see Hugo
Huegelmeier, Huegelmeyer (hill
    farmer) 67, 93
Huehner (poultry raiser) 95, 196
Huelle (swamp) 80, 122
Huellbrock (swamp brake) 80, 80
Huelskamp (marsh field) 80, 84
Huelskamp (holly field) 89, 84
Huelsmann (swamp dweller) 80,
    94
Huelsmann (dweller among the
    hollies) 89, 94

Huemmelmann, see
    Himmelmann
Huemmer, see Hubmeier
Huene (giant) 62
Huenecke (descendant of the
    giants) 118
Huenemeyer (farmer near a
    cairn) 93
Huepner, see Huber
Huerde (fence gate) 84
Huesmann, see Hausmann
Huessler, see Heussler
Hueter, Huether (keeper,
    guardian) 96
Huette, Huetter, Huettner (hut,
    workplace) 65
Huettenrauch (hut smoke,
    charcoal burner) 96
Huettig (fr Huttingen) 122
Hufeisen (blacksmith) 96
Huff (hoof, probably short for
    Huffschmidt) 96
Huff, see Hoff
Huffaker (small farm) 84
Huffbauer (farmer owning a hide
    of land) 91
Huffer, Huffert 74 (blacksmith)
    96, see Hofer
Huffines, see Hoffheintz
Huffman, Huffmann, see Huber,
    Hoffmann
Huffschmid, Huffschmidt,
    Huffschmit (blacksmith) 96
Hufmeister, see Hoffmeister
Hufnagel, Hufnail 153 (horseshoe
    nail, blacksmith) 96
Hufschmidt, see Huffschmidt
Hug 53, Hugg, Hugi < Hugo
Hugbald (thought + bold) 47
Hugel, Hugele, Hugeles 164, see
    Huegel
Hugelsheim (hill hamlet) 67, 124
Hugo (thought, mind) 47
Huhn, Huhner (chicken, poultry
    dealer) 91, 105

Huhnebein (chicken leg, chicken bone) 114

Huismann, see Hausman

Hulde (loyalty) 47, 119

Hullstein, see Holstein

Huls, Hulls, Hulst 74 (marsh, holly) 89, 80

Hulsemann, Hulsmann (marsh dweller, dweller in the holly) 80, 89

Hulsheyser (swamp houses, holly houses) 80, 89, 65, 66

Hulshoff (marsh farm) 80, 92

Hulshoff (holly farm) 89, 92

Hulslander (marsh land) 80

Hults 159, Hultz, see Holtz

Hultscher (maker of wooden shoes) 96

Humback (dirty creek) 77

Humbert (bear cub + bright) 48, 47

Humboldt (bear cub + loyal) 48, 48

Humburg (bear cub + castle) 48, 73

Humelbaugh < Hummelbach (bumble bee brook) 77

Huml, Hummel, Hummell (bumblebee, restless person) 115, 122

Hummelbaugh 159 (bumblebee brook) 77

Hummer (lobster) 106

Humpe 53 < Humbert

Humperding < Humbert, follower or descendant of Humbert 124

Humple, see Huml, Hummel

Hunbach (swamp brook) 80, 77

Hund, Hunds 164, Hundt (dog, keeper of the hounds)

Hundert (hundred) 118

Hundertmark (hundred marks) 117

Hundertpunt (hundred pounds) 114, 117

Hundeshagen (kennel) 124

Hundsberger (dog mountain) 68

Hunecker (chicken yard) 85

Hunger (hunger) 118

Hunger (Hungarian) 121

Hunger, see Huenecke

Hungerbiehler, Hungerbuehler, Hungerpiller (hunger hill, sterile hill) 67

Hungerbrunnen (intermittent spring) 79

Hungerleich (starveling) 114

Hunold (young bear + loyal) 48, 48

Hunold, see Humbold

Hunsberger, see Huntsberger

Hunt, see Hund

Hunt, Hunting (fr the Hunt River) 83

Hunter 153, see Jaeger

Huntman, Huntmann, Huntemann (keeper of the hounds) 91

Huntsberger (fr Huntsberg 122, mountain on the Hunt) 68, 83

Hupf, Hupfl (hops) 91, 106

Hupfauf (Jump up!) 116

Hupfeld, Hupsfeld, Hupfield 153 (hop field) 84

Hupfenstiel (hops pole) 113

Hupfer (hop dealer) 105

Hupfer (acrobat) 96

Hupman, Huppman (hops dealer) 105

Huppert, see Hubert

Hursh 159, Hurshman, see Hirsch, Hirschman

Hurst (thicket 122), also see Horst

Hurt (hurdle, woven fence) 84, 106, 122

Hurter, Hurther (wattle weaver) 96

Hurtig (swift, brisk) 115

Hus, see Huss

Husch (mine goblin, gremlin) 118
Husemann, see Hausmann
Husen 40, 122, see Hausen
Husener, see Hausner
Husenfeld (house field) 65, 84
Hushagen (house enclosure) 65, 124
Huskamp (house field) 65, 84
Husmann, Hussmann, see Hausmann
Huss (Czech: goose) 146
Husselbaugh 159, see Haselbach
Husserle, see Haeusler
Hussmann, see Hausmann
Hut, Huth (hat, hatter) 112, 106
Hut, Huth (herdsman) 95
Huter, Hutmann 94 (guard) 96
Huth (hat, milliner) 112, 96
Hutmacher, Huthmacher, Huthmann (milliner, hat maker) 96
Huttelmeyer (owner of irregularly shaped farm) 93
Hutter, Huetter (cotter) 118
Hutter (milliner) 96
Huttner, Huettner (cotter, metal worker) 96
Hutz, Hutzell, Hutzler (seller of dried fruit) 106
Huver, Huvar 159, see Huber
Huymaier (hay farmer) 93
Huyser, see Haeuser
Hybler 159, see Huebler
Hyde 159, Hydes 164, see Heid
Hydrick 159, see Heidrich
Hyer 159, Heyers 164, see Heuer
Hyl 159, Hylman, see Heil, Heilmann
Hynes 159, see Heinz
Hysenhood 159, see Eisenhut
Hyser 159, 66 see Haeuser, Heiser
Hyx 159

I

Iager, see Jaeger
Ibach (brook, with prehistoric name *iba* meaning brook or water) 77, 122
Ibe 159, see Eib
Iberg (water mountain) 68, 122
Ice 159, see Eis
Icenroad 159, Icenrode, see Eisenrode
Ichinger (fr Ichingen) 122
Ickel, Ickels 164 (fr *ik* meaning water)
Ickle 159, see Eickel
Idleman 159, see Edelmann, Eitel
Iermbruster 159, see Armbruster
Igel (hedgehog) 48
Igelhart (hedgehog + strong) 48, 56
Igelsbach (hedgehog brook) 48, 77, 122
Iglhaut (hedgehog skin, thick skinned) 115
Ignatz (St. Ignatius of Loyola) 133-137
Ihl, Ihle, Ihler (dweller by the Ihle) 83
Ihrich, Ihrig, see Erich
Ihrlick 159, see Ehrlich
Ikeler 159, see Eichler
Ikels 159, see Eichels, Eichholtz
Iler 159, see Eiler
Ilg, Ilgen, Illgen (St. Aegidius or St. Kilian) 135, 122
Ilgenfritz (Fritz fr Ilgen)
Ilger (fr Ilgen) 122
Illich, Illig, see Ilg
Ilmen (dweller by the Ilm) 79, 83
Ilmenau (meadow on the Ilm) 83, 84
Iln (name of river) 83, 84
Ilnau (meadow along the Iln) 79, 84

Ilrich, see Ulrich

Iltis (polecat, polecat catcher) 115

Imbach (in the brook) 69, 77, 122

Imboden (in the valley) 69, 96

Imbs (beeswarm) 91, 95, 122

Imbsweiller (beeswarm village) 127

Im Busch (in the brush) 69, 72, 122

Imdahl (in the valley) 69, 76, 122

Imdorf (in the village) 69, 124

Imel 159, see Immel

Imgarten (in the garden) 69, 84

Imhof, Imhoff (in the farmyard) 69, 92

Imhoff (bee farm, apiary)

Imke 55 < Irmin (powerful, pagan god)

Immel 53 < Emmerich

Immenhauser (fr Immenhausen 122, bee house) 65

Immer (river name) 83

Immergut (always good) 115, 139

Immermann (dweller on the Immer) 83

Imthurn (in the tower, *thurn*, fr Latin *turris*) 69

Imwald, Imwold (in the forest) 69, 71

Inderfurt, Inderfurth (in the ford) 69, 78

Indergand (in the rubble field) 69, 84

Inderly 159, see Enderle

Indermuhle (in the mill) 69, 103

Inderwiess (in the meadow) 69, 84

Indorf (in the village) 69, 124, 122

Ingber (spice dealer) 105

Ingel, Ingels 164 (swamp) 80, see Engel, Engels

Ingelhard, see Engelhart

Ingelhof (swamp farm) 80, 92, see Engelhoff

Ingelmann, see Engelmann

Inhalter (proprietor) 118

Inhoff (in the court yard) 69, 92

Insel 122, Insul (island, fr Latin *insula*)

Inselmann (island man) 94

Interlaken (between the lakes, place in Switzerland, fr Latin *interlacus*) 122

Irlbacher 159 (swamp brook) 80, 77, see Erlebach

Irrig (wrong, astray) 115

Isaac, Isaacs 164 (OT name) 135

Isberg 159, see Eisberg

Ischler (fr Ischel 122, or dweller by the Ische) 83

Ise 159, see Eise

Isemann 159, see Eisemann

Isenbart 159, see Eisenbart

Isenberg 159, Isenberger, see Eisenberg, Eisenberger

Isengard 159, see Eisengard

Isenhard 159, see Eisenhard

Isenhour 159, see Eisenhauer

Isenhut 159, see Eisenhut

Isenminger 159, see Eisenmenger

Isenring 159, see Eisenring

Isenschmidt 159, see Eisenschmid

Isensee 159 (iron lake) 82

Isenstadt 159, see Eisenstadt

Iser 159, see Eiser

Iser (dweller near the Iser) 79

Iserhut (iron helmet) 108

Isermann 159, see Eisermann, Isler 159, see Eisler

Isner 159, see Eisner

Israel (OT name) 135

Issel, Isselmann 94 (fr Issel) 122

Ittenbach (place name) 122, 77

Itzig 53 < Isaac

Iunge, see Junge

Izeley 159, see Eise, Eisele

Izlar 159, see Eisler

J

Jaac 53, 135, Jaaks 59 < Jacob
Jack 53, 135 Jacke < Jacob
Jackel 55, see Jaeck
Jacker, Jackert 74 (jacket maker) 96
Jackle 55, see Jaeck
Jackman (follower of Jack) 94
Jacob, Jacobs 59, Jacobes, Jacobus 141 (OT name) 135
Jacobi, Jacoby (son of Jacob) 142
Jacobsen, Jacobson, Jacobsohn (son of Jacob) 59
Jacobsmeyer (occupant of the Jacob farm) 93
Jaeck, Jaecks 59, Jaeckel 55, Jaekel, Jaeckle, Jaeckli, Jaecklein, Jaegli (little Jacob)
Jaegemeyer (farmer with hunting rights) 91, 93
Jaeger, Jaegger, Jaegerl 55, Jaegermann (hunter) 91
Jaegerschmidt (smith with hunting rights) 91, 96
Jaeggli 55, see Jaeck
Jaekel 55, see Jaeck
Jaenike < Johann
Jaeschke 55 < Johannes
Jaffé (OT Japhet) 135
Jag (hunt, hunter) 91
Jagdhuber (farmer with hunting rights) 91, 92
Jagdman (hunter) 91
Jagdspiess (hunting spear, hunter)
Jagemann (hunter) 91
Jagenteufel (Chase the devil!) 117
Jager, Jagerman 94, Jagmann, Jagler, see Jaeger 151
Jahn, Jahns 59 < Johann
Jahnke, Jahncke (little John) 55
Jahr, Jahren (year) 118
Jahraus, Jahrhaus < Gareis (wrought iron, smith) 96

Jahrmarkt (annual fair) 118
Jakob, see Jacob
Jakobi, see Jacoby
Jan, Jans 59 < Johann
Jandorf (John's village) 124
Janing 55, Janning, Jannings 59 < Johann
Jans, see Gans
Janse, Jansen, Janssen, Janssens 59, Janson (son of John) 59
Jantz, Jantzen, Janz (son of John) 59
Jaschke < Johann
Jasper, see Caspar
Jauch (liquid manure, peasant) 112
Jauchler (spreader of manure) 96
Jaul, see Gaul
Jauss < Josef, Jost
Jedermann (Everyman, in miracle plays) 111, 94
Jeeter 159, see Jeter
Jegelhardt 159, see Igelhard
Jeger, see Jaeger
Jehle 53 < Ulrich
Jehrling (yearling, annual) 118
Jelling (Slavic: stag, elk) 146
Jenner (January, birth or covée duty in that month) 143
Jenning 53, 55, Jennings 59 < Johann
Jensch 53, Jentzsch, Jentz < Johann
Jensel 53, 55, Jensen < Johann, see also Gensel 134
Jentsch < Johann
Jeremias (OT name, Jeremiah)
Jerg, see Joerg
Jergen 159, see Juergen
Jeschke 53, 55 < Johannes
Jeter, Jeters 59, Jetter (weeder, gatherer) 95
Jingling 159, see Juengling
Jmhof, see Imhof

Joachim, Jochem, Johen (OT name) 135

Job 153, see Hiob

Jobst 59, 74 < OT Hiob (Job) 135

Joch, Joch, Jochner (yoke, mountain pass) 68

Joder (Theodor) 135

Jodocus, see Jobst

Joel, Joell (OT name) 135

Joellenbeck (dirty brook) 77, 122

Joerg, Joerge, Joerger, Joergens 59, Joerk, Joerke (St. George) 135

Johan, Johann, Johannes, Johanness (John) 135, name of several popes 134

Johanknecht (servant John) 139

Johansen, Johannssen (son of John) 59

John 53 < Johann

Johnsen, Johnson (son of Johan) 59

Johst, see Jost

Jonas (OT Jonah) 135

Jonck, see Jung

Joncker, see Juncker

Jones, see Schantz

Jong, see Jung

Jonger, see Junger

Jontz, Jontzen < Johannes

Joost, see Jost

Jop, see Job

Joppe (jacket, jacket maker) 112, 96

Jordan (OT name) 135, 122

Jorge, Jorgen, Jorgens 59, see Joerg

Joseph, Josef (NT name) 135

Jost (St. Jodocus) 135

Jucker (swamp dweller) 80, see Junker

Jud, Jude, Judd, Judt, Judmann 94 (Jew) 121

Juda (Judah, O.T. name) 136

Judenburg (Jew castle) 73

Judi 159, see Tschudi

Judisch (Jewish) 120

Juengling (youth) 113

Juengst (youngest) 113

Juergen, Juergens 59 < Georg

Juergensen, son of Juergen 59

Juhl, Jule, Jul (Yule) 143

Juker, see Juncker

Julig (fr Juelich) 121

Julius (Latin name) 141, name of several popes 134

July (July) 143

Juncker (young lord, squire) 109

Jung, Junge (young) 113

Jungandreas (young Andrew) 113

Jungblud, Jungblut (young blossom) 89

Junge, Junges 59 (youth) 113

Junger, Jungers 59, Jungert 74 (youth, disciple) 113

Jungfer, Jungfermann (convent servant) 139

Junggust (Young Augustus) 113

Junghahn, Junghane (young rooster) 91

Junghans (John the younger) 113

Junghaus (young house) 65

Junginger (young man) 113

Jungk, see Jung

Jungling, see Juengling

Jungman, Jungmann (young man) 113

Jungreis (new branch)

Jungst (youngest) 113

Junk, see Jung

Junker, Junkermann 94, see Juncker

Junkher, see Juncker

Jupp < Joseph 135

Jurgen, Jurgens 59, Juergensen 59, see Juergen

Juss 53, Jusse < Justus, Jodocus

Just, Justus (Latin name, "just") 141, see also Jost and Jodocus

Justice 159, see Justus

K

Kaal, see Kahl

Kaas (cheese, cheese dealer) 105

Kaatz, see Katz

Kabel (cable, rope maker, river name) 83, 122, see also Gabel

Kachel, Kachele (tile, tile maker) 96, 106

Kachler, Kachner (tile maker, potter) 96

Kade (swamp) 122

Kaefer (beetle, perseverant person) 115

Kaeferstein (beetle mountain) 73

Kaegel, see Kegel

Kaehle, Kaehler, see Kehle, Kehler, Koehler

Kaelber, see Kalb

Kaemerlin 55, Kaemerling (court servant) 109

Kaemmel (occupant of house *zum Kaembel*, "to the Camel") 62

Kaemmerer (chamberlain, treasurer) 109

Kaemper, Kempf (champion) 96

Kaendel (pitcher maker) 106

Kaepel, Kaeppel (cape maker) 96

Kaercher, see Kerker

Kaes, Kaess, Kaese (cheese, fr Latin *caseus*) 105, 106, 112

Kaeseberg (cheese mountain) 118

Kaesemeyer (cheese farmer) 93, error for Casimir

Kaesmann (cheese dealer) 105

Kaessler, see Kessler

Kaestner (chest maker, revenue collector) 98

Kaestner (manager of the granary) 109

Kaeufel (second hand dealer) 105

Kaeufer (purchaser), see also Kofler

Kafer 159, see Kaefer

Kafka (Czech: jackdaw) 115, 143

Kagel (hood maker) 106

Kagle 59, see Kegel

Kahl, Kahle, Kahler, Kahlert 74, Kahlmann 93 (bald, fr Latin *calvus*) 114

Kahlbach, Kahlenbach (muddy brook) 80, 77, see Kaltenbach

Kahlbaugh 159, see Kahlbach

Kahlberg, Kahlenberg, Kahlenberger (bald mountain) 68, 122

Kahlenborn, see Kaltenborn

Kahler, see Kohler

Kahm, see Kamm

Kahn, Kahns 59 (rowboat) 96

Kahn (barge, bargeman)

Kahn, see Cohn

Kahnbach (rowboat brook) 77

Kaigler 159, see Kegler

Kail, Kailer, see Keil, Keiler

Kaiser, Kaisser (emperor, fr Latin *caesar*)

Kaiser (Kaiser, emperor, house name)

Kalb, Kalbe (calf) 91

Kalbaugh 159, see Kahlbach

Kalberer (calf raiser or dealer) 91, 105

Kalbfleisch (calf meat, veal, butcher) 96

Kalbfuss (calf foot, butcher) 96

Kalbskopf (calf's head) 114, 62

Kalcher (chalk maker, fr Latin *calcarius*) 96

Kalckbrenner, see Kalkbrenner

Kaldenbach, see Kaltbach

Kale, see Kehl

Kaler, see Kahler, Koehler

Kalichmann (chalice maker, fr Latin *calix*) 96

Kalk, Kalker, Kalkmann 94, Kalkus 141 (lime maker, fr Latin *calx*) 96

Kalkbrenner (lime burner) 96

Kalkbrunn (chalk spring) 79

Kalkreuth (chalk clearing) 126

Kalkstein (chalk) 96

Kall, Kaller, Kallert 74, Kallner, Kallman 94 (dweller by a stream)

Kallemeyer, Kallmeyer, Kallmyer 159 (farmer on a stream) 77, 93

Kallenbach 122, see Kaltenbach

Kallenberg, Kallenberger (stream mountain) 77, 68

Kallenstein (stream mountain) 77, 73

Kalman, Kahlmann, see Kall

Kalmbach, Kalmbeck, see Kaltenbach

Kalp, see Kalb

Kalteis, Kalteisen (cold iron, blacksmith) 96, 122

Kaltenbach, Kaltbacher, Kaltenbacher, Kaltenbacker, Kalterbach (cold brook) 77, 122

Kaltenbaugh 159, see Kaltenbach

Kaltenborn (cold spring) 79, 122

Kaltenhauser (cold house) 65

Kaltenschnee (cold snow) 118

Kalthof, Kalthoff (cold farm) 92, 122

Kaltreider, Kaltrider 159 (cold clearing) 126

Kaltschmidt (coppersmith, kettle smith) 96

Kaltwasser (cold water) 118

Kalwe (bald, fr Latin *calvus*) 114

Kamber (comb maker) 96

Kamerer, see Kammerer

Kamm (ridge of mountain) 68

Kamm (comb, combmaker) 96, 106

Kamman (comb maker) 96, 106

Kammer (chamber, fr Latin *camera*) 122

Kammerad, Komrad (comrad) 119

Kammerdiener (valet) 109

Kammerer, Kammerle, see Kaemmerer

Kammermann (chamberlain, administrative official) 109

Kammermann (dweller on a ridge) 68, 94

Kammeyer (farmer on a ridge) 68, 103

Kamner (comb maker) 96

Kamp, Kampe, Kamps (field, fr Latin *campus*) 84, 122

Kampenmueller, Kampfmueller (miller with a cogwheel) 84, 103

Kamper, Kampmann 94 (champion, fr Latin *campus*) 84

Kampf, Kampfer, Kampfert 74 (struggle, struggler, fr Latin, *campus)*

Kamphaus (field house) 84, 65, 122

Kamphoefner (fr the Kamphoff, field farm) 84, 92

Kampmayer, Kampmeyer (field farmer) 84, 93

Kamrath (ridge clearing) 68, 126

Kamrath (cogwheel) 96

Kandel, Kandell, Kandelin 55 (pitcher, pitcher maker) 106, 122

Kandlbinder (pitcher maker) 96

Kangiesser, see Kannengiesser

Kann, Kanne (can, pitcher, fr Latin *canna*) 106

Kannenberg (pitcher mountain) 68, 122

Kannenblei (pitcher lead, pitchermaker) 106

Kannengiesser, Kannengieser, Kannengieszer (pewterer, tinsmith) 96

Kanssel, see Kantzel

Kant, see Gand

Kantor, see Cantor

Kantzel, el, Kantzler (chancelor,
fr Latin *cancellarius*) 109
Kapaun (capon) 91
Kapfer (gazer) 118
Kapfer (dweller at a mountain
peak) 68
Kaplan, Kaplon 159 (chaplain)
110
Kapp, Kappe, Kapps,
Kappenmann 94,
Kappenmacher (cowl maker,
Capuchin monk) 96, 106, 110
Kappe (hill) 68
Kappel (chapel, place in
Switzerland) 122
Kappeler, Kappelmann (cap
maker) 96
Kappler (monk, occupant of a
chapel) 110
Kappus (cabbage farmer, fr Latin
caput) 91
Kaps, see Kappus
Karch, Karcher, Karchner
(carter, fr Latin *carruca*) 96,
see also Karg
Karg, Karger (clever, stingy) 115
Karinther (Carinthian) 121
Karl, Karle (man, Charles,
cloister servant) 139
Karlbach (Charles' brook) 77
Karleskind (child of Charles)
Karli (son of Karl) 142
Karmann 94 (basket maker) 96
Karp 53 < St. Polycarp 135
Karp, Karpf (carp, fishmonger)
115
Karsch (lively, merry) 115
Karseboom, see Kirschbaum
Karsner, see Kirschner
Karst, Karsten, Karstner,
Karstmann 94 (mattock) 106
Karst (bare alpine land) 81
Karst, Karsten (Christian) 135
Kartheuser, Karthehausen,
Kartheiser (employee of the
Carthusians) 110

Kas, Kase, Kass, see Kaes,
Kaese, Kaess
Kaschenbach (cherry brook) 89,
77
Kasekamp (cheese field) 84
Kasemann (cheese dealer) 105
Kasemeyer (folk-etymology fr
Casimir), see Kaesemeyer
Kaser, see Kasemann
Kasmann, see Kasemann,
Gassmann
Kaspar, Casper, see Caspar
Kassebaum, Kassebom,
Kasseboom (chestnut tree) 89
Kassel, Kassler, Kasselmann (fr
Kassel) 121, 122
Kasselberg (castle mountain, fr
Latin *castellum*) 68
Kastendiek, Kastendyk (chestnut
dike) 89, 81
Kastner, see Kaestner
Kastor (Latin *castor*, beaver,
Bieber) 141, 122
Kat, Katt, Katte, Kattner,
Kathmann (cotter) 94
Kather (tom cat) 115
Katterfeld (fenced field) 84
Kattermann, see Gattermann
Katz, Katzen (cat) 115
Katz (fr Hebrew *Kahenzedek*
priest) 110, 147
Katzenbach, Katzenbacher
(swamp brook) 80, 77, 122
Katzenberg, Katzenberger (cat
mountain) 68, 122
Katzenelnbogen (cat's elbow,
probably folk-etymolgy fr
Celtic) 3, 4, 122
Katzenmayer, Katzenmeyer,
Katzmeier (fr the Katzenhof,
swamp farm) 93
Katzenstein, Katzenstine 159
(cat mountain) 73, 122
Katzmann (cat man) 118
Kaub 122, Kaube, Kaubes 59

Kauder, Kauders 59 (fr Chur in Switzerland) 122

Kauf, Kauff, Kauffer (purchase, merchant, fr Latin *caupo*) 105

Kaufholtz (wood dealer) 105

Kaufler, Kauffler (inhabitant of a *Kofel*) 67

Kaufmann, Kauffman (merchant) 105

Kaul (swamp) 80

Kaulbach (swamp brook) 80, 77, 122

Kaulfuss (clubfoot) 114

Kaup, Kaupp, Kauper, Kaupert 74 (merchant) 105

Kautz, Kauz (screech owl) 115, 122

Kayler, Kaylor 159, see Kehler, Koehler

Kayley, see Kuehle

Kaylor, see Koehler

Kayser, see Kaiser

Kazmier 159, see Kaesemeyer

Keabler 159, see Kuebler

Keagle 159, see Kegel

Keane 159, see Kuehn

Keasel 159, Keasler, see Kiesel, Kiessler

Keating 159, see Gueting

Keaver 159, see Geber, Kieffer

Keber, see Geber

Kebhart 159, see Gebhard

Keck (lively) 115

Keebler 159, see Kuebler

Keefer 159, see Kieffer

Keefover 159, Kefauver, see Kiefhofer

Keehn 159, Keehner, see Kuehn, Kuehner

Keel 159, Keely, Keeler, see Kuehl, Kuehler

Keen 159, Keene, Keener, see Kuehn, Kuehne, Kuehner

Keenaple 159 < Kienappel (pine cone) 118

Keeny 159, see Kuehn, Kuehne

Kees, Keesen < Cornelius

Keesler 159, see Kiessler

Keeting 159, see Gueting

Kegel, Kegelmann (illegitimate child) 119

Kegler (ten-pin player) 118

Kehl, Kehle (throat) 114, also < Wolfskehl 122

Kehl (narrow gorge) 76

Kehler (fr Kehl, swamp) 122, see also Koehler

Kehr, Kehrs 59, Kehrer, Kehrmann 94 (dweller on the Kere) 83, 122

Kehs, see Kaes

Keibler 159, see Kuebler

Keichenmeister 159, see Kuechenmeister

Keicher (gasper, wheezer) 114

Keidel (course or misshapen person) 115

Keifer (quarreler) 115, see Kieffer 159

Keil (wedge, woodchopper) 95

Keiler (wild boar) 115, 91

Keilhauer (boar tusk) 91

Keilhauer (woodcutter) 95

Keilholtz (wedge for splitting wood, wood chopper) 95

Keillor 159, see Keiler

Keim (germ, sprout) 118

Keim 53 < Joachim 135

Keiper, Keipert 74 (fish netter) 91

Keiser, Keisser, see Kaiser

Keisersmith 159 (imperial smith) 110

Keisler, see Kessler

Keiss 159, see Kies, Geiss

Kelbaugh 159 (swamp brook) 80, 77

Kelberman (calf dealer) 91, 105

Kelch, Kelchner (chalice, calice maker, fr Latin *calix*) 96

Kell, Kelle (ladle, trowel, mason)
106, 122

Kelle (swamp) 81

Kellenberger (fr Kellenberg,
swamp mountain) 81, 68, 122

Keller, Kellers 59, Kellner (cellar,
cellar master, fr Latin
cellenarium) 102, 122

Kellerhouse 153 (cellar house) 65

Kellermann, Kellermeyer (butler,
keeper of the cellar) 102, 94,
93

Kellner, Kelner, see Keller

Kelly 159, see Kell, Kelle

Kelnoffer (swamp farmer) 81, 92

Kelsch, Koelsch (from Cologne)
122

Kelteisen, see Kalteisen

Kelter, Keltner, Keltermann
(winepress, vintner, fr Latin
calcatura) 96

Kem, Kembel, Kemele, Kemler,
Kemmler, Kemmer, Kemner,
Kemmacher (comb maker,
wool comber) 96, 106

Kemenate (room with a hearth)
118

Kemerer, Kemmerer, see
Kaemmerer

Kemmel (resident on a ridge) 68

Kemmel, see Kam

Kemp, Kempe, Kempel, Kempen,
Kempf, Kempfer, Kemper,
Kemperle, Kemphfer 159,
Kemperly 159 (champion) 84

Kempt, Kempter (fr Kempten)
122

Kendel, Kendal 159 (fr Kenel)
122

Kendig, see Kundig

Kenimer 159, Kenimar, see
Genheimer

Kenner (connoisseur) 115

Kenpf, see Kemp

Kensler 159 < Kentzler
(chancelor)

Kentner (Slavic: stand for beer
and wine barrels) 146

Kentner (fr Kenten) 122

Kentzel 159 (raised ground) 68

Kephart 159, see Gebhard

Keplinger, see Kepplinger

Keppel, Kepple 159, Keppler,
Kepler, Kepner (cap maker, fr
Kappel) 96, 106, 122

Keppelhoff (chapel court) 156

Kepplinger (fr Kepplingen)

Kerbe (notch, score, taverner) 96

Kerber (basket maker) 96

Kerch ..., Kerck, see Kirch ...

Kerchner, see Kirchner

Kerg, Kerge, Kerger, see Karg

Kerhart 159, see Gerhard

Kerker (prison, fr Latin *carcer*)

Kerkhof 92, 122, see Kirchhoff

Kerkhuis (church house) 65

Kerkner, see Kirchner

Kerl (fellow, rascal) 115

Kermes, Kermisch (kermess,
church festival) 143

Kern (kernel, grain, farmer) 91

Kern (handmill) 103, 122

Kernberg, Kernberger (mill
mountain) 103, 68, 122

Kernebeck (swamp stream) 80,
77

Kernenbeck (miller of coarse
grain) 103

Kerner (carter) 96, see also
Koerner

Kersch 122, Kerschner,
Kerschman, see Kirsch,
Kirschner, Kirschman

Kerschbaum (cherry tree) 89, 122

Kerschensteiner (cherry stone)
89, 73

Kerschner, see Kuerschner

Kerse, Kerser (Christian) 140

Kershbaum 159, see Kirschbaum

Kerst, Kersten (Christian) 139,
see also Gerst

Kertsche, see Kerzner

Kerzendocht (candle wick, candle maker) 96

Kerzner (candle maker) 96

Kesbauer, Kesemeyer (swamp farmer) 80, 91

Kese, see Kaese

Keslar, Kesler, see Kessler

Kessel, Kessell, Kessler, Kessels 59 (kettle, kettle maker or burnisher, fr Latin *cattilus*) 101

Kesselberg (kettle mountain) 68

Kesselhut (helmet maker) 108

Kesselring (kettle hook, cook) 106

Kessler (kettle maker, tinker) 96

Kestenbaum (chestnut tree) 89

Kestenberg (chestnut mountain) 89, 68

Kestenholtz (chestnut wood, cabinet maker) 89

Kester, Kesster, Kestner, Kestler, Kestermann, see Kaestner

Kester, see Kuestner

Ketchindaner 159, see Getzendanner

Ketelhut (kettle lid) 96, 106

Kettelberger (kettle mountain) 68

Kettelkamp (kettle field) 84, 118

Kettenmacher (maker of chain mail) 108

Kettenring (chain mail) 108

Ketter, Ketterer, Kettler, Kettner (chain maker, fr Latin *catena*) 96

Ketzer (heretic, fr Latin *Cathari*)

Keufer (purchaser) 96

Keul, Keuler (club, mallet maker) 96

Keusch (pure, virgin) 115

Keyl, see Keil

Keyser, Keysers 59, see Kaiser

Khunn 159, see Kuhn

Kibler 159, Kiebler, see Kuebler

Kiefer, Kiefere, Kieffer, Kiefner, Kieffner, Kiefert 74 (cooper, fr Latin *cuparius*) 96, 101

Kiefhaber, see Kiefhofer

Kiefhofer (fr the Kiefhof, pine farm) 89, 92

Kieger 159, see Geiger

Kiehl, Kuehl (cool) 118

Kiehlewein (cool wine, taverner) 96

Kiehn, Kiehner, see Kuehn

Kiehnholtz (pine wood) 89, 72

Kiehnle 55, Kienke 55 (little pine) 89

Kienappel (pine cone) 118

Kienast (pine branch) 89

Kienholdt (pine forest) 89, 72

Kienle (little pine) 89

Kienscherf (pine shavings, carpenter) 96

Kienz, Kientz 159, see Kuenz

Kienzle, Kienzel, see Kuenz

Kies, Kiesel, Kiessel, Kieseler, Kiesling, Kiessling (pebbles) 118

Kieselhorst (pebble hurst) 72, 122

Kieser, Kiesler (beverage taster, weight tester) 109

Kiesewetter (Check the weather!, weather forecaster) 116

Kiesselbach (pebble brook) 77, 122

Kiessling (dweller in the pebbles or gravel) 122

Kiester 159, see Kuester

Kifer 159, Kiffer, see Kieffer

Kihl 159, see Kuehl

Kihn 159, see Kuehn

Kilberg, see Kilchberg

Kilchberg (church mountain) 68, 122

Kilchenstein (church mountain) 73

Kilcher (chief cleric in a church) 110

Kile 159, Kiler, see Keil, Keiler

Kilgen, Kilian, Killian (St. Kilian, Irish monk) 135

Kilmer 159, see Kuehlmer

Killwaine, see Kiehlewein

Kimmel, Kimmell, Kimmelman 94, see Kuemmel

Kimmer (tub maker) 96

Kimmerle 55, see Kuemmerle

Kimpel 159, see Guempel

Kince 159, see Kuentz

Kind, Kindt, Kindl 55, Kindle 55, Kindlein 55, Kinder (child, minor)

Kindermann (schoolmaster) 96, 94

Kindig, Kindige, see Kundig

Kindsvater, Kindervater (baptismal sponsor) 119

King, see Koenig

Kinn, Kinlein 55 (chin) 114

Kinnard, see Kuehn

Kinnss 159, see Kuentz

Kinsberger 159, see Guenzberg

Kinsbrunner 159 (Guenther's well) 79

Kinsel, Kinsler 159, see Kuenzel

Kinsey, see Kuentz 151

Kinstler 159, see Kuenstler

Kintz 159, Kintzel, Kintzer, see Kuentz, Kuentzel, Kuentzler

Kinzinger (fr Kinzingen) 122

Kipp, Kippe, Kipper, Kippers 59 (dweller on the Kippe) 83

Kippenberg (marsh mountain) 80, 68

Kippenberg (mountain on the Kipper) 84, 68

Kippenbrock (brake on the Kippe) 83, 80

Kirbach, see Kirchbach

Kirberger, see Kirchberg

Kirch (church, dweller near the church) 71

Kirchbach (church brook) 77, 122

Kirchbauer (peasant on glebe land) 139, 91

Kirchberg, Kirchberger (church mountain) 68, 122

Kircheck (church field) 139, 85

Kirchenbauer (church builder) 96

Kircher, see Kirchner

Kirchgaessner, Kirchgesser, Kirchgessner (dweller on church alley) 65

Kirchhausen (church houses) 65, 122

Kirchheim (church hamlet) 139, 124

Kirchherr (church patron) 110

Kirchhof, Kirchhoff, Kirkhof, Kirchhoffer (church yard, cemetery) 8, 71, 92, 122

Kirchman (sexton) 110

Kirchmeier, Kirchmeyer (glebe farmer) 139, 93

Kirchner (employee of church, dweller near church) 71, 110

Kirchoff, Kirchhofen, see Kirchhoff

Kirck, Kircke, Kirckner, Kirkner, see Kirch, Kirche, Kirchner

Kirk... , see Kirch

Kirkenberg (church mountain) 68, 139

Kirn, Kirner (swamp) 80, see Kern, Kerner, Koerner

Kirsch (cherry, fr Latin *ceresia*) 89

Kirschbaum, Kirschenbaum (cherry tree) 89, 122

Kirschenhofer (fr the Kirschhof, cherry farm) 89, 92

Kirschensteiner (cherry stone) 89, 73

Kirscher, Kirschner, see Kuerschner

Kirschermann, Kirschenmann, Kirschman (cherry grower or dealer) 89, 105

Kirschfeld (cherry field) 89, 84
Kirschner, see Kuerschner
Kirschstein (cherry stone) 89, 73
Kirsh ... 159, see Kirsch ...
Kirsh 159, Kirshman, Kirsher,
   etc., see Kirsch etc.
Kirst, Kirsten (Christian) 135
Kirts 159, Kirtz, see Kuertz
Kiselburgh 159 (gravel castle) 73
Kiser 159, see Kaiser
Kisner 159, Kissner, see Kistner
Kisselbach (gravel brook) 77
Kissinger (fr Kissing or
   Kissingen, swamp area) 80,
   122
Kissner, see Kister
Kist, see Christian
Kister, see Kuester
Kister, Kistner, Kistler,
   Kistenmacher (chest maker, fr
   Latin *cista*) 96
Kitsintander 159, see
   Getzendanner
Kittel, Kittle, Kittelmann,
   Kittleman 159 (smock, baker,
   miller, etc.) 112, 106
Kittner, Kittler (monk, smock
   wearer, smock maker) 112, 96,
   110
Kitz, Kitzer, Kitzmann 94 (kid,
   goatherd) 91, 95
Kitzbiehl, Kitzbuel (goat hill) 67
Kitzing, Kitzinger (fr Kitzing)
   122
Kitzmiller (kid miller) 103
Kitzover (kid farm) 92
Klaas 53 < Nikolaus
Klaeger (public prosecutor) 109
Klaff, Klaffer (gossip) 115
Klaffenbach (resounding brook)
   77, 122
Klag, Klage, Klager (complaint,
   complainant) 115
Klages (Nikolaus) 135
Klaiber, see Kleiber

Klamm, Klamman 94 (dweller in
   a gorge) 76
Klang (sound) 118
Klapf (cliff) 68
Klapp (shutter, trapdoor) 118
Klapp, Klapper, Klappert 74
   (gossip) 115
Klappauf (Open up!) 116
Klapproth (clearing in the Hartz
   Mountains) 126
Klar, Klaar, Klarr, Klahr (clear)
   115
Klar (husband or son of Clara)
Klarmann (man of rectitude) 115,
   138, 94
Klas 53, Klaas, Klass, Klassen,
   Klaus < Nikolaus
Klatthaar (tousled hair) 112
Klatzkopf (bald head) 114
Klaucke (wise man) 115
Klaue (claw, cloven hoof) 114
Klauenberg, Klaunberg (claw
   mountain) 68, 122
Klaus 53, Klauss < Nikolaus 122
Klause, Klausen 122, Klauser,
   Klausener, Klausmann,
   Klaussner, Klausler (hermit's
   cell, hermit, fr Latin *clausum*)
   110
Klause (gap) 68
Klausmeyer, Klausmayer,
   Klausmeier (farmer near
   hermit's cell, in a gap) 103
Klausmier 159, see Klausmeyer
Kleamann 159, see Klehmann
Kleb, Klebe, Klebes 59, Kleber,
   Klebert 74 (dweller in a damp
   place) 80
Kleber, Klebert 74 (plasterer) 96
Kleckner, see Gloeckner
Klee 53 < Nikolaus
Klee (clover) 89
Kleebach (clover brook) 89, 77
Kleebauer (clover farmer) 89, 91
Kleeberg (clover mountain) 89,
   68, 122

Kleefeld (clover field) 89, 84, 122

Kleefisch (fr Cleves) 121

Kleemann (clover farmer) 89, 91, see also Clemens

Kleemeyer (clover farmer) 89, 93

Kleepuhl (clover pond) 89, 80

Klees 53 < Nicklas

Klef (cliff) 122

Kleger, Klegermann, see Klaeger

Klehmann (plasterer) 96, 94

Kleiber (clay plasterer) 96

Kleid, Kleidlein 55, Kleiderlein (clothing, clothier) 96, 106

Klein, Kleine, Kleiner, Kleines 59, Kleinert 74, Kleinle 55 (small)

Kleinbach (small brook) 77

Kleinbart (small beard) 112

Kleinbaum (small tree) 89

Kleinberg (small mountain) 68, 122

Kleindienst (small service, tax duty) 139

Kleinfeld, Kleinfield 153, Kleinfeldt, Kleinfelder, Kleinfelter (small field) 84, 122

Kleinhammer (small hammer, carpenter) 96, 122

Kleinhans (Little John, John the younger) 113

Kleinhauf (small heap, small troop) 107

Kleinhaus (fr Kleinhausen 122, small houses) 65

Kleinheinz (little Henry) 113

Kleinhenn (small hen) 115

Kleinjohann (small John, John the younger) 113

Kleinknecht (secondary hired hand) 95

Kleinkopf (small head) 114

Kleinlein, Kleinmann 94, Kleinmeyer 103 (small, little) 113

Kleinman (small man) 113

Kleinmichel (little Michael, Michael the younger) 113

Kleinpeter (little Peter, Peter the younger) 113

Kleinschmidt, Kleinsmith (locksmith) 96

Kleinschrot (small grain, groats, miller) 103

Kleinsteuber (fine dust)

Kleis 53, Kleiss < Nikolaus

Kleist, Kleistner (paster) 96

Klem 53, Klemm, Klement, Klementz < St. Clementius 135, 94 (name of pope)

Klemann, Kleemann, Klehmann < St. Clementius 135

Klemm, Klemme, Klemmer (penurious, stingy) 115, see Klempner

Klemmich, see Kleinmichel

Klempner (tinsmith) 96

Klenck, Klenk, Klencker, Klenkel 55 (dweller by a marsh pool) 80

Klepp, Klepper, Kleppner, Kleppert 74 (gossip, calumniator) 115

Klepper (nag, jade; tenant who pays in horses) 91

Klett, Klette (burr, bothersome person) 115

Kletter (hanger-on) 115

Kliebenschaedel (Cleave the skull!, mercenary) 116, 96

Kliebenstein (Split the stone!, quarryman) 116

Kliegel, Kleugel, see Klug

Kliem, see Clemens

Klimper, see Klempner

Klinbach 159, see Kleinbach

Klinck, Klincken, Klinkmann 94 (dweller by a marsh pool) 80

Kline 159, see Klein

Klinedienst 159, Klinedinst, see Kleindienst

Klinefelter 159, see Kleinfeld

Klinejohn 153, see Kleinjohann

Kling, Klinge, Klinges 59 (deep gorge with noisy stream) 76, 122

Klingebuhl, Klingebuehl, Klingebiel (gorge hill) 76, 84

Klingehoffer, Klingenhoffer, Klingenhofer, Klingelhofer, Klingelhoefer, Klingelover (fr the Klingehoff, gorge farm) 76, 92

Klingel, Klinkel (small bell) 106

Klingelhofer, see Klingehoffer

Klingelschmidt (bell smith) 96

Klingemann, see Klingmann

Klingemeyer, Klingenmeier (gorge farmer) 76, 93

Klingenbach (gorge stream) 76, 77

Klingenbuehl (gorge hill) 67

Klingenhagen (gorge enclosure) 76, 124, 122

Klingenhofer (fr Klingenhof 122), see Klingehoffer

Klingenschmidt, Klingensmith 153 (sword smith, cuttler) 96

Klingenstein (gorge mountain) 76, 73, 122

Klinger, Klingermann 94, Klingmann (swordsmith) 96, 108

Klinger (gorge dweller) 76

Klinghammeer, see Klinkhammer

Klinghoffer (fr Klinghof 122), see Klingehoffer

Klingkammer, see Klinkhammer

Klingler (public crier) 109

Klingmann 94, Klingmeyer 93 (occupant of a gorge) 76, 94, 93

Klingseis (May the iron sound!, blacksmith) 96, 116

Klink, Klinke, Klinker (latch, locksmith) 96

Klinkhamer, Klinkhammer (latch hammer, locksmith) 96

Klinsmith 153, see Kleinschmidt

Klipp, Klippe (shoemaker) 96

Klippenstein (craggy mountain, cliff) 73

Klob (plump coarse person) 114, 115

Klobenholtz (split fire wood, wood cutter) 96

Klock, Klocke, Klocker, see Glock, Glocke, Glocker

Klockmann (wise man) 115

Kloekner, Klocker (bell ringer) 96

Kloepfer (mallet, knocker) 118

Kloes, Kloese (dumpling, cook) 112, 96

Kloesterkamp (cloister field) 65, 84

Kloetzel 55, Kloetzli, see Klott

Kloever (wood splitter) 96

Kloosterhuis (cloister house) 110, 65

Klopfenstein (Strike the stone!, quarryman) 116, 96

Klopfer (mallet) 106

Klopfinstern (Beat your forehead in remorse, penitent) 116

Klopp (flax swingle) 106, 112

Kloppenstein (stone for sharpening scythes, see Dengler) 73

Kloppmann (flax swingler) 95

Klose (dumling) 112

Klose, see Klause

Klosmann 53, 94, Klossmann, Klossner < Nikolaus

Kloss, Klosse (lump, clump) 118

Kloss 53 < Nikolaus

Kloster, Klostermann 94 (cloister, monk, fr Latin *claustrum*) 110, 122

Klotfelder (log-strewn field) 84

Kloth (lump, clod) 113

Klothusen (log house) 65

Klott, Klotz (block, log) 115
Klotz (clumsy person) 115
Klotzbach (stream full of logs) 77
Klouser 159, see Klause
Kluckhohn (brooding hen)
Klueber (wood cleaver)
Klueg, Klug, Kluge, Kluger, Kluegel, Klugmann 94 (clever) 115
Klump, Klumpp (clumsy person) 115
Klung, Klunck, Klunk (tassel maker) 96
Kluse, see Klause
Klutz, see Klotz
Klyne 159, see Klein
Knab, Knabe, Knabbe, Knapp, Knappe (boy, miner, lumberjack) 113
Knabschneider (boy's tailor) 96
Knann, see Gnann
Knapheide, Knapheit (scarcity) 114
Knapp, Knappe (page, boy, miner) 113, 96
Knauer (course person) 115
Knauf, Knauff (nob, stub)
Knaus (niggardly) 115
Knebel (crossbar) 106
Knebel (crude person) 115
Knecht (servant, hired hand) 96
Knechtel 55, Knechtle (little servant) 97
Kneemoeller 159, see Niemoeller
Knef (shoemaker's knife, shoemaker) 96, 106
Kneip (knife, shoemaker) 106, 96
Kneip, Kneipe, Kneiper (taverner) 96
Kneiss (gneiss)
Knell, Kneller (noisy person) 115
Knepper (button maker) 96
Knie (knee) 114

Knieper, Knipper (users of pincers, such as cobblers and leather workers) 96
Knieriemen, Knierim 159 (knee strap, leather worker) 106
Knight 159, see Knecht
Knipe 159, Kniper, see Kneip, Kneiper
Knittel, Knittle 159 (cudgel, crude person) 115
Knobel (little shelter, birdcage) 118
Knobel, Knoble 159 (round elevation) 74, 122
Knoblauch, Knobeloch (garlic seller) 105, 122
Knochen (bones) 113, 122
Knochenhauer (butcher) 96
Knoechel, Knochel (knuckle) 113
Knoedler (dumpling maker) 96
Knoepfel, Knoepfler, Knoepfmacher (button maker, button seller) 96, 106
Knoll, Knolle (hill, mountain top) 67, 68, 122
Knopf, Knopfle, Knopfler, Knoepler (button, button maker) 106
Knopp 122, see Knapp, Knopf
Knor, Knorr (nob, knot, hunchback) 113
Knor (hill) 68
Knospe (gnarl, short person) 113
Knotz (gnarl) 113
Knous, Knouse 159, see Knaus
Knuell (ruffian) 115
Knuettel, see Knittel
Knuetter (net maker) 96
Knur, see Knor, Knauer
Kobarg (cow hill) 67
Kobel, Kobler (fr Kobel, swamp) 122
Kobel (cottage) 118
Koben (hut, pig pen, pig raiser) 91

Kofel, Koffel, Kofler, Koffler, Kofer (projection on slope of mountain, see Unterkofler) 67

Kofer, see Kofel

Koffer (trunk, fr Latin *cophinus*, but often corruption of *Kofler*) 96

Kofman 159, Koffman, Koffmann, see Kaufmann

Kogel, Kogler (cowl, monk, hood maker, fr Latin *cuculla*) 106, 122

Kogel, see Kugel

Kohde, see Gode

Kohl, Kohle (cabbage, cabbage dealer, fr Latin *caulis*) 105

Kohlbauer (cabbage planter) 91

Kohlbecker (cabbage brook) 80, 77

Kohlberg, Kohlenberg, Kohlenstein (coal mountain) 68, 73, 122

Kohlberg, Kohlenberg (cabbage mountain) 68, 73, 122

Kohlbrenner, Kohlenbrenner (charcoal burner, collier) 95

Kohleisen (collier's poker, collier) 95

Kohler, Koehler, Kohlerman 94 (collier, charcoal burner) 95

Kohlfelt (cabbage field) 84

Kohlhammer, see Kohlheim

Kohlhas 53, Kohlhaas < Nikolaus

Kohlhas (cabbage hare, nickname for peasant) 112

Kohlhauer (coal digger) 95

Kohlhaus, see Kohlhas 122

Kohlhaver 159, see Kohlhof

Kohlheim (cabbage hamlet, coal hamlet) 124

Kohlhof, Kohlhoff (cabbage farm) 92, 122

Kohlleppel (cabbage spoon) 106

Kohlman, Kohlmann (collier) 95, 94

Kohlmeyer (fr the Kohlhoff, cabbage farm) 93

Kohn, Kohne, Kohner, see Kuhn, Cohen

Kohnke, Kohnle (little Kuhn) 55

Kol, Kole, Koler, see Kohl, Kohler

Kolb 159, see Kalb

Kolb, see Kolbe

Kolbach (cabbage brook) 77

Kolbacher, see Kohlbecker

Kolbe, Kolby 159, Kolben (club) 122

Kolbenhauer, Kolbenheyer (cudgel maker) 96, 106

Kolemann, see Kohlmann

Kolker, see Kalk, Kalker

Kollenbach 159, see Kaltenbach

Kollenborn 159, see Kaltenborn

Koller, Kollermann (cape or jacket maker) 112, 106

Koller (giddiness, frenzy) 115

Kollman, Kollmann, Kollner, Kolman, see Kohlmann

Kolmeyer (cabbage farmer) 91

Kolpach, see Kolbach

Kolter, Koltermann (plowshare, fr Latin *culter*) 106

Kompost, see Gumpost

Konder 159, see Gunther

Kone, see Kohn

Konig 159, Konik, see Koenig

Konigsberg, see Koenigsberg

Konigsdorffer (king's village) 124

Konkel, Konkle 159, see Kunckel

Konrad, see Conrad

Konradi, son of Konrad 142

Konter, see Guenther

Konts 159, Konz, see Kuntz

Konvenz (convent) 71

Konzelman 159, see Kuenzelmann

Koobler 159, see Kuebler

Koog (polder) 84

Koogel 159, Koogle, Koogler, see Kugel

Kool 159, Kooler, see Kuhl,
  Kuhler, Kohler
Koolhoff 159, see Kuhlhoff
Koon 159, Koons 59, see Kuhn,
  Kunz
Koonce 159, Koons, see Kunz
Koons, Koontz 159, see Kuntz
Koop, Koopman, Koopmann, see
  Kauf, Kaufmann
Kopald (cobalt)
Kopf (head, cup, fr Latin *cuppa*)
  114
Kopfermann, see Kupfermann
Kopisch < Jacob
Kopp 53, 134 < Jacob, see also
  Kapp, Kopf
Kopmann, see Kaufmann
Koppel 53, 55, 134 < Jacob
Koppel (common pasture) 84, 122
Koppel (leash, leash of hounds,
  hunter) 91
Koppelberger (mountain with
  common pasture) 68
Koppelmann (farmer with rights
  to common pasture) 94
Koppenhafer, Koppenhaver,
  Koppenhofer, Koppenhoffer,
  Koppenhoefer (fr
  Koppenhoefen 122, Jacob's
  farm) 92
Koppenhoffer (farmer who pays
  rent in capons) 92
Kopper (bloodletter) 96, see
  Kupfer
Koppermann, see Kupfermann
Koppman, see Kaufmann
Korb (basket, fr Latin *corbis*,
  basket maker 106, child found
  in a basket, fr the Korb 83)
Korbach 122, Korbeck (swampy
  brook) 80, 77
Korber, Koerber (basket maker)
  96
Kordes 53 < Conrad
Kordewan (Cordovan leather,
  leatherworker) 106

Korenberg, see Kornberg
Korenblit, see Kornblit
Korff, Korfes 59, Korfmann 94
  (basket, basket maker) 96, 106
Korn (grain, wheat, grain dealer)
  91, 105
Kornblatt (corn blade) 118
Kornblit (grain blossom) 89
Kornblum (cornflower) 89
Korndorf (grain village) 124
Korner, see Koerner
Kornfeld (grain field) 84
Kornguth (grain farm) 92
Kornhaus (granary) 65
Kornhauser (granary manager)
  109
Kornhizer 159, 66, see
  Kornhauser
Kornman, Kornmann 94 (grain
  raiser, grain dealer) 91, 105
Kornmesser (official grain
  measurer) 109
Kornmeyer, Kornmayer (grain
  farmer) 93
Kornmutter (grain measurer) 109
Kornprobst (grain supervisor)
  109
Kornreich (rich in grain) 118
Kornrumpf (grain sieve) 96, 106
Kornscheuer (grain barn,
  granary) 65
Kornstein (grain mountain) 68
Korper 159, see Koerper
Korpman, see Korber
Kort, Korte, Korten, Korter,
  Korth, Kortte, Kortz, see
  Kurtz
Korthals (short neck) 114
Korthose (short pants) 112
Kortjohann (short John) 113
Kortkamp (short field) 84
Kortschenkel (short legs) 114
Kortz, Korz, see Kurtz
Kost, Koster, Kostermann 94
  (taster), see Kuester
Kotch 159, see Koch

Kotchenreuter 159,
    Kotchenreuther, see
    Kochenreiter
Koth, Kothe (mud, filth) 118
Kotmair (mud farmer) 93
Kotsch 159, see Koch
Kotschenreuther 159, see
    Kochenreiter
Kottenbach (granary creek) 77
Koubek 159, Koubik, see
    Kuhbach
Koufman 159, see Kaufmann
Kougl 159, see Kugel
Kouns 159, Kountz, see Kuntz
Kouperstein 159, see Kupferstein
Koutz 159, see Kautz
Kowellentenz 159, see Coblentz
Kraatz, see Kratz
Krabacher (crow brook) 77
Krabbe (crab, active person) 115
Krabbe (shrimp dealer) 105
Krabill, see Kraebuehl
Krach (noise) 115
Krack, Kracke (crow) 115
Krack (underbrush) 72
Kraeber, see Graeber
Kraehbuehl (crow hill) 67
Kraehe (crow) 115
Kraehenwinkel (crow corner) 69
Kraeher (crow catcher) 96
Kraemer, Kraehmer (shopkeeper,
    retailer) 105
Kraenckel, Kraenkel (sickly) 115
Kraetzer, see Kratzer
Kraeuter, Kraeuther (herbs, herb
    seller) 106
Kraff, see Graf
Kraft, Krafte, Krafft (strength)
    115
Kraft (river name) 83
Krager 159, see Krueger
Krahe 159, see Kraehe
Krahenbuhl 159, see Kraehbuehl
Krahenwinkel (crow woods) 69
Krahling 159 (little crow) 115

Krahmer, see Kraemer
Krahn, see Kran
Krahwinckel, see Krahenwinckel
Kral, Krall, Kralle (claw) 114
Kral (Czech: king, fr Carl) 146
Krallmann (fr Krall) 122, 94
Kram (retail trade, huckster's
    pack, huckster) 105, 122
Kramer, Kramers 59, see
    Kraemer
Kramp, Krampf (cramp) 118
Kran, Krane (crane) 115
Kranck (sick) 115
Kranefeld (crowfield) 84
Kranewitter, Krannewetter,
    Krannebitter (juniper forest)
    89
Kranick, Kranich (crane, proud
    person) 115
Kranitzfeld (border field, fr
    Slavic) 84, 146
Krank (sick, weak) 115
Krankheit (sickness) 118
Krantz, Kranz, Krans 159
    (wreath, rosary) 106
Kranwinckel (crow woods, crane
    woods) 72
Krapf, Krapfen, Krapfer (fritter)
    106, 112
Krapf (hooked nose, hunched
    back) 114
Krappmann (doughnut maker)
    96
Krass (crass, gross) 115
Kratz 53 < St. Pancratius 135
Kratz, Kratzer, Kratzler, Krazer
    (scraper, wool comber) 96
Kraus, Krauss, Krause, Krauser,
    Krausman 94 (curly haired)
    112
Krausam, see Grausam
Kraushaar (curlyhead) 112, 159
Krauskob, Krauskopf (curly
    headed) 112

Kraut, Krauth (greens, herbs)
106

Krauter, Krautler, Krauthman
94, Krautz, Krautze, see
Kraeuter

Krauthammer (fr Krautheim,
herb hamlet) 124, 122

Krautheim, see Krauthammer

Kraybil 159, Kraybill, Kraybell,
see Kraehbuehl

Kreager 159, see Krueger

Kreamer 159, see Kraemer

Kreatchman 159, Kreatchmann,
see Kretschmann

Krebill, Krebiel, Krebuehl,
Krebuel, see Kraebuehl

Krebs, Krebser (crab, crab
catcher, sign of zodiac) 96, 143

Krebsbach (crayfish brook) 77

Kreczner, see Kretsch

Kreek 159, see Krueg

Krefeld (swampy field) 80, 84

Kreft, see Kraft

Kreger 159, Kregar, Kreeger, see
Krueger

Kreh (crow) 115

Krehbiehl 159, see Kraebuehl

Krehmeyer (fr the Kraehoff, crow
farm) 93

Krehnbrink (crow hill) 74

Krei, see Kraehe

Kreide, Kreider, Kreidler (chalk
maker or seller, fr Latin *creda*)
96, 106

Kreider, see Kraeuter

Kreideweiss (chalk white) 112

Kreig 159, Kreigh, Kreiger, see
Krueg, Krueger

Kreiner 159, see Greiner

Kreis, Kreiss, Kreise (circle,
district), see Greis

Kreisberg (district mountain) 68,
see Kreutzberg

Kreischer (screamer) 115

Kreisel, Kreisler (spinning top)
118

Kreiter (quarreler) 115, see
Kraeuter

Kreith (cleared land) 125

Kreitz (cleared land) 126, 122,
also see Kreutz

Kreitzberg (cleared mountain),
see Kreutzberg

Kreitzer, Kreitzner, see Kreutzer

Krell, Kreller (cross-patch) 115

Krell, see Grell

Kremer, see Kraemer

Kremeyer (fr the Krehhof, crow
farm) 93

Kremp, Krempf (hat with turned
up brim) 112

Krempe (swamp) 80

Krempel (wool carder) 96

Krempel, Krempler (peddler) 96

Krenkel, see Kraenkel

Krentz, Krenzmann 94, see
Grentzel

Krepp, Krepner (dweller on a
sunken path) 65

Kreps, Krepps, see Krebs

Kress (cress, fr Latin *cresso*) 89

Kress (gudgeon, fisherman) 91

Kressmann (Christian) 135, 94

Kretsch, Kretschmer,
Kretschmar, Kretzschmar,
Kretchmer, Kretschmann 94
(tavern keeper, fr Slavic) 9, 96,
146

Kretz, Kretzer, Kretzel, Kretzler
(collector of fines) 109, 122

Kreuder, see Kreider, Kraeuter

Kreuger 159, see Krueger

Kreul, see Greul

Kreuscher, see Kreischer

Kreuth, see Gereuth, Kraeuter

Kreutz, Kreuz, Kreutziger,
Kreutzinger (crusader, dweller
on a cross road) 122

Kreutzach (cross spring) 79

Kreutzberg, Kreuzberger (fr
Kreuzberg 122, cross
mountain) 68, 122

Kreutzburg (cross castle) 73

Kreutzer, Kreuzer (a coin) 117

Kreutziger (crusader) 107

Krey, Kreye, Kreyer (crow) 113

Kreyder, see Kreider

Kreyenhagen (crow enclosure)
125

Kreymer 159, see Kraemer

Kreyss, Kreysz, see Kreis

Krick 159, see Krueck

Krickstein (crutch mountain) 73

Kridel 159, Kridler, Krideler, see
Kreidler

Kriech, Kriechbaum (blackthorn,
wild plum) 89

Krieder 159, Kriedler, see
Kreider

Krieg (war), see Krug

Krieger, see Krueger

Kriegmann, Kriegsman, see
Kruegmann

Kriegsmann (soldier) 107

Kriemhild (mask + battle) 46, 46

Kries, Kriesbaum, see Kirsch,
Kirschbaum

Krieter (querulous person) 115

Kriger 159, Krigger, Krigman,
see Kruegman

Krimm 122, see Grimm

Krimmel, Krimmell (crooked)
114, 122

Krimmelbein (crooked leg) 114

Kriner 159, see Greiner

Krings 53 < St. Quirinus 135

Kripps, see Krebs

Krise 159, see Kreis

Krisfeller, Christfelder (Christ's
field) 140

Krisler 159, see Kreisler

Krisman, Krissman, see
Kressmann

Krist, Kristian, see Christ,
Christian

Kritz 159, Kritzer, see Kreutzer

Kroat (Croat, Croatian
mercenary) 121, 107

Krob, Krobs 59, Krober, see Grob

Krock, Krocker (fr Crock or
Cracow) 122

Kroder, Kroeder, Kroeter (toad)
113

Kroebiel, see Kraebuehl

Kroeger, see Krueger

Kroeher, see Kraeher

Kroemer, see Kraemer

Krog, Kroger, Krogh, Krogman
94 (fr Krog 122), see Krug,
Krueger, Kruegman

Kroh (crow) 48, 115

Krohn, see Kron, Krahn

Krol, Kroll, Krall (Slavic for king
[Carl]) 146

Kroll (curly) 112

Kromer, see Kraemer

Kromholz, Krompholtz, see
Krumbholz

Kromm, see Krumm

Kron, Krone, Kroner, Krohne
(crown, house name) 63

Kron, see Kran

Kronau, see Gronau

Kronawetter 159, see
Krannewetter

Kronberg, Kronberger,
Kronenberg, Kronenberger,
Kroneberger (crown mountain)
68, 122

Kronburger (fr Kronburg 122,
crown castle) 73

Krone, see Kron

Kroneck (crown field) 85

Kronenschild (crown shield) 109

Kronewetter 159, see
Krannewetter

Kronfeld, Kronfeldt (royal field)
85

Kronforst (crown forest) 72

Kronhoff (crown farm) 92

Kronk 159, see Krank

Kronmaier, Kronmeyer (crown farmer) 93

Kronmueller (crown miller) 103

Kronsbehn (crane leg) 114

Kronstadt (crown city) 122

Kronwald (crown forest) 72

Kroon, see Kron

Kropf, Kropp (crop, goiter) 114

Krott (toad) 113

Krouse 159, Krouss, see Kraus, Krause

Kroushaar, Kroushour 159, see Kraushaar

Krout 159, see Kraut

Krueck (crutch) 114

Krueckeberg, Kruckeberg (fr Krueckenberg 122, crutch mountain) 68

Kreuder, see Kräuter

Krueger (tavern keeper) 63, 96

Kruegmann (tavern keeper) 63, 96, 94

Kruelle (curly) 112

Krueppel (cripple) 113

Kruesy, see Kraus

Kruetzer 159, see Kreutz

Krug, Krugs 59, Krug (pitcher, tavern, taverner) 63, 96, see Krueger

Kruger, Krugman, see Krueger, Kruegmann

Kruise 159, see Kraus

Krull (curly) 112

Krum 159, see Krumm

Krumbach (crooked brook) 77

Krumbein, Krumblebeim 159 (crooked leg) 114

Krumbhaar (curly hair) 112

Krumbholz, Krumholtz, Krummholtz (bent wood for wheel, wheelwright) 96

Krumenacker (crooked field) 84

Krumhus (crooked house) 65

Krumlauf (crooked course) 77

Krumm (crooked) 114

Krummacher (wainwright) 96

Krummeck (crooked field) 85

Krump, Krumpf (crooked, deformed) 113

Krumpholz, see Krumbholz

Krup, Krupp (croup, crupper) 113

Krus, Kruse, Krusen, Kruser, see Kraus

Kruth, see Kraut

Krutmann, Krautmann (spice dealer) 105, 94

Kruttschmer, see Kretschmer

Kryder 159, see Kreider

Kryger 159, see Krueger

Krygsman 159, see Kriegsmann

Kubach, Kubeck, see Kuhbach

Kubel 159, Kubler, see Kuebel, Kuebler

Kubel, Kubler (mountain ridge) 68

Kuche, see Kueche

Kuchenbeisser (cookie biter) 112

Kuchenmeister (chief cook) 96, 102

Kuckuck (cuckoo) 115

Kuebel, Kuebele, Kuebler, Kuebeller 159 (tub, bucket maker) 96

Kuechenmeister, see Kuchenmeister

Kuechler (cookie baker) 96

Kuefer, Kuefner, see Kieffer

Kuefus, see Kuhfuss

Kuegler, see Kugel

Kuehl, Kuehler, Kuehling, Kuehlmar, Kuehlman (dweller near a pit or mine) 94

Kuehlkopf (cool head) 115

Kuehltau (cool dew) 118

Kuehlwein, Kuehlenwein (cool wine, tavern) 63, 102

Kuehn, Kuehne, Kuehner, Kuehnert 74 (brave man) 115

Kuehnemann (brave man) 115, 94

Kuehnemund (brave + guardian)
115, 50
Kuehnholtz, see Kienholt
Kuemmel, Kuemmelmann 94
(carraway seed, fr Latin
cuminum) 106
Kuemmerle 55 (miserable
creature) 115
Kuempel, see Kump
Kuendig (knowledgeable)
Kuenholtz, see Kienholtz
Kuenkel, see Conrad
Kuenlin 55, see Kuhn
Kuenst, Kuenstler (artist,
artisan) 96
Kuenz, Kuentzel, Kuenzel,
Kuenzler, see Kunts
Kuerbis (gourd, farmer) 91
Kuerschner (furrier) 96
Kuertzer, see Kurtz
Kuessnacht (city in Switzerland)
122
Kuessner (bolster maker) 96
Kuester, Kuesterle 55 (sexton, fr
Latin *custos*) 110
Kuettner (cowl wearer, cowl
maker, monk) 96, 112, 110
Kufel, Kufler, see Kieffer
Kuffner, see Kiefer
Kugel, Kugel, Kugler,
Kugelmann 94 (cowl, cowl
maker or wearer, fr Latin
cuculla) 96, 106, 41
Kugel, Kugelberg (round topped
mountain) 68
Kuhaar (cow hair) 112
Kuhbach (cow brook) 77, 122
Kuhfuss (cow foot, club foot) 114
Kuhhirt (cowherd) 95
Kuhl, Kuhle, Kuhler, Kuhlert 74,
Kool 159 (pond, pit) 81
Kuhlau (meadow on a pond) 80
Kuhlenberg (cool mountain) 68

Kuhlmann, Kuhlman,
Kuhlemann, Kuehlemann
(dweller on a pond) 81
Kuhlmeyer (farmer at the pond)
81, 93
Kuhltau (cool dew) 118
Kuhlwein (cool wine, taverner)
96
Kuhlwetter (cool weather)
Kuhmann (cow man) 91, 94
Kuhn, Kuehn, Kuhne, Kuhnen,
Kuhns 59, Kuhner, Kuhnert
74, Kuhnke (brave) 115, also <
Konrad
Kulemann, see Kuhlmann
Kullenberg, Kullberg, see
Kuhlenberg
Kullenthal (cool valley, pond
valley) 81, 76
Kulm (peak) 68
Kulman, Kullmann, see
Kuhlmann
Kulp (carp) 115
Kumeler, see Kuemmeler
Kumet, Kummet, Kumeth,
Kumith 159 (horse collar) 106
Kummel, Kummell,
Kummelmann 94, see
Kuemmel
Kummer (sorrow) 122
Kummerbach (sorrow brook) 77
Kummerling 55, Kummerle 55
(stunted tree) 89
Kump, Kumpel, Kumper, Kumpf,
Kumps 59, Kumpermann
(barrel maker) 96, 106, 122
Kumpfmiller (miller with
overshot wheel) 103
Kumpost, Kumst (kind of
sourkraut, peasant food) 112
Kuncel 159
Kunckel, Kunkel, Kunkele
(distaff, fr Latin *conucula* 106,
relative on distaff side 119)
Kunckler (distaff maker) 96

Kunert, see Kuehnert

Kung, Kunig, see Koenig

Kunisch 53 < Conrad

Kunkel (spindle, spindle maker) 96

Kunkel, Kunkl, Kunkle 159, Kunkler, Kunkelmann 94 < Conrad, see Kunckel

Kunnert, see Kuehnert

Kuno, see Kuhn, Conrad

Kunolt, Kunoldt (brave + rule) 46, 48

Kunrad, see Conrad

Kunsman 159, see Kunstmann

Kunst (art, skill) 96, also < Constantius

Kunstler, see Kuenstler

Kunstmann, Kuntzler, Kuntzman, Kuntzmann, Kuntzelmann, Kunzelman (artisan) 96, 94

Kunts 159, Kuntz, Kuntze, Kunz, Kunze, Kundtz, Kunzle 55, Kuhns 59 < Conrad

Kuntsman 159, see Kunstmann

Kuper, Kuperman, see Kupfer, Kupfermann

Kuperberg, see Kupferberg

Kuperstein, see Kupferstein

Kupfer, Kupfermann 94 (copper dealer, fr Latin *cuprum*) 105

Kupferberg (copper mountain) 68

Kupferschmid (coppersmith) 96

Kupferstein (copper ore) 73

Kupp, Kupper, Kuppert 74 (dweller on a mountain peak) 68

Kuppenheim (town in Baden) 122

Kupperman, see Kupfer, Kupferman

Kur (fr Chur in Switzerland)

Kurad, Kurath < Conrad

Kuradi, Kunradi (son of Kurad) 142

Kurcfeld 159 (short field) 84

Kurcz, see Kurtz

Kurfurst, Kurfuerst (prince elector) 109

Kurland, Kurlander (territory on the Baltic) 121

Kursner 159, Kurstner, see Kuerschner

Kurt 53, Kurth, Kurtz 59, Kurtze, Kurz, Kurts 159 < Conrad

Kurtenbach (short brook) 77

Kurtz (short) 113

Kurtzendorf (short village) 124

Kurtzman 94, Kurtzman, Kurtzmeyer 93 (short man) 113

Kurtzweil (pastime, leisure) 115

Kurzman, see Kurtzman

Kuss (kiss), or < Dominicus 1

Kussmaul, Kusmaul, Kuszmaul (not "kiss mouth" but Czech for "tousle-haired") 112, 146

Kuster, Kustner, see Kuester

Kutler, Kuttler (maker or wearer of cowls 106, or fr Kutten 122)

Kutner 159, see Kuettner

Kutscher, Kutcher 159, Kutchermann 94 (coachman, fr Hungarian) 96

Kyle 159, Kyler, see Keil, Keiler

Kyme, see Keim 151

Kyseler, see Kies

Kyser 159, see Kaiser

Kyssel, see Kies

L

Laage, see Lage

Lach, Lack (laugh) 115

Lach (blaze on a tree) 118

Lach, Lache (puddle, lake) 80, 82, 122

Lachberg (boundary mountain) 68

Lachenicht (Don't laugh!) 116

Lachenmann, see Lachman

Lacher, see Lachner

Lacher (incanter, see Lachmann)

Lachman, Lachmann (leech, incanter) 96

Lachmann (dweller at a pond) 81

Lachmeyer (farmer on a lake) 80, 93

Lachner (dweller on a boundary or on a pond) 81

Lachs (salmon, salmon catcher) 91, 96

Lachter (laughter) 115

Lack, Lacker (laquer, laquerer) 96, 106, 122

Lacke, see Lach

Lackmann, see Lachmann

Lackner (meat pickler) 96

Lackner (dweller by a pond) 81

Lademacher (chest maker) 94, 98

Laden (window, store) 105

Lader, Ladner (loader) 96

Laderer 159, see Lederer

Laechler, Laechner (laugher) 115

Laechner, see Lachner

Laemmel, Laemmle, Laemmermann 94, Laemmer (lambs) 91

Laemmerhirt (shepherd) 91

Laendler (countryman) 118

Laerch (lark) 115

Laessig (easy-going) 115

Laeuenstein (lion mountain) 73

Laeufer (runner, deer's leg) 96, 91

Lage, Lagermann 94 (flat area between mountains, dweller there) 67, 71

Lager, Lagger (couch, lair, camp) 118

Lagerfeld (camp field, lair field) 84

Lahm, Lahme (lame) 114, 122

Lahman 159, see Lehmann

Lahn, Lahner (dweller on the Lahn) 83

Lahner, Lahners 164 (wire maker) 96

Lahr (dweller on the Lahr) 83, 122

Laib, see Leib

Laibinger (fr Laibingen) 122

Laible (baker) 96

Laicher (musician) 96

Laidig, see Ledig

Lainhart 159, see Lehnert, Leonhard

Lakemacher, Lakenmacher (blanket maker) 96

Lakmann, see Lachmann

Lallemand, see Alleman 144

Lamb, Lambb (lamb) 91

Lambard, see Lampart

Lambert, Lampert, Lambrecht, Lambrechts 59, Lamprecht (land + bright) 49, 47

Lambright 159, see Lambert

Laminit (Don't leave me!) 117

Lamm, Lamkin 55, Lamke 55, Lampke, Lammlein 55 (lamb, house name) 91

Lamp, Lampe, Lampen (lamp) 96, see also Lambert

Lampack 159, see Leimbach

Lampart, Lampert, Lombart (Lombard, banker) 96, 121, also see Lambert

Lampe (lamp) 106

Lance, see Lantz 151

Lanck, see Lang

Land, Landes (land, shortened form of certain names) 59

Landau, Landauer (name of province and cities) 121, 122

Landbeck (land brook) 77

Landborn (land spring) 79

Landeck, Landecker (name of a province) 121

Lander (picket fence) 84, 122

Landfeld, Landfelder (land field) 84

Landfried (mandate of peace) 118

Landgraf, Landgraff, Landgrebe, Landgrof (landgrave) 109

Landherr (territorial lord) 109

Landhut (regional lookout) 109

Landkammer (provincial court) 118

Landman, Landmann (countryman, compatriot) 94

Landmesser (surveyor) 96

Landolf (brave + wolf) 46, 48

Landolt (brave + loyal) 46, 47, 49

Landsberg, Landsberger 68

Landschultz (village mayor) 109

Landsknecht (lansquenet, pikeman) 107

Landskroner, Landskroener (fr Landskron) 122

Landsman, Landesman (countryman, compatriot) 94

Landsvenner (ensign, banner bearer) 107

Landwehr, Landweer, Landwehrmann (militiaman) 107

Landzberg, see Landsberg

Lane 159, see Lehn

Lanehardt 159, Lanehart, see Lehnert, Leonhard

Lang, Lange, Langer, Langert 74, Langes 59 (long, tall) 113

Langanacker, Langenacker (long field) 84

Langbaum (tall tree) 89, 113

Langbein, Langbehn (long leg) 114

Langemann (tall man) 113

Langen (short for names like Langenecker, etc.)

Langenau, Langau (long meadow) 84

Langenbach, Langenbacher, Langenbaugh 159 (long brook) 77, 122

Langenberg, Langenberger (long mountain) 68, 122

Langenbrunner (long spring) 79

Langendorf, Langendorfer (long village) 124, 122

Langenegger, Langenecker, Langeneker (fr Langeneck 122, long field) 84

Langenfeld, Langenfeldt, Langenfelder (fr Langenfeld 122, long fields) 84

Langenhagen (long hedge, enclosure) 125, 122

Langenkamp (long field) 84

Langenstrasse (long street) 65

Langenthal (long valley) 76, 122

Langenwalter (fr Langenwald 122, long forest) 71

Langer, Langermann 94 (tall mann) 113

Langereis (long journey) 118

Langfeldt 122, see Langenfeldt

Langfield 153, see Langenfeldt

Langfritz (tall Frederick) 113

Langguth, Languth (long estate) 92

Langhaar (long hair) 112

Langhage (long enclosure) 124, 122

Langhals (long neck) 114

Langhanke, see Langhans

Langhans (tall Johnny) 113

Langhaus (long house) 65, 122

Langheim (long hamlet) 124, 122

Langheinrich (tall Henry) 113

Langhirt (tall herdsman) 113, 95

Langhoff, Langhoffer, Langenhoffer (long farm) 92

Langhorn, Langhorne (long horn)

Langhorst (long hurst) 72, 122

Langhutte (long hut) 65

Langkammerer (tall chamberlain) 109

Langkopf (long head) 113

Langloh (long forest) 72

Langman, Langmann (tall man) 113, 94

Langmichel (tall Michael) 113

Langnau, Langenau, Lankenau (long meadow) 84

Langohr (long ear) 114

Langrock (long gown) 112, 147

Langsam (slow) 115

Langschmidt (tall smith) 96, 113

Langsdorf, Langstorf (Lange's village) 124

Langsdorf (long village) 127

Langohr (long ear) 113

Langut, see Langguth

Langwald (long forest) 71

Lanhart, see Lahner

Lannert, see Lahner

Lanohr (long ear) 114

Lansman, see Landsman

Lantz, Lants, Lans, Lanz 122 (spear, lance, fr Latin *lancea*) 107, 108

Lantzer (pikeman) 107

Lapp (rag, fool) 115

Lappersdorf (Luitfried's village) 124

Larcher (dweller among the larch trees) 89

Lasch (rag, rag picker) 96

Laser (Lazarus OT name) 135

Lass (serf, bondsman) 119

Lass (salmon, fisherman) 91

Lasser 53 < Lazarus 135

Last (burden carrier) 96

Laster (vice) 115

Laster (packman) 96

Lastfogel, Lastvogel (load carrier) 96

Lastinger (prunella weaver) 96

Lastner (burden carrier) 96

Lattner, Lattermann (dweller near a picket fence) 84

Latz (codpiece) 112, 106

Lau, Laue (thin forest) 72

Lau, Laue, see Leu

Laub, Laube, Lauber, Laubner (leaf, foliage, arbor) 89

Laubach (forest brook) 77, 122

Laubenstein (lion mountain) 73

Laubheim, Laubheimer (swamp hamlet) 80, 124

Lauch, see Lau

Lauch, Laucher, Lauchner (leek, leek seller) 89, 106

Lauck, Laucks (St. Luke) 135

Laudenbacher, see Lautenbach

Laudenslager 159, Laudenslayer 159, Laudenschlaeger, see Lautenschlaeger

Laue, see Lau

Lauenroth (lion clearing) 126

Lauenstein (lion mountain) 73, 122, see Loewenstein 122

Lauer, Laur, Laurer, Lauerman 94 (tanner) 96

Lauerenroth (tanner's red, tanner) 96, 106

Lauf, Laufe (course, track of game, hunter) 91, 122

Laufenberger, Lauffenburger 159 (waterfall mountain) 68

Laufenburgen, Laufenburger, Lauffenburger (waterfall castle) 73, 122

Laufenhaus, Laufinghouse 159 (house on a waterfall) 65

Laufer, Lauffer, Laufert 74 (runner) 96

Laufer (fr Lauffen) 122

Lauffen (waterfall, places in Switzerland and Wurttemberg) 122

Laug, Lauge (lye) 106

Laughner 159, see Lochner

Lauman, Laumann (forest dweller) 72

Laumann, see Lauer

Laun (mood, disposition) 115

Laupheim 122, see Laubheim

Laur, see Lauer

Lauritzen, see Lorentz

Laus 53 < Nikolaus

Lausch (Listen! hearken) 116

Lauss (boundary) 118

Laut, Lauth (loud) 115

Laut, Lauth (lute) 106

Lautenbach (swamp brook) 80, 77, 122

Lautenbach (town in Prussia, loud mountain) 122

Lautenschlaeger, Lauteschlager 159 (lute player) 96

Lauter (swamp) 80

Lauter (pure) 83

Lauter (river name) 103

Lauterbach (swampy brook) 80, 77, 122

Lautermilch (pure milk) 112

Lauterwasser (pure water) 112

Lauterwasser (swamp water) 80

Lauth, see Laut

Lauthans (noisy Johnny) 115

Lautman, Lauthman (lute player) 96

Lautringer (fr Kaiserslautern) 122

Laurentz, Lawrentz 159, see Lorentz

Lavater < Latin lavator, washer, (probably a fuller) 96, 141

Lax (salmon) 115

Layman 159, see Lehman

Lazarus (NT name) 135

Leab 159, see Lieb

Leabhart 159, Leapheart, see Lepbhard

Leader, see Lueder

Leaderer 159, see Lederer

Leaderman 159, see Ledermann
Leahman 159, see Lehman

Leap 159, see Lieb

Leapart 159, Leaphart, see Lepard

Leatherman 159, see Ledermann

Lebart, see Lepart

Lebegut (Live well!) 116, 117

Leber, Leberwurst (liver, butcher) 96

Leber (river name) 83

Leberecht (Live right!) 116, 140

Leberknight 159, see Lieberknecht

Lebermann (dweller on the Leber) 83, also see Liebermann

Lebherz (dear heart) 159

Lebkucher (cookie baker) 96

Lebolt, see Leopold

Lebsanft (Live well!) 117

Lech, Lechert 74, Lechmann 94 (dweller on the River Lech, swamp) 80, 83

Lech, Lechner, Lechnir 159, Lechman, see Lehner

Lechleiter, Lechliter 159, see Lichleiter

Lechner (tenant) 119

Leckner, see Lech

Leder, Lederer (leather, leather worker) 96, 106

Lederhos, Lederhas (leather breeches, peasant) 112, 122

Lederkremer, Lederkraemer (leather merchant) 106

Ledermann (leather worker) 96, 106, 94

Ledig (single, free) 115

Leeb 159, Leeby, see Lieb, Liebe, Loewe

Leebmann 159, see Liebmann

Leeman, see Lehman

Leer (empty) 118

Leffel, Lefler, Leffler, see Loeffler

Lefknecht, see Liebknecht

Lehder, see Leder

Lehfeld (tenant field) 84

Lehm, Lehmer (clay, ceramics worker) 96, 106

Lehman, Lehmon, Lehmann (tenant), see Lohmann

Lehmbeck (clay brook) 77, 122

Lehmberg (clay mountain) 68, 122

Lehmkuhl (clay pond) 81, 122

Lehn, Lehen (fief) 122

Lehne (steep slope) 71
Lehner, Lehnerd 74, Lehnert 74,
    Lehnerts 59, Lenerz,
    Lehninger (tenant) 109, 122
Lehnhard, see Leonhard
Lehnhoff (rented farm) 84
Lehnwald (forested fief) 71
Lehr (teaching, teacher) 96
Lehr (swamp) 80, 122
Lehrenkraus (Empty the jug!,
    drinker) 116
Lehrenkrug (Empty the jug!,
    drinker) 116
Lehrer, Lehrman 94, Lehrmann
    (teacher, minister) 96, 109
Lehrkind (pupil, apprentice)
Lehrmann (swamp dweller) 80,
    94
Leib, Leiber, Leibert 74 (body)
Leibenguth, Leibunguth (life and
    property, a serf) 109
Leibheim (fr Leipheim) 122
Leibknecht (body servant) 96, see
    Liebknecht 159
Leibnitz (Slavic place name) 122
Leibrock (body gown) 112
Leicher (minstrel) 96
Leichnam (corpse) 118
Leicht (light, lighthearted) 115
Leichtfuss, see Lichtfuss
Leidecker, Leidegger, see
    Leitecker
Leidenfrost (Suffer cold!) 116
Leider (sufferer, patient)
Leidhauser, see Leithauser
Leidhauser (taverner) 65
Leidholdt, see Leutholt
Leidig, Leidy 159, see Ledig
Leidner, see Leitner
Leidy 159, see Leite
Leier (lyre) 96, 118
Leihkauf (loan purchase, drink
    sealing a bargain) 118
Leihofer, Leihoffer (tenant) 92
Leim (clay) 118

Leimacker (clay field) 84
Leimbach, Leimbacher, Leimback
    (clay brook, swamp brook) 80,
    77, 122
Leimberg, Leimberger (clay
    mountain) 68
Leimbrok (clay brook) 77
Leimkuhler (clay pond) 80
Leinauer (clay meadow) 84
Leinbach, Leinbacher,
    Leinebacher (clay brook) 77,
    122
Leinbaugh, see Leinbach
Leinberger, Leineberger,
    Leinberry 159 (fr Leinberg
    122, clay mountain) 68
Leine (leash) 118
Leineweber, Leinweber (linen
    weaver) 96
Leinhardt, see Leonhard
Leinhass (linen trousers) 112
Leinwand (cloth, mercer) 106
Leinwater (linen weaver) 96
Leip, Leipp (fr Leipe 122), see
    Leib
Leipold, Leippold, see Leopold
Leirer (minstrel) 96
Leis, Leiss, Leise, Leiser (soft,
    softly) 115
Leisler, Leissler (wainwright) 96
Leist (last, shoemaker) 104, 106,
    122
Leite, Leitner (dweller on a
    slope) 71
Leitecker (field on a slope) 71, 84
Leitenberger (slope mountain)
    71, 68, 122
Leiter (ladder) 106
Leiter (leader) 118
Leithausen, Leithaeuser,
    Leithauser, Leitheuser
    (occupant of house on slope)
    71, 65
Leitheimer (fr Leitheim, hamlet
    on a slope) 71, 124, 122

Leither, Leitmann 94, Leitzmann (guide)

Leithiser 159, 66, Leithizer, see Leithausen

Leitinger, see Leite

Leitner, see Leite

Leitwein, see Leutwein

Lembach, Lembeck (swamp brook) 80, 77, 122

Lembchen 55, Lembke, Lembcke, Lemke, Lembeke (little lamb) 91

Lemberg, Lemberger (swamp mountain) 80, 68

Lemer, see Laemmer

Lemke, see Lembchen, also < Lamprecht

Lemmenhoffer (lamb farm) 91, 92

Lemmer, see Laemmer

Lemmer, Lemmert 74, Lemmerman 94 (shepherd) 95

Lemmlein 55 (little lamb) 91

Lempke 55, see Lembchen

Lenard 159, Lennert, see Leonhard

Lence 159, Lencz, see Lentz

Lendel, see Laendler

Lendeman 94, Lendemann, Lendermann, see Laendler

Lenden (thighs, hips) 114

Lendler, see Laendler

Lener, see Lehner

Lenert, Lennert, see Lehnert

Lenfer < *landfried* (public peace) 118

Lengefeld, Lengfelder, Lengenfelder (fr Lengfeld 122), see Langenfelder

Lenhard, Lenhardt, Lenhart, see Leonhard, Lehner

Lenhof, Lenhoff, Lennhof, see Lehnhoff

Lenk (supple) 115

Lenker (steerer, driver)

Lennebecker, see Leinbach

Lennerd 159, Lennert, Lennard, see Lenhard, Lehner

Lents 159, Lentz 122, Lenz, Lenzer, Lentzer (spring 143) or < Lorentz, St. Laurentius 13

Leo (name of several popes) 134

Leonberger (lion mountain) 48, 68

Leonhard, Leonhardt, Leonhart, Leonheart 159, Leonard 159 (lion + strong) 46, 49

Leonhardi (son of Leonhard) 142

Leonhauser (lion house) 48, 65

Leopold, Lepold (folk + brave) 46, 46

Lepart, Lepert, Lepperet, Lephardt (leopard, or lion + strong, house name) 48, 62, 46

Lepetit (French, little one) 144

Leppel (spoon) 106

Lepper, Leppert 74 (shoe repairer, clothes patcher) 96

Leppler, see Loeffel

Lerch, Lerche, Lercher, Lerge, Lerich, Lerik (lark, joyful person) 115, 122

Lerner (learner, pupil)

Lesch, Lescher, Leschert 74, Leschner (one who lives on the Lesch) 83

Leschke (Slavic, "forest dweller") 146

Leser, Lesemann (reader) 96

Lesser, Lessner (bloodletter) 96

Lessing, Lessig (Slavic for forest dweller) 146, 122

Letsch, Letscher (weak-kneed) 115

Lettermann 159, see Ledermann

Leu (lion, house name) 46

Leubecker (fr Leubeck 122, lion brook) 77

Leubolt, Leuphold, see Leopold

Leucht, Leuchter (light) 118

Leuchtenberg (bright mountain, candle mountain) 67

Leuenberg (lion mountain) 68

Leuew (lion) 48

Leuffer, Laeufer (runner, deer's leg) 96

Leupold, Leupoldt, see Leopold

Leutbrand (volk + sword) 46, 46

Leuthaeuser, see Leithaeuser

Leuthard (folk + strong) 46, 46

Leuther (folk + army) 46, 46

Leuthold (folk + dear) 46, 48

Leutner, Leuthner, see Leitner

Leutram (folk + raven) 46, 48

Leutwein (folk + friend) 46, 48

Leverenz, see Lorentz

Levering 159 < Liebering 55 (dear one)

Leverknight 159, see Lieberknecht

Levy (OT tribal name) 135

Lewald (lion forest) 48, 71, see also Lehwald

Lewenberg, Lewenberger (lion mountain) 48, 68

Lex, Lexer 53 < St. Alexius 135

Leyb, see Leib

Leybach, see Leimbach

Leybold, see Leopold

Leydeckeer, see Leidecker

Leydeman, see Luedemann

Leydiker, see Luedeker

Leyer, Leier (lyre) 96, 106

Leykauf, see Leikauf

Leypold, Leypoldt, see Leopold

Libendraut 159 (dearly beloved) 119

Liber 159, Liberman, see Lieber, Lieberman

Libert, Libhart, Lebhart (leopard, lion + strong) 48, 46

Libold, see Leopold

Liborius (name of saint) 135

Lice, see Leis 151

Lichliege (swamp marsh) 80

Lichliter, Lichtliter, see Lichtleiter

Licht, Lichte 122, Lichter (light, clearing) 126

Lichtblau (light blue) 112

Lichtenauer (cleared meadow) 126, 84

Lichtenberg, Lichtenberger (clearing + mountain) 126, 68, 122

Lichtenfeld, Lichtenfeldt (cleared field) 126, 84, 122

Lichtenfels (treeless cliffs) 68, 122

Lichtenstaig, Lichtenstaiger (fr Lichtenstaig, in the Thurgau) 122

Lichtenstein, Liechtenstein (European principality 121 and various cities 122)

Lichtenthal (cleared valley) 126, 76

Lichtenwald, Lichtenwalner (cleared forest) 126, 71, 122

Lichtfuss (light foot) 115

Lichtleiter, Lickliter 159, Licklighter 159 (cleared slope) 126, 71

Lichtmann (dweller on a slope) 71

Lidenheimer, see Leitheimer 151

Lidke 53, 55, Lidtke < Ludolf

Lieb, Liebe, Liebel 55, Lieber, Liebert 74 (dear one) 115

Liebegott (Love God!) 116, 117, 139

Liebele 55, Libley 159 (dear one)

Liebendorf (inherited village) 124

Liebengut, Liebenguth, see Leibenguth

Liebenthal (inherited valley) 127, 76

Lieber, Liebert 74 (inheritence +
army) 127, 46
Liebergott (Dear God!) 117
Liebering 55 (dear one) 115
Lieberknecht (dear servant) 139
Liebermann (dear man) 115, 94
Liebeskind (love child,
illegitimate child) 119
Liebesmann (dear man) 115, 94
Liebfeld (inherited field) 127, 84
Liebgott, see Liebegott
Liebhold (dear, fond) 115
Liebknecht (dear servant) 139
Liebman (dear man) 115
Liebrecht (Love right!) 116, 139,
see also Leberecht
Lied (damp region) 80
Liederbach (salmon stream) 77,
122
Liedtke 53, 55, Liedtzke < Ludolf
Lienenberger 159, see
Lueneberger
Lienhard, Lienhardt, see
Leonhard
Liepmann, see Liebemann
Liepold, see Leopold
Light 153, see Licht
Light 159, see Leite
Lightenberger 159, see
Lichtenberger
Lightfoot 159, see Lichtfuss
Lighthizer 159, 66, Lighthiser,
see Leithaeuser
Lightner 159, see Leitner
Lightwardt 159 (guardian of the
slope) 71, 47
Lilienfeld (lily field) 89, 84
Lilienkamp (lily field) 89, 84
Lilienthal, Lillienthal, Lilenthal
(lily valley) 89, 76, 122
Lilje (lily, house name)
Limbach, Limbaugh, Limbacker
159 (swampy brook [fr *lint*])
80, or see Leinbach

Limberger (fr Limberg 122,
linden mountain) 89, 68, see
Leimberger
Lime 159, see Leim
Limmat (Swiss river) 83
Limpert, see Lambert
Linaberry, see Leimberger
Linaweaver 159, see Leineweber
Linck, Linke, Linker, Linkert 74
(left, left-handed) 114
Lind, Lindt, Linde, Linden,
Linder, Linders 59, Lindler,
Lindner (dweller near the
linden trees) 89
Lind, Linde (gentle) 115
Lindahl (linden valley) 89, 67
Lindauer (fr Lindau, swampy
meadow) 80, 84, 122
Lindbeck (linden brook) 89, 77
Lindbeck (swampy brook) 80, 77
Lindberg (linden mountain) 89,
68
Lindblat (linden leaf) 89
Linddorf, Lindorf (linden village)
89, 124, 122
Lindeman 94, Lindemann,
Lindemeyer 93, Lindemyer
(dweller near the lindens) 89
Lindemann (dweller near the
swamp) 80, 94
Lindenauer (linden meadow) 89,
84
Lindenauer (swamp meadow) 89,
84
Lindenbaum (linden tree) 89
Lindenberg, Lindenberger
(linden mountain) 89, 68, 122
Lindencamp (linden field) 89, 84
Lindenfeld, Lindenfelder (linden
field) 89, 84, 122
Lindenhauer (linden cutter) 89,
96
Lindenhein (linden grove) 89, 72
Lindenmeyer (farmer by the
swamp) 80, 93

Lindenmuth, Lindemuth (gentle disposition) 115

Lindenschmidt, Lindenschmid (smith under the linden trees) 89, 96

Lindenstrutt, Lindenstruth (fr Lindenstruth 122, linden swamp) 89, 80

Linder, Lindner, Lindener, Lindeman 94, Lindermann (dweller near linden) 89

Linderborn (linden spring) 89, 77

Linderschmidt (smith under the linden tree) 96

Lindhorst, Lindhurst, Linhorst (linden hurst) 89, 72, 122

Lindler, Lindner, Lindt, see Lindeman

Lindmeyer (farmer by the linden) 89, 93

Lindmood 159, see Lindemuth

Lindner, see Linder

Lindober, see Lindauer

Lindorf (swampy village) 80, 124

Lindrud (linden clearing) 89, 126

Lindwurm (dragon, house name) 62

Linebarger 159, see Leinberger

Linebaugh 159, see Leinebach

Lineweaver 159, see Leineweber

Lingelbach, Lingelback (mud brook) 77, 122

Lingelmann 94, Lingelmeyer 93 (dweller by the swamp) 80

Lingenberg (muddy mountain) 68

Lingenfeld, Lingenfelder, Lingenfelter, Lingerfelt (swampy field) 84

Linger, Lingner, Lingerman (dweller near the swamp) 80

Lingert, see Linhard

Linhard 159, Linhardt, Linhart, see Leonhard

Link, Linker, see Linck, Lincker

Linkenbach (muddy brook) 77

Linnbaum, see Lindenbaum

Linneman, see Lindeman

Linnenkamp, see Lindencamp

Linnestruth, see Lindenstrutt

Lins, Linse, Linsen, Linser (lentil) 91, 106

Linsebach (lentil brook) 91, 77

Linsemann (lentil farmer or dealer) 93

Linsenmeyer, Linsenmyer (lentil farmer) 91, 93

Lintner, see Lindeman

Lintz, Linz (fr Linz) 122

Lion, Lyons (fr French *lion*) 144

Lionberger, see Leinberger 151

Lionhard 159, see Leonhard

Lipe, see Leib

Lipmann 53, Lipp, Lippmann 94 < Philipp

Lippelt, Lippolt < Leopold

Lippersdorf (Leutbrand's village) 46, 46, 124

Lippert, Lipphart, see Lebhart

Lisch 122, Lischer, see Lescher

List, Listmann 94 (intelligence, cunning, skill) 115, 122

Litfass (wine barrel) 96

Litinger (dweller on a slope), see Leitner

Little 153, see Luetzel

Litwiller (village on the slope)

Litz, Litze, Litzemann 94 (lace, lace maker) 96, 106, 112

Litzeldorf (little village) 124

Litzen 53, Litzmann 94 < Ludwig

Liveright 153, see Leberecht

Livingood 159, see Leibenguth

Loan 159, see Lohn

Lob, Lobe, Loben (praise, praiser) 118

Lobach, Lobeck (forest brook) 71, 77, 122

Lobauer (forest peasant) 71, 91

Lobaugh 159, see Lobach 77, 151

Lobedanz (Praise the dance! dance leader) 117

Lober (tanner) 96

Loberger (forest mountain) 72, 68

Lobmueller (bark miller for tanners) 72, 103

Loch, Locher (hole, ravine) 76, 122

Lochbaum (hollow tree, boundary tree) 89

Lochner (dweller by a pond) 80

Lochstampfer, Lochstamphor (hole stamper) 159

Lock (pond) 80

Lock (lure, trapper) 91, 96

Lockbaum (pond tree) 89

Lockermann (dweller by a swamp) 80

Lockhoff (pond farm) 80, 92

Lockmayer (farmer on the pond) 77, 78

Lockner, see Lochner

Loden (shag, course woolen cloth) 96, 106, 112

Lodenkemper (shag field) 84

Lodwig, see Ludwig

Loeb, Loeber, Loebl 55, Loeblein 55 (lion)

Loeb (fr Loebau) 122, see also Loew

Loebenhoffer (occupant of the Lion Farm) 122

Loebenstein, see Loewenstein

Loechel (little hole) 55

Loeff, see Loeb

Loeffel, Loeffler (spoon, spoon maker) 96, 106

Loehr, Loemann, Loehrmann, Loeher (tanner) 96

Loesch (extinguish), see Lesch

Loescher, Loeschner, Loeschke 55 (stevedore)

Loesser, see Lesser, Leser

Loew, Loewe, Loewen (lion) 48, 62, 63

Loewenbach (lion brook) 48, 77

Loewenberg (lion mountain) 48, 68, 122

Loewenhausen (lion houses) 48, 65

Loewenheim (lion hamlet) 48, 124

Loewenstein, Leuwenstein (lion mountain) 48, 73, 122

Loewenstern (lion star) 48, 148

Loewenthal, Lowenthal (lion valley) 48, 76, 122

Loffler 159, see Loeffler

Lofink (wood finch) 115

Logemann (dweller near a swamp) 80

Loh (flame) 118

Loh 122 (forest 71, swampy area 80), see Hohenloh

Lohaus (forest house) 71, 65, 122

Lohaus (tanner's shop) 65, 122

Loher, Lohgerber (tanner) 96

Lohman, Lomann (forest man, tanner) 72, 96, 94

Lohmeyer (forest farmer) 72, 93

Lohmuller (forest miller) 72, 103

Lohn, Lohner, Lohnes 59, Loner, Lohnert 74 (reward, rewarder)

Lohn, Lohner (dweller on the Lahn) 83, 122

Lohner, Lohnert 74 (day laborer) 96

Lohoefer (fr the Lohoff, forest farm) 92, 122

Lohoeffer (forest farm) 72, 92

Lohr, Lohre, Lohrman 94, Lohrmann, Lorman (fr Lohr 122, dweller on the Lohr 83)

Loman, see Lohman

Lombart, Lombarth, see Lampart

Long, see Lang

Longacker 159 (long field) 84

Longanecker 159, Longenecker, see Langenecker

Longbaugh, see Langenbach 151

Longbrake 159, see Lamprecht

Longnecker 159, see Langenecker

Longhoffer 159, see Langhoffer
Longnacker 159, see
    Langenacker
Longschade (long shadow) 159
Lookabaugh, see Luckenbach 151
Loos, Loose (lot, fate) 122
Loos 53, Loose, Looser < Ludwig
    53
Lor, see Lohr
Lorbach (laurel brook) 89, 77,
    122
Lorber (spice dealer) 105
Lorch, Lorche (place name) 122
Lorentz, Lorenz, Lorentzen,
    Lorincz (St. Lawrence) 135
Lortz 53, Lorz, see Lorentz
Losacker (field drawn by lot) 84
Losch, Losche, Loscher, Loschert
    74 (costly leather, leather
    worker) 96, 106
Loss (dweller by a swamp) 80
Lothar (loud + army) 47, 46
Lothringer (fr Lorraine) 121
Lotz, Lots, Lotse (pilot) 96
Lotze 53 < Ludwig
Lotzgeselle (pilot's assistant) 96
Loub 159, see Laub
Loudenschlager 159,
    Loudenslager, see
    Lautenschlaeger
Louderback 159, see Lauterbach
Loudermilk 159, Loudmilk,
    Loudermilk, see Lautermilch
Loudiwick 159, see Ludwig
Louge 159, see Laug
Loughman 159, see Lachman
Loughner 159, see Lachner
Louk 159, see Lauck
Loun 159, see Laun
Lovenstein 159, see Loewenstein
Lowdermilk 159, see Lautermilch
Lowe 159, see Loewe 122
Lowenhaupt 159 (lion head,
    housename) 113, 62
Lowenstein 159, see Loewenstein

Lowenthal 159, see Loewenthal
Lower 159, see Lauer
Lowman 159, see Lohman
Lowrentz 159, see Lorentz
Loy 159, see Leu
Lubbe 53 < Liutbert (people +
    bright) 46, 47, 53, 54
Lubbehusen, Lubehusen
    (Liutbert's houses) 65
Lubeck, Lubecker (fr Luebeck)
    122
Lubrecht < Liutbrecht (retinue +
    bright) 46, 47
Lucabaugh 159, see Luckenbach
Lucas, Luck, Lux (St. Luke) 135
Luchs (lynx, sly person, house
    name) 115
Lucht, see Leucht
Lucius 141, see Lutze
Luck (St. Luke) 135
Luckabaugh 159, see Luckenbach
Luckenbach (swamp brook) 80,
    77, 122
Luckenbill (swamp hill) 80, 67
Lucker, Luckert 74, Luckner,
    Luckerman 94 (swamp
    dweller) 80
Ludeke 53, 55, Luddecke,
    Lueddecke, Ludtke, Ludicke <
    Ludolf
Luden 53, Luder < Ludwig
Ludewig, see Ludwig
Ludke 55, see Ludeke
Ludman 53, 94, Ludemann <
    Ludolf
Ludmer (loud + famous) 47, 47
Ludolf, Ludolph (loud + wolf) 47,
    48
Ludowice (fr Ludowici, son of
    Ludowicus, Latin for Ludwig)
    141
Ludwig, Ludwig, Ludwick (loud +
    battle) 47, 46
Ludwin (loud + friend) 47, 48
Ludwitzke, see Ludowice

Luebbe 53, Luebber, Luebbers 59, Luebbermann 94 < Liutbert (folk + bright) 46, 47, 53, 54

Luebke 53, 55, Luepke, see Luebbe

Luechow (place name) 122

Lueck, Luecke, Luecker, Luck (St. Luke) 135

Lueder, Lueders 59, Luedemann 94 (loud + army) 47, 46

Luedge 55, 53, Luedke, Luedeke, Luetge, Luethje, Luethke, Lutjen, Luetcke, Luetke < Ludwig

Lueppert, see Lebhart

Luetkemeyer (occupant of Luetkehoff, Ludwig's farm) 93

Luetz, Luetze 53, Luetzmann 94 < Ludwig

Luetzel (little) 113

Luft, Lufft (air) 122

Lugenbeal 159, Lugenbeel, Luginbill (lookout hill) 67

Luger (deceitful) 115

Luginsland (lookout) 118

Luik, see Lukas

Luitbold, see Leopold

Lukas (St. Luke) 135

Lummel (lout, bore) 115

Lump, Lumpe (rag, ragman, tramp) 115

Luneburger, Lunenburger (fr Lunenburg) 121

Lunte, Luntz, Lunz (fuze, harquebusier) 107

Luppold, see Leopold

Lurz (awkward) 115

Lushbaugh 159 (reed brook) 81, 77

Lust (joy) 115

Lustbader (pleasure bather, bath attendant) 96

Lustgarten (pleasure garden) 84

Lustig (merry) 115

Luterman (lute player) 96

Lutgen 55, see Luedge

Luthardt (loud + strong) 47 + 46

Luthari (loud + army), etc. 53, 54, see Luther

Luther (loud + army) 47, 46, 49

Luthold, Ludholtz (retinue + loyal) 46, 48

Lutjen 53, 55 < Ludolf, Luther, etc.

Lutman, see Lauthman, Ludman

Luts 159, see Lutz

Lutter 53 < Ludwig

Lutterbeck 122, see Lauterbach

Luttich (fr Liege) 122

Luttig 53 < Ludolf

Luttman, see Lutman

Luttrodt (Ludwig's clearing) 126

Lutwycke, see Ludowice

Lutz 53, Lutze, Lutzel, Lutzens 59 < Ludwig

Lutzel (little) 113

Lux (lynx) 115

Lux (Latin, light) 118

Lux, see Lukas

Luxemburg, Luxenburg, Luxenberg 159 (a principality, little castle) 121

Luz, see Lutz

Lytchen, see Lutchen

M

Maack, Maak, Maag (kinsman) 119

Maak, see Markward

Maas, Mass (Meuse) 83

Maas < Thomas 55

Maasch (marsh) 80

Machetanz (Start the dance!, dancemaster) 96, 116

Macher 159, see Metzger

Machler, see Mackler

Machrodt (Mack's clearing) 126

Macht (power) 46

Mack 53, Mag, Mak, Make,
    Makh < Markward
Mackel, see Makel
Mackler (broker) 96
Mackrodt (Mack's clearing) 125
Madel (girl) 118
Mader, Maeder, Maehder
    (mower) 95
Mader (dyer, dye seller) 96, 106
Madreiter (meadow clearing) 125
Maehl, Maehler, see Mehler
Maeltzer, Meltzer (malt maker)
    96
Maenhart, see Meinhart
Maentler (old clothes dealer) 105
Maerker (observer, umpire)
Maerten, Maertens 74, see
    Martin
Maertz, Maerz, Mertzke 55
    (March, period of feudal
    service) 143
Maessner, see Mesner
Maeule (mouth) 114
Maeusezahl (mouse tail) 114
Mag, Magen (kinsman) 119
Magaziner (keeper of the
    magazine) 109
Magdeburger (fr Magdeburg 122,
    the Virgin's city) 122
Magenheim, Magenheimer (fr
    Magenheim 122, kinsmen
    hamlet) 124
Magenhoffer (fr Magenhof 122,
    kinsman farm) 92
Mager, Magers 59 (thin) 114
Magerfield 153 (infertile field) 84
Magerfleisch (lean meat,
    butcher) 96
Magnus (Latin, *magus*, great)
    141
Maher 159 (mower) 95
Mahl, Mahle (meal, time) 118
Mahler (miller) 103
Mahler (painter) 96
Mahlmann (miller's assistant)
    103

Mahlstedt (parliament place) 122
Mahn (admonition), see Mohn
Mahnke, Mahncke, Mahnken 53,
    55 < Mangold
Mahr, Mahrer (swamp, dweller
    by a swamp) 80
Mahrenholtz (swamp forest) 80,
    72, 122
Mai (May, month of birth or of
    corvée duty) 143
Maibaum (May tree) 89
Maiden, see Meiden
Maienshein 159, see
    Mayenschein
Maier, see Meyer
Maierhof (farm) 84
Maijer, see Meyer
Mailender (fr Milan) 122
Mainfort (Main ford) 78, 122
Mainhard, Mainhardt, see
    Meinhard
Mainz, Maintzer, Mainzer (fr
    Mainz 122) 129
Mair, Maiers 164, Maijer, see
    Meyer, Meyers
Maisel, Maizel 159, see Meisel
Maisner, see Meissner
Maiwald (May forest) 148
Makel, Makell (stain, spot, Latin
    macula)
Makler (broker) 96
Mal (boundary)
Malchior, Malcher, see Melchior
Maler (painter) 96
Mallmann, see Mehlmann
Maltheser, Maltheuser (Maltese
    knight) 107, 108, 109
Maltz, Maltzer, Malz, Maltzman
    94 (malt, brewer) 96, 106, 122
Mance 159, see Mantz
Mandel, Mandell, Manndel
    (almond) 158, see Mantel
Mandelbaum (almond tree) 89
Mandelberg (almond mountain)
    89, 68

Mandelblat (almond leaf) 89

Manfred, Manfretz 59 (man + peace or protection) 94, 47

Mangel (lack) 118

Mangold < Managwalt (great + power) 46

Manhard, see Meinhard

Manhim 159, see Mannheim

Manlich (manly) 115

Mann, Manne, Manns 59 (man, vassal) 94, or < Hermann

Mannalther (adult) 113

Mannbar (marriageable) 113

Mannheit (manhood) 118

Mannhardt, see Meinhard

Mannheim, Mannheimer (fr Mannheim, swamp hamlet) 122

Mannherz (man heart) 115

Mannlein (little man) 94, 113

Mansfeld (fr Mansfeld) 122

Mansfield 153, Mansfeild, see Mansfeld

Mansker, see Maintzer

Mantel, Mantell (coat, fr Latin *mantellum*) 112, 106, 158

Mantel, Mantell (fir tree) 89, 122

Mantler (coat dealer) 105

Mantz, Manz, Maentz < St. Manitius 135, see Mangold

Mar, Marr (swamp) 80

Marbach, Marbaker 159 (swamp brook) 80, 77, 122, see Markbach

Marburger (fr Marburg 122, swamp castle) 80, 73

Marckel 53, 55 < Markwart

Marcksteiner (boundary stone) 73

Marcus (St. Mark) 135, name of a pope 134

Marder, Marders 59 (marten) 115

Marenburg, see Marburg

Margenthaler, see Mergenthaler, Morgenthaler

Margot (famous + god) 47, 135

Margraf, see Markgraf

Marienborn (Mary's spring) 50

Marius (Roman name) 141

Mark, Marck, Marks, Marcks, Marx, Marcus (St. Mark, name of a pope) 134

Markbach (boundary brook) 77

Markel 53, 55, Markels 59, see Markwart

Markgraf (margrave) 109

Markhart, Markart (boundary + strong) 46

Markscheffel (market bushel) 118

Markstein (boundary stone) 73

Markus (St. Mark) 135

Markwart, Markward, Markword, Markwordt, Marckwart, Markwardt (guardian of the boundary) 47

Markwitz (boundary village, march village) 127

Marner (mariner) 96

Marold (famous + loyal) 47, 48

Marquard, Marquart, Marquardt, see Markwart

Marsch, Marscher, Marschke 55 (marsh) 80

Marschall, Marschalk (horse + servant, marshal) 107

Marscheck (marsh field) 80, 84

Marschuetz (horse guard) 107

Marstaller, Marsteller (horse + stall, equerry) 107

Mart, Martel 55, Marten, Martens, Martenz, see Martin

Marti 53 < Martin

Martin, Martins, Marthin (St. Martin, name of several popes) 134

Martini (son of Martinus) 142

Martinus (St. Martin) 141

Martinssen (son of Martin) 59

Martz, Marz, see Maertz

Marx, see Markus

Masbach, see Mosbach

Masbaum (mast tree such as oak or beech) 89

Maschauer (swampy meadow) 80, 84

Maschbaum (swamp tree) 80, 89

Maschmeyer (farmer at the swamp) 80

Maschke < Thomas

Mass (measure, see Thomas) 1

Masse (quantity, mass) 118

Massmann < Thomas

Massteller, see Marstaller

Mathaus, see Matthaeus

Mathes, Mathis, Matheis, Mathai, see Matthias

Matt, Matz, see Matthaeus

Matt, Matfeld (sloping meadow) 71

Matthaeus (St. Matthew) 135

Matthias, Mattheiss, Matteis, Mattis, Mattice 159 (St. Matthew) 135

Matthiesen, Matthyssen (son of Matthias) 59

Matthouse 159 (house on the slope) 65

Mattmueller (miller on the sloping meadow) 71, 84

Mattmueller (miller on the Matte) 83

Matz 53, Matzel, Matzen < Matthaeus or Mattias

Matzdorf (Matthew's village) 124

Matzger 159, see Metzger

Matzke 53, 55 (little Matz) 113

Mau (wide sleeve, dandy) 112

Mauch (glutton) 115

Mauer, see Maurer

Mauershagen (walled enclosure) 124

Maul, Maule (mouth, probably large or deformed) 114

Maul, Mauler (mule) 91

Maultasch (distorted face) 114

Maurenbrecher (battering ram) 108

Maurer, Mauer, Mauerer (mason, fr Latin *murus*) 100

Mauritz, Maurits 159, Mauriz, see Moritz

Maus, Mause, Mauss, Maeusel (mouse) 115

Mauser, Mausser (mouser) 118

Maushund (mouse dog, fraternity name) 113

Maut, Mauth, Mauthe, Maute, Mautz 59, Mautner (toll collector) 109

Max 53 < St. Maximilian 135

May (May, period of corvée duty) 143

Maybach (maybrook) 70

Maydag, see Maytag

Mayenbaum (may tree, maypole) 89

Mayenschein (as bright as May) 115, 148

Mayer, Mayers 59, see Meyer

Mayerhafer 159, Mayerhaver, see Mayerhoff

Mayerhoff, Mayerhoffer (fr Mayerhoff 122), see Meyerhoffer

Maygarden (May garden) 84

Mayhler 159, see Mehler

Maykranz (May wreath) 118

Maylender (fr Milan) 122

Maynard 159, Maynerd, see Meinhard

Mayr, see Meyer

Mayse (titmouse) 115

Maytag (Mayday) 143

Maywald (May forest) 148

Mealy 159, see Muehle

Mearkle 159, see Merkel

Mease 159, see Mies, Miess

Mechler, see Mackler

Meckel, Mechelke 55 (little Michael) 113

Meckel, Mechtel < Mechthild (power + battle) 46, 46, 53, 54

Mecklenburg (German province) 121

Meder, see Mader

Medicus (Latin for doctor) 141

Meece 159, see Mies

Meer (sea, swamp) 80

Meerholtz (swamp forest) 80, 72

Meerman (swamp dweller) 80

Mees, Meese, Meesen (swamp) 80

Meetze 159, see Muetze

Megenhardt (might + strong) 46, 46

Megenwart (might + guard) 46, 47

Meher (mower) 95

Mehl, Mehle, Mehler (meal, grist, miller) 106

Mehler, see Maler

Mehlkopf (meal head, miller) 96

Mehlman, Mehlmann (meal dealer) 105

Mehlsack (meal sack, miller) 103

Mehner, Mehnert 74, see Meinhard

Mehr 53, Mehren, Mehring < Merhold

Mehrdorf (swamp village) 80, 124

Mehrenholtz (swamp forest) 80, 72

Mehrtens, see Maertens

Meichelsbeck < am Aichelsbeck (on the acorn brook) 70, 77

Meichelweg < am Aichelsweg (on the acorn path) 70, 65

Meichler (dweller near stagnant water) 79

Meiden (horses) 91

Meidenbauer (horse farmer) 91

Meier, Meiers 59, see Meyer, Meyers

Meierhenry 159 < Meyerheinrich (farmer Henry)

Meierhofer (fr Meierhof 122), see Meyerhofer

Meijer, see Meyer

Meil, Meile (mile, Latin, *mille passum*) 101

Meilchen 55 (short mile) 101

Meineke 53, 55, Meinecke < Meinhard

Meinhard, Meinhardt, Meinert, Meiner (might + strong) 46, 46

Meinhold (might + loyal) 46, 48

Meinholtz, error for Meinhold

Meininger (fr Meiningen) 122

Meinke 53, 55, Meinken < Meinhard

Meinrad < Meginrat (power + counsel) 46 + 46

Meinrich < Maginrich (power + strong) 47, 47

Meinschein, see Meyenschein

Meinstein (mountain on the Main) 83, 73

Meinster, see Muenster

Meintzer, Meinzer, Meinz (fr Mainz) 122

Meise (titmouse) 115

Meisel, Meisels 59 (mouse hawk) 115

Meisenbacher (swamp water brook) 80, 77, 122

Meisenhalder, Meisenhelder, Meisenholder (songbird owner, songbird seller) 106

Meisenheim (swamp hamlet) 124, 122

Meisgeier (mouse hawk) 115

Meisner, Meissner (fr Meissen) 122

Meissel (chisel) 106

Meissinger (fr Meissing) 122

Meister (master, fr Latin *magister*)

Meisterjan (Master John) 118

Meitzel (power) 118

Meixner, see Meisner

Mekeburg 159, see Mecklenburg

Melber (flour merchant) 96

Melchior, Melcher, Melchers 59,
    Melchert 74, Melger, Melken
    (one of Three Kings) 111
Meltz, Meltzer, Melzer (malt
    maker, brewer) 96, 106
Memminger (fr Memming or
    Memmingen) 122
Mench 159, see Mensch
Mencken 55, Menke, Menken,
    Menkel 55 < Meinhard
Mende, see Amend
Mendel, see Mandel
Mendel < Meinhard 55
Mendelbaum, see Mandelbaum
Mendelsohn, Mendelssohn (son of
    Mendel) 59
Menge (multitude, retailer) 105
Mengel, Mengle 159, Mengele,
    see Mangel
Mengeldorff, see Mengersdorf
Menger, Mengers 59, Mengert 74
    (monger, fr Latin *mangari*)
    105
Mengersdorf (mongers' village)
    124
Menges, Mengs, Mengen (fr
    Megingoz, might + Goth) 46,
    53, 54
Menhard, see Meinhard
Menke 53, 55, Mennecke,
    Menning, see Meinhard
Menrad, see Meinrad
Mensch (human being, servant)
Menser, see Maintzer
Mensh 159, Mentch, see Mensch
Mentz, Menz, Menzer, Mentze,
    Mentzer, Mentzel, Mentzell,
    Mentzel, Mentzl, Mentzer, see
    Maintzer
Menzel < Hermann
Merbach (swamp brook) 80, 77
Mercator (Latin for Kremer,
    merchant) 9, 141
Merck 53, Merckel 55, Merckle
    159, Mercke, Merkle 159,
    Merklin 55 < Markwart

Mercker, Merker (watchman) 96
Merfart, Merfert (sea voyage,
    pilgrim) 118
Merfeld (marshy field) 80, 84,
    122
Mergardt (swamp garden) 80, 84
Mergart (son of Merigarda) 60
Mergel, Mergl, Mergels 59,
    Mergler (marl, marl supplier,
    fr Latin *margila*) 106
Mergenthaler (marl valley) 76,
    122
Merhold (famous + loyal) 47, 48
Merkel 53, 55, Merkle, see
    Markwart
Merker, Merkertz 74, 59 (fr Mark
    Brandenburg) 121
Merker (watchman) 109
Mermelstein (marble) 73
Mersinger (fr Mersing) 122
Mertel 55, 53, see Marten
Merten, Mertens 59, Merthens,
    see Martin
Merts, Mertz, Merz, see Maerz
Merwin (famous + friend) 47, 48
Mesman, see Messman
Mesmer, Mesner (sexton, fr Latin
    mansionarius) 110
Mess (mass), see Messmann
Messbach (swamp brook) 80, 77
Messenger 159, see Messing
Messer, Messerman,
    Messermann (knife, knife
    grinder, cutler) 96, 106
Messer (official measurer) 109
Messerschmidt, Messerschmied,
    Messersmith 153 (cutler, knife
    maker) 96
Messing, Messinger, Mesinger,
    Messingschlaeger (brass,
    brass worker 96, 106), or fr
    Messing 122
Messman, Messmann (attendant
    at fair, at mass) 110
Messmer, Messmers, see Mesmer
Messner, see Mesmer

Meth, Methe (mead, taverner) 96

Methaus (tavern, taverner) 96

Metscher, see Metzger

Metschke 53, 55 < Matthaeus

Metter, Mettler (mead maker) 96

Metts 159, see Metz

Metz (inhabitant of Metz 122),
see Metzger, Matthias

Metz (knife, cutler) 96

Metzbower 159 (butcher farmer)
102, 91

Metzdorf (butchers' village) 102,
124, 122

Metzdorf (Mechthild's village)
124

Metzel, Metzler (butcher, fr Latin
macellarius) 102

Metzel < Matthaeus 55

Metzer, Metzger (butcher, fr
Latin *matiarius*) 102

Meumann (swamp dweller) 80

Meurer, see Maurer

Meusel (little mouse) 115

Meuser, see Maeuser

Mewes 53, Meves < Matthaeus,
Bartholomaeus

Mey, see May

Meyer (farmer, dairy farmer, fr
Latin *major domus, major
villae*) 93

Meyerfeld (farmer's field) 84

Meyerhoffer, Mayerhofer,
Meyerhoeffer (farm managed
by bailiff) 93, 92

Meyers 59, Meyerson 59, see
Meyer

Meylaender, see Mailaender

Meyn, Meyner < Meginher
(might + army) 46, 46

Meysel, see Meisel

Meywald, see Maiwald

Mezger, see Metzger

Michael, Michaels 59, Michaelis,
Michaeles, Michel, Michele
(St. Michael) 135

Michel, see Michael

Michel, Mickeli, Michels 59,
Michler, Michener, Michelman
94, Michelman, Michelmann
(large, large fellow) 113

Michelbach (large brook) 77, 122

Michelbach (St. Michael's brook)
77, 122

Michelfelder (large fields) 84

Michelfelder (St. Michael's fields)
84

Michelsen (son of Michel) 59

Mick, Micks 59, see Mueck

Mickel, Mickle 159, see Michel

Mickley, see Michel

Middag, Middaugh 159, see
Mittag

Middeldorp, Middendorf, see
Mitterdorf

Middelkamp, Middelcamp
(middle field) 84

Middelkauf (in-between) 96

Middelman, see Mittelman

Middelstadt, Middelstaedt
(middle town)

Middendorf (dirt village) 124

Midnight 153, see Mitnacht

Miers 159, 59, see Meyer

Mies, Miess (marsh) 80

Miesbach (marsh brook) 80, 77

Mihle, see Muehle

Mil ..., mill ..., see Muehl

Milch (milk) 106

Milchberg (milk mountain) 68

Milcher, see Melchior

Milcher (milk seller) 96

Milchraum (milkroom, dairyman)
96

Milchsack (milk bag, shepherd's
purse) 106

Mild (generous) 115

Milde (river name) 83

Mildenberg (gentle mountain) 68

Milhaus, see Muehlhaus

Milheim (mill hamlet) 124

Milhizer 159, 66, Milheisler, see
Muehlhaus

Milhous 159, Milhouse 153,
Milhouser, see Muehlhaus
Millberg, Millenberg, see
Muehlenberg
Millen (place name) 122
Miller, see Mueller
Millhaus, Millhausen, Millhauser
< Muehlhaus
Millhizer 159, 66, see Millhaus,
Millhauser
Millhof (mill farm) 92
Millhouse 153, Millhouser 159,
see Muehlhaus 151
Millspaugh 159 (mill brook) 77
Millstein, Milstein (millstone) 73,
see Muehlstein
Milner, see Muehlner
Milroth (mill clearing) 126
Miltonberger 159, see
Mildenberger
Miltz (spleen) 115
Mince 159, see Muentz
Mincer 159, see Maintzer
Minch 159, Minnich, see Moench
Minchenberg 159, see
Moenkeberg
Minchhoff 159 (cloister farm) 92
Minck, see Mink
Minden (name of city) 122
Minderlein 55 (of low rank) 115
Minehart 159, see Meinhard
Mineweaser 159 < Mainwiese
(meadow on the Main) 83, 84
Mingeldorf, see Mengersdorf
Minger, Mingers 59, see Menger
Mingersdorf, see Mengersdorf
Minig, see Muench
Mink, Minke, Minken, Minkel 55
(Wendish, miller) 146
Minne (love) 118
Minnegerode, Minnigerode 159
(Minne's clearing) 126
Minnich, Minnick, Minnik, see
Moench
Minster, see Muenster

Mintz, Mintze, Mintzes 59,
Mintzer, see Muentz,
Muentze, Muentze
Mire 159, Mires 164, see Meyer
Mischle 53, 55, Mischler,
Mitschler < Michael
Misel 159, see Meisel
Misener 159, Misner, see Meisner
Mish 159, Mishler, see Mischle
Misslich (awkward, inconvenient)
114, 115
Missner 159, see Meissner 159
Mitchler 159, see Mischler
Mitnacht, Mittnacht, Mitternacht
(midnight) 143
Mittag (midday) 143
Mittelberger, Mittenberger
(middle mountain) 68, fr
Mittelberg 122
Mitteldorf (middle village) 124
Mittelholz (middle forest) 72
Mittelkamp (middle field) 84
Mittelmann, Mittleman 159
(middle man, in-between) 96
Mittelstadt, Mittelstaedt,
Mittelstetter (middle city) 122
Mittenberger (fr Mittenberg) 68,
122
Mittendorf (in the middle of the
village) 124
Mittenthal (in the middle of the
valley) 76
Mittenzwei (wood splitter) 96
Mittermeier (middle farmer) 93
Mitternacht (midnight) 143
Mittersteiner (middle stone) 73
Mittnight 153 > Mitternacht
(midnight) 143
Mitz 159, see Muetz
Mix, see Mueck
Mizel 159, Mizell, see Meisel
Moan 159, see Mohn
Mock (female wild boar, see also
Mack) 115
Moeglich (Possible!) 117

Moehle, Moehler, see Muehle,
    Muehler
Moehler, see Mehler
Moehlman, Moehlmann (miller)
    103
Moehm (aunt) 119
Moelcher (milker, dairyman) 95
Moeller, Moellers 59, Moellmann,
    Moelleken 55) 103, see
    Mueller
Moench, Moenck (monk, fr Latin
    municus) 110
Moenkeberg (monk mountain)
    68, 122
Moenkemeyer (monks' farm
    manager) 139
Moenkhof (monks' farm) 139
Moennich, see Moench
Moersberger (marsh mountain)
    80, 67
Moerschbacher (fr Moersbach
    122, swamp brook) 80, 77
Moersdorf (swamp village) 80,
    124, 122
Moeser, Moesinger (fr Moese 122,
    marsh) 80
Moessbauer (marsh farmer) 80,
    93
Moessinger, see Messing
Moessmer, see Messmer
Mohl, Mohle, Mohlberg, see
    Muehle, Muehlenberg
Mohlberg, see Muehlenberg
Mohler, Mohlmann, see Mahler,
    Mueller
Mohlhenry < Mohlheinrich
    (Henry at the mill) 103
Mohlmann, see Mehlmann
Mohn (poppy) 89
Mohnberger (poppy mountain)
    89, 68
Mohnkern (poppy seed) 89
Mohr, Mohrman, Mohrmann
    (Moor, possibly actor in
    miracle play) 111

Mohr (fen or bog) 80
Mohrmann (dweller on a fen) 80
Molden, Molder (trough maker)
    96, 100, fr Moldau 122
Moldenhauer, Mollenhauer, see
    Molden
Moler, see Mueller
Molk (milk, milk dealer) 105
Moll, Molle (heavy set) 114
Mollenhauer, Mollnauer, see
    Molden
Moller, Mollere, see Mueller
Mollman, Mollman (miller) 103
Molnar, Molner, see Mueller
Moltke (Slavic: young) 113, 146
Moltmann (earthman, Adam)
Moltmann, see Meltzer
Moltz, Moltz, Molz, Moltzer, see
    Maltz, Maltzer
Momma, see Mumma
Monat, Monath, Monnat (month,
    period of service) 143
Monbauer (fr the Monhof, poppy
    farm) 91
Monch 159, see Moench
Moncke, Monke, Monkey, see
    Moench 151
Mondorf (moon village, poppy
    village) 124
Mondschein, Monschein
    (moonlight) 148
Mondsee (moon lake) 80
Monheim (poppy village) 89, 124
Monheit, see Mannheit
Monich, Monick, Monk, see
    Moench
Monkemeier (monastery bailiff)
    110, 93
Monkmann (monastery worker)
    110, 96
Monschein, see Mondschein
Monsees, see Mondsee
Montag (Monday, day of birth or
    of some duty) 143
Moon, see Mohn

Moor 122, Moore 159, see Mohr

Moorer, see Maurer

Moos (fen, bog) 80

Moosbrugge (bridge on the fen) 80

Moosmann (dweller on a fen) 80

Morast (marsh, morass) 80

More, see Mohr

Morganstein 159, see Morgenstein

Morgen (morning) 122, 143

Morgen (acre, farmer) 84, 91

Morgenroth (morning red) 148

Morgenstein (field stone) 84, 73

Morgenstern (morning star) 148

Morgenstern (mace) 107, 109

Morgenthal, Morgenthaler (morning valley) 76, 148

Morgenthau (morning dew) 148

Morgott, see Margot

Morheim (fen hamlet) 80, 124

Moritz (St. Mauritius) 135, 122

Morman, Mormann (dweller on the fen) 80

Mornhinweg (early riser) 115

Morningstar 153, see Morgenstern

Morris 159, 148, see Moritz

Morsberger, Morstein (swamp mountain) 80, 81, 68, 73

Morsch (rotten, decayed)

Morschhauser (decayed houses) 65

Morschheimer (fr Morschheim, rotten + hamlet) 81, 124, 122

Morstadt, Morstaedter (fen city) 80

Morstorff (fen village) 80, 124

Mosbach, Mosbacker (marshy brook) 80, 77

Mosberg (marsh mountain) 80, 68, 122

Mosburg (marsh castle) 80, 73

Mosel (fr the Moselle) 83, 122

Moser, Moseman, Mosemann (dweller on a marsh) 80

Moser (place name) 122

Moses, Mose (OT name) 135

Mosmiller (marsh miller) 80, 103

Mosner (marsh dweller) 80

Moss, see Moos

Mossbach, Mossbacher, see Mosbach

Mosser, see Moser

Mosshamer (bog hamlet) 80, 124

Mossmann (dweller on a marsh) 80

Most (grapejuice, fr Latin *mustum*) 96, 112

Mott, Motte (moth) 118

Motz, see Matz

Motzenboker (Matthew's brook) 54, 77, 151

Moul 159, see Maul

Mour, see Maurer 151

Mous 159, Mouser, see Maus, Mauser

Mouterer, see Maut, Mauter

Mowl 159, see Maul

Mowrer 159, see Maurer

Much (marshy stream) 81

Mueck, Muecke, Muck, Mick, Micks 59, Mix (midge, gnat, restless person) 115

Mueckenberg (gnat mountain) 68, 122

Mueckenfuss (gnat leg) 114

Muegge, see Muecke

Mueh (trouble, effort) 118

Muehl (mill) 103

Muehlbach, Muehlebach, Muehlenbach (mill brook) 103, 77

Muehleisen, Muehlseisen (mill axeliron) 103, 106

Muehlenberg (mill mountain) 68

Muehlenkamp (mill field) 103, 84

Muehlenstein (millstone) 103, 73

Muehlenweg (mill path) 103, 65

Muehler, see Mueller

Muehlhaus, Muehlhause, Muehlhausen, Muehlhauser (mill house) 103, 65

Muehlheim (mill hamlet) 103, 123

Muehlhoff (mill farm) 92

Muehlich (annoying) 115

Muehlke 55 (little mill) 103

Muehlman (mill man, miller) 103

Muehlsteff (Stephen fr the mill) 103

Muehsam (toilsome, tedious) 115

Mueldener, see Molden

Mueller (miller, fr Latin *molinarius*) 103

Muellibach (mill stream) 103, 77

Muelliberg (mill mountain) 103, 68

Muench, see Moench

Muencheberg (monk mountain) 110, 68

Muendel 55, Muendlein 55 (little ward)

Muennich, see Moench

Muenster (minster, fr Latin *monasterium*) 122

Muensterman (worker for, or dweller near a minster) 139

Muenter, Munter (coiner, minter) 96

Muentz, Muentze, Muenz, Muenzen (coin, minter, fr Latin *moneta*) 106

Muenzenberger (coin mountain) 106, 68

Muesch (bog) 80

Muessig (vacant, leisurely) 115

Muetz (cap, cap maker) 96, 106

Muetzenberg (cap mountain) 68

Mugg, see Mueck

Muhl 159, Muhly, Muhler, see Muehle, Muehler

Muhlbach 159, see Muehlbach

Muhlbauer 159 (farmer at the mill) 91

Muhldorf 159 (mill village) 124

Muhleisen 159, see Muehleisen

Muhlenbruch 159 (quarry at the mill) 80

Muhlhaus 159, Muhlhausen, see Muehlhaus, Muhlhausen

Muhlmeister 159 (master miller) 103

Muhr (bog) 80

Mulderer, Multerer, see Molden

Mulhauser 159, see Muhlhaus

Mulinari (miller, fr Latin *molinarius*) 142

Mullendorf 159 (mill village) 124

Muller 159, see Mueller

Mullhausen 159, see Muehlhaus

Multscher (mole) 115

Mumel (aunt) 119

Mumma, Mumme (masquerader) 118

Munch, see Moench

Mund, Mundt, Mundth (guardian) 47, see Siegmund

Mund, Mundt (mouth) 114

Mundel 55, Mundelein 55, see Muendel, Muendlein

Munich, see Moench

Munk, Munck, Munke, see Moench

Munkshower 159, Munschauer, Munshower (monk's meadow) 84

Munster 159, Munsterman, see Muenster, Muensterman

Munter (lively, merry) 115

Muntz 159, Munz, Muntzer, Munzer, Munzert 74, see Muentz

Munzenmayer 159 (foreman at the mint) 96

Mur, Murer, see Murr

Murach (swamp river) 80, 79

Murbach (swamp brook) 80, 77,
   122
Murdorf (swamp village) 80, 124
Murgenstern 159, see
   Morgenstern
Murlach (swamp pond) 80, 81
Murnau, Murner (swamp
   meadow) 80, 84, 122
Murner (tom cat) 115
Murr (sullen) 115
Muschel (mussel, mussel dealer)
   105
Musculus (Latin, muscle) 141
Musiker (musician) 96
Muss < Dominicus, Hieronymus
   135
Musse (leisure) 115
Musselman, Mussellmann
   (Moslem, one who has fought
   the Moslems)
Must, see Most
Muth, Muthe (courage,
   disposition, mood) 46
Muth 53 < Helmuth
Muthart (courage + strong) 46,
   46
Muthorst (muddy hurst) 72
Mutscher, Mutschler, Mutschke
   55 (baker of long loaves) 96
Mutter (bushel) 118
Mutter (official measurer) 109
Mutzenbecher (muddy creek) 77
Myer 159, Myers 59, see Meyer
Mynhard 159, see Meinhard
Myrs 159, Myers 59, see Meyer
Myster 159, see Meister

N

Naab (river name) 83
Naas, Nass (wet), see Nas
Nabel (navel) 113
Naber, see Nachbar
Nachbar, Nachbahr, Nachbauer
   (neighbor) 119

Nachlas (legacy) 118
Nacht (night) 143
Nachtigal, Nachtigall
   (nightingale) 115
Nachtschade, Nachschatt (night
   burgler) 96
Nack 122, Nacke (nape of neck)
   114
Nack (ridge) 68
Nader (sewer) 96
Nadler, Nadeler, Nadelmann
   (needle maker) 96, 106, 148
Naegele, Naegeli (little nail,
   clove) 106
Naeter (sewer) 96
Naff, see Neffe
Nafzger, Naffzer, Naftziger
   (sleepy person) 115
Nagel, Nagell, Nagele, Nagl,
   Nagle 159, Nagler (nail, nail
   smith) 96, 98, 106
Nagengast (Gnaw the guest!,
   stingy host) 96, 115
Nahm, Name (name) 118
Nahrgan, Nahrgang (earning of
   nourishment, livelihood) 118
Nail 159, see Nagel
Nanamacher 159, see
   Nonnenmacher
Nangesser 159 (probably fr
   Nongazzer)
Napfel, Nappel (an apple) 89
Napp (bowl maker) 96
Narr (fool)
Nas, Nase, Nasemann (nose,
   promontory) 114, 74
Nass (wet), see Nase
Nassau, Nassauer (fr Nassau,
   swamp meadow) 80, 121
Nast (fr ein Ast, branch cutter)
   95
Nastvogel (nest bird) 115
Nathan (OT name) 135
Natter (adder) 115

Natz < St Ignatius

Nau, Nauer, Nauert 74, Nauerz 74, 59 (dweller near the Naue) 83

Nauman, Naumann (new man), see Neumann 34

Naumburg (new castle) 34, 73, 122

Neable 159, see Nebel

Neagley 159, see Naegeli

Neander (Greek for Neumann) 9, 143

Nease 159, see Nies

Nebel (fog) 118

Nebeling (fr land of fogs, cf. Nibelungen)

Neckel, see Nick

Needleman 153, see Nadelmann

Neef, Neefer, see Neff

Neesemann (son of Agnes) 60

Neff, Neffe (nephew) 119

Nefzger, see Nafzger

Negele, Negle, see Naegele

Neher (ferryman) 96

Nehring (nutrition, subsistence), fr Nehring or Nehringen 122

Nehrkorn (fattening corn) 91

Neibauer, Neibuhr, see Neubauer 34

Neibling, Neiblinger, Nuebling, see Nebeling

Neibrand (new clearing) 34, 126

Neid, Neider, Neidert 74 (envy, hater) 46, see also Neidhard

Neidenbach (stream brook) 83, 77

Neidenberg (place name) 68

Neidhard, Neidhart, Neidhardt (hate + strong) 46, 46

Neidig (envious) 115

Neidlinger (fr Neidling or Neidlingen) 122

Neifeld (new field) 34, 84

Neighoff 159, see Neuhoff 151

Neihart, see Neidhart

Neihoff 34, see Neuhoff

Neikirk 34, see Neukirk

Neimann 34, see Neumann, Niemann

Neimiller 34 (new miller) 103

Neischwanger 34, see Neuschwander

Neisser (dweller near the Neisse River) 83

Neiswander, Neiswender, Neiswenter, Neiswinter 159, see Neuschwander

Neithard, see Neidhard

Nelde 53 < Arnold

Nembhard (one who likes to take) 115

Nemitz (Russian for "dumb one," German)

Nemeyer, see Niemeyer

Nemth, Nemetz, Nemitz, see Nimmitz

Ness (fr Nessen) 122

Nessel (nettle) 89, 72

Nesselroth (nettle clearing) 89, 72, 125

Nessler (dweller in the nettles) 89, 72

Nester (Greek, Nestor) 143

Nestli (little nest) 54, 55

Nestler (lace maker) 96

Neter (sewer) 96

Nett, Netter, Nettman (dweller on the Nette) 83

Nettelbladt (nettle leaf) 89

Netz (net, net fisherman) 91, 106

Neu (new, new settler)

Neubach, Neubacher, Neubeck, Neubecker (new brook) 77

Neubauer, Neugebauer, Neubaier (newly arrived farmer, fr the Neuhof, new farm) 91

Neuber, Neubert 74, Neuberth, see Neubauer

Neuberger (fr Neuberg 122, new mountain) 68

Neuboerger, see Neuberger

Neuburger (fr Neuburg 122, new castle) 73

Neudorff 122, Neuendorff (new village) 124

Neuenschwander, Neuenschwand 126, see Neuschwander

Neufeld, Neufeldt (new field) 84, 122

Neugart, Neugarth, Neugarten (new garden) 84, 122

Neugebauer, see Neubauer

Neuhart, Neuharth, see Neidhart

Neuhaus, Neuhausen, Neuhauser (new house) 65, 122

Neuhof, Neuhoff (new farm) 92

Neujahr (Newyear, time of birth or time of tax duty) 143

Neukamp (new field) 84, 122

Neukirch (new church) 71, 122

Neuland, Neulander (newly cleared land) 125

Neuman, Neumann (fr the Neuhoff, new farm) 34

Neumann, see Neubauer

Neumark (new boundary marker) 122

Neumarkt (new market) 122

Neumauer (new wall) 100

Neumayer, Neumeier, Neumeyer (new farmer), or fr the Neuhof (new farm) 93

Neumeister (new master)

Neumyer 159, see Neumayer

Neun, Neuner, Neunert 74 (nine, ninth) 143

Neunuebel (Nine evils!) 117

Neupert, see Neubauer

Neurath, Neureuther (new clearing) 125

Neuremberg, see Nuernberg

Neuschaefer, Neuschafer (new shepherd) 95

Neuschwander, Neuschwender (new clearing) 125

Neuschwanger, see Neuschwander

Neustadt, Neustater, Neustadt 55 (new city) 122

Neuwahl (new choice) 118

New, see Neu

Newbauer 153, see Neubauer

Newberger 153, see Neuberger

Newfeld 153, see Neufeld

Newhagen (new enclosure) 153

Newhart 153, see Neidhart

Newhaus, Newhouse, see Neuhaus

Newhiser 153, 66, see Neuhaus

Newhof 153, see Neuhof

Newirth, see Neuwirth

Newman 153, see Neumann

Newmeyer 153, see Neumeyer

Newmister 153, see Neumeister

Newschwanger, see Neuschwander

Newstead 153, see Neustadt

Newwirth 153, see Neuwirth

Ney 34, see Neu

Neymeyer 34, see Neumeyer

Neys, see Neiss

Nibling, see Nebling

Nice 159, see Neiss

Nicewonder 159, Nicewander, see Neuschwander

Nicholas, see Nikolaus

Nicht, Nichter (not, naught)

Nick, Nickel 53 < Nikolaus

Nickel, Nickels (nickel), or < Nikolaus

Nickel (decoy owl) 115

Nickelmann (water sprite) 118

Nicklaus, see Nikolaus

Nicodemus (St. Nicodemus) 135

Nicolai, Nicolay < Nikolaus

Nicolas, Nicolaus, see Nikolaus

Nider, see Nieder

Nidorf, see Neudorf

Nie..., see Neu

Niebe (merry, lively) 115

Niebel, see Nebel

Nieber 34, see Neubauer

Niebuhr 34, Niebur, see
Neubauer

Nied, Niede (nailsmith) 96, 106

Niedenthal, Niedentohl 159 (low
valley) 76

Nieder (low) 118

Niederauer (fr Niederau 122, low
meadow) 84

Niederhaus, Niederhausen,
Niederhauser (fr
Niederhausen 122, low house)
65

Niederhof, Niederhoff,
Niederhuber (low farm) 92,
122

Niederman, see Niedermayer

Niedermayer, Niedermeyer (fr
the Niederhof, lower farm) 93

Niederreuther (lower clearing)
125

Niedhart 159, see Neidhart

Niehaus 34, see Neuhaus

Niehof 34, see Neuhof

Niel, Nielmann (swamp, swamp
dweller) 80

Nieman 34, Niemann, Niman,
see Neumann

Niemand, Niemandt (no one)

Niemeier 34, Niemeyer, see
Neumayer

Niemiller 34, see Neumiller

Niemitz, see Nimitz

Niemoeller 34 (proprietor of the
new mill) 103

Niemyer 34, 159, see Neumayer

Nierendorf (lower village) 124

Nierhaus (lower house) 65

Nierman, see Niederman

Niermeyer, Niermyer, see
Niedermayer

Nies, Niese, Nieser, Niess,
Niessler, Niessner, Niessmann
94 (usufruct, also < Dionysius
and Ananies)

Nighswander 195, Nighswonger,
see Neuschwander

Nighthart 159, see Neidhart

Niklas, Niklaus, see Nikolaus

Nikolai, see Nikolaus

Nikolaus, Nikolas (St. Nicholas,
name of several popes) 134

Nimann, see Nieman

Nimeyer, Nimmeier, see
Niemeyer

Nimitz, Nimetz, Nimtz, Niemitz
(Slavic: "the dumb one,"
German) 121

Nimmersatt (never satisfied) 115

Nimmervoll (glutton)

Nipp, Nipper, Nippert 74 (dweller
near water) 81

Nissen (lice, lice eggs) 113

Nissler 159, see Nuessler

Nissley, see Nuess 159

Niswander 159, see
Neuschwander

Niswonger 159, see
Neuschwanger

Nitchmann 159, see Nitsch

Nitsch 53, Nitszche, Nitschmann
94 < Nikolaus

Nitze 53 < Nikolaus

Niwenhous 159, see Neuhaus

Noah (OT name) 135

Nobel (noble, name of lion in
Renard cycle)

Noble 159, see Nobel

Nodhart, see Nothart

Nodler, see Nadler

Nofziger, see Nafziger

Nohrnberg 159, see Nuernberg

Nolde, Nolder, Noldner 53 <
Arnold

Noll, Nolls 59, Noller, Nollmann
(heavy, simple person) 115

Noll, Knolls 59 (hill) 68
Nollenberger (hill mountain) 68
Nollendorf (hill village) 68, 124
Nolt 53, Nolte, Nolting 55,
    Noelting < Arnold
Noman, see Naumann
Nonemacher, see Nonnemacher
Nongazzer (resident on nun
    alley) 50, 65
Nonnenmacher, Nonemaker (pig
    castrator) 95
Noppenberger (woolnap
    mountain) 68, 122
Norbeck (northern brook) 85, 77
Norberg, see Nordberg
Norbert (St. Norbert) 135
Nord, Nordt, North (north) 85
Nordahl (north valley) 85, 76
Nordberg (northern mountain)
    85, 68, 122
Nordbrook, Nordbruch (northern
    brake) 85, 80, 122
Nordbruck (northern bridge) 85
Nordhaus, Nordhauser (fr
    Nordhausen 122, north house)
    85, 65
Nordheimer, Northeimer (north
    hamlet) 85, 124
Nordhoff (northern farm) 85, 92
Nordhus, see Nordhaus
Nordlingen, Nordlinger (fr
    Nordlingen) 122
Nordman, Nordmann
    (northerner, Northman) 85
Nordorf (north village) 85, 124,
    122
Nordstrand (north beach) 85, 122
Nordstrom (north stream) 85, 77
North (north) 85
Notenbom, see Nottebom
Notestein 159, Notstein (battle
    mountain) 46, 68
Noth (plight, battle) 46
Nothard (battle + strong) 46, 46

Nothelfer (helper in need,
    helping saint) 135
Notte (nut) 89
Nottebom, Nottebohm, see
    Nussbaum
Nowack, Nowak (Slavic: new
    man) 146
Nuechterlein 55 (moderate
    drinker) 115
Nuernberg, Nuernberger (fr
    Nuremberg) 122
Nueschler (buckle maker) 96
Nuess, Nuessli 55, Nueslein,
    Nuesslein (little nut) 89
Numeyer 159, see Neumeyer
Nummer (number) 118
Nunamacher, Nunnamacher, see
    Nonnenmacher
Nungesser, see Nongazzer
Nurenberg, see Nuernberg
Nushagen (nut hedge) 125
Nusholtz (nut wood) 89
Nuss, Nusse (nut) 89, 106
Nussbauer, Nusbauer,
    Nuszbaurn (nut farmer) 91
Nussbaum, Nusbaum,
    Nussbaumer (nut tree, house
    name) 89, 62
Nusterer (maker of rosaries) 96
Nuswanger 159, see
    Neuschwanger
Nyce 159, see Neuss
Nyenhuis, see Neuhaus
Nymann, see Neumann

O

Oak 159, see Eich
Oakes 159, see Ochs
Oben (up above) 118
Obenauer (upper meadow,
    beyond the meadow) 84
Obenauf (Up and onward!) 117
Obendorf, see Oberdorf
Obenheim (water hamlet) 80, 124
    see Oberheim

Obenheyser 66 (upper houses, beyond the houses) 65

Ober (boss, superior) 119

Oberbeck (upper creek, across the creek) 77

Oberberger (fr Oberberg 122, upper mountain, beyond the mountain) 68

Oberdahlhof (upper valley farm) 76, 92

Oberdorf, Oberdoerfer (fr Oberdorf 122, upper village, beyond the village) 124

Oberfehl, Oberfell (beyond the swamp) 80

Oberfeld, Oberfeldt, Oberfelder (upper field, beyond the field) 84, 122

Oberhaus, Oberheuser (upper houses) 65

Oberheim (upper hamlet) 124

Oberholtz, Oberholtzer (beyond the forest) 72

Oberkamp (upper field) 84

Oberkirch, Oberkirche (upper church) 71

Oberkofler (upper monticule) 67

Oberkuhn (temerarious) 115

Oberlaender, Oberlander (highlander, fr Oberland) 122

Oberle 55, Oberlin 55 < Albrecht

Oberman, Obermann (boss, superior)

Obermayer, Obermeyer, Obermeier (chief bailiff) 93

Obermiller, Obermueller, Obermuller 159 (chief miller) 103

Oberndorf, see Oberdorf

Oberscheimer, Obersheimer (upper hamlet) 124

Oberst (colonel) 107

Oberthaler (fr Oberthal, upper valley) 76, 122

Obitz, see Opitz

Obman, Obmann (steward) 96

Obrecht < Albrecht

O'Bright 159, see Obrecht

Obrist, see Oberst

Obser, Obster (fruit grower or dealer) 89, 105, 143

Ochs (ox) 91, 149

Ochsenbacher (fr Ochsenbach 122, ox brook) 77

Ochsenberger (fr Ochsenberg 122, ox mountain) 68

Ochsenfuss (ox foot) 114

Ochsenhirt (ox herder) 95

Ochsenreiter, Ochsenreuter (ox clearing) 125

Ochsenreiter (ox rider) 115

Ochsenschwantz (ox tail) 112

Ochsner (ox raiser or seller) 91, 96

Ochswald (ox forest) 72

Odenwald, Odewalt, Odewaelder (swamp mountains, mountain range along Rhine) 121

Oechsele 55, Oechsle, Oechslein, Oechslin, Oechselin, Oexli (little ox, carter) 96, 149

Oechsener, see Ochsner

Oechsler, see Ochsner

Oechsli 55, see Oechsele

Oefner, Oeffner (oven tender, oven maker) 96

Oehl (oil, oil dealer, fr Latin *oleum*) 105

Oehlenschlager, Oehlenschlaegel, see Ohlenschlager

Oehler, Oehlers 59, Oehlert 74, Oehleret, see Ulrich, Eyler

Oehli (OT Eli) 135

Oehlkuch (oil cake, baker) 96

Oehlstrom (eel stream) 77

Oelberg (Mount of Olives) 122

Oelhaf, Oelhafer (oil pitcher, oil dealer) 105

Oelken, Oelker (oil dealer) 105

Oelkrug (oil pitcher, oil dealer) 105

Oellen, Oeller, Oelmann,
Oellenschlaeger (oil maker) 96

Oertel, see Ortolf, Ortwin,
Ortlieb

Oesch, Oescheler, Oeshler, see
Esch, Eschelmann

Oesler (fr Oesel) 122

Oeste, Oester 122, Oesterle 55,
Oesterlein 55, Oesterlin,
Esterling, Oestermann
(easterly, man fr the east) 85,
see Oster

Oestreich, Oestreicher,
Oesterreicher (Austrian) 121

Oestrike, see Oestreich

Oetken 55 (little otter) 115

Oetting, Oettinger (fr Oettingen)
122

Oexler, see Ochsner

Ofenstein (oven stone) 73

Offenbach, Offenbacker 159
(swamp brook) 80, 77, 122

Offenhauser (fr Offenhaus 122,
swamp house) 80, 65

Offenstein (open stone) 73

Offer, Offerman, Offermann, see
Opfermann

Offner, Ofner, see Oefner

Oheim (uncle) 119

Ohl, Ohle < Odal (inherited
property 47), see also Ahl

Ohl, see Oehl

Ohl, Ohd, Old ..., see Alt

Ohlbach 122, see Ahlbach

Ohlbrecht, Ohlbrich (estate +
bright) 47

Ohldermann, see Aldermann

Ohlendorf, see Altdorf

Ohlenschlaeger, Ollenschlager
(oil maker) 96

Ohler (oil dealer) 105

Ohlhausen (old houses) 65

Ohlhausen (swamp houses) 80,
65

Ohlhaver (last year's oats, oat
dealer) 105

Ohlhoff (old farm) 92

Ohlhausen (old houses) 65

Ohli, Ohliger, Ohlinger (oil
dealer) 105

Ohlmacher (oil maker) 96

Ohlmann (old man) 113

Ohlmeyer (proprietor of the
Ohlhoff) 93

Ohlschlaeger, see Ohlenschlaeger

Ohlweiler (old village) 124

Ohlwein < Odalwin (inherited
property + friend) 46, 48

Ohm, Oheim, Ohms 59 (mother's
brother) 119

Ohm (river name) 83

Ohne (without, see Ahn) 122

Ohnemann (without a husband)
115

Ohnemuss, see Hieronymus

Ohnesorg, Ohnisorg 159 (without
worry) 115

Ohnfeld (without a field) 84

Ohnhaus (without a house) 65

Ohnmacht (weakness) 115

Ohnschild (without a shield) 114

Ohr (ear) 114

Ohrbach, see Auerbach

Ohrenschall (ear-deafening noise)
115

Ohrle 55 (little ear) 114

Ohrndorf, Orendorf (village on
the Oren) 83, 124

Okner 153, see Eichner

Olbrich, see Albrecht

Oldach, see Altag

Oldekamp (old field) 84

Oldenburg (old castle, German
province) 73, 121

Oldendorf, Ollendorf (old village)
124, 122

Oldermann, see Aldermann

Oldhouse 153, see Althaus

Oldhuis, see Althaus

Olenschlaeger, see
  Ohlenschlaeger
Olinger, Ollinger (fr Ollingen)
  122
Oliver (friend of Roland) 18
Ollrich, Olrick, see Ulrich
Olm, Olmert 74, see Ulm
Olthaus, see Althaus
Olthof, see Althoff
Omeis, see Ameis
Omwake 159, see Amweg
Onangst, Ohnangst (without
  fear) 115
Onimus, see Hieronymus
Opdebeek (on the brook) 69, 77
Openbrink (on the hill) 69, 74
Opfer, Opher (sacrifice, fr Latin
  operari)
Opfermann (sexton) 110
Opfertuch (sacrificial cloth) 118
Opitz 53 < Albrecht
Oppenheim, Oppenheims 59,
  Oppenheimer (open hamlet)
  124, 122
Oppermann, see Opfermann
Oppert 53 < Albrecht
Oppitz, see Opitz
Oppmann, see Obmann
Ord, see Ort
Ordemann, see Ortmann
Ordner, see Ortmann
Orebaugh 159, see Auerbach
Oremus (Latin, "Let us pray,"
  name for clerics) 116, 117, 110
Orendorf, Orndorf (village on the
  Oren) 124
Orendorf (swamp village) 80, 124
Orff 53 < Ordolf (sword point +
  wolf) 46, 48
Orgelfinger (organ finger,
  organist) 96
Orgelmann, Orgler (organ player,
  or maker) 96
Orndorf, see Arndorf
Ornhold, see Arnold

Ornstein, Orenstein, see Arnstein
Ort, Orth, Ord, Oertli 55 (place)
  122
Ort, Orth (point of sword or
  spear 46, point of land)
Ortel 53, 55, Ortell < Ortlieb,
  Ortwin, etc.
Ortlieb, Ortlip (point of sword +
  dear) 46, 48
Ortman, Ortmann, Orthmann,
  Ortmeyer, Ortner (dweller at
  the end of the village) 94, 93
Ortner, see Ortmann
Ortolf (sword point + wolf) 46, 47
Ortwein, Ordwin (sword point +
  friend) 46, 48
Ortwig, Orwig (point of sword +
  battle) 46, 46
Oslager 159, see Ohlenschlager
Osmann, see Ostmann
Osmer < Osmar (gods + famous)
  51, 47
Osmund (gods and protection) 51,
  47
Ossenecker (ox field) 84, 85
Ossenfort (ox ford) 78
Ost (east) 85
Ostberg (east mountain) 85, 68,
  122
Ostendorf (east village) 85, 124,
  122
Oster (easter, easterner, time of
  birth, period of corvée duty)
  143
Osterberg, Osterberger (east
  mountain) 85, 68, 122
Osterhaus, Osterhouse 153
  (eastern house) 85, 65
Ostericher (Austrian) 121
Osterkerze (Easter candle,
  candle maker) 96
Osterle, see Oesterle
Osterling (easterner) 85
Osterloh (eastern forest) 85, 72
Osterloh (Easter fire) 122

Osterman, Ostermann, see
　Ostmann
Ostermayer, Ostermeier,
　Ostermeyer (eastern farmer)
　85, 93
Ostermueller (eastern miller) 85,
　103
Ostertag (Easter) 143
Osterweil (eastern village) 127
Osthaus (eastern house) 85, 65
Ostheim (eastern hamlet) 85,
　124
Ostmann (eastern man) 85
Ostreicher (Austrian) 121
Oswald, Ostwalt, Osswald (god +
　rule, English saint) 47, 71,
　135, 137
Otfried (treasure + protection)
　47, 47
Otmar, Othmar (treasure +
　famous) 47, 48
Ott, Otte, Odt, Utt (treasure) 47
Otten, Ottens 59 < Otto
Ottenbach (Otto's brook) 77
Ottendorf, Ottendorfer (Otto's
　village) 124, 122
Ottenheim, Ottenheimer (Otto's
　hamlet) 124
Otter (otter, otter hunter) 91
Otterbach (swamp brook) 80, 77
Otterbein (otter bone, otter leg)
　113
Ottersheim (otter hamlet) 123
Ottnand (treasure + brave) 47,
　46
Otto (treasure) 47
Ottwein (treasure + friend) 47,
　48
Otweil (treasure village) 127
Over, see Ober
Overbeck (beyond the brook) 77
Overdieck (beyond the dike) 82
Overhizer 159, see Oberheuser
Overholser 159, see Oberholtzer
Overholt, see Oberholtz

Overlack (beyond the lake) 80
Overstoltz (overly proud) 115
Oxley, see Ochsner

P

Paap, Paape, see Pape
Paasch, see Pasch
Pabst (pope, fr Latin *papa*) 110,
　134, 143
Pabstmann (member of papal
　party) 110, 94
Pach, Pacher, Pachmann 94,
　Pachmeyer 93 (tenant farmer)
　119
Pacht, Pachter, Paechter (tenant)
　119
Packenkopf (horse head) 113
Packer, Packert 74, Packard 74,
　see Bacher
Packer (wholesaler) 105
Packheiser 66 (bake houses) 65
Pader, see Bader
Paebke 55 (little priest) 110
Paetz, see Betz
Paetzsch 53, Paetsch < Petrus
Paff, Paffen, see Pfaff
Paffenbach (priest's brook) 110,
　77
Paffenroth (priest's clearing) 110,
　125
Pagel, Pagels < Paulus
Pagenhart (horse herder) 91
Pahnke 55 (Slavic, young lord)
　146
Painter (dweller in a fenced
　inclosure) 84
Pallmert < Baldemar
Palm, Palmer (palmer) 110
Palzgraf, see Pfalzgraf
Palsgrove 159, see Pfalzgraf
Pamberg, see Bamberg
Pancer 159, see Pantzer
Panebaker 159, Pannabaker,
　Pannabecker, see
　Pfannenbecker

Pangratz (St. Pancratius) 135

Pantel, see Bandel

Pantel (panther, house name) 62

Pantel, Pantel < St Pantaleon 135

Pantzer, Panzer (breastplate, fr Latin *pantex*, armorer) 108

Pape (priest, Latin *papa*) 110

Papel (poplar) 89

Papelbaum (poplar tree) 89

Papenberg, see Pappenberg

Papendorp (priest's village) 110, 124

Papp, Pappe, see Pape

Pappenberg, Pappenberger (priests' mountain, swamp mountain) 80, 110, 68

Pappendiek (swamp dike) 80, 82

Pappenheim (swamp hamlet) 80, 122, 123

Pappenheimer (priests' hamlet) 110, 124

Pappler (dweller by the poplars) 89

Paproth (priest's clearing) 110, 125

Papst, see Pabst

Parchenter, Parkent, Parmenter (fustian dealer) 105

Paris, Paries, Pariser (Parisian, journeyman who trained in Paris) 122

Parr (pair, couple) 118

Parr (parish) 118

Parris, Paries, see Paris

Part, Parth, Partz 59, see Bart

Partsch, see Bartsch

Pasch, Pasche (Easter 143), also fr French dice game

Paschke 53, 55 < Paulus

Passaw, Passauer (fr Passau, Latin *castra batava*) 122

Passmann (dweller in a pass) 68

Pasternack (parsnip) 91, 112, 105, 114

Pastorius (Latin for Schaefer) 141

Pate, Path, Pathe (godfather, fr Latin *pater*) 119

Paternoster (Our Father, maker of rosaries) 96

Pates 159, see Betz

Patz 53, Patzer < Balthasar

Pau, Paue, see Pfau

Paur, Pauer, see Bauer

Pauck, Paucker, Pauckner (drummer) 96

Paul, Pauls, Paulus (St. Paul, name of pope) 134

Pauli, Pauly (son of Paulus) 142

Paulig, Pauling 53, 55, Paulinger, Paulmann < Paulus

Paulitsch 53 < Paulus

Paulus (St. Paul, name of several popes) 134

Pausch, see Baus

Pause (pause)

Pawel, see Paul

Pawl 159, Pawlus, see Paul

Paynter 159, see Painter

Peagler 159, see Buegler

Peal 159, Pealer, see Buehl, Buehler

Pech, Peche, Pecher (pitch, tar maker) 96; see also Beck

Pechmann, Peckmeyer 93 (tar maker) 95

Pechtle, see Bechtle

Peck, see Beck

Peckinpaw 159, see Beckenbach

Peel 159, Peeler, see Buehl, Buehler

Peffer, Peffers 59, see Pfeffer

Peheim, see Boehm

Peifer, Peiffer, see Pfeiffer

Peightel 159, see Bechtel

Peil, see Pfeil

Peinter, see Painter

Peiper, see Pfeiffer

Pelgrim, Pelegrim, Pellegrin, see Pilgrim

Pelican, Pelikan (pelican, house name) 62, 148

Pelter, see Peltz

Peltz, Pelz, Peltzer, Peldner, Peldtmann (pelt, hide worker, fr Latin *pelis*) 96

Pence, see Bentz

Pennecker (little bear) 48

Penner (salt maker) 96

Pennypacker 159, Pennybaker, see Pfannenbecker

Pens, Pentz, see Bentz

Peper, Pepper, Peppermann, see Pfeffer, Pfeffermann

Perdt (horse, horse dealer, carter) 105, 96

Perger, see Berger

Perle (pearl, jeweler) 96

Perlman (pearl dealer, possibly Ashkenazic metronym for "Pearl's husband") 105

Perlmutter (mother of pearl, jeweler) 105

Perlroth (pearl red) 148

Permenter, Pergamenter (parchment maker) 96

Perner, see Berner, Bernher

Pershing 159, Persing, Persinger, see Pfirsich

Pertsch, Pertz < Berthold

Pesch (grassy field, fr Latin *pascuum*) 84

Peter, Peters 59, Peterlein 55, Peterke 55, Petrus (St. Peter) 135, name of a pope 134

Peterly (son of Peter) 59, 142

Petermann (follower of Peter) 119

Petersen, Peterson, Petersohn (son of Peter) 59

Petri, Petry (son of Petrus) 59, 141

Petrus (Latin for Peter) 141

Petsch 53 < Peter

Petz, Petts 159 (bear) 48, also < Peter

Petzold, Pezold 53 < Peter

Peukert (drummer, person fr Peuker in Silesia) 96, 122

Peyer, see Bayer

Peysel 159, see Beisel

Pfaar, see Pfarr

Pfadenhauer (thread maker) 100

Pfaeffer (priest) 110

Pfaeffikon (priest village) 110, 127

Pfaf, Pfaff, Pfaffe (priest, fr Latin *papa*) 110

Pfaffenbach (priests' brook) 110, 77

Pfaffenberger (fr Pfaffenberg 122, priests' mountain) 110, 68

Pfaffenmeier (priests' farmer) 139

Pfaffmann (priest's man) 110

Pfaffroth (priest's clearing) 110, 139, 126

Pfahl (stake, fr Latin *palus*) 118

Pfaltz, Pfaltzer (Rhenish Palatinate, from Latin *palatium*) 121

Pfalzgraf (palgrave, fr Latin *palatium* + *graf*) 109

Pfann, Pfanne, Pfanner (pan, pan maker, fr Latin *panna*) 106

Pfannebecker (cake baker) 96

Pfannenstiel, Pfanstiel (pan handle) 118

Pfanner (pan maker) 96

Pfannkuchen (pancake, baker) 96

Pfannstiel, see Pfannenstiel

Pfarr (pastor, pastorate, fr Latin *parrochia*) 110

Pfarrer (pastor) 110

Pfattenhauer, Pfadenhauer (thread maker) 96

Pfau (peacock) 115

Pfeffer, Pfeffermann (pepper, seller of pepper, fr Latin *piper*) 105

Pfefferkorn (pepper corn, spice dealer) 105

Pfeidler (shirt maker, dealer) 105

Pfeifenberger, Pfeiffenberger (pipe mountain) 68

Pfeifer, Pfeiffer, Pfeiffers 59, Pfeifere (fifer, fr Latin *pipa*) 96

Pfeil, Pheil, Pheyl (arrow, fr Latin *pilus*, a javelin) 109

Pfeiler (arrow maker, fletcher) 109

Pfennig, Pfenning (penney) 117

Pfetzer (rag man) 96

Pfingst, Pfingstag, Pfingsten (Pentecost, Whitesuntide) 143

Pfirsich, Pfersich (peach, fr Latin *malum persicum*) 89

Pfister, Pfistner, Pfisterer (baker, fr Latin *pistor*) 102

Pfitz, Pfitze, Pfitzer, Pfitzel (flagellant)

Pfitzner, see Pfuetzner

Pflanz, Pflantz (plant, fr Latin *planta*) 89, 101

Pflaum (plumb, fr Latin *pluma*) 89, 101

Pflaumenbaum (plum tree) 89

Pfleger (guardian, fosterer, judge) 109

Pflueger (plowman) 91, 46

Pflug (plow, plowman) 91

Pflug (a measure of plowland, farmer) 92

Pflugfelder (arable field) 84

Pfoersching, see Pfirsich

Pfoertner, Pfortner (gate keeper, fr Latin *porta*) 96

Pfontz, see Puntzius

Pfort (gate, fr Latin porta) 71

Pfortzheim (town in Baden) 122

Pfriendtner, Pfruendner (prebendary) 110

Pfuetzner, Pfutzner (dweller by a pond) 80

Pfuhl (puddle) 80

Pfund (pound, fr Latin *pondus*)

Pfuntz, see Puntzius

Pfutzner, see Pfuetzner

Pfyfer, see Pfeiffer

Ph ..., look under Pf

Pheidler (shirt maker) 96

Pheifer, Phifer, Phieffer, see Pfeifer

Philip, Philips 74, Philipp (St. Philip) 135

Philipi (son of Philip) 142

Philips, Philipson (son of Philip) 59

Phister, see Pfister

Phyffer, see Pfeifer

Pichler 41, see Buehler

Pickel, Pickler, Pickelman (pick, pickax) 106

Pickli (little pick) 106

Piefer, see Pfeiffer

Piehl, Piel, Pihl, see Buehl

Piehler, see Buehler

Pielmeyer, see Buehlmeyer 151

Pieper, see Pfeifer

Pieters 59, Pieterse, see Peter

Pietsch (St. Peter) 133-137

Pifer 159, see Pfeifer

Pilger, Pilgrim, Pilgram (pilgrim, fr Latin *peregrinus*) 110

Pilgrim < Biligrim (sword + helmet) 46, 46

Piller (sword + army) 46, 46

Piltz (mushroom, fr Latin *boleta*) 106

Pinder, Pindar, see Binder

Pinsel (artist's brush, fr Latin *penicillus*)

Piper 159, see Pfeifer

Pirsch (hunter) 91

Pister, Pistor 159, see Pfister

Pitner, Pittner, see Buettner

Pitsenberger, Pitzenbarger (dweller near mountain peak) 68

Plage (marshy grassland) 80

Plank, Planck (white) 112

Planckenhorn (white peak) 72

Plate, Plathner, see Platner

Platner, Plattner (sheet metal worker, armor maker) 108

Platte (small plateau) 68

Platz (place, village green, fr Latin *platea*)

Plechner, see Blech

Pless 53, Plesse, Plessi < St. Blasius 135

Plessing 53 < St. Blasius 135

Pletsch, Pletscher, Pletcher, see Platner

Plette, see Platner

Pletz (clothes patcher) 96

Pleyer, see Blei

Plocher, see Blocher

Plock, see Block

Ploeg, see Pflug

Plotz, see Platz

Pluecker, Plucker (plucker) 96

Plug, see Pflug

Plum, see Blum, Pflaum

Plum 153, see Zwetschen

Plumenstein (flower stone) 73

Poechler, see Beck, Bechler

Poehlman, Poehlmann, see Pohlmann

Poehmer, see Boehmer

Poertner, see Pfoetner

Poetzel 53, Poetzold, Poetsch < Peter

Poffenberger, see Pfaffenberger

Pogener, see Bogener

Pohl, Pohlner (Pole) 121

Pohl (pool, pond, swamp) 80

Pohl 53, Pohle, Pohler, Pohling < Paulus

Pohl (stake, fr Latin *palus*)

Pohlhaus (fr Pohlhausen 122, pond houses) 80

Pohlman, Pohlmann (dweller near a pool) 80

Poland, Polander (fr Poland) 121

Poldermann (occupant of a polder) 80

Pollak (Pole) 121

Pollinger, see Bollinger

Polmann, Pollmann, Pollner, Polner, see Pohlmann

Polster, Poelster (polster maker) 106

Polther 53, Poltermann < St. Hippolytus 135

Poltz, see Boltz

Pomgarddiner, see Baumgaertner

Pommer (Pomeranian) 121

Pommer (place name) 121

Pool, Poole 159, Poole, see Puhl

Pope, see Pape

Popp, Popps 59, Poppe, see Papp, Pappe

Poppelmann (dweller among the poplars) 89, 94

Porcher, see Burckhard

Porkholder 159, 151 see Burghalter 151

Portmann, Portner, see Pfoertner

Portz (place name) 122

Poser, Posner (fr Posen) 121

Possart, Possert, see Bosshart

Posthumus (posthumous)

Pot 159, Pott, Potts 59, see Bote

Potasch (potash maker) 96

Poth, see Bote

Pothe, see Pot

Potsdammer (fr Potsdam) 122

Potter (potter) 96

Pottgiesser (potter) 96

Potthast (pot roast, meat and vegetable stew) 112

Potts 159, see Batz

Powledge 159, see Paulitsch

Pracht (splendor) 118

Praetorius (Latin for Schultheiss) 9, 141

Praeuner, see Braeuner

Prag, Prager (fr Prague) 122

Prahl, Prall (splendor, luxury) 115

Pramschufer, Pramschuefner (boat poler) 96

Prang, Prange (claw) 114

Prang, Prange (quarreler, brawler) 115

Pranger (pillory) 118

Praslaw (fr Breslau) 122

Prass, Prasse (glutton, gourmet) 115

Praun, see Braun

Praunmueller, see Braunmueller

Precht, see Brecht

Prechtel 53, 55 < Helmbrecht

Prediger (preacher, fr Latin *predicare*) 109

Preidenback 159, see Breitenbach

Preis, Preiss, Preise, Preisz (praise, price, prize, fr Latin *pretium*)

Preising, Preisinger (fr Preisingen) 122

Preissle, Preissmann (shoelace maker) 96

Preller (shouter) 115

Presl (fr Breslau) 122

Presser, Pressler (fr Breslau) 122

Pressly, see Bresler

Presster 159, Prester, see Priester

Pretorius, see Praetorius

Pretzel (pretzel maker) 96

Pretzer, see Brett

Preusch, Preuscher, see Preuss

Preuss, Preussner (Prussian, North German) 120

Prevost, Prevot, see Probst

Price 159, see Preiss, Preuss

Pricker, see Bruecker

Prieber, Pryber < Pribislav (Slavic) 146

Priest, Priester (priest, fr Latin *presbyter*) 110, 101

Pright 159, see Brecht

Printz, Prinz (prince, fr Latin *princeps*) 109, 101

Probst, Propst (provost, fr Latin *praepositus*) 109, 101

Profrock, Prufrock (Test the rye! market official) 116, 109

Prophet (prophet, fr Latin *propheta*) 101

Prost (simple) 115

Prost (*Prosit*, a Latin toast) 117

Proth (bread, baker) 96

Protmann 159, see Brotmann

Pruder, see Bruder

Pruegel (whip) 106

Prunder (prebend, prebendary)

Pruner, Prunner, see Brunner

Prysing 159, see Preising

Pryss 159, see Preis

Pub 159, see Bube

Puehl (pillow, fr Latin *pulvinus*) 106

Puetzbach (pond brook) 80, 77

Puhl (pool) 80

Puhlhoffer (farm by a pool) 80, 92

Pulgram, see Pilgrim

Pullmann, see Pulvermacher

Pulver (powder, powder maker) 108

Pulvermacher, Pulvermann 94 (powder maker) 108

Pulvermueller (gunpowder maker) 108

Punchoer (French for *Bonjour*) 144

Pundschuh, see Bundschuh

Pundt, see Pfundt

Puntzius (Pontius Pilate, actor in morality play) 111

Pupper (doll maker) 96

Purpur (purple) 112

Pursch, Bursch (lad, youth) 151

Putsch, Putscher, Putch (rioter) 115

Putz (finery, cleaning) 115

Pyle, see Peil, Pfeil 151

Q

Quade (wicked, dirty) 115

Qualbrink (agony hill) 67

Quandmeyer (rascal) 115, 93
Quandt, Quante (rascal) 115
Quarengesser, Quarngesser (path along the Quern) 83, 65
Quark (cottage cheese) 112
Quart (quart) 118
Quartz (quartz, miner) 96
Quasebarth (glutton) 115
Quast (tassel, bather's whisk, bath attendant) 96
Queck (lively) 115
Quell (spring) 79
Quenzer (card player) 96
Querfurth (fr Querfurth, city at a ford on the Querne) 83, 122
Querne (name of river) 83
Quetschenbach (plum brook) 89, 77
Quick (alive, lively) 115
Quint < St Quentin 135
Quirmbach (fr Quernbach) 122
Quitman (quince dealer) 89, 105
Quittenbaum (quince tree) 89

R

Raab, Raabe, Raap, see Rab
Raasch, see Rasch
Rab, Rabb, Rabe, Raben (raven) 115
Rab, see Rapp
Rabanus (Latin for Rabe) 141
Rabbe 55, see Ratbold
Rabenau (raven meadow) 48, 84
Rabenecke (raven field) 48, 85,
Rabenhorst (ravens' eyrie) 48, 72
Rabenolt (raven + loyal) 48, 48
Rabenstein (raven crag) 48, 73
Rach, Rache (vengeance) 115
Rachbach (muddy stream) 80, 77
Rackensperger (muddy mountain) 80, 68
Radabaugh 159, Radebaugh (marshy brook) 80, 77
Radebach, see Rautebach

Radecke (marshy field) 80, 84
Radehose (red pants) 112
Radekopf (red head) 112
Rademacher, Radermacher, Radmacher (wheelright) 96
Rademan, Radman, Radmann (marsh dweller) 80, see also Rathmann
Rademann (councillor) 96, 109
Rader, Radner, Raderman, see Rademan
Radick 53, 55 < Radolf (counsel + wolf) 47, 48
Radke 53, 55 Radtke < Conrad
Radmer < Ratmar (counsel) 47
Raeck, see Reck
Raeder, see Reeder
Raedermacher, see Rademacher
Raff, Raffer (scrawny person) 113
Raff (raven) 48
Raffensberger, Raffensbarger (raven mountain) 48, 68
Raffschneider, see Reifschneider
Rafkamp (raven field) 48, 84
Ragle 159, see Regel
Rahder, see Rader
Rahl, see Rall
Rahm, Rahmm (cream) 112, 122
Rahman, Rahmann (marsh dweller) 80
Rahn (slender) 113
Rahn (brunet) 112
Rahnfelder, perhaps for Rheinfelder
Raiber, see Reiber
Raibold < Raginbold (counsel + bold) 46, 46
Raich, see Reich
Raichert, see Reichert
Raifeisen (hoop maker) 96
Raiffschneider, see Reiffschneider
Raimund < Reginmund (counsel + protection) 46, 46
Rainard, see Reinhart
Rainer, see Reiner

Raisbeck, Raischbeck (rapid stream) 77

Raiser, see Reiser

Rakebrandt (stoker) 96

Rall (water rail) 115

Rall (noisy) 115

Ram (ram, wether) 91

Rambach, Ramsbach (swamp brook) 80, 77, 122

Ramberg, Ramberger, Ramsberg (raven mountain) 68, 122

Rame, Rahme, Ramm, see Rahm

Ramelmeier (fr the Rammelhof, wether farm) 93

Ramer (creamer) 96

Ramhoff (wether farm) 92

Ramhorst (wether hurst) 72

Ramler, Rammler (wether, male hare) 115

Ramm (bear leek, *allium ursinum*) 89

Rammelfanger (ram catcher) 117

Rammelkamp (wether field) 84

Rampmeyer, see Ramelmeier

Ramsau, Ramsaur, Ramsauer, Ramsayer (meadow with bear leek, *allium ursinum*) 89, 84, 122

Ramsberg (raven mountain, or mountain with bear leek *allium ursinum*) 89, 68, 122

Ramsburg (raven castle) 48, 73

Ramsland (raven land) 48

Ramspacher, see Rambach

Ramstein (raven mountain) 48, 68

Ranck, see Ranke

Rand, Randt (edge of the shield, shield) 46

Randolf (shield + wolf) 46, 48

Ranft (bread crust, baker) 96

Rang, Rank (rank)

Ranke (tendril, climber, agile person) 115

Ranzenbach (rancid brook) 77

Rap, see Rapp

Raper, Rapert 74 < Ratbrecht (counsel + bright) 47, 47

Raphael (an archangel) 135

Rapp, Rappe (black horse) 91

Rapp (raven) 48

Rappel, see Rappold

Rappert < Radbrecht (counsel + brilliant) 36, 46, 47

Rappolt < Ratbold (counsel + bold) 47, 46

Rasbach, Rashpacker 159, see Raschbacher

Rasch, Rasche (swift) 115

Raschbacher, Raschpacker (fr Raschbach 122, swift brook) 77

Raskop (hot head) 115

Rast (rest) 118

Rast (swamp) 80

Rat, Rath (counsel) 47

Ratbold (counsel + bold) 47, 47

Ratenmacher, see Rademacher

Rather, Ratherr (councilman, adviser) 109, 159

Rathgeb, Rathgeber (advice giver) 115

Rathhauser (city hall) 65

Rathmacher, see Rademacher

Rathschild 159, see Rothschild

Ratmann, Rathmann, Rattmann (councilman) 109

Ratner, Rattner, see Radner

Ratschlag (advice) 18

Rattenauer (rat meadow) 84, see Reitenauer

Rattenzahl (rat tail) 113

Ratz, Ratze (rat) 115

Ratzenberger (rat montain) 68

Rau, Raue, Rauh, Rauher (rough, hairy) 115, 114

Raub, Rauber (robbery, robber) 109

Raubach 122, Raubaugh 159, see Rautebach, Rohbach

Raubenstine 159, see Rubenstein

Rauch (towsel haired) 112

Rauch (fish and meat smoker) 96, 106

Rauchfass (incense burner) 106

Rauchhaus (smokehouse, meat or fish smoker) 96

Raudabaugh 159, see Rautebach

Raudenbach (Slavic river name) 83

Raudenbusch (rue bush, fr Latin *ruta*) 89

Rauer, see Rau

Rauff (brawl) 115

Raugh 159, see Rau

Rauh, see Rau, Rauch

Rauhut (fur cap, milliner) 112, 96

Raum (room, space) 118

Raun, Rauner (mystery, whisperer) 115

Raup, Raupp, see Raub

Raup, Raupe (caterpillar) 118

Raupach, see Raubach

Rausbach, see Rauschbach

Rausch, Rauscher (rush, intoxication) 115

Rauschbach, Rauschenbach (bullrush stream) 81, 78

Rauschberg, Rauschenberg, Rausenberger (bullrush mountain) 81, 68

Rauscher, Rauschert 74 (illegitimate child) 119

Rauschkorb (reed basket) 106

Rauth (rod) 118

Raven (raven) 48

Rawn 159, see Rahn

Raymund, see Raimund

Rayser, see Reiser

Raysinger, see Reisinger

Reach 159, see Reich

Read 159, see Ried

Reagle 159, see Riegel

Reahl 159, see Riehl

Ream 159, Reamer, see Riem, Riemer

Reaser 159, see Rieser

Reasoner 159, see Rieser, Riesner

Reb, Reber, Rebert 74 (grapevine, vintner) 106

Reback 159, Rehbeck, see Rehbock

Reber (vintner) 96

Reberg (roe mountain) 68

Rebhahn, Rebhan, see Rebhuhn

Rebholtz (grapevine) 72

Rebhoon 159, see Rebhuhn

Rebhuhn, grouse 115

Rebmann, Rebner (vine dresser) 96, 102

Rebsamen (grapeseed) 102, see Ruebsamen

Rebstock (grapevine, vintner) 102

Rebuck, see Rehbock

Rechenberg (rake mountain, roebuck mountain) 68, see Reckenberger

Rechenmacher (rake maker) 96

Rechner (accountant) 96

Recht (Right!) 117

Rechter 159, Righter 159, see Richter

Rechthand (right hand) 118

Reck, Recke (hero) 42

Reckenberger (fr Reckenberg 122, marsh mountain) 80, 68

Reckenwald (marsh mountain) 80, 71

Recker, Reckers 59, Reckert 74, Reckman (dweller by a marsh) 80

Reckhaus (marsh house) 80, 65

Reckmeyer (swamp farmer) 80, 91

Reckner, see Rechner

Reckziegel (Pull the bridle!, horseman, groom) 96, 116

Rector (Latin, rector, headmaster) 109, 141, see also Richter

Reddick, see Radick

Redeke, Redecker (cartwright) 96

Redeman, Redemann (swamp
dweller) 80, see also
Rademann

Redenbaugh 159 (swamp stream
80, 77, 122), see also
Reitenbach

Reder (councilman, see also
Reeder) 109

Redlich (honest) 115

Redmann, see Redemann

Ree ..., see Rie...

Reeb, see Reb

Reece 159, see Riess

Reed 159, see Riet

Reeder (ship owner) 96

Reem 159, Reemer, Reemsnyder
159, see Riem, Riemer,
Riemenschneider

Reep, Reeper, Reepschlaeger
(rope, rope maker) 106

Rees 159, Reese, see Ries

Reeser 159, Reezer, see Rieser

Reffner (censurer, rebuker) 115

Refsnyder 159, see Reifschneider

Regel (rule, fr Latin *regula*) 118

Regenbogen (rainbow) 118

Regenhardt, Reginhardt, see
Reinhard

Regenhold, see Reinhold

Regensburg (castle on the River
Regen) 83, 73, 122

Regenstein (rain mountain, rock
on the Regen River) 83, 73,
122

Regenthal (Regen valley) 83, 76,
122

Reger, Regert 74 (heron, thin
person) 114, 115

Reger (restless person) 115

Regler (monk in orders, fr Latin
regula) 110

Regner (dweller on the Regen) 83

Regters 159, 59, see Richter

Regul, see Regel

Reh (roe, roebuck) 48, 115

Rehbach, Rehbacher (roe brook)
77

Rehbein (roe bone, roe leg) 113

Rehberg, Rehberger (fr Rehberg
122, roebuck mountain, see
Reberg) 68

Rehbock (roebuck) 115, 91

Rehder, see Reeder

Rehfeld (roe field) 84

Rehfus, Rehfuss (roe foot) 114

Rehkemper (roebuck field) 84

Rehkopf (roebuck head) 114

Rehling, Reehling, Reeling
(railing) 122

Rehm, Rehmer, Rem (strap
cutter) 106, see also Reinmar

Rehman, Rehmann (marsh
dweller) 80, see Raimann

Rehmer, see Roemer

Rehmeyer (marshland farmer)
80, 93

Rehmus (latinized Rehm) 141,
see Adoremus

Rehorn (roebuck horn) 106

Rehwalt, Rehwoldt (roebuck
forest) 71

Rehweg (roebuck path) 65

Rehwinckel (roebuck forest) 72

Reiber, Reibert 74 (bath
attendant, masseur) 96

Reibetanz (dance leader) 96

Reich, Reiche (empire, of the
imperial party) 109

Reich, Reicher, Reichert 74 (rich)
115

Reichard, Reichhardt, Reichart,
Reicharz 59 (rule + strong) 46,
46

Reich auf (Reach up!) 117

Reichburg (imperial castle) 73

Reichel, Reichl, Reichle 159,
Reichelt 74, Reichler <
Reichard

Reichelderfer 159 (Reichel's
village) 124

Reineck 122, Reinecke, Reineke, Reinecker, Reinicker, see Reinke

Reinemann, see Reiman

Reiner, Reiners 164, Reinert 74 < Reinher (counsel + army) 47, 46

Reinfeld, Reinfelder 122, see Rheinfeld

Reinfried (counsel + peace) 47, 47

Reinhard, Reinhardt, Reinhart, Reinheardt 159 (counsel + strong) 47, 46, 49

Reinheimer 159, see Rheinheim

Reinhold, Reinholdt, Reinholt, Reinholtz 164 (counsel + loyal) 47, 46

Reinig 53, 55, Reining, Reininger < Reinhard, Reinhold

Reinke 53, 55, Reinicke, Reineke, Reininck < Reinhart, Reinhold, etc.

Reinknecht (stable boy, horse breeder) 96

Reinman (Rhinelander) 121

Reinmar, Reimar (counsel + famous) 47, 47

Reinmuth (pure disposition) 115, 138

Reinmuth (counsel + disposition) 47, 46

Reinninger (fr Reining) 122, see Reinig

Reinohl, Reinoehl (pure oil, oil dealer) 105, see Reinhold

Reinsch 53 < Reinhold, Reinhard

Reinsfelder, Reinsfeller (fr Reinsfeld) 122, see Reinfeld

Reinstein 122, see Rheinstein

Reinthaler, see Rheinthaler

Reints 53, 159, Reintzel 55, Reintzell, see Reinsch

Reinwald < Reginwald (counsel + rule) 47, 46, see Rheinwald

Reip, see Reif

Reis, Reiss (branch, faggot gatherer) 95

Reis, Reise (journey, traveler) 96

Reisberger (faggot mountain) 68

Reisenweber, see Reusenweber

Reiser, Reisser, Rizer 159 (traveler, mercenary) 107

Reiser (dweller by a stone slide) 71

Reiser (wood carver) 96

Reiser, Reisig (brushwood, faggot) 72

Reisfeld (stone slide field) 84, 122

Reisig, Reisiger, Reisinger (dweller in the brush) 95

Reisig, Reisiger, Reissig (armed for war) 107, see Reissiger

Reising, Reissing, Reisinger (knight on horseback) 107, 122

Reisinger, Reissiger, Reissiger, Reissmann (cavalryman) 107

Reisman, Reissman, Reisner, Reisler (soldier) 107

Reiss, see Reis

Reissenkittel (Take the smock!, robber) 109

Reist, Reister (fr Reiste) 122

Reitberger (fr Reitberg 122, bullrush mountain) 81, 68

Reitemeyer (clearing farmer) 125, 93

Reitenauer (fr Reitenau, bullrush meadow) 81, 84

Reitenbach, Reitenbaugh 159 (bullrush brook) 81, 77

Reiter, Reiterman (rider, cavalryman) 107

Reiter (sieve) 106

Reiter (dweller in a clearing) 126

Reith (clearing) 125, 122

Reitman (dweller in a clearing) 125

Reitmeyer, see Reitemeyer 125, 93

Reitmueller (clearing miller) 125, 103

Reitnauer, see Reitenauer

Reitz, Reitzer (provocateur) 115

Reitz, Reiz (fr Reitz) 122

Reitzel (fowler's lure, fowler) 91

Reizer 159, see Reiser, Rieser

Rekenthaler (marsh valley) 80, 76

Rembold, see Reinbold

Remmensperger, see Riemensperger

Remmer, Remmert, see Reimbrecht

Remp, Rempe, Rempt, see Reimbert

Remsber 159, Remsburg, see Ramsberg, Ramsburg

Remshard (marsh forest) 80, 72, 122

Remsnyder 159, see Riemschneider

Remy < St. Remigius 135

Renchler, see Rensch

Renck (vendace, a kind of fish, fish monger) 96, 105

Renecke, see Reinecke

Rennenkampf (Run into battle!, aggressive person) 115, 116

Renner, Rennert 74 (mounted courier) 96

Renninger 53, 55, Reninger < Reinhard

Renninger (place name) 122

Rennweg (path on mountain ridge) 68, 65, 122

Renold, see Reinhold

Rensch 53, Renschler < Reinhard, Lorentz

Rentner (pensioner) 118

Rentsch, Rentschler, see Rensch

Rentz, Rentzel, Renz, see Rensch

Reper, Rebschlaeger (rope maker) 96

Rephann, see Rebhun

Repp, Reps 59, Reppe, Reppert 74 (marsh dweller), see Reb

Repphun, see Rebhuhn

Requardt < Rickward (rule + guardian) 46, 47

Resch, Resh 159, Roesch, see Rasch

Reser 159, see Rieser

Ress, Resse, Resse (swamp dweller) 80

Ressmeyer (proprietor or occupant of the Resshoff, swamp farm) 93

Rest (resting place) 116

Rester (fr Resten) 122

Restar 159, Resta, see Rester

Reth (rushes) 81

Rethman, Rettmann (dweller at the rushes) 81

Rethmeyer, Rettenmeyer, Rettmayer (farmer in the marsh) 81, 93

Rettberg (marsh farmer) 81, 68

Rettenbaugh (swamp creek) 80, 77, 151

Rettenburg (castle on the rushes) 81, 73

Rettenmeyer (swamp farmer) 81, 93

Retter, Reter (saver, savior) 118

Rettig (radish, fr Latin *radix*) 91, 106

Retz, Rez (dweller near swamp water) 80

Reu (remorse) 115

Reuber, see Rauber

Reucher, Reuchert 74 (meat or fish smoker) 96

Reuchlin (little smoke, blacksmith) 55, 96

Reudenauer, see Reitenauer

Reus, Reuss, Reuse (eel trap) 106

Reusch, Reuschler, Reuschling (dweller in the reeds) 81, 122

Reusenweber (eel trap maker) 96

Reuss (Swiss river) 83

Reuss (Russian) 121

Reuss (cobbler) 96

Reutenbach, see Reitenbach

Reuter, Reuther (cavalryman) 107

Reuter, Reuther (dweller in a clearing) 125

Reuter, Reutter, see Reiter

Reuthnauer, see Reitenauer

Reutlinger (fr Reutling) 122

Rewald, Rewold, see Rehwald

Rex (Latin for king) 109, 141

Rey ..., see Rei and Rhei

Reybold, see Reinbold

Reydenauer 159, Reydenhower 159, see Reitenauer

Reyder 159, see Reiter

Reylandt, Reylender, see Rheinland

Reymann, see Rheinmann

Reyngold, see Reingold

Reynhart, see Reinhard

Reynolds 59, 159, see Reinhold, Reinol

Reys, see Reiss

Reyser, see Reiser

Reytenar 159, see Reitenauer

Reyter, see Reiter

Rezer 159, see Rieser

Rhein (Rhine) 83, 122

Rheinauer (meadow on Rhine) 83, 84

Rheinert, see Reinert

Rheinfeld (field on Rhine) 83, 84, 122

Rheinfels (Rhine cliffs) 83, 68

Rheingold (Rhine gold) 83

Rheinhard, Rheinhardt, see Reinhard

Rheinheim (hamlet on the Rhine) 83, 123

Rheinlaender, Rheinlender (Rhinelander) 121

Rheinstein (Rhine mountain, rhinestone) 83, 73, 121

Rheinstettler (fr Rheinstadt) 121

Rheinthal, Rheinthaler (Rhine valley) 83, 76, 121

Rheinwald (Rhine forest) 83, 71

Rhine 159, see Rhein

Rhinehart 159, see Reinhard

Rhinelander 159, see Rheinlander

Rhoads 159, see Roth

Rhodaback 159, see Rhodabaugh

Rhode, Rhodes 159, see Roth, Rode

Rhymer 159, see Reimer

Rhyner 159, see Reiner

Rhynhard 159, see Reinhard

Rice 159, see Reiss

Rich 159, see Reich

Richard 159, Richards 59, Richert, Richerdt, see Reichhard

Richburg 159, see Reichburg

Richman 159, see Reichmann

Richter, Richters 164 (judge) 109

Richtersweil (judge's village) 109, 127

Richwein, Richwin, Richwien 159, Richwiene (rule + friend) 46, 48

Rick 53, Ricke, Ricker, Rickerds, Rickers 59, Rickert 74 < Richard, Henrik

Rickabaugh 159, see Rickenbacker

Rickel 53, 55, Ricker, Rickert 74 < Reichhard

Rickenbacher, Rickenback 159, Reickenbaker (fr Rickenbach 122, swamp brook) 80, 77, 122, see Reichenbach

Rickhoff (ridge farm) 68, 84

Rickmann (ridge dweller) 68

Rickter 159, Ricktor, Rictor, see Richter

Rickwin, see Richwein

Ridder, see Ritter

Ridel 159, see Riedel

Ridelsberg 159, Riddleberger 159, Riddlespurger 159, see Riedelsperger

Ridenauer 159, Ridenhour, Ridener, see Reitenauer

Ridenbaugh 159, see Reitenbach

Rider 159, see Reiter

Rieb, Riebe, Riep 122, see Rueb

Riebau (turnip field) 84

Riebel, see Ruebel

Riebman (turnip man) 91, 105, 112

Riebsame, see Ruebsamen

Riech 53, Riecher, Riechert 74, Riechner < Richard

Rieck 159, Riecke, Rieckert < Richard

Ried, Riedt, Riede, Reed 159 (reed, marshland) 81, 122

Riedel 53, Riedl, Riedal 159, Riedling 55, Ridelinger < Rudolf, Ruediger

Riedelbauer (fr Riedel's farm), see Riedel

Riedelsperger (Rudolf's mountain) 53, 68

Rieder, Riedner, Riedeman (marsh dweller) 81

Rieder (fr Rieden) 122

Riedesel (marsh donkey) 81, 115

Riedheim (marsh hamlet) 81, 123

Riedheim (clearing hamlet) 81, 123

Riedmann (dweller by the reeds) 81, 93

Riedmueller, see Riethmueller

Riefenstahl (Rub the steel!, armorer) 109

Riegel, Riegle 159, Riegelmann (bolt, locksmith) 106

Riegel (ridge) 68

Rieger 122, Riegger, Riegert 74 (censurer), also < Ruediger

Riegler, Riegelman, Riegelmann (locksmith, night watchman) 96, 109

Riehl 53, Riel < Rudolf

Riehm, Riehme, see Riem, Riemen

Riem, Riemen, Riemer (strap, strap cutter) 97, 106

Riemann (Rhinelander) 121

Riemenschneider, Riemensnyder 159, Riemenschnitter, Riemschneider (strap cutter) 97

Riemensperger (strap cutter mountain) 97, 68

Riemer (strap cutter) 97

Rienhard 159, see Reinhard

Rienhof (farm on the Rhine) 83, 92

Riepe, see Ruebe

Rieper, see Reeper

Ries, Riese (giant, house name) 63

Ries, Riese, Riess (timber slide) 95

Riesberg (giant mountain) 68

Riesberg (timber slide mountain) 95, 68

Riesch 53 < Rudolf

Rieschel (little Rudolf) 53

Riesenbeck (brook used for logging) 77, 122

Riesenfeld (logging field) 95, 84

Riesenfeld (giants' field) 84

Rieser, Riesner, Riesser, Reezer 159 (logger) 95

Riesinger 159, see Reisinger

Riet 122, Rieth 122, see Ried

Riethmueller (miller on the marsh) 81, 103

Rietweill (reed village, marsh village) 81, 127

Rietwiese (marshy meadow) 81, 84

Rietz 53, Rietze < St. Mauritius

Right 159, see Recht

Righter 159, see Richter

Rightmeyer 159, see Reitmeyer

Rightnour 159, see Reitenauer
Rightor 159, see Richter
Rigler 159, see Riegler
Rilke, see Ruediger, Rudolf
Rimbach, Rimback (swamp water creek) 80, 122
Rimer 159, see Riemer
Rinde (bark, bark collector) 95
Rinder (cattle) 91
Rinderer (cattle dealer) 105
Rindfleisch (beef, butcher) 96
Rindfuss (cow foot, club foot) 114
Rindknecht (cow hand) 91, 96
Rindlaub (cattle foliage) 91, 62
Rindskopf (cow head, house name) 114, 62
Rindt (cattle, cow) 91, 106, 115
Rine 159, see Rhein
Rinecker 159, see Reinecker
Rinehard 159, Rinehart, Rinehardt, Rineheart, see Reinhard
Rinehimer 159, see Rheinheimer,
Rineholt 159, see Reinhold
Riner 159, see Reiner
Rinestein 159, see Rheinstein
Rinfret, see Reinfried
Ring, Ringe, Rings 59, Rinck, Rink (finger ring, city wall) 106
Ringel, Ringle, Ringler 159, Ringeler, Rinkler (ring maker) 96
Ringelstein (place name) 122
Ringer, Ringers 59, Ringger (ring maker) 96
Ringgold, Ringold, see Rheingold
Ringler, see Ringer
Ringold < Ringholdt (council + loyal) 47, 46
Rinman 159, see Rheinmann
Ringsdorf (circular village) 124
Ringwald (encircling forest) 72
Rink, Rinker, Rinkert 74, Rinkler (clasp maker) 106

Rink, Rinker, Rinkert 74 (round hill) 68
Ripke 53, 55, see Ruprecht
Ripley 53, 55, 159, Ripli < Ruprecht
Rippel 55 < Ruprecht
Rippert, Rippart < Ruprecht
Rippe (rib) 114
Rippe (swamp grass) 81
Rippel 53, 55 < Ruprecht
Ripple 159, see Rippel
Risberg, see Riesberg
Risch (swamp, reeds) 80
Rischel (swamp dweller) 80
Rischenbeck (swampy brook) 80, 77
Rischhof (swamp farm) 80, 92
Rischstein (marsh stone) 80, 73
Riser 159, see Reiser, Rieser
Risinger 159, see Reisinger
Rismiller, Rissmiller (swamp miller) 80, 103
Riss, Risse (gap, gorge) 67
Riss (swamp) 80, 122
Risterholtz (bullrush forest) 81, 72
Ritenour 159, see Reitenauer
Riter 159, Rither, see Reiter, Ritter
Ritger, Ritgert 74, see Rutger
Ritmueller, Rittmiller (miller on the marsh) 80, 103
Ritschard (fr Old French Richard)
Ritt (reeds) 80, 89
Rittenauer (reed meadow) 81, 84
Rittenbach (reed brook) 81, 77
Rittenberger, Rittenberry 159 (reed mountain) 81, 67
Rittenhaus (reed house) 81, 65
Rittenhouse 153, see Rittenhaus
Rittenour 159, see Reitenauer, Ritter, Riter 159 (knight) 107
Ritter (knight) 107
Ritterbusch (knight's crest) 107, 112

Ritterbush 159, Ritterpush, see
　Ritterbusch
Ritterhaus, Rittershaus (knight's
　house, castle) 107, 65
Ritterhoff (knight's court) 107, 92
Ritterman, Rittermann (trooper)
　107
Ritterscamp (knight's field) 107,
　84
Rittmeister (cavalry captain) 107
Rittmeyer (reed farmer) 81, 93
Ritz 53, Ritzel 55 (St. Euricius,
　St. Moritius, Henricius) 135
Ritzenberg (St. Moritz Mountain)
　135, 68, 122
Ritzenthal, Ritzendollar 159 (St.
　Moritz Valley) 135, 76
Ritzheim (St. Moritz hamlet) 135,
　124
Ritzman, Ritzmann (servant of
　St. Moritz convent) 139
Rizer 159, see Reiser
Road 159, see Roth
Robacher, Robach, Robacker, see
　Rohback
Roberg, Roberge, see Rohberg
Robertus (Latin for Robert) 141
Robke 53, 55, Robken < Robert
Robling, see Roebling
Robrecht, see Ruprecht
Rock (gown) 112, 106
Rockefeller < Roggenfelder (rye
　fields) 91, 84
Rockemann (rye dealer) 105
Rockenbach (rye brook) 77, 122
Rockenbauch (potbelly) 114
Rockenbaugh 159, see
　Rockenbach and Rockenbauch
Rockenbrod, see Roggenbrod
Rockenstihl (rye stalk, tall thin
　person) 114
Rockmueller (rye miller) 103
Rockstroh (rye straw) 106
Rodabaugh 159, Rodebaugh
　(clearing brook) 125, 77

Rodberg, Rodenberg (cleared
　mountain) 125, 68
Rode (clearing) 125
Rode, see Roth
Rodefeld (cleared field) 125, 84
Rodeheaver 159, Rodehaver <
　Rodehoffer (clearing farmer)
　125, 92
Rodel, see Rudel
Rodejan (Red John) 112
Rodemann (forest clearer) 125
Rodemeier, Rodemeyer (clearing
　farmer) 125, 93
Rodemund (red mouth) 122, 112
Roden (clearing) 125, 125
Rodenbach, Rodenbaugh 159
　(clearing brook) 125, 77, 122
Rodenberg (cleared mountain)
　125, 68, 122
Rodenhauser (fr Rodenhausen,
　clearing houses) 125, 65
Rodenhiser 66, 159, Rodenizer,
　see Rodenhauser
Rodenstein 122, see Rotenstein
Roder (forest clearer) 125
Roder < Rodhari, famous + army)
　47, 46
Roder (place name) 122
Rodermel 159, see Rothermel
Rodewald (cleared forest) 125,
　71, 122
Rodman, Rodner (clearing
　dweller) 125
Rodweller < Rodewaelder, see
　Rodewald
Roeber, Roebler, see Reber
Roebling 53, 55 < Robert
Roebling (fr Roeblingen, swamp
　water) 80, 122
Roedeger, see Ruediger
Roedel (scribe, fr Latin *rotula*) 96
Roeder < Rother (famous + army)
　46, 47
Roeder, see Reeder
Roediger, see Ruediger

Roefer (robber) 109

Roehl 53, Roehlke < Rudolf

Roehm, see Rehm

Roehmer, see Roemer

Roehn, Roehner (rune) 122

Roehr, Roehre, Roehrig (rushes) 81

Roeker (skirt maker) 96

Roemer (bragger) 115

Roemer (loving cup) 106

Roemer (Rome pilgrim) 110

Roenike 53, 55, Roennecke < Hieronymus (Jerome) 135

Roentgen, see Reinhart

Roeper, Roper (town crier) 96

Roepke 53, 55 < Robert

Roes (swampy ground) 80, 122

Roesberg, Rossberg (swamp mountain) 80, 68, 122

Roesberg (horse mountain) 68

Roesch, Roescher, see Rasch

Roeser, Roesser (swamp dweller) 80

Roesler, Roessler, Roessel, Roesselmann, Roesemann (carter) 96

Roesli, Roesslein (little horse) 91, 115

Roess, Roesser, Roessner, see Roes, Roeser

Roessler (horse dealer) 105

Roetenbach (red brook) 77, 122

Roettger, see Ruediger

Roffeld, see Rohfeld

Roger (French, fr *Hrodoger*, famous + spear) 47, 46, 144

Rogge, Roggemann (rye, rye dealer) 91, 105

Roggenbaugh 159 (rye creek) 77

Roggenbrod (rye bread, baker) 96

Roggenfeld, Roggenfelder (rye field) 84

Roggenkamp (rye field) 91, 84, 122

Roggensuess (rye sweet) 118

Roh, Rohe (raw) 118

Rohauer (cleared meadow) 126, 84

Rohback 159 (clearing brook) 126, 77

Rohde, see Rothe, Rod

Rohfeld (cleared field) 126, 84

Rohland, see Roland

Rohleder (rawhide, tanner) 96, 106

Rohlehr, see Rohleder

Rohlff, Rohlfs 59, Rohlfing 55, see Rolf

Rohling 53, 55 < Rudolf

Rohm, Rohme, see Rahm

Rohman, Rohmann (dweller in a clearing) 126

Rohmer, see Roemer

Rohn 53, Rohner < Hieronymus (St. Jerome) 135

Rohn, see Rahn

Rohr, Rohrs 164 (reed, pipe) 81, 122

Rohrbach, Rorbach, Rohrback, Rohrbacher, Rohrbeck (reed brook) 81, 77, 122

Rohrbaugh 159, see Rohrbach

Rohrer (dweller by rushes) 81

Rohrig (swampy, covered with reeds) 81

Rohrmann (marsh dweller) 81

Rohrmoser (dweller on the reedy marsh) 81, 80

Roisch 159, see Reusch

Rojan, see Roderjan

Rokenbaugh, see Roggenbaugh

Roland, Rolandt, Rolland < hrodo + land (illustrious + courage) 47, 47

Roland (cleared land) 125, 126

Rolf 53, Rolfe, Rolff, Rolfs 59, Rolfes, Rolfers, Rolfing 55 < Rudolf

Roller (carter) 95

Rollwagen (stagecoach) 96

Roman (speaker of Romance language) 145

Romberg, see Ronberg

Romelfanger, see Rammelfanger

Romer 159, see Roemer

Romerstein 159 (Roman mountain, Roman stone) 73

Romisch 159 (Roman) 121

Rommel, see Rummel

Rompf, see Rumpf

Romshower 159, 100 (tree trunk cutter) 95

Ronbach (fallen tree brook) 89, 77

Ronberg (fallen tree mountain) 89, 68

Roner (dweller among the fallen trees) 89

Roof 159, see Ruf

Rook, see Rauch

Rookstul 159, see Rueckstuhl

Roorig, see Rohrig

Roos, Roosen, see Rose

Ropach, see Rohbach

Rorbach, Rorbaugh, Rorabaugh 159, Rorapaugh, see Rohrbach

Rorich, see Rohrig

Rormann, see Rohrmann

Rosa, Roos, see Rose

Rosbach, Rosbeck (swamp brook) 80, 77, 122

Rosdorf (swamp village) 80, 124, 122

Rose, Rosen (rose) 89

Rosecrans 159, see Rosencrans

Rosefeld 159, see Rosenfeld

Rosemann, see Rossmann

Rosenau, Rosenauer (swamp meadow) 80, 84, 122

Rosenbach, see Rosbach

Rosenbalm (rose balm) 89, 148

Rosenbauer (rose farmer) 89, 91

Rosenbauer (horse farmer) 91

Rosenbaum, Rosenboom, Rosenbohm (rose tree, house name) 62, 89, 148

Rosenberg, Rosenberger, Rosenberry 159 (swamp mountain) 80, 68, 148, 122

Rosenblat, Rosenblatt (rose leaf) 89, 148

Rosenblit, Rosenbluth (rose blossom) 89, 148

Rosenblum, Rosenbloom (rose blossom) 89, 148

Rosenbohm, Rosenboom, see Rosenbaum

Rosenbower 159, see Rosenbauer

Rosenbrock (swamp brake) 80, 80

Rosenbusch (rosebush) 89, 148

Rosenbush 159, Rosennbush, see Rosenbusch

Rosencrans, Rosecrantz, Rosencranz, Rosekranz, Rosenkrantz (rosary, house name) 62, 106

Rosendahl, Rosendale 155, Rosendall 122, see Rosenthal

Rosendorf (swamp village) 80, 124

Rosenfarb (rose color) 89, 148

Rosenfeld, Rosenfelder, Rosenfeldt (horse field) 84, 122

Rosenfeld (rose field) 89, 84, 148

Rosenfield 153, see Rosenfeld

Rosengarden, Rosengarten, Rosengart (rosegarden) 89, 84, 122

Rosenhagen (rose hedge, rose enclosure) 89, 124

Rosenhain, Rosenshein (rose grove) 89, 72, 122

Rosenhauer 159, see Rosenauer

Rosenhaupt (rose head) 89, 114, 148, see Rosskopf

Rothman, Rothmann (clearing dweller) 125, see also Ratmann

Rothmeyer, Rothmeier (clearing farmer) 125, 93

Rothmund (red mouth) 112

Rothrock (red gown) 112

Rothschild, Rothscheld 159 (red shield, a house name) 62, 109

Rothstein 122 (red mountain) 73, see Rotenstein

Rothut (red hat) 112

Rotschuh (red shoe) 112

Rott 122, Rotte, Rottman, Rottmann (troop, trooper) 107

Rotter (harpist) 96

Rottmund, see Rothermund

Rotwax 159 (red wax) 118

Rotz, Rotzer (flax processor) 96

Roudenbach 159, see Rautebach

Rouf 159, see Rauf

Rouland 159, see Roland

Rous 159, Roush, see Rausch

Roushenbacht 159, see Rauschenbach

Routh 159, see Rauthe

Rowe 159, see Rau

Rowland 159, see Roland

Royce 159, see Reuss

Rozen 159, see Rosen

Rozencwaig 159, Rozencweig, see Rosenzweig

Rubenstein (ruby) 73

Rubenstien 159, see Rubenstein

Rubenthal (turnip valley) 76

Rubert, see Ruprecht

Rubi, Ruby, Rubin, Rubins 59 (ruby), see Rubinstein

Rubincam, Rubincamp (turnip field) 84

Rubinstein, Rubenstein (ruby) 73

Rubrecht, see Ruprecht

Rubright 159, see Ruprecht

Rubsam, see Ruebsamen

Ruch, see Rauch

Ruch (unkempt) 112

Ruck, see Rueck

Rucker 53, Ruckert 74, see Ruecker, Rueckert

Ruckhaus (house on a ridge) 67, 65

Ruckstuhl (chair with back) 106

Rude 53 < Rudolf

Rudegaire 159, see Ruediger

Rudel, Rudell (pack, herd, keeper of the hounds) 91, 96

Rudi 53, 55, Rudy < Rudolf, Ruediger

Rudiger, see Ruediger

Rudmann, Rudemann (leader of hounds, hunter) 91, or < Rudolf

Rudolf, Rudolph (illustrious + wolf) 47, 48

Rudolphi (son of Rudolf) 142

Rueb, Ruebener (turnip eater, turnip raiser or dealer) 112, 105

Ruebeck (turnip brook) 77

Ruebel (rape cultivator, fr Latin *rapum*) 91

Ruebenacker (turnip field) 84

Ruebenzahl (turnip tail, Silesian spook) 118

Ruebsamen (turnip seed) 96

Rueck (jerk) 118

Rueckdeschel (backpack, rucksack) 106

Rueckenbrot, see Roggenbrot

Ruecker, Rueckert 74 (dweller on ridge) 67

Ruecker see Ruediger

Rueckheiser (houses on a ridge) 66, 65

Rueckstuhl (back chair) 106

Ruede (large hound) 112

Ruediger (illustrious + spear) 38, 47, 46, 39

Rueg, Rueger (reproof, reprover) 115

Ruehl 53, Ruehle, Ruel < Rudolf

Ruehmer (boaster) 112

Ruemstall (Empty the stall!, horse thief) 116, 117

Rueppel 53, 55 < Ruprecht

Ruessel (trunk, snout) 114

Rueter (land clearer) 125, also error for Reuter

Ruetiger, Ruettiger, Ruettger, see Ruediger

Ruetsch (slide) 67

Ruf, Ruff, Roof 159 (call), or < Rudolf 53

Ruger, see Rueg

Ruh, Ruhe (rest) 115

Ruhl 53, Ruhle, Ruhling 55, Ruhlmeyer 103 < Rudolf

Ruhland, Ruland, see Roland

Ruhm (fame) 118

Ruhrwein (Stir the wine!) 116

Ruhsam (restful) 115

Rukeyser (dweller in a ridge house) 67, 65

Rule, see Ruhl

Rulmann 53, 94, Rullman < Rudolf

Rum, Rumpep (heavy-set) 112, 113

Rumbacker 159 (fr Rumbach 122) 77

Rumbarger, see Ramberger

Rumbaugh 159, see Rambach

Rummel, Rummler (hurly-burly) 115

Rump, Rumpf, Rumph (sieve in a gristmill) 106

Rumpel, Rumple 159 (noise maker) 115

Rumpf (torso) 113

Rund (round) 118

Rundberg (round mountain) 68

Rung, Runge (wainwright) 96, 106

Runke (wrinkle) 114

Runkel, Runckels 59, Runckel (marsh root) 81, 122

Runkelstein (reed mountain) 81, 73

Runkhorst (swamp hurst) 81, 72

Runner, see Renner 151

Runz (wrinkle) 112, 114

Ruoff, see Ruff

Rupert, Ruppert, Rupertus 141, see Ruprecht

Rupp 53, Ruppel 55 < Ruprecht

Ruppertsberger, Ruppersberger (Ruppert's mountain) 68, 122

Ruprecht, Rupprecht (famous + bright) 47, 47

Rurapaw 59, see Rohrbach

Russ, Russe (rust), or < Rudolf 53

Russ (Russian) 121

Russel, see Ruessel

Rust (reeds, rushes) 81, 122

Rust (rest, calm) 115

Rutger, see Ruediger

Ruth, Rute (rod) 118

Ruth < Hrodomar (famous + famous) 47, 47

Rutmann, Ruttmann, see Rudmann

Rutsch 53, Rutschi < Rudolf

Rutschild 159, see Rothschild

Rutschman 53, 94 < Rudolf

Ruttger, see Ruediger

Ruyter, see Reiter

Ryder 159, see Reiter

Ryecart 159, see Reichard

Ryland, Rylander, see Rheinlander

Rymer 159, see Reimer

Rynert 74, see Reiner

Rynhart, see Reinhart

Rynthal (Rhine valley) 83, 76

Ryser 159, see Reiser, Rieser

Rysling 159, see Reisling

Ryther 159, see Reither, Reuther

Rytter 159, see Ritter

S

Saal (hall) 122
Saalig, see Selig
Saalwechter (hall waker) 96
Saar (fr the Saarland) 121
Saas (Saxon) 120
Saat (seed, newly planted grain field) 91
Saatfeld (newly planted grain field) 84
Saatkampt, see Saatfeld
Sabath (Sabbath) 118
Sabel, Sable 159 (saber) 108
Sabelhaus, Sablehaus (sable house, house name) 62
Sach (thing, cause) 118
Sachmann, see Sackmann
Sachs, Sachse (Saxon) 120
Sachtleben, see Sanftleben
Sack (sack, trapper's net, Latin *saccus*) 96
Sackman, Sackmann (member of baggage train) 107
Sackreiter (clearing on a deadend road) 126
Sacks, see Sachs
Sadler, Saddler, Sadtler, see Sattler
Saefried, see Siegfried
Saeger (sawyer) 96
Saegermueller (saw miller) 103
Saeli 53, 55 < Salomo, OT name
Saemann (sower) 95
Saemanshaus (sower's house) 65
Saemueller, see Seemueller, Saegemueller
Saenger (singer, cantor) 96
Saettler, see Settelman
Saeuberlich (clean) 115
Saffold, see Siegbald
Saffron (saffron dealer) 105
Saft (juice) 118
Sagebiel (sedge field) 84
Sager, Sageman, Sagenmann (minstrel) 96

Sager (sawyer) 91, 106
Sagmiller 159, see Saegemueller
Sahl, see Saal
Sahli, see Sali
Sahn (cream) 91
Saidel, see Seidel
Saidemann, see Seideman
Sailer, see Seiler
Saks, see Sachs
Salb (salve dealer) 105
Salbeck (swamp brook) 80, 77
Salberg (swamp mountain) 80, 68
Sali 53, Salli, Sally (little Salomo) 113
Salinger 53, 55 < Salomo, also fr Salingen 122
Salm (salmon, fisherman, fish dealer) 105
Salman < Salomon (OT name) 135
Salman, Salmann, Sallmann, Sahlman (trustee, custodian) 109
Salmann (hall man) 109
Salmar, see Selmer
Salomo, Salomon, Salomon (OT name) 135
Saltmann, see Salz
Saltner (forester, fr Latin *saltarius*) 109, 96
Salz, Saltzer, Salzer, Saltzman, Saltzmann, Saltsman (salt seller) 105, 122
Saltzberg, Salzberg (salt mountain) 68, 122
Saltzer, Salzer (salt dealer) 105
Saltzgaver 159, Saltzgiver (salt dealer) 105
Salzman, see Salz
Samann 159, see Saemann
Samenfink (seed finch) 115
Samet, Sameth, Sammet, Sammeth (velvet dealer, tailor) 105, 104
Samler, Sammler (collector) 118
Sammet, see Samet

Sampson, Samson (OT name)
135

Samstag (Saturday, day of birth
or day of tax or service) 143

Samuel (OT name) 135

Sanbower 159, see Sandbauer

Sand, Sander, Sanders 164 <
Alexander, fr Sand 122

Sandau (swamp meadow) 80, 84

Sandbauer, Sandbower 159
(swamp peasant) 80, 91

Sandberg (swamp mountain) 80,
68

Sanderson (son of Sander) 59

Sandhaus (swamp house) 80, 65

Sandhofer (fr Sandhof 122,
swamp farm) 80, 92

Sandkuhler (fr Sandkuhl 122,
swamp pool) 80, 80

Sandmann (swamp dweller) 80

Sandmeier, Sandmeyers 164,
Sandmyer 159 (fr the Sandhof,
swamp farm) 80, 93

Sandrock, Sandroch (sand rye) 91

Sanft (gentle) 115

Sanftleben (carefree life, bon
vivant) 115

Sanftmut (gentle disposition)
115, 139

Sanger, see Saenger

Sangmeister (choir leader) 96

Santen (fr Xanten) 122

Santer 53 < Alexander, or fr
Xanten

Santmeyer, Sandmeyers 164, see
Sandmeier

Sarazin (Saracen, fighter against
the Saracens) 107, 120

Sartor, Sartory, Sartorius (Latin
for tailor) 9, 141

Sas, Sass, Sasse, Sassen, Sasser,
Sassman, Sassmann (Saxon)
120, 122

Sattel (saddle) 106, 122

Sattelthaler (saddle valley) 76

Sattler (saddler) 96, 98

Sattler (dweller on mountain
pass) 68

Sauber, Sauberlich (clean, fr
Latin *sobrius*) 115

Sauer, Saur, Sauers 164, Saure
(river name, spring, swamp)
80, 83

Sauer (sour) 112

Sauerbach, Sauerborn (sour
brook, sour spring) 77, 79

Sauerbach, Sauerborn (southern
brook, southern spring) 85, 77,
79

Sauerbier (sour beer) 112

Sauerbrei, Sauerbrey (sour
pottage) 112

Sauerhammer (southern hamlet)
85, 123

Sauerhoff (southern farm) 85, 92

Sauerland (southern land,
mountain range in
Westphalia) 121

Sauermann (southerner) 118

Sauermilch (sour milk) 112

Sauerteich (sourdough, baker) 96

Sauerwald (southern forest) 85,
72

Sauerwein, Saurwein (sour wine)
112

Saul (OT name) 135

Saulpaugh 159 (swamp brook,
see Salbeck)

Saum (hem, boundary) 106

Saum (load, pack animal, fr
Latin *suma*)

Saur, Saure, see Sauer

Saus, Sause (confusion, noise)
155

Sauter, Sautter, see Sutter,
Schuster

Saylor 159, see Seiler

Sax, Saxen, see Sachs

Saxman, see Sackmann

Saxonhouse 159 (fr
Sachsenhausen) 120, 65

Sayler 159, see Seiler

Scammele, see Schemel

Schaab, see Schabbe

Schaadt, see Schad

Schaaf, see Schaf

Schaal, see Schall

Schaar, see Schar

Schabbe (shabby, skinflint) 115

Schaber (scraper) 106

Schablein 55, see Schaeberle

Schach (checkmate, wooded area) 72

Schacht (mine shaft, gorge) 76, 122

Schacht, Schachtschneider (shaft maker) 96

Schacht (reed-bank) 81

Schachtel (box, case) 106

Schachter, Schachtner, see Schaechter

Schad, Schade, Schaden, Schadt (swamp water) 80

Schad, Schaedlein 55 (loss, damage) 118

Schadel, Schadle 159, see Schaedel

Schadenfroh (full of malicious joy) 115

Schaeberle (scrapings, carpenter) 96

Schaech, Schaecher (thief) 109

Schaechter (butcher) 96

Schaedel, Schadel 159 (skull) 114

Schaedlich (harmful) 118

Schaefenacker (sheep field) 84

Schaefer, Schaefers 59, Schaeffer (shepherd) 95

Schaeffler, see Scheffler

Schaefknecht (sheep hand) 96

Schaeflein 55 (little sheep) 91

Schaefner, see Schaffner

Schaemel, see Schemel

Schaenck (taverner) 118

Schaener 159, see Schoener

Schaenkel (leg) 114

Schaerer, see Scherer

Schaerf (sharp, sharpness) 115

Schaerzer, see Scherzer

Schaeufele, see Schaufel

Schaf, Schaff (sheep) 95

Schafer, Schaffer, Schafers 164, see Schaefer

Schaffeld (sheep field) 84, 122

Schaffer, Schaffermann, see Schaefer, Schaffner

Schaffhauser, Schaffhausen (fr Schaffhausen, sheep fold) 65, 122

Schaffner, Schafner (steward, manager) 109

Schaffroth, Schafrath (sheep clearing) 126

Schaffuss (sheep foot) 114

Schafhirt (shepherd) 95

Schafstall (sheep fold)

Schaible, Schaibler, see Scheibel

Schaide, see Scheide

Schait, Schaiteler (split log, wood chopper) 95

Schalabaugh 159, see Schallenbach

Schaler, see Schaller

Schalk, Schalck (servant) 96

Schall (loud sound) 115

Schall (noise) 115

Schallenbach (resounding brook) 77

Schallenberg 122, Schallenberger (resounding mountain) 68

Schaller, Schallert 74 (noise maker, public announcer) 109

Schalter (shutter, window, shop keeper) 105

Schaltheis, see Schultheiss

Scham (shame, modesty) 115

Schambach (short brook) 77, 122, see also Schaumbach

Schamberger (short mountain) 68, see Schaumberg

Schamburg, see Schaumburg

Schamel, Schammel, see Schemel

Schamroth (red with embarrassment) 115

Schanberger (reed mountain) 81,
see Schoenberger
Schanck, Schank, see Schenk
Schande (disgrace) 115
Schane, see Schoen
Schank, see Schenk
Schantz, Schantze, Schanz,
Schanze (redoubt,
entrenchment) 107
Schantzenbaecher,
Schantzenbecker (redoubt
creek) 77
Schanz (peasant jacket) 112
Schap, Schappes, see Schaf
Schaper (scoop, laddle) 96, 106
Schaper 39, Schapper, Schappert
74, see Schaeffer
Schar (crowd, troop) 107
Schard, Schardt, Schart (crack,
embrasure, shard) 118
Scharf, Scharfe, Scharff, Scharpf
(sharp, keen) 115
Scharfenberg, Scharfenberger
(sharp mountain) 68, 122
Scharffschmidt (knife grinder,
cutler) 96
Scharfstein (sharp stone) 73
Scharlach (scarlet, a fabric, from
Latin *scarlatum*) 105, 106, 122
Scharman, see Scharrmann
Scharnagel (shingle nail) 106
Scharnhorst (muddy hurst) 72
Scharp, Scharpe, Scharpf,
Scharpp, see Scharf
Scharr (troop, band) 107
Scharrer (wool carder) 96
Scharrmann (trooper) 107
Schart, see Schard
Scharte (pass) 68
Schartner (dweller in a pass) 68
Scharwaechter (night watchman)
109
Schatt, see Schad
Schatz (treasure, dear one) 115,
122

Schatzle 53, 55, Schatzlein 55
(little treasure) 119
Schatzmann (treasurer) 96
Schau (Look!) 117
Schaub, Schauber (sheaf, farmer)
91, see Schub
Schaubach, Schaubacher, see
Schaumbach
Schauber, Schaubner (jacket
maker, thatcher) 96
Schauder (shudder) 115
Schauer, Schauerman,
Schauermann (shiver, shower)
118
Schauer (market inspector) 109
Schaufel, Schaufle 159,
Schaufler, Schaufele (shovel,
shovel maker) 96, 106
Schaufelberger (shovel mountain)
68
Schaum (scum, foam, skimmer)
96
Schaumbach (foam brook) 77
Schaumburg (lookout mountain)
68, 122
Schaumenkessel (cauldron for
skimming, cook) 106
Schaumloeffel (skimming spoon)
106
Schazel 55 (little treasure) 119
Scheafer, Scheffer 159, see
Schaefer, Schiefer
Schechter, Schecter (Yiddish:
slaughterer) 96
Scheck (dappled horse) 118
Scheck (coat of mail) 109
Schedel, see Schaedel
Schedtlin, see Schaedel
Scheef (crooked) 113
Scheel 159, Scheele, Scheeler, see
Schiel, Schiele, Schieler
Scheeper, see Schaeffer
Scheer, Scheerer, Schehr, see
Scher, Scherer
Scheermann, see Schermann

Scheermesser (shearing knife) 106

Scheesler 159, see Schuessler

Scheetz 159, see Schuetz

Schef, Scheff, see Schief, Schiff

Scheffel (bushel) 106

Scheffer, Scheffers 164, see Schaefer

Scheffler (barrel maker) 96

Scheffner, see Schaffner

Scheib, Scheibe, Scheibel 55 (disc, round pane) 106, 122

Scheibe (common pasture) 84

Scheid (watershed, ridge, boundary) 68, 122

Scheide, Scheidt (sheath) 106

Scheidecke, Scheidekke, Scheidegger (dweller on a watershed or boundary) 122

Scheidel, Scheidler (arbitor) 109

Scheidemnn (arbitor, judge) 96, 109

Scheider, Scheidemann, Scheidmann (umpire) 109

Scheidt, see Scheit

Scheif, Scheiffler (crooked, askew) 114

Scheimer, Schaeumer (skimmer, cook) 96

Schein ..., see Schoen ...

Scheinberg 159, see Schoenberg

Scheinemann 159, see Schoenemann

Scheinholtz 159, see Schoenholtz

Scheiss (feces), surely an American error for Schiess

Scheit, Scheidt, Scheiter, Scheitlein 55 (split log, woodcutter) 95

Scheitel, Scheitele (crown of the head) 113

Scheithauer (log splitter) 95

Schelb (squinter) 113

Scheldt (river name) 83

Scheler, Schelbert 74 (squinter) 113

Scheler (bark peeler) 95

Schell (bell, manacles) 106

Schell (noisy person) 115

Schellberg, Schellenberg, Schellenbarg, Schellenberger (swamp mountain) 80, 68, 122

Schellenbach (swamp brook) 80, 77

Schellenschloeger, Schellenschlaeger (bell ringer) 96, 109

Scheller (bell ringer, see Schaller) 96

Schellhaas, Schellhas, Schelhase (flushed, startled hare) 114

Schellhammer (fr Schellheim, swamp hamlet) 80, 123, 122

Schellhaus, Schelhaus, Schelhause, Schelhouse 159 (swamp house) 65

Schellhorn (trumpet, trumpeter) 96, 122

Schelling, see Schilling

Schellkopf (noisy person) 115

Schellmann, Schellschmidt (bell maker) 9

Schelm (rascal) 115

Schelter (scolder) 115

Schemel, Schemmel (footstool, cripple, fr Latin *scamillus*) 106, 114

Schenck, see Schenk

Schene, see Schoen

Scheneberg (reed mountain) 81, 68, see Schoenberg

Schenefeldt (reed field) 81, 84, 122, see Schoenfeld

Scheneman, Schenemann, see Schoenemann

Schenfeld, see Schenefeldt

Schenk, Schenck, Schenke, Schenker (cup bearer, taverner) 96

Schenkbier (Serve beer!) 116, 96

Schenkel, Schenckel (thigh) 114

Schildhauer (shield maker) 100,
  108
Schildknecht, Schildtknecht
  (squire) 107
Schildkraut (thyssum) 89
Schildmacher (shield maker) 108
Schildwachter, Schiltwaechter
  (sentry) 107
Schilf (bullrushes) 81
Schiller (redish wine) 96
Schiller (squinter) 114
Schilling (shilling) 117
Schilling (freedman) 92
Schillkneth 159, see
  Schildknecht
Schiltz, see Schultz
Schimel, Schimmel (white horse)
  118
Schimmel (mildew) 118
Schimmelmann (greybeard) 112
Schimmelpfenig (miser) 115
Schimmelreiter (rider of a white
  horse)
Schimpf, Schimpff (play,
  amusement, entertainer) 96
Schinckel, see Schenkel
Schindel, Schindler (shingle,
  Latin *scindula*) 96, 106
Schindeldecker, Schindelmann
  (roof shingler) 96
Schinder (skinner) 96, 109
Schindler (roofer) 96
Schine 159, see Schein
Schinkel 159, see Schenkel
Schipp (boat) 62
Schipper, Schippert 74, see
  Schiffer
Schirach (Wendish: George) 146
Schirm, Schirmer (protector) 169
Schirmacher, Schirrmacher
  (harness maker) 96
Schirra < Girard (French) <
  Gerhard (Germanic)
Schisler 159, Schissler, see
  Schuessler

Schlabach 159, see Schlebach
Schlachte (battle) 107
Schlachter, Schlacter 159
  (slaughterer) 96
Schlade (reed-bank) 81, 122
Schlaechter (butcher) 96
Schlaegel, see Schlegel
Schlaf, Schlaff, Schlaffer (sleeper,
  sleepy person) 115
Schlafhorst (muddy hurst) 72
Schlag (blow) 118
Schlag (forest, cf. Kahlschlag)
  126
Schlagel, see Schlegel
Schlagenteufel (Strike the devil!)
  116
Schlager (hitter, beater) 115
Schlaich, see Schleich
Schlang, Schlange (snake,
  dragon, house name) 115, 63,
  149
Schlatter (swamp or marsh
  dweller) 80
Schlatterbach (swamp brook) 77
Schlauch (wine bag, tube, hose)
  106, 122
Schlayer, Schlair, see Schleier
Schlebach (sloe brook) 89, 77
Schlebohm (sloe tree, wild plum
  tree) 89
Schlecht (simple, slight,
  straightforward) 115, 122
Schlechter, Schlechtermann
  (butcher) 96
Schlee, Schlehe (sloe) 89
Schleeweiss (sloe white) 114
Schlegel, Schlegl (mallet) 106,
  122
Schlegel (turnkey) 109
Schlegemilch (buttermilk, milk
  dealer) 112, 105
Schlehdorf (wild plum village) 89,
  123, 122
Schlei, see Schley

Schleich, Schleicher, Schleichert 74 (one who sneaks about or else walks in a stately fashion) 115, 122

Schleich (muddy place) 122

Schleier (veil maker) 106

Schleiermacher (veil maker) 96

Schleife, Schleiff (slipknot) 106, 122

Schleifer, Schleifner (grinder) 96

Schleigh 159, see Schleich

Schleimer (glue maker) 96

Schlemmer (gormand, guzzler) 115

Schlencker, Schlenker (shambler) 115

Schlesien, Schlesing, Schlesiger, Schlesinger, Schlessinger (Silesian) 121

Schleucher, see Schleicher

Schleuder (sling shot) 107

Schley (fish dealer) 105, see Schlee

Schleyer, see Schleier

Schlicht, Schlichter, Schlichtman (simple, smooth-haired) 112

Schlicht (high flat area) 72

Schlick (mud, slime) 118

Schlieb (grinder, sharpener) 96

Schliemann (seller of freshwater fish) 105

Schliesser, Schliessers 164, Schliessmann (keeper of the keys, of the stores)

Schlimm, Schlimme (slight, simple) 115

Schlimp (diagonal) 118

Schlindwein (Drink wine!, wine bibber) 115, 116

Schlitt (sled, sled maker) 96

Schlitz (muddy stream) 80

Schlitz (slit, slash) 112

Schloegel, Schlogel 159, see Schlegel

Schloemer, see Schlemmer

Schloetel, see Schluessel

Schloss, Schlos 159 (lock, castle, locksmith) 106, 122

Schlossbach (castle brook) 73, 77

Schlossberg, Schlossberger (castle mountain) 73, 68

Schlossburg (castle) 73

Schlosser, Schloesser (locksmith) 96

Schlossherr (castellan) 109, see Schlosser

Schlossnagel (locknail, locksmith) 96, 106

Schlott, Schlotte, Slot (castle) 73

Schlotter, Schlottman, Schlottmann (locksmith) 96

Schlotterbach, Schlotterback, Schlotterbeck (swamp brook) 80, 77

Schlotterer (wobbler, doddering) 115, see also Schlatter

Schlotthauer (reed cutter) 96

Schlough 159, see Schlauch

Schluecker, Schlucker (swallower, guzzler) 115

Schluesser (keeper of the keys, house keeper) 119

Schlueter, Schlueters 74 (locksmith, keeper of the keys) 119

Schlumberger (gorge mountain) 68

Schlund, Schlundt (gorge) 76

Schlusemeyer (sluice warden) 96, 109

Schlussel, Schlussler (key, turnkey) 96

Schluter, see Schlueter

Schmach (disgrace) 115

Schmaehling (slender person) 113

Schmaek, see Schmeck

Schmaeussner, see Schmeiser

Schmahl, Schmahle, see Schmal

Schmal, Schmale, Schmall (narrow) 114

Schmalbach (narrow stream) 77

Schmaltz, Schmalz, Schmalz (lard, tallow, candler) 106, 105

Schmaus (banquet) 115

Schmeck (gourmet, taster) 115

Schmeckefeffer (spice dealer) 105

Schmeichel, Schmeichler (flatterer) 115

Schmeiser, Schmeissner (thrower, slinger) 118

Schmeling (slender, slight) 114

Schmeltz, Schmelz (enamel 106, 122, fr Schmeltz 122), see Schmaltz

Schmeltz (iron foundry) 96

Schmeltzer (melter, smelter, enameler) 96, fr Schmeltz 122

Schmerbauch (lard belly) 114

Schmerz (pain) 118

Schmetzer (gossip) 115

Schmick 159, Schmicke, see Schmuek

Schmid, Schmide, Schmids 164, Schmidt, Schmidte, Schmidts 164, Schmidtt, Schmidtz, Schmit, Schmith 153, Schmitt, Schmitte, Schmitz (smith) 96

Schmidhauser (smithy) 65, 96

Schmidlein, see Schmittlein

Schmidt, Schmitt (smith) 96

Schmidtbauer, Schmidtmeyer (smith farmer) 96, 92

Schmidtknecht (smith's helper) 96

Schmied, Schmiedt (smithy) 96

Schmiedekamp (smithy field) 84

Schmieg (cuddle) 118

Schmierer (laugher, smiler) 115

Schmiltz, see Schmeltz

Schmink, Schminke (make-up, cosmetics) 106

Schmit, Schmitt, Schmitz, see Schmid

Schmittlein 55 (little smith) 96

Schmoke 159, see Schmueck

Schmoll (fat person) 112

Schmoller (pouter, sulker) 115

Schmollinger (tar boiler) 95

Schmueck, Schmuck, Smuckers 164 (adornment, jeweler) 96, 106

Schmuecker (adorner) 96

Schmuecker (fr Schmueck, swamp) 122

Schmutz (dirt, filth) 115

Schnaack, Schnack (chitchat, nonsense) 115

Schnaack (deer fly) 115

Schnabel, Schnable 159 (snout, talkative person) 114, 115

Schnackenberg, Schnachenberg (deer fly mountain) 68

Schnader, see Schnatter

Schnaebele (little snout) 114

Schnaid (trail cut through woods) 122

Schnaider, see Schneider

Schnall, Schnalle (buckle) 106

Schnap, Schnaps (brandy) 96, 106, 115

Schnatter (chatterer, gabbler) 115

Schnauber (snorter) 115

Schnauffer (snorter) 115

Schnautz (snout) 114

Schnebel, Schnebele, Schnebly, see Schnaebele

Schneberger (fr Schneeberg 68, 122), see Schneeberg

Schneck, Schnecke (snail, snake, slow poke) 115

Schneckenburg (snail castle) 73

Schnee (snow) 43

Schneebaum (snow tree) 89

Schneeberg, Schneeberger (fr Schneeberg 122, snow mountain) 68

Schneeganz (snow goose) 115

Schneehagen (snow enclosure) 123

Schneemann (snowman) 118

Schneeweiss (snow white) 112

Schneewind (snow wind) 118
Schneewolf (snow wolf) 48
Schnegel (snail) 115
Schneibly 159, see Schnaebele
Schneickburger, see
Schneckenburg
Schneid, Schneiden (mountain
ridge, boundary, trail cut
through woods) 68, 65
Schneider, Schneyder, Schnider,
Schnyder (tailor) 104
Schneiderjohann (tailor John)
104
Schneidermann, see Schneider
Schnel, Schnell (swift, active) 115
Schnellbacher (fr Schnellbach
122, rapid brook) 77
Schnellenbach (rapid brook) 77,
122
Schnellewind (strong wind) 118
Schnellmann (fast man, active
man) 115
Schnepf, Schnepfe, Schnepp,
Schneppe (snipe, weakling)
115
Schnetter, see Schnitter
Schneyder, see Schneider
Schnider 159, see Schneider
Schnierle, see Schnuerle
Schnitter (reaper) 95
Schnitzel (chip, wood carver) 106
Schnitzer, Schnitzler, Schnizler
(cutter, wood carver) 96
Schnock (pike, house name) 63
Schnor, Schnorr (cadger, peddler)
105
Schnuck (small sheep) 91
Schnuerle (little string, heavy
raindrops) 118
Schnur (daughter-in-law) 119
Schnur, Schnurr, Schnurer,
Schnurman (string, string
maker) 96, 106
Schober, Schobert 74 (barn, barn
builder) 96
Schoch (hay stack) 118

Schock, Schoek, Schockmann
(swamp) 80
Schoder (stunted) 113
Schoedel, see Schaedel
Schoeff (assessor) 109
Schoeffer, see Schaefer
Schoeffler, see Scheffler
Schoeler, see Schueler
Schoelkopf, see Schellkopf
Schoemaker 159, see
Schumacher
Schoemburg (beautiful castle) 73
Schoen, Schoene, Schoener,
Schoenert 74, Schoenemann
(beautiful, handsome) 115
Schoenau, Schoenauer (beautiful
meadow) 84, 122
Schoenbacher, Schoenback 159
(fr Schoenbach 122, beautiful
brook) 77
Schoenbaum (beautiful tree) 89
Schoenberger (fr Schoenberg 122,
beautiful mountain, shiny
mountain) 68, 157
Schoenbild (beautiful picture)
118
Schoenblum (beautiful flower) 89
Schoenborn (beautiful spring) 79
Schoenbrot (beautiful bread,
baker) 96
Schoenbruck (beautiful bridge)
71
Schoendorf (beautiful village)
123, 122
Schoeneck, Schoeneker (beautiful
field) 85, 122
Schoenemann, Schoenmann
(beautiful man) 115
Schoener (fr Schoeningen) 122
Schoener, Schoenert 143
(handsome) 115
Schoenfeld, Schoenfeldt,
Schoenfelder (beautiful field)
84, 122
Schoenfuhs (beautiful foot) 112
Schoenhaar (beautiful hair) 112

Schoenhals (beautiful throat) 112
Schoenhardt (beautiful forest) 72
Schoenherr (handsome
gentleman) 112, see
Schoenhaar
Schoenhof (beautiful farm) 92
Schoenholtz, Schoenholtzer
(beautiful forest) 72
Schoenhut (beautiful hat,
miliner) 96, 106
Schoenkind (beautiful child) 112
Schoenkopf (beautiful head) 112
Schoenknecht (beautiful servant)
112
Schoenleben (the good life) 115
Schoenleben (the beautiful
estate) 127
Schoenmann, see Schoenemann
Schoenmannsgruber (fr
Schoenmann's valley) 76
Schoenrock (beautiful dress,
tailor) 96
Schoenrock (beautiful barley,
barley dealer) 91, 105
Schoenthal (beautiful valley) 76,
122
Schoenwald, Schoenewalt
(beautiful forest) 71
Schoenwand (clothmaker) 96
Schoenweiss (beautiful white)
112
Schoepf (scoop, place for drawing
water) 77
Schofer, Schoffer, see Schaefer
Schoff (shed) 65
Schoffstal (sheep fold) 65
Schofner, see Schaffner
Schol, Scholl, Scholle, Schollen
(soil, clodhopper) 91, 115
Scholler (farmer, clodhopper) 91,
115
Schollmeyer (dirt farmer) 93
Scholt, Scholten, Scholtz, see
Schultz
Schomaker, Schomakers 164, see
Schumacher

Schomann, Schooman 159, see
Schumann
Schombach, see Schoenbach,
Schaumbach
Schomberg (beautiful mountain)
68
Schomburg 122, Schomburger,
see Schoemburg, Schaumburg
Schon 159, Schone, see Schoen
Schon ... , see under Schoen ...
Schonbach 159, see Schoenbach
Schonberg 159, see Schoenberg
Schonfeld (beautiful field) 84
Schonfield 153, see Schonfeld
Schop, see Schopp
Schopf (shock of hair) 112
Schopp 122, Schoppe (measure of
wine) 106, 102
Schorbach (dirty stream) 77, 122
Schornstein (chimney, chimney
sweep) 96
Schorsch (fr French: Georges)
144
Schorstein, see Schornstein
Schott, Schotte (curds) 112, 105
Schott (bulkhead) 118
Schott (Scot) 122
Schottenheimer (Scots hamlet)
121, 123
Schotter (gravel) 118
Schotthofer (dairy) 92
Schoultz 159, see Schultz
Schoumacker 159, see
Schumacher
Schoumburg 159, see
Schaumburg
Schour 159, Schouwer, see
Schauer
Schouster 159, see Schuster
Schraag, Schrag (slanting)
Schrader 159, Schraeder, see
Schroeder
Schram, Schramm, Schramme
(scratch, scar, abrasion,
wound) 114

Schranck, Schrank (cupboard, wardrobe) 106

Schranne (crack in glacier) 118

Schrantz (split, sycophant) 115

Schraub (screw) 106

Schrecengost 159, Schreckengaust, Schrengost (Frighten the guest!) 116

Schreck (jump, fright) Schreck (muddy ground) 80

Schreder, see Schroeder

Schrei, see Schreier

Schreiber, Schreiver (scribe) 96

Schreibfeder (writing plume, scribe) 96

Schreier, Schreyer (town crier) 96, 109

Schrein, Schreiner (cabinet maker, fr Latin *scrinarius*) 99

Schrempff (cut, wound) 114

Schreter, see Schroeder

Schreyder (gristmiller) 96

Schreyer, see Schreier

Schriber 159, Schriver, see Schreiber

Schriftgiesser (type founder) 96

Schroder, Schroader 159, see Schroeder

Schrodt, Schroth, see Schrott

Schroeck, see Schreck

Schroeder, Schroeter, Schroter 159, Schroder (tailor) 104

Schroepfer (bleeder, cupper) 96

Schroff (rugged) 115

Schroll (clod, clodhopper) 91, 115

Schrott (bruised grain, groats) 106, 122

Schroyer, see Schreier

Schu (shoe, shoemaker) 96, 104

Schub (shove) 115

Schubart, see Schubert

Schubdrein (Shove it in!) 116

Schubert, Schuberth, Schubart (shoemaker) 104

Schubisser (shoe repairer, cobbler) 104

Schuch, Schuchard, Schuchart 74, Schuchardt (shoe, shoemaker) 96, 104

Schuchman, Schuchmann (shoemaker) 104

Schuck, Schucks 164, Schucker, Schukert 164, Schuckermann 94 (shoe, cobbler) 96, 104

Schude, Schuder, Schudt, Schudy, see Schutt

Schuebel, Schueble 159 (bushel) 118

Schuele, Schuelle, see Schule

Schueler, Schuehler, Schueller, see Schuler

Schuenemann, Schuenmann, see Scheunemann

Schuerenbrand (Stir the fire!, troublemaker)

Schuerer, Schuermann (scourer) 96

Schuerholtz, Schuerholtz (firewood) 106

Schuerholtz, Schuerholz (poker, baker, etc.) 96

Schuessel, Schuessler (bowl, bowlmaker, fr Latin *scutella*) 96, 106

Schuett, Schuette (rubble) 122, see Schuetz

Schuetz, Schuez (marksman) 107

Schuh (shoe, shoemaker) 106, 104

Schuhknecht (shoemaker's assistant) 104

Schuhl, see Schule

Schuhmacher (shoemaker) 104

Schuhmann, see Schumann

Schuhriem, Schuhriemen (shoestrap, shoe lace) 96, 104, 106

Schul (school) 71

Schuhwerk (footwear, cobbler) 104

Schulberg (school mountain) 68

Schuld, Schuldt (guilt, debt) 115
Schuldenfrei (debt free) 115
Schulder 159, see Schulter
Schuldheis, see Schultheiss
Schule, Schull (school,
	synagogue, fr Latin *scola*)
Schulenberg (hidden mountain)
	68, 122
Schulenburg (hidden castle) 73,
	122
Schuler, Schuller (pupil) 118
Schulhoff (school yard) 92
Schulius (Latin for Schule) 141
Schulkind (school child) 118
Schullehrer (school teacher) 96
Schulmann, Schulmeister
	(teacher, synagogue sexton) 96
Schult, see Schuld
Schult, Schulte, Schultes, see
	Schultheis
Schulteis, see Schultheis
Schulter, Schulther, Schulters
	164 (shoulder) 114
Schulter (debtor)
Schultheis, Schultheiss (village
	magistrate) 109
Schultz, Schulz, Schulze, see
	Schultheis
Schumacher, Schumaker, see
	Schuhmacher
Schuman, Schumann, see
	Schuhmacher
Schumer (skimmer of millk, etc.,
	cheat) 96, 115
Schumm, see Schuhmacher
Schumpeter (Cobbler Peter) 104
Schunemann 159, see
	Scheunemann
Schunk, Schunke (shank, thigh)
	114
Schupp (scale) 118
Schuppen (shed) 65
Schuppehauer (maker of wooden
	ladles) 106

Schurman, Schurmann (dweller
	by a pond 80), see also
	Scheuermann
Schurtz, Schurz (apron, skirt,
	shirt, blacksmith, baker, etc.)
	96, 106
Schuss, Schusz (shot) 107
Schuss (very steep slope) 71, 122
Schussele 55, see Schuessel
Schuster (shoemaker, fr Latin
	sutor) 104
Schut, Schutt, Schutte (rubbish,
	rubble) 118
Schutz, Schutze, Schutzman
	(watchman, guard) 109, see
	Schuetz
Schwaab, Schwab, Schwabe,
	Schwaber (Swabian) 120
Schwabeland, Schwabenland,
	Schwabland (Swabia) 120
Schwabline 55, 159 (little
	Swabian) 120
Schwach (weak) 114
Schwaegerin (sister-in-law) 119
Schwaeher (brother-in-law) 119
Schwager (brother-in-law) 119
Schwahn, see Schwan
Schwaiger, see Schweiger
Schwaizer, see Schweizer
Schwalb, Schwalbe (swallow) 115
Schwalb (dweller near the
	Schwalb, swamp) 83
Schwalbach (swamp brook) 80,
	77
Schwall, Schwalls 74 (swamp) 80
Schwalm (name of river, swamp
	water) 80, 83
Schwamb, Schwamm, Schwam
	(sponge) 106
Schwan, Schwann (swan, house
	name) 48, 62
Schwander, Schwandner,
	Schwandter, Schwandtner,
	Schwaner (occupant of a
	clearing 126, fr Schwand 122)

Schwandt (clearing, see Schwander) 126, 122

Schwanebeck, Schwanenbeck (swan creek) 48, 77, 122

Schwanfelder (fr Schwanfeld 122, swan field) 48, 84

Schwanger (pregnant) 115

Schwank, Schwanke (swing, farce) 118

Schwantz (tail) 118

Schwarm (swamp) 80, 122

Schwarm (bee swarm, apiarist) 96

Schwart, see Schwarte, Schwartz

Schwarte (bristled hide, peasant's scalp) 114

Schwartz, Schwartze (black, brunet, blacksmith) 112, 96

Schwartzbach, Schwarzenbach (fr Schwartzbach 122, black brook) 77

Schwartzbart (black beard) 112

Schwartzberg (black mountain) 68

Schwartzenfeld (blackfield) 84

Schwartzhaubt (black head) 112

Schwartzkopf (black head) 112

Schwartzman (brunet) 112

Schwartzschild, Schwarzschild (black shield) 62, 149

Schwartzwelder 159, Schwarzwaelder, Schwartzweller 159 (fr the Black Forest) 121

Schwarz, see Schwartz

Schwarzman, Schwarzmann, see Schwartzman

Schwarzschild, see Schwartzschild

Schwarzwalder 159, Schwarzwald, see Schwartzwelder

Schwatz (gossip, chatter) 115

Schwebel, Schwefel (sulphur) 106

Schwebel (little Swabian) 120

Schwegler (flutist, bagpiper) 96

Schweich (Be silent!) 116

Schweiger, Schweigert 74, Schweickhard, Schweigerts 74, 164, Schweighart 74 (fr a cattle farm) 91, 92, 143

Schweighof (cattle farm) 91, 92, 122

Schweighoff, Schweigerhoff (cattle farm) 91

Schweighoffer, Schweighoefer (cattle farmer) 91, 92

Schweighouser (fr a Schweighof) 159

Schweigstill (Be quiet!) 116

Schweiker, Schweicker < Schwindger (swift + spear) 46, 46

Schweikert 74, Schweikhart, Schweickhart < Schweiger

Schwein (swine, swineherd) 91

Schwein (swamp water) 80, 91, 115

Schweinfurt, Schweinfurth (swamp water ford, a city) 80, 122

Schweinhard (swineherd) 91

Schweinhart (wild boar + strong) 46, 46

Schweinle (little swine) 114

Schweinsberg (boar mountain) 48, 68

Schweinschneider (pig castrator) 96

Schweiss (sweat, blood) 118

Schweisshelm (blood + helmet) 46

Schweitz, Schweitzer, Schweizer, Schweizzer (Swiss) 120

Schweller (drunkard) 115

Schwemmer (rafter) 96

Schwenck, Schwenk, Schwenker (brandisher) 118

Schwend, Schwender, Schwendemann (dweller in a clearing) 126

Schwenkel, Schwengel (swingbar, clapper) 106

Schwentke 55, see Schwend

Schwentzel (little tail) 55

Schwentzer (idler) 115

Schwer (heavy), see Schwaeher

Schwerd, Schwerdt, Schwert (sword) 41, 45, 108

Schwerdfeger, Schwerdtfeger (sword burnisher) 108

Schwerdtle, Schwertlein 55 (little sword) 96, 107, 108

Schwerdtner, Schwertner (sword maker) 108

Schwermann 119, see Schwaeher

Schwicker, see Schweiker

Schwickert, see Schweiger

Schwieger, Schwiegert 74 (in-law, mother-in-law) 119

Schwind, Schwindt (a clearing) 126, 122

Schwind, Schwindt (swift, tumultuous) 115

Schwindel, Schwindler (swindler) 115

Schwing (swamp) 80, 122

Schwingel (fescue grass) 89

Schwingenschloegel (Swing the mallet!, cooper) 116

Schwingschwert (Brandish the sword!) 116

Schwitzer, see Schweitzer

Schwizerhoff (Swiss farm) 92

Schwob, see Schwab

Schwoerer (swearer, conspiritor) 115

Schwol, see Schwall

Schwyzer, see Schweitzer

Schynder 159, see Schinder

Schyner 159, see Scheunemann

Schyre 159, see Scheuer

Scriber 159, see Schreiber

Scrivers 159, 164, see Schreiber

Seabaugh, see Seebach

Seabald 159, Seabold, Seaboldt, see Siegbald

Seacrist 159, see Sigrist

Seafred 159, Seafret, Seafrett, see Siegfried

Seager 159, see Sieger

Seagle 159, see Siegel

Seaholz 159, Seaholz, see Seeholtz

Seaman 159, see Siemen, Saemann

Sebald, see Siegbald

Sebastian (St. Sebastian) 135

Sebeniecher 159, see Siebeneichen

Sebert, see Siegbrecht

Sebold, Seboldt, see Siegbald

Sechrist 159, see Sigrist

Sechter (bushel) 96, 106

Seckel 55, Seckler (satchel, satchel maker) 106

Seckel 53, 55 (little Isaac, OT name) 135

Seckinger (person fr Seckingen) 122

Secrest, Secrist, see Sigrist

Sedlmayer 159, see Sattelmeyer

See (lake) 80

Seebach, Seebacher (lake brook) 80, 77, 122

Seeberg, Seeberger (lake mountain) 80, 68, 122

Seebold 159, see Siegbald

Seeburg (lake castle) 80, 73

Seefeld, Seefeldt (lake field) 80, 84, 122

Seefret 159, Seefried, see Siegfried

Seegel 159, Seegal, see Siegel

Seeger 159, Seegar, Seger, see Sieger

Seegmiller (sawmiller) 103, 151

Seehausen (lake house) 80, 65

Seehaver 159, Seehofer (lake farm) 80, 92

Seegrist 159, see Sigrist

Seeholtz (lake forest) 80, 72

Seehousz 159, see Seehausen

Seekamp (lake field) 80, 84, 122

Seel (soul) 118

Seel (swamp) 80

Seel, see Seil

Seelaender (fr Seeland, Zeeland) 121

Seelbach (swamp brook)

Seelhorst (swamp hurst) 80, 72

Seelig, see Selig

Seelmann (swamp dweller) 80

Seemann (seaman) 96

Seemann (dweller near a lake) 80

Seemueller (miller on the lake) 80, 103

Seethaler (fr Seethal, lake valley) 80, 67

Seets 159, see Seitz

Seewald (lake forest) 80, 71

Sefeldt, see Seefeld

Sefret, Seffret, see Siegfried

Sefues 53 < Josephus 135

Segbolt < Siegbald

Segebrecht, see Siegbert

Segel (sail) 106

Segel 159, Segal, Segall, see Siegel

Segeler, Segler (sailor, sail maker) 96

Segenreich (rich in blessing) 139, 148

Seger 159, Segers 164, see Sieger

Segfried 159 < Siegfried

Segmueller (sawmiller) 96, 103

Segrist, Segrest, see Sigrist

Sehl (swamp) 80, see also Seel

Sehlhorst (swamp hurst) 80, 72

Sehlmeyer (swamp farmer) 80, 93

Sehlsted (swamp place) 80

Sehr (scorch, burn) 118

Seib (sieve) 106

Seibald, see Siegbald

Seibel, see Siegbald

Seibert, Seipert < Siegbert

Seibold < Siegbald (victory + bold) 47, 46

Seibrandt < Siegbrand

Seidel, Seidl, Seidell (mug, pint) 106

Seideler, Seidler, Seidelmann (mug maker) 96

Seidemann, Seidenman, Seidman, Seidenspinner (silk worker) 96

Seidenader (silk sewer) 96

Seidenband, Seidenbaender, Seidenbender (silk ribbon maker)

Seidenberg (silk mountain) 68

Seidenfaden (silk thread, silk reeler, spinner) 96

Seidenfrau (silk woman) 96

Seidenschnur (silk thread) 106

Seidenschwanz (silk train, elegant person) 115

Seidenstricker (silk knitter) 96

Seider (silk dealer) 105

Seidl, Seidler, see Seidel

Seidner (silk worker) 96

Seif, Seifensieder (soap boiler) 106, 96

Seifarth, see Seifert

Seifert, Seiffert, Seifahrt, Seiffert < Siegwart

Seifried, Seifrit < Siegfried

Seig 159, see Sieg

Seigel 159, see Siegel

Seigler 159, see Ziegler

Seil, Seile, Seils 164, Seiler (rope maker) 106

Seilback 159 (fr Seilbach 122, rope brook), see Selbach

Seiler (rope maker) 96

Seip 53, Seipel, Seipell, Seippel, Sippel, Seifold < Siegbald

Seippert < Siegbert

Seiss (scythe) 106

Seissenschmidt (scythe maker) 96

Seitz 53, Seiz, Seitzer < Siefried

Seivert, see Siegfried, Siegwart

Seivold, see Siegbald

Sekler (sack maker) 96

Selbach (swamp brook) 80, 77, 122

Selde (house, shelter) 65

Seldenreich (fortunate) 115, see Seltenreich

Selder, Seldner (cottager, peasant) 91

Seldomridge 159, see Seltenreich

Selhorst (marsh hurst) 80, 72

Selig, Seliger (fortunate, blessed) 115, 139, 148

Seligman, Seligmann (blessed man) 115, 139, 148

Selkman 159, Selkmann, see Seligman

Sell, Selle 122, Seller, Sellner, Selman, Sellmann (marsh land) 80

Sellmayer, Sellmeyer (farmer on the marsh) 80, 93

Selmer < Salmar (hall + famous) 47

Selpert < Salbrecht (hall + bright) 47

Seltenreich (seldom rich) 115, see Seldenreich

Selter, Seltz, Seltzer, Selzer (salt merchant, meat and fish salter) 105, 106

Seltmann, see Selter

Seman 159, Semans 164, see Saemann, Seemann, Sieman

Semmel, Semmler, Semler (blond) 112

Semmel, Semmler, Semler (white roll baker) 96

Senck, Senk, Senkler (inhabitant of a burned off clearing) 126

Sendeck (swamp field) 80, 84

Sendel, Senderling (swamp dweller) 80

Sender 53 < Alexander

Sender (dweller in a burned clearing) 126

Sendldorfer (swamp village) 80, 124

Senecker 159, Senneca, see Schoenacker

Senf (mustard, mustard dealer) 105

Senfelder, Senffelder, Sennfelder (mustard field) 84

Senft (gentle) 115

Senftleber, see Sanftleben

Seng, Senge (burned off land) 84, 125

Sengebusch (burned shrubland) 72, 125

Senger (singer) 96

Sengeysen (scorching iron) 106

Sengmueller (miller on a clearing) 125, 103

Sengstake (Burn the poker!, stoker) 116, 96

Senkel (lace) 106

Senn, Senner (Swiss shepherd) 95

Sennhauser (occupant of shepherd's hut) 95, 65

Sennwald (shepherd's forest) 91, 71

Sens (reed grass) 81

Sensabaugh 159, Sensebaugh, Sensibaugh, Sinsabaugh, Sensebach (reed brook) 81, 77

Sense (scythe) 106

Sensenbrenner (reed burner) 96

Sensenmann (reaper) 95

Senske (little sickle) 106, 54, 55

Senstack, see Sengstake

Sentheim, see Sontheim

Sentz 53 <St. Vincent 135

Seohnlein 159, 55, see Soehnlein

Seppel 53, 55, Seppler, Seppi < Josef, Giuseppi

Sermatt 159 (fr Zermatt) 122

Servas < St. Servatius 135

Sessler (chair maker) 96

Setmayer, see Sattelmeyer

Settelman, Settleman, Settle 159, Settler (dweller on a mountain saddle) 68

Settelmeyer, see Sattelmeyer

Settmacher (maker of bowls or baskets) 96

Setzepfand (spendthrift) 115

Setzer, Setzler, Setser (compositor) 96

Seuberlich, see Saeuberlich

Seubert, Seuberth < Siegbert

Seubold < Siegbald

Seuer, see Saeuer

Seufer, Seuffert (tipler) 115

Seuffert, Seufried < Siegfried

Seuter, Seutter (shoemaker, fr Latin *sutor*) 104

Sevalt < Siegbald

Sevart, Severt, Sewert < Siegwart

Severin (St. Severin, name of a pope) 134

Sewalt 159, see Seewald

Seybel < Siegbald

Seybert, Seybert < Siegbert

Seybold, Seybolds 164 < Siegbald

Seybold, see Siegbold

Seybrecht, see Siegbert

Seydel, Seydeler, see Seideler

Seydelmann, see Seideler

Seydelmann (silk worker) 96

Seydenbender, see Seidenband

Seydler, see Seydelmann

Seydt, see Seide

Seyer (sower) 91

Seyfer, Seyfers 164, Seyfert 74, Seyvert, Seyferth, Seyfarth, Seyfardt < Siegwart

Seyfreet 159, see Siegfried

Seyfrid, Seyfrit, Seyfritz 164, Seyfried, Seyfriedt < Siegfried

Seyl, Seyle, Sylar 159, see Seiler

Seymond < Siegmund, Sigismund

Seyppel < Siegbalt

Sh ..., see under Sch ... (Only a small sample given here)

Shade 159, Shadlein 55, see Schad, Schadlein

Shach 159, see Schach

Shadle 159, see Schaedel

Shafer 159, Shaffer, Shaefer, Shaeffer, see Schaeffer

Shaffner (estate manager)

Shalk, see Schalk

Shallenberg 159, see Schallenberger

Shaller 159, see Schaller

Shambaugh 159, see Schaumbach

Shane 159, Shaner, see Schoen, Schoener

Shanebacker 159, see Schoenbacher

Shaneberger, see Schoenberger

Shanefelter 159, see Schoenfelder

Shaneour 159, see Schoenauer

Shaner 159, see Schoener

Shank 159, see Schenk

Shants 159, see Schantz

Sharp 159, see Scharf

Sharpstein 159, see Scharfstein

Sharsmith 159, fr Scharschmidt (plow smith) 96

Shats 159, see Schatz

Shaub 159, see Schaub

Shauder 159, see Schauder

Shauer 159, see Schauer

Shaumloffel 159, see Schaumloeffel

Shaver 159, see Schaber

Sheaffer 159, see Schaeffer, Schiefer

Shealy 159, see Schiele

Shear 159, Shearer, Shearman, see Scher, Scherer, Schermann

Shearer, see Scherer

Sheats 159, Sheets, Sheatsen, see Schuetz, Schuetzen

Sheeler 159, Sheely, see Schieler, Schiele

Sheets 159, see Schuetz
Sheib 159, see Scheib
Sheildknight 159, Scheldknight,
    see Schildknecht
Shelhamer 159, Schellheimer
    (bell hamlet) 123
Shelhouse 159, see Schellhaus,
    Schellhaas 151
Shellenberger 159, see
    Schellenberger
Shelley 159, see Schiele
Shellman, see Schellmann
Shelmire 159 (occupant of the
    Schelhof, swamp farm) 80, 93
Shendler 159, see Schindler
Shenk 159, see Schenk
Shepherd 153, Shepperd, see
    Schaefer
Sher 159, see Scher
Sherer, see Scher
Sherman 159, see Schermann
Sherouse 159, see Scheraus
Shertz 159, see Schertz
Shetzline 159, see Schatzle 55
Sheuer 159, see Scheuer
Shewmaker 159, see Schumacher
Shieldmaker 159, see
    Schildmacher
Shieldnight 159, see
    Schildknecht
Shiller 159, Shilling, see Schiller,
    Schilling
Shilnite 159, see Schildknecht
Shimelman, see Schimmelmann
Shimer 159, see Schaeumer
Shindle 159, see Schindel
Shine 159, see Schein, Schoen ...
Shinebach 159, see Schoenbach
Shipe 159, see Scheib
Shirer 159, see Scheurer
Shissel 159, Shissler, Shislor, see
    Schuessel, Schuessler
Shively 159, see Scheib
Shmal 159, Shmall, see Schmal
Shnaveli 159, see Schnaebele

Shnyder 159, see Schneider
Shoemaker 153, see Schumacher
Shoff, Schoff 159, see Schaf
Shoffroth, see Schaffrath
Sholl 159, see Scholl
Shoney 159, see Schoene
Shonfeld 159, see Schoenfeld
Shonik 159, see Schoeneck
Shonts 159, see Schantz
Shools 159, see Schultz
Shots 159, see Schatz
Shoup 159, see Schaub
Shrader 159, see Schroeder
Shriner 159, see Schreiner
Shriver 159, see Schreiber
Shroder 159, see Schroeder
Shrontz 159, see Schrantze
Shroyer 159, see Schreier
Shugart 159, see Schuch
Shuler 159, see Schueler
Shults 159, see Schultz
Shumaker 159, see Schumacher
Shuman 159, see Schumann
Shupe, see Schub
Shwab, see Schwab
Shwegler 159, see Schwegler
Shweyart, see Schweiger
Shy 159, see Scheu
Shyd 159, see Scheidt
Sibert < Siegbert
Sible 159, see Seibel
Sibold < Siegbald
Sichel (sickle, fr Latin *sicilis*) 106
Sichelstiel (sickle handle) 106
Sicher (secure, fr Latin *securus*)
    115
Sickafoos 159 < Ziegenfuss
    (goatfoot)
Sickler 159, see Ziegler, Sichel
Sidell, Sidle 159, see Seidel
Sides 159, see Seitz
Sidnor 159, see Seidner
Sieb, Siebe, Sieber (sieve, sieve
    maker) 106
Siebelt < Siegbald

Sieben (seven) 118

Siebenbuergen (place in Hungary, seven castles) 73, 121

Siebeneichen (seven oaks) 89, 122

Siebenhaar (seven hairs, balding) 112, 114

Siebenheller (seven pence) 117

Siebenrock (seven coats, tailor) 96, 112

Siebensohn (seven sons) 118

Sieber, Siebers 74 (strainer, siever) 106

Siebert < Siegbert

Siebold, Sieboldt < Siegbald

Siebrand (victory + flame) 47

Siebzehenriebel (seventeen turnips, farmer) 112

Sieck (sick) 114

Sieck (marsh) 80, 122

Sieckman (marsh dweller) 80

Siecrist 159, see Sigrist

Siedel, Siedler (settler)

Siedel, Siedler (salt boiler) 96

Siedenkamp (low lying hill) 84

Siedentop (boiling pot) 106

Sieder (salt boiler) 96

Siefer, Sieffert, Siefferts 74, Sieverts, Sievers, Siewers, see Siegwart

Siefreit, see Siegfried

Sieg (victory) 47, 122

Sieg (river name, swamp) 80, 83

Siegbald (victory + bold) 47, 46

Siegbert, Siegbrecht (victory + bright) 47, 46

Siegbrand (victory + sword) 46, 46

Siegehrist 159, see Sigrist

Siegel, Siegal 159, Siegler, Siegle 159, Siegelman (seal, fr Latin *sigillum*) 106

Siegel 53, 55, Siegle 159 < Siegfried, Siegward, etc.

Siegenthaler, Siegenthahler (victory valley) 47, 76

Sieger, Siegert 74 (winner) 118

Siegfried, Siegfreit 159 (victory + protection) 47, 47

Sieghart (victory + strong) 47, 46

Siegler, see Siegel, Ziegler

Siegman, Siegmann (victor) 47

Siegmeyer (farmer in the swamp) 80, 93

Siegmund, Sigismund (victory + guardian) 47, 47

Siegnand (victory + brave) 47, 46

Siegrist, see Sigrist

Siegwald (victory + rule) 47, 46

Siegwart, Siegworth 159 (victory + guardian) 47, 47

Siegwein (victory + friend) 47 48

Siehdichum (Look around!) 116

Siek, Sieker, Siegmann (swamp, swamp dweller) 80

Sieman, Siemann, Siemanns 74, see Siegman

Siemann (henpecked man, uxorious husband) 115

Siemer, Siemering 55 < Siegmar (victory + famous) 47, 47

Siemund, see Siegmund

Sieppert < Siegbert

Siess, see Suess

Sievers 74, Sievert, Sieverts 74 < Siegwart

Sievold, see Siegbald

Sifert, see Siegfried

Sigafoose 159 < Ziegenfuss (goat foot)

Sigel 159, Sigal, Sigler, see Siegel, Siegler

Sigfried, Sigfritz < Siegfried

Sigman, Sigmon 159, see Siegman, Siegmund

Sigmund, Sigismund, see Siegmund

Sigrist, Sigerist (sexton, fr Latin *sacrum*) 110

Sigwalt, Siewald < Siegwald
Sigwart, see Siegwart
Silbaugh 159, see Selbach
Silber, Silbers 164, Silbert 74,
　　Silver, Silvers 164 (silver,
　　silver smith) 96, 106
Silberberg, Silverberg 153 (silver
　　mountain) 68, 148
Silbergeld (silver money) 117
Silberholz (silver forest) 72
Silberhorn (silver horn) 106
Silbermann, Silverman 153
　　(silver smith) 96
Silbernagel, Silvernail 153 (silver
　　nail) 106
Silbersack (silver bag) 117, 106
Silberstein, Sillverstein 159
　　(silver stone, silver mountain,
　　litharge, silversmith) 73, 122
Silberzahn (silver tooth) 114
Siler, see Seiler
Silver ..., see Silber ...
Silvernail 153, see Silbernagel
Silvester (name of Pope) 134
Simeon (OT name) 135
Simmel (baker of white rolls) 106
Simmermann 159, see
　　Zimmermann
Simon, Simons 164 (NT name)
　　135
Simprecht < Sindbercht (journey
　　+ brilliant)
Simrock, see Siebenrock
Singer, Singert 74, see Saenger
Singhaus (concert house) 65
Singmaster 153, see Sangmeister
Singvogel (song bird) 115
Sinn (mind, idea) 118
Sinn (swamp water) 80
Sinnig (wise) 115
Sintenis (St. Dionysius) 135
Sipart, see Siegbert
Sipe 159, Sipes 164, see Seib
Sipp, Sippen (kinsman) 119
Sippel, Sipple 159 < Siegbald

Sirach (OT name) 135
Sirch (millet) 91
Sis, Siss, see Suess
Siskind, see Suesskind
Sites 159, see Seitz
Sittig (well mannered) 115
Sitzer (sitter) 118
Sitzwohl (Sit well!) 116
Siverd, Sivert < Siegwart
Siwald 159, see Seewald,
　　Siegbald
Six, Sixt (St. Sixtus, name of a
　　pope) 134
Sl ..., see under Schl .... Only a
　　sample is given here.
Slaback, Slabaugh 159, see
　　Schlebach
Slagle, Slagel, see Schlegel
Slater 159, see Schlatter
Slaubaugh 159 (meadow brook)
　　84, 77
Slauch 159, see Schlauch
Slaugenhoup 159 <
　　Schlagdenhaupt (Hit the
　　head!) 116
Slaughter 159, see Schlechter
Slaybaugh 159, Slayback, see
　　Schlebach
Slaymaker 159, see
　　Schleiermacher
Slechter 159, see Schlechter
Sleeman 159, see Schliemann
Slegel 159, see Schlegel
Sleifer 159, see Schleifer
Slemaker 159, see Schleirmacher
Slemmer 159, see Schlemmer
Slicher 159, see Schleicher
Slick 159, see Schlick
Sligh 159, see Schley
Slimm 159, see Schlimm
Slomann (swamp dweller) 80
Slosser 159, see Schlosser
Slotman, see Schlosser
Slotter 159, see Schlatter
Slotterbach 159, Slotterback, see
　　Schlatterbach

Slouk 159, Slough 159, see
  Schlauch
Slund 159, see Schlund
Sly 159, see Schley
Sm ..., see Schm ... 43. Only a
  sample is given here.
Small 159, see Schmal
Smalts 159, see Schmaltz
Smearcase 159 < Schmerkaes
  (soft cheese) 91, 112
Smelser 159, Smeltz, see
  Schmeltzer
Smick 159, see Schmueck
Smit, Smitz 159, see Schmidt
Smith 153, see Schmidt
Smithmeyer 153, see
  Schmidtbauer
Smithpeter 152 < Schmidtpeter
  (Peter the smith)
Smitsdorf < Schmidtsdorf
  (smith's village)
Smoke, Smoker 159, see
  Schmuck, Rauch
Smoller 159, see Schmoller
Smoltz 159, see Schmaltz
Smook, see Schmueck
Smouse 159, see Schmauss
Smucker 159, see Schmucker
Smyser 159, see Schmeisser
Sn ..., see under Schn ...43. Only
  a sample is given here.
Snader 159, see Schneider
Snatterbeck (chatterer, gossip) 115
Snavel 159, see Schnabel
Snavely, Snaveley 159, see
  Schnaebele
Snay 159, see Schnee
Snek (snail) 113
Sneckenberger 159, see
  Schneckenberger
Snee 159, see Schnee
Sneider 159, see Schneider
Snell 159, see Schnell
Snider 159, Sniders 164, see
  Schneider

Snively 159, see Schnaebele
Snook, see Schnuck
Snowberger 153, see
  Schneeberger
Snurr 159, see Schnur
Snyder 159, Snyders 164, see
  Schneider
Sockriter 159, see Sackreiter
Socks 159, see Sachs
Soeder, see Soeter
Soehnlein 55 (little son) 119
Soeldner, Soellner (mercenary, fr
  Latin *solidarius*) 107
Soeller (fr Soell) 122
Soeller (balcony, fr Latin
  solarium)
Soelter (salt dealer) 105
Soetebier (sweet beer, brewer) 96
Soeter (shoemaker) 104
Sohl (swamp) 80
Sohn, Sohns 164 (son) 119
Sol, Soll (mud, bog) 80
Solberg (mud mountain) 68
Soldan, see Soltan
Soldat (soldier, mercenary) 107
Soldier 153, see Soeldner
Soldner 159, see Soeldner
Sollenberg, see Solberg
Solms (swamp water) 80, 122
Solomon 153, see Salomo
Soltan (sultan, perhaps actor in
  miracle play) 111
Solter, see Saltzer
Soltz, Soltmann, see Salz, also
  inhabitant of Solt 122
Sommer, Sommers 164, Somer,
  Somers 164 (summer) 118
Sommerfeld 122, Sommerfeldt,
  Sommerfelt (summer field) 84
Sommerfield 153, see
  Sommerfeld
Sommerhausen (summer house)
  65
Sommerkamp (summer field) 84

Sonderegger (swamp field) 80, 85

Sonderman, Sondermann (swamp dweller) 80

Sondersorge (carefree) 115

Sondheim (swamp hamlet) 80, 123, 122, see Sontheim

Sonn, Sonne (sun) 118

Sonnabend (Saturday) 143

Sonneborn (sun spring) 79

Sonnefeld, Sonnenfeld (sun field) 84, 122

Sonnenberg (sun mountain) 68, 122

Sonnenleiter, Sonnelitter 159 (fr Sonnenleite, sunny slope) 71

Sonnenschein (sunshine, happy person) 115

Sonnenthal (sun valley) 76

Sonntag, Sontag (Sunday, birth date or time of service) 143

Sontheim (southern hamlet) 85, 123, 122

Sooter 159, see Sutter

Sorber (Sorbian) 121

Sorg, Sorge, Sorgen (care, worrier) 115, 122

Sorgenfrei, Sorgenfrey (care free) 115

Souter 159, see Suter

Sower, Sowers 159, see Sauer

Sowerbier 159, see Sauerbier

Sowers, see Sauer

Sowerwine 159, see Sauerwein

Sox 159, see Sachs

Spaatz, see Spatz

Spaengler, see Spengler

Spaenhauer (kindling splitter) 96

Spaeth, Spaet, Spaete, Speth (late, tardy) 115

Spahn (swamp) 80

Spahn (shavings, carpenter) 96

Spahr (sparrow) 115

Spaight 159, see Spaeth

Spainhour 159, Spainhower, see Spanhauer

Spalt, Spalter, Spalder (wood splitter) 96

Span, see Spahn

Spange, Spangemacher (buckle, bracelet) 106

Spangenberg, Spangenberger (swamp mountain) 80, 68, 122

Spangenthal (swamp valley) 76

Spangler 159, see Spengler

Spanhauer (chip hewer) 95, 100

Spanier, Spanierman (Spaniard) 121

Spann, see Span

Spanner (bale binder) 96

Spar, see Spahr

Sparber, see Sperber

Sparbier (Save beer!, taverner) 116

Sparenberg (sparrow mountain) 68

Sparkuhl (sparrow pond) 81

Sparr (rafter, carpenter) 96

Sparrenburg (sparrow castle) 73

Spath, see Spaeth

Spatz (sparrow, urchin) 115

Spealman 159, see Spielmann

Speas 159, see Spiess

Specht, Spaecht (woodpecker) 115

Speck (lard, pork seller) 105

Speck, Speckmann (raised path through a bog, corduroy road) 65, 122

Speece 159, Speas, see Spiess

Speelmann, see Spielmann

Speer 41, Speers 164, Speert 74 (spear, spearmaker) 107, 108

Spegel, see Spiegel

Speice 159, see Speiss

Speicher, Speichert 74 (granary, fr Latin *spicarium*) 122

Speidel (woodcutter's wedge) 95, 106

Speier, see Speyer

Speigel 159, see Spiegel

Speight 159, Speights 74, see
   Spaeth
Speis, Speiss, Speise, Speiser
   (food, victualer) 106
Speishaendler (food handler) 106
Speismann (victualer) 96, 106
Speker 159, see Spieker
Spellerberg, see Spielberg
Spelmann, Spellmann, see
   Spielmann
Spener (kindling splitter) 96
Spener (needle and pin maker)
   96
Spengler, Spengel (tinsmith,
   plumber) 96
Sperber (sparrow hawk) 115
Sperl, Sperling 55, Sperlein 55
   (sparrow) 115
Sperlbaum (sparrow tree) 89
Sperre, Sperry 159 (barricade,
   closing) 118
Spervogel (sparrow) 115
Spessart, Spessard (mountain
   range, swamp forest) 80, 72,
   122
Speth 159, see Spaeth
Speydel, see Speidel
Speyer (city on Rhine) 122
Spice 159, Spicer, see Speiser
Spidel 159, Spidelle, see Speidel,
   Spiecher, Speicher
Spiegel, Spiegler (mirror, fr Latin
   speculum) 106
Spieker (large nail, spike) 106
Spieker (granary, granary guard)
   96
Spielacker (field drawn by lot) 84
Spielberg (lookout mountain, fr
   Latin *specula*) 68, 122
Spieler (player, gambler) 115
Spielholtz (parish forest, glebe
   woodland) 72
Spielmann, Spillman (minstrel)
   96
Spier, Spiers (Speyer) 74

Spierling (smelt, fish dealer) 105
Spies, Spiess (spear, spit,
   spitshaped field) 108, 106
Spies (swamp) 80
Spiesman, Spiessman (pikeman)
   107
Spieth (swift) 115
Spigel 159, Spigler, see Spiegel,
   Spiegler
Spigelmire 159 (fr the Spiegelhof,
   mirror farm) 93
Spiller, Spillman, see Spieler,
   Spielman
Spindel, Spindler (distaff,
   spinner, distaff maker) 106
Spingler 159, see Spengler
Spinnenweber, Spinneweber
   (spinnerweaver) 96
Spinner, Spinnler (spinner) 96
Spittel, Spital (hospice) 118
Spittelmayer (hospice overseer)
   93
Spittler, Spitler (worker in a
   hospice) 96
Spitz, Spitzer, Spitzler, Spitzner
   (point, dweller near a peak) 68
Spitzberg (sharp peaked
   mountain) 68
Spitzfaden (tailor) 96
Spitznagel, Spitznagle 159 (sharp
   nail) 106
Spitznas (pointed nose) 114
Spitzweg (pointed role, baker) 96
Spohn, see Span
Spohr, Spor (spur, spur maker)
   96, 106
Sponheimer (city name) 122
Spoon 159, Spohn, see Span
Spoonhour 159, 100, see
   Spanhauer
Spott, Spotz 74 (ridicule) 115
Sprecher (speaker, reciter of
   rhymes) 115
Spreckels 164 (marsh dweller)
   80

Sprengel (diocese) 110
Sprengel (grasshopper) 115
Sprenkel, Sprenkle 159, see
    Sprengel
Spring, Springer (dweller near a
    spring) 77
Springel, see Sprengel
Springer, Sprenger, Springmann
    (jumper, dancer 96, fr
    Springen 122)
Springfeld (spring field) 84
Sprinkel, Sprinkle 159 (freckles)
    112, 113
Spritz, Spritzer (spray, sprayer)
    96
Sproll (carp, fish dealer) 105
Spuecher, see Spiecher
Spuhler, Spuehler (spool maker)
    96
Spund, Spunt (bung, taverner) 96
Spur (spoor) 118
Spyker, Spycher, see Spieker
Staab, see Stabe
Staadt, see Stadt
Staal, see Stahl
Staar, see Stahr
Stabe (staff)
Stablein 159, 55 (little staff)
Stabler 159, see Staebler
Stach < St Eustachius 135
Stack 53, Stach < St. Eustachius
    135
Stackhouse 153, see Stockhaus
Stackman 159, Stackmann, see
    Stockmann
Stadel, Stadeli (stable, barn) 65
Stadelman, Stadelmann (barn
    supervisor) 96
Stadelmayer, Stadelmeier (barn
    steward) 96, 93
Stader (dweller at a landing) 118
Stadfeld (field at the landing) 84
Stadler, Stadtler, Stattler (barn
    supervisor) 96

Stadt, Stadter, Stadtler,
    Staedtler, Statler (townsman)
    118
Staeblein (little staff) 55
Staebler (staff-carrying official)
    109
Staeheli, Staehle, Staehli,
    Staehler, Steheli, Steely 159,
    Stelly 159 (steel, blacksmith)
    96
Staempfli 55, see Stempel
Staengel, see Stengel
Staerk (strength) 115
Staetler (townsman) 118
Staffel (step, rung) 118
Stahl, Stahle, Stahler, Stahley
    159, Stahlmann, see Staehli
Stahlkopf (steel merchant) 96
Stahlschmit (steel smith) 96
Stahr (starling, bird catcher) 115
Staiger, see Steiger
Staigerwald (footpath forest) 65,
    72
Stain, see Stein
Stainbach, see Steinbach
Stalbach (steel brook) 77
Stalcupp, see Stahlkopf
Stalden (steep path) 65
Staley 159, see Staeheli
Stall, Stallmann, Stalling 55,
    Stallings 74 (stall, barn,
    stableman) 96, 122
Stalley, see Staehli
Stallknecht (groom) 96
Stalmaster 153 < Stallmeister
    (equerry) 96
Staltzfus 159, see Stoltzfus
Stambach, Stambaugh 159
    (stump brook) 77
Stamberg, Stammberger (stump
    mountain) 68
Stambler, see Stammler
Stamgast (regular guest) 118
Stamitz, see Steinmetz
Stamm, Stam (stem, trunk) 118

Stammbach, see Steinbach

Stammer, Stammler, Stamler (stutterer) 114

Stampf, Stampfel, Stampfl (stamp, tamper) 106

Stampf (steep path) 65

Stanback, Stanbaugh 159, see Steinbach

Stance 159, see Stantze

Stand, Stand, Stant (condition) 118

Standauf (Stand up!) 116

Stang, Stange, Stanger (pole, stick, spear) 106

Stantze (stamp, die) 106

Stapel (warehouse) 65

Stapf, Stapp (step)

Star, Stahr, Starr (starling) 115

Starck, Stark, Starke, Starker (strong) 115

Starkand (strong hand) 115

Startz 159, see Stortz

Startzbach, see Sturtzbach

Stassen 53 < St. Anastasius 135

Stattler, see Stadtler

Staub, Staube, Stauber (dust, miller) 103

Staubach (dammed up stream) 77

Stauch (jolt) 118

Staud, Staude, Staut, Staudt, Stauder (shrubs, underbrush) 72

Staudacker (brush field) 84

Staudehauer (brush clearer) 72, 100, 95

Staudemeyer, Staudenmaier (fr the Staudehoff) 72, 93

Stauffer (mug maker) 96

Stauffer (crag dweller) 68

Staup, see Staub

Stauss, see Steiss

Stautberg (brush mountain) 72, 68

Stautt, see Staud

Stayner, see Steiner

Steagall 159, see Stiegel

Stealy 159, see Staeheli 151

Stearn 159, Stearns 74, see Stern

Stebbins < St. Stephan 135

Stecher, Stechler (engraver) 96

Stecher (castrator) 96

Steckel, Stecker (swamp) 80

Steckmetz (dagger) 108

Stedler, Stedeler, see Stadtler

Steeg, see Steg

Steely 159, see Staeheli

Steen, see Stein

Steenfeld, see Steinfeld

Steer 159, Steere, see Stier

Steermann 159 (cattle raiser) 91

Steffen, Steffel, Steffens, Steffy, see Stephan

Steg, Steger, Stegmann (footbridge, dweller by steep footpath) 71, 65

Stegel 159, see Stiegel

Stegman (dweller by a footpath) 65

Stegmeyer, Stegmaier, Stegmeier (farmer by the footpath, or footbridge) 93, 65

Stegmueller, Stegmiller (fr a mill with facilities for other activities) 103

Stegreif (stirrup) 96, 106

Stehfest (Stand fast!) 116

Stehle, Stehli, Stehlig, Steheli, Stehlin, Stehll, see Staeheli

Stehman, see Steinmann

Stehr (grain measure) 106

Stehr (wether, ram) 91

Steidel (dweller in the brush) 72

Steier, see Steyer

Steif (stiff, brave) 112, 113

Steiful 159, see Stiefel

Steig, Steiger, Steigler, Steigman (dweller by a footbridge, footpath) 65

Steigauf (Climb up!) 116

Steiger, Steigler, Steigman
(climber)
Steigerwald, Steigerwalt
(footpath mountain) 65, 68
Steigleder (stirrup strap) 106
Steil, Steile (steep) 118
Steimetz, see Steinmetz
Stein (stone, stone worker) 73, 96
Steinach (stone terrain) 73, 79
Steinacker (stone field) 73, 84
Steinau, Steinauer (stone
meadow) 73, 84, see also
Steinhauer
Steinbach, Steinbacher,
Steinback (stony brook) 73, 77
Steinbeck, Steinbecker (stony
brook) 73, 77
Steinbeiss, Steinbeisser (stone
etcher, lithographer) 96
Steinberg, Steinbergen,
Steinberger (stone mountain)
73, 68
Steinbock, Steinboeck (ibex,
house name) 63
Steinborn, Steinbronn (stone
spring) 73, 79
Steinbrech, Steinbrecher,
Steinbrecker (stone crusher,
quarryman) 96, 100
Steinbrenner (brickmaker) 100
Steinbrickner, Steinbrueckner
(dweller by stone bridge) 71
Steinbrink (stone hill) 67
Steinbronn, see Steinbrunner
Steinbrook 159, see Steinbrueck,
Steinbruch
Steinbruch 122, Steinbruechel
(quarry, quarryman) 73
Steinbrunner, Steinebrunne 159
(fr Steinbrunn, stone spring)
79
Steinburg (stone castle) 73, 73
Steindecker (slater) 96
Steinegger (stony field) 84
Steiner, Steinert 74 (stone
worker) 73, 143

Steinfeld, Steinfeldt, Steinfelder
(stone field) 73, 84, 122
Steinfuhrer (stone hauler) 73, 96
Steingart (stone garden) 73, 84
Steingass (stone road, stone
street) 73, 65
Steingoetter (stone drains) 118
Steinhag (stone enclosure) 73,
123, 122
Steinhard, Steinhart (stone hard)
115
Steinhardt, Steinharter (fr
Steinhardt, stone forest) 73,
72
Steinhauer (stone cutter) 73, 100
Steinhaus, Steinhauser,
Steinhaeuser (fr Steinhaus
122, stone house) 73, 65, 66
Steinheimer (fr Steinheim 122,
stone hamlet) 73, 123
Steinheiser 66, see Steinhaus
Steinhice 159, Steinheiser, see
Steinhauser
Steinhof, Steinhoff, Steinhoeffel
(stone farm) 73, 84, 122
Steinhorn (stone peak) 73, 68
Steinhorst (stone hurst) 72
Steinhour 159, Steinour, see
Steinhauer
Steinhuebel (stone hill) 73, 67
Steiniger, Steinigger, Steininger
(fr Steiningen) 122
Steiningen, see Steininger
Steinkamp, Steinkampf (stone
field) 73, 84
Steinkirchner (fr Steinkirchen
122, stone church) 73, 71
Steinkoenig (wren) 115
Steinkohl (coal) 118
Steinkopf (stone head) 115
Steinkopf (earthenware mug) 96,
106
Steinlein 55 (little stone) 73
Steinler (stony place) 73
Steinman, Steinmann (stone
cutter) 96

Steinmaur (fr Steinmauren 122, stone wall, mason, dweller by a stone wall) 100

Steinmetz, Steinmets 164 (stone cutter) 96, 100

Steinmeyer, Steinmeier (fr the Steinhoff) 93

Steinocher, Steinocker, see Steinacker 151

Steinour 159, see Steinauer, Steinhauer

Steinrucken (stone ridge) 73, 68

Steinschneider (stone cutter) 96

Steinseiffer, Stainsayfer (stony brook) 73, 77

Steinthal (stone valley) 73, 76

Steinwald (stone forest) 73, 71

Steinwand, Steinwaender (stone wall) 73

Steinway 159, see Steinweg

Steinwedel (stony ford) 73, 78

Steinweg (stony path) 73, 65, 122

Steinwehr (stone defense, stone weir, stone mason) 73, 96

Steinwerker (stone mason) 96

Steinwinder, see Steinwand

Steinwyk (stone village) 73, 123

Steiss (rump) 114

Steitz (fuller, cloth cleanser) 96

Steli 159, see Stelly

Stell (frame, holder) 118

Steller, Stellmach, Stellmacher, Stellman, Stellmann (wainwright, cartwright) 96

Stelling (marsh dweller 80, fr Stellingen 122)

Stellmach, see Steller

Stellpflug (wheeled plow) 91, 96, 106

Stellwagen, Stellvagen 159 (stage coach) 118

Stelly 159, Stelley, see Staeheli

Stelmach, Stelmack, see Steller

Steltz, Stels 159, Selzer, Stelzner (stilts, walker on stilts or crutches) 114, 106

Steltzfuss (wooden leg) 114

Stemm, Stemmer, Stembler, Stemler, Stemmler (marsh dweller) 80

Stempel, Stemple 159 (stamp) 106

Stenabaugh 159, Stenbaugh, see Steinbach

Stendal 122, see Steinthal

Stender (carpenter) 96

Stendorf (stone village) 73, 124

Stenert, see Steiner, Steinert

Stengel, Stengle 159, Stenglein 55 (stalk, thin person) 114

Stenhouse 153, Stenkamp, see Steinhaus, Steinkamp

Stentz 53, Stenzer < Polish: Stanislaw 146

Step, Stepf, see Stapp, Stapf

Stephan, Stephann, Stephans, Steffen, Steffe, Stephanus (St. Stephen, name of several popes) 134

Stephani, Stephany, son of Stephan 142

Steppe (quilt) 106

Sterb (Die!) 116, 117

Sterchi, Sterki, Sterkee 159 (strength) 115, see Stuerki

Stern, Sterne (star, house name) 62

Sternberg, Sternberger (swamp mountain) 73, 80, 68

Sternburg (swamp castle) 73

Sterner (swamp dweller) 80

Sternfeld (swamp field) 80, 84, 122

Sternglass (telescope, astrologer) 96, 106

Sternheim, Sternheimer (swamp hamlet) 80, 123

Sternkamp (steer field) 84

Sternschuss (comet) 118

Sternsdorf (swamp village) 80, 124

Sternthal (swamp valley) 80, 76

Stertzenbach (dirty brook) 77

Stettiner, Stettinius (fr Stettin) 9, 122, 142

Stettler (townsman) 118

Steubesand (fine sand for drying ink, scribe) 96, see Streusand

Steuer (dowry, steering, tax, tax collector) 109

Steuernagel (tiller, helmsman) 96

Steurer, Steuermann, Steuersmann (steersman) 96

Steyer, Steyert 74 (fr Styria, Steiermark) 121

Steyerwald, see Steigerwald

Steyger, see Steiger

Stich (stitch, tailor) 104

Stichel, Stichler (engraver, stylus) 106

Stichel (steep path) 65

Stichling (stickleback) 115

Stichter (founder) 96

Stick, Stickeler (embroiderer) 106, 122

Stickelbach (stickleback brook) 115, 77

Stiebel (dust) 118

Stief (steep, rigid)

Stiefel, Stieffel, Stieffler (boot, boot maker) 104, 106

Stiefvater (stepfather) 119

Stieg (staircase) 118

Stiegel, Stiegler, Stiegman, Stiegmann (stile, dweller near a stile) 118

Stiehler (chair maker) 96

Stiel, Stiehl (handle, helve) 96, 106

Stienes (St. Augustine) 135

Stier, Stierle (bull, steer) 91

Stierhoff (steer farm) 92

Stierlin 55, Stierlin (little steer) 91

Stiermann (keeper of breeding bulls) 91

Stiernkorb (beggar's basket) 118

Stiersdorfer (bull village) 124

Stiffler, Stifler, Stiffler, see Stiefel

Stifter (occupant of a church institution) 139

Stigall 159, Stigler, see Stiegel

Stiger 159, see Steiger

Stile 159, Steiler, see Steil

Still, Stille, Stilling, Stillmann (tranquil person) 115

Stillwagon 159, Stillwagoner, see Stellwagen

Stimits 159, see Steinmmetz

Stimmel, Stimmell (stump of log, etc.)

Stine ..., see Stein ...

Stinebaugh 159, see Steinbach

Stindler (fisherman) 96

Stinefield 159, see Steinfeld

Stiner 159, see Steiner

Stinnes 53 < Augustinus 135

Stirn (forehead) 114

Stob, Stober (bath attendant) 96

Stobaugh 159, see Staubach

Stock (stick, tree trunk) 114

Stockfisch (fish monger) 105

Stockhausen (tree trunk hamlet) 65

Stockmann, Stockmeister (jailor) 109

Stockmann, see Stuckmann

Stockschlaeger, Stockslager 159 (whipper) 96

Stockstill (stockstill, very quiet) 115

Stoehr, Stoer, Stoerr, Sterr 159 (sturgeon catcher 91 or dealer 105), see also Stehr

Stoekel 55, Stoeckl, Stoeckle, 159 Stoecklein, Stoeklin (little stick)

Stoerzbach, see Sturzbach

Stoessel (pestle) 106

Stoff (stuff) 118

Stoffel 53, Stoffels 164 <
Christoff

Stoffer 159, see Stauffer

Stoffregen (downpour) 118

Stohldreyer (chair maker) 106

Stolberg (mined mountain) 68

Stoll (mine gallery, miner) 96

Stoll (loaf, slice, baker) 96

Stoller, Stollman (miner) 96

Stollfuss (club foot) 114

Stolte (proud) 115

Stoltfus, Stoltzfuss (limper) 114

Stoltz, Stoltze, Stoltzer, Stolz
(proud) 115

Stoltzenbach (proud brook) 77,
122

Stoltzenberg (proud mountain)
68

Stolz, see Stoltz

Stombaugh 159, see Stambach

Stombler 159, see Stammler

Stone 153, Stoner, see Stein,
Steiner

Stonebach 153, see Steinbach

Stonebraker 153, see
Steinbrecher

Stoneburner 159, see
Steinbrenner

Stonecipher 159, Stonecypher,
see Steinseiffer

Stonefield 153, see Steinfeld

Stoneking 153, see Steinkoenig

Stoner 159, see Steiner

Stonesifer 153, see Steinseiffer

Stong 159, see Stang

Stoots 159, see Stutz

Stoppelbein (stubble leg) 114

Storbeck (dirty water) 77

Storch, Storich, Storck, Stork
(stork, house name) 114, 63

Storm 153, see Sturm

Stortz (tumble, crash) 118

Stoss (sword thrust) 107

Stotler 159, see Statler

Stottlemeyer 159, Stottlemire
159, Stottlemyer 159, see
Stadelmeyer

Stotz (log, clumsy person) 115

Stoudemeyer 159, Stoudemaier,
see Staudemeyer

Stoudt 159, Stout, see Staude

Stouffer 159, Stoupher, see
Stauffer

Stoup 159, see Staub

Stout, see Staud

Straatmann, see Strattmann

Strabel, see Strobel

Strack (stiff, inflexible) 115

Strackbein (stiff leg) 114

Straecker, see Strecker

Straehler (comb maker) 96

Strahl, Strahle, Strale (ray of
light, arrow) 118

Straif, see Streif

Straight 159, see Streit

Strait 159, see Streit

Strand, Strant (beach) 72

Strang, Strange (leash, strip of
land) 84

Strang (rope, rope maker) 96

Strasbaugh 159 (road brook) 65,
77

Strasberger, Strassberger
(highway mountain) 65, 68,
see Strassburger

Strasburg, Strasburger,
Strassburger (fr Strassburg)
122

Strass (road, highway, fr Latin
strata) 65, see Strasser

Strasser, Strassler, Strassner,
Strassman (dweller on a
highway, fr Latin *strata*) 65

Stratemeyer, Stradtmeyer
(farmer on the road, fr Latin
strata) 65, 93

Strattmann, Stratmann,
Strathmann (dweller on the
street or road) 65

Straub, Straube, Strauber
(tousled, disheveled) 112

Strauch (bush, shrub, forest) 72

Straumann, see Strohmann

Straup, see Straub

Straus, Strauss (bouquet) 118

Straus, Strauss (fight) 115

Straus, Strauss (ostrich, often a
house name, fr Latin *struthio*)
62

Strausbaugh 159 (ostrich brook),
see Strasbaugh

Strawsburg 159, see Strassburg

Streagle 159, see Striegel

Streber, Strebel (striver) 115

Streck, Strecker (stretcher,
stretch of land)

Strecker (torturer) 96

Streckfuss (Stretch a leg!) 116

Stregels 159, 164, see Striegel

Strehler (comb maker) 96, 106

Streif, Streiff (stripe, campaign)
107

Streif (mounted patrol) 107

Streigel 159, see Striegel

Streight 159, see Streit

Streisand, see Streusand

Streisgut (Scatter wealth!,
spendthrift) 115, 116

Streit 122, Streith, Streiter,
Streitz 164, Streitman
(struggle, struggler) 115

Strempel (pestle) 106

Streng, Strenger (strict) 115

Streusand (blotting sand, scribe)
96

Strick, Stricker, Strickert 74,
Strickler, Strickman,
Strickmann (knitter) 96

Strick (snare, trapper) 91

Stricker, see Strick

Stricker (poacher) 91

Strickler, see Strick

Strider 159, see Streiter

Striegel, Strigel 159, Striegler
(curry comb, fr Latin *strigilis*)
106

Strite 159, see Streit

Strobar, Strohbart (straw beard)
112

Strobel (unkempt) 112

Strodtmann, see Stradtmann

Stroebel, Strobel, Stroble 159,
Strobell, Stroblich (disheveled)
115

Stroessner, see Strassner

Stroh, Stro (straw) 118

Strohacker, Strohhecker (straw
field) 84

Strohbach, Strohbaugh 159,
Strohbeck (straw brook) 77

Strohbank (straw bench) 118

Strohkorb (straw basket, basket
maker) 96

Strohm, see Strom

Strohmann, Stromann,
Strohmayer 93, Strohmeyer,
Stromier 159 (straw man,
straw dealer) 105

Strohsacker (maker of straw
sacks) 96

Strohscher (straw cutter) 96

Strohschneider (straw cutter) 96

Strom, Strohm (stream, current,
river) 79

Stromann, see Strohmann

Stromberg, Stromberger (stream
mountain) 79, 68

Stromenger, Strominger (straw
dealer) 105

Stromer, see Strohmann

Stromyer 159, see Strohmann

Strosnider 159, Stroosnyder, see
Strohschneider

Strossner, see Strasser

Strotman, Strothmann, see
Straatmann

Strouber 159, see Strub

Strough 159, see Strauch

Styne, Styner 159, see Stein,
  Steiner
Suchenwirt (Seek a host!) 116
Sucher, Suchman (searcher,
  hunting assistant) 91
Sudbrink (muddy hillock) 74
Sudbrok, Sudbrook (muddy
  brake) 80
Sudeck, Sudek (south field) 85,
  84
Suder, Sudermann (one dwelling
  toward the south) 85, 94, or
  name shortened fr one of the
  following three:
Suderode (south clearing) 85,
  126, 122
Sudheim (south hamlet) 85, 123,
  122
Sudhoff (south farm) 85, 92, 122
Sudler (slovenly worker) 115
Sudler (southerner) 85
Sudman, Sudmeyer (southerner)
  85
Suehle (wild boar wallow) 118
Suehn (penitence, penance,
  reconciliation) 138
Suender, Sunder (sinner) 138
Sues, Suess 122, Suesse (sweet)
  115
Suesskind (sweet child) 115
Suessmann (sweet man) 115
Suessmuth (sweet disposition)
  115
Suestrunk (sweet drink,
  taverner) 106
Suetterlin 55, see Suter
Sugarman 153, Sugerman, see
  Zuckerman
Suhr (sour) 115
Sukop (sow head) 114
Sulander, Sulender (southerner)
  85
Sulhe, see Suehle
Sultan, see Soldan

Sultzbach, Sulzbacher,
  Sultzbaugh 159, Sulsbach
  (swampy brook) 80, 77, 122
Sultzbach, Sultzbaugh 159 (salt
  lick brook) 77
Sulz, Suls 159 (salt lick, salt
  worker) 96
Sulzenbach, see Sultzbach
Sulzenbach, see Sultzenbach
Sulzer, Sulser 159, Sulzmann
  (maker of jellied meat) 96
Summer, Summers (sumpter) 96
Sumwald 159, Sumwalt, see
  Zumwald
Sundberg (southern mountain)
  85, 68
Sunder, see Suende
Sundermann (southerner) 85
Sundheim (south hamlet) 85,
  123, 122
Sundmacher (healer) 96
Sundstrom, Sunstrom (southern
  river) 85, 77
Sunschein 159, see Sonnenschein
Surbaugh 159, see Sauerbach
Surland 159, see Sauerland
Suskind, Sussman, see
  Suesskind, Suessman
Suss, see Suess
Susstrunk, Susztrunk (sweet
  drink, taverner) 96
Suswein (sweet wine) 106, 112
Suter, Sutor, Sutter (shoemaker,
  fr Latin *sutor*) 104
Sutorius (latinization of *sutor*)
  141
Sutter (swamp) 80, see also Suter
Sutterlin 55 (little shoemaker)
  104
Sutterlin 55 (little swamp) 80
Sw ..., see under Schw ... 43.
  Only a sample given here.
Swab, see Schwab
Swaggert 159, see Schweiger
Swanger 159, see Schwanger

Swank 159, see Schwank
Swantner 159, see Schwander
Swantz 159, see Schwantz
Swapp 159, see Schwalb, Swab
Swarthout (dark skin) 114
Swarts 159, Swartz, see
    Schwartz
Swartsback 159, Swarzbaugh
    159, see Schwartzbach
Swarzwelder 159, see
    Schwartzwaelder
Swauger 159, see Schwager
Swearer 153, see Schwoerer
Sweetman 153, see Suessman
Sweetser 159, see Schwytzer,
    Schweitzer
Swegler, see Schwegler
Swek 159, see Zweck
Sweiger 159, Sweigert 74,
    Sweigart, see Schweiger
Sweitzer 159, see Schweitzer
Swerdlin 159, 55, see
    Schwertlein
Swiger 159, Swigger, Swiggert
    74, see Schweiger
Swindel 159, Swindle 159,
    Swindler, Swindell, Swindall
    159 (swindle, swindler) 151
Swinehart 159 < Schweinhart
    (strong as a wild boar) 48
Swinghammer (Swing the
    hammer!, blacksmith) 96
Switzer 159, Swietser, Switzer,
    see Schweitzer
Swob 159, Swope, Swoope,
    Swopes 164, see Schwab
Swonk, see Schwank
Swyger 159, Swygert 74, see
    Schweiger
Sybel, Seybold < Siegbold
Sybert, see Siegbert
Syder 159, Sydnor, see Seider,
    Seidner
Syfrett, Syford 159, see Siegfried
Sygrist, see Sigrist

Syler 159, see Seiler
Sylvester 159, see Silvester
Symon, see Simon
Synder 159, see Suender

T

Tabb, Taber, Tabbert < Dietbert
    (people + famous) 46, 47
Taeger (day laborer) 96
Taenzer, Tenzler, see Tants
Taescher (purse maker) 96
Taeuber, Teubert 74, see Teuber
Tafel (table) 118
Taffner (fr Taffingen, marsh
    village) 80, 122
Tafner (panel maker, painter) 96
Tag, Tage, Tagg (day) 118
Taich, see Teich
Tallebach, Telebach (muddy
    brook) 80, 77
Tanbusch (forest bush) 89, 72
Tanhauser (forest house, fir
    house) 89, 65
Tanhof, see Tannhoeffer
Tanne (fir tree) 89
Tannebaum, Tannenbaum (fir
    tree) 89
Tannenberg, Tannenberger (fr
    Tannenberg 122, fir mountain)
    89, 65
Tannenzapf (pine cone) 89
Tanner (dweller among the firs)
    89
Tannhauser, see Tanhauser
Tannhoeffer (fr Tanhof 122, farm
    among the firs, forest farm)
    89, 92
Tants 159, Tantz, Tantzer,
    Tanzer (dance, dancer) 96
Tapfer (brave) 115
Tapp, Tapper (tap maker,
    taverner) 96, 106
Tappert (wearers or makers of
    long coats, fr Latin *tabardum*)
    106

Tarnkappe (invisible cloak) 118

Tasch, Tascher, Taschner, see Taescher

Tatelbaum, Dattelbaum (date tree) 62, 89

Tau (dew) 118

Taub, Taube, Tauber (deaf, deaf man) 114

Taub, Taube (dove, pigeon) 115

Taubemann (dove keeper) 96

Taubenfeld (dove field) 84

Taubenheim (dove hamlet) 123

Taubenslag 159 (dove cote, dove keeper) 96

Tauber, Taubert 74, Taubermann (cock pigeon, pigeon raiser or seller) 105, 143

Tauber (name of river) 83

Taubner, Taubman, Taupmann, see Tauber

Tauchinbaugh 159 (Jump in the brook!) 116, 77

Tauhauer (hawser maker) 100

Tauler (dove raiser) 96

Tausch (barter, trickster) 118

Tausendschoen (thousand beautiful [thanks]) 117

Taxler (badger hunter) 91

Taylor 153, see Schneider

Teagle 159, see Tiegel

Teale 159, see Thiel

Tederick < Dietrich

Teel 159, see Thiel

Teeter 159, see Dieter

Teets 159, see Dietz

Tegler, Tegele (tyler, brickmaker, fr Latin *tegula*) 96

Teich, Teichner, Teichler, Teichman (pond, dweller by a pond) 82, 122

Teich (dough, baker's helper) 96

Teichgraeber (pond digger, ditch digger) 82, 96

Teichholtz (forest by a pond or dike) 82, 72

Teichmann (fish farmer) 91

Teichmueller, Teichmoeller (miller on the pond) 82, 103

Teitelbaum, see Dattelbaum

Teitz 159, see Dietz

Telebach, see Tallebach

Telge (branch, small bush) 89

Teller, Tellermann, Tellert 74 (dish, dishmaker, fr Latin *talea*) 106

Tempel, Tempelman (temple, synagogue) 118

Tenberg, Tennenberg, Tennenbaum, see Tanberg, Tannenberg, Tannenbaum

Tenberg, Tenberge, see Zumberg

Tenkler, see Dengler

Tenner, see Danner

Tenser 159, see Tants

Teobald 159, see Theobald

Tepel 53, Teppel < Theobald

Tepper, Tepperman (potter) 96

Terkeltaub 159, see Tuerkeltaub

Terkuhle (at the pool) 70, 81

Termoehlen (at the mill) 69, 103

Terr, see Duerr

Tesch 159, Tesche, see Taescher

Tessiner, Tesener (fr the Tessin in Switzerland) 121

Tessler, see Tischler

Tester 159, Testor, see Textor

Teubel, see Teufel

Teuber, Teubler, Teubner, see Tauber

Teufel, Teufell (devil) 131

Teufelbiss (the devil's bite) 131

Teufer (baptist) 110

Teutsch, see Deutsch

Textor, Textur (Latin for Weber) 141

Thal (valley) 76, 122

Thalacker (valley field) 76, 84

Thalberg, Thalberger (valley mountain) 76, 68

Thaler (coin from Joachimsthal) 117

Thaler (valley dweller) 76

Thalheim (valley hamlet) 76, 123

Thalhofer (valley farm) 76, 92

Thalmann (valley man) 76, 94

Thalmueller (valley miller) 76, 103

Thanhouser 159, see Tannhauser

Thankappan 159, see Tarnkappe

Thede < Dietrich 53

Theil (part) 118

Theis 53, Theiss 6, Theissen < Matthias

Theobald, Thebald < Dietbald (folk + bold) 46, 46

Theodor (Greek, gift of God) 143

Theologus (Latin, theologian) 141

Therman 159, see Thurmann

Theuerkauf (expensive purchase) 118

Theus 53 < Matthaeus or Timothaeus

Thiel 53, Thiele, Thielemann, Thielman < Dietrich

Thieman, see Dietman

Thiemer < Dietmar

Thier (animal) 118

Thierfelder 122 (animal field) 84, 122

Thiergarten (zoo, animal park), 84, 122

Thies, Thiess 53, Thiesse, Thiessen 122 < Matthias

Thiessenhusen (Mathew's houses) 65

Thilo 53 < Dietrich

Thiringer, Thieringer, see Thueringer

Thirry 159, see Dietrich

Thoene 53 < Antonius

Tholde 53 < Berthold

Thom 53, Thoma, Thome < Thomas

Thomas, Tomas (St. Thomas) 135

Thomburn (at the spring) 69, 79

Tommen, see Thomas

Thomsen (son of Thomas) 59

Thon (clay, potter) 96

Thon 55, Thons 59, Thonis, Thonges < St. Anthonius 135

Thor (door) 118

Thorbruggen, see Zurbrueck

Thormann (gate keeper) 96

Thorwart (door keeper) 96

Thron 122, Throne (throne)

Thueringer (Thuringian) 120

Thuermann (door man) 96

Thurm (tower, fr Latin *turris*) 118

Thurmherr (lord of the tower) 109

Thurneck (tower field) 85

Thussing, see Tussing

Thyssen 53 < Matthias

Tibbet < Theobald, Dietbald

Tice 159, see Theiss

Tidbal, see Dietbald

Tiebendorf, see Tiefendorf

Tiebinger, see Tuebingen

Tiede 53, Tiedebohl, Tiedeman 94, Tiedemann, Tidemann < Dietbald

Tiefel, see Teufel

Tiefenbach, Tieffenbach (deep brook) 77

Tiefendorf, Tiebenderf 159 (deep village) 124

Tiefenwerth, Tieffenwert, Tiefenworth (deep river island) 79

Tieffenbrunn (deep well) 79

Tiegel (saucepan, crucible, fr Latin *tegula*) 106

Tiegler, see Ziegler

Tielmann 53, 94, Tilman, Tillman < Dietrich

Tieman, see Dietman

Tienken 53, 55, see Martin

Tier (animal) 118

Tierdorf (animal village) 124
Tiess 53 < Matthias
Tietjen 53 < Dietrich
Tietz 53, Tietzer, Tietzen <
  Diedrich
Tiffenderfer 159, Tiffendarfer, see
  Tiefendorf
Tigel, see Ziegel
Tilgen < St. Ilgen 135
Till, see Diehl
Tillich 53 < Dietrich
Tillinger, see Dillinger
Tillmann, see Tilgen
Tilly 53 < Dietrich
Tilo 53 < Dietrich
Timke (little Thimothaeus), 53,
  55
Timmer (timber, carpenter) 98,
  106
Timmerman, Timmermann,
  Timberman, see Zimmermann
Timothaeus, Thimothee (St.
  Timothy) 135
Tinnemann (dweller by a bog) 80
Tiringer, Thieringer, see
  Thueringer
Tischbein (joiner) 96
Tischer, Tischler, Tischner,
  Tischmann (cabinet maker, fr
  Latin *discus*) 106, 98
Tisher 159, see Tischler
Titus (Latin name) 141
Tobel, Tobler (wooded gorge) 122
Tobias (OT name) 135
Tochtermann (son-in-law) 119
Tod, Todt (death) 118
Tod, Todt (godfather) 119
Toellner (customs collector) 96
Toennies 53 < St. Anthonius
Toepfer, Toepfner (potter) 96
Toeplitz (Slavic place name) 146
Toericht (foolish) 115
Toerrenberger, see
  Duerrenberger
Togend, see Tugend

Tohr, see Thor
Tokayer (wine seller) 106, 96
Told 53, Tolde < Berthold
Toll, Tolle (mad) 115
Toll 53 < Berthold
Tollboom (custom's gate, toll
  collector) 109
Toller, Tollmann, Tolman, Tolner,
  Tollner (toll collector) 109
Toltzmann, Tolzman, see Tolde
Tombaugh 159 (at the brook) 69,
  77
Tomforde (at the ford) 70
Tonne, Tonnemacher (barrel,
  barrel maker) 96
Tonner, see Donner
Tonnewan (barrel, cooper) 106
Tontz 159, see Tantz
Toor, see Thor
Toothackers 159 < Todenacker
  (cemetery)
Topf (pot, potter) 96
Topfer (potter) 96
Topp (forelock, pigtail) 112
Topper (potter) 96
Torbeck (at the brook) 69, 77
Torfstecker (peat digger) 95
Torgler, Torkler, Torkel (wine
  presser, fr Latin *torculare*) 96
Tormoellen (at the mill) 69, 103
Torsch, see Dorsch
Tote, Toth (Death, in morality
  play) 111
Totenberg (swamp mountain) 80,
  68
Totenberg (godfather's mountain)
  119, 68
Toth, see Tod
Toth, Thote, Totman (godfather)
  119
Toubman 159, see Taubman
Towler 159, see Tauler
Trabant (fr Czech, infantryman)
  107
Traber, Trabert 74 (trotter) 118

Trache, see Drache

Trachsler, see Drechsler

Trachtehengst (packhorse, drayman) 106

Trachtenberg (funnel mountain, fr Latin *tractarius*) 68

Traffley 159, see Trefflich

Trager 159, Traeger (porter, carrier) 96

Tran (whale oil) 106

Tranck (drink, taverner) 96

Trapp (bumpkin) 115

Trapp (bustard) 115

Tratz, see Trotz 151

Traub (grape, vintner) 89, 96

Traugott (Trust God!) 116, 140

Traurig (sad) 115

Traut, Traud, Traudt, Trauth (dear) 48, 115

Trautmann (confidant) 48, 115

Trautwein (dear friend) 48, 48, 115

Trautwig (friend + battle) 48, 46

Traver, see Traber

Traver (dweller near the Trave) 83

Traxel, Traxler, see Drechsler

Trayer, see Dreier

Trefflich (Excellent!) 117

Trefouse 159, see Dreifuss

Treger, see Trager

Treibel (mallet, cooper) 106

Treiber (drover) 91

Treier, Treyer (from Trier)

Treitl, Treitel, see Treutel

Tremoehlen, see Termoehlen

Trepp, Treppe (stairs) 118

Trescher, Treschner, Treshman 159, see Drescher

Tresp (broom plant) 89

Tressler, see Drechsler

Tretler (treader or treadmill) 118

Treu (loyal) 119

Treulieb (loyal and dear) 119

Treumann (loyal man) 119

Treut, Treuth (confidant) 119

Treutel, Treuttle (sweetheart) 48, 119

Treutlen, see Treutel 25

Trew 159, see Treu

Trexler 159, see Drechsler

Trieber (driver) 96

Triesler, see Drechsler

Trimbach (place name) 122

Trinkauf (Drink up!) 116

Trinkaus (Drink up!) 116

Trinker (drinker) 115

Trinkhaus, Trinkaus (tavern) 96

Tritt (step) 118

Trockenbrod, see Truckenbrodt

Trockenmiller (dry miller) 103

Troeger, see Trager

Troester (draff) 118

Troester (comforter) 115

Troll (goblin) 118

Trommer, Trommler (drummer) 96

Trompeter, Trumpeter (trumpeter) 96

Trootman 159, see Trautmann

Tropf (drop, simple person) 115

Tross (pack train) 107

Trost, Trostl 55, Trostle 159 (helper, comfort) 115

Trott, Trotter, Trottman (wine presser) 96

Trotz (defiance) 115

Troum 159 (dream) 118

Trout 159, see Traut

Troutman 159, see Trautmann

Troxel 159, Troxell, Troxler, see Drechsler

Troy 159, see Treu

Truckenberg (dry mountain) 68

Truckenbrodt (dry bread, baker) 96

Truckenmiller, see Trockenmiller

True 153, see Treu

Trueb (sorrowful) 115

Truhe (chest, trunk) 106

Truman 159, Trueman, see
Treumann
Truman (drummer) 96
Trumbauer, Trumbower 159
(farmer at the end of the field)
91
Trumm (end of field) 84
Trump, Trumph (trump,
drummer) 96
Trumpeter, see Trompeter
Trunk (drink, drunkard) 115
Trupp (troop) 107
Trutmann, see Trautmann
Tsahn 159, see Zahn
Tschantz, see Schantze
Tschudi (judge) 109
Tschudi (foolish, tense person)
115
Tsvetshen 159, see Zwetschen
Tuch, Tuchman, Tuchmann,
Tucher, Tuchner (mercer) 105
Tuchmantel (cloth coat, tailor) 96
Tuchscherer (cloth shearer) 96
Tuebingen (German city)
Tuefel 159, see Teufel
Tuerenberger, see Duerrenberger
Tuerk (Turk, one who has fought
the Turks) 107
Tuerkeltaub (turtledove) 115
Tuerner (tower keeper, fr Latin
turris) 109
Tullius (Latin name) 141
Tulman, Tulner, see Tollman,
Tollner
Tulp (tulip) 89
Tunkel, see Dunkel
Turban 53 < St. Urbanus 135
Turc, Turk, Turkman, see Tuerk
Turinger, Thurringer, see
Thueringer
Turkeltaub, see Tuerkeltaub
Turman, see Thuermann
Turn, see Thurm
Turnau (tower meadow) 84
Turnbach (tower brook) 77

Turnbaugh 159, Turnbough, see
Turnbach 151
Turner (tower keeper) 109
Turnipseed 153, see Ruebsamen
Tussing (French, Toussaints) 144
Tutweiler, see Dutweiler
Tyce 159, see Theiss
Tyll, see Diehl
Tysen 159, Tyssen, Tyson, see
Theissen

U

Uberhoff (upper farm) 69, 92
Uebel (evil, irascible obstinate
person) 115
Uebelmann (wicked man) 115
Ueber (over) 118
Ueberall (everywhere,
ubiquitous) 115
Ueberholtz (upper forest, beyond
the forest) 69, 72
Ueberroth (upper clearing,
beyond the clearing) 69, 126
Uebersax (beyond Saxony, Upper
Saxony) 121
Ueberwasser (beyond the water)
83
Uehlein 55 (little owl) 115
Ufer, Uffer, Ufermann, Ufner
(dweller on the shore)
Uhl, Uhle, Uhll (owl) 115, see
Ulrich
Uhland < Udalnand (wealth +
courage, lancer) 107
Uhlefelder, Uhlfelder (swamp
field) 80, 84
Uhlenbeck (swamp brook) 80, 77
Uhlenberg (swamp mountain) 80,
68
Uhlenkamp (swampy field) 84
Uhler, see Aulmann
Uhlfelder (swampy field) 84
Uhlich 53, Uhlig, Uhlik, Ulich,
Uly < Ulrich

Uhlmann, Ullmann (dweller near the elms) 89

Uhlshafer (swamp farm) 89, 84

Uhrich, Urich, see Ulrich

Uhrmacher (clock maker) 96

Ulbrich < Uodalbrecht (inheritance + bright) 46, 47

Ulbright 159, see Ulbrich

Uli 53 < Ulrich

Ullman 53, 55, Ullmann, see Ulrich

Ulm, Ulmer (dweller by the elms) 89

Ulm, Ulmer (inhabitant of Ulm) 122

Ulrich, Ullrich, Ulrik (inherited property + rule) 47, 46, 54

Umbach 159, see Ambach

Umbaugh 159, see Umbach

Umberger 159, see Amberger

Umbreit 159, Umbright (unwilling, incapable) 115

Umholtz 159 (at the forest) 69, 72

Umstad 159, Umstead < Amstad (at the landing) 71

Unangst 159, see Ohnangst

Unbescheiden (indiscrete, unknowledgeable) 115

Unbewusst (unconscious) 115

Unclebach 159, see Unkelbach

Underberg, see Unterberg

Underkoffler, Underkofler, Underkaufer (middleman), see Unterkofler

Underweg (underway) 118

Unfried (disturber of the peace) 115

Unfug (mischief, impropriety) 115

Ungeheuer (monster) 115

Ungemach (inconvenient, unpleasant) 115

Ungenade (merciless) 115

Ungenannt (unnamed, nameless) 115

Unger, Ungerer (Hungarian) 121

Ungerleider, see Hungerleide

Ungethum (monster) 115

Ungewitter (storm) 115

Unglaub (disbeliever) 115

Unkel, Unkle (toad) 115

Unkelbach (toad brook) 77, 122

Unkenholz (toad forest) 72

Unmut (anger, discontent) 115

Unold, Unhold (monster, fiend) 115

Unrat, Unrath (rubbish) 118

Unrau, see Unruh

Unruh (disquiet) 115

Unselt, Unseldt, Unsoeld, Unsoelt (tallow dealer) 105

Unsinn (nonsense) 115

Unstruth (swamp on the One) 83, 79

Unterberg, Unterberger (below the mountain) 68, 122

Unterdenerd (under the earth) 69

Unterkofler (lower monticule) 67

Unterwalden (among the forests, below the forests) 69, 71, 122

Unterweger (the lower path) 65

Unverferth (unafraid) 115

Unversagt, Unferzagt 159, Unverzogt (undaunted) 115

Uphoff (on the farm) 69, 92

Upperman, see Obermann

Upperman, see Obmann

Upright 159, see Obrecht

Urbach 122, see Auerbach

Urban (St. Urbanus, name of several popes) 134

Urich, Urick, see Ulrich

Urlaub (leave) 118

Urman, Urmann, see Uhrman

Utermohle, see Ausdermuehle

Utli 53, 55, Utley < Ulrich

Utterbach, Utterbaugh 159, see Otterbach

Uts 53, Utz, Utze < Ulrich

V

Vogelhut (bird hat) 112
Vogelhut (bird watch) 118
Vogelius (latinized Vogel) 141
Vogelmann (fowler) 115
Vogelpohl (bird pool) 80, 122
Vogelsang, see Vogelgesang
Vogelstein (bird mountain) 68
Vogler (fowler) 91
Vogt, Vogts 164, Voegt, Voigt, Voight 159, Vogtmann (governor, fr Latin *advocatus*) 109
Volbrecht, see Volkbrecht
Volk, Volck, Volcks 164 (nation, folk) 46
Volkbrecht, Vollbrecht (folk + illustrious) 46, 47
Volkel 55, Voelkel < Volkmar
Volkenstein 159, see Wolkenstein
Volker, Volcker, Volkert 74, Volkner (people + army) 46, 46
Volkhart, Volkert (folk + strong) 46, 46
Volkmann (people + man) 46, 94
Volkmar, Volkmer (people + famous) 46, 47
Volkwein (folk + friend) 46, 48
Voll, Volle, Voller, Vollers 164 (full) 118
Vollbert, Vollbrecht, see Volkbrecht
Vollenweide, Vollenweider, see Fuellenweide
Voller, see Volkhard
Vollmer, Volmer, Volmar, see Volkmar
Vollmerhausen (Volkmar's houses) 65
Vollprecht, Volpert, see Volkbrecht
Vollrat, Volrath < Folkrat (folk + counsel) 46, 47
Voltz, Volz, see Foltz
Vom Berg (fr the mountain) 69, 70, 68

Vom Hoff (fr the court) 69, 92
(In seeking a name preceded by *von*, look under the base name. Von Hagen appears under Hagen.)
Von Aesch, von Esch (from the ash trees)
Von Berg (fr the mountain) 69, 70, 68
Von Burg (fr the castle) 69, 70, 73
Von Busch (fr the bush), see Busch 69, 70, 72
Vonderheid, Vonderheide (from the heath) 69, 70, 84
Vonderhorst (fr the hurst) 69, 70, 72
Von der Lind (fr the linden) 69, 70, 89
Vonderschmidt (fr the smithy) 69, 70, 96
Von der Weyt (fr the meadow) 69, 70, 84
Vonhagen (fr the enclosure) 69, 70, 123
Vonhoff (fr the farm) 69, 70, 92
Vonholt (fr the forest) 69, 70, 72
Vonniederhauser, Von Niederhaeuser (fr the lower houses) 69, 70, 65
Von Paris (Parisian, journeyman who trained in Paris) 69, 70
Vonwald (fr the forest) 69, 70, 71
Vorberge, Vordemberge (before the mountain, piedmont) 69, 70, 68
Vorderbruggen (before the bridge) 70, 71
Vorgang (process, proceedings) 118
Vorhenne (trout) 115
Vorhoff (atrium, before the farm) 69, 70, 92, 122
Vorkamp (before the field) 69, 70, 84

Vorkauf (speculation) 118
Vorm Walt (in front of the forest) 69, 71
Vorman, see Fuhrmann
Vorn Holt (before the forest) 69, 71
Vornfeld (before the field) 69, 84
Vorspann (added team of horses) 118
Vosburg, Vosburgh (fox castle) 73
Voss (fox) 115
Vossberg (fox mountain) 68
Vosse 53 < Volkmar
Vosshage (fox enclosure) 123, 122
Vossloh (fox forest) 71, 72
Vought 159, see Vogt
Vrees, see Vries
Vries (Frisian) 121
Vroman, see Fromann
Vulkner, see Volkner
Vulpius (Latin for fox) 115, 141

W

Waag, Waage (scales) 106, see Wage
Waber, Waeber, see Weber
Wache (watch) 107
Wachenhut (sentry, guard) 96
Wachenschutz (guard) 107
Wachholtz (boggy woods) 81, 72
Wachs, Wax, Wachsmann (wax dealer) 105
Wachsmuth (bright mind) 115
Wacht, Wachter, Wachtman, Wachterman (watchman) 96
Wachtel (quail) 115
Wachter, see Waechter
Wacker (brave, watchful) 115
Wadsack, see Watsack
Waeber, see Weber
Waechter, Wachter (watchman) 96
Waeger, Waegermann (official weigher) 109

Waesche (washing, bleaching) 106
Waffenschmidt (armorer) 108
Waffler, Wafler, Waffelaer (armorer) 108
Wage (scales) 106
Wageman (official weigher) 109
Wagener, see Wagner
Wagenfuehr (carter) 96
Wagenheim (marsh hamlet) 123
Wagenhorst (marshy hurst) 80, 72, 122
Wagenknecht (carter's helper) 96
Wagenmann (wainwright) 96
Wagenseil (wagon rope, carter) 106
Waggener, Waggner, Waggoner 159, see Wagner
Wagner, Wagener, Waagner, Wagenaar (wainright) 96
Wagschal (scale, official weigher) 109
Wahl, Wahle, Wall, Waal (choice) 118
Wahlberg (marsh mountain) 80, 68
Wahlenfeld (marsh field) 80, 84
Wahrheit (truth, informant, guarantor) 115
Wahrlich (honest) 115, 117
Waibel, see Weibel
Waiblinger (fr Waibling) 122
Waid 122, Waidner, see Weid, Weidner
Waidmann, Waitmann, see Weidmann
Wain, Wainberg, Wainstock, see Wein, Weinberg, Weinstock
Wais, Waisman, see Weis, Weissmann
Waitz, see Weitzen
Waitzbauer, see Weitzbauer
Waitzenegger (wheat field) 80
Wajbel, see Weible
Wajer, see Weiher

Waker, see Wacker

Waksmann, see Wachsmann

Walbach, Walbeck (swamp brook) 80, 77

Walbaum (walnut tree) 89

Walber, Walberd, Walbert, Walbrecht (battlefield + bright) 46, 47

Walbrecher (wall breaker) 118

Walburg (battlefield + protection) 46, 47, see also Waldburg

Walch, Walcher (foreigner, non-German) 145

Walchensee (foreigners' lake) 145, 80

Walcker, see Walker

Wald, Waldt, Walde, Walt (forest) 71, or < Oswald or Walther

Waldbauer (forest farmer) 71, 91, 94

Waldbaum (walnut tree) 72, 89

Waldberg (forest mountain) 71, 68

Waldbrand (forest clearing) 71, 126

Waldburg, Waldburger (fr Waldburg 122, forest castle) 71, 73

Waldeck, Waldecker (fr Waldeck 122, forest place, German province) 71, 85

Walden (forests) 71

Waldenberger (forest mountain) 71, 68

Walder (forest dweller) 71

Waldhauer (wood cutter) 96

Waldhaus, Waldhausen, Waldhauser (fr Waldhausen 122, forest houses) 71, 65

Waldheuer, Waldheyer (wood chopper) 96

Waldhorn (French horn) 106

Waldhuber (farmer in the forest)

Waldhutter (forest guard) 96, 109

Waldhutter (forest cotter) 71

Waldkirch (forest church) 71

Waldkoenig (forest king, a bird) 118

Waldman, Waldmann, Waldner (forest dweller, forester) 71

Waldmann (giant, house name) 63

Waldmeier, Waldmayer (forest farmer, fr the Waldhof) 71, 93, 94

Waldmueller (forest miller) 71, 103

Waldo < Waldau (forest meadow) 72, 84

Waldorf, Waldrop (forest village) 71, 124

Waldschmidt, Waldschmitt (forest smith, one who smelts his own ore) 71, 96

Waldsee (forest lake) 71, 80

Waldspecht (forest jay) 115

Waldt, see Wald

Waldvogel (forest bird, carefree person) 71, 115

Walheim (swamp hamlet) 80, 123

Walk, Walker, Walkeman (fuller) 96

Wall (rampart, fr Latin *vallum*) 101

Wallach (gelding) 91

Wallenborn (marsh spring) 80, 79

Wallendorf (marsh village) 80, 124

Wallenhorst (marsh hurst) 80, 72

Wallenser (Waldensian, fr Wallensen) 122

Wallenstein (fortified mountain) 73

Wallenstein (foreigners' mountain) 145, 73

Waller, Wallner (pilgrim) 118

Wallerstein (pilgrims' mountain) 73

Walliser (Swiss fr Valais) 145, 121

Wallner (forest warden) 71, 109
Wallrodt (marsh clearing) 80, 126
Walpert (battlefield + brilliant) 46, 47
Walrath, Walrot, see Wallrodt
Walrath (battlefield + counsel) 46, 47
Walsch (Romanic) 145
Walser, see Walliser
Walstein, see Wallenstein
Walt, see Wald
Waltaich (fr Waldteich, forest pond) 71, 80
Walter, Walters 164, see Walther
Walther, Walthers 164 (rule + army) 46
Waltmann, see Waldmann
Waltmeyer, Waltimyer 159, Waltemire 159 see Waldmeyer
Walts, Waltz, Walz, Waltze 122, Waltzer, Walzer (roll, roller), or < Walther
Wambach, Wambaugh 159 (marsh brook) 80, 77
Wambold (hope + bold) 46, 122
Wamp (belly) 114
Wamser, Wambescher (jerkin maker) 96
Wanamaker 159, see Wannamacher
Wand (cliff, bluff) 68
Wandel (Vandal) 121
Wandel (change) 115
Wanderer (wanderer) 115
Wandschneider (clothier, mercer) 96, 105
Wangenheim (sloping hamlet) 123
Wanger (fr Wangen, damp sloping meadow) 71, 122
Wankel (fickle) 115
Wankmueller (miller off the beaten path) 103
Wann, Wanne (vat, vat maker) 96

Wannamacher, Wannemacher, Wannermacher, Wannamaker 159 (winnowing basket maker, vat maker, fr Latin *vannus*) 96
Wanner (tub maker) 96
Wantz (bedbug) 118
Wapner, see Waffner
Wapp, Wappe, Wappner (weapon, armorer) 108
Wappaus (armory) 108, 65
Wardmann (watchman) 96
Warfel 159, see Wuerfel
Warkmeister, see Werkmeister
Warm (warm) 118
Warmbier (warm beer, brewer) 92, 112
Warmkessel (warm kettle, cook) 106
Warmuth, see Wermuth
Warner (warner) 47
Warnke 53, 55, Warnecke, Warneche, Warnek, Warneke < Wernher
Warnold (guard + loyal) 47, 48
Warschauer, Warshauer 159 (fr Warsaw) 122
Wartburg, Wartenburg, Wartz (lookout, castle) 47, 73
Warth, Warthmann, Wartmann, Wartz, Wartzmann 74 (lookout) 47
Wasch, see Weschler
Waschbaugh 159, Washabaugh, see Weschebach
Wascher, see Wescher
Waschke < Slavic: Vadislav 146
Waschnicht (Don't wash!) 116
Wasmut, see Wachsmut
Wasp (wasp, annoying person) 115
Wasser (water) 118
Wasserbach (water brook) 77
Wasserkrug (water jug) 106

Wasserman, Wassermann
(waterman, water carrier) 96,
also Aquarius 143
Wasserstrom (water stream) 79
Wassertraeger (water carrier) 96
Wasserzieher (bath attendant) 96
Waterman 153, see Wassermann
Watsack (clothes bag) 106
Watte (wadding, padding) 118
Wattenbach (swamp stream) 80,
77
Wattenberg (swamp mountain)
68
Waughtel 159, see Wachtel
Waxler 159, see Wechsler
Waxmann, Wassmann, see
Wachs, Wachsman
Waydmann, see Weitmann
Wayer, see Weiher, Weyer
Weabel 159, see Webel, Weibel
Weaber 159, Weaver 153, see
Weber
Wease 159, see Wiese
Weatherholtz, see Wedeholz
Weaver, see Weber
Webel (sergeant) 107, see Weibel
Weber, Webert 74, Webber 159,
Webner, Webling (weaver) 96
Wechsler (money changer) 96
Weck, Wecker, Weckerle 55,
Weckler, Weckerli, Weckerlin,
Weckerling (baker or seller of
rolls) 96
Weckesser (roll eater) 112, 115
Wecter 159, see Waechter
Wedeholz (forest wood) 72
Wedekind (forest child) 72
Wedel, Weddel (whisk) 106, 122
Wedemann, Wedemeyer,
Wedemayer (forest dweller,
forest farmer) 72, 93
Weeber, see Weber
Weelhalm, see Wilhelm
Weesenbeck 159, see Wiesenbach
Weesner 159, see Wiesner

Wefer, see Weber
Weg, Wege (way) 65, 122
Wegand, see Weigand
Wegbrot (viaticum, traveler) 118
Wegel, see Wagner
Wegener, Wegner, see Wagner
Weger, Wegerlein 55 (weigher)
109
Wegmann (dweller on a roadway)
65
Wegner, see Wagner
Wegstein (guide post) 65, 73
Weh, Wehe (woe, pain) 117
Wehmeyer, see Weidemeyer
Wehn 53, Wehner < Werner 122
Wehner, Wehnert 74, see Wagner
Wehr, Wehrs 164 (defense) 118
Wehrhan (weather vane) 118
Wehrli 53, Wehrle 55, Wehrly
159 < Werner
Wehrmann (defender) 108
Wehrstedt (fortified place)
Weibel, Weible 159 (village
authority) 109, 107
Weich (soft) 115
Weichbrot (soft bread, baker) 96
Weichert < Wighard (battle +
brave) 46, 46
Weichseldorf (Vistula village) 83,
123
Weichseler (fr the Vistula) 83, see
Wechsler
Weicker, Weickert, see Weichert
Weid, Weit, Weidt, Weide
(pasture) 84
Weidebach (brook through
meadow or willows) 84, 77
Weidemueller (miller on the
meadow) 84, 103
Weidemann, Weidemeyer
(meadow man) 84, see also
Weidmann
Weidenauer (fr Weidenau 122,
pasture meadow) 84, 84

Weidenbacher (fr Weidenbach
122, meadow brook) 84, 77

Weidenbaum (willow tree) 89

Weidenfeld (willow field) 89, 84

Weidenhammer, Weidenhamer (fr
the willow hamlet) 89, 123

Weidenhaus (meadow house,
house in the willows) 84, 89,
65

Weidenhoefer (fr the Weidenhoff,
willow farm, pasture farm) 89,
92

Weidenmeyer (pasture farmer)
84, 93

Weidenmueller (miller at the
willows, at the pasture) 89,
103

Weiderholt 159, see Wiederholt

Weidmann, Wideman 159
(hunter) 91

Weidner (hunter) 91

Weier, see Weiher

Weierbach (fish pond brook) 77

Weiermiller (fish pond miller) 77,
103

Weigand, Weygant (warrior) 107

Weigel, Weigels 164, Weigelt 74,
Weigle 159 < Weigand

Weigert, see Weichert

Weihaus, see Weinhaus 102, 65

Weiher (fish pond, fr Latin
vivarium) 101

Weiherbach (fish pond stream) 77

Weihermann (dweller at a fish
pond) 101

Weihnacht (Christmas, day of
birth or of service obligation)
143

Weihrauch (incense) 106

Weikert, see Weichert

Weil, Weile, Weill (village, fr
Latin *villa*) 127, 148

Weiland, see Wieland

Weilbach (village brook) 127, 77

Weiler, Weilert 74 (inhabitant of
a villa) 127

Weiman, see Weinmann

Weimar, Weimer, Weimert 74 (fr
Weimar 122, holy spring) 79

Weimaster 159, Weinmeister
(vintner) 96, 102

Wein, Wyn (wine, wine dealer)
102, 105

Weinacht, see Weihnacht

Weinbaum (wine tree, grape
vine) 89, 102

Weinberg (vineyard) 102, 68, 122

Weinberger (vintner) 102, 68

Weinblatt (grape leaf) 102, 89

Weinbold (friend + brave) 48, 46

Weinbrecht (friend + brilliant)
48, 47

Weinbrenner (brandy distiller)
102, 96

Weiner, Weiners 164, see Wagner

Weinfeld (vine field) 102, 84

Weinflasch (wine flask, bottle)
106

Weingard, Weingarden,
Weingart, Weingarten 122,
Weingartz 74 (vineyard) 102,
84

Weingartner, Weingaertner,
Weingertner, Weingartman
(vintner) 102

Weinglass (wine glass) 106

Weinhandl (wine dealer) 102, 105

Weinhard (friend + strong) 48, 46

Weinhauer (cartwright) 96

Weinhaus (tavern) 102, 65

Weinheimer (fr Weinheim 122,
swamp hamlet) 80, 102, 123

Weinholt, Weinhold (friend +
loyal) 48, 48

Weinhouse 153, see Weinhaus

Weininger (fr Weiningen) 122

Weinkauf, Weinkop (wine seller,
drink to confirm a sale) 102,
106

Weinknecht (vineyard worker) 96

Weinland (wine country) 102

Weinmann (wine merchant) 102, 106

Weinmueller (miller who serves wine) 102, 103

Weinreb (grape) 102

Weinreich, Weinrich (friend + rule) 68, 46

Weinschenk (taverner) 96

Weinstein (tartar in wine barrels, vintner) 96

Weinstock (grape vine) 102, 62

Weintraub, Weintrob (grape, wine dealer) 102, 62, 149

Weintraut (friend + dear) 48, 48

Weinzweig, Weintzweig (grapevine twig) 89

Weir, see Weiher

Weirauch, see Weihrauch

Weis, see Weiss

Weisaecker, Waisacker (white field) 84, 85

Weisbacher, Weissbacher, Weisbeck, Weissbecker (fr Weissbach 122, white brook) 77

Weisbeck, see Weissbeck

Weisberg (white mountain) 68

Weisborn, Weisborrn (white spring) 79

Weisbrod, Weisbord, see Weissbrot

Weise (wise) 115

Weiselberger 159, see Wieselberger

Weisenborn 159, see Wiesenborn

Weisenmiller, Weissmeller 159, see Weissmiller

Weiser (guide, wise man) 115

Weisfeld, Weisfeldt (white field) 84

Weisgarber, Weisgerber, see Weissgerber

Weisgrau (white grey) 112

Weishaar, see Weisshaar

Weishampel (white ram) 91

Weishart, see Weisshart

Weishaupt, Weisshaupt (blond, white hair) 112

Weisheit, see Weissheit

Weismantel, see Weissmantel

Weiss, Weisse, Weisser, Weissert 74, Weisz (white, blond) 112

Weissbach, Weissenbach (white brook) 77

Weissbart (white beard) 112

Weissbek, Weissbecker (baker of white bread) 96

Weissberg, Weissenberg, Weissberger (white mountain) 68

Weissbrot, Weissbrodt (white bread, baker) 106, 96

Weissburg (white castle) 73, 122

Weissenauer (white meadow) 84

Weissenbacher (white brook) 77

Weissenberger (fr Weissenberg 122, white mountain) 68

Weissenborn (white spring) 79, 122

Weissenburg (white castle) 73

Weissencamp (white field) 84

Weissenfeld (white field) 84

Weissenstein (white mountain) 68, 73

Weisser (whitewasher) 96

Weissgerber, Weissergerber (tanner of white leather) 97

Weisshaar (white hair, blond hair) 112

Weisshardt, Weisshart (white forest) 72

Weissheit (wisdom) 115

Weisskep (white cap, miller, baker) 96

Weisskirch (white church) 71

Weisskittel (white smock, miller, baker) 96

Weisskopf (white head, blond
  head) 112
Weissman, Weissmann (white
  man, white-haired man) 112
Weissmantel, Weissmantle 159
  (white cloak) 106
Weissmueller, Weissmiller,
  Weissmeller 159 (miller of
  white flour) 103, 162
Weissmut (wise disposition) 115
Weitekamp (wheatfield) 84
Weitenauer (fr Weitenau 122,
  broad mead) 84
Weitenfeld (broad field) 84
Weithenbach (broad brook) 77
Weitmann, see Weidmann
Weitz, Weitzman (wheat dealer)
  105
Weitzbauer (wheat farmer) 91
Weitzel, Weitzell, Weitsal 159
  (wheat seller) 106
Weitzen (wheat, wheat dealer)
  105
Weitzenfeld (wheat field) 84
Weitzenkorn (wheat grain, wheat
  dealer) 105
Weitzman, Weitzmann (wheat
  dealer) 105
Wejner, Wejnert 74, see Weiner,
  Weinert
Weksler 159, see Wechsler
Welck, Welk (faded, withered)
  115
Welcker, see Walker
Welder 159, see Schwarzwaelder
Welenbach (swampy brook) 80,
  77
Welhoeltzer (swampy forest) 80,
  72
Wellbrock (swamp brake) 80, 80
Welle, Wellen (well, faggot,
  faggot gather) 95
Welle (marshy ground) 80, 122
Wellemeyer (marsh farmer) 80,
  93

Weller, Wellner, Wellmann (clay
  or loam mason) 96
Wels, Welss (catfish) 115
Welsch, Wellisch, Welser, Welsh
  159, Welch 159 (Romanic) 145
Welschhan (turkey) 145
Welter, Weltner, Weltz (fr Welt
  122), see Walther
Weltmer (world sea, traveler) 118
Wemming (fr Wemmingen) 122
Wenberg, see Weinberg
Wendel, Wendl (Vandal, Wend)
  121
Wendelmuth (vacillating) 115
Wendelspiess (Turn the spit!,
  cook) 96
Wengel (little cheek) 115
Wenger 122, Wengert 74, see
  Wanger
Wenholt, see Weinholt
Wenig (few, small)
Weniger (fewer, less)
Wenner 53, Wennert 74 < Werner
Wenrich, see Weinreich
Wentz 53, Wentzel 55, Wenz,
  Wenzel, Wentzle 159 < Werner
Wentzke (little Werner) 54, 55,
  see Wentz
Weppler (armed soldier) 107
Weppner (armorer) 108
Werbel (legendary minstrel) 96
Werber (entrepreneur, recruiter)
  96, 109
Werdebaugh 159 (river island
  creek) 79, 77
Werdmann, see Wertmann
Werdmueller (miller on river
  island) 79, 103
Werele 53, 55, Werle, Werli,
  Werlin, Werlein < Werner
Werfel 159, see Wurfel
Werkman (craftsman, artisan) 96
Werkmeister (foreman) 96
Werley, see Wehrli
Wermuth (vermouth) 105

Wernegerode (swamp clearing) 80, 126, 122

Werner, Wernher, Warner (protection + army) 47, 46

Wernick, Wernicke, Wernecke < Werner 53, 54

Wernsdorfer (Werner's village) 124

Wert, Werth (island in river) 79

Werthamer, Wertheimer (German city, hamlet on river island) 79, 124

Werthmann (man of worth) 115

Wertmann, Werthmann (dweller on river island) 79

Wertmueller (miller on river island) 79, 103

Werts 159, see Wuertz, Wirtz

Wertsch, see Wirtsch

Wertz 159, see Wuertz

Wesbrot, see Weissbrot

Weschenbach (laundry creek) 77

Wescher, Weschler (fuller) 96

Wesenbach, 159, see Wiesenbach

Wess, Wessberg, see Weiss, Weissberg

Wessel 53 Wessels 164, Wessell < Werner

Wesselhof (Werner's farm) 92

Wessler, see Wescher, Wechsler

Wessner, 159, see Wiessner

West, see Wuest

Westbrock (west brake) 85, 72

Westenberg, see Westerberg

Westencamp (west field) 85, 84

Westdorf, Westendorf, Westendorfer (west village) 85, 124

Westenfeld, Westerfeld, Westerfield 152 (west field) 85, 84

Westerberg, Westerberger (western mountain) 85, 68

Westerheide (western heath) 85, 84

Westerkamp, Westkamp (west field) 85, 84

Westerlaken (western lakes) 85, 77

Westerman, Westermann (westerner) 85

Westermeyer (fr the Westerhof, western farm) 85, 84, 93

Westfal, Westfalen (fr Westphalia) 121, 85

Westhafer 159, Westheffer, see Westhoff

Westheim (western hamlet) 85, 123

Westhoff (west farm, now sometimes Westcourt in America) 85, 84

Westholt (west forest) 85, 71

Westinghouse 153 (house toward the west) 85, 65

Westkamp (west field) 85, 84

Westphal, Westphale, see Westfal

Westreich (western empire) 85

Wetstone 159 (whetstone) 106

Wetter (weather, river name meaning "swamp") 80, 83

Wetterau (meadow on the Wetter) 83, 84

Wettstein, see Wetzstein

Wetzel 53, 55, Wetzler < Werner

Wetzelberger (Werner's mountain) 68

Wetzikon (Werner's village) 127

Wetzler (knife grinder) 96

Wetzstein, Wettstein (whetstone, knife grinder) 73, 106

Wexler 159, see Wechsler

Wey ..., see Wei ...

Weyand, Weyandt, Weygant, see Weigand

Weydenhauer (willow cutter) 89, 95, 100

Weydenmeyer, see Weidemeyer

Weydmann, see Weidmann

Weydner, see Weidner

Weyer, Weyher, Weyerman, see
Weiher

Weyerhausen (house on fish
pond) 65

Weygand, Weygandt, Weygant,
see Weigand

Weygel, see Weigel

Weyhinger, see Vaihinger

Weyhkamp (holy field) 84

Weyl, see Weil

Weyland, see Weiland

Weyman, see Weinman

Weyrauch, Weyhrauch, see
Weihrauch

Weys, Weyss, see Weiss

Weytzel, see Weitzel

Whetsell 159, Whetsler, see
Wetzel

Whetstone 152, see Wetzstein

White 153, Whitey, see Witt,
Weiss

Whitebread 153, see Weissbrot

Whitehard 159, see Weishard

Whiteman 159, see Wittmann,
Weidmann

Whitescarver 159, see
Weissgerber

Whitesel 159, Whitesell,
Whytsell, see Weitzel

Whitman 159, see Widemann

Whitmoyer, see Weidemann 151

Wibel, see Weibel

Wice 159, see Weiss

Wichert 164, Wichart, Wichhardt
< Wighard (battle + strong)

Wichmann, see Wiechmann

Wicke (vetch, fr Latin *vicia*) 89

Wickenhoffer, Wickenhaffer
(vetch farm) 89, 92

Wickenmeyer (vetch farmer) 89,
103

Wicker, Wickert 74, see Wichert

Wickesser (vetch eater) 112

Wickheiser (vetch house) 89, 65,
66

Wickram (battle + raven) 46, 48

Wickwier (vetch pond) 89

Wickes 53 < Ludowicus

Widder (ram) 91, 62

Widderkind, see Wederkind

Wideman 159, Widman, see
Weidemann, Weidmann

Widemeyer 159, Widemayer,
Widmaier, see Weidemeyer

Widener 159, Widenor 159, see
Weidner

Widenhouse 153, see Weidenhaus

Widerholt 159, see Wiederholt

Widmann, Wideman 159, see
Wittmann, Weidmann

Widmer, see Wittmann

Widmeyer, see Weidemeyer

Widner 159, see Weidner

Wieboldt < Wicbald (battle +
brave) 46, 46

Wiechert < Wighard

Wiechmann < Wigman (battle +
man) 46, 94

Wied, Wiede (withe, willow tree)
89

Wiedbach (swamp brook) 80, 77

Wiedeck, Wiedecker (swamp
field) 80, 84

Wiedefeld (swamp field) 80, 84

Wiedeman, Wiedenmann (dweller
among the willows) 89, 94

Wiedenfeld 159, see Weidenfeld

Wiedenheft, Wiedenhoeft (willow
farm) 89, 92

Wiedenmeyer 159, see
Weidenmeyer

Wieder, see Widder

Wiederholt (repeated, opponent)
115

Wiederkehr (return) 118

Wiedersprecher (gainsayer) 115

Wiedkamp (pasture field) 84, 84

Wiedman, Wiedmann, see
Weidmann, Weidemann

Wiedmayer, Wiedmaier, see
  Weidemeyer
Wiedner < see Weidner
Wiedorfer (wine village) 102, 124
Wiedorfer (swamp village) 80,
  124
Wiegaertner, see Weingaertner
Wiegand, Wigand, see Weigand
Wiegard, Wieghard (battle +
  strong) 46, 46
Wieger, Wiegert 74, Wiegner
  (official weigher) 109
Wiegman, Wiegmann, Wiegner
  (weigher) 109
Wiehoff (willow farm, swamp
  farm) 89, 92
Wiel, Wiele (marsh) 80
Wieland (name of legendary
  smith) 96
Wieman, Wiemann, see
  Wiechmann
Wiemer, Wiemers 164 < Wigmar
  (war + famous) 46, 47
Wien, Wiener, Wieners 164,
  Wienert 74 (fr Vienna,
  Viennese) 122
Wienand < Wignand (battle +
  brave) 46, 46
Wiener, see Weiner
Wienhold, Wienholt, see Weinholt
Wienke 53, 55 < Wignand (battle
  + brave) 46
Wienkoop, see Weinkauf
Wieprecht < Wigbrecht (battle +
  brilliant) 46, 47
Wier 159, see Weyher
Wies, Wiese (meadow) 84
Wiesbaum (hay pole) 84, 89
Wiesel, Wieseltier (weasel) 115
Wieselberger (fr Wieselberg 122,
  weasel mountain) 68
Wiesenbacher (fr Wiesenbach
  122, meadow brook) 84, 77
Wiesenfeld (meadow field) 84, 84

Wiesenhoffer (meadow farm) 84,
  92
Wiesent, Wiesendt (bison) 115
Wiesenthal (meadow valley) 84,
  76, 122
Wiesenthal (bison valley) 115, 76
Wiesenthauer (bison meadow)
  115, 84
Wiesman, Wiesler, see Wiesner
Wiesner, Wiessner (dweller on
  the meadow) 84
Wiess, see Wiese, Weiss
Wiest (fr Wieste 122), see Wuest
Wigand, see Weigand
Wigener < Weigand
Wighard (battle + strong) 46, 46
Wightman 159, see Weidmann
Wigle 159, see Weigel
Wike 159, see Weich
Wikman, see Wiechmann,
  Wiegman
Wiland, see Wieland
Wilberger, see Wildberg
Wilbert (determination + bright)
  46, 47
Wilcke (little William) 53, 55
Wild, Wilde, Wilder (wild, game)
  115
Wildbach (wild brook) 77
Wildberg, Wiltberger,
  Wildenberger (wild mountain)
  68
Wildbrett, Wildprett (game,
  hunter) 96
Wilde (river name) 83
Wildeman, Wildemann (wild
  man) 115
Wildener, Wildner (poacher) 109
Wildenmut, Wildermuth (wild
  disposition) 115
Wilder, Wilderer (hunter,
  poacher) 91, 109
Wilderbach (wild stream) 77
Wildermuth (high spirits) 115

Wildfang, Wilfong 159 (tended forest, game, prey, tomboy) 115

Wildhauer, see Waldhauer

Wildhengst (wild stallion) 91

Wildheyt (wildness) 115

Wildhorn (hunting horn) 106

Wildner (poacher) 91, 109

Wildschuetz (hunter, poacher) 91, 109

Wildt (game, hunter) 91

Wile 159, see Weil

Wilfong, see Wildfang

Wilgar, Wilger (determination + spear) 46, 46

Wilhauer, see Wildhauer

Wilhelm, Wilhelms 164, Wilhelmus 141 (determination + helmet) 46, 46, 136

Wilhelmi (son of Wilhelm) 142

Wilhelmsen (son of Wilhelm) 59

Wilhide 159, Wilhite, Wilhoit, see Wildheyt

Wilk 53, Wilke 55, Wilkes 74, Wilkens, Wilkins, Wilkie, Willikin < Wilhelm

Will, Wille (will, determination) 46

Willbach (village brook), see Wildbach

Willem, Willems 164, Willemsen 59 < Wilhelm

Willheim (village hamlet) 123, 123

Willhide 159, Willhite, see Wilhide

Willich, Willig, Willik, Willing (willing) 115

Willikon (Wilhelm's hamlet) 127

Williram (will + raven) 46, 48

Willkom (Welcome!) 117

Willmann, Willmanns 164 (determination + man) 46, 94

Willmer, Willmers 164, Wilmer, Wilmers (determination + famous), 46, 47

Willner, see Wildner

Willoch 53 < Wilhelm

Willowby 159, see Wilderbach

Willpert (determination + bright) 46, 47

Wilmann, see Willmann

Wilner, see Wildner

Wilpers 164, see Wilbert

Wilt, see Wild

Wiltrout 159 < Wiltraut, Wiltrud (determination + beloved) 46, 48

Wimert 74, Wimmer, Wimmers 164, see Widmer

Wimmler (marsh dweller) 80

Win, Wine, see Wein

Winacker, Winecker (grape field, vineyard) 102, 84

Winberg, see Weinberg

Winblat, see Weinblatt

Winburger 159, see Weinberger

Winchel 55, 159, see Wuensch

Winckler, Winckelmann, see Winkler

Wind (wind) 118

Wind, Winde (hunting dog, greyhound) 91

Windemuth, Windermuth, see Wendelmuth

Winder, Winders, see Winter, Winters

Windesheim (wind hamlet) 123

Windfeld (wind field) 84

Windheim, see Windesheim

Windhoffer (windy farm) 92

Windhorst (wind hurst) 72

Windisch (Wendish, Slavic) 121, 146

Windmiller, Windmueller (windmiller, dweller by a windmill) 103

Windstein (wind mountain) 73

Winebarger 159, see Weinberger

Winebrener 159, Winebrenner, Wineburner, see Weinbrenner

Winecoff 159, see Weinkauf

Winegard 159, Winegeard, see Weingard

Wineholt 159, see Weinhold

Wineman 159, see Weinman

Winfelder, see Weinfeld

Winfelder 159, see Weinfelder

Winfurth (fr Weinfurth) 122

Winhart (friend + strong) 48, 46

Winholt (friend + loyal) 48, 48

Winkel (corner, angle, wooded valley) 69

Winkelbauer (farmer in a wooded valley) 69, 91

Winkelmeyer (farmer in wooded valley) 69, 93, or fr Winkel 122

Winkelstein (wooded mountain) 69, 73

Winkler, Winkelman, Winkelmann, Winklemann (corner storekeeper) 105

Winland, see Weinland

Winrich, see Weinreich

Winter, Winters 164 (winter)

Winter, see Wintzer

Winterberg (winter mountain) 68

Winterberg (vintners' mountain) 102, 68

Wintercorn (winter grain) 105

Winterheimer (winter hamlet) 118

Wintermantel (winter coat, coatmaker) 112, 106

Wintermeyer (vintner) 102, 93

Winterroth (winter clearing, vintner's clearing) 126

Winterstein (winter mountain) 73, 122

Winterstein (vintners' mountain) 102, 73

Wintner, Wintzer (vintner) 102

Wintsch 159, see Wuensch

Wintz, Winz, Winzer (vine dresser) 102

Winzell (tiny) 113

Wipbold, Wippel < Wigbald (battle + bold) 46, 46

Wipert, Wipprecht < Wigbert (battle + bright) 46, 47

Wirbel (whirl, vertebra) 118

Wireback 159, see Weiherbach

Wireman 159, see Weiherman

Wirt, Wirth (host, proprietor) 63, 96

Wirthlin 55 (little host) 96

Wirtsch < Wirt

Wirtz, Wuertz (spice) 106

Wisbrod, see Weissbrod

Wisch, Wischel (wiper) 96

Wise 159, see Wiese, Weiss

Wisebroad, see Weissbrot

Wiseburg 159, see Weissburg

Wisel, see Wiesel

Wiseman 159, see Weissmann

Wisenauer (dweller on a meadow) 84

Wisenbaker 159, see Wiesenbacher, Weissenbacher

Wishard, Wishart, see Weisshart

Wisman, Wismann, see Weissman

Wismar (place name) 122

Wismatt (white meadow) 84

Wisner, Wissner, see Wiessner

Wissant (bison, auerochs) 115

Wissel 53, Wissels 164 < Werner

Wissler, see Wechsler

Wist, Wister, Wistar, see Wuest, Wuester

Wisterfeld (abandoned field), see Wuest

Wisthoff (wilderness, uncultivated farm) 84

Withaar (white hair) 112

Witt, Witte (white) 112

Witenberger, see Wittenberg

Witkop, see Weisskopf

Witsel 159, see Witzel, Weitzel

Witt, Witte (white) 112

Wittbecker (fr Wittbeck 122, white brook, forest brook) 77

Wittbrod (white bread, baker) 92, 12

Wittcamp (white field) 84

Wittekind, see Wedekind

Wittenbach (white brook, or forest brook) 77, 122

Wittenberg (white mountain) 68, 122

Wittenmeyer, Wittemeyer 159, see Widmeyer

Wittfeld (white field) 84

Wittgerber, see Weissgerber

Witthauer (woodchopper) 95, 100

Witthof (forest farm) 72, 92

Witthuhn (white chicken, poultryman) 96

Witthuhn (grouse, forest hen) 91

Wittich, Wittig (legendary hero) 118

Wittkamp (white field) 84

Wittkopf (white head) 112

Wittmann, Wittmer (manager of church property) 110, 139, or see Weidmann

Wittmayer, Wittmayer, Wittmyer 159 (manager of glebe land) 93, 110, 139

Wittrock (white coat) 112

Wittstadt (white city) 122

Wittstein (white stone, white mountain) 73

Wittvogel (white bird, house name) 63

Wittwer (widower) 119

Witz, Witzig (wit, intelligence) 115, or < Witu, forest 72

Witzel 53, 55 < Ludwig, Wiegand

Witzthum (manager, fr Latin *vicedominus*) 109

Wizeman 159, see Weissmann

Wizenbaker 159, see Weissenbacher

Wocher, see Wucher

Wockenfuss (spindle leg) 114

Woeber, Wobner, Woebner see Weber

Woefel 55, Woefele, Woelffle (little wolf) 48, see Wolfhart

Woehrle, see Wehrl

Woehrmann (dweller on a dike) 81

Woellenweber, see Wollenweber

Woelpert (wolf + bright) 48, 47

Woelpert (rule + bright) 46, 47

Woerbel, see Werbel

Woerner, see Werner

Wohl (well-being) 115

Wohlfart, Wohlfahrt, Wohlfhard, Wohlfert (welfare) 115

Wohlfart, Wohlfahrt, Wohlfort < Wolfhart

Wohlfeil (inexpensive) 115, 105

Wohlgemut, Wohlgemuth, Wohlmut (happy disposition) 115, 117

Wohlleben, Wohleben (the good life) 115

Wohlmut, Wohlmuter, see Wohlgemuth

Wohlschlaegel, Woleslagel 159 < Woolschlaegel (wool cleaner) 106

Wohlust (joy) 115

Wohner (occupant) 118

Wolbert < Walbrecht

Wold, see Wald

Woldhouse 159, see Waldhaus

Woldorf, see Waldorf

Wolf 122, Wolfe, Wolff, Wolfs 164 (wolf) 48, or < Wolfgang, Wolfhart

Wolfart, Wolfarts 164, Wolfahrth, see Wohlfart

Wolfer, Wolfers 164, Wolfert 74 < Wolfher (wolf + army 48, 46), or Wolfhart

Wolffanger, Wolfanger (wolf catcher) 91

Wolfgang (wolf + gait, name of a saint) 48
Wolfger (wolf + spear) 48, 46
Wolfhart (wolf + strong) 48, 46
Wolfisch < Walfisch (whale) 118
Wolfkamp, Wolfkampf (wolf field) 48, 84
Wolfram (wolf + raven) 48, 48
Wolfshagen (wolf's enclosure) 48, 123
Wolfsheimer (wolf hamlet, Wolf's hamlet) 48, 123
Wolfskehl, Wolfskill 159 (wolf's throat) 48
Wolgemuth, see Wohlgemut
Wolhandler (wool dealer) 105
Wolk (cloud) 118
Wolkam (wool comb) 106
Wolkstein, see Wolkenstein
Wollenhaupt (wool head) 112
Wollenmacher (woolmaker) 96
Wollenschlaeger, Woolslager (wool beater) 96
Wollenweaver 159, see Wollenweber
Wollenweber, Wolweber (wool weaver) 96
Woller, Wollert 74, Wollner, see Wollenschlaeger
Wolff, see Wolf
Wollhuter (maker of wool hats) 96
Wollmershausen, see Vollmershausen
Wolpert < Walbrecht
Wolter, Wolters 164, see Walther, Walthers
Woltman, Woltmann, see Waldmann
Woltz, see Waltz
Wombacher, see Wambach
Wonderly 159, see Wunderlich
Wool, Wolle (wool) 105, 106
Woole (wool) 106
Woolmaker 153, see Wollenmacher

Woolman, Wolman (wool dealer) 105
Woolsleger, see Woolenschlaeger
Woost 159, see Wuest
Workman 153, see Werckmann
Workmester 159, see Werkmeister
Worms, Wormser (fr Worms) 122
Worst, see Wurst
Wrangel (querulous) 115
Wrighter 159, see Reiter
Wrights 159, 164, see Reitz
Wucher, Wucherer (usurer) 96
Wueller, Wuellner, see Wollner
Wuensch (wish) 118
Wuensch (Wendish) 146
Wuenschel < Wuenschelrute (divining rod) 106
Wuepper (river name) 83
Wuerfel (dice, gambler) 115
Wuergler (strangler) 115
Wuertemberger, Wuerttemberger (fr Wurttemberg) 121
Wuertz (spice) 106
Wuest, Wueste (desert, wasteland, abandoned farm) 118
Wuestenberg (desert mountain) 68
Wuetrich (maniac) 115
Wulf, Wulff, see Wolf, Wolff
Wulfhart, see Wolfhart
Wulfhorst (wolf horst) 72
Wullenweber (wool weaver) 96
Wuller (woolworker) 96
Wullschlaeger, see Woolenschlaeger
Wullwever (wool weaver) 96
Wund (wound, wounded) 118
Wunder (wonder, miracle) 118
Wunderlich, Wunderlick 159, Wunderli, Wonderlich (quaint, odd, eccentric) 115
Wunsch, see Wuensch
Wurdeman (man of dignity) 115
Wurfel (dice) 118

Wurm (dragon, house name) 149

Wurmser, see Wormser

Wurst, Wurste (sausage) 106

Wurster (sausage maker) 96

Wurttemberger, Wurttenberger
(fr Wurttemberg 121, reed
mountain) 81, 68

Wurtz, Wurts, see Wuertz

Wurtzbach, Wurtzbacher,
Wurtzbaugh 159 (spice brook)
77

Wurtzer (spice dealer) 105

Wurz 122, see Wuertz

Wurzburg, Wurtzburger (fr
Wurtzburg 122, swamp castle)
80, 73

Wurzel, Wurzell (root) 118

Wust 159, see Wuest

Wusterwald (deserted forest) 71

Wustfeld (waste field) 84

Wut (anger) 115

Wycoff, Wyckoff (wine seller) 102,
105

Wydman, see Weidmann

Wygand, see Weigand

Wygart, see Weingard

Wyl, Wyler, see Weil

Wyland, see Wieland

Wyman, see Weinmann

Wynberg, Wynberger, see
Weinberg

Wyner, see Weiner

Wyngarde, Wyngartner,
Wyngaarden, see Weingard,
Weingaertner

Wynkoop, see Wycoff

Wyrauch, Wyrouch, see
Weihrauch

Wys, Wyss, see Weiss

X

Xander < Alexander

Y

For Y see also under J.

Yackley 159, see Jaeck

Yaeger 159, Yager, Yagermann,
see Jaeger

Yaeter 159, see Jeter

Yahn 159, Yanke 55, see Jahn,
Jahnke

Yahr 159, see Jahr

Yakel 159, 55, Yakeley, see
Jaeckli

Yan 159, see Jan

Yancey 159, see Jantz

Yantz 159, see Jantz

Yauch 159, see Jauch

Yeager 159, Yager, see Jaeger,
Yeaterman, see Jeter

Yeakley 159, see Jaeck

Yenny 159, see Jenny

Yergens 159, see Juergen

Yerke 159, Yerkes, see Joerg 151

Yerrick 159, see Joerg

Yetter 159, see Jeter

Yingling 159, see Juengling

Yingst 159, see Juengst

Yoder 159, see Joder

Yohn 159, see John

Yon 159, see Jahn

Yonce 159, see Jantz

Yongman 159, see Jungman

Yonker 159, see Junker

Yoos 159, see Jost

Yorden 159, see Jordan

Yost 159, see Jost

Young 159, see Jung

Youngblood 153, see Jungblut

Youngheim 159, < Jungheim
(young hamlet) 123

Younginger 159, see Junginger

Yssenhut 159, see Eisenhut

Yuengling 159, see Juengling

Yung 159, Yunger, see Jung,
Junger

Yunginger 159, see Junginger

Yungmann (young man) 159

Yungmeyer (young farmer, heir to the farm) 159, 93

Yunker 159, see Junker

Yustus 159, see Justus

Yutsi 159, see Uts

Z

Zabel (board game, fr Latin *tabula*) 101

Zaber, Zaberer (fr Zaben) 122, 129

Zach, Zacher 53, see Zacharias

Zacharias (NT name) 135, (name of a pope) 134

Zachringer, Zaehringer (Swiss dynastic name)

Zachs 159, Zaks, see Sachs

Zaehringen (fr Celtic Tarodunum) 129

Zagel (tail, penis) 118

Zaharias, see Zacharias

Zahl (number) 118

Zahler, Zaehler (teller, payer, debtor) 96

Zahm (tame, domestic) 118

Zahn, Zahner (tooth, dentist) 114, 96

Zahringer, see Zachringer

Zaiss, see Zeiss

Zaitman 159, see Seideman

Zaller, Zalner, see Zahler

Zander, see Alexander

Zane, see Zahn

Zang, Zange, Zanger (tongs, torturer, tooth puller) 106

Zanger 159, see Saenger

Zangmeister 159 (choir master) 96

Zank, Zanck, Zanker (quarrel, quarreler) 115

Zant (tooth) 114

Zapf (tap, taverner) 106

Zarcher 159, see Zuericher

Zaring, see Zehr

Zarncke (Slavic: black) 146, 112

Zart (tender) 115

Zassenhaus 159 (Saxons' house) 121, 65

Zauber (magician) 96

Zauberbuehler, Zouberbuhler, see Zuberbiller

Zauberman (bucket maker) 96

Zaubermann (magician) 96

Zaun, Zauner, Zuner (fence, fence maker) 96, 122

Zaydel 159, see Seidel

Zeagler 159, see Ziegler

Zech, Zecher, Zechman (tippler) 115, 122

Zeder (cedar) 89

Zedler (scribe) 96

Zeender, see Zehender

Zegel 159, Zegal, see Siegel

Zeger 159, see Sieger

Zeh (toe) 114

Zehenbauer (tithe farmer) 91

Zehender, Zehnder, Zehnter (tithe collector) 109

Zehler, see Zahler

Zehn, Zehner (ten, tenth) 143

Zehntbauer, see Zehenbauer

Zehr (nourishment) 106

Zeichner (draftsman) 96

Zeidel 159, see Seidel

Zeiderman 159, see Seideman

Zeidler (honey gatherer) 95

Zeidner 159, see Seidner

Zeigenfuss, Zeigenfuse < Ziegenfuss (goat foot) 114

Zeiger (hand of clock) 118

Zeigler 159, see Ziegler

Zeil, Zeile (line) 118

Zeiler 159, see Seiler

Zeiss (gentle, tender) 115

Zeit (time) 118

Zeitler, see Zeidler

Zeitung (tidings, announcement) 118

Zeits 159, Zeitz, see Seitz

Zelik 159, Zelikman, see Selig, Seligman

Zell (cell, fr Latin *cella*) 122
Zeller, Zellner, Zellmann (dweller near a shrine or cell) 71
Zellhofer (farm near a shrine or cell) 92
Zellner, see Zoellner
Zelt, Zelter, Zeltner (tent, tentmaker) 96
Zelter (palfrey) 92
Zeman 159, see Siemann
Zemel 159, see Semmel
Zenger (lively person) 115, see Saenger
Zenker (quarreler) 115
Zenner 159, see Zentner
Zentgraf, Zentgraft (village magistrate) 109
Zentmyer 159 (tithing farmer) 93
Zentner (hundredweight) 114
Zents 53, Zentz < St. Vincentius 135
Zepp, see Zapf
Zepperfeld, Zeppenfeldt (threshing floor) 84
Zerbrock, see Zurbruek
Zercher, see Zuericher
Zering, Zehrung (nourishment, victualer) 106, 96
Zerkel 159, see Zirkel
Zermatt (to the meadow, Swiss village) 69, 84, 122
Zetel (marsh) 80
Zetrower 159, see Zittrauer
Zettel (scrap of paper, note, scribe) 96
Zettelmeyer 159, Zettlemoyer, see Sattelmeyer
Zettler, see Zedler
Zeumer (bridle maker) 96
Zeuner (fence maker) 96
Zevenbergen 159 (seven mountains), see Siebenbuergen
Zibel (onion) 91, 105

Zickafoose 159, Zickefoose (Shake a leg!) 116, 151
Ziebenbuergen 159, see Siebenbuergen
Ziebli, Zieblin, see Zuebli
Ziebolt 159, see Siegbald
Zieg, Ziege, Ziecke (goat) 91, see Sieg
Ziegaus 159 < Zeughaus (armory) 65, 108
Ziegeheaver 159, see Ziegenhoff
Ziegel, Zieggel, see Zuegel
Ziegel 159, see Siegel
Ziegenbein (goat leg) 114
Ziegenfuss, Ziegenfoos 159 (goat foot) 114
Ziegenhard (goat herder)
Ziegenheim (goat hamlet) 123
Ziegenhoff, Ziegenhoffer (goat farm) 92
Ziegenmeyer (goat farmer) 93
Ziegenmilch (goat milk) 106, 122
Ziegfeld, Ziegfield (goat field) 84
Ziegler, Zieglar, Zieglert 74 (tile setter or maker, fr Latin *tegulum*) 96, 101
Ziegman 159, see Siegmann
Ziel, Ziehl (goal), 118
Zielke (little goal), 55
Zieman 159, see Sieman
Ziepold 159, see Siegbald
Zier (decoration) 115, 106
Zigel 159, see Siegel, Zuegel
Zigenfuss 159, see Ziegenfuss
Zigler 159, see Ziegler
Zilber 159, see Silber
Zile 159, see Seil
Zimelman 159, see Semmel
Zimmer, Zimmerli, Zimmerli 55 (timber, carpenter) 96, 105
Zimmermann, Zimermann (carpenter) 96, 98
Zindel, see Zuendl
Zinder (silk worker) 96
Zinder, see Zuender